CATALAN:
A COMPREHENSIVE GRAMMA

Catalan: A Comprehensive Grammar is a complete reference guide to modern Catalan grammar, presenting an accessible and systematic description of the modern language.

The *Grammar* reflects the current reality of Catalan by acknowledging regional diversity and features Balearic and Valencian varieties alongside the language used in the Barcelona region.

The combined specialist knowledge of the author team ensures a balanced coverage of modern Catalan.

Features include:
- comprehensive coverage of all parts of speech
- a wealth of authentic examples illustrating language points
- attention to areas of particular difficulty for those whose first language is English
- full cross-referencing
- detailed index

Catalan: A Comprehensive Grammar will remain the standard reference work for years to come.

Max W. Wheeler is Reader in Linguistics at the University of Sussex. **Alan Yates** is 'Illes Balears' Professor of Catalan at the University of Sheffield. **Nicolau Dols** is Professor Titular d'Escola Universitària at the University of the Balearic Islands.

CATALAN:
A COMPREHENSIVE
GRAMMAR

Max W. Wheeler, Alan Yates and
Nicolau Dols

London and New York

First published 1999
by Routledge
2 Park Square, Milton Park, Abingdon , Oxon, OX14 4RN

Simultaneously published in the USA and Canada
by Routledge
270 Madison Ave, New York NY 10016

Routledge is an imprint of the Taylor & Francis Group

Transferred to Digital Printing 2006

Typeset in Times by RefineCatch Limited, Bungay, Suffolk

British Library Cataloguing in Publication Data
A catalogue record for this book is available from the British Library

Library of Congress Cataloging in Publication Data
Wheeler, Max.
    Catalan: a comprehensive grammar / Max W. Wheeler, Alan Yates and
Nicolau Dols.
      p.   cm.—(Routledge grammars)
    Includes bibliographical references and index.
    1. Catalan language—Grammar.   I. Yates, Alan.   II. Dols.
Nicolau, 1967– .   III. Title.   IV. Series.
    PC3823.W44   1999   98–47194
    449'.982421—dc21   CIP

ISBN 0–415–20777–0 (hbk)
ISBN 0–415–10342–8 (pbk)

Publisher's Note
The publisher has gone to great lengths to ensure the quality of this reprint
but points out that some imperfections in the original may be apparent

We dedicate this volume to the memory of Joan Gili (1907–1998)

CONTENTS

Preface   ix
Acknowledgements   xvii
Map of Catalan-speaking areas and dialects   xviii

PART I: NOUN PHRASE CONSTITUENTS

 1   Gender of nouns   3
 2   Plural of nouns and formation of derived nouns   30
 3   Articles   43
 4   Adjectives   71
 5   Comparison   95
 6   Demonstratives   106
 7   Possessives   114
 8   Miscellaneous adjectives and pronouns (quantifiers and indefinites)   121
 9   Nominalizations via articles   143
10   Numerals   150
11   Personal pronouns (stressed)   160
12   Pronominal clitics (weak object pronouns)   167

PART II: ADVERBS, PREPOSITIONS, AND CONJUNCTIONS

13   Adverbs and adverbials   221
14   Prepositions   242
15   Conjunctions   268

PART III: VERBS

16   Morphology of the verb   283
17   Use of indicative (non-continuous) verb forms   340
18   Progressive constructions and other verbal periphrases   363
19   The subjunctive   373
20   The infinitive   393
21   Participles   407
22   The gerund   416
23   Pronominal verbs   427

PART IV: SENTENCE TYPES: SIMPLE AND COMPLEX

24	Interjections and ideophones	449
25	Simple sentences and grammatical relations	458
26	Negation	474
27	Interrogation and exclamation	486
28	Imperative utterances	501
29	Passive and impersonal sentences	505
30	Copular sentences (**ser**, **estar**, etc.)	521
31	Relative clauses	532
32	Complement clauses	550
33	Adverbial clauses	557
34	Conditional sentences	575

PART V: INFORMATION STRUCTURE AND WORD ORDER

35	Cleft sentences	591
36	Word order	599
37	Spelling, accent rules, and punctuation	610
	Further reading	621
	Bibliography	623
	Index	625

PREFACE

This book is designed to provide an up-to-date, systematic description of the morphology and syntax of the modern standard Catalan language. In preparing it we have had in mind the needs of pre-university and university students, teachers, translators and those with a private or professional interest in the language as it is currently used by Catalan speakers in educated conversation and in the normal range of written registers. We note with pleasure the appearance of Jenny Brumme's *Praktische Grammatik der katalanischen Sprache* (Wilhelmsfeld: Egert, 1997); we coincide with the aims and scope of this work in offering a substantial grammar of Catalan, in a language other than Spanish or Catalan itself, designed expressly for non-natives. Brumme's work was published when the present volume was in the final stages of preparation, so we have been unable to make use of it in our own work. We have, of course, relied considerably on the extensive existing literature on Catalan grammar, though we have developed some topics which have not previously been covered in depth. We have also given particular emphasis to areas of usage which are likely to be difficult for users starting from English.

One assumption with which we have worked is that those who use this book, whether for reference or for systematic study, will already have acquired some basic familiarity with Catalan, either through immediate contact and 'total immersion' or, more probably, through working with various methods (in the medium of English, Spanish or Catalan itself) for induction in the language. This Comprehensive Grammar is thus conceived as an extension or complement to a fairly wide repertoire of basic study materials, a sample of which is provided in the Further reading list. Another, related, assumption is that users of this book will be acquainted with basic traditional grammatical concepts and terminology; we aim to explain any more specialized concepts and terms as we go along. Such explanations can be located via the index.

Catalan is a member of the Romance family of languages which are modern forms of the Latin language which spread from Rome to much of Europe in the wake of the Roman empire around the beginning of the common era. As its geographical position might suggest, Catalan shares several features with its nearest Romance neighbours: Italian, Sardinian, Occitan, Spanish, while being distinct in several respects from all of them. The map on page xviii shows where Catalan is spoken and identifies the main dialect divisions. The second section of this Preface briefly discusses 'normative' and 'standard' Catalan in relation to the position of the language in the twentieth century and insofar as these important concepts affect criteria and procedures followed in the body of this book. We do not attempt to supply here any history of Catalan as a member of the Romance family of languages, or any discussion of the mightily complex issues of Catalan as a stateless language in post-Renaissance Europe, in contact/conflict with more powerful linguistic neighbours (primarily Spanish, but also French, and Italian). These sociolinguistic and politico-linguistic factors have been of great moment in shaping the historical evolution of Catalan and, especially in the twentieth century, in affecting the politics associated with community self-awareness centred in linguistic difference.

The territories where Catalan is natively spoken are:

(1) The Principality of Andorra.
(2) In France: almost all of the *département* of Pyrénées-Orientales.
(3) In Spain:
    (i)   Catalonia (under the autonomous government, the *Generalitat*, of Catalonia), except for the Gascon-speaking Val d'Aran.
    (ii) The eastern fringe of Aragon.
    (iii) Most of the *Comunitat Valenciana*, excepting some regions in the west and south which have been Aragonese/Spanish-speaking since at least the eighteenth century.
    (iv) El Carxe, a small area of the province of Murcia, settled in the nineteenth century.
    (v) The Balearic Islands: Majorca and Minorca (Balearic *stricto sensu*), Ibiza (*Eivissa*) and Formentera (strictly *Illes Pitiüses*).
(4) In Italy: the port of Alghero in Sardinia.

A conservative estimate of the number of native speakers of Catalan is about 6.5 million (based on the 1991 census in Catalonia, Valencia, and the Balearics, with estimates for the remaining territories). Within Spain a further three million claim to understand Catalan. Partly as a result of the incorporation of Catalan locally into the education system, there are within Spain increasing numbers of second-language speakers.

STATUS OF CATALAN

The status, situation, and prospects of the Catalan language are significantly different in each of the territories enumerated above, though each of those in Spain shares, in some way, the consequences of Catalan's having been for centuries an oppressed minority language. For a multiplicity of reasons, cultural decline and loss of prestige affected Catalan from the sixteenth century onwards. The defeat of the Catalans in the war of the Spanish Succession (1714) initiated a series of measures extending throughout the eighteenth and nineteenth centuries, imposing the use of Spanish in public life, for example, in accounts, in preaching, in the theatre, in the criminal courts, in education, in legal documents, in the civil registers, on the telephone. In the twentieth century these measures were mostly repeated, and supplemented by the imposition of Spanish in the catechism, by prohibition of the teaching of Catalan, and by sanctions against persons refusing to use Spanish. The Second Republic (1931–39) to a large extent removed these restrictions, but Franco's victory in the Spanish Civil War was followed in 1940 by a total ban on the public use of Catalan. This ban was subject to a series of relaxations from the 1950s onwards, allowing (subject to censorship applied generally in Spain) the publication of increasing numbers of Catalan books from the 1960s, though Catalan remained excluded from nearly all public institutions until Spain's adoption of a democratic constitution in 1978.

That constitution enjoins respect for and protection of Spain's 'other' languages, and opened the way for statutes of autonomy in the various regions. In the early 1980s, Catalonia, Valencia, and the Balearics obtained their respective autonomy statutes, involving co-officiality for Spanish and Catalan. All of these statutes promote 'language normalization', the goal of which is universal bilingualism without diglossia. In Catalonia the expressed aim of the Generalitat goes much further than this: to make the local language the normal medium of public life, with Spanish having a secondary role as an auxiliary language, or a home language for its native speakers. In Valencia and the Balearics, the de facto policy has been to promote effective knowledge of Catalan and to enhance its status, although complex socio-political factors, differentially in each area, continue to hinder progress towards full and normal integration of Catalan in public life.

In Catalonia, Catalan is co-official and its knowledge and use are actively promoted by the autonomous government and by local government. Teaching of Catalan is obligatory in all schools, and primary and secondary education through the medium of Catalan reaches in the 1990s about 60 per cent of the population. The provision includes, since 1993, some Catalan immersion programmes in Spanish-speaking suburbs. There are two Catalan-language television stations, with wide audiences, and numerous radio stations. Catalan is still clearly in a minority position in the periodical press, in advertising, in cinema/video, and in the administration of justice, but a gradual advance is noted here too. The January 1998 Language Normalization Act is designed to build upon progress achieved under the previous Act of 1983, especially as regards extending the use of Catalan in the commercial and judicial fields, where the predominance of Spanish has been obstinate.

In the Aragon fringe, Catalan has no official status, though the Aragonese autonomy statute speaks of protection and support of minority languages. In the towns and villages in question there are many cultural associations promoting Catalan (not necessarily by that name), and in many cases the local administration supports Catalan teaching in schools. Radio and television from Catalonia are accessible, of course. Language shift (except through emigration) is minimal.

The language situation in the Community of Valencia is extremely complex, politically, culturally, and geographically. Catalan has been strongest in the countryside and among the urban working classes. The language policy of the Generalitat Valenciana, responding to popular pressure, has largely concentrated on education, and Catalan is available in around 80 per cent of state schools. A shortage of teachers has hindered advance here up to now. Teaching through Catalan is available in a minority of schools. A Valencian state television station broadcasts bilingually. Catalan is quite prominent in cultural life; it is present in administration and in commerce, and there is evidence of popular demand for, and expectation of, a greater use of Catalan.

Though the Balearic Islands Council passed a linguistic normalization law in 1986, relatively little has been done to put it into effect. Spoken Catalan is predominant except in Palma and in Ibiza (Eivissa), where immigration is highest, and where there is recent evidence of some inter-generational language shift to Spanish. Catalan has some place in local broadcasting, TV and radio, and Catalan television stations from the mainland have a wide following. Since 1996 there has been a Palma-based Catalan-language daily newspaper, with a wide distribution, and outside Palma the local press is largely Catalan. In schools, Catalan as a subject is widely available, responding to pressure from parents and from local administrations (though in Ibiza one fifth of pupils does not receive the prescribed hours of Catalan teaching). In 1990–91 17 per cent of pupils had Catalan as their medium of education, in whole or in part; this trend is strongest in Minorca. In advertising and commerce Spanish predominates, but with Catalan increasing its role somewhat.

In Valencia and in the Balearic Islands, there is in some sectors a preference for using the terms '*valencià*' and '*mallorquí*', respectively, to refer to the variants of the language used there. This feature (which we refer to again below in discussing normative and standard Catalan) is susceptible to political manipulation, and it strongly affects debate on the linguistic unity of the Catalan-speaking territories.

In Andorra, Catalan has always been the sole official language, though until recently secondary education was provided by the French and Spanish states, in their standard, monolingual, model. Spanish-speaking immigrants account for almost 40 per cent of the population of about 50,000. Spanish and French are widely used in commerce, but Catalan predominates in other areas of public life. In 1993 Andorra adopted a new constitution, and the government has been pursuing an active 'Andorranization' policy, involving education through a medium of Catalan.

The status and position of Catalan in North Catalonia is closely parallel to that of the other traditional minority languages in France. Language shift was all but universal after the Second World War, so that most native speakers are over fifty years old. Catalan has at best an occasional, decorative, role in public life. In primary schools, some 30 per cent study Catalan (as a foreign language), and some 15 per cent in secondary schools.

In Alghero, in 1987, it was estimated that about 58 per cent of the population of 37,000 understood *alguerès*. However, inter-generational language shift to Italian is proceeding apace, despite the recent declaration of co-officiality for Catalan and Italian in the city. Stimulated in part by Catalan revival further west, a certain pro-Catalan cultural movement can be observed, evident in local associations and local television and radio. As elsewhere in Italy, the local language has no official role in the education system.

DIALECTS

Though there are significant dialect differences in Catalan, the dialects are to a very high degree mutually intelligible. They are conventionally divided into two groups, on the basis of differences in phonology as well as in some features of verb morphology; there are some interesting lexical differences, too. The eastern dialect group covers North Catalan (including *rossellonès* in French Catalonia), Central Catalan (in the eastern part of Catalonia), Balearic, and *alguerès* (in Alghero). The western group consists of North Western (NW) Catalan (western and southern Catalonia and eastern Aragon) and Valencian. The principal dialect divisions are shown in the map on page xviii.

NORMATIVE AND STANDARD CATALAN

A unified literary Catalan koine had already become well established by the fifteenth century. With the subsequent cultural decline in the sixteenth to eighteenth centuries, awareness of the conventions of this koine, and of the linguistic and cultural unity of the Catalan territories it reflected, was gradually dissipated, so that, by 1800 or so, writers had in mind only a regionally limited audience for works in a local idiom. One of the goals of the nineteenth-century *Renaixença* ('Rebirth') movement was the restoration or reconstruction of a Catalan standard language. The standardization process crystallized in the work of Pompeu Fabra (1868–1948), whose orthographic norms (1913), grammar (1918), and dictionary (1932) were immediately adopted by official institutions in Catalonia, and quickly became accepted elsewhere. The bases of Fabra's standard Catalan were the medieval koine, current educated usage in Catalonia, particularly in Barcelona, the contemporary dialects, and the removal of 'barbarisms'. Fabra's intention was that the standard language should be open to development, and to further incorporation of non-Barcelona usage, but the circumstances of the Spanish

Civil War (1936–39) and the Franco period (1939–75) had the effect of turning Fabra's works into an orthodoxy, deviation from which was regarded by Catalan nationalists as unpatriotic. It is only since the 1980s that the Institut d'Estudis Catalans and associated institutions have regained the authority to expand and modernize standard Catalan, introducing recommendations for terminology, for spoken usage in the mass media, and for regional parastandards.

In fact, in addition to the Barcelona-based norm which is used throughout Catalonia and to some extent elsewhere, de facto standards for Valencian and Balearic had already grown up, largely through the practice of a few major publishers. These parastandards diverge from the Barcelona norm only in retaining some regional differences of vocabulary and morphology which were part of the literary tradition. The differences are comparable to those between British and American English; one may easily read a page of text before coming on a feature which marks it as of one regional standard variety rather than another. In recent years some writers and publishers in Catalonia have argued for, and practised, modifications of the standard language to reflect more popular usage, especially that of Barcelona, in vocabulary and syntax. The vehemence of the polemic surrounding these deviations is out of proportion to the rather modest scope of the innovations proposed.

A potentially much more serious trend since the 1980s has been one associated with the claim that Valencian is not just a regional variety of Catalan but a separate language. This has led to the development by the Reial Academia de Cultura Valenciana of a different orthography, grammar, and vocabulary, reflecting more closely (but by no means entirely consistently) the popular speech of Valencia; this alternative standard has won some official backing – in the city government of Valencia and under the regime currently (1998) controlling the Generalitat Valenciana – but has generally been opposed by educational institutions, publishers, and most creative writers in Catalan.

TYPE OF LANGUAGE COVERED IN THE GRAMMAR

Our approach to presenting a systematic description of modern Catalan is one which takes into account the issues discussed above. We endeavour to reflect the current reality of the language by acknowledging regional diversity.

Both our descriptions and the examples supplied refer primarily to the established prescriptive norms, with their inclination towards the standard status and standardizing influence of the Central dialect, in particular. However, in areas of use where differences are marked (e.g. weak object pronouns, verbal morphology, demonstratives, etc.), we follow the practice of describing regional or dialect differences from the General variety (as we label it in this context), with examples correspondingly supplied and explained. Elsewhere, in discussing general normative features, we regularly include without comment examples which contain recognized dialect features (e.g. Valencian **et porte esta carta** for Central-based norm **et porto aquesta carta** 'I am bringing you this letter'; Balearic **t'ho pos aquí** for **t'ho poso aquí** 'I'm putting it here (for you)'). Proportionally, though, the example material supplied reflects the prevalence of the Central norm, for the reasons explained above.

Where we make mention of 'the Dictionary', reference is principally to the *Diccionari de la llengua catalana*, published in 1995 under the aegis and with the authority of the Institut d'Estudis Catalans. The Institut, through its Philological Section, is the acknowledged and legally recognized ultimate authority in matters concerning the formal lexical and grammatical rules of Catalan, throughout the Catalan-speaking area. The 1995 *Diccionari* incorporates the contents and various revisions of the *Diccionari general de la llengua catalana* which first appeared in 1932 under the direction of Pompeu Fabra (see p. xiii). Until 1995 the *Diccionari general* was complemented by the *Diccionari de la llengua catalana* (1982), published by Enciclopèdia Catalana, which retains its usefulness for coverage of recent and specialized terminology.

A corpus might have been established to provide authorized and published illustration of each and every point discussed. Selected quotations from written sources have been used, but we have rejected using a corpus base as our main method. Several practical and theoretical reasons have determined this decision. In the first place we wished to break with the reference grammar convention of prioritizing literary usage. Second, establishing a corpus of authorities would have meant imposing certain criteria of selectivity regarding normative status which, in the context of modern Catalan publishing, is subject to outside constraints, house styles, subjective preferences and the vagaries of correction. Third, genuine quotations in many cases bring the disadvantage of details which are irrelevant to the point under discussion, making it harder to see the wood for the trees. Our examples, some of which have been adapted from complementary linguistic sources, are intended to be both realistic and practical. This procedure is consistent with our main team approach to the preparation of this volume, combining our individual competences, namely those of a theoretical linguist with a particular interest in the structures of Catalan, a specialist in teaching Catalan grammar to advanced students of languages, and a Catalan-speaker (incidentally of Majorcan origin) who supplies an internal perspective based on both native competence and professional expertise.

In addition to remarking on dialect differences within the standard language, we give considerable attention to levels of formality, both in speech and writing. That is, we draw attention to the fact that not everything that is accepted as standard is equally appropriate in all contexts; furthermore, many features that are categorized as non-standard are characteristic at least of the spontaneous spoken usage of many educated speakers.

CONVENTIONS AND PRESENTATION

An asterisk (***hem comprar pa**, ***vull de veure**) indicates an ungrammatical form, that would be instinctively rejected by a native speaker. A question mark before an example (**?Era envejada per mi**, **?Li ho direm al teu germà**) indicates a form that would not be accepted as natural or genuine by all speakers. Widespread colloquial non-standard variants are systematically referred to as such.

Where the English translation of an example departs markedly from the wording or structure of the Catalan original, we supply in parentheses, thus (lit. . . .), a more literal version to accompany the communicative equivalent of the original.

The English translations that we give, whether of words or whole sentences, are not intended to cover the whole range of possible meanings (or to substitute for a dictionary). They are designed to identify the items in question, or to illustrate the point at issue, drawing attention to similarities and differences between Catalan and English. Among other things, a Catalan third person singular verb such as **pren** might well correspond to 'she takes', 'he takes', 'it takes', 'you take', 'she is taking', 'he is taking', 'it is taking', 'you are taking', and so on. We select just one of the possibilities without comment. Alternatives have been indicated (usually by a diagonal stroke /: thus, **vam/vàrem cridar** 'we shouted', **camioneta** 'van'/'light truck') where the difference is noteworthy or significant, but for the sake of clarity we have not attempted to be comprehensive in showing all alternatives wherever they might be possible.

Max W. Wheeler (Falmer)
Alan Yates (Sheffield)
Nicolau Dols (Palma)
April 1999

ACKNOWLEDGEMENTS

We are grateful to all the Catalan-speakers, too numerous to mention individually here, who have helped us, knowingly or not, to exemplify or clarify points of grammar and usage. Special thanks are due, though, to Joaquim Martí i Mainar for his good advice; to Pere Santandreu Brunet, Puri Gómez i Casademont and Josep A. Grimalt Gomila for reading and sensitively commenting on drafts of some chapters; and to Louise Johnson for intellectual and technical support. The final version has benefited from the detailed observations of an anonymous reader, to whom we also express our gratitude.

One particular axis of our collaboration has benefited from support for joint research given by the Universitat de les Illes Balears and the University of Sheffield.

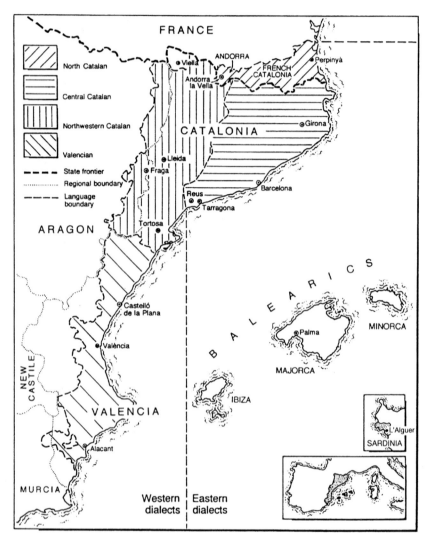

Catalan-speaking areas and dialects

PART I: NOUN PHRASE
CONSTITUENTS

1 GENDER OF NOUNS

Catalan displays the phenomenon of grammatical gender agreement found in many European languages (and elsewhere). Every noun is either of masculine or of feminine gender; adjectives which modify the noun, as well as pronouns which cross-refer to it, are required to take the same, 'agreeing', gender. For example:

Aquell armari vell era ple, i el vam haver de
that (*m.*) cupboard (*m.*) old (*m.*) was full (*m.*), and it (*m.*) we-had to
buidar.
empty
That old cupboard was full, and we had to empty it.

Aquella caixa vella era plena, i la vam haver de buidar.
that (*f.*) box (*f.*) old (*f.*) was full (*f.*), and it (*f.*) we-had to empty
That old box was full, and we had to empty it.

As is the case in most languages, the masculine gender is semantically 'unmarked', in that it is also used when referring to groups of mixed biological gender or to persons of unknown or unspecified gender:

els italians (*m.*)	Italian males *or* Italians in general
els professors (*m.*)	male teachers *or* teachers of either sex
els pares (*m.*)	fathers *or* parents
els fills (*m.*)	sons *or* sons and daughters (male and female) *or* children (sex unspecified or unknown)
Si algú arriba d'hora, feu-lo (*m.*) **esperar.**	If anyone arrives early, have them wait.
but **les professores** (*f.*)	female teachers

In addition to masculine and feminine gender, Catalan is unusual among Romance languages in having a special neuter agreement pronoun **ho**, used when no noun has been mentioned or is in mind. Its use is explained in section **12.5**.

1.1 GENDER OF NOUNS REFERRING TO HUMANS AND FAMILIAR ANIMALS

As a very general rule nouns referring to female humans and female familiar/domestic animals are of feminine gender (e.g. **tia** 'aunt', **xinesa** 'Chinese girl/woman', **gallina** 'hen'), and those referring to male humans and male familiar/domestic animals are of masculine gender (e.g. **oncle** 'uncle', **xilè** 'Chilean boy/man', **gall** 'cock') which is, of course, the source of the names masculine and feminine for the two agreement classes. There are a few exceptions, to be mentioned below (**1.1.6**).

Generally we find pairs of nouns, one of masculine and one of feminine gender, for the corresponding male and female referents; these pairs are morphologically related in a number of possible ways. In the majority of cases, human males and females and males and females of familiar/domestic animals are denoted by distinct word forms. In the case of words denoting professions that were traditionally exercised only by men, the morphologically related feminine form is used to denote 'wife of . . .' such as **alcaldessa** 'mayoress'; currently such forms are used mostly of women who exercise the profession in their own right. With professions that are even now exclusively male (e.g. military) the former convention may survive.

1.1.1 DERIVATION OF FEMININES WITH -a

The commonest pattern is that in which a feminine noun is derived from the corresponding masculine one by the addition of the feminine gender suffix -a (replacing any unstressed final -e or -o of the masculine). Thus:

fotògraf (*m.*)	**fotògrafa** (*f.*)	photographer
noi (*m.*)	**noia** (*f.*)	boy/girl
company (*m.*)	**companya** (*f.*)	companion
fill (*m.*)	**filla** (*f.*)	son/daughter
pediatre (*m.*)	**pediatra** (*f.*)	paediatrician
monjo (*m.*)	**monja** (*f.*)	monk/nun
etc.		

In many cases there are consequential modifications to the spelling or pronunciation (or both).

(i)   A different written accent may be required (according to the general accentuation rules – see **37.5**; these modifications apply to all parallel cases):

avi (*m.*)	**àvia** (*f.*)	grandfather/grandmother
pagès (*m.*)	**pagesa** (*f.*)	farmer
Lluís (*m.*)	**Lluïsa** (*f.*)	(Louis, Louisa – given name)
etc.		

(ii)   Those ending in a stressed vowel add **-na** in the feminine:

germà (*m.*)   **germana** (*f.*)   brother/sister
beduí (*m.*)   **beduïna** (*f.*)   Bedouin
etc.

Also, irregularly, **rei** (*m.*) 'king' → **reina** (*f.*) 'queen', **orfe** (*m.*) → **òrfena** (*f.*) 'orphan'.

(iii) Those ending in **-òleg** have **-òloga** in the feminine:

cardiòleg (*m.*)   **cardiòloga** (*f.*)   cardiologist
sociòleg (*m.*)   **sociòloga** (*f.*)   sociologist
etc.

(iv)   A few of the nouns ending in **-s** double the **s** in the feminine:

gos (*m.*)   **gossa** (*f.*)   dog/bitch
ós (*m.*)   **óssa** (*f.*)   bear

Similarly **bordegàs/bordegassa** 'lad/lass', **capatàs/capatassa** 'foreman', 'overseer', **possés/possessa** 'someone possessed by the devil', **profés/ professa** 'one who has taken vows', **rus/russa** 'Russian', **suís/suïssa** 'Swiss', **talòs/talossa** 'dolt'.

(v)   A few of those ending in **-l** have **-l·la** in the feminine:

gal (*m.*)   **gal·la** (*f.*)   Gaul
pupil (*m.*)   **pupil·la** (*f.*)   ward

And likewise with the given names **Marcel, Camil, Ciril,** feminines **Marcel·la, Camil·la, Ciril·la.**

(vi)   Some masculine nouns which end in a voiceless consonant preceded by a vowel replace the consonant with the corresponding voiced one (**-c** → **-ga, -p** → **-ba, -t** → **-da**):

amic (*m.*)   **amiga** (*f.*)   friend   **nebot** (*m.*)   **neboda** (*f.*)   nephew/niece
llop (*m.*)   **lloba** (*f.*)   wolf   etc.

Likewise **borrec/borrega** 'yearling lamb', **cec/cega** 'blind person' **dormilec/dormilega** 'sleepyhead', **enemic/enemiga** 'enemy', **gallec/gallega** 'Galician', **grec/grega** 'Greek', **llec/llega** 'lay person', **manyac/manyaga** 'sweetheart' (addressed to a small child), **noruec/noruega** 'Norwegian'. The great majority of nouns ending in **-t** (many of which are nominalized adjectives) thus have corresponding feminines in **-da. Serf/serva** 'serf' is the sole example showing **-f** alternating with **-va.**

(vii) Most nouns ending in semi-consonant **-u** have feminines in **-va**; such as:

detectiu (*m.*)	**detectiva** (*f.*)	detective	**jueu** (*m.*)	**jueva** (*f.*)	Jew
esclau (*m.*)	**esclava** (*f.*)	slave	etc.		
eslau (*m.*)	**eslava** (*f.*)	Slav			

Hereu (*m.*) 'heir' has feminine **hereua** or **hereva**; **romeu** (*m.*) 'pilgrim' has **romeua** or **romeva**. Note given names **Andreu/Andreua, Pompeu/Pompeia, Pau/Paula**. To **reu** (*m.*) 'accused person', 'culprit' corresponds **rea** (*f.*); likewise **arameu/aramea** 'Aramaean', **ateu/atea** 'atheist', **caldeu/caldea** 'Chaldean', **fariseu/farisea** 'Pharisee', **filisteu/filistea** 'Philistine', **galileu/galilea** 'Galilean', **hebreu/hebrea** 'Hebrew', **indoeuropeu/indoeuropea** 'Indo-European', **maniqueu/maniquea** 'Manichean', **pigmeu/pigmea** 'Pigmy'.

1.1.2   FEMININES DERIVED WITH OTHER SUFFIXES

In some cases the feminine form has another suffix (before which may be found the same types of change affecting final consonants or vowels as mentioned above). The commonest such suffix is -**essa**:

abat (*m.*)	**abadessa** (*f.*)	abbot/abbess
alcalde (*m.*)	**alcaldessa** (*f.*)	mayor/female mayor/mayoress
baró (*m.*)	**baronessa** (*f.*)	baron/baroness
comte (*m.*)	**comtessa** (*f.*)	count/countess
déu (*m.*)	**deessa** or **dea** (*f.*)	god/goddess
diable (*m.*)	**diablessa** (*f.*)	devil
diaca (*m.*)	**diaconessa** (*f.*)	deacon/deaconess
druida (*m.*)	**druïdessa** (*f.*)	druid
duc (*m.*)	**duquessa** (*f.*)	duke/duchess
hoste (*m.*)	**hostessa** (*f.*)	lodger, host/hostess
jutge (*m.*)	**jutgessa** (*f.*)	judge
metge (*m.*)	**metgessa** (*f.*)	doctor, physician
ogre (*m.*)	**ogressa** (*f.*)	ogre/ogress
poeta (*m.*)	**poetessa** (*f.*)	poet
profeta (*m.*)	**profetessa** (*f.*)	prophet/prophetess
tigre (*m.*)	**tigressa** (*f.*)	tiger/tigress
etc.		

To refer to a female poet or prophet, **poeta** (*f.*) and **profeta** (*f.*) are now preferred.

A few nouns take -**ina**:

gall	cock	**heroi**	hero	**tsar**	czar
gallina	hen	**heroïna**	heroine	**tsarina**	czarina

A few nouns in -**tor** or -**dor** replace these with -**triu** or -**driu** respectively:

actor	actor	**emperador**	emperor
actriu	actress	**emperadriu**	empress
institutor	tutor	**ambaixador**	ambassador
institutriu	governess	**ambaixadriu** (now more usually **ambaixadora**)	ambassadress

1.1.3   MASCULINES DERIVED FROM FEMININE

In the following instances a masculine noun is derived from a feminine one via the suffix -ot:

abella (*f.*)	**abellot** (*m.*)	bee/drone
fura (*f.*)	**furot** (*m.*)	ferret
guatlla (*f.*)	**guatllot** (*m.*)	quail
guilla (*f.*)	**guillot** (*m.*)	vixen/fox
merla (*f.*)	**merlot** (*m.*)	blackbird
perdiu (*f.*)	**perdigot** (*m.*)	partridge
bruixa (*f.*)	**bruixot** (*m.*)	witch/wizard
dida (*f.*)	**didot** (*m.*)	wet nurse/wet nurse's husband

1.1.4   IRREGULAR OR SUPPLETIVE GENDER PAIRS

Some gender pairs are expressed with unrelated, or irregularly related, nouns:

amo (*m.*)	**mestressa** (*f.*)	master/mistress
gendre (*m.*)	**jove** or **nora** (*f.*)	son-in-law/daughter-in-law
hereu (*m.*)	**pubilla** (*f.*)	heir/heiress of family fortune
home (*m.*)	**dona** (*f.*)	man/husband/woman/wife
marit (*m.*)	**muller** (*f.*)	husband/wife
oncle (*m.*)	**tia** (*f.*)	uncle/aunt
príncep (*m.*)	**princesa** (*f.*)	prince/princess
ase (*m.*)	**somera** (*f.*)	stallion donkey/jenny (female donkey)
boc/cabró/cabrot (*m.*)	**cabra** (*f.*)	billy goat/nanny goat
cavall (*m.*)	**egua/euga** (*f.*)	stallion/mare
gall dindi or **indiot** (*m.*)	**polla díndia** (*f.*)	turkey
marrà (*m.*)	**ovella** (*f.*)	ram/ewe
porc (*m.*)	**truja** (*f.*)	pig/hog/sow
toro or **brau** (*m.*)	**vaca** (*f.*)	bull/cow
bou (*m.*)		ox

1.1.5   NOUNS OF COMMON GENDER

There is a considerable number of nouns of common gender referring to humans. The same form is used with both masculine and feminine articles, for example, **una asteca** 'a female Aztec', **un asteca** 'a male Aztec'/'an Aztec (sex unspecified)'.

There is a substantial number of common gender nouns ending in **-a**; the following are a representative sample:

asteca (*m./f.*)	Aztec	**extra** (*m./f.*)	(film) extra
belga (*m./f.*)	Belgian	**ganàpia** (*m./f.*)	childish person
carca (*m./f.*)	reactionary	**gimnasta** (*m./f.*)	gymnast
col·lega (*m./f.*)	colleague	**hipòcrita** (*m./f.*)	hypocrite
demòcrata (*m./f.*)	democrat	**indígena** (*m./f.*)	native
dormilega (*m./f.*)	sleepy-head	**judoka** (*m./f.*)	practitioner of judo
Note **dormilec** (*m.*) is also found		**pastifa** (*m./f.*)	botcher
electricista (*m./f.*)	electrician	**terapeuta** (*m./f.*)	therapist

Metaphorical/metonymic transfers

Certain nouns ending in **-a**, regularly feminine and denoting inanimates in their literal sense, are also applied metaphorically or metonymically to humans; many of these are pejorative. Dictionaries record some as masculine only (in their transferred sense); others as masculine or feminine. These assignments are recorded below. There is little doubt that all of them can in fact be feminine if required.

barra (*m.*)	shameless person < **barra** (*f.*) impudence
canalla (*m.*)	cad < **canalla** (*f.*) (arch.) riff-raff
consueta (*m./f.*)	prompt < **consueta** (*f.*) book of rituals
cràpula (*m.*)	drunkard, debauchee < **cràpula** (*f.*) drunkenness
estafa (*m./f.*)	swindler < **estafa** (*f.*) swindle
fanfàrria (*m./f.*)	braggart < **fanfàrria** (*f.*) bluster
fava (*m./f.*)	indecisive person < **fava** (*f.*) broad bean
guàrdia (*m./f.*)	police officer < **guàrdia** (*f.*) protection, police force
mala pinta (*m./f.*)	rotter < **mala pinta** (*f.*) bad blotch
mandra (*m./f.*)	lazybones < **mandra** (*f.*) sloth, disinclination
manta (*m./f.*)	lazybones < **manta** (*f.*) blanket
marieta (*m.*)	poof < **marieta** (*f.*) ladybird
maula (*m./f.*)	fraud < **maula** (*f.*) dirty trick, fraud
ordenança (*m.*)	batman < **ordenança** (*f.*) ordinance
paleta (*m./f.*)	bricklayer, building worker < **paleta** (*f.*) trowel
peça (*m./f.*)	bad sort < **peça** (*f.*) piece
poca-solta (*m./f.*)	idiot < **poca solta** (*f.*) little sense
pocavergonya (*m./f.*)	shameless person < **poca vergonya** (*f.*) little shame
policia (*m./f.*)	police officer < **policia** (*f.*) police
trafica (*m./f.*)	con-man < **trafica** (*f.*) trick
etc.	

A few words similar in meaning to some of those above seem to be derived directly from verbs of Conjugation I, such as:

bada (*m./f.*)	look-out	< badar	open (eyes, etc.)
guaita (*m./f.*)	watchman	< guaitar	look out
guarda (*m./f.*)	guard	< guardar	guard
mossega (*m./f.*)	profiteer	< mossegar	bite, look for profit
espia (*m./f.*)	spy	< espiar	spy
guia (*m./f.*)	guide	< guiar	guide
llepa (*m./f.*)	bootlicker	< llepar	lick
pispa (*m./f.*)	pickpocket	< pispar	pinch, steal

Just as **consueta** and **paleta** (see above) are applied both to the objects and the persons who habitually use them, so nouns denoting performers may also be derived directly from the name (feminine noun) of the musical instruments they play:

viola (*m./f.*)	viola player	trompeta (*m./f.*)	trumpeter
trompa (*m./f.*)	horn player	flauta (*m./f.*)	flautist
corneta (*m./f.*)	bugler		

Compound nouns

A compound noun which denotes a human can be used in the same form as either masculine or feminine, whatever its structure, or whatever the underlying gender of any noun(s) it contains. For example:

un/una adobacadires	a person who repairs chairs
un/una guardabarrera	a level-crossing gate keeper
un/una llepafils	a fussy eater
un/una mastegaparaules	a person who talks with their mouth closed
un/una portaveu	a spokesperson
un/una somiatruites	a dreamer
un/una tastaolletes	a dilettante

Similarly:

pell-roja (*m./f.*)	redskin	pocatraça (*m./f.*)	bungler
setciències (*m./f.*)	know-all	plats-i-olles (*m./f.*)	crockery seller
malànima (*m./f.*)	villain	vetesifils (*m./f.*)	haberdasher
passavolant (*m./f.*)	occasional customer	capicausa (*m./f.*)	instigator
		etc.	

Nouns in -aire

The common agent suffix -**aire** is invariable, for example:

captaire (*m./f.*)	beggar	terrissaire (*m./f.*)	potter	etc.

Nouns in -ant, -ent

The vast majority of nouns referring to humans ending in -ant or -ent are also invariable, such as:

gerent (*m./f.*)	manager	**vianant** (*m./f.*)	pedestrian
televident (*m./f.*)	(television) viewer	etc.	

A couple of dozen do form feminines in -a however. These feminines are:

-ant

acompanyanta	companion, accompanist	**dibuixanta**	draughtsman, designer
ajudanta	assistant	**estadanta**	resident
berganta	rascal	**estudianta**	student
comedianta	comedian, hypocrite	**figuranta**	walk-on part
		geganta	giantess
comercianta	trader	**infanta**	princess
congreganta	member of congregation	**santa**	saint
		viatjanta	traveller

-ent

aprenenta	apprentice	**parenta**	relative
assistenta	attendant, social worker	**presidenta**	president
clienta	client	**pretendenta**	pretender, claimant, suitor
dependenta	shop assistant	**regenta**	manager
intendenta	supervisor	**serventa**	servant

Nouns in -al, -ar, -ble

The majority of nouns ending in stressed -al, -ar, or -ble are also invariable, such as: **el/la corresponsal** '(newspaper) correspondent', **esquimal** 'Eskimo', **el/la rival** 'rival', etc.; **auxiliar** 'assistant', **balear** 'native of the Balearic islands', **escolar** '(primary-school) pupil', etc.; **comptable** 'accountant', **doble** 'double', **noble** 'noble', etc. There are only a few exceptions where -a is added to these endings to make a feminine, namely:

-al

col·legiala	(secondary) schoolgirl	**manescala**	vet
		menestrala	artisan
generala	mother superior; general's wife	**mariscala**	wife of marshal or major-general
majorala	steward, overseer	**oficiala**	official, clerk

-ar

avara   miser

-ble

deixebla   disciple, student   condeixebla   fellow student

Other nouns of common gender, denoting humans

The number of other common gender human nouns is not large; the following is a fairly comprehensive list:

afí (*m./f.*)	relation by marriage	hindú (*m./f.*)	Hindu
almohade (*m./f.*)	Almohad(e)	ianqui (*m./f.*)	yankee
almoràvit (*m./f.*)	Almoravid(e)	intèrpret (*m./f.*)	interpreter
amateur (*m./f.*)	amateur	iogui (*m./f.*)	yogi
àrab (*m./f.*)	Arab	jove (*m./f.*)	young man/ woman
artífex (*m./f.*)	craftsman, artificer	lladre (*m./f.*)	thief
banau (*m./f.*)	nincompoop, sucker	manxú (*m./f.*)	Manchu
		màrtir (*m./f.*)	martyr
bengalí (*m./f.*)	Bengali	miop (*m./f.*)	short-sighted person
berber (*m./f.*)	Berber		
bus (*m./f.*)	diver	model (*m./f.*)	model
cafre (*m./f.*)	brutal person	mossàrab (*m./f.*)	Mozarab
cap (*m./f.*)	head, chief	mudèjar (*m./f.*)	Mudejar
còmplice (*m./f.*)	accomplice	muladí (*m./f.*)	(descendant of Hispano-gothic convert to Islam)
cònjuge (*m./f.*)	spouse		
conserge (*m./f.*)	concierge		
consort (*m./f.*)	consort		
contralt (*m./f.*)	contralto, alto	muslim (*m./f.*)	Muslim
daixonses (*m./f.*)	so-and-so	negroide (*m./f.*)	negroid
dallonses (*m./f.*)	so-and-so	nyau-nyau or nyeu-nyeu (*m./f.*)	hypocrite
esnob (*m./f.*)	snob		
etíop (*m./f.*)	Ethiopian	nyicris (*m./f.*)	weakling
extraterrestre (*m./f.*)	extraterrestrial	orfebre (*m./f.*)	goldsmith
fan (*m./f.*)	fan	papú (*m./f.*)	Papuan
golafre (*m./f.*)	glutton	partícip (*m./f.*)	participant, partaker
hemeralop (*m./f.*)	sufferer from day blindness		
		pilot (*m./f.*)	pilot
nictalop (*m./f.*)	sufferer from night blindness	ramarol (*m./f.*)	fidget
		rebel (*m./f.*)	rebel
		repòrter (*m./f.*)	reporter
heretge (*m./f.*)	heretic	salvatge (*m./f.*)	savage

sequaç(*m./f.*)	follower, partisan	**testimoni** (*m./f.*)	witness
	(Note *f.pl.* is	**tiple** (*m./f.*)	treble, soprano
	sequaces)	**víking** (*m./f.*)	Viking
soprano (*m./f.*)	soprano	**zulu** (*m./f.*)	Zulu

1.1.6   NOUNS OF FIXED GENDER

A very few nouns referring to people are of fixed gender, that is, they retain the same form and grammatical gender whether a male or a female is referred to. Some (i) are basic nouns; others (ii) are terms applied metaphorically to humans, as are (iii) titles of address.

(i)	**bebè** (*m.*)	baby	**persona** (*f.*)	person
	criatura (*f.*)	baby	**personatge** (*m.*)	character, personage
	individu (*m.*)	individual	**víctima** (*f.*)	victim
(ii)	**àngel** (*m.*)	angel	**geni** (*m.*)	genius
	celebritat (*f.*)	celebrity	**patum** (*f.*)	celebrity
	desastre (*m.*)	disaster	**visita** (*f.*)	visitor
	estrella (*f.*)	star		
(iii)	**altesa** (*f.*)	Highness	**majestat** (*f.*)	Majesty
	eminència (*f.*)	Eminence	**santedat** (*f.*)	Holiness
	excel·lència (*f.*)	Excellency	**senyoria** (*f.*)	Lordship

When these terms are applied to a human whose biological gender is known, the agreement of a predicative adjective or pronoun will typically follow the biological gender: **Sa santedat el Papa està malalt** 'His Holiness the Pope is ill', **Ses alteses reials els prínceps estan molt complaguts del viatge** 'Their Royal Highnesses the Prince and Princess are very pleased with their trip', **Quina criatura! Que és petit!** 'What a (nice) baby! How small he is!', but **Les víctimes foren hospitalitzades** 'The victims (sex unknown) were taken to hospital'.

1.1.7   GENDER OF ANIMAL NAMES

For the most part, only familiar or domestic animals and birds have separate forms for the male and the female of the species. Some of these, where the masculine and feminine words are unrelated, such as **cavall** (*m.*) 'horse', 'stallion', **egua** (*f.*) 'mare', have been mentioned above (**1.1.4**). Those where the masculine form is derived from the feminine with the suffix -**ot** were listed at **1.1.3**, and feminines with special suffixes at **1.1.2**. The remaining cases of animal names where a regularly formed masculine and feminine pair exists are these:

ànec (*m.*)	**ànega** (*f.*)	duck
cérvol (*m.*)	**cérvola** (*f.*)	stag/doe
colom (*m.*)	**coloma** (*f.*)	pigeon, dove

conill (*m.*)	conilla (*f.*)	rabbit
elefant (*m.*)	elefanta (*f.*)	elephant
garrí (*m.*)	garrina (*f.*)	piglet
gat (*m.*)	gata (*f.*)	cat
gos (*m.*)	gossa (*f.*)	dog/bitch
jònec (*m.*)	jònega (*f.*)	bovine under two years old
lleó (*m.*)	lleona (*f.*)	lion/lioness
lleopard (*m.*)	lleoparda (*f.*)	leopard
llop (*m.*)	lloba (*f.*)	wolf
mul (*m.*)	mula (*f.*)	mule
ós (*m.*)	óssa (*f.*)	bear
paó (*m.*) or pavó (*m.*)	paona (*f.*) pavona (*f.*)	peacock/peahen
poll (*m.*)	polla (*f.*)	chick, chicken (not **poll** (*m.*) 'louse')
pollí (*m.*)	pollina (*f.*)	young ass
porcell (*m.*)	porcella (*f.*)	piglet
primal (*m.*)	primala (*f.*)	sheep or goat between one and two years old
ruc (*m.*)	ruca (*f.*)	ass
vedell (*m.*)	vedella (*f.*)	calf (under one year old)
xai (*m.*)	xaia (*f.*)	lamb

A few apparent gender pairs may be misleading. The masculine and feminine words either denote different creatures, or are used equivalently, without regard to biological gender:

cuc (*m.*)	worm, maggot	cuca (*f.*)	bug, insect
llagost (*m.*)	locust	llagosta (*f.*)	1 locust (= **llagost**), 2 grasshopper, 3 lobster
falcillot (*m.*)		= falcilla (*f.*)	swift
granot (*m.*)		= granota (*f.*)	frog
rat (*m.*)		= rata (*f.*)	rat
talp (*m.*)		= talpa (*f.*)	mole

If you want to distinguish the sex of any other animal you add **mascle** 'male' or **femella** 'female' to the invariable noun, for example, **un lloro mascle** 'a male parrot', **un lloro femella** 'a female parrot', **una rata mascle** 'a male rat', **una rata femella** 'a female rat'.

1.2 GENDER OF NOUNS REFERRING TO NON-DOMESTIC ANIMALS AND INANIMATE OBJECTS

The grammatical gender of nouns referring to non-domestic animals and inanimate objects or concepts is largely unpredictable on semantic grounds alone. From the phonological or orthographic form, though, it is often possible to infer what the gender will be. As a broad generalization, we can say that nouns ending in unstressed -a are feminine; the rest are masculine. However, there is a significant number of exceptions, on both sides; some guidance can be given on these, in terms of form, meaning, or structure.

1.2.1 NOUNS ENDING IN -a

Most nouns ending in unstressed -a are feminine. As seen above, the affix -a is also the major one used to derive feminine nouns and adjectives from masculine ones. Thus:

capsa (*f.*)	little box	**França** (*f.*)	France
història (*f.*)	history, story	**Tarragona** (*f.*)	Tarragona
cama (*f.*)	leg		

Curiously, feminine names of towns, cities, and countries are preceded by invariant **tot** 'all', **mig** 'half' rather than the feminine forms **tota**, **mitja**: **tot Catalunya** 'all Catalonia', **Mig Girona va quedar a les fosques** 'Half Girona was in darkness'.

1.2.1.1 Nouns ending in -ma

But many nouns ending in -ma are masculine (mostly words borrowed from Greek, often with the same or similar form in English). For example:

drama (*m.*)	drama
melodrama (*m.*)	melodrama

Specifically, all those ending in -**grama** are masculine, such as:

anagrama (*m.*)	anagram	**programa** (*m.*)	programme,
diagrama (*m.*)	diagram		program
epigrama (*m.*)	epigram	etc.	

And all those ending in -**orama** are masculine, such as:

panorama (*m.*)	panorama
etc.	

Most of those of three or more syllables ending in -**ema** are masculine, such as:

cinema (*m.*)	cinema	**estratagema** (*m.*)	stratagem
dilema (*m.*)	dilemma	**poema** (*m.*)	poem
emblema (*m.*)	emblem	**problema** (*m.*)	problem
ènema (*m.*)	enema	etc.	
esquema (*m.*)	outline, draft		

But half a dozen in -**ema** are feminine, of which **diadema** (*f.*) 'diadem' and **verema** (*f.*) 'grape harvest' are reasonably common.

Those ending in **-gma** are mostly masculine, such as:

diafragma (*m.*)	diaphragm	**estigma** (*m.*)	stigma
paradigma (*m.*)	paradigm	**dogma** (*m.*)	dogma
enigma (*m.*)	enigma	etc.	

but **flegma** 'phlegm' is feminine.

Those of three or more syllables in **-oma** are mostly masculine, such as:

axioma (*m.*)	axiom	**idioma** (*m.*)	language
carcinoma (*m.*)	carcinoma	**símptoma** (*m.*)	symptom
diploma (*m.*)	diploma	etc.	

But feminine are: **aroma** (*f.*) 'aroma', **coloma** (*f.*) '(female) dove', 'pigeon', **majordoma** (*f.*) '(female) house keeper', **maroma** (*f.*) 'thick rope', **paloma** (*f.*) 'parasol mushroom'.

Most of those ending in **-sma** are masculine (mostly technical), such as:

cisma (*m.*)	schism	**plasma** (*m.*)	plasma
fantasma (*m.*)	phantom	**prisma** (*m.*)	prism
miasma (*m.*)	miasma	etc.	

But several in **-sma** are feminine, namely:

asma (*f.*)	asthma	**maresma** (*f.*)	salt marsh
esma (*f.*)	instinct	**morisma** (*f.*)	Moorish crowd
desesma (*f.*)	dismay	**onosma** (*f.*)	saxifrage
cinquagesma (*f.*)	quinquagesima	**xusma** (*f.*)	rabble
quaresma (*f.*)	Lent		

Of those ending in **-auma** or **-euma**, **trauma** 'trauma', **reuma** 'rheumatism' and a number of technical words are masculine; but **catabauma** 'den' and **fleuma** 'ribbonfish' are feminine.

Of those ending in **-erma**, **derma** 'corium' and words derived from it are masculine. **Esperma** 'sperm' is feminine, as are **angiosperma** and **centrosperma**; however **episperma** and other compounds of **-sperma** are masculine.

1.2.1.2   The suffix -cida

The suffix **-cida** '-cide' is masculine if it refers to a product. (It has regular common gender when it denotes humans, as in **suïcida** '(person who commits) suicide'):

herbicida (*m.*)	weed killer	**raticida** (*m.*)	rat poison
insecticida (*m.*)	insecticide	etc.	

1.2.1.3   Unexpected masculine nouns in -a

There are a few other non-human nouns ending in -a which are of masculine gender. Firstly some exotic animals:

equidna (*m.*)	spiny anteater	**puma** (*m.*)	puma
goril·la (*m.*)	gorilla	**tamàndua** (*m.*)	lesser anteater
llama (*m.*)	llama		

The remainder are semantically miscellaneous:

abracadabra (*m.*)	abracadabra	**hosanna** (*m.*)	Hosanna
		ioga (*m.*)	yoga
afores (*m.pl.*)	outskirts	**mapa** (*m.*)	map
al·leluia (*m.*)	Hallelujah/Alleluia	**nirvana** (*m.*)	nirvana
bocabarra (*m.*)	cavity in windlass for inserting lever	**passa-passa** (*m.*)	sleight of hand
		pijama (*m.*)	pyjamas;
clima (*m.*)	climate		Neapolitan
còlera (*m.*)	cholera		ice-cream
cometa (*m.*)	comet	**planeta** (*m.*)	planet
cremallera (*m.*)	rack railway	**quilowatt-hora** (*m.*)	kilowatt-hour
delta (*m.*)	delta		
dia (*m.*)	day	**terra** (*m.*)	ground, floor
migdia (*m.*)	midday	**titella** (*m.*)	puppet
gàmeta (*m.*)	gamete	**tramvia** (*m.*)	tram
glòria (*m.*)	the Gloria (of the Mass) (**glòria** otherwise feminine)	**visca** (*m.*)	cheer, cry of '*visca!*'

1.2.2   GENDER OF NOUNS ENDING OTHER THAN IN -a

Nouns which end in anything except unstressed -a are typically masculine, for example: **ferro** (*m.*) 'iron', **sofà** (*m.*) 'sofa', **gra** (*m.*) 'grain', **judici** (*m.*) 'judgement', **mitjó** (*m.*) 'sock', **segle** (*m.*) 'century', **te** (*m.*) 'tea', **tipus** (*m.*) 'type', **tret** (*m.*) 'feature', and so on.

1.2.2.1.   Feminines in -o

The ending -o is regarded as a prototypically masculine one: in fact it occurs as a specific masculine gender marker in certain nouns and adjectives like **amo** (*m.*) 'master', **maco** (*m.*) 'handsome', 'pretty', **fondo** (*m.*) 'deep', and in masculine noun and adjective plurals like **discos** 'records', **feliços** 'happy (*m.pl.*)'. There are very few feminine nouns ending in -o: the following is a complete list:

dinamo (*f.*)	dynamo	**foto** (*f.*)	photo	**Gestapo** (*f.*)	Gestapo

libido (*f.*)	libido	**pòlio** (*f.*)	polio	**soprano** (*f.*)	soprano
magneto (*f.*)	magneto	**ràdio** (*f.*)	radio	**Unesco** (*f.*)	Unesco
moto (*f.*)	motorbike				

1.2.2.2   Typical feminine endings other than -a

There are a score or so of word endings other than -a which are nearly always feminine (V stands for any vowel, C for any consonant): **-tud**, **-VCide**, **-ie**, **-cele**, **-ole**, **-si** (not -ssi), **-xi**, **-ció**, **-nió**, **-sió**, **-tió**, **-xió**, **-lis**, **-tis**, **-edat**, **-etat**, **-itat**, **-ltat**. Words with these endings are nearly always abstract nouns. Where there are exceptions, the words which are masculine, despite these endings, tend to be concrete nouns. We give a couple of examples of each:

-tud

altitud (*f.*)	altitude	**inquietud** (*f.*)	worry

etc. (no exceptions)

-VCide

piràmide (*f.*)	pyramid	**probòscide** (*f.*)	proboscis

etc. (two exceptions: **àpside** (*m.*) 'apsis', **ràfide** (*m.*) 'raphide')

-ie

sèrie (*f.*)	series	**superfície** (*f.*)	surface

etc. (no exceptions)

-cele

hidrocele (*f.*)	hydrocele	**varicocele** (*f.*)	varicocele

etc. (no exceptions)

-ole

hipèrbole (*f.*)	hyperbole	**prole** (*f.*)	progeny

etc. (no exceptions)

-si (not -ssi)

catarsi (*f.*)	catharsis	**hipòtesi** (*f.*)	hypothesis
dosi (*f.*)	dose		

etc. (nine exceptions: **cesi** (*m.*) 'caesium', **dicasi** (*m.*) 'dichasium', **èxtasi** (*m.*) 'ecstasy', **Gènesi** (*m.*) '(the book of) Genesis', **indusi** (*m.*) 'indusium', **magnesi** (*m.*) 'magnesium', **oasi** (*m.*) 'oasis', **parèntesi** (*m.*) 'parenthesis', 'round bracket', **prasi** (*m.*) 'prase')

-xi

profilaxi (*f.*)	prophylaxis	**sintaxi** (*f.*)	syntax

etc. (one exception: **taxi** (*m.*) 'taxi')

-ció

> **acció** (*f.*)   action, share   **nació** (*f.*)   nation
> etc. (very numerous, but there is one exception: **alció** (*m.*) 'halcyon', 'kingfisher')

-nió

> **unió** (*f.*)   union   **comunió** (*f.*)   communion
> etc. (one exception: **anió** (*m.*) 'anion')

-sió

> **concessió** (*f.*)   award   **inclusió** (*f.*)   inclusion
> etc. (very numerous, no exceptions)

-tió

> **digestió** (*f.*)   digestion   **qüestió** (*f.*)   question, issue
> etc. (four exceptions: **bastió** (*m.*) 'bastion', **catió** (*m.*) 'cation', **llantió** (*m.*) 'fairy light', **tió** (*m.*) 'burning log')

-xió

> **reflexió** (*f.*)   reflection   **connexió** (*f.*)   connection
> etc. (no exceptions)

-lis

> **bilis** (*f.*)   bile   **sífilis** (*f.*)   syphilis
> etc. (four exceptions: **melis** (*m.*) (a kind of resinous pinewood), **pròpolis** (*m.*) 'propolis', 'bee glue', **rosolis** (*m.*) 'rosolio', **xeflis** (*m.*) 'feast')

-tis

> **diabetis** (*f.*)   diabetes   **artritis** (*f.*)   arthritis
> and many others, mostly inflammations or diseases. (There are five exceptions: **cutis** (*m.*) 'cutis', 'complexion', **frontis** (*m.*) 'façade', **hidrastis** (*m.*) 'hydrastis', **mutis** (*m.*) '(stage) exit', **plumetis** (*m.*) (type of cotton cloth).

-edat

> **netedat** (*f.*)   cleanness   **fosquedat** (*f.*)   darkness
> etc. (three exceptions: **emparedat** (*m.*) 'sandwich (British style)', **refredat** (*m.*) 'cold' (affliction), **vedat** (*m.*) 'preserve')

-etat

> **varietat** (*f.*)   variety   **seguretat** (*f.*)   security

etc. (three exceptions: **acetat** (*m.*) 'acetate', **emboetat** (*m.*) 'tongue-and-groove boarding', **empaquetat** (*m.*) 'pack(ag)ing')

-itat

meitat (*f.*)   half   **veritat** (*f.*)   truth

etc., very numerous examples, largely abstract nouns derived from adjectives: e.g. **intensitat** 'intensity', **impossibilitat** 'impossibility'. (There are five exceptions: **acolitat** (*m.*) 'rank of acolyte', **hàbitat** (*m.*) 'habitat', **palmitat** (*m.*) 'palmitate', **precipitat** (*m.*) 'precipitate', **recitat** (*m.*) 'recitative'.)

-ltat

lleialtat (*f.*)   loyalty   **facultat** (*f.*)   faculty

etc. (one exception: **resultat** (*m.*) 'result')

1.2.2.3   Less predictable endings

Certain other frequent word endings are less predictably assignable to one gender or the other.

Nouns in -al

There are some 340 nouns ending in **-al**, of which 77 per cent are masculine. Among the commonest feminine ones are:

canal (*f.*)	channel, gutter, and see **1.2.4**.	**espiral** (*f.*)	spiral
capital (*f.*)	capital (city), and see **1.2.4**.	**moral** (*f.*)	morality
		postal (*f.*)	postcard
		sal (*f.*)	salt
catedral (*f.*)	cathedral	**sucursal** (*f.*)	branch (office)
central (*f.*)	head office, power station	**terminal** (*f.*)	terminal building
		vocal (*f.*)	vowel, and see **1.2.4**
editorial (*f.*)	publisher, publishing house, and see **1.2.4**.	etc.	

Nouns in -oide

There are in the *Diccionari General de la Llengua Catalana* about fifty-six nouns, of a technical nature, ending in **-oide** of which about 75 per cent are masculine, including **cel·luloide** (*m.*) 'celluloid' and **solenoide** (*m.*) 'solenoid'. Among the feminines are **hemorroide** (*f.*) 'haemorrhoid' and **sinusoide** (*f.*) 'sine curve'. (**-oide** is also an adjective ending; many **-oide** nouns are substantivized adjectives, for example, with ellipsis of the head noun whose identity (or gender) may no longer be evident.)

Nouns in -or

The gender of the numerous nouns with two or more syllables ending in -**or** depends to a considerable extent on their meaning or derivation.

(i)   Nouns ending in -**or** denoting animals or concrete objects are for the most part masculine: **castor** (*m.*) 'beaver', **decor** (*m.*) 'decor', 'decoration', **encenedor** (*m.*) 'lighter', **licor** (*m.*) 'liqueur', **motor** (*m.*) 'motor', 'engine', **obrador** (*m.*) 'workbench', **païdor** (*m.*) 'stomach', **retrovisor** (*m.*) 'rear-view mirror', **tambor** (*m.*) 'drum', **tumor** (*m.*) 'tumour', **voltor** (*m.*) 'vulture', and so on.

But three concrete nouns in -**or** are feminine:

llavor (*f.*)	seed	**volior** (*f.*)	flock of birds in flight
llacor (*f.*)	sludge		

(ii)   Abstract nouns derived from verb stems with the suffix -**or** are feminine, for example:

escalfor (*f.*)	warmth (from **escalfar** 'warm')
picor (*f.*)	itch (from **picar** 'itch')
pudor (*f.*)	stink (from **pudir** 'stink')
suor (*f.*)	sweat (from **suar** 'sweat')
tardor (*f.*)	autumn (from **tardar** 'be late')
coïssor (*f.*)	burning feeling (irregular derivative of **coure** 'sting', 'burn')

etc.

There are a few exceptions: **tremolor** (*m.*) 'trembling' is masculine (cf. **tremolar** 'tremble'); **clamor** (*m.* or *f.*) 'shout', 'outcry' (cf. **clamar**), **temor** (*m.* or *f.*) 'fear' (cf. **témer**), **valor** (*m.* or *f.*) 'value' (cf. **valer**) resemble the more usual non-derived abstract -**or** nouns (see v(c) below) in being usually masculine, though they may also be feminine.

(iii)   Likewise, abstract nouns derived from adjectives with the suffix -**or** are feminine:

claror (*f.*)	light (from **clar**)
dolçor (*f.*)	sweetness (from **dolç**)
frescor (*f.*)	freshness (from **fresc**)
morenor (*f.*)	darkness of complexion (from **moreno/morè**)

etc.

(iv)   There are also a few such feminine abstract nouns derived from other nouns:

avior (*f.*)	ancestry, antiquity (from **avi** 'grandfather')
bafor or **bavor** (*f.*)	whiff (from **baf** '(bad) breath')
borinor (*f.*)	distant thunder, hum (from **borinot** 'bumble bee')
germanor (*f.*)	brotherhood (from **germà** 'brother')
verinor (*f.*)	poisonousness (from **verí** 'poison')

(v)   Non-derived abstract nouns ending in -or fall into three groups:

(a) A few are always masculine:

enyor (*m.*)	longing	**pudor** (*m.*)	shame (not = **pudor** (*f.*) 'stink')
factor (*m.*)	factor	**vector** (*m.*)	vector

(b) Several are always feminine; these include words which denote smells (mostly unpleasant), and words associated with atmospheric heat:

bovor (*f.*)	sultriness, stuffiness	**olor** (*f.*)	smell
calor (*f.*)	heat	**xafogor** (*f.*)	closeness, sultriness
fetor (*f.*)	putrid smell	**xardor** (*f.*)	stifling heat
fortor (*f.*)	stench		

and the following miscellaneous ones:

albor (*f.*)	whiteness, dawn light (not = **albor** (*m.*) (a freshwater fish))	**resplendor** (*f.*)	radiance
		rabior (*f.*)	itch, stinging
		bonior (*f.*)	buzz, hum
		remor (*f.*)	murmur, rustle
esplendor (*f.*)	splendour	**torpor** (*f.*)	torpor

(c) The third group includes some very common abstract nouns, which may be feminine, but are predominantly masculine in current prose usage:

amor (*m./f.*)	love	**furor** (*m./f.*)	fury
desamor (*m./f.*)	indifference	**honor** (*m./f.*)	honour
ardor (*m./f.*)	zeal	**horror** (*m./f.*)	horror
candor (*m./f.*)	candour, guilelessness	**humor** (*m./f.*)	humour
		rancor (*m./f.*)	rancour, grudge
color (*m./f.*)	colour	**rigor** (*m./f.*)	rigour
dolor (*m./f.*)	pain	**rubor** (*m./f.*)	blush
error (*m./f.*)	error	**rumor** (*m./f.*)	rumour
estridor (*m./f.*)	raucousness	**sabor** (*m./f.*)	taste
estupor (*m./f.*)	stupor	**dessabor** (*m./f.*)	tastelessness
favor (*m./f.*)	favour	**sopor** (*m./f.*)	drowsiness
desfavor (*m./f.*)	disagreeableness	**terror** (*m./f.*)	terror
fervor (*m./f.*)	fervour	**vigor** (*m./f.*)	vitality
fragor (*m./f.*)	din	(**en vigor** 'in force', 'in effect')	
fulgor (*m./f.*)	glow	**xamor** (*m./f.*)	charm

Note, with reference to abstract nouns ending in -**or**, that except in Valencian the final -**r** is usually silent in feminine nouns but pronounced in masculine ones.

1.2.2.4   Other unexpectedly feminine nouns

There remain over 250 feminine nouns which do not end in unstressed -a, and which are not covered by the principles mentioned so far (**1.2.2.1–3**). The names of the letters of the alphabet: **a, be, ce, de**, etc. are feminine, including **xeix**, the name for the letter **x** when it sounds 'sh'; likewise the letters of the Greek alphabet: **alfa** 'alpha', to **omega**. (Notes of the scale, however, are masculine: **do, re, mi**, and so on.)

The majority of the remainder of 'exceptionally feminine' nouns are everyday, or fairly common, words, though a few are technical terms from rhetoric, botany, and so on. The following list includes the commonest words, in alphabetical order.

allau or **llau**	avalanche	**enemistat**	enmity
amistat	friendship	**falç**	sickle
anemone	anemone	**fam**	hunger
arrel or **rel**	root	**fase**	phase, stage
art	art	**fe**	faith
base	basis	**febre**	fever
beixamel	bechamel	**fi**	end (not = **fi** (*m.*)
bici	bike		'objective')
bondat	goodness	**flor**	flower
breu	breve	**font**	spring, fountain
calç	lime	**frase**	phrase, clause
cançó	song	**gent**	people
carn	meat, flesh	**germandat**	fraternity,
catàstrofe	catastrophe		sisterhood
cicatriu	scar	**gla**	acorn
circular	circular	**grip** (also *m.*)	influenza
ciutat	city	**guineu**	fox
classe	class, kind	**hèlice**	spiral, propeller
clau	key (not = **clau**	**higiene**	hygiene
	(*m.*) 'nail')	**imatge**	image
clímax (also *m.*)	climax	**imperdible**	safety-pin
col	cabbage	(also *m.*)	
coliflor	cauliflower	**invariant**	invariant
consonant	consonant	**joventut**	youth
constant	constant	**lent**	lens
cort	court, sty	**llar**	home, fireplace
creu	cross	**llebre**	hare
cristiandat	Christendom	**llei**	law
dent	tooth	**llet**	milk
deu	spring, source	**llibertat**	liberty
el·lipse	ellipse	**lliçó**	lesson

llum	light (not = **llum** (*m.*) 'lamp')	**post**	plank, ironing board
mà	hand	**potestat**	authority, jurisdiction
majestat	majesty	**presó**	prison
maldat	wickedness	**processó**	(religious) procession
mar (also *m.*)	sea	**psique**	psyche
marató	marathon	**pubertat**	puberty
matriu	womb	**raó**	reason
mel	honey	**rebel·lió**	rebellion
ment	mind	**sal**	salt
mercè	favour, benefit	**salut**	health (not = **salut** (*m.*) 'greeting')
metròpoli	metropolis	**sang**	blood
molar	molar	**serp**	snake
mort	death	**set**	thirst
mortaldat	death toll	**seu**	cathedral
nau	ship	**síndrome**	syndrome
neu	snow	**son**	sleepiness
nit	night	**sort**	luck
nou	nut, walnut	**talent**	appetite (not = **talent** (*m.*) 'skill, gift')
oblivió	oblivion		
ordre	order, command	**tele**	television, telly
orfandat	orphanhood	**tempestat**	storm
paret	wall	**Tet**	(river in North Catalonia)
part	part		
patent	patent	**torre**	tower
patum	(figure representing a fabulous animal, which is paraded through the streets during popular festivals), big shot	**tos**	cough
		tribu	tribe
		vall	valley (not = **vall** (*m.*) 'trench')
		variable	variable
		variant	variant
pell	skin	**veu**	voice (note **altaveu** (*m.*) 'loudspeaker')
pelvis	pelvis		
perdiu	partridge	**virtut**	virtue
pols	dust (not = **pols** (*m.*) 'pulse')	**voluntat**	will
		voluptat	sensual pleasure
por	fear		

1.2.3   THE GENDER OF COMPOUND NOUNS

1.2.3.1   *Verb + noun compounds*

A frequent type of compound is that composed of a verb and a noun, referring to the person or animal or plant that does such-and-such, or the instrument with which it is done. The important point to bear in mind is that the gender of the compound is not normally related to the gender of the noun it contains. Those that denote humans can, as usual, be of either gender (**1.1**). The remainder are masculine, such as:

eixugamà (*m.*)	hand-towel	**portamonedes** (*m.*)	purse
enganyabadocs (*m.*)	booby-trap	**rentamans** (*m.*)	washbasin
escuradents (*m.*)	toothpick	**rentaplats** (*m.*)	dishwasher
passaport (*m.*)	passport	**xuclamel** (*m.*)	honeysuckle
picaporta (*m.*)	door-knocker	etc.	

There are a very few exceptions, in all of which the included noun element is itself feminine singular in **-a**, where the whole compound is feminine, such as:

lligacama (*f.*)	garter
tornaboda (*f.*)	celebration on the day after a wedding or holiday

1.2.3.2   The gender of endocentric compounds

If the compound is endocentric, that is, it consists of a head noun basically denoting the object in question together with a modifier (which may also be a noun), then the gender of the compound is the gender of the head noun. The head is normally the element on the left when the elements are written with a hyphen or space. In the rest, the sense is the only guide to which is the head element (indicated in italics in the examples):

camió cisterna (*m.*)	tanker lorry	**ferro*carril*** (*m.*)	railway
ciutat estat (*f.*)	city state	***fil*ferro** (*m.*)	wire
decret llei (*m.*)	order in council	***marededéu*** (*f.*)	image of the Virgin
ocell lira (*m.*)	lyre-bird	**plena*mar*** (*f.*)	high water
òpera ballet (*f.*)	opera ballet	**terra*trèmol*** (*m.*)	earthquake
paper ceba (*m.*)	onion-skin paper	**vor*avia*** (*f.*)	pavement,
planta pilot (*f.*)	pilot plant		sidewalk
***rata*pinyada** (*f.*)	bat	etc.	

The following, however, are exceptionally masculine; note that the adjectival elements fail to mark feminine agreement with **aigua** (*f.*) 'water' and **vora** (*f.*) 'edge':

aiguacuit (*m.*)	glue	**aigua-ros** (*m.*)	rose-water
aiguamoll (*m.*)	marsh	**aiguanaf** (*m.*)	orange-flower
aiguafort (*m.*)	dilute nitric acid,		water
	etching	**salfumant** (*m.*)	hydrochloric acid
aiguardent (*m.*)	eau-de-vie	**voraviu** (*m.*)	hem

1.2.3.3   Other types of compound nouns

In the case of other types of exocentric compounds (other than those in
1.2.3.1), which denote something different from what either of the individual
elements denotes, and in the case of noun + noun compounds where both
elements contribute equally to the meaning, the principle seems to be that a
compound that contains a feminine singular noun and no masculine nouns is
feminine (i), otherwise the compound is masculine (ii):

(i)				
aiguaneu (*f.*)	sleet	**coliflor** (*f.*)	cauliflower
avemaria (*f.*)	Hail Mary	**enhorabona** (*f.*)	congratulations
bonaventura (*f.*)	fortune-telling,	**giravolta** (*f.*)	turn, revolution
	palmistry	**marialluïsa** (*f.*)	lemon verbena
cama-roja (*f.*)	flamingo	etc.	

and also **semprevival** 'everlasting flower' which contains a feminine adjective but no noun.

(ii)				
adéu (*m.*)	farewell	**culdellàntia** (*m.*)	vignette
aiguapoll (*m.*)	dummy egg,	**estira-i-arronsa**	give and take
	infertile egg	(*m.*)	
capicua (*m.*)	palindromic	**forabord** (*m.*)	outboard motor
	number	**llargmetratge** (*m.*)	feature-length
cara-sol (*m.*)	part facing		film
	the sun	**no-sé-què** (*m.*)	*je-ne-sais-quoi*
colinap (*m.*)	turnip (for	**trespeus** (*m.*)	tripod
	fodder) (*f.* in	etc.	
	some sources)		

Milfulles 'yarrow', which ought to be masculine by the above principles,
is given as (*f.*) in some sources, including the Institut d'Estudis Catalans
Diccionari de la llengua catalana. The following are also unexpectedly
masculine.

bona-nit (*m.*)	goodnight	**milengrana** (*m.*)	goosefoot
cinc-en-rama (*m.*)	cinquefoil	**semprenflor** (*m.*)	alyssum

1.2.4   HOMONYMS OF DIFFERENT GENDER

There is a relatively small number of nouns which have a homonymous form
of the opposite gender, with a different meaning:

	Masculine	*Feminine*
alambor	scarp	luxuriance
albor	(freshwater fish)	dawn light
baboia	scarecrow, foolish man/boy	fib
breu	(papal) brief	breve

canal	canal	channel, gulley
capital	capital, assets	capital (city/letter)
clau	nail	key
còlera	cholera	anger
coma	coma	comma, mountain hollow
cometa	comet	(*pl.*) inverted commas
consonant	vowel rhyme	consonant
contra	organ pedal, argument against	opposition, obstacle
cremallera	rack railway	zip
delta	(river) delta	(Greek letter) delta
deu	ten	source, spring
editorial	editorial	publishing house
extra	bonus, extra item, (male) film extra	(female) film extra
fe	hay	faith
fi	objective	end
fleuma	dope, fool (male)	ribbonfish, dope, fool (female)
frau	fraud	gorge, defile
Gènesi	book of Genesis	genesis
guia	(male) guide	guidebook, guidance, (female) guide
habilitat	paymaster	skill
levita	Levite	frock coat
llama	llama	lamé
llum	lamp	light (radiation)
marieta	poof	ladybird, *Russula sanguinea* mushroom
mel	cheekbone	honey
mofeta	(male) leg-puller	(female) leg-puller, firedamp, skunk
mort	(male) dead person	death
necessitat	needy man	need, necessity
neula	(male) twit/fool	(female) twit/fool, mist, wafer
ordre	order, orderliness	command
paleta	(male) bricklayer	(female) bricklayer, trowel, palette, paddle
part	childbirth	part
pau	simpleton, mug	peace
pi	pine	pi
planeta	planet	(a person's) destiny
pols	pulse	dust
post	(military) post	plank, ironing board
pudor	shame, modesty	stink
salut	greeting	health
set	set, seven	thirst
setge	siege	figwort

son	sleep	sleepiness, desire to sleep
talent	talent	appetite
terra	ground	earth, Earth
tos	occiput	cough
vall	trench	valley
vocal	(male) committee member	(female) committee member, vowel

1.2.5 NOUNS OF VARIABLE OR DOUBTFUL GENDER

The case of some abstract nouns ending in **-or**, where either gender may be found, has been mentioned above (**1.2.2.3**). There are a few others where either gender is regarded as correct, or where the two genders are found in slightly different uses.

The following are nowadays predominantly masculine: **aglà** 'acorn' (but the alternative form **gla** is feminine), **crin** 'horsehair', **èmfasi** 'emphasis', **esfinx** 'sphinx', **pivot** 'pivot', **serpent** 'serpent'.

The following are predominantly feminine: **crisma** 'chrism', 'holy oil', **grip** 'influenza', **idus** (*f.pl.*) 'Ides', **sarment** 'vine shoot'.

For some there is no clear preference: **aviram** 'domestic fowls', **bricbarca** 'barque', **laude** 'arbitrator's decision', **vodka** 'vodka'. **Fel** 'gall', 'bile' may be feminine in Balearic and Valencian, but is masculine elsewhere.

Art is masculine in the sense 'fishing net'; in the sense 'art', 'skill' it is masculine in phrases such as **Viure bé és un art** 'Good living is an art', **el dubtós art de la guerra** 'the doubtful art of war', **exercitar un art** 'practise a skill', **art dramàtic** 'dramatic art', **art figuratiu** 'figurative art', **art grec** 'Greek art'; feminine in **belles arts** 'fine arts', **arts gràfiques** 'graphic art', **arts mecàniques** 'manual skills', **art poètica** 'Ars Poetica', 'poetics', **males arts** 'trickery'.

Mar is usually masculine in its literal sense, when occurring unqualified, as in **D'allí podíeu veure el mar** 'From there you could see the sea', **la superfície del mar** 'the surface of the sea'. But we find both **el mar Mediterrani** and **la mar Mediterrània** 'the Mediterranean'. When talking about the state of the waves or tide, **mar** is feminine: **l'estat de la mar** 'the state of the waves', **mar grossa/brava/desfeta** 'heavy sea', **mala mar** 'heavy sea', **mar calma** 'calm sea', **fer-se a la mar** 'put to sea'; and metaphorically: **una mar de/la mar de** 'a lot', 'a large quantity' as in **Vam estar la mar de contents** 'We were extremely pleased', **Estic en una mar de dubtes** 'I am in a great deal of doubt'. In Balearic **mar** is feminine in all senses.

Vessant is masculine in the sense 'valley side', but either masculine or feminine in the sense 'slope' (of roof, hillside, where rainwater runs down) and in the figurative sense 'facet' (of an issue).

1.2.6 METONYMIC GENDER

Some of the examples in previous sections illustrate instances where one noun has acquired the gender of another associated with it which has been suppressed. This pattern accounts for some apparent gender anomalies, e.g. **el Psicosi** = **el bar 'Psicosi'** (**la psicosi** 'psychosis'), **el Gran Via** = **el cine 'Gran Via'**, **una EBRO** = **una camioneta EBRO** 'an EBRO light van', **la Model** = **la presó Model** 'Model prison', **un Ibiza** = **un cotxe SEAT «Ibiza»**; **un Alella** = **un vi d'Alella** 'Alella wine', **el Barça** = **el club de futbol «Barça»** 'Barcelona FC', **el Plata** = **el riu Plata** 'the River Plate' (but note that Catalan rivers whose names end in **-a** are feminine: **la Valira, la Sènia**).

Through ellipsis of this kind names of companies are feminine: **la (companyia) SEAT, la IBM, la Hertz**; likewise roads: **la (carretera) N2, l'(autopista) A-1**.

1.2.7 GENDER OF ABBREVIATIONS AND ACRONYMS

This is determined by the gender of the head noun:

el BUP (*m.*) (**Batxillerat Unificat Polivalent**)	(approx. GCSE)
la CEE (*f.*) (**Comunitat Econòmica Europea**)	EEC
els EUA (*m.pl.*) (**Estats Units d'Amèrica**)	USA
la Fecsa (*f.*)	
(**la (companyia) Forces Elèctriques de Catalunya, SA**)	
l'IVA (*m.*) (**Impost sobre el Valor Afegit**)	VAT
l'ONU (*f.*) (**Organització de les Nacions Unides**)	UN
l'OTAN (*f.*) (**Organització del Tractat de l'Atlàntic Nord**)	NATO
ovni (*m.*) (**objecte volant no identificat**)	UFO
la SIDA (*f.*) (**Síndrome d'Immunodeficiència Adquirida**)	AIDS
la UIB (*f.*) (**Universitat de les Illes Balears**)	

When the abbreviation or acronym denotes an institution named in a foreign language, the gender either derives from an associated Catalan word if there is one, or is masculine by default: **la Unesco** 'UNESCO' (cf. **ONU** (*f.*)), **la Unicef** 'UNICEF', **l'FBI, l'IRA** (*m.*).

1.2.8 GENDER OF FOREIGN WORDS

Words borrowed from Spanish, French, Italian, and Latin typically bring with them the gender they have in the source language (with Latin neuter > Catalan masculine); words from other languages tend to be masculine, unless they are closely associated semantically with a Catalan word which is feminine. Even so there are some anomalies. The following examples are taken from Terenci Moix's novel *Lleonard, o el sexe dels àngels* (1992): *allure* (*f.*), *alma mater* (*f.*), *aloha* (*m.*), *best-seller* (*m.*), *blue-jeans* (*m.*) de

color blanc 'white jeans', ***boom*** (*m.*), ***boutade*** (*f.*), ***cassette*** (*m.*) 'cassette recorder', ***charme*** (*m.*), ***contestazione*** (*f.*), **les** *élites* (*f.pl.*), ***entente cordiale*** (*f.*), ***flipper*** (*m.*) 'pin-ball machine', ***kitsch*** (*m.*), ***knack*** (*m.*), ***els mass media*** (*m.pl.*), ***milieu*** (*m.*), ***minishorts*** (*m.*), ***modus vivendi*** (*m.*), ***no-man's land*** (*f.*), ***ñángara*** (*m.*) 'guerrilla fighter', ***partouze*** (*m.*) 'orgy', ***puente del diálogo*** (*m.*) 'bridge of discussion', ***sancta sanctorum*** (*m.*), ***trattoria*** (*f.*), ***travelling*** (*m.*) 'pan shot'.

2 PLURAL OF NOUNS AND FORMATION OF DERIVED NOUNS

In **2.1** and **2.2**. we discuss plural formation and the use of plurals. Section **2.3** introduces diminutive, augmentative, and evaluative suffixes in nouns, especially those that are productive. Some orthographic features mentioned at various points in this chapter are summarized in Chapter 37.

2.1 PLURAL FORMATION

There are five, related, patterns for forming the plural of nouns (and adjectives) in Catalan. These are (i) the addition of **-s** to the singular form (the predominant pattern), (ii) the replacement of final **-a** by **-es**, (iii) the addition of **-ns**, (iv) the addition of **-os**, (v) invariable form (plural identical with singular). Pattern (iv), the addition of **-os**, is unique to masculine nouns; the other patterns are found with nouns of both genders.

2.1.1 BASIC PLURAL FORMATION RULE

The normal pattern for words which end in a consonant or semiconsonant (other than **-ç**, **-s**, or **-x**), or an unstressed vowel (other than **-a**), consists in the addition of the suffix **-s**. (Words which end in **-ig**, **-sc**, **-st**, or **-xt** optionally follow this pattern; see below **2.1.5.4**.)

ou → ous	eggs	**crisi → crisis**	crises
got → gots	tumblers	**moto → motos**	motorbikes
arbre → arbres	trees	etc.	

Nouns which end in unstressed **-en** require the addition of a written accent in the plural, e.g. **examen → exàmens** 'examinations', **fenomen → fenòmens** 'phenomena', **origen → orígens** 'origins' (see **37.5.1**).

2.1.2 PLURAL OF WORDS ENDING IN -a

Words which end in unstressed **-a** in the singular replace this with **-es** in the plural. There are some consequential regular orthographic changes when the stem ends in **-c-**, **-ç-**, **-g-**, **-gu-**, **-j-**, or **-qu-** (see **37.3**).

cama → cames	legs		psicòloga →	(female)
fantasma →			psicòlogues	psychologists
fantasmes	phantoms		llengua → llengües	tongues
idea → idees	ideas		taronja → taronges	oranges
papa → papes	popes		platja → platges	beaches
taula → taules	tables		pasqua → pasqües	Christmas
boca → boques	mouths			period
plaça → places	squares, places		etc.	

2.1.3 PLURAL OF WORDS ENDING IN A STRESSED VOWEL

Most nouns that end in a stressed vowel (for historical reasons) add -ns in the plural (losing any written accent; a diaeresis will be required over syllabic -i- preceded by another vowel).

cinturó → cinturons	belts		pi → pins	pines
do → dons	gifts		veí → veïns	neighbours
mà → mans	hands			

Names of the letters of the alphabet, and notes of the scale (music), are exceptions, which add just -s: bes 'Bs', kas 'Ks', dos 'Cs', etc. Likewise, grammatical words: perquè/perquès 'whys'/'reasons', sís 'yeses', nos 'noes', peròs 'buts'. There are around a hundred other exceptions which add -s only, the great majority of them words borrowed from other languages and which usually have a similar form in English. The following list includes the indigenous examples, and the commonest of the rest, grouped according to the final vowel.

lilà	*pl.* lilàs	lilac
mamà	*pl.* mamàs	mum
panamà	*pl.* panamàs	Panama hat
papà	*pl.* papàs	dad
rajà	*pl.* rajàs	rajah
sofà	*pl.* sofàs	sofa
tarannà	*pl.* tarannàs	character
xa	*pl.* xas	shah

abecé	*pl.* abecés	ABC, *pl.* = rudiments
calé (fam.)	usually used in *pl.* calés	lolly, cash
clixé	*pl.* clixés	photographic plate, cliché
consomé	*pl.* consomés	consommé
pagaré	*pl.* pagarés	promissory note
peroné	*pl.* peronés	fibula
plaqué	*pl.* plaqués	gold or silver plate

puré	*pl.* purés	purée
quinqué	*pl.* quinqués	oil lamp
ximpanzé	*pl.* ximpanzés	chimpanzee
bebè	*pl.* bebès	baby
cafè	*pl.* cafès	coffee
canapè	*pl.* canapès	couch
comitè	*pl.* comitès	committee
fe	*pl.* fes	faith
mercè	*pl.* mercès	reward, favour; (plural also = thanks)
oboè	*pl.* oboès	oboe
bengalí	*pl.* bengalís	Bengali
bisturí	*pl.* bisturís	scalpel
esquí	*pl.* equís	ski
frenesí	*pl.* frenesís	frenzy
juí (Val.)	*pl.* juís	judgement
perjuí (Val.)	*pl.* perjuís	damage
dominó	*pl.* dominós	mask, disguise
rondó	*pl.* rondós	rondo
pro	*pl.* pros	pro, argument for
bambú	*pl.* bambús	bamboo
hindú	*pl.* hindús	Hindu
menú	*pl.* menús	table d'hôte menu
nyu	*pl.* nyus	gnu
tabú	*pl.* tabús	taboo
tatú	*pl.* tatús	armadillo

2.1.4   PLURAL OF WORDS ENDING IN UNSTRESSED -e

In Valencian, NW Catalan, and some other areas (Ibiza, Alghero) a few
words that end in unstressed -e may form plurals in -ns (entailing a written
accent on the stressed syllable). **Hòmens** and **jóvens** are well established in
standard Valencian.

home	Val/NW *pl.* hòmens, elsewhere homes	man
jove	Val/NW *pl.* jóvens, elsewhere joves	youth
ase	Val/NW *pl.* àsens or, as elsewhere, ases	ass
cove	Val/NW *pl.* còvens or, as elsewhere, coves	conical basket
freixe	Val/NW *pl.* fréixens or, as elsewhere, freixes	ash tree
marge	Val/NW *pl.* màrgens or, as elsewhere, marges	edge, margin
orfe	Val/NW *pl.* òrfens or, as elsewhere, orfes	(male) orphan

rave	Val/NW *pl.* **ràvens** or, as elsewhere, **raves**	radish
terme	Val/NW *pl.* **térmens** or, as elsewhere, **termes**	boundary, term
verge	Val/NW *pl.* **vèrgens** or, as elsewhere, **verges**	virgin

2.1.5 PLURAL OF NOUNS ENDING IN -ç, -s, -x; -sc, -st, -xt; -ig

2.1.5.1 Feminine nouns

Feminine nouns ending in -s are invariable: **les tos** 'the coughs', **les càries** 'the caries (*pl.*)', **les ics** 'the Xs', etc. Feminine nouns ending in one of the other letters or sequences mentioned add -s in the regular way (though the **s** is silent after -ç or -x): **les falçs** 'the sickles', **les xeixs** 'the Xs', **les hèlixs** 'the spirals', **les larinxs** 'the larynxes', **les posts** 'the planks', **les forests**, 'the forests', etc.

2.1.5.2 Plural of masculine nouns ending in -s or -x (unstressed)

Masculine nouns ending in -s or -x whose final syllable is unstressed follow the rule just given for feminines: **un atles** 'an atlas': **els atles** 'the atlases', **divendres** 'Friday': **els divendres** 'the Fridays', and so on for **Adonis** 'Adonis', **clítoris** 'clitoris', **albatros** 'albatross', **termos** 'thermos flask', **síl·labus** 'syllabus', **focus** 'spotlight', **fòrceps** 'forceps'; **índex** 'index': **índexs** 'indices', 'indexes', **apèndix** 'appendix': **apèndixs** 'appendices', **càrritx** 'reed': **càrritxs** 'reeds', etc. (Before a spelling reform of 1984 some masculine words were written with unstressed -as in the singular, but with -es in the plural, such as **atlas** 'atlas', **galimatias** 'nonsense', **Judas** 'Judas', **pàncreas** 'pancreas'; the reform introduced invariable -es into all such words.)

2.1.5.3 Plural of masculine nouns ending in -ç, -s, or -x (stressed)

Masculine nouns whose stressed final syllable ends in -ç, -s, or -x add -os in the plural. (Written accents indicating stress will be suppressed.) Thus:

braç	*pl.* **braços**	arm	despatx	*pl.* **despatxos**	office
calaix	*pl.* **calaixos**	drawer	marquès	*pl.* **marquesos**	marquis
comerç	*pl.* **comerços**	trade	peix	*pl.* **peixos**	fish
curs	*pl.* **cursos**	course	reflex	*pl.* **reflexos**	reflection, reflex

Many nouns ending in -s double the **s** in the plural. This is true of the majority of those where the preceding vowel is **a**, **i**, **o** or **u**. So we have: **fas** 'palm branch' *pl. fassos*, **sedàs** 'sieve' *pl.* **sedassos**, **ris** 'curl', 'loop' *pl.* **rissos**, **passadís** 'corridor' *pl.* **passadissos**, **os** 'bone' *pl.* **ossos**, **ós** 'bear' *pl.* **óssos**, **arròs** 'rice', 'paella' *pl.* **arrossos**, **esbós** 'sketch' *pl.* **esbossos**, **rus** 'Russian' *pl.* **russos**, **gaús** 'horned owl' *pl.* **gàssos**. However, a reasonable number of mostly common words with these stressed vowels retain single -s- (pronounced [z]) in the plural. These are:

-as (-às)   *pl.* **-asos**

as	ace	**gimnàs**	gymnasium	**ras**	open country
cas	case	**hipocràs**	mulled wine	**ucàs**	ukase, edict
entrecàs	chance	**madràs**	madras (cloth)	**vas**	tumbler
envàs	container	**mas**	farmhouse		
gas	gas	**ocàs**	setting (of sun)		

-is (-ís)   *pl.* **-isos**

avís	announcement	**maravedís**	(old Spanish coin)
bis	Pacific mackerel	**matís**	shade, nuance
comís	confiscation, confiscated goods	**narcís**	daffodil
decomís	confiscation	**país**	country
divís	discord	**paradís**	Paradise
encís	charm	**permís**	permit
desencís	disenchantment	**pis**	storey, flat
fideïcomís	trust	**quirguís**	Kirghiz
fris	frieze, wainscot	**sis**	six
gris	grey; cold wind	**somrís**	smile
incís	parenthetical phrase	**tamís**	sieve
llassís	press	**vis**	screw, bolt
macís	mace (herb)	**tornavís**	screwdriver

-os (-òs, -ós)   *pl.* **-osos**

All masculine nouns which are nominalizations of adjectives ending in **-ós** have, like the adjectives, **-osos** in the plural, such as **religiós** 'monk' *pl.* **religiosos**, **gomós** 'fop', 'toff' *pl.* **gomosos**, etc. The other exceptions to the doubling of **s** after **o** are:

aigua-ros	rose-water	**nualós**	comfrey
clos	enclosure	**peresós**	sloth
dos	two	**peuterrós**	clodhopper
entredós	decorative panel	**repòs**	rest, repose
espòs	husband, spouse	**respòs**	refrain

-us (-ús)   *pl.* **-usos**

andalús	Andalusian	**obús**	howitzer, shell
autobús	bus	**reclús**	recluse, prisoner
fus	spindle	**refús**	refusal
nus	knot	**ús**	use
entrenús	section between two knots	**abús**	abuse
		desús	disuse

-es (-ès, -és)

In the case of masculine nouns ending in stressed -es (-ès, -és), the majority do not double the -s: **mes** 'month' *pl.* **mesos, maltès** 'Maltese' *pl.* **maltesos** (similarly hundreds of nouns with the suffix -ès denoting geographic origin, and so on), etc. The following are the exceptional nouns with this ending which do double the -s to give -essos:

abscés	abscess	**reingrés**	re-entry
accés	access	**insuccés**	failure
aiguavés	slope, run-off	**interès**	interest
aprés	milking parlour	**desinterès**	disinterest
bes	strip of canvas in sail	**procés**	process
bres	cradle	**progrés**	progress
calcés	masthead	**recés**	retreat
confés	confessor	**regrés**	return
congrés	congress	**retrocés**	backward movement
decés	decease	**revés**	reverse
excés	excess	**sargués**	osier, willow
exprés	special messenger;	**ses**	anus
	express (train)	**succés**	event
fes	fez	**través**	width
ges	plaster	**xerès**	sherry
ingrés	entrance, admission (plural also 'income')		

A few masculine nouns ending in -s or -x do not add -os in the plural, but follow the rule for feminines given in **2.1.5.1**. A significant group consists of compound nouns whose final element already contains a plural -s; they are invariable in the plural, for example: **enganyapastors** 'nightjar(s)' (lit. deceives shepherds), **parallamps** 'lightning conductor(s)', **centpeus** 'centipede(s)' (lit. 100 feet), **vuit-cents** '800', **els vuit-cents** 'the 1800s'. The remainder of the masculine nouns in -s or -x that do not add -os in the plural are these:

bis	encore(s)	**fons**	bottom(s), funds
blocaus	blockhouse(s)	**gneis**	gneiss(es)
calamars	squid(s): a singular **calamar** and a plural **calamarsos** are also used	**plus**	bonus(es)
		pus	pus(ses)
		reps	rep (cloth)
		socors	assistance: *pl.* also **socorsos**
dijous	Thursday(s)		
dilluns	Monday(s)	**temps**	time(s), weather (and compounds such as **passatemps** 'pastime(s)')
dimarts	Tuesday(s)		
edelweiss	edelweiss(es)		
ens	entity/-ies, body/-ies		

tris-tras		bee-line(s)	**linx**	*pl.* **linxs** lynx
zas		whizz(es)	**matx**	*pl.* **matxs** match
dux	*pl.* **duxs**	doge	**ponx**	*pl.* **ponxs** punch (drink)
esfinx	*pl.* **esfinxs**	sphinx		

2.1.5.4 *Plural of masculine nouns ending in -sc, -st, -xt, or -ig*

Masculine nouns ending in **-sc**, **-st**, **-xt**, or **-ig** form their plurals either in **-s** or in **-os**: **disc** 'disk' *pl.* **discs** or **discos**, **gust** 'taste' *pl.* **gusts** or **gustos**, **text** 'text' *pl.* **texts** or **textos**. The addition of **-os** after **-ig** entails some orthographic changes: **-ig** becomes **-j-** in some words (basically those with **-j-** in related forms) but becomes **-tj-** in others (basically those with **-tj-** in related forms): **passeig** 'walk' *pl.* **passeigs** or **passejos** (cf. **passejar** 'to walk'), **desig** 'desire' *pl.* **desigs** or **desitjos** (cf. **desitjar** 'to desire'), etc. The tendency in the standard language has been to prefer **-os** in the first three types (**discos, gustos, textos**), but **-s** in the last type (**passeigs**). More recently, in line with pronunciation, forms such as **assajos** 'rehearsals', **marejos** 'nauseas', **bojos** 'madmen' are increasingly found in print. In Valencia and the Balearic Islands forms like **discs, gusts, texts** are current both in speech and in writing. Against the general trend, **test** 'test', **raig** 'ray', and **puig** 'hill' nearly always have **-s** plurals: **tests, raigs, puigs**.

2.1.6   THE PLURAL OF COMPOUND WORDS

Most compounds form their plurals according to the rules already given, bearing in mind that an additional plural suffix is not added to a compound that already ends with one: so **altaveu** 'loudspeaker' *pl.* **altaveus**, **capicua** 'palindrome number' *pl.* **capicues**, **celobert** 'courtyard', 'light well' *pl.* **celoberts**, **escanyapobres** 'miser(s)', **passaport** 'passport' *pl.* **passaports**, **poca-solta** 'fool' *pl.* **poca-soltes**, **rentamans** 'washbasin(s)', **tornavís** 'screwdriver' *pl.* **tornavisos**. All compounds written joined together (without hyphen) follow this pattern.

Compounds consisting of two nouns (written with hyphen or space) generally pluralize only the head element, which is the part which also determines the gender of the compound (see **1.1.3.3**). So **el camió cisterna** 'the tanker lorry' *pl.* **els camions cisterna**, **la ciutat dormitori** 'the dormitory town' *pl.* **les ciutats dormitori**, **el decret llei** 'the order in council' (approx.) *pl.* **els decrets llei**, **la deessa mare** 'the mother goddess' *pl.* **les deesses mare**, **l'hora punta** 'the rush-hour' *pl.* **les hores punta**.

2.1.7   PLURALS WITHOUT SINGULARS (*PLURALIA TANTUM*)

Catalan (like English) has a considerable number of nouns used only in the plural. This is more or less the rule for the names of articles with two matched parts like **alicates** 'pliers', **bragues** or **calces** 'knickers', **calçotets** 'underpants',

molls 'tongs', **pinces** 'tweezers', 'tongs', **pantalons** 'trousers', **prismàtics** 'binoculars', **setrilleres** 'set of oil and vinegar bottles', **sostenidors** 'bra', **tenalles** or **estenalles** 'pincers', **texans** 'jeans', **tisores** 'scissors', **ulleres** 'spectacles'. To speak of 'a pair of' such things one uses the plural of the number 'one': **unes bragues** 'a pair of knickers', **unes tisores** 'a pair of scissors' (see **3.2.4iii**). There are also many *pluralia tantum* associated with the concept 'left-overs', 'leavings', such as **acaballes** 'last stages (of an event)', 'tail end', **deixalles** 'left-overs', 'rubbish', **endergues** 'junk', **escombraries** 'rubbish', **serradures** 'sawdust'. A few other common ones are **afores** 'outskirts', **comicis** 'hustings', 'election campaign', **diners** 'money', **escacs** 'chess', **(es)tovalles** 'tablecloth', **ganes** 'desire', 'fancy', **pessigolles** 'tickle', **postres** 'dessert', 'sweet course', **queviures** 'food', 'groceries', **vacances** 'holiday(s)'.

2.1.8 PLURAL OF PROPER NAMES

When referring to several members of the same family, the usual practice is to leave the surname invariable: **els Solà** 'the Solà family', **els Riquer** 'the Riquers'. Plural forms of surnames are found, though they are not obligatory, when referring to famous historical dynasties, such as **els Àustries** 'the house of Austria', **els Borbons** 'the Bourbons', **els Borges** 'the Borgias' (see **3.3.2**).

2.2 USES OF THE PLURAL

2.2.1 NUMBER AGREEMENT WITH COLLECTIVE NOUNS

Collective nouns, grammatically singular, such as **gent** 'people', **colla** 'group', **nombre** 'number', **sèrie** 'series', **parell** 'couple', **majoria** 'majority', **resta** 'remainder' may take either singular or plural verb agreement, as in British English, according to whether the activity of the collective or of its individual members is predominant. Thus **La resta anava amb un tren especial** 'The remainder went (sg.) by a special train'; but a plural verb is more likely in **La resta dels viatgers anaven . . .** 'The remainder of the passengers went (*pl.*) . . .' That is, Catalans have no hang-ups about formal number agreement rules in cases like these, though singular verb agreement is likely to be preferred if the collective noun is adjacent to the verb: **Va entrar un grup de taxistes** 'A group of taxi-drivers came (*sg.*) in'.

2.2.2 DISTRIBUTIVES (ONE EACH)

Whereas in English we normally say e.g. 'They all put their hands on their heads' (several people, thus several hands and several heads) Catalans will say **Tots es van posar les mans al cap** 'They all put their hands (two each) on their head (one each)'. Thus also **tres turcs amb passaport alemany** 'three Turks with German passports' (lit. with German passport, i.e. one each).

2.2.3 COUNT NOUNS AND MASS NOUNS

Count nouns refer to countable items like 'fingers', 'eggs', 'journeys'; mass nouns refer to non-countable items like 'bread', 'justice'. Though we can in English use mass nouns (especially in the plural) to mean 'types of . . .' or 'instances of . . .', e.g. 'French wines', 'her fears', this is rather more common in Catalan. More generally, mass and count terms in the two languages may not match:

amistat	friendship	**les amistats**	friends, acquaintances
atenció	attention	**les atencions**	courtesies, acts of kindness
carn	meat, flesh	**les carns**	fleshy parts
informació	information	**les informacions**	news items
un negoci	a deal, a business	**negocis**	business, trade
pa	bread, loaf	**pans**	loaves of bread
progrés	progress	**els progressos**	advances
torrada	piece of toast	**torrades**	pieces of toast
tro etc.	thunder	**els trons**	thunderclaps

2.3 DIMINUTIVE, AUGMENTATIVE, AND EVALUATIVE SUFFIXES

There are a number of suffixes which, as well as carrying connotations of size, can give an affective note to the basic meaning of the root word. The principal ones are -et/-eta (diminutive), -às/-assa (augmentative), -ot/-ota (pejorative). The use of such suffixes in adjectives is dealt with in **4.1.5**. Addition of a suffix may entail some morphological change in the root word, of the kind described above at **2.1.3** and elsewhere (**5.3.2**, etc.): **home** 'man', **homenet** 'little man'; **mà** 'hand', **manassa** 'big hand'.

In some cases these suffixes convey no affective colouring, creating derived forms which are independent lexical items. Such derived forms may occasionally be of different gender from the base: **avió** (*m.*) 'aircraft', **avioneta** (*f.*) 'light aircraft'; **camió** (*m.*) 'lorry', **camioneta** (*f.*) 'van', 'light truck'; **vagó** (*m.*) 'wagon', 'coach', '(railway) carriage', **vagoneta** (*f.*) 'small wagon', 'open railway truck'; **maleta** (*f.*) 'suitcase', **maletí** (*m.*) 'attaché case'. The ending -ot (see below) is used for the masculine of certain species nouns that are feminine: **abella** 'bee', **abellot** 'drone'.

Otherwise these suffixes occur frequently in speech and in informal written registers, and they are (especially the diminutives) very productive. They can communicate a wide range of nuances – affection, condescension, contempt, admiration, irony, repugnance, and so on – and they are observed to be instinctively deployed by native speakers with considerable subtlety. Sensitivity and resourcefulness are required in their interpretation and translation: **Posi'm dos enciams, si us plau** is the straightforward way of asking politely for two lettuces, whereas **Posi'm dos enciamets** could imply a certain friendliness between speaker and hearer as well as a mild appreciation of the (required or observed) quality of the lettuces (understood as well to be smaller rather than larger). As another example, **llibrot** (from **llibre** 'book') could, according to context, be either an unwieldy and unattractive book, or a relatively large one whose size is subjectively emphasized. There is a degree of regional variation in the kinds of derived words that are produced, and in their usage. Moreover, while most nouns could in theory take any suffix, many theoretically possible derivations are blocked in practice. An account like that provided by Anthony Gooch, in *Diminutive, Augmentative and Pejorative Suffixes in Modern Spanish* (Oxford 1970), is much needed for Catalan.

2.3.1 DIMINUTIVE SUFFIXES

The most productive diminutive suffix is **-et, -eta**:

peu	foot	**peuet**	**cadira**	chair	**cadireta**
bastó	stick	**bastonet**	**gos/gossa**	dog/bitch	**gosset/gosseta**
estona	short time	**estoneta**	**capsa**	box	**capseta**
moment	moment	**momentet**	etc.		

As indicated above, the diminutive may give an intimate or friendly note to the use of a particular word as well as implying (relative) smallness of size or importance:

Ha pronunciat un discurset que ha vingut molt a tomb.
He made a (nice) little speech which was very appropriate.

Haurà d'esperar una estoneta.
You will have to wait just a short while.

The diminutive may have a differentiated or specialized meaning:

pit	chest	**pitet**	bib
ull	eye	**fer l'ullet**	to wink
cara	face	**careta**	mask
vara	rod/staff	**vareta**	wand
finestra	window	**finestreta**	small window (in vehicle, box office)
llengua	tongue	**llengüeta**	tongue (of shoe)/tab
mentida	lie	**mentideta**	white lie

Gender change (as in **avió** 'aircraft', **avioneta** 'light aircraft'; **camió** 'lorry', **camioneta** 'light truck', 'van'; **furgó** 'truck', 'trailer', **furgoneta** 'van') is seen in specialized **llibreta** (*f.*) 'notebook', 'bank book', 'rent book' from **llibre** (*m.*)

with **llibret** (*m.*) available for 'small book'. Both **cigarret** (*m.*) and **cigarreta** (*f.*) 'cigarette', the former much more common, are derived from **cigar(ro)** 'cigar'.

Almost all personal names admit the diminutive -et/-eta: **Estevet** 'little/ young Esteve', **Ramonet/Ramoneta**, **Quimet** (from abbreviation of **Joaquim**). **Una marieta** (from **Maria** 'Our Lady') is 'a ladybird'.

Other diminutives

These include **-ó/-ona**, **-ol/-ola**, **-eu/-eva**, **-etxo/-etxa** and **-oi/-oia**, all more limited in application than **-et/-eta**.

Diminutive **-ó/-ona** (often with gender change) is quite productive: **un cafetó** would be used when ordering 'a nice (little) cup of coffee'; **pessetones** is an affectionate diminutive of **pessetes**; note also **un paretó** 'a low wall', **un cadiró** 'a small chair', **el cordó** 'string', 'shoe-lace' (from **corda** 'rope'). Many common derivations with **-ó/-ona** are specialized in meaning:

carrer	street	**carreró**	(urban) lane/narrow street
caixa	box	**caixó**	small box/casket
carro	waggon/car	**carretó**	trolley
carbassa	pumpkin	**carbassó**	courgette
pinya	pineapple	**pinyó**	pine nut
finestra	window	**finestró**	shutter
sella	saddle	**selletó**	(bicycle) saddle
llebre (*f.*)	hare	**llebretó** (*m.*)	levret
llop	wolf	**llobató**	wolf cub
etc.			

In a few cases there is no difference in meaning between the root word and derivative: **company/companyó** 'companion', **espia/espió** 'spy', **fura/furó** 'ferret'.

The suffix **-ol/-ola** makes basically diminutive versions of a limited number of root words, e.g., **bandera** 'flag', **banderola** 'pennant'; **bèstia** 'beast', 'animal', **bestiola** 'small creature'; **estany** 'pond', **estanyol** 'small pond'; **vent** 'wind', **ventijol** 'light wind', or it can create a related word with a distinct meaning, e.g., **fulla** 'leaf', **fullola** 'veneer'; **fill(a)** 'son', 'daughter', 'child', **fillol(a)** 'godson', 'goddaughter', 'godchild'; **llenç** 'canvas', **llençol** 'sheet'.

Formations with **-oi/-oia** and **-eu/-eva** are even fewer: **nas** 'nose', **nassoi** 'cute little nose'; **camí** 'track', **caminoi** 'country lane', 'footpath'; **caseva** 'small house', 'hovel'; **tassoneu** 'small glass' (from **tassó**, mainly Balearic).

A diminutive may occasionally carry pejorative connotations: **politiquets manefles** 'small-time, busybody politicians', **la cultureta** 'culture with a small 'c''. The suffix **-etxo/-etxa** is exclusively pejorative: **un homenetxo** 'an odd little bloke', **un caminetxo** 'a narrow track that's hard to follow', **una barquetxa** 'an inadequate little boat'.

2.3.2   AUGMENTATIVE SUFFIXES

The most productive augmentative suffix is -às/-assa:

peu	foot	**peuàs**		**mare**	mother	**marassa**
casa	house	**casassa**		**home**	man	**homenàs**
vapor	steam/vapour	**vaporàs**		etc.		
boira	fog	**boirassa**				

Gender change can occur, as in **paper** (*m.*) 'paper', **paperassa** (*f.*) 'lot of paper with writing on'.

As remarked in **2.3.1**, imagination and ingenuity are often called for in translation of these suffixally derived forms:

Era un gegantàs de gairebé dos metres d'alt.
He was a big strapping fellow (lit. a big giant) well over six feet tall.
Tenia una marassa que el mimava molt.
His mother spoilt him to death.

The following are examples of words with specialized meaning formed with -às/-assa:

cànem	hemp	**canemàs**	canvas
barca	boat	**barcassa**	barge/pontoon
pi	pine	**pinassa**	pine needles
cuiro	leather	**cuirassa**	cuirass/carapace
gallina	hen	**gallinassa**	hen droppings
mar	sea	**maregassa**	heavy sea/swell
etc.			

Whereas -às/-assa is generally appreciative (as in **gegantàs**, **marassa** above) the augmentative suffix -arro/-arra is distinctly (and rather crudely) pejorative: **homenarro** 'ungainly big bloke', **peuarro** 'clumsy great foot', **veuarra** 'loud and raucous voice', **cotxarro** 'ponderous old jalopy', **hotelarro** 'rambling pile of a hotel', etc. (Translations given are approximate and would vary according to context.)

2.3.3   SUFFIXES WITH MARKED EVALUATIVE FORCE

The most productive pejorative suffix is -ot/-ota:

cadira	chair	**cadirota**		**ocell**	bird	**ocellot**
peu	foot	**peuot**		**paper**	paper	**paperot**
xicot	boy/youth	**xicotot**		**anglès**	Englishman	**anglesot**
home	man	**homenot**		etc.		

See the general comment, made in **2.3** above, on the force of -ot. The celebrated author Josep Pla created a series of biographical sketches of public figures he admired, entitled *Homenots*, where the depreciative connotations of the suffix are outweighed by positive ones of 'larger than life'. The more usual, fully pejorative force is seen in examples like:

Haurem de sofrir la invasió dels alemanyots. (Nadal Batle)
The dreadful Germans will come and invade us.

No m'ho toquis pas amb aquestes manotes brutes!
Don't go and touch it with those horribly dirty hands.

No sé què hi feia aquella donota.
I don't know what that awful woman was doing there.

Gender change (*f.* to *m.*) occurs quite regularly as in, e.g., **sabata** 'shoe', **sabatot; barraca** 'shack', 'hovel', **barracot; pila** 'pile', 'heap', **pilot; ala** 'wing', **alot,** etc.

Specialization is seen in, e.g., **paraula** 'word', **paraulota** 'swear word'; **ungla** 'finger nail', **unglot** 'claw', 'talon', **pebre** (*m.*) 'pepper (spice)', **pebrot** 'capsicum'. Also to be noted in this context is the use of -**ot** to supply the masculine of certain nouns for which the feminine form generally denotes the species: **merla** 'blackbird', **merlot; guatlla** 'quail', **guatllot; perdiu** 'partridge', **perdigot; abella** 'bee', **abellot;** also **bruixa** 'witch', **bruixot** 'wizard' (see **1.1.3**).

The suffix -**ot** had a diminutive sense in old Catalan, and this is reflected in the survival of a couple of diminutive names, **Pere – Perot, Jaume – Jaumot,** and also in **illa** 'island' – **illot** 'islet'.

The only other pejorative suffix, with application to a very limited number of items, is -**all/-alla: espantall** 'scarecrow', **gentalla** 'unpleasant/undesirable people', **jovenalla** 'ignorant young people'.

3 ARTICLES

The use of definite and indefinite articles in Catalan is on the whole comparable with the use of the corresponding forms in English; we shall draw special attention to the most important differences. One general point worth making at the start is that a noun in a noun phrase which is the subject of a clause and precedes the verb nearly always has an article, definite or indefinite (if it has no other determiner):

Venien protestes de molts sectors (not *__Protestes venien . . .__).
Protests came from many sectors.

Les protestes venien de tots el sectors.
The protests came from many sectors.

There are two main differences of usage. The first is that in generic noun phrases Catalan uses the definite article not only with singular count nouns, but with singular mass nouns and plural nouns also (**3.1.4.2**). The second is that, rather more often than in English, a singular indefinite noun phrase may lack an article or determiner altogether (**3.2.3**).

Catalan also uses a 'personal article' before proper names of people (**3.3**). Nominalization via articles is discussed separately in Chapter 9, and in **9.2** we deal with the so-called neuter article **el/lo**.

3.1 DEFINITE ARTICLES

There are two series of definite article forms in Catalan: the standard article and the forms based on **s** (*article salat*, see **3.1.2** below). The standard article is the most commonly used (almost exclusively in written language).

3.1.1 MORPHOLOGY OF THE DEFINITE ARTICLE

Standard definite article

	singular		*plural*
	before consonant	*before vowel or **h-***	
masculine	**el**	**l'**	**els**
feminine	**la**	**l'**	**les**

Use of apostrophized **l'**, especially as a reduction of feminine singular **la**, requires special comment. When followed by a vowel the singular articles, both masculine and feminine, are reduced to **l'**: **l'all** 'the garlic' (*m.*), **l'elefant** 'the elephant' (*m.*), **l'idiota** 'the idiot' (*m.* or *f.*), **l'ou** 'the egg' (*m.*), **l'ull** 'the eye' (*m.*), **l'ànsia** 'the anxiety' (*f.*), **l'illa** 'the island' (*f.*), **l'olla** 'the pot' (*f.*).

This also applies when the vowel is preceded by **h** (which is silent): **l'home** 'the man' (*m.*), **l'hora** 'the hour' (*f.*), **l'herba** 'the grass' (*f.*). The same form **l'** is also used, as a special case, when the noun begins with **s-** followed by a consonant. This is only found in words borrowed from foreign languages: **l'Stradivarius** 'the Stradivarius', etc. (actually pronounced with an initial **e-**).

Exceptionally, in the standard written language, reduction of the feminine singular definite article **la** to **l'** does not apply in the following cases:

(i)   When the noun begins with an unstressed **i** or **u** (which may be preceded by **h**): **la indústria** 'the industry', **la ullada** 'the glance', **la història** 'the story', **la humanitat** 'humanity', etc. (cf. **l'única possibilitat** 'the only possibility', **l'hidra de la revolució** 'the hydra of revolution', etc. where initial **i/u** is stressed).

(ii) When the noun is the name of a letter: **la ena** 'the N', **la erra** 'the R', **la efa** 'the F'.

(iii) When the noun begins with the negative prefix **a-** and its pronunciation without a pause could cause confusion with its opposite: **la anormalitat** 'the abnormality': compare **la normalitat** 'the normality'; **la asimetria** 'the asymmetry': compare **la simetria** 'the symmetry', etc.

(iv) Before the three nouns **ira** 'anger', **host** 'host', **una** 'one (o'clock)': **la ira**, **la host, la una**. (The numeral adjective **una** 'one' behaves normally: **L'una era blanca i l'altra negra** 'One of them was white and the other, black', etc.)

Northwestern Catalan retains in the spoken language the older forms of the masculine article **lo/los** for **el/els**. **Lo** also appears in eastern dialects in a few fixed expressions: **per lo senyal de la Santa Creu** 'by the sign of the Cross', **tot lo dia** 'all day', **tot lo món** 'the whole world'. It also appears in folk songs.

Contraction of the definite article with prepositions

The masculine article forms **el** and **els** placed after the prepositions **a**, **de**, and **per** and the word **ca** (= **casa**) are contracted with them:

preposition	definite article	
	el	els
a	al	als
de	del	dels
per	pel	pels
ca	cal	cals

Contraction does not occur when the article has been reduced to **l'**:

al nen 'to the boy' but **a l'home** 'to the man'
del camp 'from the field' but **de l'hort** 'from the market garden'
pel mes 'through the month' but **per l'any** 'through the year'
per al pare 'for father' but **per a l'avi** 'for grandfather'
cal dentista 'the dentist's' but **ca l'adroguer** 'the grocer's'

3.1.2   ARTICLE SALAT

The *article salat* refers to a special set of forms of the definite article which are most commonly used in the Balearic Islands. Its use there is typical of the spoken language (and printed versions of folk tales and popular literature); it is not used in very formal speech.

	singular		plural
	before consonant	before vowel or **h-**	
masculine	es	s'	es
feminine	sa	s'	ses

The singular articles are reduced to **s'** when a noun beginning with a vowel or with **h** follows. The exceptions pointed out in **3.1.1** for **la → l'** are applied to the *article salat* only when **sa** precedes the name of a vowel **sa i** 'the *i*', **sa u** 'the *u*'.

In masculine noun phrases preceded by the preposition **amb**, special forms **so** and **sos** are used in Majorca, Ibiza, and Formentera: **amb so martell** 'with the hammer', **amb sos amics** 'with the friends'.

In Majorca and Minorca **es** (plural) is pronounced like **ets** when a vowel follows; in this context **ets** used to be found in writing. Currently **es** is the recommended spelling, whatever the pronunciation.

Certain words in the Balearic dialects do not accept the use of the *article salat*. Although there is no simple rule governing this feature, it can be said that many of the words affected refer to objects or institutions which are unique or socially salient: **el cel** 'the sky' not *es cel, **la mar** 'the sea' not *sa mar, **el rei** 'the king', **la reina** 'the queen', **el senyor** (followed by a name) 'Mr', **el doctor** (followed by a name) 'Dr', **el professor** (followed by a name) 'Professor', **el Palau** 'the Palace', **la Sala** 'the town hall', **la Cúria** 'the Curia', **el bisbe** 'the bishop', **el Papa** 'the Pope', **la Mare-de-Déu** 'the Virgin Mary', **el rosari** 'the rosary', **l'església** 'the church', **la Seu** 'the Cathedral', **el Bon Jesús** 'the Christ child', **el dimoni** 'the devil', **l'infern** 'Hell', **el purgatori** 'Purgatory', **la parròquia** 'the parish (church)', **els passos** (floats representing scenes from the Passion of Christ carried in Holy Week processions), **el sagrari** 'the tabernacle', **el cor** 'the choir'. When uniqueness is not foremost, the *article salat* appears: **es papes que jo he conegut** 'the Popes I have known', **ses esglésies que ha visitat el Papa** 'the churches that the Pope has visited'. Many cases challenge the generalization made above: **es sol** 'the sun', **sa lluna** 'the moon', **es Parlament** 'the (Balearic) Parliament', **es Govern** 'the (Balearic) Government', **es president** 'the (Balearic) president', **es àngels** 'the angels', etc. Expressions of time require the standard article: **les nou, les deu, les onze i vint**, etc. The standard article is also obligatory in prayers (**en nom del Pare** . . . 'in the name of the Father . . . ') and in many idioms: **com anell al dit** 'like a glove' (lit. 'as ring to the finger'), **l'any passat** 'last year', **l'any que ve** 'next year', including those with **la** preceding an adjective, mentioned in **3.4**.

Contraction of the article salat with prepositions

The masculine article form **es** placed after the prepositions **a**, **de**, and **per** and the word **ca** (= **casa**) contracts with it:

	es (singular and plural)
a	**as**
de	**des**
per	**pes**
ca	**cas**

Vaig trobar mil pessetes as mig des carrer.
I found 1000 pesetas in the middle of the street.

Van tornar a cas ferrer pes camí més curt.
They went back to the blacksmith's by the shortest route.

Contraction does not occur when the article has been reduced to **s'**.

3.1.3 SYNTAX OF THE DEFINITE ARTICLE

In a list of nouns, each preceded by its own article, repetition of the article can be avoided, but it must be borne in mind that, whereas the masculine article can include feminine nouns, the feminine article can only appear before feminine nouns. Thus, the article preceding a masculine noun placed first in the enumeration can affect the rest of the nouns, masculine or feminine:

les escoles i les guarderies = les escoles i guarderies
the schools and (the) day nurseries

els nens i les nenes dels col·legis i les escoles = els nens i nenes dels col·legis i escoles
the boys and (the) girls of the secondary and (the) primary schools

but not *__les nenes i nens de les escoles i col·legis.__

Pairs of animate nouns of different sex are given with the corresponding article for each noun: **el pare i la mare** 'the father and mother', **l'avi i l'àvia** 'the grandfather and grandmother' (cf. **els pares** 'the parents' and **els avis** 'the grandparents' which present the pairs as units; see Chapter 1), **el porc i la truja** 'the boar and the sow'. Although articles may be omitted in lists of nouns considered to be synonymous or to be part of a single idea (**els resultats i conclusions de l'experiència** 'the results and conclusions of the experiment'), the safest option is always to retain the article with each noun, as in **Porta els plats i les copes** 'Bring the plates and (the) glasses'.

3.1.4 PRESENCE OR ABSENCE OF THE DEFINITE ARTICLE

Despite the generalization with which this chapter opens, concerning the general parallels between article usage in English and Catalan, it is difficult to draw up hard and fast rules for the behaviour – use or omission – of definite articles in Catalan as generated through 'native competence'. As often, the devil is in the detail. A couple of general observations may provide some foundation for working with the description provided in **3.1.4.1–5**.

(i)   With two exceptions the definite article is used in Catalan whenever it appears in English: 'the magnitude of the tragedy' → **la magnitud de la tragèdia**, 'the beginning of the third act' → **el començament del tercer acte**:

La feina més difícil ha estat explicar el problema al cap de departament.
The most difficult job has been explaining the problem to the head of department.

Exceptions, where the definite article is used in English but not in Catalan, are:

(a)   Ordinal numbers with monarchs, popes, etc.: **Carles III** (pronounced

Carles tercer) 'Charles the Third', **Joan XXIII** (pronounced **Joan vint-i-tres**) 'John the Twenty-third', etc.

(b)   Some set adverbial phrases which do not take the article in Catalan while the English counterpart usually does: **carrer amunt/avall** 'up/ down the street', **a llarg/curt termini** 'in the long/short run', **a vo-luntat de** 'at the discretion of', **en ple estiu** 'at the height of the summer', **de plantilla** 'on the payroll', **en nom de** 'in the name of', etc. (see **3.1.4.4iv(d–f)**).

(ii)   The most obvious contrast between Catalan and English concerns use of the article with nouns used generically (**3.1.4.2**), including its 'unfamiliar' (for English speakers) appearance before abstract nouns. For example, **La carn és més cara que el peix** 'Meat is more expensive than fish', **la intel·ligència** 'intelligence', **la vida i la mort** 'life and death'.

3.1.4.1 *Definite article with definite noun phrases*

The main role of the definite article in Catalan, as in English, is to indicate that the listener or reader is expected to be able to identify uniquely, in their mental model of the current world of discourse, the referent of the noun phrase in question. By contrast, an indefinite noun phrase (**3.2.3**) is used in order to establish a new referent in the hearer's mental model, or when no specific individual or group is intended.

The expectation that the reference of a noun phrase can be uniquely iden-tified arises fundamentally from one of three reasons. First the referent may already have been mentioned previously:

El piset **tenia tres peces diminutes ... Una gàbia amb una cadernera i un quadre de cromos eren tot l'ornament** *del pis.*
The little flat had three tiny rooms ... A goldfinch in a cage and some colour prints in a frame were the only decoration of *the flat.*

Such a previous mention may well be via a paraphrase rather than with the same word or words:

Estengué *la mà* **com per afrontar tota la misèria del lloc amb** *el seu gest.*
She put out her hand as if to confront with *her gesture* all the wretchedness of the place.

Much more commonly the identity of the referent of the definite noun phrase is derived by inference (and is expected by the speaker to be so derived) from general or specific knowledge of scenes or situations:

... el piset tenia tres peces diminutes. *El* **menjador a***l* **mig, on s'obria directament** *la* **porta de fora ...**
... the flat had three tiny rooms. *The* dining room in *the* middle, into which *the* front door opened directly ... (by inference from general knowledge

one knows that a flat will have a dining room and a front door; similarly, if there are three rooms, one will be in the middle, approximately anyway).

In some instances the recognition of a particular referent by inference is virtually unavoidable; the reference of the noun phrase is taken to be unique for everybody: **la lluna** 'the moon', **el Papa** 'the Pope', **el mar** 'the sea'.

The third way of establishing definiteness is through an explicit modifying phrase, such as a relative clause, or a prepositional phrase complement:

–**Em fa vergonya**– **va dir ella amb** *l'***accent obert de** *la* **gent de***ls* **pobles de Lleida.**
'I am ashamed,' she said with *the* open accent of *the* people from *the* villages of Lleida.

Here we have a series of interlocking phrases which are definite via explicit modification: **l'accent . . . de la gent, la gent dels pobles, els pobles de Lleida.**

3.1.4.2 *Generic noun phrases and the definite article*

With the exceptions noted below (and **3.1.4.3–4**), the definite article is used before all Catalan nouns used generically, whether they are singular or plural, countable or mass (i.e. uncountable) nouns. This contrasts with English usage, where in a generic sense only singular count nouns may have the definite article:

El **nen segueix un llarg procés d'aprenentatge.**
The child undergoes a lengthy learning process.

Els **nens segueixen un llarg procés d'aprenentatge.**
Children undergo a lengthy learning process.

Els **polítics han de ser alhora cauts i atrevits.**
Politicians have to be cautious and bold at the same time.

*L'***elefant és un mamífer herbívor.**/*Els* **elefants són mamífers herbívors.**
The elephant is an herbivorous mammal./Elephants are herbivorous mammals.

Reivindiquem els drets de *la* **mare soltera/de** *les* **mares solteres.**
We stand up for the rights of the unmarried mother/of unmarried mothers.

This rule covers

(i)   abstract nouns used generically:

La castedat és una condició envejable.   Chastity is an enviable condition.

Feu l'amor i no la guerra.   Make love not war.

(ii)   Mass nouns denoting a substance understood generically:

La mel és bona per a la salut.   Honey is good for health.
M'agrada la cervesa més que el vi.   I like beer more than wine.

(iii) Count nouns used (generically) to refer to all the members of their class:

Les dones tenen més sentit comú que els homes.
Women have more common sense than men.

Els llibres ocupen molt d'espai.
Books take up a lot of room.

No m'agraden els menjars picants.
I don't like spicy food. (lit. Spicy food is not pleasing to me.)

3.1.4.3   Generic or indefinite?

An English mass or plural noun phrase without an article may be either generic or indefinite. If the sense is generic, a definite article will be needed in Catalan; if it is indefinite, an indefinite article (**un**), some other indefinite quantifier (such as **algun** 'some'), or a noun phrase with no determiner will be required.

Els especialistes alemanys han refutat aquesta teoria.
German specialists have refuted this theory.

Especialistes alemanys han refutat aquesta teoria./Aquesta teoria ha estat refutada per especialistes alemanys.
(Some) German specialists have refuted this theory.

The definite article in the first sentence has a generic function and conveys that 'all German specialists (in the context of discourse)' are referred to: absence of the article corresponds to the indefinite sense of the noun phrase in the second sentence. (As we mention below a subject noun phrase with no article, as in the first alternative here, is stylistically marked; **3.2.3**.)

More often than not a mass or plural count noun as the object of a verb will be indefinite:

No tens paciència.   You have no patience.
El director fa visites.   The boss is making calls.
La premsa té reaccions exagerades.   The press has extreme reactions.
**Ara que s'ha jubilat escriu tractats   Now he has retired he writes treatises
   d'astronomia.**   on astronomy.
Menja patates fregides.   She's eating chips./She eats chips.

In the last example, although there is a kind of generic sense to 'chips' (in the second translation, at least), the important thing is that the sense 'all' is not appropriate, and it is this sense 'all' which is part and parcel of the definite generic noun phrase.

Verbs of consumption, desire, use, or production show a strong tendency to govern noun phrases used indefinitely:

No mengen ni carn ni peix.
They eat neither meat nor fish.

Volem pa amb oli, pa amb oli volem. (children's refrain)
We want bread with oil; bread with oil we want.

Compon simfonies i música de cambra.
He composes symphonies and chamber music.

Faig servir massatge facial i desodorant *Floïd.*
I use *Floïd* aftershave and deodorant.

On the other hand, verbs which express preference, taste, emotion, prohibition, censure, etc., tend to refer to their objects as totalities or total inclusive sets, whence the appearance of the generic definite article:

Odio les patates fregides.	I hate (all) chips.
Adoro les muntanyes.	I love mountains.
M'han prohibit el cafè i el te.	I've been forbidden to drink coffee and tea.
Temo les reaccions exagerades.	I'm afraid of extreme reactions.
No entenc els tractats d'astronomia.	I do not understand treatises on astronomy.

In sentences like these 'all' is understood. This is also true for **agradar** translating 'like' (**M'agrada la cervesa** 'I like beer') although **la cervesa** is not the object but the subject of **agradar**.

Nominal complements of prepositions appear with the definite article when what they denote is either definite or generic:

Han parlat de les vagues.
They spoke about the strikes/about strikes.

No es preocupa gens pels altres.
He's not at all concerned about the others/other people.

les meves opinions sobre el desarmament
my opinions on disarmament/the disarmament (in a context where some specific disarmament can be understood)

As in English, indefinite noun phrases after a preposition will often have no article at all.

Lloguen apartaments per a turistes.
They rent out apartments for tourists.

Organitzen classes sobre literatura anglesa contemporània.
They run classes on contemporary English literature.

In the last example **classes sobre la literatura anglesa contemporània** would mean 'classes covering the whole of contemporary English literature'. Presence or absence of the definite article in a context like this will reflect the perspective of the speaker or writer: **quatre conferències sobre arquitectura romànica** implies 'four lectures on (aspects of) Romanesque architecture', whereas **. . . sobre l'arquitectura romànica** would imply the scope was the total phenomenon.

3.1.4.4   *Other aspects of presence or absence of the definite article*

We can summarize other aspects of presence or absence of the definite article under the following headings: (i) with nouns combined with **de**, (ii) with nouns restricted by a qualifier, (iii) dates and days, (iv) miscellaneous.

(i)   *Nouns joined with* **de**

When two nouns are joined by **de** to form what is effectively a compound noun, the definite article does not appear before the second noun (effectively indefinite here):

una/la bola de neu	a/the snowball
la carn de vedella	veal
(cf. **la carn de la vedella**	'the meat from the calf')
un/el mal de ventre	a/the stomach ache
cursos de lingüística aplicada	courses in applied linguistics

Note, however, **la parada de l'autobús** 'the place where the bus stops/the bus stop' but **una parada d'autobús** 'a bus stop', **la nit de la festa** 'the night of the party' but **una nit de festa** 'a party night', **el dia de la festa** 'the day of the festivity' but **un dia de festa** 'a holiday'.

(ii)   *Nouns restricted by a qualifier*

As in **cursos de lingüística aplicada** above, or **classes sobre literatura anglesa** in **3.1.4.3**, the presence of a qualifier does not always make a noun definite. Qualified nouns often function thus as compounds, without an article in the complement phrase:

aquell llibre de tapes de cuiro	that leather-bound book
exercicis de meditació transcendental	transcendental meditation exercises

The following examples illustrate how, as in English, a noun which lacks an article when used indefinitely may be definite (and used with a definite article) when it is qualified or restricted by a following word or phrase (**3.1.4.1**):

Portaven regals.
They brought presents.

Portaven els regals que havien comprat a Portugal.
They brought the presents they had bought in Portugal.

Desitjo pau i tranquil·litat.
I desire peace and tranquillity.

Desitjo la pau de la meva llar i la tranquil·litat de la rutina familiar.
I desire the peace of my own home and the tranquillity of familiar routine.

A similar effect occurs with proper names, which may have a definite article when used with a qualifying phrase:

la Barcelona de la postguerra
post-war Barcelona

El Verdaguer èpic és més imponent que el Verdaguer líric.
Verdaguer is more imposing as a writer of epics than as a lyric poet.

(iii)   Definite article in time expressions

The definite article (with no preposition) introduces a year, either with the noun **any** following it or directly followed by the number (see **10.11** for more detail on expressing years):

Mossèn Alcover morí l'any 1932. = Mossèn Alcover morí el 1932.
Mossèn Alcover died in 1932.

The same happens with the names of months:

El mes de maig de 1968 ells estudiaven a París. = El maig de 1968 ells estudiaven a París.
In May 1968 they were studying in Paris.

A year qualifying a month may also be introduced by **del**: **31 de març de(l) 1998** '31 March 1998'; the article is never omitted after **de** when the year has been abbreviated: **el juliol del 36**, 'July '36' (*****el juliol de 36). Similarly with days: **el dia X, el X**:

El dia 20 de març ens vam trobar a Londres.
On March 20th we met in London.

El dia de Nadal ens vam llevar molt tard.
On Christmas Day we got up very late.

With centuries **a** is used with the definite article:

Al segle XX hi ha hagut dues guerres mundials.
In the 20th century there have been two world wars.

The singular definite article introduces the names of the days of the week when the sense is generic: **El dilluns vaig a pescar** 'I go fishing every Monday', but **Dilluns aniré a pescar** 'I will go fishing on Monday', **Dissabte no va venir a veure'm** 'He did not come to see me last Saturday'. See **13.3** for more detailed exemplification of time expressions.

Note the optional absence of the definite article after the preposition **a** when indicating the age of persons:

A tres anys ja sabia llegir./Als tres anys . . .
At three years I could already read.

A divuit anys ja poden votar./Als divuit anys . . .
At eighteen they have the vote.

(iv)   Miscellaneous

Cases (a)–(h) below relate to absence of an expected definite article; (j) and (k) are perhaps unexpected cases of the presence of the definite article.

(a)   In many proverbs, with generic phrases:

Mules i dones, garrot les fa bones.
Mules and women only understand a good hiding. (lit. Mules and women, stick makes them good!)

(b)   The definite article is absent in vocatives, that is, when addressing a person directly, but the definite article is used before a title in a referring expression:

Sí, senyor Mates.	Yes, Sr Mates.
El senyor Mates dinarà amb nosaltres.	Sr Mates will have lunch with us.
Vostè és molt astut, doctor Ferrer.	You are very shrewd, Dr Ferrer.
El doctor Ferrer és molt astut.	Dr Ferrer is very shrewd.

The same applies when addressing relatives: **Sí, papà/mamà** 'Yes, daddy/mummy', **Que tens foc, mare?** 'Have you got a light, mother?' Observe, however, that the article is used when talking *about* relatives:

El pare arribarà aviat.	(Your) father will arrive soon.
La iaia està malalta.	Granny is ill.
l'oncle Pau	Uncle Pau

(c)   The (generic) definite article is optional in the case of **parlar** 'speak' + the name of a language (and likewise with **entendre** 'understand', **escriure** 'write', **estudiar** 'study'):

No sap parlar el rus. = No sap parlar rus.
She can't speak Russian.

But note:

Comparat amb l'euskera el català és poc complicat.
Compared with Basque, Catalan is uncomplicated.

Domina perfectament l'alemany.
She has a complete command of German.

(d) The definite article is absent before the following nouns in prepositional phrases depending on verbs of location or movement: **casa** 'home', **classe** 'class', **escola/estudi** 'school', **missa** 'Mass', **plaça** 'market', **muntanya** 'mountain', **terra** (*m.*) 'floor'. Notice that in some, but not all, cases the English corresponding expressions also lack an article:

Sóc a casa.	I'm at home.
Vaig a classe.	I'm going to school.
Vinc d'escola.	I'm coming from school.
Són a estudi.	They are at school.
Visc a muntanya.	I live in the mountains.
Vas a plaça?	Are you going shopping?
Seu a terra.	She is sitting on the ground.
etc.	

(e) The definite article is absent in prepositional phrase idioms like: **en teoria** 'in theory', **en definitiva** 'in short', **en lloc de** 'instead of', **en benefici de** 'in favour of', **en concepte de** 'by way of', **per part de** 'on the part of', **per raó de** 'by reason of', **de part de** 'on behalf of', **a càrrec de** 'within the responsibility of', **a expenses de** 'at the expense of', **a força de** 'by dint of', etc.

(f) The definite article is absent in certain other idiomatic expressions (where again the noun phrase is object of a verb or a preposition): **nedar, llençar(-se), caure** or **ésser dins mar** 'swim, jump, fall, be in the sea', **seure a taula** 'sit at (the) table', **parar/desparar taula** 'lay/clear the table'; **per terra** 'by land', **per mar** 'by sea', **per aire** 'by air', with names of games after **jugar a**: **jugar a cartes** 'play cards', **jugar a futbol** 'play football', **jugar a tennis** 'play tennis', etc.

(g) In signs: **Entrada** 'Way In', **Sortida** 'Exit', **Excusat** 'Toilet', etc.

(h) In simple apposition the definite article is normally absent:

Grècia, terra de filòsofs, fou el bressol de la civilització occidental.
Greece, (the) land of philosophers, was the cradle of western civilization.

una biografia de Prat de la Riba, primer President de la Mancomunitat
a biography of Prat de la Riba, the first president of the Catalan *Mancomunitat*

The definite article is retained, however, if apposition serves to individuate the noun in question (in practice by use of a comparative or superlative, or by a restrictive qualification):

en Ferran, el més llest d'aquell grup
Ferran, the cleverest in that group

Josep Carner, el 'Príncep dels poetes'
Josep Carner, the 'Prince of poets'

Fleming, el científic que va descobir la penicil·lina
Fleming, the scientist who discovered penicillin

The article also appears if apposition is used to avoid possible confusion of reference, as in: **Franklin, el polític i filòsof** 'Franklin, the politician and philosopher (not the explorer)'.

(j) To be noted is use of the definite article with numbered nouns: **una disposició de l'article 69 de la Constitució** 'a provision in Article 69 of the Constitution'; **Això s'explica en el capítol IV** 'This is explained in Chapter IV'; and after first- and second-person plural pronouns in phrases like **nosaltres els valencians** 'we Valencians', **vosaltres els rics** 'you wealthy people'.

(k) The masculine singular definite article always introduces the name of a sports team: **el Barça** 'Barcelona FC', **el València, el Sheffield Wednesday**.

Section **3.4** describes other idiomatic expressions involving articles. Further coverage of the definite article is given elsewhere as follows: in nominalization of adjectives, etc., **9.1**; before an infinitive, **20.5**; followed by a relative clause, **31.6.2**; as the neuter article, **9.2**.

3.1.4.5   The definite article with geographical names

Rather more commonly than in English, Catalan geographical names contain the definite article. It occurs in many local place names, with most mountains and volcanoes, and also with Heaven (**el cel**) and Hell (**l'infern**).

When the definite article is part of a place name, the rules given above (**3.1.1**) concerning contractions apply. Except when the name appears on its own (in signs: **L'Hospitalet, Les Borges Blanques**), the article is written with lower-case initial, and this means that capitalization is different in the two languages when English versions of Catalan place names are being given: **l'ajuntament de la Garriga** 'the town hall of La Garriga', **quan passàvem pel Vendrell** 'as we were going through El Vendrell'.

The names of rivers always have the definite article (as they do in English): **l'Ebre** 'the Ebro', **el Tàmesi** 'the Thames', **el Ter, la Noguera**, etc. Likewise for mountains (**el Pirineu** 'the Pyrenees', **l'Everest, el Cadí, l'Aneto, el Montseny**) with the exceptions of **Montserrat, Montjuïc**.

Most names of the Catalan **comarques** (traditional territorial divisions) contain the definite article: **el Vallès, l'Empordà, el Barcelonès, l'Horta d'Alacant, les Garrigues**, etc., but **Anoia, Garraf, Osona** are used without the article.

The majority of names of villages, towns, and cities have no article: **València**, **Blanes**, **Puigcerdà**, **Madrid**, **Nova York** 'New York'. Some that do are: **l'Argentera**, **les Borges Blanques**, **l'Escala**, **el Masnou**, **es Mercadal**, **s'Arenal**. Noteworthy are some foreign cities with the definite article: **el Caire** 'Cairo', **l'Alguer** 'Alghero', **la Meca** 'Mecca', **l'Havana** 'Havana'. There is no rule to predict the presence or absence of the article in this sort of name, though the article is often found when the place name is also (or begins with) a common noun, as in **l'Ametlla**, **es Camp de Mar**, **l'Estany**, **la Figuera** (but **Figueres**), **el Prat de Llobregat**, **la Vila Joiosa** (but **Vilafranca**, **Vilanova**), **la Palma d'Ebre** (but **Palma**, Majorca).

In the names of foreign countries and geographical regions the use of the definite article is quite a complex matter. We can state a number of principles, most of which have some exceptions. Generally speaking compound names contain the definite article: **l'Alemanya Federal** 'The Federal Republic of Germany', **l'Amèrica Central** 'Central America', **l'Amèrica del Nord** 'North America', **l'Amèrica del Sud** 'South America', **l'Aràbia Saudita** 'Saudi Arabia', **l'Àsia Menor** 'Asia Minor', **els Estats Units** 'the United States', **els Països Baixos** 'the Netherlands'. (**El Regne Unit** 'the United Kingdom' always appears with the article but use is optional for (**la**) **Gran Bretanya** 'Great Britain'.) Major exceptions: **Corea del Nord** 'North Korea', **Corea del Sud** 'South Korea', **Irlanda del Nord** 'Northern Ireland', **Nova Guinea** 'New Guinea', **Nova Zelanda** 'New Zealand'.

Names of island groups bear the definite article: **les Balears**, **les Canàries**, **les Filipines**, **les Hawaii**.

Most names ending in **-a** have no article: **Alsàcia** 'Alsace', **Armènia**, **Croàcia** 'Croatia', **Gascunya** 'Gascony', **Mongòlia**, **Sibèria**, etc.; but note with the article **l'Argentina**, **l'Índia**, **l'Indo-xina** 'Indochina', **la Xina** 'China', and usually **l'Aràbia**, **l'Àsia**, **l'Arcàdia**, **la Campània** 'Campania'; variably (**l'**)**Àfrica**, (**la**) **Florida**, (**la**) **Llombardia** 'Lombardy', (**la**) **Xampanya** 'Champagne'.

Most names of countries or regions ending other than in **-a** do have the article: **el Brasil**, **el Canadà**, **l'Equador**, **el Iemen** 'Yemen', **l'Iran**, **l'Iraq**, **el Japó** 'Japan', **el Marroc** 'Morocco', **el Paraguai**, **el Perú**, **el Piemont** 'Piedmont', **el Sudan**, **el Tibet**, **el Tirol**, **el Txad** 'Chad', etc. Variable are: (**l'**)**Aragó** 'Aragon', (**el**) **Vietnam**. Examples without the article are: **Lleó** 'León', **Luxemburg**, **Portugal**, **Xile** 'Chile'.

Names of countries and regions which are generally used with the definite article may appear without the article in lists, and on labels or addresses, and so on: **Canadà**, **Uruguai**, **Xina**; but the article will appear when the name is used in a phrase: **els habitants del Canadà** 'the inhabitants of Canada', **les exportacions de l'Uruguai** 'Uruguay's exports', **un viatge a la Xina** 'a trip to China'.

Use of the definite article in urban geography also deserves comment. The article does not appear in street signs: **Plaça de la Revolució** 'Revolution

Square', **Carrer d'Aribau** 'Aribau Street', **Ronda de la Universitat**, etc., but it is used when talking about these streets, squares, avenues, etc.:

> **Abans vivia al carrer Balmes però s'ha traslladat fa poc a la plaça del Pi.**
> He used to live in Balmes Street but he recently moved to Pi Square.

3.2   INDEFINITE ARTICLES

As with the definite article, there is general correspondence between the behaviour of the Catalan indefinite article and 'a/an' in English. Divergence is most noticeable in relation to:

(i)   The fact that the Catalan indefinite article **un/una** can appear in the plural:

> **Són uns ganduls.**
> They are lazy people.

> **Tens unes idees ben rares.**
> You have (some) very strange ideas.

(ii)   The fact that in some contexts the indefinite article is not used before singular count nouns:

> **Tinc passaport.**
> I have a passport.

> **S'escriu sense guionet.**
> It's written without a hyphen.

> **És broma.**
> I'm only teasing. (lit. It's a joke.)

(iii)   A plural indefinite subject, in preverbal position, usually requires an article.

These features are covered in detail below (**3.2.3**).

3.2.1   MORPHOLOGY OF THE INDEFINITE ARTICLE

	singular	*plural*
masculine	**un**	**uns**
feminine	**una**	**unes**

3.2.2   SYNTAX OF THE INDEFINITE ARTICLE

The indefinite article is usually needed before each noun given in a list:

L'acompanyaven un nen i una nena.
A boy and (a) girl came with him.

Encara hi han d'instal·lar una dutxa i un bidet.
They still have to install a shower and (a) bidet in here.

This does not apply when the nouns have the same referent:

Ho ha fet amb una elegància i delicadesa extraordinàries.
He did it with extraordinary elegance and delicacy.

un poeta i periodista complert
an accomplished poet and journalist (one person)

The restrictions on the combination of masculines and feminines pointed out for the definite article (**3.1.2**) apply here as well:

uns nens i unes nenes d'uns col·legis i unes escoles
some boys and some girls from some secondary and some primary schools

uns nens i nenes d'uns col·legis i escoles
some boys and girls from some secondary and primary schools

but not: *****unes nenes i nens d'unes escoles i col·legis**
          some girls and boys from some primary and secondary schools

Also observed is the rule that requires subject nouns before the verb usually to have some kind of determiner (**3.2.3**):

Uns amics vindran a saludar-te. (not *****Amics vindran a saludar-te.**)
Some friends will come to say hello to you.

Options are available when the subject comes after the verb, or when the noun concerned is not the subject of the sentence:

Vindran (uns) amics a saludar-te.	Some friends will come to say hello to you.
T'he vist amb uns amics.	I saw you with (some) friends.
T'he vist amb amics.	I saw you with friends.

Some subtleties of **uns/unes** are covered in **3.2.4**. The use of **un/una** as impersonal subject is discussed in **29.3**.

3.2.3   PRESENCE AND ABSENCE OF THE INDEFINITE ARTICLE

As mentioned above, preverbal indefinite subjects, whether singular or plural, generally have an indefinite article; a postverbal indefinite plural subject may have no article.

> **Unes propostes han sorgit per regularitzar la posició dels estudiants estrangers.**
> approx. = **Han sorgit propostes per regularitzar la posició dels estudiants estrangers.**
> Proposals have come up for regularizing the situation of foreign students.

> **Sonaven trets a tot arreu.** (not *Trets sonaven a tot arrreu.)
> Gunfire could be heard all around.

> **Van venir col·legues de tots els països.**
> Colleagues came from every country.

The expected indefinite article before a preverbal plural subject may optionally be omitted in enumerations:

> **Homes, dones, criatures, tothom va sortir a rebre'ls.** (Fabra)
> Men, women and children, everyone came out to greet them.

Also in proverbs, such as:

> **Hostes vingueren que de casa ens tragueren.**
> lit. Guests came who removed us from home. (approx. They ate us out of house and home.)

Another exception is observed in a sentence like:

> **Idees com aquestes només se t'acuden a tu.**
> Ideas like this only occur to you.

This exceptional usage is not possible with a singular indefinite noun phrase:

> *Idea com aquesta només se t'acut a tu.
> *Aigua s'escampava pertot arreu. → S'escampava aigua pertot arreu.
> Water spread everywhere.

Where there is an option the difference between the indefinite article (**amb uns amics**) and zero (**amb amics**) is rather difficult to define. In the plural, as here, it can be said that **uns/unes** corresponds to **alguns/algunes** 'some'/'certain'; it tends to suggest a more specific, usually small, number. To some degree the choice between 'some' and zero in plural noun phrases in English is similar for example, 'with some friends', 'with friends'. In Catalan a similar choice may occur also with singular indefinite phrases. **Hi haurà examen de final de curs** 'There will be an end-of-year exam' makes a statement differing slightly from **Hi haurà un examen de final de curs**, which has the same translation but which is specific about the number of examinations.

Against this general background, in the following sections we approach the question of particular uses involving the presence or absence of the indefinite article.

(i)   Absence of the indefinite article before predicative nouns denoting profession, status, and so on

No article is used before nouns in predicate position which identify the subject as a member of a class (profession, occupation, social status or sex):

El germà gran és metge i els altres són enginyers.
The elder brother is a doctor and the others are engineers.

El seu oncle era professor de matemàtiques.
His uncle was a maths teacher.

La meva veïna és vídua.
My neighbour is a widow.

Em preguntava si la persona que mirava era home o dona.
I wondered whether the person I was looking at was a man or a woman.

A predicative noun used metaphorically, however, entails the use of the indefinite article: **És un inquisidor** 'He's an inquisitor' (by nature, not profession), **Ets un pispa** 'You're a sneak thief' (e.g. said when someone has 'borrowed' something not theirs). The article is also retained if the meaning is 'one of . . .':

–Qui és aquell? –No ho sé; deu ser un jardiner.
'Who is that?' 'I don't know; he must be a gardener' (i.e. 'one of the gardeners' not 'a gardener by profession').

If the predicative noun is qualified or restricted by an adjective or adjective phrase, the article is required:

És una actriu famosa.
She is a famous actress.

És un arquitecte que ha fet molta feina a l'estranger.
He is an architect who has done a lot of work abroad.

This kind of construction with a qualified noun, entailing use of the article, is not to be confused with compound noun phrases (like **professor de matemàtiques** above) that in themselves denote an identifiable profession or general category: **Havia estat entrenador de cavalls** 'He had been a horse trainer'. This principle applies to a wider category of predicates of **ser**: in **Tu ets (un) home seriós** 'You are a serious man', the absence of the indefinite article places the person referred to in a pre-existing category of 'serious people', whereas the presence of the article makes the qualification **seriós** more descriptive than categorizing.

(ii)   Absence of the indefinite article in certain other circumstances after ser

The indefinite article may be absent in some common set expressions where a noun is complement of the verb 'be':

Era qüestió de . . .	It was a question of . . .
Són víctimes d'un equívoc.	They are victims of a mix-up.
És broma.	I'm only kidding.
Ha estat pura casualitat.	It was (a) sheer coincidence.
És llàstima.	It's a pity.
És part del nostre deure.	It's (a) part of our duty.
És norma de la casa no admetre menors d'edat.	It's a house rule not to admit minors.

No hard and fast rule governs this behaviour and many other similar expressions retain the indefinite article:

És una pena.	It's a pity.	**Ha estat un error.**	It was a mistake.
És un problema.	It's a problem.	**Serà un èxit.**	It'll be a success.
És un desastre.	It's a disaster.		

This is an area of usage in which omission is optionally allowed for stylistic effect:

És obligació dels rics fer obres caritatives.
It is an obligation of the wealthy to do charitable works.

És axioma que el peix gros es menja sempre el peix petit.
It is axiomatic that the big fish always swallows the little fish.

Under this heading we can also consider use of the indefinite article to distinguish nouns from adjectives:

En Pere és presumit.	Pere is presumptuous.
En Pere és un presumit.	Pere is a presumptuous person.
Sou idealistes.	You are idealistic.
Sou uns idealistes.	You are idealists.

(iii)   Absence of indefinite article before objects of certain verbs

Catalan does not use the indefinite article before count nouns acting as objects of the verbs **tenir** 'have', **portar/dur** 'wear' (clothes, etc.), **buscar/cercar** 'look for', **trobar** 'find', **comprar** 'buy', and others. The common denominator of the object nouns in question is that they are items which are normally had or used one at a time: **Tenc cotxe** 'I have a car', **Té clau de l'apartament** 'He has a key to the flat', **Abans duia barba** 'He used to have a beard', **Cercam pis al centre** 'We are looking for a flat in the town centre', **Troba taxi sempre que vol** 'She finds a taxi whenever she wants one'.

When the indefinite article is used after the verbs under discussion it is with an object, often qualified, that is seen as specific and as having particularized relevance:

Portava una brusa blanca i uns pantalons de ratlles grogues i blaves.
She was wearing a white blouse and (a pair of) yellow and blue striped trousers.

Tenia un aspecte de gueriller vençut.
He had the look of a defeated warrior.

Compare **tenir aspecte (de)** which means, much more generally, 'look': **Això té bon aspecte** 'This looks good', **El teu amic té aspecte de setciències** 'Your friend looks like a know-all'.
The point is reinforced by comparing

Tenia dona i fills.
He had a wife and children.

with

Tenia una dona manyaga i uns fills obedients.
He had a loving wife and obedient children.

(iv)   Absence of indefinite article after prepositions **amb**, **sense**, *and* **en**

The principle explained in (iii) above also operates in this case. The indefinite article is absent when no need is felt to underline that the object (even when a singular count noun) is specific:

Ha vingut sense cartera.	He came without a briefcase.
un bar amb terrassa	a bar with outside tables
un ca sense cua	a dog without a tail
Si surts sense paraigua, segur que plourà.	If you go out without an umbrella, it's bound to rain.

Even when the noun is qualified the article may be absent:

Escriu amb bolígraf negre.	She writes with a black ballpoint.

But compare **Escriu amb un bolígraf negre que li va regalar un cosí seu**, 'She writes with a black ballpoint that a cousin of hers gave her', where the complement is now distinctly individuated. The article is also retained if the idea of '(a single) one' is emphasized: **sense un duro** 'without a single *duro* (five-peseta coin)'.
The article is not used after **en** with nouns expressing a means of transport: **Han vingut en tren/en avió/en cotxe** 'They came by train/by plane/by car', etc. The article does appear after **en** when the noun is qualified: **Han arribat en un avió militar** 'They arrived in a military aircraft'. Central dialects substitute

amb for **en** in this context, systematically when the noun is unqualified (**anar amb cotxe, amb tren, amb avió**, etc.), less frequently when the noun is qualified. Note also **parlar en veu baixa/alta** 'speak in a low/loud voice'.

(v)   Absence of indefinite article with nouns in apposition

The indefinite article is normally absent in appositive phrases (which are, we note, a feature much more of the written than of the spoken language):

la poesia èpica, gènere poc conreat en la literatura del segle XX
epic poetry, a genre little cultivated in twentieth-century literature

Va néixer a Reus, ciutat que ha produït molts fills famosos.
He was born in Reus, a town that has produced many famous sons.

In less formal language the article need not be suppressed before the noun in apposition:

Comentàvem el partit amb en Jaume, un fan incondicional d'aquell club.
We were discussing the game with Jaume, an unconditional fan of that club.

els tomàquets i el cogombre, uns bons ingredients per a una amanida d'estiu
tomatoes and cucumber, good ingredients for a summer salad

(vi)   Other expressions contrasting with English

The indefinite article does not appear:

(a)   After **com a** 'in the capacity of' or 'by way of' (see **14.3**) nor after **a manera de** (nor the more elevated synonym **a guisa de**):

Anirà a la cerimònia com a amic de la núvia.
He'll go to the ceremony as a friend of the bride's.

Dóna-li mil pessetes com a paga i senyal.
Give him 1000 pesetas as a down payment.

Considerem, com a exemple d'això . . .
Let us consider, as an example of this . . .

A manera d'introducció us explicaré aquest acudit.
By way of an introduction I'll tell you this joke.

(b)   After **quin/quina** 'What a . . .' in exclamations:

Quin miracle!	What a miracle!
Quina manera de guanyar-se la vida!	What a way to earn a living!

(c)   Before **tal** 'such a' and **mig/mitja** 'half (a)'.

A notional distinction is made between **un tal** 'of such a kind' and, without the article, **tal** 'such a = similar', the examples usually given being:

Jo no he emprat mai un tal llenguatge.
I have never used language of that kind.

Ella no ha dit mai tal cosa.
She never said such a thing.

Note also **un tal Sugranyes** 'a certain (Mr) Sugranyes', **un tal Martí** 'some Martí or other'/'somebody called Martí'.

English expressions involving 'a half'/'half a' are translated by the adjective **mig** (see **10.9**): **mitja taronja**, 'half an orange', **mitja horeta** 'less than half an hour', **mig quilo** 'half a kilo'; note that with the indefinite article **un mig quilo** corresponds to 'about half a kilo'.

The influence of Spanish is said to be responsible for non-standard omission of the article with indefinite adjectives **altre** 'other' and **cert** 'certain' (see **8.3**):

Ho hauries de fer d'una altra manera. (non-standard . . . d'altra manera)
You ought to do it another way.

Un color indefinible que té un cert to groguenc. (non-standard . . . té cert to groguenc)
An indefinable colour that has a certain yellowish hue.

3.2.4   SPECIAL USES OF **uns/unes**

The plural indefinite article in Catalan covers various shades of meaning that may require special glossing in English translation:

(i)   *Uns/unes before numbers, meaning 'approximately'*

unes sis-centes cinquanta pàgines
about 650 pages/some 650 pages

La pesta va afectar la regió durant uns quinze anys.
The plague affected the region for some fifteen years.

(ii)   *Uns/unes 'a few'*

Anem a fer unes copes.
Let's go and have a few drinks.

Encara tinc unes mínimes esperances d'aconseguir-ho.
I still have a few slight hopes of achieving it.

The idea conveyed may be vaguer than 'a few', expressing a limited quantity sometimes put across with connotations of restraint on the part of the speaker, like 'a couple of' or 'one or two':

Hi ha uns detalls que voldria aclarir.
There are one or two details I'd like to clarify.

This moderating function can be so subtle, or so weak, that it merges with the normal use of **uns/unes** as plural indefinite article:

Hem escoltat unes coses que ens han esgarrifat.
We have listened to (some) things which have horrified us.

(iii)   Uns/unes: symmetrical pairs

The plural indefinite article occurs with the meaning of 'a pair of' (symmetrical and joined) objects always conceived of as a pair (see **2.1.7**), the commonest being: **unes tisores** '(a pair of) scissors', **une pinces** '(a pair of) tweezers', **unes alicates** '(a pair of) pincers', **unes pantalons** '(a pair of) trousers', **uns calçotets** '(a pair of) underpants', **unes calces** '(a pair of) knickers', **uns pantis** '(a pair of) tights', **unes ulleres** '(a pair of) spectacles', **uns prismàtics** '(a pair of) binoculars', **uns auriculars** '(a pair of) earphones', and also **unes cortines** '(a pair of) curtains'. Footwear (**uns mitjons** 'socks', **unes mitges** 'stockings', **unes botes** 'boots', **unes sabates** 'shoes') and **uns guants** 'gloves' can be presented thus, but they can also be preceded by **un parell de** 'a pair of'.

(iv)   Emphatic or metaphorical use of uns/unes

As with the singular indefinite article (**3.2.3**, especially **iii**) the plural form may be retained, where normally not expected, to show that an indefinite noun is being used emphatically or metaphorically:

Són uns fills de puta.	They're real bastards.
Sou uns pallassos.	You're behaving like clowns.

3.2.5   APPRECIATIVE USE OF THE INDEFINITE ARTICLE

Emphatic use of the indefinite article: in sentences like **Allí fan un vi!** or **He vist uns cotxes!** the indefinite article emphasizes admiration by underlining the uniqueness in its class of the object referred to by the noun. Contrasted with the normal statements **Allí fan vi** 'They make wine there' and **He vist cotxes** 'I saw cars', the versions with the indefinite article might be translated 'What wine they make there!', 'The cars that I saw!'.

With singular mass nouns qualified by an adjective or a relative clause the use of the indefinite article is emphatic: **Allí serveixen cafè molt bo** or **Allí** serveixen un cafè molt bo 'They serve very good coffee there'; **Duc llenya sequíssima** or **Duc una llenya sequíssima** 'I've brought some very dry firewood'. It must be said that when an intensifier (e.g. **molt, ben**) or a superlative is involved in the adjectival qualification, the presence of the indefinite article is more normal than its absence.

3.3 THE PERSONAL ARTICLE

Proper names of persons, both given names and surnames, are often introduced by an article; in many varieties the standard definite article (**el, la**) has taken over from the original personal article forms.

The personal article is not used at all in Valencia and southern Catalonia.

3.3.1 MORPHOLOGY OF THE PERSONAL ARTICLE

	before consonant	*before vowel*
masculine	en (el)	n' (l')
feminine	na (la)	n' (l')

Contraction occurs between **ca** (but not **a, de**, or **per**) and the personal article **en**. The circumstances and resulting forms follow the model of those for **el**: **can Joan, ca n'Enric** (see below, in conjunction with the section in **3.1.1** on contractions).

3.3.2 USAGE OF THE PERSONAL ARTICLE

Four patterns of usage of the personal article can be identified:

(i)   **En, Na, N'**
(ii) **en, na, n'**
(iii) **en, la, l'**
(iv) **el, la, l'**

Pattern (i), with initial capital letter, is an honorific title used in formal written style, preceding given name + surname. It corresponds very roughly to the use of Esq. in English: **En Miquel Ferrer, N'Antònia Salvà i Pérez**. It cannot be combined with other titles like **Senyoreta, Doctor**, etc.

Pattern (ii) is found in the Balearic Islands. There the personal article is used very widely, before given names or surnames, of individuals personally known or not, current or historical: **en Nicolau Dols/en Nicolau/en Dols, na Lourdes Urquidi, n'Eiximenis, na Mercè Rodoreda**. Only names of persons in the Bible or in Classical antiquity appear without the article: **Maria, Pilat, Aristòtil, Ciceró**.

Pattern (iii) is current in Catalonia generally, with pattern (iv) more usual in colloquial Barcelona speech. In Catalonia the personal articles (patterns (iii) and (iv)) are typically used when the speaker expects the hearer will recognize, from the context or from shared assumptions, who is being spoken about. In this respect the personal article resembles the definite article with more prototypical noun phrases; thus **En Max m'ho va explicar** 'Max told me', **Vas a veure l'Alan?** 'Are you going to see Alan?', **Ho vaig consultar amb la Rigau** 'I discussed it with Rigau', **L'Oriol Pi és qui ho porta** 'Oriol Pi is the one who is dealing with it'. The personal article is not typically used in Catalonia when a name identifies someone who is taken to be well known to everybody, that is, for public figures or historical figures. So **Ha cantat Raimon** 'Raimon sang' (where Raimon is the well-known protest singer-songwriter), **Montserrat Caballé cantarà divendres al Palau de la Música** rather than **La Montserrat Caballé . . .** 'Montserrat Caballé sings on Friday at the Palau de la Música', **Beethoven va tornar sord** 'Beethoven went deaf', **Gaudí projectà la Sagrada Família** 'Gaudí planned the Sagrada Família'. The personal article *can* be used with the surname of a public figure, **en Pujol, la Caballé**; the article gives a connotation of familiarity or solidarity, that is, it invites the listener to consider the person identified not on the basis of unique salience but on the basis of mutual knowledge. In this context, the article used with a famous name can be slightly derogatory, as possibly **la Thatcher** 'Thatcher (the person of that name that we all know about)'.

Within Catalonia, where the personal article is always **l'** before names beginning with a vowel, and **la** before other feminine names, **en** and **el** are in variation before consonant-initial masculine names. Where both are found alongside one another, outside Barcelona, **el** seems to be more used before given names, such as, **el Miquel, el Pere**, while **en** is preferred before surnames: **en Ballester, en Garriga**. Pattern (iii), with **en** in both cases, is regarded as more 'correct'.

The personal article does not appear in vocatives: **Miquel, vine aquí!** 'Miquel, come here!' (never ***En Miquel, vine aquí!**).

The Catalan equivalent of English 'the Smiths', 'the Wilkinsons', etc. uses the plural article **els**, but without making the family name plural: **els Oliver** = **la família Oliver** 'the Olivers', 'the Oliver family', **els Porta** = **la família Porta**, etc. (**2.1.8**).

3.4   IDIOMS WITH FEMININE ARTICLES

Feminine articles figure in a variety of idiomatic expressions in Catalan:

(i)   Idiomatic adverbial phrases with **a la/a les**

When the feminine definite article is preceded by preposition **a** and followed by an adjective (often an adjective denoting geographical origin) the noun **manera** can be understood between article and adjective (cf. French *à la*):

Com t'estimes més que et preparin el sopar, a la (manera) francesa o a la (manera) russa?
How do you prefer your supper to be prepared, in the French or the Russian style?

Dinarem de pop a la mallorquina.
We'll have Majorcan-style octopus for lunch.

Several idioms, which are adverbial phrases unrelated to geographical origin, also begin with **a la/a les**:

a la babalà	crazily	**a les clares**	plainly, openly
a la puta	carelessly (vulgar)	**a les fosques**	in the dark
a la torta	twistedly	**a les palpentes**	by touch
a les bones	willingly	**a les totes**	really well/quickly

Some of the glosses given above are very approximate; English equivalents may be variously idiomatic, according to context:

Es va haver de vestir a les palpentes.
She had to feel her way into her clothes.

Si no m'ho dóna a les bones, li ho prendré a les males.
I'll get it out of him one way or the other/whether he likes it or not.

Parla alemany a les totes.
He can jabber away in German.

*(ii)   Idiomatic use of **la de/una de** expressing quantity*

In colloquial language the feminine singular articles (strongly emphasized in pronunciation) occur in admirative expressions of quantity, roughly equivalent to 'loads/tons of':

N'hi havia una d'estrangerots, i no vam poder banyar-nos enlloc.
There were all these horrid foreigners, and we couldn't get a swim anywhere.

La de vegades que t'he hagut de dir això!
The times I've had to tell you this!

Amb la d'empreses que es dediquen a això, la competència és fortíssima.
With ever so many firms doing this line, competition is fierce.

(iii) *Idiomatic feminine articles without visible antecedents*

A number of quite lively idioms contain the feminine article with no antecedent:

La que s'armarà si ton pare ho sap!
There'll be one hell of a to-do if your father finds out!

No vulguis saber la que em va dir.
You can't imagine what he said to me.

We may suppose that the understood noun here is **cosa** 'thing' or **feta** 'deed', as in

N'ha dites unes de grosses.	He came out with some really rich ones.
Me n'ha passat una com un cove.	Something really bizarre has happened to me.

This implicit feminine referent can also be detected in various idioms involving other parts of speech:

passar-les magres	have a lean time
portar-ne alguna de cap	have a bee in one's bonnet
Se les sap totes.	She doesn't miss a trick.
Aquesta me la pagaràs.	I'll get my own back (on you for that).
Se la/les dóna d'expert.	He reckons he's an expert.

4 ADJECTIVES

Attributive adjectives in Catalan agree in gender with the head of the noun phrase they appear in (expressed or understood): **la meva estimada muller** 'my (*f.*) dear (*f.*) wife (*f.*)'. Predicative adjectives agree with their subject noun phrase: **Aquelles taronges no són pas madures** 'Those (*f.pl.*) oranges (*f.pl.*) are not ripe (*f.pl.*)'. Most adjectives have distinct forms for masculine and feminine, in the singular at least, and are referred to here as 'adjectives with two endings'. There is no direct relation between word ending and gender, although it is true that consonant endings and -**e**/-**o** endings tend to represent the masculine, while -**a** tends to represent the feminine. Exceptions to this 'rule' are so many (see **4.1.2**) that it cannot be taken for granted. Adjectives showing no distinction between the masculine singular and feminine singular form are referred to as 'adjectives with one ending'. Our main discussion of morphology (**4.1.1**–3) concentrates on this distinction between singular adjectives with one and with two endings; formation of plural adjectives is covered in **4.1.4**.

The typical position of attributive adjectives in Catalan is following the noun which they qualify. This is true of all specifying adjectives (**les arts pictòriques** 'pictorial arts', **una escala metàl·lica** 'a metal ladder'), but for other types position can be affected by various factors of sentence structure and pragmatics. The question is considered in **4.2.1**.

4.1 MORPHOLOGY OF ADJECTIVES

4.1.1 FEMININE SINGULAR ADJECTIVES: THE BASIC TWO-ENDING PATTERN

The normal way to form the feminine singular of an adjective in Catalan is by adding the morpheme -**a** to the stem. It is a convenient simplification to say that feminine forms of adjectives are based on masculine forms. (In many cases, though not always, the masculine form is indeed the bare stem.) Since masculine forms (rather than stems) are what are given in dictionary entries, we shall adopt this convenient simplification here (as we did for the corresponding gender formation of nouns; see **1.1.1**).

The commonest pattern is that in which a feminine adjective is derived from the corresponding masculine one by the addition of the feminine gender suffix -**a** (replacing any unstressed final -**e**, or -**o** of the masculine). Thus:

bonic (*m.*)	bonica (*f.*)	pretty
malèvol (*m.*)	malèvola (*f.*)	spiteful
prim (*m.*)	prima (*f.*)	thin
fort (*m.*)	forta (*f.*)	strong, loud

baix (*m.*)	baixa (*f.*)	short, low
pobre (*m.*)	pobra (*f.*)	poor
flonjo (*m.*)	flonja (*f.*)	spongy
etc.		

In many cases there are consequential modifications to spelling (**37.3** and **37.5**):

tebi (*m.*)	tèbia (*f.*)	lukewarm
danès (*m.*)	danesa (*f.*)	Danish

vague (*m.*)	vaga (*f.*)	vague
etc.		

4.1.2   MORE COMPLEX ALTERNATIONS IN ADJECTIVES WITH TWO ENDINGS

4.1.2.1   *Adjectives ending in a stressed vowel*

Adjectives ending in a stressed vowel add **-na** for the feminine singular; this **-n-** appears in the plural forms also (see **4.1.4** and cf. **2.1.3**):

m.sg.	*f.sg.*	*m.pl.*	*f.pl.*	
sa	sana	sans	sanes	healthy
bo	bona	bons	bones	good
ple	plena	plens	plenes	full
amè	amena	amens	amenes	pleasant
genuí	genuïna	genuïns	genuïnes	genuine
etc.				

Exceptions to this rule are **cru/crua/crus/crues** 'raw', and **nu/nua/nus/nues** 'naked'.

4.1.2.2   *Adjectives whose masculine singular ends in -t or -c preceded by a vowel*

As a final voiced plosive (**-b**, **-d**, **-g**) is unpronounceable in Catalan, many masculines whose underlying stem ends in one of these consonants have them written as **-p**, **-t**, **-c** respectively (though there happen to be no adjectives illustrating the **p–b** alternation): **buit** 'empty' (but **buidar** 'to empty'), **menut** 'tiny' (but **menudesa** 'tininess'), **cec** 'blind' (but **ceguesa** 'blindness'), **antic** 'ancient' (but **antiguitat** 'antiquity'), etc. All these adjectives show the voiced consonant in their feminines: **buida, menuda, cega, antiga**, etc. There are very many instances of the **t–d** alternation, including the great majority of past participles.

adequat (*m.*)	adequada (*f.*)	adequate
eixerit (*m.*)	eixerida (*f.*)	smart

enfeinat (*m.*)	enfeinada (*f.*)	busy
humit (*m.*)	humida (*f.*)	damp

mut (*m.*) **muda** (*f.*) dumb	**temut** (*m.*) **temuda** (*f.*) feared	
	etc.	

There is a considerable number of adjectives displaying the **c–g** alternation such as:

feixuc (*m.*)	**feixuga** (*f.*)	heavy	**gallec** (*m.*)	**gallega** (*f.*)	Galician
feréstec (*m.*)	**feréstega** (*f.*)	wild	**groc** (*m.*)	**groga** (*f.*)	yellow
				etc.	

Contrasting with the last two sets are masculine adjectives ending in **-t** or **-c** which is already present in the stem. In such cases these stem consonants are maintained in the feminine.

(i)   *Adjectives ending in -t with feminine in -ta:*

All those ending in **-et** (including words containing the diminutive suffix; see **4.1.5**):

abstret (*m.*)	**abstreta** (*f.*)	preoccupied
analfabet (*m.*)	**analfabeta** (*f.*)	illiterate
complet (*m.*)	**completa** (*f.*)	complete
contrafet (*m.*)	**contrafeta** (*f.*)	counterfeit
estret (*m.*)	**estreta** (*f.*)	narrow/tight
estretet (*m.*)	**estreteta** (*f.*)	nice and tight
net (*m.*)	**neta** (*f.*)	clean
secret (*m.*)	**secreta** (*f.*)	secret
etc.		

All those ending in **-ot**:

devot (*m.*)	**devota** (*f.*)	devout
remot (*m.*)	**remota** (*f.*)	remote
tot (*m.*)	**tota** (*f.*)	all, whole

etc. with the exception of **got–goda** 'Gothic' and its compounds **ostrogot** 'Ostrogothic' and **visigot** 'Visigothic'.

All those ending in unstressed **-it**:

inèdit (*m.*)	**inèdita** (*f.*)	unpublished
insòlit (*m.*)	**insòlita** (*f.*)	unusual
pretèrit (*m.*)	**pretèrita** (*f.*)	past
etc.		

There follows a list of most of the adjectives ending in **-at**, **-it**, or **-ut** in which **t** is retained in the feminine:

absolut	absoluta	absolute	fortuït	fortuïta	fortuitous
barat	barata	cheap	grat	grata	pleasing
beat	beata	blessed	gratuït	gratuïta	free of
beneit	beneita	simple, holy			charge,
brut	bruta	dirty			gratuitous
carabrut	carabruta	dirty-faced	hirsut	hirsuta	hirsute
caut	cauta	wary	immediat	immediata	immediate
confit	confita	preserved	imperit	imperita	inexpert
contrit	contrita	contrite	impol·lut	impol·luta	unpolluted
convolut	convoluta	convoluted	inaudit	inaudita	unheard-of
cuit	cuita	cooked	infinit	infinita	infinite
diminut	diminuta	diminutive	ingrat	ingrata	ungrateful,
dissolut	dissoluta	dissolute			disagree-
eixut	eixuta	dry			able
erudit	erudita	learnèd	innat	innata	innate
escrit	escrita	written	insensat	insensata	senseless
		(compounds	lat	lata	broad
		of escrit	manuscrit	manuscrita	handwritten
		inflect the	perit	perita	skilled
		same way)	petit	petita	small
favorit	favorita	favourite	sensat	sensata	sensible
finit	finita	finite	susdit	susdita	aforesaid
fit	fita	fixed	timorat	timorata	God-fearing

(ii)   *Among adjectives ending in -c, the following endings retain c unaltered*

-aic

arcaic (*m.*)	arcaica (*f.*)	archaic
laic (*m.*)	laica (*f.*)	lay
etc.		

-ac (unstressed)

elegíac (*m.*)	elegíaca (*f.*)	elegiac
maníac (*m.*)	maníaca (*f.*)	maniacal
etc.		

-ic (unstressed)

bàsic (*m.*)	bàsica (*f.*)	basic
màgic (*m.*)	màgica (*f.*)	magic
etc.		

This -ic/-ica group is quite large, with only two exceptions: **aràbic/aràbiga** 'Arabic' and **místic/místiga** 'faded'.

-oc (unstressed)

equívoc (*m.*)	equívoca (*f.*)	ambiguous
unívoc (*m.*)	unívoca (*f.*)	unambiguous

The following examples complete the list of adjectives ending in invariable -c:

eslovac	eslovaca	Slovak	sec	seca	dry
flac	flaca	lean	suec	sueca	Swedish
opac	opaca	opaque	txec	txeca	Czech
quec	queca	stammering	txecoslovac	txeco-	Czecho-
rebec	rebeca	obstinate		slovaca	slovakian

The adjectives **inic** 'iniquitous', **oblic** 'oblique', **propinc** 'neighbouring', and **ventríloc** 'ventriloquous' derive from stems ending in /-kw/ and, therefore, their feminine correlatives are **iniqua**, **obliqua**, **propinqua** and **ventríloqua**.

4.1.2.3 *Adjectives ending in -s*

A voiced sibilant [z] is also unpronounceable in word-final position in Catalan. For this reason masculine forms of adjectives whose stem ends in this sound turn it into its unvoiced correlative [s]. It is then unpredictable on the basis of the masculine singular form alone, ending in -s, whether its feminine form will contain intervocalic [s] (written ss) or [z] (written s). See **37.3.2**. The majority of adjectives whose masculine ends in s preceded by a vowel also show single -s- (pronounced [z]) in the feminine (and plural). For example:

abundós (*m.*)	abundosa (*f.*)	abundant	(*pl.* **abundosos/-es**)
cortès (*m.*)	cortesa (*f.*)	polite	(*pl.* **cortesos/-es**)
francès (*m.*)	francesa (*f.*)	French	(*pl.* **francesos/-es**)
gris (*m.*)	grisa (*f.*)	grey	(*pl.* **grisos/-es**)
precís (*m.*)	precisa (*f.*)	precise	(*pl.* **precisos/-es**)
etc.			

The alternation -s (*m.*)/-ssa (*f.*) – with *m.pl.* -ssos and *f.pl.* -sses – is found in adjectives containing the augmentative suffix -às (**4.1.5**) or the derivational suffix -ís:

-às:

dolçàs (*m.*)	dolçassa (*f.*)	sickly sweet
grandàs (*m.*)	grandassa (*f.*)	great big
etc.		

-ís:

oblidadís (*m.*)	oblidadissa (*f.*)	forgetful
massís (*m.*)	massissa (*f.*)	solid
etc.		

The following is a comprehensive list of the remaining adjectives showing an unvoiced [s] in the feminine (-ssa) (and in the plural -ssos/-sses):

aglòs	aglossal	**malaltús**	sickly
confés	confessed	**mestís**	half-caste
cras	gross	**mus**	blunt
escàs	scarce	**naquis**	tiny
esmús	blunt	**obsés**	obsessed
espès	thick	**postís**	false
exprés	express	**profés**	professed
gras	fat	**revés**	complicated
gros	big (the compounds of	**ros**	fair
	gros, e.g. **bocagròs**	**cella-ros**	with fair eyebrows
	inflect in the same	**rus**	Russian
	way)	**suís/suïssa**	Swiss
hipoglòs	hypoglossal	**talòs**	dull-witted
inconcús	unshakable		
las	weary		

4.1.2.4   *Adjective stems in -l·l-*

With l·l being unpronounceable in final position, it reduces to -l in masculine singulars, but it remains in feminines, before the -a ending: gal/gal·la 'Gaulish', nul/nul·la 'null', tranquil/tranquil·la 'calm'. Apart from this set, though, the majority of adjectives ending in -l are of the 'one ending' type, that is, have no distinct feminine singular form (see **4.1.3**).

4.1.2.5   *Adjectives ending in -ig*

A voiced palatal fricative [ʒ] (represented in other positions by g/j) is unpronounceable in Catalan in word-final position and is replaced by an affricate (written -ig). It is impossible to determine from the masculine singular form if the stem ended originally in a fricative or in an affricate and, therefore, whether the feminine will have a final -ja (fricative) or -tja (affricate).

feminines ending in -tja: lleig/lletja 'ugly', mig/mitja 'half'
feminines ending in -ja: boig/boja 'mad', roig/roja 'red(-haired)'

4.1.2.6   *Adjectives ending in semiconsonantal -u*

Adjectives whose masculine singular ends in semiconsonantal -u follow one of three different patterns in the feminine. The commonest is for -u to alternate with -va as in:

blau (*m.*)	blava (*f.*)	blue		nou (*m.*)	nova (*f.*)	new
còncau (*m.*)	còncava (*f.*)	concave		tou (*m.*)	tova (*f.*)	soft
efectiu (*m.*)	efectiva (*f.*)	effective		etc.		
viu (*m.*)	viva (*f.*)	living				

This pattern accounts for all adjectives ending in -au or -ou, and the vast majority of those in -iu. The second pattern retains semiconsonantal -u- in the feminine; it is found in four adjectives in -iu which do not follow the more general pattern above:

geliu (*m.*)	geliua (*f.*)	icy		nadiu (*m.*)	nadiua (*f.*)	native
joliu (*m.*)	joliua (*f.*)	dainty		soliu (*m.*)	soliua (*f.*)	solitary

The third pattern is found only among adjectives in -eu, but accounts for the majority here; u is cut off and is replaced by -a in the feminine:

ateu (*m.*)	atea (*f.*)	atheist		plebeu(*m.*)	plebea(*f.*)	plebeian
europeu (*m.*)	europea (*f.*)	European		etc.		
hebreu (*m.*)	hebrea (*f.*)	Hebrew				

Two adjectives in -eu have -eua in the feminine: **garneu/garneua** 'crafty' and **moreu/moreua** 'dark'; two have -eva in the feminine: **jueu/jueva** 'Jewish' and **sueu/sueva** 'of the Suevi'. The possessive adjectives **meu** 'my', **teu** 'your', **seu** 'his/her/their/your' have in the feminine **meva** or **meua**, **teva** or **teua**, **seva** or **seua**.

4.1.2.7 Other adjective alternations

Anàleg 'analogous' has **anàloga** in the feminine; similarly **homòleg/homòloga** 'homologous', **heteròleg/heteròloga** 'heterologous'; **sacríleg/sacrílega** 'sacrilegious' is regular.

A few adjectives ending in -or have, alongside a regular feminine ending in -ora, an alternative irregular form. These are: **motor** 'motive' and its compounds, which has both **motora** and **motriu**; **accelerador** 'accelerative' has **acceleradora** and **acceleratriu**; **retardador** 'decelerative' has both **retardadora** and **retardatriu**. The irregular -triu forms of these adjectives seem most often used with the noun **força** 'force' , e.g. **força electromotriu** 'electromotive force'. The mathematical term **osculador** 'osculatory' has feminine **osculadora** and **osculatriu**.

4.1.3 ADJECTIVES INVARIABLE FOR GENDER (ADJECTIVES WITH ONE ENDING)

Many adjectives show the same form for masculine and feminine singular. There are several word endings which generally indicate an invariable adjective: -a, -e, -al, -el, -il, -ar, -ant, -ent (for -ç see **4.1.3.4**). However, there are some exceptions for most of these endings.

4.1.3.1 Adjectives with one ending: vowel endings

All adjectives whose masculine ends in unstressed -a are invariable: **celta** 'Celtic', **cosmopolita** 'cosmopolitan', **feixista** 'fascist', **hipòcrita** 'hypocritical', **idiota** 'idiotic', **indígena** 'indigenous', **persa** 'Persian', etc. (with invariable plurals **celtes, cosmopolites, feixistes, hipòcrites, idiotes, indígenes, perses**, etc.).

The great majority of adjectives ending in unstressed -e are invariable, including all those ending in -ble, and all those with the suffix -aire. Thus: **bilingüe** 'bilingual', **celeste** 'celestial', **enorme** 'enormous', **feble** 'weak', **jove** 'young', **lliure** 'free', **noble** 'noble', **possible** 'possible', **salvatge** 'savage', **unànime** 'unanimous', etc. (and plural **bilingües, celestes**, etc.).

A significant minority of adjectives in -e do vary for gender, however, and should be noted. Among adjectives ending in a consonant + **re** most have -**a** in the feminine:

altre	**altra**	other	**neutre**	**neutra**	neutral
nostre	**nostra**	our	**pobre**	**pobra**	poor
negre	**negra**	black	etc.		

Those with one ending despite terminating in consonant + **re** are:

-**membre** '-membered' (**bimembre, trimembre**)
-**estre** (e.g. **alpestre** 'alpine', **campestre, eqüestre, pedestre, rupestre, silvestre, terrestre**)
-**rostre** (e.g. **brevirostre** 'short-billed')

acre	bitter	**il·lustre**	illustrious
alegre	cheerful	**lacustre**	lake-dwelling
cafre	kaffir	**mediocre**	middling
cèlebre	celebrated	**salubre**	salubrious
diedre	dihedral	**insalubre**	insalubrious
fúnebre	funereal	**triquetre**	triangular
golafre	gluttonous	**lúgubre**	mournful

The remaining exceptions to the principle that adjectives in -e are invariable are the following:

ample	**ampla**	broad	**probe**	**proba**	upright
còmode	**còmoda**	comfortable	**prompte**	**prompta**	quick
culte	**culta**	cultured	**univalve**	**univalva**	univalve
ímprobe	**ímproba**	dishonest	**bivalve**	**bivalva**	bivalve
lledesme	**lledesma**	legitimate	**vague**	**vaga**	vague
omnímode	**omnímoda**	all-encompassing			

Adjectives with other unstressed vowel endings show the regular 'two endings' in the singular, with addition of -**a** in the feminine: **propi/pròpia** 'own', **fenici/fenícia** 'Phoenician', **vacu/vàcua** 'vacuous', etc. Of adjectives ending in unstressed -**i** only two are invariable: **cursi** 'affected', and **ianqui**

'Yankee'; likewise there are two in **-u**: **bantu** 'Bantu' and **zulu** 'Zulu'. (Note the forms **bantú** and **zulú** are no longer current.) No adjectives ending in unstressed **-o** are invariable, thus **flonjo/flonja** 'spongy', and so on.

Almost all adjectives whose masculine singular ends in a stressed vowel add **-na** in the feminine; see above **4.1.2.1**. The following only are invariable:

afí	related	**hindú**	Hindu
bengalí	Bengali	**manxú**	Manchu(rian)
carmí	carmine	**papú**	Papuan
rococó	rococo		

4.1.3.2 Adjectives with one ending: consonantal endings

The following endings generally indicate an adjective invariable for gender in the singular:

-al e.g. **global** 'global', **igual** 'equal', **mundial** 'world', **verbal** 'verb', 'verbal' and hundreds of others, with the single exception of **mal/mala** 'bad'.

-el **cruel** 'cruel', **fidel** 'faithful', and **rebel** 'rebellious'. Exception: **paral·lel/ paral·lela** 'parallel' (and **antiparal·lel**).

-il stressed and unstressed, e.g. **humil** 'humble', **subtil** 'subtle', **fàcil** 'easy', **inútil** 'useless'; exceptions are: **tranquil/tranquil·la** 'calm' (see above, **4.1.2.4**), and those adjectives ending in **-dàctil** (such as **monodàctil/ monodàctila** 'having one finger'), in **-òfil** (such as **catalanòfil/catalanòfila** 'Catalanophile') and in **-stil** (**hipòstil/hipòstila** 'hypostyle', **pròstil/ pròstila** 'prostyle').

-ant e.g. **constant** 'constant', **pedant** 'pedantic', **semblant** 'similar', etc. There are the following exceptions: **gegant/geganta** 'giant', **quant/quanta** 'how much?'/'how many?', **sacrosant/sacrosanta** 'sacrosanct', **sant/santa** 'holy', **tant/tanta** 'so much'.

-ent e.g. **decent** 'decent', **obedient** 'obedient', **prudent** 'careful', etc. The exceptions are **atent/atenta** 'attentive', **content/contenta** 'happy', **cruent/ cruenta** 'bloody', and all those ending in **-lent** (including **lent/lenta** 'slow', **dolent/dolenta** 'bad', **calent/calenta** 'hot', **valent/valenta** 'bold', and so on) except for **equivalent** 'equivalent' which is invariable.

A number of adjectives in **-ant/-ent** which in the standard language are invariable in the singular have a feminine in **-a** in colloquial (non-standard) usage, e.g. **amargant** 'bitter', **bullent** 'boiling', **picant** 'hot (to taste)': (non-standard: **amarganta, bullenta, picanta**, then corresponding non-standard feminine plurals **amargantes, bullentes, picantes**).

-ar stressed, e.g. **familiar** 'family', **regular** 'regular', **similar** 'similar', **titular** 'titular', etc., except for the following: **avar/avara** 'miserly', **car/cara** 'dear', **clar/clara** 'clear', **entreclar/entreclara** 'partly clear', **ignar/ignara** 'ignorant', **preclar/preclara** 'illustrious', **rar/rara** 'rare'.

-or   Among the adjectives ending in **-or** most have feminines in **-a**, such as **sonor/sonora** 'sonorous', **prometedor/prometedora** 'promising', **opressor/ opressora** 'oppressive'.

Exceptions are:

(i)   those ending in **-erior**, such as **superior** 'superior', **anterior** 'previous';

(ii)   the synthetic comparative adjectives **millor** 'better', **pitjor** 'worse', **major** 'greater', **menor** 'less(er)';

(iii)   most compounds of **-color** 'colour', such as **multicolor** 'multi-coloured', **unicolor** 'of one colour', but not **incolor/incolora** 'colourless'.

4.1.3.3   *Other adjectives with one ending*

The list of remaining exceptions is not large. Sources differ on precisely which items to mention here (mostly because various sources include in the list one or more nouns, which may be used appositively). Some of these, like **breu, gran, greu, suau**, are extremely frequent. They are arranged by termination:

àrab	Arab	**nictalop**	nyctalopic	**suau**	gentle
núvol	cloudy	**ametrop**	ametropic	**insuau**	ungentle
sublim	sublime	**mudèjar**	Mudejar	**lleu**	light
gran	large	**púber**	pubescent	**breu**	short
partícip	participant	**impúber**	under the age	**greu**	serious
miop	short-sighted		of puberty	**procliu**	prone
etíop	Ethiopian	**ligur**	Ligurian	**cloc-piu**	downcast
hemeralop	hemeralopic	**mat**	matt		

Note that, for all these adjectives with consonantal endings, an invariable singular form is matched by an invariable plural:

m. and *f.sg.*	*m.* and *f.pl.*	*m.* and *f.sg.*	*m.* and *f.pl.*
global	**globals**	**superior**	**superiors**
cruel	**cruels**	**major**	**majors**
fàcil	**fàcils**	**multicolor**	**multicolors**
semblant	**semblants**	**suau**	**suaus**
prudent	**prudents**	**breu**	**breus**
similar	**similars**	etc.	

Those presented as exceptions (consonant-final words with more than one ending in the singular) show the corresponding 'two endings' in the plural:

m.sg.	*f.sg.*	*m.pl.*	*f.pl.*
mal	**mala**	**mals**	**males**
tranquil	**tranquil·la**	**tranquils**	**tranquil·les**

quant	quanta	quants	quantes
lent	lenta	lents	lentes
clar	clara	clars	clares
sonor	sonora	sonors	sonores
blau	blava	blaus	blaves
etc.			

Formation of plural adjective forms is reviewed more fully in **4.1.4**.

4.1.3.4 Adjectives invariable in the singular, but gender-marked in the plural

In contrast with all the patterns shown so far, all adjectives ending in -ç are invariable in the singular but mark gender in the plural. For example:

m. and *f.sg.*	*m.pl.*	*f.pl.*	
capaç	capaços	capaces	capable
eficaç	eficaços	eficaces	effective
feliç	feliços	felices	happy
atroç	atroços	atroces	atrocious
etc.			

4.1.4 FORMATION OF THE PLURAL OF ADJECTIVES

Some principles affecting the formation of plurals (notably stem changes) have been introduced in the preceding sections **4.1.1–3**. Formation of the plural of adjectives follows the same rules as for nouns (see **2.1**), that is, -s is added both to masculines and feminines; in the case of masculines ending in a sibilant consonant, -o- is inserted between the stem and the plural inflection. Another general point to be noted is that a final -a (typical ending for a feminine) is changed into an -e- before the final -s.

The basic pattern (corresponding to sections **2.1.1** and **2.1.2** for nouns) can be shown as:

m.sg.	*f.sg.*	*m.pl.*	*f.pl.*
un nen dolent	**una nena dolenta**	**uns nens dolents**	**unes nenes dolentes**
a bad boy	a bad girl	bad boys	bad girls

Corresponding to section **2.1.3** (nouns ending in a stressed vowel) we have, e.g. in the adjective **sa**:

un home sa	**una dona sana**	**uns homes sans**	**unes dones sanes**
a healthy man	a healthy woman	healthy men	healthy women

Adjectives ending in a stressed vowel which do not have an **n** in their feminine form (either because the feminine just adds -a as in **cru/crua** 'raw', or because their feminine is identical to the masculine, as in **rococó** 'rococo') do not have

n in the plural either: thus **crus** (*m.pl.*)/**crues** (*f.pl.*), **rococós** (*m./f.pl.*). **Afí** (*m./f.sg.*) 'related' is an exception here; its plural is **afins** (*m./f.pl.*). As in **2.1.4**, the words **jove, orfe, verge** as adjectives – 'young', 'orphan', 'virgin' respectively – have alternative plurals in Valencian, Northwestern Catalan, and some other areas: **jóvens, òrfens, vèrgens**. (Note *f.sg.* **òrfena** *f.pl.* **òrfenes**.)

Corresponding to the case of **2.1.5**, nouns ending in sibilants, we have, among adjectives, the following. Notice that when a variation of the stem appears before the feminine ending, the same variant appears before **-o-** in the masculine plural:

un jersei gros	**una casa grossa**	**uns jerseis grossos**	**unes cases grosses**
a large sweater	a large house	large sweaters	large houses
el mateix gos	**la mateixa gossa**	**els mateixos gossos**	**les mateixes gosses**
the same dog	the same bitch	the same dogs	the same bitches
un gat lleig	**una gata lletja**	**uns gats lleigs/lletjos**	**unes gates lletges**
an ugly cat (*m.*)	an ugly cat (*f.*)	ugly cats (*m.*)	ugly cats (*f.*)
un noi audaç	**una noia audaç**	**uns nois audaços**	**unes noies audaces**
a daring boy	a daring girl	daring boys	daring girls

As illustrated here with **lleig**, and as mentioned for nouns in **2.1.5.4**, masculine words ending in **-sc**, **-st**, and **-ig** have alternative masculine plural forms. Thus **frescs** or **frescos** (*m.pl.*) 'fresh', **etruscs** or **etruscos** 'Etruscan', **vasts** or **vastos** 'vast', **injusts** or **injustos** 'unjust'. The forms without **-o-** tend to be preferred in Valencia and in the Balearics, except that **aquests** 'these' (pronounced [əkɛts]/[əkets]) is generally preferred to **aquestos**. **Mig** 'middle', **boig** 'mad', and **roig** 'red-haired' conform basically to the pattern of **lleig**, maintaining the contrast between **-tj-** and **-j-** which is explained above (**4.1.2.5**):

*m.*sg.	*f.sg.*	*m.pl.*	*f.pl.*
lleig	**lletja**	**lleigs/lletjos**	**lletges**
mig	**mitja**	**migs/mitjos**	**mitges**
boig	**boja**	**boig/bojos**	**boges**
roig	**roja**	**roigs/rojos**	**roges**

4.1.5   DIMINUTIVE, AUGMENTATIVE, AND EVALUATIVE SUFFIXES

The following is to be read in conjunction with the discussion of diminutive, augmentative, and evaluative suffixes applied to nouns, in **2.3**. The basic range of this type of suffix available for adjectives is the same as for nouns. As already explained, the boundaries between augmentative and diminutive, pejorative and appreciative are rather unstable in this area of usage, and are made more fuzzy by subtle questions of subjective attitude and pragmatics. For adjectives the following merged schema shows, approximately, how the dimensions are related:

	augmentative	diminutive
appreciative	-às/-assa	-et/-eta, -ó/-ona, -eu/-eva
pejorative	-ot/-ota, -arro/-arra	-et/-eta, -etxo/-etxa, -eu/-eva

The endings above are added to the adjective stem, with morphological or spelling modification as required: **seriós/serioset** 'serious', **bonic/boniquet** 'pretty', **bo/bonet** 'good', **jove/jovenet** 'young', etc. Observe that **gran** 'big' (invariable singular) has stem **grand-**, whence **grandot, grandet, grandàs** (or **grandolàs**). In **grassonet/-eta** 'plump'/'chubby' we see double suffixation: **gras → grassó → grassonet**. The use of these suffixes is widespread, particularly in familiar speech, and diminutive **-et/-eta** is especially common. The suffixed forms are produced according to discourse circumstance and are not separately recorded in dictionaries. As remarked in **2.3** proficient imitation is by no means easy for non-natives, and translation of shades of meaning can be extremely elusive.

Examples:

-às/-assa: **M'ha vingut a veure aquell noi tan gras i vermellàs de cara.**
That chubby lad with the red face came to see me.

-ot/-ota: **A mi no em sembla gens educat, el trobo més aviat grollerot.**
He doesn't seem at all polite to me; in fact I think he's rather crude.

-arro/-arra: **No facis cas de res del que digui, és tan beneitarro.**
Don't take any notice of him, he's a jerk.

-eu/-eva: **Ara està molt grassa, però quan va néixer era maca i petiteva.**
Now she's quite fat, but when she was born she was cute and tiny.

-ó/-ona: **És lletjó, però molt simpàtic.**
He's no picture, but he's very nice.

-et/-eta: **Compri'm a mi, que ho tenc tot baratet.**
Buy from me, you won't find better prices. (lit. I have it all a little cheap.)

-etxo/-etxa: **És un carrer ben lleig, tan fosc i estretetxo.**
It's an ugly little street, so dark and narrow.

See **5.3.2** on the absolute superlative, involving the intensifying suffix **-íssim/ -íssima**.

4.1.6 FORMATION OF ADJECTIVES BY CONVERSION

Conversion is the process by which an element (a word or a phrase) changes its grammatical category without adding any morpheme. The adjectival use of the Catalan past participle (discussed in **21.1**) is a very clear case in point:

El cotxe fou robat ahir a la nit.
The car was stolen last night.

El cotxe robat ahir a la nit ha aparegut.
The car stolen last night has appeared.

Thus **un cotxe robat** 'a stolen car', **una illa abandonada** 'an abandoned island', **penes compartides** 'shared suffering', and so on.

Of considerable relevance in the present context is noun–adjective conversion. Nouns are used as qualifiers by adjunction in certain compounds. The most typical examples of this use are nouns designating certain tonalities of colours, the reason being that many colours are originally nouns referring to objects: **lila** 'lilac', **rosa** 'pink', **carabassa** 'pumpkin', **violeta** 'violet', **safrà** 'saffron', **avellana** 'hazel', etc.: thus **blau cel** 'sky blue', **gris perla** 'pearl grey', **gris marengo** 'dark grey', **verd turquesa** 'turquoise', **verd poma** 'apple green', **groc cadmi** 'cadmium yellow', **merda d'oca** 'dirty beige' (lit. goose shit), **ala de mosca** 'greyish' (lit. fly's wing), **color de gos com fuig** 'indeterminate dark colour' (lit. dog fleeing). These adjectives by conversion, simple and compound, sometimes introduced by explanatory **color (de)**, are invariable in gender and number, thus: **un gelat rosa** 'a pink ice cream', **unes cortines verd poma/unes cortines color (de) verd poma** 'apple green curtains'.

An adjoined noun can limit or explain the meaning of another noun in the same way as an adjective might: **carta bomba** 'letter bomb', **cotxe bomba** 'car bomb', **festa sorpresa** 'surprise party', **pare director** 'headmaster of religious school', **curs pont** 'bridging course', **jutge àrbitre** 'main referee' (in sport), **nen proveta** 'test-tube baby', **llibreta habitatge** 'building society account', **hores punta** 'peak times', **qüestions clau** 'key questions', etc. Most of the examples of this type of construction in the Romance languages are relatively recent, and probably reflect the influence of English, where nouns can be 'converted' to adjectives almost without limit. Such is the relative unfamiliarity of these constructions that Catalan grammarians debate whether they are formed with a noun in adjectival function, or whether they refer to a mixed reality (two nominal elements equally applicable), as the following more clearly do: **cafè teatre** *'café-theatre'*, **sofà llit** 'sofa bed', **sala menjador** 'living/dining room', **home llop** 'werewolf', **aigua-sal** 'brine' (cf. **aiguaneu** 'sleet'), etc. Independently of this question, syntactic apposition shows how a noun or noun phrase can develop an adjectival function:

Parles de Barcelona ciutat o de Barcelona província?
Are you talking about Barcelona city or Barcelona province?
(cf. **Barcelona, ciutat industrial a la vora del mar, gaudeix de bones comunicacions.**
Barcelona, an industrial city on the coast, enjoys good communications.)

La corbata objecte de regal masculí ha deixat pas a la corbata disseny d'elecció personal.
The tie (as) masculine gift object has given way to the tie (as) personal design choice.
(cf. **La corbata, objecte de regal masculí per excel·lència, persisteix com a complement de roba obligatori.**
The tie, a masculine gift object par excellence, remains an obligatory clothing accessory.)

El Miquel Àngel escultor i arquitecte ha deixat a l'ombra el Miquel Àngel poeta.
Michelangelo sculptor and architect has left Michelangelo poet in the shadows.
(cf. **Miquel Àngel, escultor i arquitecte del Renaixement, també va deixar una obra poètica interessant.**
Michelangelo, Renaissance poet and sculptor, also left an interesting body of poetry.)

Classificatory nouns like **tipus** 'type', **classe** 'class', **marca** 'brand', **raça** 'breed' can be adjoined to the head noun with an optional **de** preceding them and a noun indicating which particular class, type, etc., following them. It is also possible to use the class name directly as an uninflected adjective:

un cotxe (de) marca Renault = un cotxe Renault	a Renault car
dos cotxes Renault	two Renault cars
una poma (de) classe reineta = una poma reineta	a pippin apple
dues pomes reineta	two pippin apples
hepatitis (de) tipus B/hepatitis B	hepatitis (type) B
un gos (de) raça bòxer = un gos bòxer	a boxer dog
dos gossos bòxer	two boxer dogs

When the semantic head noun is absent (by ellipsis) the class name, becoming the main noun in the phrase, can take inflection:

Han xocat dos Renaults.	Two Renaults collided.
Compra'm dues reinetes.	Buy me two pippins.
Amb aquest ja hem tingut tres bòxers.	This is the third boxer we have had.

Otherwise it is important to stress that Catalan cannot create noun + adjectival noun combinations at will. The equivalent of most such constructions, which are so frequent in English, will be noun + prepositional phrase (**de** + noun), or noun + adjective phrase in Catalan: **un partit de futbol** 'a football match', **un camió militar** 'an army lorry', **vacances d'estiu/vacances estivals** 'summer holidays', etc.

The noun–adjective conversion just discussed has its counterpart in the much more extensive adjective–noun conversion available in Catalan. Any adjective can become a noun by the simple adjoining of the definite article or another determiner (see **9.1**):

> –**Quin d'aquests dos cotxes t'agrada més? –El blau m'agrada més que el vermell.**
>
> 'Which of these two cars do you prefer?' 'I prefer the blue one to the red one.'

4.1.7   COMPOUND ADJECTIVES INVOLVING A NOMINAL

Catalan has a number of noun + adjective compound adjectives. These compounds usually refer to parts of the body, physically described or metaphorically used. They correspond roughly to English adjective + noun '-ed' compounds. Here are a few examples: **alatrencat** 'broken-winged', **barbablanc** 'white-bearded', **bocaample** 'wide-mouthed', **camallarg** 'long-legged', **capbuit** 'empty-headed', **caragirat** 'turncoat' (lit. face-turned), **cuallarg** 'long-tailed', **peugròs** 'big-footed'. These compound adjectives inflect exactly like the contained adjective element: thus *m.pl.* **camallargs**, *f.*sg. **camallarga**, *f.pl.* **camallargues**, etc. Some existing adjectives are clearly the result of combining two independent adjectives: **blauverd** 'blue-green' (*m./f.pl.* **blauverds**), **agredolç** 'bitter-sweet' (*m.pl.* **agredolços**), **sordmut** 'deaf and dumb' (*m.pl.* **sordmuts**).

4.2   ADJECTIVE SYNTAX AND USAGE

4.2.1   WORD ORDER

Although it can be said that the *usual* position of the adjective in Catalan is after the noun it modifies, the matter is rather more complex than that and is best addressed from first principles. Adjectives in Catalan noun phrases may in fact be found *before* or *after* head nouns. The position depends in part on which kind of adjective is involved – quantifiers and demonstratives normally precede, for example – and in part on the discourse function of the adjective in relation to the referent of the modified noun. The typical place for a 'restrictive' adjective in Catalan is immediately after the head noun. The underlying principle is that this kind of adjective specifies *which* X, or *which kind* of X, (X being the head noun or, more precisely, what it denotes). The function of such an adjective is similar to that of a restrictive relative clause (see **31.1.2**), as demonstrated in the examples below:

Visc a la casa buida.
I live in the empty house (= the house which is empty).

El cotxe és aparcat al carrer ample.
The car is parked on the wide street (= the street which is wide).

Els llibres gruixuts són mals de llegir.
Thick books (= books which are thick) are hard to read.

M'agrada molt la pintura medieval.
I am very fond of medieval painting (= painting which is medieval).

L'any següent va cobrar una herència.
The following year (= the year which followed) she inherited some money.

Coneixien un noi americà.
They knew an American boy (= a boy who was American).

If the noun has a specifying prepositional phrase complement, any descriptive adjective which agrees with the head noun follows the complement: **una casa de pagès buida** 'an empty farmhouse', **màquines d'escriure antigues** 'old typewriters'. Note, however, that this arrangement is blocked if the complement is itself modified by an adjective: 'a long tradition of folklore activity' is not *una tradició d'activitats folklòriques llarga** but rather **una llarga tradició d'activitats folklòriques.**

The alternative order, adjective + noun, is appropriate when the function of the adjective is not to identify more specifically, but rather to perform one of three other (overlapping) functions: (i) to convey some additional information, as does a non-restrictive relative clause (**31.1.2**), (ii) to emphasize or bring to prominence some (already assumed) aspect of what the noun refers to, or (iii) to express the speaker's attitude towards what is referred to. Examples:

(i)	**l'odiosa premsa**	the hateful press (= the press, which is hateful)
	una mera hipòtesi	a mere hypothesis (= a hypothesis, which is nothing more than a hypothesis)
(ii)	**la grisa quotidianitat**	(the) dull routine
	la llunyana Índia	distant India
	l'astuta guineu	the crafty fox
(iii)	**el blau oceà**	the blue ocean (= the ocean, which is blue, *not* the blue ocean in contrast to the green one)
	les altes estrelles	the lofty stars
	la seva increïble presumpció	his incredible presumption
	el meu estimat col·lega	my esteemed colleague

What is seen in (iii) above also lies behind the characteristic adjective + noun + adjective arrangement such as **els magnífics temples tailandesos** 'the magnificent Thai temples', **la inspirada adaptació teatral de la novel·la** 'the inspired theatrical adaptation of the novel'. In such cases (see **4.2.2**) it is as though a single unit were formed by the noun and the restrictive adjective together, with the other adjective having a descriptive/evaluative function.

An adjective may express a speaker's attitude and at the same time identify which kind of X is referred to. In such a case, either position may be found, though on the whole noun + adjective (the second in the following pairs) is preferred in ordinary usage.

> **Assagen solucions agosarades./Assagen agosarades solucions.**
> They are attempting bold solutions.

> **Va fer un discurs brillant./Va fer un brillant discurs.**
> She gave a brilliant speech.

Adjectives which would normally be postposed by the principles given above often precede nouns in poetry or similar registers. The effect of this inversion of the usual order is to supply specially emphasized or emotive information:

> **Vénen la flota i el fibló // i del fantàstic horitzó . . .** (J. Alcover)
> There comes the fleet and the tornado, and from the fantastic horizon . . .

> **Conserva de ses branques l'eterna primavera.** (M. Costa)
> It retains the eternal spring of its branches.

> **Sol i de dol i amb vetusta gonella . . .** (J.V. Foix)
> Alone and grieving and wearing an ancient tunic . . .

Prenominal position of an adjective is nonetheless impossible in three cases:

(i) With attributive adjectives equivalent to a de + noun phrase complement of the head noun, of the kind **la vida de família** = **la vida familiar** 'family life'.

> **equip ministerial** (= **equip del ministeri**) *ministerial equip** ministerial team
> **món universitari** (= **món de la universitat**) *universitari món** university world
> **cerimonial eclesiàstic** (= **cerimonial de l'església**) *eclesiàstic cerimonial** church ceremonial/ecclesiastical ceremonial
> **parc automobilístic** (= **parc d'automòbils**) *automobilístic parc** car fleet
> **tècniques discursives** (= **tècniques del discurs**) *discursives tècniques** discourse techniques/discursive techniques

(ii) With restrictive-specifying adjectives:

He trobat una pedra groga.
*He trobat una groga pedra.
I found a yellow stone.

Fes l'examen amb un bolígraf negre.
*Fes l'examen amb un negre bolígraf.
Do the test with a black ballpoint.

No vull tractes amb gent impuntual.
*No vull tractes amb impuntual gent.
I don't wish to deal with unpunctual people.

(iii) With an adjective that has itself a degree modifier, or a complement. Thus while **un famós cantant** 'a famous singer' may occur in appropriate circumstances, neither *un força famós cantant nor *un famós pels seus discos cantant is possible. It must be **un cantant força famós** 'a very famous singer', **un cantant famós pels seus discos** 'a singer famous for his recordings'.

In the case of a few adjectives, position before or after the noun they modify is associated with a distinct meaning difference. In line with what we have seen above, the preposed adjectives tend to be figurative or evaluative, the postposed ones, specifying.

grans persones	**persones grans**
great people	old/adult people
la pobra família	**la família pobra**
the poor family (= which inspires pity)	the poor (= needy) family
un simple oficinista	**un oficinista simple**
a mere clerk	a simple-minded clerk
una trista història	**una història trista**
a sorry tale	a sad story
la pura casualitat	**la casualitat pura**
sheer chance	chance alone
un cert interès	**un interès cert**
a certain (amount of) interest	a definite interest
un vell amic	**un amic vell**
an old friend (= of many years)	an elderly friend
la mateixa idea	**la idea mateixa**
the same idea	the idea itself

Notice that when standing as predicates these adjectives can only have the sense seen in the postposed modifiers: **La família era pobra** 'The family was poor (= needy)'. The above differences in meaning are not necessarily identifiable in every case. **Una gran distància** 'a great distance' means the same as **una distància gran** and, in fact, the former is more usual.

The adjectives **mal** and **dolent** 'bad' have essentially the same meaning; **mal** occurs only before a noun; **dolent** occurs after, and in predicate position: **una mala proposta** = **una proposta dolenta** 'a bad suggestion'. The adjective **bo** 'good' (**bona** (*f.*), **bons** (*m.pl.*), **bones** (*f.pl.*)) irregularly has a special form **bon** for the masculine singular when it precedes a noun: **un bon dinar** 'a good lunch', but **un dinar bo**.

Bo, dolent, petit, gran (or gros)

All these very common adjectives follow the noun when they are restrictive, indicating objective quality. Preceding the noun, they usually express a subjective evaluation.

(objective)
Va ser després que van venir els maldecaps grossos.
It was later that the big headaches came.

Porta la plata petita.
Bring the small serving dish.

(subjective)
Ens ha sortit una petita dificultat.
We've come across a minor difficulty.

És un gran escriptor/mentider.
He is a great writer/liar.

It is to be observed that **gros** is preferred to **gran** (both meaning 'big'/'large') when what is referred to is physical volume:

Porta la plata grossa. (preferable to **la plata gran**)
Bring the large serving dish.

Aquestes caixes grosses no ens cabran aquí.
We won't be able to fit those large boxes in here.

4.2.2   NOUNS WITH MORE THAN ONE ADJECTIVE

Two basic patterns are observed when a noun is complemented by two adjectives:

(i)   when both adjectives carry equal weight they are normally joined by the conjunction **i** and are positioned together, either before or after the noun, according to the principles explained in **4.2.1**.

Això obeeix a la més rigorosa i ineluctable lògica.
This conforms to the strictest, most inescapable logic.

Més enllà es distingien uns edificis miserables i raquítics.
Further away some sordid, rickety buildings could be made out.

El senador féu una intervenció contundent i decisiva.
The senator made a sharp, decisive intervention.

Tot plegat formava un quadro de desbridada i sorollosa alegria.
The whole scene was one of unbridled, noisy merriment.

The conjunction may be suppressed to give separate emphasis to each adjective:

Penso en aquelles converses animades, interminables, que fèiem al Casino.
I have in mind those lively, endless conversations we used to have in the Casino.

(ii) When one of the two adjectives is restrictive this will take its usual position after the noun, with the non-restrictive adjective preceding the noun. Note that in English it is the absence of the comma that indicates this relationship between the adjectives:

els poètics paisatges pirinencs
the poetic Pyrenean landscapes

Era filla d'un obscur advocat provincià.
She was the daughter of an obscure provincial lawyer.

Se sentí un desconcertant xiscle agut.
A disconcerting shrill scream rang out.

This pattern is sometimes broken by **tan** used to introduce the non-restrictive modifier placed after the first (restrictive) one:

Agraeixo aquestes paraules introductòries tan simpàtiques. =
Agraeixo aquestes simpàtiques paraules introductòries.
I am grateful for those kind opening words.

When the restrictive adjective and noun are so closely allied as almost to form a compound noun, a second adjective qualifying the quasi-compound noun phrase usually follows, producing thereby a kind of mirror image of the normal English word order:

un estudi sobre la poesia italiana contemporània
a study on contemporary Italian poetry

l'empresa privada francesa
French private enterprise

More than two adjectives

When a noun is qualified by more than two adjectives these are distributed according to the principles explained in (i) and (ii) above. If all the adjectives carry equal weight they go together either before or after the noun:

Van explicar-se amb la pura, tradicional i primitiva senzillesa de l'home del camp.
They spoke with the countryman's pure, traditional, primitive simplicity.

Em va semblar un personatge complex, neuròtic i violent.
He struck me as a complex, neurotic, violent character.

If a noun + adjective quasi-compound is involved other qualifying adjectives invariably precede:

Hi va haver una sola, trista i insegura veu discrepant.
There was just one sad, hesitant, dissident voice.

Departure from the norm in the positioning of adjectives may be determined by subjective considerations of style. This is particularly true of poetry, but it also applies to prose and to diverse speech registers. In general, the more unusual the positioning of the adjective, the more the writer/speaker wishes to draw attention to it or secure for it an other than purely literal value:

Alguns arcs, algunes columnes, inscripcions borroses, sepulcres destrossats, mutilades estàtues, semblen les restes d'un gran naufragi, les desferres d'una immensa i cataclísmica tempesta.
Some arches, some columns, faint inscriptions, shattered tombs, mutilated statues, looking like the flotsam of a great shipwreck, the debris of an immense, cataclysmic storm.

4.2.3   GENDER AGREEMENT OF ADJECTIVES WITH COORDINATED NOUNS

When a combination of more than one noun of different genders occurs, an attributive or predicative adjective will appear in the masculine plural form:

Els plàtans i les peres ja són madurs. (*Els plàtans i les peres ja són madures.)
The bananas and pears are ripe now.

autopistes amb accessos i sortides adequats
motorways with adequate approaches and exits

Hi havia cotxes de cavalls i carrosses molt ben guarnits.
There were finely decorated horse-drawn coaches and carriages.

(**Hi havia cotxes de cavalls i carrosses molt ben guarnides** means that only the carriages were finely decorated.)

However, when two coordinated nouns are very close in meaning, an attributive adjective may be used in the singular, agreeing in gender with the nearer: **fàstic i repulsió instintiva** 'instinctive disgust and revulsion'.

4.2.4   COMPLEMENTS OF ADJECTIVES

Many adjectives can have a complement which is a prepositional or infinitive phrase. The complement is normally introduced by **de**:

orgullosa de les seves obres	proud of her works
atacs difícils de suportar	attacks hard to endure
cadires cobertes de pols	chairs covered in dust
Va restar malalta del cor.	She suffered from a heart condition.

Certain adjectives may have a preposition other than **de** with their complement, e.g. **content amb** 'happy with' (**content de** is also used), **fidel a** 'faithful to':

Estàvem contents amb el professor/del professor.
We were happy with the teacher.

un gos fidel al seu amo
a dog faithful to its master

A finite sentential complement of an adjective has, in the standard language, no introducing preposition before the complementizer **que** (see **32.3–5**):

Està orgullosa que el seu fill estudiï per al doctorat.
She is proud that her son is studying for a doctorate.

Pronominalization of adjective phrases by **ho**, **en**, or **hi** is discussed in **12.5**, **12.6vi**, and **12.7iv** respectively.

4.2.5   ADVERBIAL USE OF ADJECTIVES

An adjective may appear in predicate position, that is, after a verb and ostensibly qualifying that verb, for example: **Ho mirava tota preocupada** 'She was looking at it quite worriedly'. Although formally the adjective here expresses a characteristic of the subject (as is confirmed by the number–gender agreement), the communicative effect is virtually the same as that of an adverb modifying the verb, and the English equivalent is often an adverb:

Els antics competidors avui es tracten benèvols (approximately = benèvolament).
The former competitors nowadays behave in a kindly way towards each other.

Ell sempre actuava recelós (approximately = **recelosament**).
He always behaved apprehensively.

En aquesta casa elles dues vivien tranquil·les (approximately = **tranquil·lament**).
In this house the two of them lived at peace.

See also **13.1.2.**

4.2.6   TRANSLATING THE NEGATIVE PREFIX 'UN-'

Catalan has a negative prefix **in-**, which is used with adjectives and generally coincides with English adjectives taking negative 'in-': **increïble** 'incredible', **inseparable** 'inseparable', **innombrable** 'innumerable', etc. However, Catalan does not replicate the frequency with which adjectives in English can be given a negative sense with 'un-'. For some words **in-** corresponds to 'un-': **inimaginable** 'unimaginable', **intocable** 'untouchable', **insociable** 'unsociable', **inintel·ligible** 'unintelligible', **indigne** 'unworthy', **irreal** 'unreal', **indesitjable** 'undesirable'. The dictionary must be consulted to see whether a form with **in-** exists, as they cannot be created at will. Where the **in-**—'un-' match is not allowed, equivalents have to be formed with **anti-** (occasionally), or, more regularly, with **poc, no,** or **sense:**

antinatural	unnatural	**no retornable**	non-returnable
antieconòmic	uneconomic(al)	**no autoritzat**	unauthorized
poc convincent	unconvincing	**sense principis**	unprincipled
poc profesional	unprofessional	**sense llegir**	unread
poc atractiu	unattractive	**sense provar**	untried
poc favorable	unfavourable	**sense obrir**	unopened
poc freqüentat	unfrequented	etc.	
poc intel·ligent	unintelligent		

5 COMPARISON

Traditional grammars often have a section on 'the comparison of adjectives and adverbs', but it is by no means only adjectives and adverbs that participate in comparative constructions. Here our discussion and examples will take a broader view, looking in general at how Catalan expresses concepts like 'more . . . than', 'less/fewer . . . than', 'as (many/much) . . . as', 'the more . . . the more', 'most', 'least', and so on.

The first term of a comparison, the element compared, can be a noun, an adjective, an adverb, a prepositional phrase or a clause: **més sucre que no acostumo a posar-hi** 'more sugar than I normally use', **tan fondo com el mar** 'as deep as the sea', **menys fàcilment que no creus** 'less easily than you suppose', **més a la dreta que això** 'more to the right than that', **T'estima més que no penses** 'She loves you more than you think'. The quantifiers or degree words in comparisons are **més** 'more', **menys** 'less', 'fewer', **tan** 'so', 'as', **tant** 'as much/many'. There are synthetic comparative forms of certain adjectives (see **5.2.1**). **Com**, in comparisons of equality, and **que (no (pas))**, **de**, and **del que** in comparisons of inequality are the pivots introducing the standard of comparison. The standard of comparison – the complement of 'than' in English – may be an element from a wide range of categories: a noun (**més ample que el Nil** 'wider than the Nile'), a pronoun (**menys feliç que tu** 'less happy than you'), an adjective (**més genial que segur** 'more ingenious than reliable'), an adverb (**menys que mai** 'less than ever'), a complement clause or infinitive (**millor que no pas que els n'informem nosaltres** 'better . . . than that we should inform them', **més que no deixar-l'hi** 'more than lending it to him'), a relative clause (**més estrany del que creuries** 'stranger than you would credit'), and so on. Notice that whereas English may optionally include a verb in the standard of comparison, Catalan avoids doing this where the verb would be the same (and in the same tense) as one already mentioned.

5.1 COMPARISON OF EQUALITY

Equality is normally expressed by the terms **tan . . . com** 'as . . . as'/'so . . . as', **tant/tanta . . . com** 'as much as', **tants/tantes . . . com** 'as many . . . as', or **igual de . . . que** 'just as . . . as'. **Tant** is a quantifier pronoun, or an adjective which takes gender and number agreement (and which may be used pronominally). As a degree adverb **tan** is used when it precedes what is qualified; **tant** is used elsewhere (see **13.6**). That is to say, **tan** occurs before an adjective, an adverb, or an adverbial prepositional phrase.

> **No n'he menjat tant com en volia. (tant** quantifier pronoun)
> I didn't eat as much (of it) as I wanted.

> **Vendré tantes parcel·les com podré.**
> I will sell as many plots as I can.

> **Té tants amics francesos com jo en tinc d'alemanys.**
> She has as many French friends as I have German ones.

> **No són tan llestos com es pensen. (tan** degree adverb modifying **llestos)**
> They are not so clever as they think.

> **M'agradava tant com l'altre. (tant** degree adverb modifying **m'agradava)**
> I liked it as much as the other one.

In the following examples, observe, as mentioned above, that Catalan avoids repeating a verb in the standard of comparison, where English may repeat the verb or substitute an auxiliary.

> **El teu fill ja és tan alt com tu.   ? . . . com tu ets/ . . . com ets tu**
> Your son is already as tall as you (are).

> **L'edifici és tan alt com llarg.**
> The building is as tall as it is long.

> **He viatjat tantes vegades a Àfrica com a Àsia.**
> I have travelled to Africa as often as (I have travelled) to Asia.

> **Ningú no llegeix tant com ell.**
> Nobody reads as much as he (does).

> **S'ha comprat un pis igual de vell que el que ja tenia.**
> She has bought a flat just as old as the one she had before.

> **S'aixequen igual de prest que quan feien feina a la fàbrica.**
> They get up just as early as when they worked in the factory.

Omission of **tant** (adverb but not adjective) and **tan** in comparisons is probably explained as an overlap with **com** as a manner adverbial:

> **Ningú no llegeix com ell.**
> Nobody reads like (= as much as) he does.

> **És alt com un Sant Pau.**
> He's a giant of a man. (lit. . . . as tall as a Saint Paul)

> **Aquest noi és divertit com ningú.**
> This boy is as amusing as anything. (lit. as nobody/anybody)

5.2 COMPARISON OF INEQUALITY

Inequality is typically expressed by the formula **més . . . que** 'more . . . than' or **menys . . . que** 'less than'. These patterns are the same whether what is compared is an adjective, an adverb, or another category. **Més, menys** themselves are primarily degree adverbs, though they can also be used as quantifier adjectives in noun phrases, and as quantifier pronouns (see **8.2**). **Manco** 'less' is used in informal styles in the Balearics and in Valencia. In the Balearics **pus** is an alternative to **més** after a negative.

Avui tens un dinar més suculent que el dels altres dies.
Today you're having a more tasty lunch than on the other days.

El lladre va actuar més astutament que la policia.
The thief behaved more cleverly than the police.

Fa més fred a dins que a fora.
It is colder inside than outside.

La poesia és menys comercial que la prosa.
Poetry is less commercial than prose.

Aquest camí mena a la catedral menys directament que l'altre.
This road leads less directly to the cathedral than the other.

Menys . . . que can occasionally be replaced by **més poc . . . que**:

Hi ha menys cadires que (no (pas)) gent. = Hi ha més poques cadires que (no (pas)) gent. (see **5.2.2** on expletive **no/no pas**)
There are fewer chairs than people.

La poesia és més poc comercial que (no (pas)) la prosa.
Poetry is less commercial than prose.

Més and **menys** can themselves be modified by degree expressions like **molt** 'much', 'a lot', **força** 'a lot', **un poc** 'a little', **una mica** 'a bit', **poc** 'little' (not = **un poc** 'a little') or other expressions.

Em va parlar força menys violentament que l'altre dia.
He spoke to me a good deal less violently than the other day.

El teu mecànic sembla (molt/un poc/una mica) més hàbil que (no (pas)) el meu.
Your mechanic seems (a lot/a bit) more skilful than mine.

Aquest cotxe és poc més ràpid que el nostre.
This car is hardly any faster than ours.

Compare:

Aquest cotxe és un poc més ràpid que el nostre.
This car is a little faster than ours.

And notice the following, where Catalan, unlike English, logically uses a comparative of inequality:

si fos dues vegades més gran que no és
if it were twice as big as it is (lit. . . . twice bigger than . . .)

Un poc més, una mica més, un poc menys, una mica menys take partitive **de** before a noun in quantitative comparisons of this kind; **molt** before **més** or **menys** + a noun agrees in number and gender with the noun.

Hi ha un poc més de gent que (no (pas)) ahir.
There are a few more people here than yesterday.

Hi ha moltes més cadires que (no (pas)) persones.
There are a lot more chairs than people.

Tenc moltes menys pel·lícules de vídeo que (no (pas)) llibres.
I have a lot fewer video films than books.

Més poc seems to admit only **molt** as its own degree modifier:

Aquesta versió m'agrada molt més poc que (no (pas)) la primera.
I like this version a lot less than the first one.

Inequality can, of course, also be expressed by means of the negative **no** with the comparative of equality (**5.1**). In many instances this alternative is preferred.

Té menys anys del que sembla. = No té tants anys com sembla.
She is less old than she looks. = She is not as old as she looks.

**Era menys complicat del que ens havien explicat. = No era tan complicat com
  ens havien explicat.**
It was less complicated than had been explained to us. = It was not as
  complicated as had been explained to us.

When the standard of comparison is a numeral **de** is generally used as the pivot in place of **que**.

Hi havia més de cent parades a la fira.
There were more than a hundred stalls at the fair.

But note a contrast of meaning in a negative context between:

No hi havia més que cinquanta parades.
There were only fifty stalls. (**més** as quantifier pronoun)

and

No hi havia més de cinquanta parades.
There were not more than fifty stalls. (**més** as quantifying adjective)

5.2.1 SYNTHETIC COMPARATIVES

Major 'bigger', **menor** 'smaller', **millor** 'better', **pitjor** 'worse' are irregular synthetic comparative forms for **més gran, més petit, més bo** and **més dolent/ més mal**. However, the analytic forms are not only correct, but even preferred:

Dels dos nens, aquest és el major. = Dels dos nens, aquest és el més gran.
Of the two boys, this is the bigger one.

Era una qüestió d'una importància menor que l'altra. = Era una qüestió d'una importància més petita que l'altra.
It was an issue of lesser importance than the other.

Va ser millor el plat cuinat a casa que no al restaurant. = Va ser més bo el plat cuinat a casa que no al restaurant.
The home-made dish was better than the restaurant one.

Aquesta obra de teatre és pitjor que l'altra. = Aquesta obra de teatre és més dolenta que l'altra.
That play is worse than the other.

Millor and **pitjor** are also adverbs, commonly substituted by the analytic forms (**més bé, més malament**):

Avui ha tocat la sonata millor/més bé que ahir.
Today she played the sonata better than yesterday.

Ahir va tocar la sonata pitjor/més malament que avui.
Yesterday she played the sonata worse than today.

Major and **menor**, on the other hand, are only adjectives. (They also mean 'major' and 'minor' respectively: **Fou una omissió major** 'It was a major omission'.) The adverb **majorment** does exist, but with the independent meaning of 'generally': **La gent majorment prefereix les platges d'arena** 'People generally prefer sandy beaches'.

The second term of constructions with the lexical comparatives **inferior** and **superior** is introduced by **a**:

La qualitat del treball d'aquest actor és superior a la de la resta de la companyia.
The quality of this actor's work is superior to the rest of the company's.

Llurs esforços resultaren inferiors a les exigències de la comesa.
Their efforts proved inferior to the demands of the undertaking.

5.2.2   EXPLETIVE **no/no pas** IN COMPARATIVE CONSTRUCTIONS

Provided that the main clause is positive, the sense of inequality can be emphasized using an expletive **no** or **no pas** after **que**, with no fundamental difference in meaning:

Aquell cotxe és més ràpid que (no/no pas) el nostre.
That car is faster than ours is.

Aquesta vegada va demanar la paraula i va parlar menys vehementment que (no/no pas) abans.
This time she intervened and spoke less vehemently than before.

És millor moure-les empenyent-les que (no/no pas) estirant-les.
It is better to move them by pushing than by pulling.

When the standard of comparison is a finite clause introduced by **que**, the verb in the subordinate is obligatorily preceded by **no** standing immediately after **que**. (There is some difference of opinion about whether **pas** is possible here directly before a verb; it may be acceptable only when **més**, **menys** is a pronominal quantifier, as in the second example below.)

Són més ràpids que no t'imagines.   ? . . . **que no pas t'imagines.**
They are faster than you suppose.

Ofereixen més que no (pas) donen.
They offer more than they give.

D'aquests se'n trobaran més que no tinc jo cabells al cap.
More of these will be found than the number of hairs on my head.

He vist més accidents que no heu tingut vosaltres malsons.
I have seen more accidents than you have had hot dinners (lit. nightmares).

Expletive **no (pas)** is also obligatory when both what is compared and the standard of the comparison are finite complement clauses (to avoid cacophonous **que que** 'than that', so grammarians say):

Més s'estima que ho llencis que no (pas) que m'ho donis.
She would rather you threw it away than that you gave it to me.

Serà millor que t'ho expliqui jo que no (pas) que t'ho llegeixis a la premsa.
It will be better for me to explain it to you than for you to read about it in the press.

However, when the standard of comparison involves a non-finite verb, expletive **no** can in principle be confused with ordinary negative **no**, as in:

Més m'estimo quedar a casa avui que no veure el partit.
I would rather stay at home today than (not) see the match.

Val més equivocat que no intentat.
Better mistaken than (not) attempted.

If the intended sense in the standard of comparison is really positive, one can leave out the expletive **no**. If the intended sense is negative, one can use **no pas no**, where the first **no** is the expletive, and the second the true negative.

M'estimo més empassar-me l'orgull que no pas no tornar a parlar-hi mai més.
*****M'estimo més empassar-me l'orgull que no no tornar a parlar-hi mai més.**
I had rather swallow my pride than not talk to them ever again.
(cf. **M'estimo més empassar-me l'orgull que (no (pas)) tornar a començar de nou.**
I had rather swallow my pride than start all over again (i.e, where the second term is not negative).)

Notice that when the *main clause* is negative, either **que** alone introduces the standard of comparison, or, with a finite verb, the construction with **del que** (**5.2.3**) will be used:

No és més ràpid que el nostre. ***. . . que no (pas) el nostre**
It is not faster than ours.

No són més ràpids del que t'imagines. ***. . . que no t'imagines**
They are not faster than you imagine.

When the main clause is negative, a complement clause may also form the standard of comparison:

Aquest exercici no ofereix pas menys dificultats teòriques que l'anterior n'oferia de pràctiques.
This exercise presents no fewer theoretical difficulties than the practical difficulties found in the earlier one.

Que t'ho expliqui jo no serà pitjor que que t'ho llegeixis a la premsa.
For me to explain to you will not be worse than your reading about it in the press.

In the last example each case of **que** corresponds to one function. The first **que** is the pivot of the comparison and the second **que** is the complementizer that heads the complement clause. While the result is grammatically correct, most native speakers would recast the sentence to avoid **que que . . .** , for example **. . . que si t'ho llegeixes a la premsa** ' . . . than if you read it in the press'. Because the first clause is negative **que que** cannot be replaced by *****que no pas que**.

5.2.3 Del que 'THAN'

When the standard of comparison is a phrase containing a finite verb, **que no** can be replaced by **del que** (strictly 'than that which', 'than (the amount) which'):

> **Ofereixen més del que donen.** = **Ofereixen més que no (pas) donen.**
> They offer more than they give.

> **Treballa més del que us penseu.** = **Treballa més que no us penseu.**
> She does more work than you think.

> **És molt més intel·ligent del que sembla.** = **És molt més intel·ligent que no sembla.**
> She is more intelligent than she seems.

When the compared element is a (quantified) noun, **del que** varies in form to display number and gender agreement.

> **Aparenta més serenitat de la que té per dins** (= . . . **més serenitat que no té . . .**).
> He displays more calm than he feels inside.

> **Presenten menys feina feta de la que havien promès** (= . . . **menys feina feta que no havien promès**).
> They offer less completed work than they promised.

Notice that this construction is not entirely logical; to take the last example, it appears to say 'less completed work than the (work) they promised', whereas the intended sense is 'less completed work than the (amount of work) they promised'.

As mentioned above, there is no alternative to the **del que** construction when the main clause is negative and the standard of comparison contains a finite verb:

> **No sé cantar més afinadament del que et pensaves.**
> I can't sing more in tune than you supposed.

5.3   SUPERLATIVES

5.3.1 RELATIVE SUPERLATIVE

There is, strictly speaking, no superlative degree of comparison in Catalan. That is, there is nothing corresponding to, say, 'fairest' in 'the fairest of the three' which is different from 'fairer' in 'the fairer of the two'. Catalan says **la més bella de les tres** just like **la més bella de les dues**. In both cases the construction involves using the definite article. In attributive position, the article precedes the noun, and the compared adjective may precede or follow (see

4.2.1): **la deessa més bella/la més bella deessa** 'the fairest goddess'. In predicative position the article comes before the degree word: **Venus fou la més bella** 'Venus was the fairest'. As the second term of the relation, the group within which an individual excels is introduced by **de**, or the context is expressed by a relative clause.

No vull ser el més ric del cementiri.
I don't want to be the richest person in the graveyard.

És la persona menys seriosa de totes les que conec.
He is the least serious of all the people I know (lit. the least serious person of all those that I know).

És la història més increïble que mai hagi sentit.
It is the most incredible story I have ever heard.

Això és el millor que podies fer.
That is the best thing you could do.

In the standard language, at least, adverbs cannot be preceded by articles. For 'Speak the slowest that you can' both (non-standard) **Parla el més lentament que puguis** and (non-standard) **Parla lo més lentament que puguis** are rejected in favour of the construction with **tan . . . com**:

Parla tan lentament com puguis.   Speak as slowly as you can.

Alternatively, to express something corresponding to a superlative of an adverb we can use a comparative with an extreme standard of comparison.

Enguany ha plogut més abundosament que mai.
This year we have had more rain than ever.

Aquí estava més bé que enlloc.
It was best here of anywhere./It was better here than anywhere (else).

This pattern is not restricted to adverbs. We can also say:

És menys seriós que ningú.
He is less serious than anyone. (= He is the least serious of everyone.)

És menys seriós que cap altre.
He is less serious than anyone else (lit. than any other).

5.3.2   ABSOLUTE SUPERLATIVE

The absolute superlative sense 'X to an extreme degree' can be expressed using the suffix **-íssim (-a, -s, -es)** added to an adjective stem (which will show morphological variation as before other suffixes that begin with a vowel):

Les platges del sud són netes. →	**Les platges del sud són netíssimes.**
The southern beaches are clean.	The southern beaches are very/extremely clean.
Hi va caure una boira espessíssima.	A very dense fog came down.
Això és complicadíssim.	This is extremely complicated.

The superlative of an adverb derived from an adjective consists of the already superlative feminine adjectival form with the adverb-forming suffix **-ment** (**clara** → **claríssima** → **claríssimament**):

> **Va educar els seus infants rectíssimament.**
> He brought up his children in a most upright manner.

Molt (as an adverb) also admits **-íssim**:

> **Aquesta òpera m'agrada moltíssim.**
> I like that opera very much indeed.

Especially in Balearic dialects **-íssim** can also be added to some lexical adverbs and adverbial expressions: **bé** → **beníssim** 'very well', **prest** → **prestíssim** 'very soon', **aviat** → **aviadíssim** 'very quickly', **a prop** → **a propíssim** 'very near', **enfora** → **enforíssim** 'very far', **a poc a poc** → **a poc a poquíssim** 'very slowly', **tard** → **tardíssim** 'very late', etc.

5.4 CORRELATIVE COMPARISON: 'THE MORE . . . THE MORE . . .', 'THE LESS . . . THE LESS . . .'

Correlative comparison is expressed in Catalan with **com més/menys . . . més/menys . . .** or **quant més/menys . . . més/menys . . . .** Quant més/menys is felt to be archaic.

> **Com menys te'n preocupis, menys te'n sortiràs.**
> The less you worry about it the less you'll succeed.

> **quant menys a prop més bé**
> the further away the better

> **Com més serem, més riurem.** (proverbial)
> the more the merrier

> **Com més insistia ell, més s'hi resistia ella.**
> The more he insisted the more she resisted.

> **com més aviat millor**
> the sooner the better/as soon as possible

For quantitative proportionality **quant més/menys . . . (tant) més/menys** is used, with appropriate agreement of the adjectives. This construction is very formal:

Quantes més hores treballaràs, (tants) més diners guanyaràs.
The more hours you work, the more money you will earn.

Quants més dies s'hi quedi, més li agradarà el poble.
The more days he spends there, the more he'll like the village.

6 DEMONSTRATIVES

6.1 GENERAL

The demonstrative adjectives and pronouns in Catalan are identical in form, that is, **aquest** followed by a (*m.sg.*) noun means 'this', while standing alone it means 'this one' (*m.*); likewise, **aquelles** means 'those' or 'those ones' (*f.pl.*) (see **6.4**). In this respect demonstrative adjectives resemble other adjectives in Catalan, which can be used pronominally. The neuter demonstrative pronouns **açò**, **això**, and **allò** are discussed in **6.5**.

Modern Catalan has a binary system of demonstratives with a basis somewhat different from that found in modern English (where 'this'/'these' indicates closeness to the speaker and 'that'/'those' indicates remoteness). It is convenient to see this in relation to the three 'persons' of verbal conjugation. The standard language differentiates between **aquest**, referring to something close, in time or space, to the speaker (first person) *and* to the person addressed (second person). **Aquell**, resembling old English 'yonder', refers to something remote from both speaker and hearer/reader. Thus, in the sentence **No m'agrada aquest abric** 'I don't like this/that overcoat', the demonstrative **aquest** could indicate the overcoat worn by either the speaker or the hearer. (Where context did not make the meaning clear, clarification would be supplied by gesture or by supplementary comment like **que portes avui** 'that you are wearing today'.) The point to be observed is that **aquest** translates 'this' and also 'that' where the latter refers to something close to a second person. **Aquell**, on the other hand, conveys the idea of 'that' when remoteness from the speaker and hearer/reader is involved, either in space (**aquell abric que porta en Xavier** 'that overcoat which Xavier is wearing') or in time (**aquell abric que portava (jo)/portaves (tu) l'altre dia** 'that overcoat which I was/you were wearing the other day'). Detailed discussion is given at **6.3**.

Section **6.3.1** covers exceptions to the normal positioning of a demonstrative adjective, in front of the noun it qualifies: **aquest gos** 'this dog', **aquelles coses** 'those things'.

6.2 DEMONSTRATIVE ADJECTIVES: FORMS AND FUNCTIONS

The basic system of demonstrative adjectives in modern standard Catalan can be represented thus:

	this	*that (near)*	*that (far)*
masculine	aquest	aquest	aquell
feminine	aquesta	aquesta	aquella

	these	*those (near)*	*those (far)*
masculine	aquests	aquests	aquells
feminine	aquestes	aquestes	aquelles

In most of the eastern Catalan area the **s** of masculine singular **aquest** is not pronounced except before a noun beginning with a vowel sound: thus **aquest noi** sounds **aque[t] noi** (cf. **aquest home** contrasted with **l'home aque[t]**); **aquest moment** sounds **aque[t] moment** (cf. **aquest incident** contrasted with **l'incident aque[t]**). The first **s** of the plural **aquests** is similarly silent (but in all positions/ combinations): **aquests moments/els moments aquests/aquests orígens**, etc., pronounced **aque[t]s moments/els moments aque[t]s/aque[t]s orígens**, etc. Observe that this feature does not affect the spelling.

6.2.1 DIFFERENT FORMS AND FUNCTIONS OF THE DEMONSTRATIVES

In the older language and in some dialects an alternative system coexists with the one explained above. The principal difference concerns a particular form to express proximity to the hearer, i.e. 'that'/'those' (near) in the tables above. The full system (resembling the three-member system of Castilian) appears thus:

	this	*that (near)*	*that (far)*
masculine	aquest/est(e)*	aqueix/eix(e)*	aquell
feminine	aquesta/esta	aqueixa/eixa	aquella

	these	*those (near)*	*those (far)*
masculine	aquests**/estos	aqueixos/eixos	aquells
feminine	aquestes/estes	aqueixes/eixes	aquelles

Note: *The masculine singular variants **est** and **eix** are classical and literary, while **este** and **eixe** are characteristic of colloquial speech in Valencian Catalan.
The form **aquestos also occurs, to avoid the **sts** group, but is not frequent even colloquially.
Balearic dialects also have **aqueixs** as plural of **aqueix**.

The above scheme permits the distinction to be made between the two functions expressed by English 'that'. Referring to the example given in **6.1**, the sentence **No m'agrada aqueix/eixe abric** would unambiguously denote the coat worn by the hearer, 'that coat'. Similarly a distinction can be made between **en aquestes circumstàncies** 'in these circumstances' (that I or we are referring to), **en aqueixes/eixes circumstàncies** 'in those circumstances' (that you refer to, or that we recently referred to) and **en aquelles circumstàncies** 'in those (remote) circumstances'.

Administrative language has been recently displaying a (rather artificial) tendency to mark the difference between the first two levels (**aquest** and **aqueix**) of the three-level deictic model:

> **Hem rebut en aquesta secretaria la comunicació enviada per aqueixa direcció.**
> We have received in this secretariat the communication from your directorate.

6.3 FURTHER DISCUSSION OF THE USE OF DEMONSTRATIVES

The English-speaking learner of Catalan must be careful to observe the usage of the Catalan demonstratives, especially in view of the overlaps in function in relation to 'this'/'that'. **Aquell** referring to something remote presents few problems, particularly when it is seen as indicating the most distant in a set of things:

> –**De qui és aquest** (or **aqueix**) **cotxe?**   'Whose car is that?'
> –**Vols dir aquest d'aquí?**   'Do you mean this one (here)?'
> –**No, aquell d'allà.**   'No, that one over there.'

Aquell also indicates remoteness in time:

> **Recordes aquell dia que vam anar al museu?**
> Do you remember that day we went to the museum?

> **En aquells temps la gent vivia més bé.**
> In those times people lived better.

When an event has been located in the distant past, subsequent references to it may be made by **aquest**, or by **aqueix/eixe** where the system described in **6.2.1** is used: **Estava pensant en l'any 63. Doncs jo en aquesta/aqueixa època començava la carrera** 'I was thinking about '63. Well, at that time, I was starting university'.

Aquell will not be used in association with the historic present, because of the contradiction between remoteness and immediacy: thus we do not say **Aquell any Oller escriu *L'escanyapobres* 'In that year Oller writes

L'escanyapobres', but either **Aquest any Oller escriu . . .** or **Aquell any Oller va escriure . . . .**

This last point can also be related to the way in which **aquest**, etc. is frequently the marker (**aquest matí, aquesta tarda**, etc.) that determines the use of the perfect tense as opposed to the preterite, similar to English (see **17.1.2.1, 17.2.2**):

En aquest segle s'han produït grans progressos tecnològics.
In this century there has been great technological progress.

The logic defining what **aquest** and **aquell** refer to, as described in **6.1**, extends quite naturally to the area of telephone conversation. Even though speaker and listener are physically separated, **aquest** may still indicate something near to the listener at the other end of the line. Thus, for example, if A has sent B a book (and B has it in her possession while talking on the phone), A will refer to it consistently as **aquest llibre** (e.g. **Aquest és l'únic exemplar que n'ha quedat** 'That is the only copy that was left'). Likewise the enquiry **Què fan aquests nens teus?** addressed by A to B would translate 'How are those children of yours?' The use of **aquells** here would convey the understanding that the children are not in B's vicinity. Other examples:

No et trobes bé? Amb aquesta veu no et coneixia.
Aren't you well? I didn't recognize you with that voice.

Des d'aquest hotel puc venir amb taxi fins al bar aquest d'on em truques.
From this hotel I can come by taxi to that bar you are phoning from.

(For these last two cases Valencian Catalan would have **amb eixa veu** and **al bar eixe** respectively.)

The same applies to use of the adverb **aquí** 'here' in telephone exchanges. For example, phoning from any distance away (including abroad) A might ask B **Quin temps fa aquí a Solsona?** 'What's the weather like there in Solsona?' Similarly **Vols dir que aquí no hi ha vingut cap Pere?** 'Do you mean that nobody called Pere has come there?' (As in face-to-face conversation, **allí/allà** 'there' in this context would indicate remoteness from both speaker and listener.)

6.3.1 POSITION OF DEMONSTRATIVE ADJECTIVES

Demonstrative adjectives normally precede the nouns they determine, as in most of the examples given in the preceding sections. In colloquial and less formal registers, however, it is not unusual to find the demonstrative placed after a noun introduced by its definite article (or other determiner) or by a possessive: **aquest disc** = **el disc aquest** 'this record', **aquelles revistes** = **les revistes aquelles** 'those magazines', **aquestes tres llaunes** = **les tres llaunes aquestes** 'these three tins', **aquell company nostre** = **el nostre company aquell** 'that companion of ours' (on the position of possessive adjectives, see **7.1.1**). This postposing of the demonstrative may connote a degree of intimacy between speaker and hearer, and also a slight pejorative sense, (but this may be no more than the effect of informal style):

Aquestes teories no convencen.	These theories are not convincing.
Les teories aquestes no convencen.	These theories (just) aren't convincing.

6.4   DEMONSTRATIVES AS PRONOUNS

As already remarked, the demonstratives can be used pronominally meaning 'this (one)'/'that (one)'/'these (ones)'/'those (ones)'.
Examples of pronominal demonstratives:

Dóna'm un altre boli –aquest no guixa.
Give me another biro –this one doesn't write.

Aquesta no s'assembla gens a la seva mare.
This one (*f.*) isn't at all like her mother.

Aquelles eren les condicions en què operàvem.
Those were the conditions in which we were operating.

Use of the demonstrative to refer to someone present can be humorous or mildly offensive: **Pregunta-li-ho a aquest** 'Ask this one here' (e.g. a woman pointing to her husband), **Aquest, rai!** 'It's all right for *him* to talk'.
Where the Catalan demonstrative stands alone, and a noun cannot be supplied from context, a person is meant:

Aquest t'ho dirà.	This man/person (*m.*) will tell you.
Aquelles no cantaven tan bé.	Those girls/women didn't sing so well.

Although Catalan subject pronouns are used only for emphasis, contrast or clarity (see **11.5.1**) a demonstrative occasionally occurs as the equivalent of an English subject pronoun:

En Ramon ens va presentar les seves filles. Aquestes eren dues criatures molt entremaliades.
Ramon introduced his daughters to us. They were two very mischievous kids.

Another 'independent' function of demonstratives is as antecedent of a relative clause (see **31.6** and **6.5**):

Aquells que ho van veure no se n'oblidaran mai.
Those who saw it will never forget it.

As **aquell** denotes remoteness and **aquest** proximity, they can be conveniently used (almost invariably in written texts) to refer to the order in which things have been previously mentioned, conveying the idea of 'the former' and 'the latter' respectively:

> **Consulta la pàgina 26 i després la 73, i veuràs que l'autor contradiu en aquesta el que diu en aquella.**
> Have a look at page 26 and then at 73, and you will see that on the latter the author contradicts what he says on the former.

Also to be observed is the way that adverbial **així** 'thus', 'like this' placed after a noun can replace an adjectival phrase composed of **com** + demonstrative:

> **Amb un refredat així (= com aquest) no hauries de sortir.**
> With a cold like that you ought not to go out.

> **Mai més no tornaran a fer discos així (= com aquells).**
> Never again will they make records like those.

6.5   NEUTER DEMONSTRATIVES

There is a small set of genderless (neuter) demonstrative pronouns:

això	this/that (first or second person demonstrative; see **6.1**)
allò	that
ço	that

The members of the small set of neuter pronouns, together with the neuter pronominal clitic **ho** (dealt with in **12.5**), have two functions. They may refer to objects as yet unidentified, or not specific enough to be identified by a noun with a gender:

Què és això?	What is that?
Allò no ens interessa.	That doesn't interest us.
D'on has tret això?	Where have you got that from?

Or they may refer to a proposition, situation or event.

> **Allò no podia redundar en benefici nostre.**
> That could not have turned out to our advantage.

> **Això és el que vaig dir.**
> That is what I said.

(Observe that **això** is picked up by the 'neuter' definite article **el**, which is the same as the masculine form of the article; see **9.2**.)

Atén-lo en tot allò que desitge.	Serve him in whatever he requires.

In Valencian, where the three-term demonstrative system is in use (**6.2.1**), the corresponding neuters are **açò** (first person, corresponding to **este** 'this', **ací** 'here'), **això** (second person, corresponding to **eixe** 'that', **aquí/ahí** 'there'), and **allò** (third person, corresponding to **aquell** 'that', **allí** 'there'). In other varieties (except in Minorca, where it replaces **això**) **açò** is scarcely used.

The pronoun **ço** is largely obsolete, though it can be found in a few expressions: **ço del meu**, etc. 'my possessions', 'what is mine', **ço és (a saber)** 'that is to say', 'namely', 'that is'; **ço que** (neuter relative):

Li ha dit que sí, ço que li ha plagut molt.
He said yes to her, which pleased her a great deal.

6.6 DEMONSTRATIVES: SYNTAX AND PROBLEMS OF TRANSLATION

Catalan demonstratives can stand as antecedents of a relative clause in expressions like 'that which', 'the one which/who', 'those which/who', etc. An identifying function or an element of comparison may be prominent:

El meu rellotge no és tan bo com aquest que tens tu.
My watch is not as good as that one that you have.

Aquells que ens critiquen no han comprès el dilema.
Those who criticize us have not appreciated the dilemma.

Era una situació ben diferent d'aquella en què es van conèixer.
It was a very different situation from the one in which they first met.

D'acord amb allò que preveu la llei.
In accordance with what (lit. that which) the law stipulates.

–Qui va pagar tot allò que vam consumir? –Ho va pagar en Màrius.
'Who paid for everything that we consumed?' 'Màrius paid for it.'

In cases like the first two above (but not the third, where a preposition governs the relative), the appropriate definite article can be used instead of the demonstrative: thus we could have ... **el que tens tu, els que ens critiquen** ... but not *__la en què__.

Corresponding to the English demonstrative in the relative constructions 'those of us', 'those of you (*pl.*)', 'those of them', Catalan uses the definite article, not the demonstrative:

els que vivim a Reus
those of us who live in Reus/we who live in Reus

Vull dir les que viviu lluny.
I mean those of you (*f.*) who live far away.

els que no s'hagin matriculat
those (of them/you) who have not registered

See Chapter 31 for further discussion (especially **31.6.1–2**).

7 POSSESSIVES

7.1 FORMS OF THE POSSESSIVES

Apart from the cases considered in **7.1.1** and **7.2**, possessives are normally introduced by the corresponding definite article. For each person there are thus four forms, whose usual position is initial within a noun phrase:

	singular		plural	
	masculine	*feminine*	*masculine*	*feminine*
my, mine	**el meu**	**la meva**	**els meus**	**les meves**
your(s) (sg.)	**el teu**	**la teva**	**els teus**	**les teves**
*his, her(s)**	**el seu**	**la seva**	**els seus**	**les seves**
our(s)	**el nostre**	**la nostra**	**els nostres**	**les nostres**
your(s) (pl.)	**el vostre**	**la vostra**	**els vostres**	**les vostres**
*their(s)**	**el seu**	**la seva**	**els seus**	**les seves**
their(s) (see **7.1.2.1**)	**llur**	**llur**	**llurs**	**llurs**

Note 1: *When the **vostè(s)** mode of address is used, possession is indicated by third-person forms, **el seu**, etc. When the **vós** mode of address is used, possession is indicated by second-person plural forms, **el vostre**, etc.

Note 2: Valencian Catalan consistently uses the feminine variants **meua, teua, seua** (*sg.*) and **meues, teues, seues** (*pl.*). These forms also occur in other dialects of Catalonia and the Balearics, and are entirely acceptable in all styles of language.

Agreement in possessives

Number and gender agreement of the possessives is determined by the number and gender of what is possessed: **el meu amic** 'my friend (*m.sg.*)', **la teva millor amiga** 'your (*sg.*) best friend (*f.sg.*)', **els seus cosins** 'his/her/their cousins (*m.pl.*)', **els nostres bons consells** 'our best advice (*m. pl.*)', **les vostres relacions íntimes** 'your (*pl.*) intimate relationships (*f.pl.*)', **els seus problemes** 'their problems (*m.pl.*)'.

7.1.1 POSSESSIVE POSITION AND USE WITH OTHER DETERMINERS

Possessives usually precede the noun (as above) but may sometimes follow, and determiners other than the definite article may be used.

(i) Possessives with the indefinite article: **un meu llibre/un llibre meu** 'a book of mine', **un seu parent/un parent seu** 'a relative of his/hers/theirs', **unes vostres amigues/unes amigues vostres** 'some friends (*f.*) of yours'.

(ii) Possessives with a demonstrative adjective: **aquest meu gos/aquest gos meu** 'this dog of mine', **aquell seu fill petit/aquell fill petit seu** 'that younger son of his/hers/theirs', etc.

Whether it stands before or after a noun a possessive adjective is always accompanied by a determiner (typically an article or demonstrative), with the following exceptions only where the possessive follows the noun:

(a) The set expression **casa meva** 'my house/home', **casa teva**, etc.

(b) vocative formulae:

Tot això, fill meu, algun dia serà teu.	All this, my son, one day will be yours.
La vida és molt dura, amic meu.	Life is very hard, my friend.

(c) Indefinite noun predicates:

–Per què ho fa així? –Manies seves.
'Why does he do it like that?' 'He has these quirks.'

Allò eren aspiracions nostres; ben diferent de les meves aspiracions personals.
Our aspirations were one thing; quite another thing are my personal aspirations.

The presence of the definite article is what, generally, differentiates between a possessive adjective predicate and a possessive used pronominally. In the sentence **Aquesta calculadora és la meva** 'This calculator is mine' the possessive is pronominal, standing for a specific noun, so that the meaning is 'this (and not any other) calculator is mine'. It might also be translated '*This* is my calculator' or 'This calculator is my one'. The same sense might be expressed in **Aquesta (calculadora) és la meva calculadora**. As a predicate without the article, on the other hand, **Aquesta calculadora és meva** is a general statement of possession, glossed as 'This calculator is mine' or 'This calculator belongs to me', where **meva** is a predicate adjective referring back to the noun **calculadora**, like **japonesa** 'Japanese', for example, or **potent** 'powerful' might be in this same context. The distinction is further illustrated in the alternatives possible in a sentence like: **És difícil saber quines fotos són (les) nostres i quines**

són (les) vostres 'It is hard to tell which photos are ours and which are yours'. **Les nostres** presupposes that there are some photos which are ours. Without the article the sentence suggests that your and our photos may be hard to tell apart in principle, without presupposing any particular set of mixed-up photos.

7.1.1.1   *Llur* 'their'

The archaic possessive **llur(s)** 'their' stands without the definite article when it introduces a noun: **llur (= la seva) incomprensió** 'their lack of understanding'. This form has disappeared from all spoken dialects (except in North Catalonia where its use is supported by the model of French *leur*). However, it has been artificially reinstated in the normative formal repertoire of modern Catalan, where it sits rather uncomfortably (a favourite Aunt Sally for critics of stilted or hypercorrect expression). Use of **llur** can be justified, and retains viability, in educated discourse, to avoid confusion with the singular possessor **el seu**, etc. In speech and less formal writing, though, the ambiguity of **la seva cosina** 'his/her/their/your cousin' is more likely to be resolved by **la cosina d'ells** 'their cousin', **la cosina d'ell** 'his cousin', **la cosina d'ella** 'her cousin', **la cosina de vostè** 'your cousin', etc. Cases of **llur(s)** with the definite article are occasionally recorded, exemplifying the most rarefied level of style:

> **Els arquitectes i llurs col·laboradors (els llurs col·laboradors/els col·laboradors llurs) mereixen els màxims elogis.**
> The architects and those who worked with them deserve the highest praise.

7.2   UNSTRESSED POSSESSIVE ADJECTIVES

Corresponding to **el meu**, **el teu**, **el seu**, there are the following alternative weak or unstressed forms:

	singular		*plural*	
	masculine	*feminine*	*masculine*	*feminine*
my	mon	ma	mos	mes
your	ton	ta	tos	tes
his/her/their	son	sa	sos	ses

Before a feminine noun beginning with a vowel or **h** + vowel, **mon, ton,** and **son** replace **ma, ta, sa**, respectively:

son àvia   his/her grandmother

These unstressed forms have no equivalents for first- and second-person plural subjects, they never appear preceded by the definite article or other determiner, and they are not used pronominally.

In most varieties of Catalan the unstressed possessives have a restricted use, accompanying only names of relatives and the nouns **casa** 'house', 'home' and **vida** 'life': **mon avi** 'my grandfather', **ta mare** 'your mother', **ses nétes** 'his/her/their granddaughters' (for each of which **el meu, la teva, les seves**, respectively, would be more common), **Vine a ma casa** 'Come to my house', **En ma vida no havia vist un espectacle semblant** 'Never in my life had I seen such a sight'. The third-person forms are also found in certain formulas of respect (note capitals): **Sa Majestat** 'His/Her Majesty', **Sa Excel·lència** 'His/Her Excellency', **Ses Alteses Reials** 'Their Royal Highnesses', **Sa Sante-dat** 'His Holiness'. In this formulaic use, **Sa** not ***Son** is used before a feminine noun beginning with a vowel. The weak system of possessives is frequent in older texts and in certain styles of poetry.

In Balearic, probably due to identity between *f. sg.* possessive **sa** and *f. sg.* article **sa**, a redundant use of the third-person weak possessive can be observed as in **sa mare d'en Miquel**, 'Miquel's mother', **son pare d'en Miquel** 'Miquel's father'.

7.3 POSSESSIVE PRONOUNS

Possessives which take the definite article (i.e. all except **llur(s)** and the weak forms) can, like any adjectives, be used pronominally. The distinction between the adjectival or pronominal function depends on whether, in context, the possessive stands for a specific noun, as discussed in **7.1.1**:

Quin paraigua agafem, el meu o el teu?
Which umbrella shall we take, mine or yours?

Les vostres (e.g. **cortines**) **no són les blanques?**
Aren't yours the white ones?

Aquesta cartera és la meva.
This wallet is mine/my one.

In some cases context alone is sufficient to indicate which noun is implied, and the English translation will be more explicit:

Acabo de rebre la teva del 18 de juliol.
I have just received your (letter) of July 18.

els nostres
our relatives, members of our group

There are a number of idiomatic expressions involving pronominal posses-sives, where the reference is to a notional **cosa** 'thing'. For example: **sortir-se** amb la seva 'to have one's way', **dir la seva** 'to have one's say', **Ja n'has feta una de les teves** 'You've been up to your usual tricks'; see **3.4**.

The possessive is occasionally introduced by the neuter article **el** or demonstrative **això/allò** (see **6.5** and **9.2**):

Que cadascú pagui el seu.	Let everybody pay their own share.
Tot el meu és vostre.	Everything of mine is yours.
Allò teu va ser molt divertit.	What you did/said was very amusing.

7.4   POSSESSION: OTHER EXPRESSIONS

A Catalan possessive adjective does not occur on every occasion where one would be used in English:

quan vaig obrir els ulls	when I opened my eyes
un home que maltracta els fills	a man who mistreats his children
Sempre arriba puntual al despatx.	She always arrives punctually at her office.

To supply **seves** at either * or ** in a statement like **Caminava amb les * mans a les ** butxaques** 'He was walking along with his hands in his pockets' would be considered obtrusive or excessive. Where possession is obvious or inherent, as in the examples just given, the article is sufficient to convey it, as again in this variation on the previous example: **Caminava amb una mà a la butxaca** '. . . with one hand in his pocket'. Similarly, **On he deixat les claus?** could be 'Where have I left the keys?' but could also imply the possessive meaning of 'Where have I left my keys?' Compare then: **Parlava amb els ulls fixats en la meva cara** 'He was speaking with his gaze fixed on my face', and the difference between **Anem a casa** 'Let's go home' (i.e. to our house) and **Anem a casa teva** 'Let's go to your house'.

Constructions with the verb **tenir** 'to have' may likewise bypass the use of possessive adjectives:

Tenia els ulls blaus.	His eyes were blue.
(better than **Els seus ulls eren blaus.**)	
Heu tingut una paciència exemplar.	Your patience has been exemplary.
(**La vostra paciència ha estat exemplar.**)	

7.4.1   POSSESSIVE FUNCTIONS OF THE DATIVE

Often it is an indirect object pronoun (**12.3.2.3** and **25.4**) that corresponds to an English possessive:

M'he tallat el dit.	I've cut my finger.
Li van robar el cotxe.	They stole his car./His car was stolen.
No sap fer-se el nus de la corbata.	He can't tie the knot in his own tie.

This applies, as illustrated, both to 'reflexive' actions (**23.2**) and to actions done to others:

Renta't les mans.	Wash your hands.
Treu-te l'abric.	Take your coat off.
Renta-li la cara.	Wash his/her face.

This dative construction is usual with parts of the body, clothing, and other personal effects. In the case of personal effects and clothing, alternative use of the possessive adjective is possible:

He deixat la teva cartera a l'armari./T'he deixat la cartera a l'armari.
I've left your briefcase in the cupboard.

The possessive adjective may also be used when the thing possessed is emphasized or particularized by context, by an adjective or other words, or when ambiguity is to be avoided:

Vaig agafar la seva mà tremolosa.   I took hold of her trembling hand.

Note that a part of the body, etc., is expressed in the singular if only one per person is meant (**2.2.2**):

Recomanem que us tragueu l'americana.
We recommend you to take off your jackets.

Compare:

Li vaig estrènyer les mans amb les meves.
I grasped his two hands in mine.

7.4.2   INANIMATE OR NON-PERSONAL 'POSSESSORS'

There is a strong tendency for the possessive not to be used when the possessor is inanimate or impersonal and is not the subject of the sentence:

Vam considerar el problema i vam concloure que la solució seria massa costosa.
We considered the problem and concluded that its/the solution would be too costly.

While the presence of the possessive in **Els arbres deixaven caure les (seves) fulles** 'The trees were shedding their leaves' is tolerable to the native ear (with the inanimate noun as sentence subject), it would be avoided in **Va sacsejar l'arbre per fer-ne caure els fruits** 'He shook the tree to bring down its fruit'. Sometimes a phrase involving a possessive concept is more naturally expressed by an alternative construction: **La casa està arruïnada, i la (seva) reconstrucció costarà dos milions de pessetes** 'The house is in ruins, and its reconstruction will cost two million pesetas' might preferably be rephrased as

La casa està arruïnada, i costarà dos milions de pessetes de reconstruir-la
'. . . to restore it will cost . . .'.

A factor influencing 'avoidance' of the possessive in this area is the availability of the Catalan adverbial pronoun **en** (see **12.6**) with its anaphoric possessive function (= **de** + pronoun), referring to the object of a transitive verb:

Va agafar la capsa i en va aixecar la tapa.
He took hold of the box and raised its lid.

Quan estudiïs el text, en comprendràs la complexitat.
When you study the text you will understand its complexity.

7.5   POSSESSIVES AFTER PREPOSITIONS AND PARTICIPLES

Compound prepositions (principally those expressing position) can be followed by the possessive substituting **de** + the prepositional object pronoun (see **14.2.3**):

En Mateu està amagat darrere seu (= darrere d'ell/ella/ells/elles/vostè/ vostès).
Mateu is hidden behind him/her/them/you.

Posa't davant meu (= davant de mi).
Stand in front of me.

Volen seure a prop/a vora teu (= a prop de/a vora de tu).
They want to sit near you.

S'han declarat a favor nostre (= a favor de nosaltres).
They have spoken out in our favour.

Associated with this construction, and with the fact that agents can in some cases be introduced by **de**, is the use of the possessive instead of **per** + a strong pronoun to express the agent in a limited range of passive sentences (see **29.1.2**).

Tot això és fet meu (= fet per mi).
All this has been done by me.

No he localitzat la versió en disquet del capítol X, però n'he trobat una versió corregida teva en paper (= corregida per tu).
I haven't located the disk version of Chapter X, but I have found a version of it corrected by you on paper.

8 MISCELLANEOUS ADJECTIVES AND PRONOUNS (QUANTIFIERS AND INDEFINITES)

8.1 GENERAL AND MORPHOLOGY

Quantifiers occupy an intermediate area of meaning between numerals and indefinites, as is seen in the relationship between **dos dies** 'two days' (numeral), **uns quants dies** 'a few days' (quantifier), **alguns dies** 'some days' (indefinite; compare **uns dies** (indefinite article)). The distinction between quantifiers and indefinites is hard to establish, and is perhaps more conventional than real.

Like adjectives in general, both quantifiers and indefinites can have pronominal uses: **N'he agafat uns quants/alguns** 'I have taken a few/some (e.g. books)'. There is also a discrete set of indefinite pronouns, e.g. **algú** 'someone', **ningú** 'no one', etc. (see **8.5**). Some quantifiers are used adverbially, e.g. **bastant/prou** 'enough', **força** 'a lot' (see **8.2.2** and **13.6**).

Certain quantifying and indefinite adjectives are inflected, agreeing both in number and gender (**molt/molta/molts/moltes** 'much'/'many', **algun/alguna/alguns/algunes** 'some'); some are variable without having all four differentiated forms (**bastant** *m.sg.* and *f.sg.*, **bastants** *m.pl.* and *f.pl.* 'enough', **altre** *m.sg.*, **altra** *f.sg.*, **altres** *m.pl.* and *f.pl.* 'other'). Others are invariable, showing no number–gender agreement: **força** 'much/many', **prou** 'enough', **més** 'more', **cada** 'each'; the colloquial forms **bastanta** and **bastantes** (*f.sg.* and *f.pl.*), **forces**, **prous** and **masses** (*m.pl.* and *f.pl.*) are avoided in formal contexts.

For easy reference quantifiers and indefinites are discussed under single headings, arranged alphabetically, at **8.2** and **8.3** respectively.

8.2 QUANTIFIERS

bastant 'enough', marked only for number:

> **He llegit bastants diaris per avui.**
> I've read enough newspapers for today.

> **–Tenim pomes? –Sí, encara ens en queden bastants.**
> 'Have we got any apples?' 'Yes, we've still got a good few left.'

In the last example it can be seen that **bastant** may convey the idea of 'a certain amount or quantity' of something, as well as of sufficiency: see below under **prou**.

força 'very much/many', 'a lot (of)', invariable:

M'agrada l'amanida amb força ceba.	I like salad with plenty of onion.
Han sorgit força dificultats.	A lot of difficulties have arisen.

gaire '(not (very)) much/many', marked only for number:

This word occurs only in negative constructions (see **8.4**), or after **si** 'if' or in interrogatives (that is, it is a negative polarity item; see **26.1.5**):

No té gaire paciència.
She hasn't got much patience.

No sé si hi haurà gaires complicacions.
I don't know if there'll be many complications.

Tens gaire interès a fer-ho?
Are you very interested in doing it?

Gaire is invariable in Balearic: **No sé si hi haurà gaire complicacions.**

gens (de) 'none (at all)', 'any':

Strictly a degree adverbial, **gens** can stand on its own; otherwise it is almost invariably followed by **de**, in negative (see **8.4**) or interrogative contexts, or after **si** 'if'. See **8.6iii** for the distinction in usage between **gens** and **cap**. **Gens de** introduces a singular non-count noun:

Si teniu gens de compassió m'escoltareu amb atenció.
If you have any compassion at all you'll listen to me carefully.

–On és el sucre? –No ens n'ha quedat gens.
'Where's the sugar?' 'We've none left.'

Anaphoric constructions relating to **gens (de)** involve pronominalization with the clitic **en**, as in the first and last examples above. See **12.6v**.

massa 'too much', 'too many', invariable:

Tenia massa pressa per saludar-me.
She was in too much of a hurry to say hello to me.

Ens han donat massa maldecaps.
They have given us too many headaches.

manco Bal. 'less', 'fewer', invariable (see **menys** below, and **5.2**).

menys 'less', 'fewer', invariable (see **5.2**):

La versió censurada provocava menys escàndol.
The censored version provoked less outcry.

Menys is often replaced by a negative periphrasis containing **tant/-a** 'so much', **tants/-es** 'so many' (see below):

Posa-hi menys oli./No hi posis tant d'oli.
Put less oil in./Don't put so much oil in.

Aquest plat porta menys calories/ . . . no porta tantes calories.
This dish has fewer calories/ . . . doesn't have as many calories.

més 'more', invariable (see **5.2**):

–Vols més vi? –Sí, ja en pots demanar més.
'Do you want more wine?' 'Yes, you can order some more.'

Hem de treballar més hores que abans.
We have to work more hours than before.

Both **més** and **menys** can combine in the comparative expression **com més/ menys . . . més/menys** 'the more/less (fewer) . . . the more/less (fewer)' (see **5.4**).

mig 'half', marked for gender:

Note the absence of the indefinite article in Catalan: **mitja milla** 'half a mile', **mig quilòmetre** 'half a kilometre', **mig got de vi** 'half a glass/a half glass of wine', **una hora i mitja** 'an hour and a half' (but **la mitja hora que vam esperar** 'the half hour that we waited' with definite article). As with **tot** (see below) invariant **mig** usually precedes the name of towns, regions, and countries:

Mig Catalunya/Mig Estats Units ho sap.
Half Catalonia/Half the United States knows about it.

molt 'much', 'many', marked for number and gender:

Parlava amb molta sinceritat.	She spoke very sincerely.
Molts (= moltes persones) ho han vist.	Many (people) have seen it.

Except in Valencia (where **gaire** is not used in everyday speech), there is a preference for **gaire** over **molt** corresponding to 'much'/'many' in the negative, conditional, and interrogative contexts discussed above under **gaire**:

Ho ha fet sense gaire (= molt (d'))) esforç.
He did it without much effort.

Si has esperat gaire (= molta) estona, és perquè ho has volgut.
If you've waited a long time it's because you wanted to.

The pronoun/adverb **molt** 'a lot', 'a large amount' does not agree with a preceding noun:

Cinc-centes mil lliures, dius? És molt.
£500,000, did you say? That's a lot.

Compare the adjective construction:

Set-centes paraules per pàgina són moltes.
Seven hundred words a page are a lot (of words).

poc '(a) little', *pl.* 'few', marked for number and gender:

Ens queda poc temps./Ens queden poques hores.
We don't have much time left./We only have a few hours left.

Pocs (= **poques persones**) **s'ho creurien.**
Few (people) would believe it.

The general functioning of **poc** is parallel with that of **molt**, as discussed above. The **no gaire** periphrasis frequently substitutes for expressions with **poc** (cf. English 'not much/many' = 'a little'/'few'):

Tenen pocs amics./No tenen gaires amics.
They have few friends./They haven't got many friends.

prou 'enough', invariable:

Has menjat prou carn/patates?
Have you eaten enough meat/potatoes?

No tenim prou temps ni prou recursos.
We haven't enough time or enough resources.

Although in the sense of 'enough' **prou** is interchangeable with **bastant(s)**, it does not convey the meaning of 'a certain amount/quantity' and so a distinction is observable in cases like:

Ha guanyat bastants diners, però encara no en té prou.
He has earned a fair amount of money but he still hasn't got enough.

Hem collit bastants mòres, potser prou per fer un pastís.
We've picked a good few blackberries, perhaps enough to make a pie.

pus Bal. '(any) more', invariable:

This word occurs, in Balearic varieties, only in negative polarity contexts (**26.1.5**).

Vols pus vi?
Do you want any more wine?

No s'atreviren a intentar res pus.
They did not dare to attempt anything else.

Note that **més** is used, not **pus**, in a comparison with an explicit standard.

No hauríem de fer més hores que abans.
*No hauríem de fer pus hores que abans.
We wouldn't have to work more hours than before.

que 'what a lot (of)', invariable:

Used only in exclamations (more details in **27.2.2.2**), with the same meaning as **quant** (see below).

Que gent!	What a lot of people!
Que n'has vistes, de coses!	What a lot of things you have seen!

When a verb follows a **que** + noun phrase, another **que** is inserted:

Que gent que hi ha!	What a lot of people there are!
Que neu que queia!	How it snowed!

quant 'what a lot (of)', 'how much/many', marked for number and gender:

Quant pa (que van menjar)!
What a lot of bread (they ate)!

No sé quantes caixes han dut.
I don't know how many boxes they have brought.

See **27.1.3.3** on interrogative patterns with **quant**.

Preceded by the indefinite article, the plural **uns quants, unes quantes** translates 'a few', an indefinite (small) amount, differentiated from **pocs, poques** which stresses limitation of number (see above). **Uns quants** is not radically different in meaning from **alguns** (see **8.3**):

Hauràs d'esperar uns quants dies més.
You'll have to wait a few more days.

Potser que hi trobaràs unes quantes errades d'ortografia.
Perhaps you'll find a few spelling mistakes.

(cf. **Hi vam trobar poques errades.**
We found few mistakes.)

El president vol afegir unes quantes paraules de clausura.
The chairman wishes to add a few closing words.

tant 'as much'/'as many', 'so much'/'so many', marked for number and gender:

As this word expresses 'the same amount/number (as)', a notion of comparison (**5.1**) is always present:

Es va posar histèric de tantes interrupcions.
He became hysterical at so many interruptions.

Un dia, trobant-me dormint com he dormit tantes i tantes vegades . . .
(P. Calders, *Cròniques de la veritat oculta*)
One day, being asleep like I have been so very many times . . .

–Tens gaires diners? –Tants com tu.
'Have you got much money?' 'As much as you.'

Tant is used pronominally in the expression **un tant per cent** 'a percentage'. For more detailed discussion of comparison and for the **tant** vs. **tan** distinction, see **5.1**; for **tant de**, see **8.2.1**.

tot 'all', 'every', marked for number and gender:

(i)   Except for the cases considered below in this section and in **8.3**, **tot** will be followed by an article or other determiner (numeral or demonstrative):

tot el matí/tota la tarda
all morning/afternoon

Ni en Martí, amb tota la seva erudició, no pogué aclarir la qüestió.
Not even Martí, with all his erudition, could clarify the matter.

Hi haurem d'aplicar tots els nostres esforços.
We shall have to apply all our efforts to it.

Ja han tornat tots quatre.
All four (of them) have come back.

Tots aquests papers s'han de llençar.
All these papers have to be thrown away.

Referring to periods of time **tots** with the article can translate 'every', overlapping with the indefinite **cada** 'each' (see **8.3**):

Ens reunim tots els diumenges.
We meet every Sunday.

The singular **tot** followed by an article translates 'the/a whole . . .':

Vam passar tot el dia a la platja.
We spent the whole day on the beach.

Va sorgir tota una sèrie de problemes.
A whole series of problems arose.

Tot without the article is used with singular nouns:

(a)   To introduce a singular (indefinite) mass noun:

T'ho dic amb tota sinceritat.   I'm telling you in all sincerity.

(b) To express 'each and every':

Tota regla té excepcions.	Every rule has its exceptions.
Hi havia gent de tota mena.	There were people of every kind.

(See also **8.3**.)

(ii) Unlike other quantifiers (and indefinites), **tot** cannot take **de** 'of' when introducing a noun phrase. Compare **tots els socis** 'all (of) the members' with **bastants/moltes/algunes de les nostres amigues** 'a good few/many/ some of our female friends'. This last feature is also observed when **tots** precedes a subject pronoun:

Tots nosaltres et desitgem bona sort.	All of us/We all wish you good luck.
Havíem de saludar-los a tots.	We ought to greet them all/all of them.

Tots can be separated from its noun phrase and relocated in the sentence (as can 'all' in English), so that:

Tots els veïns d'aquest barri han protestat contra el projecte.
All the residents of this district have protested against the plan.

could be recast as:

Els veïns d'aquest barri han protestat tots contra el projecte.
The residents of this district have all protested against the plan.

(iii) **Tots dos/totes dues** is the most common way of expressing 'both', although this can also be done with the somewhat more formal **ambdós/ ambdues**:

Val la pena d'escoltar totes dues/ambdues cares del disc.
It's worth listening to both sides of the record.

(iv) There is no gender agreement when **tot** precedes the name of a city, region, nation that does not begin with an article: **tot Tarragona** 'all (of) Tarragona', **tot Catalunya** 'all (of) Catalonia'/'the whole of Catalonia', but **tota la Pobla de Segur**. (Usage before plural names beginning with an article is problematic.)

(v) Note relative clauses involving **tot** as an antecedent (**31.6.2**) corresponding to English 'all who', 'everyone who', 'whoever', etc.:

tots els que hi érem	all of us who were there
tots aquells que llegeixin això	anyone/everyone who reads this

(vi) **Tot** is also used pronominally as a neuter 'everything':

Tot li agrada.   She likes everything.
Tot és possible.   Everything is possible.

When standing as direct object **tot** 'everything' is supported by the neuter clitic **ho** 'it' (cf. English 'it all'):

Ho hem de preparar tot./Hem de preparar-ho tot. *Hem de preparar tot.
We've got to get everything ready.

Li ho has explicat tot?
Have you explained everything/it all to her?

As antecedent of a relative clause **tot** combines with neuter **el que** 'that which' (see **9.2.2**).

Apuntaré tot el que m'has explicat.
I'll note down everything you've told me.

Tot el que lluu no és or.
All that glisters is not gold.

8.2.1   QUANTIFIERS WITH de

While the main quantifiers can introduce a noun phrase directly (**Fa molt fred** 'It's very cold', **Quant pa vols?** 'How much bread do you want?'), there is an alternative pattern in which (except for **massa**, **força**, **mig**, **que** and **tot**) they take an intercalated **de**, particularly before a masculine singular noun. This pattern is typical of a more formal style, although it is more common in Majorca. (Majorcan use, however, avoids **de** after **gaire**, **manco/menys**, **més/pus**, **prou** and **poc**).

Tinc molt de fred/molta (de) calor.
I'm very cold/hot.

Hi havia poca (de) llum.
There wasn't much light.

No hauries de fer tant (d')exercici físic.
You shouldn't take so much physical exercise.

Quantes (de) cullerades hi has posat?
How many spoonfuls have you put in?

No tenia bastant (d')/prou energia per fer-ho.
He hadn't enough energy to do it.

As remarked above, **gens** always introduces a noun with **de** in all varieties and styles:

No ha quedat gens de nata.   There's no cream left at all.
*No ha quedat gens nata.

8.2.2   QUANTIFYING ADVERBS (DEGREE ADVERBS)

All of the quantifiers discussed above, except **quant**, have adverbial uses (as degree words), in which function their form is almost always invariable. This topic is taken up in **13.6**.

8.3   INDEFINITE ADJECTIVES

algun 'some', marked for number and gender:

The fact that this word can be used in the singular with the meaning of 'some' indicates how it differs in meaning from the indefinite article (discussed below and at **3.2**). **Algun** and **un** may often be interchangeable, but **algun** conveys the clear nuance of 'one or perhaps more', 'the odd . . . ', 'some or other':

(i)   **algun** as adjective:

Només es veia per les platges abandonades algun turista abatut.
All one could see on the empty beaches was the occasional glum tourist.

Era l'única manera de fer-ho amb alguna garantia d'èxit.
It was the only way of doing it with some guarantee of success.

In the plural **alguns/algunes** may correspond to 'a few', 'certain', as well as 'some':

Han estat a casa alguns dies.
They have been staying with us for a few days.

En alguns casos s'ha de pitjar l'altre botó.
In certain cases you have to press the other button.

Alguns sí, d'altres no.
Some are/do, (but/and) some aren't/don't.

(ii)   **algun** used pronominally (noun understood):

–Et van donar instruccions? –Bé, alguna, sí.
'Did they give you instructions?' 'Well, just one or two, yes.'

Amb alguns del meu grup, no hi ha manera d'entendre-t'hi.
It's impossible to get through to some of the ones in my group.

When pronominal **algun** is linked with a plural personal pronoun, person/number agreement of any associated element may be with either **algun** (third person) or the pronoun:

Si alguna de vosaltres ho sabeu . . . /Si alguna de vosaltres ho sap . . .
If any of you (*f.*) know . . . /If any one of you knows . . .

A algun de vosaltres ja m'agradaria de veure-us/veure'l en un embolic així.
I'd like to see one of you in a pickle like this.

altre 'other', marked for gender in the singular, invariable in the plural:

A definite or indefinite article will normally precede the singular adjective **altre**, whose meaning coincides with most aspects of English 'other':

Viu a l'altra banda del poble.
He lives on the other side of town.

Deixa'm un altre llibre; és que ja he llegit aquest.
Lend me another book; I've already read this one.

Una altra vegada, fes-ho amb més cura.
Another time do it more carefully.

una vocal altra que la 'u'
a vowel other than 'u'

T'hauries de posar els altres pantalons.
You ought to put your other trousers on.

L'altre dia translates 'the other day', but compare **l'altre mes/l'altra setmana** 'last month/week', and also **aquesta parada que ve, no; l'altra** 'not the next stop, the one after'. **Els altres** is the normal way of saying 'the rest', 'the others (of a set)':

França, a diferència dels altres (= la resta dels) països de la Unió Europea
France, unlike the other countries in the European Union

Pronominal use of **altre** presents no complications:

L'havia pres per un altre.
I'd mistaken him for another/someone else.

Aquestes tisores no són pas tan bones com aquelles altres que tenies.
These scissors aren't as good as those other ones you used to have.

S'han mirat l'un a l'altre.
They looked at each other/one another.

cada 'each', 'every', invariable:

Van entrevistar cada alumne, l'un darrere l'altre.
They interviewed every student, one after the other.

Cada vegada que truca . . .
Every time he telephones . . .

With periods of time **cada** is heard more frequently than the construction **tots els**:

L'inspector passa cada tres mesos.	The inspector calls every three months.
Em dutxo cada dia.	I take a shower every day.

Note that, unlike English 'each', **cada** cannot be used pronominally. In this role **cada un/cadascun** is required.

cada un or **cadascun** 'each (one)', marked for gender (**cada una, cadascuna**):

Like its English equivalent this word has no plural form and, unless used pronominally (see **8.5**), invariably introduces a noun with **de** 'of'. The form **cada un** is more commonly used:

He marcat amb una creu cada una (cadascuna) de les pàgines que has de copiar.
I have marked with a cross each (one) of the pages you are to copy.

Va portar regals per a cada un dels seus nebots.
She brought presents for each (one) of her nephews (and nieces).

cap 'not one', '(not) any', invariable:

This word is a negative polarity item like **gaire** and **gens** (see below **8.4**, also **26.1.5**) in that it can stand alone in interrogative or conditional contexts as well as forming a negative construction with **no**:

Si arriba cap visita, digue-li que s'esperi.
If any visitor arrives, tell them to wait.

Cap d'ells no ho ha entès.
Not one of them has understood.

For the difference between **cap** and **gens** see **8.6iii**.

cert 'certain', marked for number and gender:

Used as an indefinite **cert** precedes the noun. In the singular it is preceded, as in English, by the indefinite article:

L'equívoc es pot atribuir a una certa tendència seva a exagerar.
The misunderstanding is attributable to a certain tendency of his to exaggerate.

Hi ha certes persones amb qui val més no tractar.
There are certain people that it is better to have nothing to do with.

Preceding the name of a specific person 'a certain' is translated by **un tal** (see below). Used absolutely or placed after the noun **cert** means 'accurate', 'true' or 'sure':

És cert que no vindran.
It's true they're not coming.

Estic cert del que et dic.
I'm certain about what I'm saying.

Encara no tenim notícies certes sobre aquests fets.
We still don't have accurate news about these events.

diversos 'several', 'various' (plural), marked for gender:

Es pot fer de diverses maneres.
It can be done in various ways.

Li ho vaig haver d'explicar diverses vegades.
I had to explain it to her several times.

In the sense of 'several' **diversos** usually precedes the noun, although it may occasionally follow: **problemes diversos relacionats amb el cas** 'several problems related to the case'. In this position the meaning of 'diverse' comes into view, overlapping with the synonymous **varis** (*pl.* **vàries**):

Van provar remeis varis/diversos.
They tried various/several different remedies.

per raons vàries/diverses
for various reasons

The use of **varis** instead of **diversos** before the noun, in the sense of an indefinite number, is deemed non-standard. When 'several' implies a rather large number **nombrosos** can be used:

Hi hagué nombroses abstencions.
There were several/a good number of abstentions.

igual (a/de) '(the) same (as)':

Viu en una casa igual de/a la que vàrem visitar.
He lives in a house the same as the one we visited.

Em sembla que té un quadern igual del/al que jo vaig perdre.
I think she's got a ring-binder the same as the one I lost.

Igual a, not **igual de** occurs before an indefinite or a possessive:

Aquesta planta és igual a una de tropical que em van regalar.
This plant is the same as a tropical one that I was given as a present.

Tenia un pis igual al meu.
She had a flat just like mine.

mant 'many a', marked for gender:

Used only in the singular, with a plural meaning, this word is confined to very formal contexts:

El text ho descriu detingudament, amb manta observació oportuna.
The text describes it in detail, with many an opportune observation.

mateix 'same', 'selfsame', marked for number and gender:

(i) Meaning 'same' **mateix** always stands before the noun or noun phrase that it qualifies:

Teníem els mateixos gustos.
We had the same tastes.

Ja no treballen amb les mateixes eines que abans.
They don't work with the same tools as they used to.

M'ha regalat el mateix llibre que li vaig regalar jo per Nadal.
She has given me the same book as the one I gave her at Christmas.

Aquests nois no són els mateixos que varen venir a la botiga.
These boys aren't the same ones that came to the shop.

El mateix is used pronominally to mean 'the same (thing)' (see **9.2**):

Avui et dic el mateix que et vaig dir ahir.
I'm telling you today the same as I told you yesterday.

Sempre fas el mateix, i amb el mateix resultat.
You always do the same thing, and with the same result.

(ii) Placed either before or after a noun **mateix** has the emphatic meaning of 'selfsame', 'very', 'right' and likewise emphasizes any strong pronoun after which it is placed, e.g. **jo mateix** 'I myself', **ella mateixa** 'she herself':

No el reconeixeria ni el seu mateix pare/el seu pare mateix.
Not even his own father himself would recognize him.

Aquestes són les seves mateixes paraules.
These are her very words.

Aquest quadre, l'he pintat jo mateix ((*f.*) jo mateixa).
I painted this picture myself.

Where there could be ambiguity, **mateix** comes after the noun if it means 'selfsame': **la mateixa reina** could translate 'the queen herself' or 'the same queen', while **la reina mateixa** means only 'the queen herself'. **Mateix** occurs in conventional formulations when someone is asked to identify themselves, as on the telephone –**El senyor Planes? –Jo mateix** 'Mr Planes?' 'Speaking'/'That's me', or in an encounter –**Vostè és la senyora Planells? –La mateixa** 'Are you Mrs Planells?' 'I am indeed' (lit.

the same). It is also frequently used, after the relevant subject pronoun, as a way of telling someone else that they can choose or decide for themselves:

Pots quedar-te aquí o venir amb nosaltres: tu mateix.
You can stay here or come with us; it's up to you/as you prefer.

ningun 'no', 'any', singular only, marked for gender:

Ningun is used in Valencian only, and corresponds in usage to **cap** (see above).

propi 'own', marked for number and gender:

Ho ha fet amb les seves pròpies mans.
He did it with his own hands.

Ho hauries de veure amb els teus propis ulls.
You ought to see it with your own eyes.

Because of the reflexive meaning of 'belonging to oneself', the use of **propi** overlaps with that of **mateix** (as discussed at (ii) under **mateix**):

Aquestes són les seves pròpies paraules.
These are her own words./These are her very words.

Propi, however, will not qualify a pronoun: **nosaltres mateixos** 'we ourselves', never *****nosaltres propis.**

qualque 'some', singular only, not marked for gender:

Synonymous with **algun**, this adjective has wide currency in Balearic dialects and in North Catalonia. Elsewhere its use is confined to literary contexts, except in the phrase **qualque cosa = alguna cosa** 'something' (see **8.6**). The corresponding pronominal is **qualcun** 'someone', marked for number and gender.

qualsevol 'any', marked for number:

There is an alternative form **qualsevulla**. This compound word is analysed as **qual-se-vol/vulla** 'whichever might be wanted', which explains why the plural appears with double **ss** in the middle as **qualssevol (qualssevulla)**. The indefinite meaning of 'any at all', 'whichever' is prominent:

Podria haver esclatat en qualsevol moment.
It could have exploded at any moment.

Inventa qualsevol pretext per marxar.
Invent some pretext or other for leaving.

Pots agafar qualsevol d'aquestes cintes.
You can take any one of these tapes.

qualsevol que sigui la conseqüència d'aquesta acció
whatever the consequence of this action may be

Qualsevol diria que ets un milionari.
Anyone would say you're a millionaire.

The plural **qualssevol** is nowadays infrequent, being substituted by a singular construction, as the meaning is virtually the same, e.g.:

qualsevol membre de la junta que no hi estigui d'acord
any member/members of the board who isn't/aren't in agreement

Qualsevol normally precedes the noun: **Pots pagar amb qualsevol moneda** 'You can pay in any currency'. The idea of indefiniteness or randomness is strengthened, though, if it is placed after the noun:

Tracem un triangle qualsevol; no cal que sigui rectangle.
Let us draw a triangle, any triangle; it need not be right-angled.

When postposed **qualsevol** is used of people, the effect is often pejorative, equivalent to English 'any old':

No és una cantant qualsevol; és una autèntica artista.
She's not just any old singer; she's a real artist.

Used pronominally with the indefinite article, the term can be insulting: **un qualsevol** 'a nobody', **una qualsevol** 'a trollop', 'a slut'.

sengles 'one each', invariable:

This adjective exists only in the plural, with the meaning of 'one for or belonging to each of two or more persons or things':

Venia acompanyada de tres guardaespatlles, muntats en sengles motocicletes potents.
She was accompanied by three body-guards, each riding a powerful motorbike.

tots aquests casos, amb sengles peculiaritats
all of these cases, each with its own peculiarity

In everyday usage the function of **sengles** is performed by a more current indefinite word or construction, in the first example above ... **muntat cada un en una motocicleta potent**, and in the second, ... **amb les seves peculiaritats** ...

tal 'such', marked for number:

Serà millor que no ens emboliquem en tals operacions.
It will be better if we don't get involved in such operations.

In the singular **tal** alone usually corresponds to English 'such a':

Ella no hauria dit mai tal cosa.
She would never have said such a thing.

Vaig dir-li que vindria tal dia i a tal hora.
I told him I'd come on such and such a day at such and such a time.

An indefinite article sometimes precedes **tal**, though, when the comparative idea of 'similar' is uppermost:

Jo no he emprat mai un tal llenguatge.
I have never used such language/language like that.

Tal com 'just like', 'just as' can be adjectival or adverbial:

Era tal com ens l'havien descrit.
It was just like they had described it to us.

Ho faré tal com dius.
I'll do it just as you say.

Tal is also used to refer to an indefinitely identified person:

S'ha casat amb una tal Glòria.
He has married some Glòria or other/somebody called Glòria.

en tal i en tal altre
so-and-so and what's-his-name

Archaic **aital** (marked for number) occurs as a synonym for **tal** in deliberately elevated style.

tot 'every', 'any', marked for gender (singular):

Tot is used in the singular in contexts where it can be considered an indefinite rather than a quantifier (see **8.2**):

Tot mallorquí se n'hauria d'alegrar.
Every Majorcan ought to be pleased about this.

Cal rebutjar tot producte que no porti aquesta etiqueta.
Any product not bearing this label should be rejected.

un indefinite article, marked for number and gender:

For discussion of the indefinite article **un**, see **3.2.3-4**. In the present context attention is to be paid to problems involved in translating 'some' (see **8.6**) and to use of the plural **uns** before a numeral to express an approximate quantity:

Fa unes tres hores que s'espera.
She has been waiting for three hours or so/about three hours.

Aquest model val uns tres mil duros.
This model costs about 15,000 pesetas (**un duro** = five-peseta coin).

8.4 FUNCTIONS OF **cap**, **gaire**, **gens**

These words (together with **ningú** and **res**, covered in **8.5**) belong to a set of items used in negative constructions in Catalan. The description of negation given in **26.1.5** is complemented by considering the 'positive' value of the quantifiers **gaire** and **gens** and indefinite **cap** when they are used in interrogatives or after **si** 'if'. Compare:

Portaven gaire equipatge?
Were they carrying much luggage?

No sé si portaven gaire equipatge.
I don't know if they were carrying much luggage.

with the corresponding negative construction:

No portaven gaire equipatge.
They weren't carrying much luggage.

Likewise:

Ha fet gens de sol?
Has the sun shone at all?

Si fa gens de sol, anirem tots a la platja.
If the sun shines at all, we'll all go to the beach.

compared with negative:

No ha fet gens de sol.
The sun hasn't shone at all.

and

Has rebut cap carta?
Have you received any letters?

Em pregunto si ha rebut cap carta.
I wonder if he has received any letters.

compared with negative:

No han rebut cap carta.
They haven't received any letters.

8.5 INDEFINITE PRONOUNS

In addition to those indefinite adjectives which can be used pronominally, there are some words which have the exclusive function of an indefinite pronoun. Examples are given of each one, listed alphabetically:

algú 'someone', 'somebody', 'anybody':

Algú ho deu saber.
Somebody must know.

Si hi ha algú a fora, digue-li que se'n vagi.
If there's anybody outside, tell them to go away.

'Someone else' can be translated by **algú altre**, although **un altre** frequently suffices. This observation combines with the further point that when gender is a significant part of the message 'someone' can be translated by **un/una** or by a specific noun, as in:

Ara surt amb una altra.
He's going out with someone else (= a different girl) now.

M'ha saludat una que no coneixia.
Somebody (*f.*)/Some woman I didn't know said hello.

És una (dona/noia) en qui pots confiar.
She is somebody in whom you can trust.

altri 'someone else':

Altri is invariably the object of a preposition. In colloquial registers it is less commonly used than periphrastic equivalents like **un altre, una altra persona, algú altre, els altres**, according to sense.

El degueren prendre per altri.	They must have taken him for somebody else.
Treballem pel bé d'altri.	We are working for the good of others.

cada u or **cadascú** 'each', 'everyone':

Cada u és lliure d'emetre la seva opinió.
Everyone is free to voice their opinion.

The meaning of **cada u/cadascú** is close to that of absolutely indefinite **tothom** 'everybody', and it is differentiated from the pronominal adjective **cada un/cadascun** (see **8.3**) which refers to individuals from a specific group in the mind of the speaker. This can be seen by comparing:

Cadascú (= tothom) cobra el mateix.
Everybody is paid the same.

Hi treballen nou empleats i cadascun (d'ells) cobra el mateix sou.
Nine clerks work there and every one (of them) is paid the same salary.

Consequently, unlike **cada un/cadascun** (as in **cadascuna de les germanes** 'each of the sisters', **cadascun de nosaltres** 'each (one) of us'), **cadascú** cannot be followed by a **de** + noun phrase.

ningú 'no one', 'nobody', 'anyone', 'anybody':

> **No s'ho creurà ningú.**   No one will believe it.

While occurring principally in negative constructions (see **26.1.5**), **ningú** can mean indefinite 'anyone' in interrogative contexts and after **si**:

> **Mira si es veu arribar ningú.**
> Have a look to see if anybody is arriving.

> **Hi ha ningú que gosi contradir-me?**
> Is there anybody who dares to contradict me?

In practice **algú** will be found more frequently in such expressions.

qualcú 'someone' = **algú**

quelcom 'something':

> This form is strongly embedded in all formal styles. Colloquially, however, in most varieties and across the range of written registers it is substituted by **alguna cosa, una cosa**:

> **Això és quelcom que haurem de tenir en compte.**
> This is something we shall have to bear in mind.

> **Aquí hi ha alguna/una cosa que no va bé.**
> There is something wrong here.

> **T'explicaré una cosa que t'esgarrifarà.**
> I'll tell you something that will horrify you.

> The use of **qualque cosa**, synonymous with **quelcom, (alg)una cosa**, has extended beyond the Balearic dialects where its use is universal:

> **Hauries de menjar qualque cosa.**
> You ought to have something to eat.

> **Quelcom** takes **de** before a masculine adjective in translating English 'something + adjective': **quelcom de meravellós** = **una cosa meravellosa** 'something marvellous'.

res 'nothing', 'something', 'anything':

> For **res** in negative constructions see **26.1.5**. The observations made in **8.4** and above on **ningú** apply also to **res** used interrogatively and after **si** 'if':

> **Si us sobra res, doneu-ho als pobres.**
> If you've anything left over, give it to the poor.

> **Els falta res?**
> Are you short of anything?

Cal dir-hi res més?
Need anything more be said?

tothom 'everyone', 'everybody':

Tothom hi està d'acord.
Everybody is in agreement.

Saluda a tohom de part meva.
Say hello to everybody for me.

Tothom que ha signat el document en rebrà una còpia.
Everybody who has signed the document will receive a copy of it.

Plural **tots** 'all', 'everybody' and **tot el món** (cf. French *tout le monde*) are generally acceptable synonyms for **tothom** (which in some dialects, notably Valencian, is not deeply rooted); similarly **tots aquells qui/que** is equivalent to **tothom qui/que**:

Tots volien escoltar-la.
Everybody wanted to listen to her.

Tot el món sap que és veritat.
Everybody/The whole world knows it is true.

8.6   TRANSLATING 'SOME', 'ANY', AND 'SOMETHING'

Guidelines are given here for contrasting Catalan and English usage in these two primary areas of meaning of quantifiers and indefinites.

(i)   **Algun** does not translate 'some' or 'any' before a mass noun, or before a plural count noun. Unmodified nouns are used for this:

Teniu farina integral?
Have you got any wholemeal flour?

Hem de comprar llet.
We've got to buy some milk.

Vols més maduixes?
Do you want some/any more strawberries?

No han tingut escrúpols a l'hora de fixar els preus.
They didn't have any scruples when it came to setting the prices.

(ii) The plural indefinite article **uns/unes** expresses 'some' in the sense of 'a number of', that is a limited but vague quantity. This overlaps with the use of **alguns**, but the latter can carry reference to indefinite identity as well as quantity:

M'han visitat uns amics de Vic.	I've had a visit from some friends from Vic.
Alguns convidats hi van passar la nit.	Some guests spent the night there.

(iii) **Cap** introduces count nouns while **gens (de)** introduces non-count nouns where English uses 'some'/'any', in negative, interrogative, or conditional contexts:

Tens cap intenció d'anar-hi?	Have you any intention of going?
Us queda gens de paper?	Have you got any paper left?

This difference is maintained for 'any' in negative expressions:

No hi van fer cap objecció.	They didn't raise any objection.
No té gens de paciència.	He hasn't any patience.

Constructions with **cap** and **gens** frequently entail use of anaphoric **en** (see **12.6**) referring to the element that is quantified:

Entrades per a aquest vespre? Ja no en queda cap.
Tickets for this evening? There aren't any left.

Comptava que em sobraria espai, però, de fet, no me n'ha quedat gens.
I reckoned I'd have space to spare, but, in fact, I didn't have any left at all.

In cases like the last two **cap** or **gens** may be suppressed, so that the resulting construction is in line with examples given in (i) above: **Ja no en queden** 'There aren't any left', **No me n'ha quedat** 'I didn't have any left'. In standard Catalan **cap** (Val. **ningun/-a**) are used only before singular nouns. However, a tendency is observed in colloquial Catalan for **cap** to also precede *pluralia tantum* nouns:

(non-standard)	**Que has vist cap pantalons que t'agradin?**
	Have you seen any trousers you like?
(non-standard)	**No tinc cap ganes d'anar al circ.**
	I have no desire to go to the circus./I don't fancy going to the circus at all.

In the standard language something like **parell** 'pair' or **conjunt** 'set' is preferred in a case like the former:

Que has vist cap parell de pantalons que t'agradin?
Have you seen any pair of trousers you like?

In the second case **gens de** is preferred:

No tinc gens de ganes d'anar al circ.

(iv) **Qualsevol** corresponds to 'any' in the sense of 'any at all', 'it doesn't matter which . . .'. It can be contrasted with **algun** in a sentence like:

Tria qualsevol d'aquests vídeos; n'hi ha d'haver algun que t'agradi.
Choose any one from these videos; there must be one (or more) that you'll like.

(v) Catalan is elastic in rendering 'something'/'anything'. Negative expressions involve **res** (**No en sap res** 'He doesn't know anything about it') which also figures in interrogative contexts and after **si**:

Em pregunto si ella ens en dirà res.
I wonder if she will tell us something/anything about it.

Hi ha res de nou?
Is there anything new?/Is there any news?

The Castilianism **algo** 'something' (non-standard) remains widespread in uneducated speech, although it can be expected to recede as 'standards' are enforced in Catalan-language schooling and the media. **Quelcom** 'something', long favoured by purists, has been only minimally assimilated, and much the same is true, except in the Balearic Islands, of **qualque cosa**. The foreign learner of Catalan will have no difficulty in imitating native use of **alguna cosa** or **una cosa** for 'something'; these are standard and current.

9 NOMINALIZATIONS VIA ARTICLES

9.1 NOMINALIZERS

Any adjective in Catalan can function as a noun simply by becoming the head of a noun phrase; this often involves it following an article or a demonstrative (but not necessarily so). We deal separately below with one product of this process: nominalization of an adjective when a noun is suppressed (**9.1.1**). Constructions using the 'neuter' article **el/lo** with adjectives are discussed at **9.2.1** and 'intensification' of adjectives with **el/lo** at **27.2.3**. Many cases in the first category are as familiar as nouns as they are as adjectives: **els grecs** 'Greek people', **un cec** 'a blind man'/'a blind person', **un boig** 'a madman', **els vells i els joves** 'the young and the old', **els exiliats** 'exiles', etc.

9.1.1 TRANSLATING 'THE ONE(S)': OMISSION OF THE NOUN

In **–Quin llibre has llegit? –El vermell** 'Which book have you read?' 'The red one' we can see the adjective **vermell** becoming the head of a noun phrase with its own definite article. The same occurs with the italicized phrases in the following sentences:

> **No sé si m'he de posar els mitjons prims o *els gruixats*.**
> I don't know whether to wear my thin socks or my thick ones.

> **D'aquests dos nens *el petit* sembla més despert.**
> Of these two children the younger one seems more wide-awake.

When an indefinite article is involved the nominalized adjective is preceded by **de**. (An exception to note is **un altre** 'another (one)', not ***un d'altre**.)

> **–Vols un gelat? –Sí, però un de molt petit.**
> 'Do you want an ice cream?' 'Yes, but a very small one.'

This construction is related to the partitive use of **en**: see **12.6v**.

> **–Vols un gelat? –Sí, però compra-me'n un de molt petit.**
> 'Do you want an ice cream?' 'Yes, but buy me a very small one.'

> **M'agrada aquest rellotge teu; jo abans en tenia un d'igual.**
> I like that watch of yours; I used to have one like it.

The nominalized adjective can, naturally, be preceded by a preposition:

–En quina capsa penses? –En la vermella.
'Which box are you thinking of?' 'The red one.'

Hem de decidir si hi anem amb el meu cotxe o amb el teu.
We must decide whether we are going in my car or in yours.

Likewise a nominalized adjective itself can be followed by an adjectival qualifier or complement. So, in answer to the question En quina capsa penses? 'Which box do you have in mind?', we could have en la vermella ratllada 'the red one with stripes' (adjective), en la vermella que hi ha al segon prestatge 'the red one on the second shelf' (adjectival relative clause) or en la vermella del segon prestatge 'the red one on the second shelf' (prepositional phrase complement).

Nominalization of prepositional phrase complements

Just as adjectival modifiers can be nominalized, so also can prepositional phrase complements introduced by de ('that/those/the one(s) of/from'):

L'aigua de la font és més bona que no la de l'aixeta.
The water from the spring is better than that from the tap.

Aquest abric que duc és el del meu pare.
This overcoat I'm wearing is my father's.

En lloc de menjar-me el pa d'avui m'he menjat el d'ahir.
Instead of eating today's loaf I have eaten the one from yesterday.

This solution is not available for prepositional phrases introduced by any other preposition, for which alternative constructions are generated, sometimes involving replacing another preposition with de.

*M'agrada més el pa amb oli que no l'amb mantega.
M'agrada més el pa amb oli que no amb mantega/que no el pa amb mantega.
I like bread with oil on it more than bread and butter.

*És més noble l'afany per ajudar que el per enriquir-se.
És més noble l'afany per ajudar que el d'enriquir-se/que l'afany per enriquir-se.
More noble is the urge to help than (the one/the urge) to get rich.

*Qui has vist, l'home amb ulleres o el sense ulleres?
Qui has vist, l'home amb ulleres o el que no en duia?
Who did you see, the man with glasses or the one without (glasses)?

*Has de triar entre el pagament a tres mesos o l'a un any.
Has de triar entre el pagament a tres mesos o el d'un any.
You must decide between monthly or yearly payments.

Nominalization of (adjectival) relative clauses

The same pattern seen above can apply to adjectival relative clauses (see **31.6.2**).

Quin és el teu cotxe, el que hi ha a l'aparcament o el que retira la grua?
Which is your car, the one in the parking lot or the one being towed away?

És amic del professor de matemàtiques i del que ensenya història.
He is a friend of the mathematics lecturer and of the one who teaches history.

De tots els llocs possibles has triat el que és més lluny.
Of all the possible places you have chosen the one which is furthest away.

When a prepositional phrase or a relative clause is nominalized using the article, general rules for word order (**36.4.2.1**) are followed for the addition of new adjectives. As 'simple' synthetic adjectives will precede phrasal modifiers (that is, prepositional phrases or relative clauses), it is the adjective standing immediately after the article that assumes the function of head of the noun phrase (with possible following qualifiers). The limitations of the English system of nominalization are revealed in this area.

L'aigua de la font és més bona que no la infecta de l'aixeta.
Spring water is better than the filthy stuff from the tap.

Observe how the word order **L'aigua de la font és més bona que no la de l'aixeta infecta** could only mean something different: 'Spring water is better than the water from the filthy tap'.

En lloc de menjar-me el pa d'avui m'he menjat el petit d'ahir.
Instead of eating today's loaf I've eaten the small one from yesterday.
(***En lloc de menjar-me el pa d'avui m'he menjat el d'ahir petit.**)

Quin és el teu cotxe? El que hi ha a l'aparcament o el vell que retira la grua?
Which is your car? The one in the parking lot or the old one being towed away?

És amic del professor de matemàtiques i del malparit que ensenya història.
He is a friend of the mathematics lecturer and of the bastard who teaches history.

Something different occurs in a sentence like **Els problemes d'avui són els d'ahir engrandits** 'Today's problems are yesterday's writ larger', where **engrandits** 'enlarged' has an independent explicative function and cannot refer to **ahir**. Such constructions also contain an adversative perspective:

Els problemes d'avui són els (mateixos) d'ahir, però engrandits.
Today's problems are yesterday's writ large.

9.2   NEUTER ARTICLE

9.2.1   ABSTRACTION OF AN ADJECTIVE

The definite article **el** (**l'** before a vowel or **h** + vowel) can be used to turn an adjective into a sort of abstract noun, expressing the general quality conveyed by that adjective without reference to any specific noun, **el** becoming thus a 'neuter article'. Translation into English often involves 'the thing':

No és estrany que faci tard, l'estrany és que no hagi trucat.
It's not strange that he's late; the strange thing is that he hasn't phoned.

L'increïble de vegades esdevé creïble.
The incredible sometimes becomes credible.

L'important és que ara actuïn amb rapidesa.
The important thing is that they should now take swift action.

However, this construction tends to be limited to use with adjectives, like those in the examples above, whose meaning is clearly abstract. Other solutions are often used in order to prevent confusion between **el** as neuter article and **el** as masculine definite article. The sentence **El verd m'agrada** seems most likely to refer to an elided noun, 'I like the green one' (similar to examples in **9.1.1**), rather than to 'greenness'. Preference, then, in the case of an abstraction, is for a periphrastic solution like **Tot el que és verd m'agrada** 'I like everything that is green' or **Les coses verdes m'agraden** 'I like green things'. Similarly **El fàcil és més atractiu** is appropriate for comparing known objects ('The easier one (e.g. **camí** 'route') is more attractive') rather than for referring to 'easiness' as a generalized quality, so that for this concept the preference is for **Les coses fàcils són més atractives** 'Easy things are more attractive' or for the relative construction (see **9.2.2**) **El que és fàcil és més atractiu** 'That which is easy is more attractive'.

The neuter demonstratives (**això, allò**) are occasionally used to stand in for the neuter article:

Això nostre és un assumpte complicat.
This business of ours is a complicated matter.

Hauríem de parlar d'allò altre.
We ought to discuss that other business.

However, **això** and **allò** have a demonstrative value which limits their capacity for 'abstraction' of any item (especially proper adjectives) to which they refer. The utterance **Allò negre indica que porta dol** 'The black shows that she is in mourning' seems to point at a black garment rather than just to the fact that she is dressed in that colour. Similarly **Això rodó rodola** is more likely to refer to an object which can be contemplated during the conversation, 'That round thing is rolling about', rather than to be a general statement that 'Whatever is round will roll'.

The existence of **lo** (= **el**) as masculine definite article in certain dialects of Catalan has been adduced to support the acceptability of constructions that make this word a nominalizer: **Lo bonic és que . . .** 'The nice thing is that . . . ', **Lo més interessant vindrà després** 'The interesting part will come later'. However, it is much more conceivable that the influence of Castilian (which makes wide use of neuter article *lo*) is what lies behind generation of this kind of construction in colloquial Catalan. In other words, the frequent appearance of constructions with **lo** in the spoken language of many Catalans derives less from the traditional structures of their own language than from direct (if unconscious) influence of the close neighbour. In summary, standard Catalan does not have a distinctive neuter form of the article (see Chapter 3), and the masculine form **el** has limitations in this function. As shown above, it is easy to work with the more 'genuine' solutions of **la cosa/les coses** 'the thing'/'the things', **el que és . . .** and other simple semantic substitutions (readily available via English, more often than not):

> **Lo bonic és que . . .** (colloquial, non-standard) → **La cosa bonica és que . . ./**
> **El que és bonic és que . . .** (genuine)
> **Lo més interessant vindrà després** (colloquial, non-standard) → **La part més interessant vindrà després.**
> **Lo dolç li agrada menys que lo salat** (colloquial, non-standard) → **Les coses dolces li agraden menys que les salades.**
> He likes sweet things more than savoury (things).

For **el/lo** + adjective expressing a form of indirect exclamation, see **27.2.3**.

9.2.2   THE NEUTER RELATIVE PRONOUN

El que 'what (= that which)' has the neuter article **el** as the antecedent of relative pronoun **que** (see **31.6.2**). Here **el** stands for a non-specific antecedent, and it may be replaced in some contexts by **allò** or, occasionally, by **això**:

> **Per què no escoltes el que et dic?**
> Why don't you listen to what I'm saying?

> **Van dir allò que esperàvem.**
> They said what we expected.

> **El que em preocupa es pot resumir així.**
> What worries me can be summed up as follows.

On the relationship between the neuter article **el** and the demonstrative pronoun **allò** in such constructions, normative grammar recommends use of the latter (or **la cosa que**) to resolve the possible ambiguity of a sentence like **És el que et deia** 'It's the man I was telling you about' (**el** = masculine definite article) or 'It's what I was telling you about' (el = neuter article). In such a case **És allò que et deia** or **És la cosa que et deia** would be unambiguous.

A non-restrictive relative clause, placed in apposition to another clause, may make use of the expression **la qual cosa** 'which thing':

> **Perdries moltes nits, la qual cosa no va bé per a la salut.**
> You'd lose a lot of nights' sleep, which isn't good for your health.

> **Al final, per molt que havia dit que no hi aniria, va acudir a la cita; de la qual cosa dedueixo que l'afer no li era tan indiferent com pretenia fer creure.** (Lacreu, 1990)
> Finally, despite all his talk about not going, he turned up for the appointment, from which I deduce that the affair wasn't so unimportant to him as he tried to make out.

This, however, is a rather archaic solution, virtually confined to literary language, and the spoken standard prefers **cosa que** '(a) thing which' for this kind of relativization, or resorts to alternative constructions:

> **La reunió no comença fins les nou, cosa que em permet de fer abans algunes consultes.**
> The meeting doesn't begin until 9 o'clock, which allows me to make some enquiries beforehand.

> **Després d'això no va tenir altre remei que dimitir.**
> After which he had no alternative but to resign.

> **Em va acusar que era impacient i que posava en perill l'operació total; i jo li vaig respondre que . . .**
> He accused me of being impatient and of jeopardizing the whole operation, to which I responded . . .

> **Hem tingut molta ajuda i molta sort; si no, no ho hauríem aconseguit.**
> We've had a lot of help and a lot of luck, without which we never would have managed it.

> **Crea complicacions d'horari, i això s'ha d'evitar.**
> It creates timetabling problems, which is to be avoided.

> **Remodelaran aquest sector, i tots ens n'aprofitarem.**
> They'll reorganize this sector, from which we'll all take advantage.

Non-standard Catalan frequently uses **lo que** as a neuter relative pronoun in all the above constructions.

9.2.3   ABSTRACTION OF A PREPOSITIONAL PHRASE

Prepositional phrases headed by **de** may be found nominalized with neuter **el** (non-standard **lo**), but here other constructions are preferred in all styles.

?**Val més tractar ara el de més importància.** = **Val més tractar ara el que té/ això que té més importància.** = **Val més tractar ara les coses de més importància.**
It will be better to deal now with the most important matter.

?**Farem el de costum?** = **Farem el que fem de costum?** = **Farem les coses de costum?**
Shall we do the usual?

?**El de lluny no es veu gaire clar.** = **El que hi ha lluny/El que és lluny no es veu gaire clar.** = **Les coses de lluny no es veuen gaire clares.**
What is in the distance can't be seen very clearly.

In all such cases **això de** or **allò de** also seems preferable to **el de**: hence **això de més importància, allò de lluny,** etc.

10 NUMERALS

10.1 CARDINAL NUMBERS

Cardinal numbers are those used in counting ('one', 'two', 'three', etc.) as opposed to ordinal numbers which place items in numerical order ('first', 'second', 'third', etc.).

0	zero	29	vint-i-nou
1	un/una, u	30	trenta
2	dos/dues	31	trenta-un/una, trenta-u
3	tres	32	trenta-dos/dues
4	quatre	33	trenta-tres
5	cinc	34	trenta-quatre, etc.
6	sis	40	quaranta
7	set	41	quaranta-un/una, quaranta-u
8	vuit (Val. huit)		
9	nou	42	quaranta-dos/dues, etc.
10	deu	50	cinquanta
11	onze	60	seixanta
12	dotze	70	setanta
13	tretze	80	vuitanta (Val. huitanta)
14	catorze	90	noranta
15	quinze	100	cent
16	setze	101	cent un/una, cent u
17	disset (Bal.,Val. desset, Val. dèsset)	102	cent dos/dues
		103	cent tres, etc.
18	divuit (Bal. devuit, Val. díhuit)	200	dos-cents/dues-centes
19	dinou (Bal., Val. denou, Val. dènou/dèneu)	201	dos-cents un/dues-centes una, dos-cents u
20	vint	300	tres-cents/tres-centes
21	vint-i-un/una, vint-i-u	400	quatre-cents/ quatre-centes, etc.
22	vint-i-dos/dues		
23	vint-i-tres	1000	mil
24	vint-i-quatre	1001	mil un/mil una, mil u
25	vint-i-cinc	1100	mil cent
26	vint-i-sis	2000	dos mil/dues mil
27	vint-i-set	3000	tres mil, etc.
28	vint-i-vuit	100,000	cent mil

200,000	**dos-cents mil/ dues-centes mil**	1,000,000,000,000	**un bilió** (i.e. a European billion)
1,000,000	**un milió**		
1,000,000,000	**mil milions** (i.e. an American billion)	a trillion	**un trilió**

Deu és un nombre parell.	Ten is an even number.
Set és un nombre imparell/senar.	Seven is an odd number.
47 és un nombre primer.	47 is a prime number.

Forms corresponding literally to English 'twelve hundred', 'fifteen hundred', etc. are not used in Catalan. So 1858 is read as **mil vuit-cents cinquanta-vuit**, whether as a year or in any other context. Nor does Catalan use the abbreviated manner of reading numbers over one hundred which we use in English for items (years, hotel rooms, house numbers, bus routes, etc.) which are numbered in sequence:

476 AD	four-seven-six/four-seventy-six	**quatre-cents setanta-sis**
1905	nineteen-O-five	**mil nou-cents cinc**
Room 251	two-five-one	**l'habitació dos-cents cinquanta-u**

Telephone numbers, however, are normally broken up into groups of two digits (starting from the end), which are then read as numbers, if possible:

236 55 80	**dos trenta-sis cinquanta-cinc vuitanta**
(093) 509 31 22	**zero noranta-tres cinc zero nou trenta-u vint-i-dos**

Other numbers given as an arbitrary identification code (account numbers, vehicle registration numbers, ID card numbers) can be pronounced one digit at a time.

10.2 GENDER AGREEMENT OF NUMERALS

Un/una 'one', **dos/dues** 'two', and the compounds of **cent** (i.e. **dos-cents/dues-centes, tres-cents/-centes** 'two hundred', etc., but not **cent** 'one hundred' itself) agree in gender with the noun counted (expressed or understood):

(i)   **250.872 ptes = dues-centes cinquanta mil vuit-centes setanta-dues pessetes**
(ii) **22.131 persones = vint-i-dues mil cent trenta-una persones**
(iii) **81.000 tones = vuitanta-una mil tones**
(iv) **$22.131 = vint-i-dos mil cent trenta-un dòlars**

In examples (i–iii) above all the numbers which can agree in gender are feminine because **pessetes** 'pesetas', **persones** 'persons', and **tones** 'tons' are feminine; in (iv) they are masculine because **dòlars** 'dollars' is masculine.

10.3   PUNCTUATION IN NUMERALS

Note that **-i-** 'and' is used only between **vint** 'twenty' and following units. Hyphens are used to link tens and units (e.g., **seixanta-sis** 66) and to link the multiples of **cent** 'hundred' (e.g., **vuit-cents/vuit-centes** 800). The hyphen remains in the ordinal numbers derived from these (see below **10.8**), but is not used in the adjectives derived from the 'hundreds' with the suffix **-ista**, which are used to refer to centuries:

el vuit-cents	the eighteen-hundreds
la prosa vuitcentista	nineteenth-century prose

In numerals written in figures a full stop or a space (rather than a comma) separates the thousands from the hundreds, the millions from the hundred thousands, and so on; a comma, read as **coma** or as **amb**, is used for the decimal point (see **10.9**).

10.4   MILLIONS, BILLIONS, TRILLIONS

Milió, bilió, trilió (*pl.* **milions,** etc.) are masculine nouns, and are connected with **de** to the noun or noun phrase which is counted (unless another number follows 'million'/'billion'/'trillion').

El projecte va costar gairebé tres bilions de pessetes.
The project cost nearly three billion pesetas.

L'enciclopèdia contindrà mig milió d'entrades.
The encyclopedia will contain half a million entries.

£2.409.500 = dos milions quatre-centes nou mil cinc-centes lliures esterlines

S'estima que el SIDA tindrà molts milions de víctimes abans de l'any 2010.
It is estimated that AIDS will have several million victims before the year 2010.

10.5   THE FORM u 'ONE'

When referring to the names or forms of numbers (rather than counting objects), **u** 'one', **vint-i-u, trenta-u,** etc., are used, instead of **un, vint-i-un, trenta-un,** and so on.

el número u
number one

–Quin número tens? –El vint-i-u.
'Which number have you got?' 'Twenty-one.'

Cent quatre s'escriu amb un u, un zero i un quatre.
One hundred and four is written with a one, a nought and a four.

Similarly **u** occurs when using cardinals, in place of ordinals, for items in a series:

el dia trenta-u de març	the 31st of March
el quilòmetre u	the first km mark/the 1 km mark
el despatx número 141 = el despatx	office number 141
número cent quaranta-u	

However, **un**, etc., can be used in counting, in arithmetic, in giving scores, even when what is being counted is not explicitly mentioned.

El Barça ha guanyat dos a u(n).	Barcelona won 2–1.
Dos per u(n) és dos.	Twice one is two.

10.6 GENDER OF NUMBERS

The names of the numbers themselves are masculine in gender (unlike the letters of the alphabet which are feminine); they can be pluralized.

Ja no ens queden quaranta-tresos.	We haven't got any (size) forty-threes left.
Ens van sortir tres dosos.	Three twos turned up.
Hi havia cents de joves.	There were hundreds of young people.

10.7 ARITHMETICAL EXPRESSIONS

$2 + 5 = 7$	**Dos i cinc són/fan set.**
$12 \times 5 = 60$	**Dotze per cinc són seixanta.**
$14 - 3 = 11$	**Catorze menys tres són onze.**
$108 \div 12 = 9$	**Cent vuit dividit per dotze són nou.**

L'arrel segona/quadrada de 16 és 4.	The square root of 16 is four.
El quadrat de 8 és 64.	The square of 8 is 64.
3 és l'arrel terça/cúbica de 27.	3 is the cube root of 27.
El cub de 2 és 8.	The cube of 2 is eight.

10.8 ORDINALS

For the numbers above four, the ordinals are formed by adding the suffix **-è/-ena** (*pl.* **-ens/-enes**) to the cardinal number.

primer/-a	first	**vintè/-ena**	twentieth
segon/-a	second	**vint-i-unè/-ena**	twenty-first
tercer/-a	third	**vint-i-dosè/-ena**	twenty-second
quart/-a	fourth	**vint-tresè/-ena**	twenty-third
cinquè/cinquena	fifth (dial. also quint/-a)	**vint-i-quatrè/-ena** etc.	twenty-fourth
sisè/-ena	sixth (dial. also sext/-a)	**trentè/-ena** **trenta-unè/-ena**	thirtieth thirty-first
setè/-ena	seventh (dial. also sèptim/-a)	**quarantè/-ena** etc.	fortieth
vuitè/-ena	eighth (dial. also octau/octava)	**centè/-ena** **dos-centè/-ena**	hundredth two-hundredth
novè/-ena	ninth	**milè/-ena**	thousandth
desè/-ena	tenth	Note:	
onzè/-ena etc.	eleventh	**darrer/-a,** **últim/-a**	last last
dinovè/-ena	nineteenth	**enèsim/-a**	nth, umpteenth

The ordinals from 'first' to 'tenth' are in everyday use; they generally precede the noun referred to:

la primera comunió
first communion

el tercer mes
the third month

Ja és la cinquena vegada que ho sento contar.
That's the fifth time I've heard that story.

However, ordinals indicating sequences of monarchs, popes, centuries, etc., follow the noun:

Jaume I (read **Jaume primer**)	James I
Pau VI (read **Pau sisè**)	Paul VI
Elisabet II (read **Elisabet segona**)	Elizabeth II
el segle IV (read **el segle quart**)	the fourth century

For the days of the month, ordinals are used, except for 'first' where ordinal and cardinal are optional alternatives:

el primer de juliol/l'u de juliol	the 1st of July
el (dia) quinze d'agost	the 15th of August

The phrase **el/la qui/que fa x** (x = cardinal) can be used with the same meaning as an ordinal:

–Qui és el quart? –No ho sé, jo som el qui fa cinc.
'Who is fourth?' 'I don't know; I am fifth.'

The ordinals above tenth are used only in official or legal language. In other styles cardinal numbers are used, following the noun (with **u**, not **un**, for first, etc., see **10.5**). In this context the cardinal numbers do not vary for gender.

–A quin capítol es troba? –Al quinze.	'Which chapter is it in?' 'The 15th'/'15.'
el segle XVIII (read el segle divuit)	the eighteenth century
Alfons XII (read Alfons dotze)	Alfonso XII
la pàgina 301 (read la pàgina tres-cents u)	page 301
la fila 22 (read la fila vint-i-dos)	row 22

10.9   FRACTIONS

Mig/mitja 'half' is an adjective. **Meitat** 'half' is a feminine noun, generally definite. **Mig** is also used adverbially, as is the phrase **a mitges**.

mig pa	half a loaf
mitja taronja	half an orange
tres hores i mitja	three and a half hours (note word order; **mitja** (*f.*) because **hora** 'hour' is understood)
mig milió de pessetes	half a million pesetas
un milió i mig de pessetes	1½ million pesetas (**mig** (*m.*) because **milió** is understood)
Dóna-me'n la meitat.	Give me half (of it).
La meitat de sis és tres.	Half of six is three.
La meitat del temps dorm.	He's asleep half the time.
La sala només estava mig plena.	The room was only half full.
mig omplir un got	to half fill a glass
L'han fet només a mitges.	They've only half done it.

Other names of fractions in normal use are: **terç** 'third', **quart** 'quarter', **dècim** 'tenth', **centèsim** '100th', **mil·lèsim** '1000th':

dos terços	two thirds
tres quarts	three quarters
sis dècims	six tenths

For the remaining fractions it is possible to use nouns derived from the masculine ordinals, e.g. **quatre quinzens** 'four fifteenths'. Except in arithmetic, it is more usual to use the feminine noun **part** 'part' with an ordinal adjective preceding:

quatre quinzenes parts	four fifteenths

un quart dels seus béns/una quarta part   one quarter of his property
dels seus béns

Musical intervals

For musical intervals above 'fourth' some special terms are used: **segona** 'second', **tercera** 'third', **quarta** 'fourth', **quinta** 'fifth', **sexta** 'sixth', **sèptima** 'seventh', **octava** 'octave'.

Cantava una octava més alt.   She sang an octave higher.
harmonitzat a base de quintes   harmonized on a pattern of fifths

Percentages

In percentages normally an article is used, the indefinite article implying a less precise figure than the definite:

El 15 per cent dels ciutadans no saben el català/no sap el català.
15 per cent of the inhabitants do not know Catalan.

La inflació ha pujat a un 150 per cent anual.
Inflation has risen to some 150 per cent a year.

tant per cent
so much per cent

un tant per cent no gaire alt
a not very high percentage

Decimal fractions

3,43 (read **tres coma quaranta-tres/tres amb quaranta-tres**)
0,25 (read **zero coma vint-i-cinc/zero amb vint-i-cinc**)
Aquesta habitació fa 2,75 (dos coma setanta-cinc) per 3,5 (tres coma cinc) metres.
This room measures 2.75 by 3.5 metres.

10.10 COLLECTIVE NUMERALS

There is a series of words for approximate or round numbers; the commonest are: **parell** 'pair', 'couple', **desena** 'ten', **dotzena** 'dozen', **vintena** 'score', **trentena** 'thirty', **centenar** 'hundred', **miler**, **milenar** 'thousand'.

una vintena d'anys   a couple of decades
Hi havia una trentena d'assistents.   There were about thirty people present.
molts milers de persones   thousands of people

Note **la trentena, la quarantena**, etc., 'the (approximate) age of thirty, forty, etc.', **una quinzena** 'a fortnight':

Li manca mig any per a arribar a la norantena.
She is six months short of her ninetieth birthday.

Hi passarem la segona quinzena de juliol.
We shall spend the second half of July there.

Note also **centenes** 'hundreds', **desenes** 'tens', **unitats** 'units' in referring to arithmetical expressions:

367 són tres centenes, sis desenes i set unitats.
367 contains three hundreds, six tens and seven units.

10.11 NUMERALS IN TIME EXPRESSIONS

The hours are expressed with the feminine definite article: **la una** 'one o'clock', **les dues** 'two o'clock', **les tres** 'three o'clock', etc., up to twelve. Quarter hours are expressed in one of two ways:

(i)   By counting quarters to the next hour: **un quart de tres** lit. 'one quarter of three', i.e. 'a quarter past two', **dos quarts de cinc** lit. 'two quarters of five', i.e. 'half past four', **tres quarts de dotze** lit. 'three quarters of twelve', i.e. 'a quarter to twelve'.

(ii) By means of **x i quart** 'x and a quarter', i.e. 'a quarter past x', **x i mitja** 'x and a half', i.e. 'half past x', and **x menys quart** 'x less a quarter', i.e. 'a quarter to x'; note **falta un quart per a les x** 'it is a quarter to x'.

The first method (i) is popular in Catalonia, but is less common in Valencia and the Balearic islands.

Fractions of quarter hours are usually expressed as **x i y (minuts)** 'y (minutes) past x', **x menys y (minuts)** 'y (minutes) to x': **les sis i cinc (minuts)** 'five (minutes) past six', **la una menys divuit (minuts)** 'eighteen minutes to one'. A traditional system of counting in 'half quarters' is now not very commonly used. Approximate times are expressed with **cap a** or **devers** (Bal.) lit. 'towards', or **sobre** lit. 'over'/'about'. **A quarts de x** refers to an approximate time 'between a quarter past x and a quarter to x'. Times written in the 24-hour system may be read (**la/les) x hora/es y minuts**, or simply **la/les x y**; see the examples below. When the twelve-hour clock is used, as is normally the case in spontaneous speech, a.m. or p.m. is indicated by specifying the part of the day: **matinada** 'early morning', **matí** 'morning', **migdia** 'midday', 'noon', **tarda** (Bal. **horabaixa**, Val. **vesprada**) 'afternoon' , **vespre** 'evening', **nit** 'night'. The boundaries between these periods are not precisely fixed.

–Quina hora és? –És la una/Són la una.	'What time is it?' 'One o'clock.'
Són les dues en punt.	It is two o'clock exactly.
–Quina hora té? –Les nou i vint (minuts).	'What time do you make it?' '9.20.'
El concert comença a 2/4 de 9 (read dos quarts de nou).	The concert begins at 8.30.
Són tres quarts de deu. (Bal., Val. Falta un quart per a les deu.)	It is a quarter to ten.
dos quarts i mig de set	6.37 or thereabouts/nearly twenty to seven
Arriba a les cinc menys cinc.	It arrives at five to five.
Falten cinc minuts per a les onze.	It is five to eleven.
Vindrà sobre les onze/cap a les onze.	She will be coming at about 11.
Vam quedar que ens trobaríem a quarts de set.	We agreed to meet at around half past six (any time between 6.15 and 6.45).
12.45h (read as les dotze quaranta cinc (minuts), or un quart d'una, or la una menys quart)	a quarter to one

2.30h les dues trenta (minuts) = dos quarts de tres = les dues i mitja
14.50h (les) catorze hores cinquanta minuts = les tres menys deu (minuts) = falten deu (minuts) per a les tres
8.25h les vuit i vint-i-cinc

la una de la nit	1 a.m.	les set de la vesprada	7 p.m.
la una del migdia	1 p.m.	dos quarts de nou del vespre	8.30 p.m.
les tres de la matinada	3 a.m.		
les tres de la tarda	3 p.m.	les dotze de la nit	midnight
les sis del matí	6 a.m.	les dotze del migdia	noon

Writing the date:

15 d'abril de(l) 1992	15 April, 1992/April 15th, 1992
dijous, 3 de maig de(l) 1870	Thursday, May 3rd, 1870

Referring to years:

Això va passar el 1955/en 1955/l'any 1955.	That occurred in 1955.

Decades:

els anys vint	the twenties
els anys quaranta or els anys quarantes	the forties

Centuries:

el segle XV	the 15th century

(Note Roman numeral normally in Catalan.)

el quatre-cents	the 1400s
un arc del segle XIV/un arc trescentista	a 14th-century arch

Anniversaries:

There is a series of words derived from numerals for referring to anniversaries: **cinquantenari** '50th anniversary', **centenari** 'centenary', (**cinquè centenari**, etc. '500th anniversary'), **mil·lenari** '1000th anniversary'.

10.12 MEASUREMENTS

The most frequent way of expressing measurement in space uses a noun referring to the dimension measured: **alçària/alçada** 'height', **llargària/ llargada, extensió** 'length', **amplària/amplada** 'width', **gruix/gruixa/gruixària** 'thickness', **profunditat/fondària** 'depth', **volum** 'volume', **velocitat** 'speed':

Aquí el riu fa una amplada de trenta metres/fa trenta metres d'amplada.
Here the river is thirty metres wide.

Tots aquests cims tenen una alçada de més de mil metres/fan més de mil metres d'alçada.
All these peaks are higher than 1000 metres/are more than 1000 metres high.

L'autobús anava a una velocitat de 90 km per hora.
The bus was going at a speed of 90 kph.

Similarly with **temperatura** 'temperature':

La temperatura és de 31 graus.   The temperature is 31 degrees.

For weight, the verb **pesar** 'weigh' is used:

Quant pesa el seu paquet?   How much does your packet weigh?
Jo pesava 85 kilos.   I used to weigh 85 kilos.

Similarly, for time, with the verb **durar** 'last':

La conversa va durar només quatre minuts.
The conversation was only four minutes long.

11 PERSONAL PRONOUNS (STRESSED)

GENERAL

In this Chapter we cover subject pronouns and strong pronouns used after prepositions. Object pronouns are covered in Chapter 12, and possessive pronouns in Chapter 7.

Catalan is characterized, like Spanish, Italian, and Portuguese, but unlike French, by the way in which subject pronouns accompany verbs only for particular emphasis. Non-personal subjects ('it', 'they') have no corresponding stressed pronominal form. The form of the verb itself is usually sufficient to indicate the subject: **canto** 'I sing', **cantem** 'we sing'. The personal subject pronoun is used to make emphasis or clarification where required:

> **O sigui, jo portaré les begudes i vosaltres prepararreu el menjar.**
> So *I*'ll bring the drinks and *you*'ll prepare the food.

These points are expanded in **11.5**.

Apart from first-person singular **mi** and reflexive **si** the stressed pronouns used after prepositions are the same as the ordinary subject pronouns (**11.4**).

11.1 MORPHOLOGY OF THE PERSONAL PRONOUNS: CLASSIFICATION

(i) By meaning:

	person			subject		prep. object
singular	1st		I	jo/nós		jo/mi/(nós)
	2nd		you		tu/vostè/vós	
	3rd	*m.*	he	ell		ell/si
		f.	she	ella		ella/si
plural	1st		we		nosaltres	
	2nd		you		vosaltres/vostès	
	3rd		they	ells/elles		ells/elles/si

(ii) By morphosyntax:

	person	subject		prep. object
	1st	jo		mi/(jo)
singular	2nd		tu	
	3rd	ell/ella/vostè		ell/ella/vostè/si
	1st		nosaltres/nós	
plural	2nd		vosaltres/vós	
	3rd	ells/elles/vostès		ells/elles/vostès/si

11.2 MORPHOLOGY OF THE PERSONAL PRONOUNS: INFLECTION

Only the third-person pronouns show the normal number and gender agreement: **ell** 'he', **ella** 'she', **ells** 'they (*m.*)', **elles** 'they (*f.*)'. **Vostè** 'you (polite)' displays alternation only in number: **vostè/vostès**. All the other forms are invariable for gender, and number alternations rely on lexical differences (e.g., singular **tu** → plural **vosaltres**, and not ***tus**).

11.3 PRAGMATICS OF THE PERSONAL PRONOUNS

The tables (i) and (ii) shown in **11.1** above refer respectively to the semantics of the communicative situation and to formal classification based on agreement with verbal forms. Observe that there is not a one-to-one match between the two schemas:

(i) **Nós** is the majestic form (royal 'we') of the first person singular, although referring to one person (the speaker) it takes the first person plural form of the verb: **Nós, bisbe de Vic, hem resolt de concedir l'autorització sol·licitada** 'We, bishop of Vic, have resolved to grant the permit requested'. Use of this form is confined to ceremonial contexts.

(ii) **Vostè(s)** is a polite form referring to the person that the speaker is addressing. This pronoun is used to express respect, or deference; traditionally it was used when addressing professional people (doctors, lawyers, teachers, etc.). It goes with verbs and other elements (weak pronouns, possessives) in the third person:

Vostè ha dit que la seva (= de vostè) dona no li (= a vostè) explicava aquestes coses.
You said that your wife didn't explain these things to you.

(iii) **Vós** is also a polite form of address (cf. French *vous*). It reflects respect, but not as distant as **vostè**. It is normally used: with elderly or senior persons (e.g. **Com esteu, avi?** 'How are you, grandfather?'), with strangers (**Que em podríeu dir quina hora és?** 'Could you tell me the time (please)?'), on notices (**Empenyeu** 'Push'), in business and administrative correspondence, (**Benvolgut senyor, en resposta a la vostra del mes passat, us recordem que . . .** 'Dear Sir, In reply to yours of last month, we beg to remind you that . . . '), and when answering the phone (**Digueu?** 'Hello'). Systematic use of **vós** was encouraged in education before the Civil war of 1936–39 and it is encountered regularly in literary texts from that period; nowadays it is confined to the contexts mentioned. **Vós** goes with the second-person plural verbal forms (and other adjuncts), even though it refers to only one person:

Vós cobreu la jubilació cada mes.
You are paid your pension every month.

Escriviu en aquest full, si us plau, la vostra adreça i firmeu tots els altres documents que us hem lliurat.
Write your address on this page, please, and sign all the other documents we have given you.

The plural of **vós** is **vosaltres**, which is to say that the distinction in style of address in the second-person singular, between **tu** and **vós**, is not maintained in the plural.

Within the last thirty years there have been major changes in conventions of address in common spoken usage. Currently the tendency is to revert more or less to the etymological pattern, using **tu** for all singular addressees and **vosaltres** for all groups of addressees. (**Vós** is the common polite form in North (French) Catalonia, probably due to French influence.)

Other than in North Catalonia, for **vós** to be used in speech nowadays, certain conditions are required: the addressee must be older, or a stranger of equal status to the speaker, and participants must be either Balearic, or elderly rural people in Catalonia, or members of the 'intelligentsia'. The spontaneous spoken use of **vós** is declining rapidly.

For **vostè** to be used, the conditions are: a non-intimate or formal context (such as an occasional commercial or bureaucratic transaction), and usually, in addition, some perceived difference of age or status.

Vós and **vostè** are virtually always used reciprocally, that is, by both parties in the interchange, except that children are always addressed as **tu**, even when they address an adult as **vostè**. When a child becomes an adult, in this respect, is a moot point.

11.4   SYNTAX – PERSONAL PRONOUNS AS PREPOSITIONAL OBJECTS

Most of the subject pronoun forms can also appear after a preposition:

Ho han fet per tu, per vostè(s), per vosaltres, per ell, per ella, per nosaltres, per ells, per elles.
They have done it for you, for him, for her, for us, for them.

The exceptions to this are the special form **mi** for the first-person singular, and optional **si** for the third-person (singular or plural) when this is reflexive.

11.4.1   FIRST-PERSON SINGULAR OBJECT

Mi is used after all simple and compound prepositions except **segons** 'according to':

Pots venir amb mi si vols.
You can come with me if you want.

No sé si ho han portat per a mi o per a tu.
I don't know if they've bought it for me or for you.

Segons jo, no pot funcionar.
According to me, it cannot work.

(When a compound preposition ends with **de**, the sequence **de mi**, interpreted as though it were a genitive, can become **meu**; the corresponding applies to all personal pronouns after compound prepositions which include **de** (see **7.5** and **14.2.3**): **No gosarien dir això davant de mi/davant meu** 'They wouldn't dare say that in front of me'.)

When a preposition introduces conjoined elements, **jo** appears instead of **mi**:

entre tu i jo	between you and me
contra jo i vosaltres	against me and you
Es mofava de jo i tot el que defenso.	She mocked me and everything I support.

In Balearic dialects it is very common to hear **jo** after any preposition. This usage is regarded as acceptable in informal speech:

A jo no m'agrada sa carn molt poc feta.	I don't like meat that is very rare.
Aquest jove ha vengut amb jo.	This young fellow has come with me.

11.4.2   THIRD-PERSON REFLEXIVE OBJECT si

For the third person, singular and plural, after a preposition, **si** can be used reflexively, that is, when the noun governed by the preposition refers to the same person as the subject of the verb in that clause (see **23.2**). In this function **si** is followed more often than not by **mateix** (agreeing in number and gender with the subject):

(Ella) només pensa en si mateixa.
She thinks only about herself.

No ho feien per als altres, sinó per a si mateixos.
They weren't doing it for others but for themselves.

As well as reflexivity, reciprocity (see **23.3**) can also be expressed by **si**:

Parlaven entre si.   They were talking among themselves.

In all these cases reflexive **si** can be substituted by the non-reflexive third-person stressed pronouns (**ell/ella/ells/elles**), again, usually reinforced with **mateix**. The latter option is, in fact, generally preferred in everyday language:

Aquests dos treballen per a ells (mateixos). = Aquests dos treballen per a si (mateixos).
Those two work for themselves.

(Both reflexive: cf. non-reflexive **Ja no treballo per a ells** 'I don't work for them any more'.)

The expression **fora de si** 'beside himself/herself/oneself/themselves', however, appears not to allow **ell**, etc.

11.5   STYLE – USE AND OMISSION OF PRONOUNS

11.5.1   SUBJECT PRONOUNS

As mentioned above, subject pronouns are not used in Catalan as often as in English or French. The form of the verb normally suffices to identify the subject. There are some cases, however, in which the verbal forms for first- and third-person singular coincide, namely in imperfect and conditional tenses (**jo cantava – ell/ella/vostè cantava; jo dormia – ell/ella/vostè dormia; jo dormiria – ell/ella/vostè dormiria**) and the context may require the pronouns to be used to avoid confusion.

More generally third-person forms may relate to 'real' third-person subjects 'he/she/it, they' or they may correspond to 'you (polite)', that is, **vostè/vostès**. It is probably only **vostè** and **vostès** that are used significantly more often than other subject pronouns: **Com te dius?** 'What is your name?' (familiar address pronoun), **Com se diu vostè?** 'What is your name?' (polite address pronoun); **Com se diu?** could mean 'What is your name?', but can also mean, e.g., 'What is it called?', as well as 'What is his/her/its name?'

If subject pronouns are used in other cases it will be to convey an emphasis or contrast:

Jo canto bé; tu desentones.
I am singing fine; *you* are out of tune.

The presence of the pronoun becomes necessary when the verb is elided, of course.

Alguns potser ho aprovaran, però nosaltres mai.
Some people will perhaps approve of it, but we never will.

Despite Catalan's natural tendency to avoid subject pronouns except in the instances discussed above, there are cases where the subject is reinforced by the use of a demonstrative (see **6.4**) as subject pronoun, where English might just use the normal subject pronoun:

Aquesta era especialitzada en física nuclear.
She/This woman was a specialist in nuclear physics.

Ho vam anunciar públicament però aquells no en van fer cas.
We announced it publicly but they took no notice.

11.5.2   PRONOUNS AND INANIMATE NOUNS

Use of **ell/ella/ells/elles** as subject pronouns almost invariably implies human referents; these third-person stressed pronouns cannot generally refer to things or abstract nouns. The general principle explained in **11.5.1**, concerning elision of subject pronouns, applies exclusively here, i.e. an inanimate subject is never expressed by a personal pronoun.

He vist molts cotxes. Eren blancs.   I saw a lot of cars. They were white.

The sentence **Ells eren blancs**, in any context, would be taken to refer to a human subject. The use of the third-person pronouns for inanimate prepositional objects is scarcely more common, though not absolutely ruled out. Catalan has several strategies which reinforce this aversion.

(i)   In writing, demonstratives may stand for inanimates (subjects or objects), often when a contrast is made:

Ha hagut de triar entre les seves conviccions i els seus sentiments: aquelles eren republicanes, i aquests, llibertaris.
He has had to choose between his convictions and his feelings: the former were republican and the latter libertarian.

(ii) The underlying structure of preposition + third-person pronoun is substituted by adverbial pronouns **en** or **hi** (**12.6** and **12.7**):

Tinc una ploma d'aquelles d'abans però no m'agrada escriure-hi (not ***no m'agrada escriure amb ella**).
I've got one of those old-fashioned fountain pens but I don't like writing with it.

Ja estic fart de sentir aquestes coses. No me'n parlis més (not ***No em parlis més d'elles**).
I'm fed up with hearing these things. Don't talk to me any more about them.

(iii) Many prepositions can be used as adverbs, making the use of the pronoun redundant, as optionally in English:

–Has portat el cotxe? –No, he vingut sense (not ***sense ell**).
'Did you bring the car?' 'No I came without (it).'

Vaig veure la pila de llibres i, damunt (not ***damunt d'ella**), **una flor.**
I saw the pile of books and, on top (of it), a flower.

Va obrir el calaix i, dins (not ***dins d'ell**), **hi havia la pistola.**
He opened the drawer and, inside, was the pistol.

The same applies with **darrere** 'behind', **davant** 'in front', **davall** 'under', 'beneath', and all compound prepositions ending in **de**: **fora de** 'outside', **lluny de** 'far from', **a prop de** 'near (to)', etc.:

La plaça era davant l'església i el Carrer Major darrere (not ***darrere d'ella**).
The square was in front of the church and the high street behind (it).

Sobre la taula vaig veure un gerro i, davall (not ***davall d'ella**), **un parell de sabates.**
On the table I saw a jug and, underneath (it), a pair of shoes.

12 PRONOMINAL CLITICS (WEAK OBJECT PRONOUNS)

12.1 GENERAL

The Catalan pronominal clitics, also generally referred to as weak object pronouns, are unstressed elements which, while having a distinctive grammatical function (expressing verbal complements), are nevertheless reduced phonetically to forming a single unit with the verb that governs them: **Me mana** 'He orders me' behaves phonetically like the word **mamaire** 'suckling', **Veta'ls** 'Veto them' behaves like **pètals** 'petals'. These weak pronouns can stand either (proclitically) before a verb or are attached (enclitically) after a verb: proclitic: **M'ajudes** 'You help me', **Em pots ajudar** 'You can help me'; enclitic: **Ajuda'm** 'Help me', **Has d'ajudar-me** 'You must help me'.

The examples above show one of several features – here variations (in form and spelling) according to point of contact with the verb – that make this the most intricately exacting aspect of Catalan grammar. It is worth identifying at this stage what the other principal factors are, both formal and functional, that contribute further to this complexity:

(i) the range and subtleties of functions (see especially **12.3.2**);

(ii) non-standard forms, and phonetic and dialectal variations (see **12.1.2**, **12.3.2.2**, and **12.9.3.2** to **12.9.3.5**);

(iii) discrepancies between widespread colloquial habits and formal, written conventions, combined with some instability of normative grammar applied to this area;

(iv) the integration of pronominal and reflexive verbs (Chapter 23, **12.4**, and **12.9**);

(v) the integration of the pronominal adverbs **en** and **hi** in the total system of pronominal clitics (**12.6**, **12.7** and **12.9**);

(vi) the increased complication of orthographic detail when two or more clitics combine with a verb (**12.9**).

12.1.1 FORMS OF SINGLE PRONOUNS

Forms shown in brackets in the table below are those which appear when there is no specific variant for that particular pronoun corresponding to the column heading: e.g. the full form **li** occurs in contexts where other pronouns would display reinforced, elided, or reduced forms.

			before the verb		*after the verb*	
			A *reinforced*	*B* *elided*	*C* *full*	*D* *reduced*
singular	*1st person*		em	m'	-me	'm
	2nd person		et	t'	-te	't
	3rd person	*m. DO*	el	l'	-lo	'l
		f. DO	(la)	l'*	-la	(-la)
		IO	(li)	(li)	-li	(-li)
		reflexive	es	s'	-se	's
		neuter	(ho)	(ho)	-ho	(-ho)
plural	*1st person*		ens	(ens)	-nos	'ns
	2nd person		(us)	(us)	-vos	-us
	3rd person	*m. DO*	els	(els)	-los	'ls
		f. DO	(les)	(les)	-les	(-les)
		IO	els	(els)	-los	'ls
		reflexive	es	s'	-se	's
	adverbial		en	n'	-ne	'n
			(hi)	(hi)	-hi	(-hi)

A = verb beginning with consonant	*D* = verb ending with vowel
B = verb beginning with vowel	*DO* = Direct Object
C = verb ending with consonant or **u**	*IO* = Indirect Object

Note: *In accordance with fluctuation in pronunciation, **la** before unstressed **i-** or **u-** (or **hi-/hu-**) may be written with the reinforced or the elided form: **la inquieta/ l'inquieta** 'troubles her'; prescriptive norms prefer the former.

Observe that when used enclitically all the pronouns are attached to the preceding verb by a punctuation mark, either the hyphen or the apostrophe.

Information from the above table can be represented differently to show how these clitics variously display all or some of the form variations (reinforced, elided, full or reduced):

reinforced	em	et	el	es	en	ens	els	us	la
elided	m'	t'	l'	s'	n'	(ens)	(els)	(us)	l'
full	-me	-te	-lo	-se	-ne	-nos	-los	-vos	(-la)
reduced	'm	't	'l	's	'n	'ns	'ls	(-us)	(-la)

Li, les, ho and **hi** are invariable (except for the hyphen which always affixes them to a preceding verb). When the variable items appear in dictionaries, word lists, etc., or when they are mentioned in grammatical discussion, it is conventional to refer to them by the reinforced form, as in the top row of the preceding table.

It is common for the full form **se** to be used instead of reinforced **es** before verbs beginning with [s] (**s-** or **ce-**, **ci-**): **No se sentia res** 'Nothing could be heard'. The full forms **me, te, se, ne**, are often used also instead of reinforced forms before a verb, after one of a small list of adverbs/pronouns: **tant** 'so much', **quant(s)** 'how much', 'how many', **com** 'how', **on** 'where', **quan** 'when':

Com te trobes?	How do you feel?
Quants ne vols?	How many (of them) do you want?
Tant se val.	It makes no difference.
Tant me fa.	I don't care.
Com se diu?	What is he called?

In some varieties, especially Balearic and in certain parts of Valencia, it is common to use the full forms **me, te, se, ne**, in sentence-initial position, as in **Me sembla que . . .** 'It seems to me that . . .', and sometimes in other contexts where the more general tendency is to favour the 'reinforced' form.

An underlying pattern of morphological structure can be discerned in the above written conventions. Explaining this may help to make sense of the apparent complexity of the system. Firstly the marker **s** figures in all plural forms. Then it can be seen that there is a single morphemic base for the third-person and each of the first- and second-person forms, singular and plural. This pattern also incorporates the [s] base of the reflexive/reciprocal clitic (singular and plural) **es**.

		morphemic base	*pronoun forms*
first person	*singular*	/m/	**em, me, m**
	plural	/n/ + /s/	**ens, nos, ns**
second person	*singular*	/t/	**et, te, t**
	plural	/u/v/ + /s/	**us, vos**
third person	*singular*	/l/	*m.*: **el, lo, l**; *f.*: **la, l** indirect object *m.* and *f.*: **li**
	plural	/l/ + /s/	*m.*: **els, los, ls**; *f.*: **les** indirect object *m.* and *f.*: **els, los, ls**
	reflexive	/s/	**es, se, s**

The first-person singular morpheme **m** is extended to the plural form by many dialects which have **mos** for **ens/nos**. Historical affinities between /u/ and /v/

account for the fact that these same dialects (principally Balearic and Valencian) have **vos** for the central standard **us**.

The wide variety of forms of the Catalan pronoun system is reducible to the bases described above. In what follows, while we make reference as appropriate to the principal dialectal variations, the main description refers to the standard language based on the eastern Central (Barcelona) variety.

12.1.2   NON-STANDARD FORMS

The unstressed phonetic value of the pronominal clitics makes them particularly susceptible to erosion and transformation in pronunciation. This feature produces certain abbreviated forms which are widespread in colloquial registers, and which are conventionally represented in written reproduction of such registers. Comprehension of everyday spoken Catalan requires some grasp of these non-standard patterns, because the weak pronouns carry so much of the grammatical information of utterances. The instances of **vos** for **us** and full **me, te, se, ne** for reinforced **em, et, es, en** (mentioned at **12.1** above) are well established and retain a certain prestige as archaisms. Other main instances of deviation from the standard are as follows:

(i)   Voiced sibilant [z] replaces **ens** or **us** before a vowel sound. The same [z] followed by an unstressed support vowel [ə] (that is, [zə], written **se/s'/-se** in conventional representation of non-standard speech) replaces **-nos** or **-vos** after a consonant.

  Després s'hem (for ens hem) estat una estona xerrant al bar i s'hem (for ens hem) assegut amb la colla. (R. Solsona)
  Afterwards we were chatting in the bar for a while and then we sat with our gang.

  Asseiem-se (for asseiem-nos) aquí.
  Let's sit here.

  Estàvem rentant-se (for rentant-nos) les mans.
  We were washing our hands.

  Feu-se (for feu-vos) maquillar.
  Have your make up put on.

  Porteu-se (for porteu-vos) bé.
  Behave yourselves.

(ii) Non-standard **-use** [-wzə] and **'nse** [-nzə] occur after an infinitive form ending in a stressed vowel. (Here the [ə] sound can be understood to 'support' the reduced **'ns** normally used after a vowel.) Thus **arreglâ-use** can be used instead of **arreglar-vos**, and **introduî'nse** for **introduir-nos**, etc. (Note that in the non-standard speech represented here the **-r** of the standard infinitive is pronounced only before those enclitic pronouns containing not more than one consonant.) Forms without the support [ə] occur before another vowel-initial clitic.

Hem de trobâ'nse (for **trobar-nos**) **a les vuit.**	We're to meet at 8 o'clock.
Hem de trobà'ns-hi (for **trobar-nos-hi**).	We're to meet there.
per arreglà-use-la (for **arreglar-vos-la**)	to fix it (*f.*) for you
per arreglà-us-el (for **arreglar-vos-el**)	to fix it (*m.*) for you

(iii) Analogously the support vowel [ə] occurs also when **'ls** is used instead of **-los** in dialects which do not pronounce the final **-r** of an infinitive with an enclitic pronoun:

No calia fê'lse (for **fer-los**) **venir.**	There was no need to make them come.
per endú'ls-en (for **endur-los-en**)	to take them away

(iv) The final **r** of second-conjugation verbs ending in unstressed **-er** is generally not pronounced before any enclitic pronoun. Forms reflecting the most widespread pronunciation, as in **Volen convence'ns** (for **Volen convèncer-nos** 'They want to convince us') or **Pots coneixe'l** (for **Pots conèixer-lo** 'You can get to know him') are nowadays deemed acceptable in writing, though they are regarded as somewhat informal; see **16.5.1**.

(v) Pronouns beginning with [i] or [u] are colloquially reshaped as diphthongs as in [əj] for **hi**, [əw] for **ho**, [əws] for **us**. Thus **hi ha** 'there is' is commonly pronounced [əja]; **hi havia** 'there was' is pronounced [əj] **'via**; **ho confessa** 'he confesses it' is pronounced [əw] **confessa**; **us veig** 'I can see you' is pronounced [əwz] **veig**. None of these non-standard diphthongized forms appears in written texts.

(vi) A particular treatment given to pronominal clitics in the Balearic dialects can be mentioned here. Stress is displaced to the enclitic pronoun itself, or, if this has been reduced to a single consonant because the verb ends in a vowel, to the final syllable of the verb in question. This phonetic variation does not affect spelling, but only pronunciation, as indicated in these examples where the mark ' precedes the syllable on which the stress falls:

indicar-me	[indikaɾ'mə]/[indikəɾ'mə]
incloure'ls	[iŋklɔw'ɾəls]/[iŋklɔw'ɾəls]
incloure-les	[iŋklɔwɾə'ləs]/[iŋklɔwɾə'ləs]
aturant-me	[əturam'mə]/[əturəm'mə]
agafa'l	[əɣa'fəl]/[əɣə'fəl]
cantau-la	[kəntaw'lə]/[kəntəw'lə].

Other alterations and significant dialect particularities will be remarked on at the appropriate points in what follows, e.g., **12.3.2.2** and, regarding pronouns in combination, **12.9.3.2**, **12.9.3.4**, **12.9.3.5**, and **12.9.3.8**.

12.2   POSITION OF THE PRONOUN WITH A VERB

The form taken by an individual weak pronoun depends upon whether it precedes or follows a verb, and on whether the verb has a vowel or a consonant at the point of contact. A weak pronoun follows an imperative, and infinitive, or a gerund, and precedes any other verb form. These forms are tabulated in the schema in **12.1.1**. We consider first those cases where the pronoun stands before the verb.

12.2.1   PRONOUN BEFORE THE VERB

The weak object pronoun stands before the verb in all cases except those mentioned below in **12.2.2**, with the additional consideration covered in **12.2.3**.

When the verb begins with a consonant the reinforced (*A*) form of the pronoun appears:

Em parlen.	They speak to me.
Et crida.	She is calling you.
El convidem.	We invite him.
La coneixíem.	We used to know her.
Es desperta.	She wakes up.
Es posava la corbata.	He was putting his tie on.
No li fan il·lusió.	She doesn't like them.
Ho reciclen.	They recycle it.
No ens convenceren.	They did not convince us.
Us cridarem d'hora.	We'll call you early.
Els/Les venen.	They sell them.
Es pentinen.	They comb their hair.
Els va fer por.	It frightened them.
No en tenim.	We don't have any (of them).
Hi passem la nit.	We spend the night there.

Dialects frequently use the full forms (**me**, etc.) in this context, especially at the beginning of an utterance; the Balearic preference for **vos** over **us** has already been observed.

When the verb begins with a vowel sound (including **h** + vowel) elided forms (*B*) are used if these exist:

M'han vist.	They have seen me.	**S'aixeca.**	He gets up.
T'admiren.	They admire you.	**N'hem parlat.**	We have talked
L'odien.	They hate him/her.		about it.

If no elided form is available, we find reinforced **ens** and **els**, reduced **us**, and the full forms of **li, les, ho** and **hi**:

Ens admetran.	They will admit us.	**Les organitzem.**	We organize them (*f.pl.*).
Us estimen.	They love you.	**Ho arreglarem.**	We will sort it out.
Li agradaran.	He will like them.	**Hi hem anat.**	We have been there.

As remarked in the note to the table given in **12.1.1**, normative grammar prefers **la** to elided **l'** when this feminine singular direct object pronoun precedes *unstressed* (**h**)**i**- or (**h**)**u**-:

La irriten.	They irritate her.	**La ungeix.**	She anoints her.
La hipnotitzen.	They hypnotize her.	**La humilieu.**	You humiliate her.

Otherwise, this pronoun elides before a vowel sound. Note **L'odien** 'They hate her': elision here even in those dialects where the unstressed **o** is pronounced [u]; **L'hissen** (**la bandera**) 'They raise it (the flag)': elision here because the initial **i** is stressed. Western Catalan dialects insistently retain in prununciation the distinction between **L'insultaven** 'They were insulting him' and **La insultaven** 'They were insulting her'.

Also to be noted here is the fact that phonetic elision of reinforced clitics with a preceding vowel sound is not registered in orthography:

Ara el castigaran. (pronounced as if *aral castigaran*)
Now they will punish him.

No et preocupis. (pronounced as if *not preocupis*)
Don't worry.

Què em dius ara? (pronounced as if *quèm dius ara*)
What are you trying to tell me?

Tu els has vist. (pronounced as if *tuls has vist*)
You have seen them.

Ja ens coneixem. (pronounced as if *jans coneixem*)
We've already met.

Així es convenceran. (pronounced as if *aixís convenceran*)
This is how they'll be convinced.

A casa en tinc un d'igual. (pronounced as if *a casan tinc . . .*)
I've got one like it at home.

No ho vol fer. (pronounced as if *nou vol fer*)
She doesn't want to do it.

Ja hi aniré demà. (pronounced as if *jai aniré demà*)
I'll go there tomorrow.

Note that in cases like the last two above, the vowel sounds [i] and [u] of the pronouns **hi** and **ho** do not disappear but rather become semivowels forming a diphthong with the preceding vowel sound.

12.2.2   PRONOUNS AFTER THE VERB

Weak pronouns are enclitically attached after the verb when this is an infinitive, a gerund, or a (positive) imperative.

If the verb ends in a consonant or a semiconsonant **-u** (in the diphthongs **-au**, **-eu**, **-iu**, **-ou**, **-uu**) the full forms (C: hyphenated) are used: **mirar-me** 'to look at me', **pintant-los** 'painting them', **Oblideu-la** 'Forget her'. If the verb ends in a vowel (other than **-u**) reduced forms (D: with apostrophe) are used where these exist; otherwise the full (hyphenated) forms are used:

	reduced	*full*
Put it there.	**Posa'l** (*m.sg.*) **aquí.**	**Posa-la** (*f.sg.*) **aquí.**
		Posa-ho (neuter) **aquí.**
Put them here.	**Posa'ls** (*m.pl.*) **aquí.**	**Posa-les** (*f.pl.*) **aquí.**
Pick it up.		**Recull-lo/recull-la.**
Pick them up.		**Recull-los/recull-les.**
Get up.	**Aixeca't** (*sg.*).	**Aixequeu-vos** (*pl.*).
Buy some.	**Compra'n.**	**Compreu-ne.**
You must buy some.		**Has de comprar-ne.**
He won't receive us.	**No vol rebre'ns.**	
He won't receive you.		**No vol rebre-us.**
He is looking at us.		**Està mirant-nos.**
He is looking at you.		**Està mirant-vos.**
Take me to the bar.	**Porti'm al bar** (vostè).	**Portin-me al bar** (vostès).
	Porta'm al bar (tu).	**Porteu-me al bar** (vosaltres).

It is worth repeating the observation that all enclitic pronouns are attached to the verb with either a hyphen (where no elision occurs) or an apostrophe (where there is elision).

12.2.3   MOBILE OBJECT PRONOUNS: CLITIC RAISING

When an infinitive or gerund is governed by a conjugated verb, any individual pronoun may, in a large number of cases, either precede the conjugated verb (as in **12.2.1** above) or be affixed enclitically to the infinitive/gerund (as in **12.2.2** above). The proclitic forms are less formal. The frequency with which the (periphrastic) preterite tense and other verbal periphrases occur (see Chapter 18, especially **18.2.1.1**) means that this option (called clitic raising) is regularly exercised:

No van viure-hi gaires anys. = No hi van viure gaires anys.
They did not live there for many years.

Estava arreglant-lo/arreglant-la. = L'estava arreglant.
He was mending it.

Heu d'ajudar-me. = M'heu d'ajudar.
You must help me.

In addition to the periphrases illustrated in the last three examples, the commonest verbs that that allow this clitic raising are: **voler** 'want', **poder** 'can', **acabar de** 'have just', **saber** 'know how to', **començar a** 'begin to', **acostumar a/de** 'be accustomed to', **deure** 'must', **gosar** 'dare', **pensar** 'intend', **fer** 'make', **deixar** 'let', **tornar a** 'do again', **anar a** 'be going to', **venir a** 'come to' and verbs of perception (**veure** 'see', **sentir** 'hear', etc.). Examples:

No volem molestar-te. = No et volem molestar.
We don't want to inconvenience you.

Encara no he començat a llegir-lo. = Encara no l'he començat a llegir.
I haven't started reading it yet.

No tornis a fer-ho. = No ho tornis a fer.
Don't do it again.

Acostumàvem a parlar-ne en veu baixa. = N'acostumàvem a parlar en veu baixa.
We usually talked about it in low voices.

No acabava de veure-ho clar. = No ho acabava de veure clar.
I couldn't quite work it out.

No puc atendre-la en aquest moment. = No la puc atendre en aquest moment.
I can't attend to you at the moment

Has intentat (de) trucar-li? = Li has intentat (de) trucar?
Have you tried phoning him?

M'ha fet repetir-ho. = M'ho ha fet repetir.
He made me repeat it.

(On mobility affecting pronoun groups, see **12.9.4.**)

Many verbs that govern an infinitive, however (with or without a preposition), do not allow clitic raising:

Han insistit a convidar-nos.	They have insisted on paying for us.
Va decidir comprar-lo.	She decided to buy it.
Han evitat haver-ho de fer. = Han evitat haver de fer-ho.	
***Ho han evitat haver de fer.**	They have avoided having to do it.

Some hesitation, or controversy, exists among native speakers as to which verbs do or do not allow clitic raising. Authentic usage is assured if one remembers that the enclitic form is always possible (if more formal). The question of clitic raising is related to that of valency, which is discussed in **25.5**.

Further information on clitic raising

Clitic raising does not occur:

(a) If the main verb is pronominal (see Chapter 23 for definition and examples): e.g. **Es va afanyar a acabar-ho** 'He strove to finish it', not ***S'ho va afanyar a acabar**; **Ens penedim d'haver-la insultada** 'We regret having insulted her', not ***Ens la penedim d'haver insultat**. Compare the mobility available with non-pronominal verbs: **Ens ha vist fer-ho = Ens ho ha vist fer** 'He saw us do it', **Ens deixaran entrevistar-la = Ens la deixaran entrevistar** 'They will let us interview her'.

(b) If another word or words intervene between the main verb and the dependent infinitive: **Havia intentat mil vegades de rectificar-ho** 'He had tried a thousand times to rectify it', not ***Ho havia intentat mil vegades de rectificar**; **Voldria no fer-ho** 'I'd rather not do it', but not ***Ho voldria no fer**.

   This rule is not always observed in the colloquial language: **No li tinc res a dir** for **No tinc res a dir-li** 'I've nothing to say to him/her/you'. Another exception is found when the post-verbal negative element **pas** (see **26.1.8**) is present in the sentence: **pas** itself can stand after the main verb or the infinitive, and clitic mobility is not affected in any arrangement: **No puc pas rebre'ls avui = No els puc pas rebre avui = No puc rebre'ls pas avui = No els puc rebre pas avui** 'I cannot receive them/ you today'.

(c) If the main verb is a positive command: **Mira de corregir-ho** 'Make sure you correct it', **Procureu evitar-ho** 'Try to avoid it'. But see **Deixa'm fer-ho = Deixa-m'ho fer** 'Let me do it'.

If more than one infinitive is involved, several solutions are possible (with the first generally being the most reliable for foreigners, in that it will always be correct, if not always the most colloquial):

No puc tornar a visitar-los. = No puc tornar-los a visitar. = No els puc tornar a visitar.
I can't visit them again.

Ja pots començar a copiar-ho. = Ja pots començar-ho a copiar. = Ja ho pots començar a copiar.
You can start copying it now.

12.3 PRONOMINAL CLITICS IN USE

12.3.1.1 First- and second-person object pronouns

First- and second-person object pronouns combine with the verb as explained in **12.1.1**. For both the first and the second persons the forms are undifferentiated for the accusative (direct object) and for the dative (indirect object) functions. The direct object in Catalan is easily identified (Chapter 25) and its function conforms to that of its counterpart in English: **M'han vist** 'They have seen me', **Heu de creure'ns** 'You must believe us'. The Catalan indirect object, on the other hand, covers a range of meanings beyond the simple function of dative (see **25.4**).

12.3.1.2 Reflexive and pronominal clitics

A particular category is that in which the object pronoun refers to the subject of the verb (as indicated by the verb ending): **Em dutxo** 'I'm having a shower', **M'estic rentant les dents** 'I'm cleaning my teeth', **T'has equivocat** 'You were mistaken', **No us emboliqueu en aquest assumpte** 'Don't get involved in this matter'.

These reflexive or pronominal verbs are discussed in detail in Chapter 23; the third-person reflexive clitic **es** is considered at **12.4**.

12.3.2 THIRD-PERSON OBJECT PRONOUNS

Third-person object pronouns pronouns correspond to **vostè(s)** 'you (polite)' as well as to third-person (animate and inanimate) objects:

Senyor comissari, li asseguro que no el tornaré a molestar.
Inspector, I assure you I won't trouble you again.

El vaig veure ahir.
I saw him/it/you yesterday.

Els vaig veure ahir.
I saw them/you yesterday.

12.3.2.1 Third-person direct objects

Third-person direct objects are differentiated for masculine and feminine (both animate and inanimate), combining variously with the verb as shown in **12.1.1**. The following examples illustrate all the different forms:

Quin dia! El recordaré sempre./No l'oblidaré mai./No podré oblidar-lo.
What a day! I'll always remember it./I'll never forget it./I shan't be able to forget it.

Treu-lo (el cotxe) del garatge i aparca'l a la cantonada.
Take it (the car) out of the garage and park it on the corner.

Seran uns bons col·laboradors. Posa'ls/Inclou-los/Els hem d'incloure/Hem d'incloure'ls a la llista.
They'll be good collaborators. Put them/Include them/We must include them in the list.

És una bona oportunitat: no la perdis/no l'hauries de perdre/no hauries de perdre-la.
It's a good opportunity: don't miss it/you ought not to miss it.

Si arriben les meves nebodes, les acompanyaràs/acompanya-les/les pots acompanyar/pots acompanyar-les al saló.
If my nieces arrive, you will show them/show them/you can show them to the drawing room.

In all of these cases the object pronouns agree in number and in gender with the noun the speaker has in mind. Where 'it' refers not to an identifiable noun but to something non-specific, to an idea or to a whole sentence (to something that might be represented by the neuter pronouns **això/allò** 'that'), then **ho** is used, as described in Chapter 9 (and later in **12.5**).

12.3.2.2 Third-person indirect objects

Li in the singular and **els** (**-los**, **'ls**) in the plural stand for both masculine and feminine indirect objects:

Ja li demostraré com s'ha de fer.
I'll demonstrate to him/her/you how it's to be done.

Si veus els meus pares, digue'ls/els pots dir/pots dir-los que els escriuré aviat.
If you see my parents, tell them/you can tell them I'll write (to them) soon.

A persones com aquestes, els hem de retre/hem de retre'ls el màxim homenatge.
We must pay the highest homage to people like these.

The indirect object plural form **els** (**-los**, **'ls**) is replaced in many spoken dialects (including the influential one of the Barcelona region) by an element which is pronounced [əlzi]. This widespread variant can be explained starting from a popular reanalysis of the singular indirect object pronoun, **li**, as consisting of a third-person singular element {l} (see second table in **12.1.1**) followed by an indirect object element {i}. On this basis speakers have constructed [əlzi] from the third-person plural {ls}, together with the element {i}, as in the singular. The innovation allows differentiation between third-person plural masculine direct object **els** and third-person plural indirect object [əlzi] where the standard language has only undifferentiated **els**. (The same tendency is detected in the substitution of the indirect object full form **-los** by (non-standard) **-lis**, which is found in speech particularly in Valencia and Minorca.) In recognizing this phenomenon, and even in spontaneously reproducing it in informal conversation, foreign learners need to be aware that it is a colloquial variant. In writing that attempts to represent popular speech, [əlzi] is generally written as **els hi**, as if the two pronouns **els** and **hi** were involved (as discussed in **12.9**, especially **els hi** considered at **12.9.3.5**). The standard form of indirect object plural **els** (**-los**, **'ls**) is used in educated speech and in nearly all kinds of written texts. The following sentences show how colloquial [əlzi], reproduced according to formal orthographic convention, would replace the correct form of indirect object **els** in examples already shown above:

> (non-standard) **Si veus els meus pares, digue'ls-hi/els hi pots dir/pots dî'ls-hi que els (hi) escriuré aviat.**

> (non-standard) **A persones com aquestes els hi hem de retre/hem de retre'ls-hi el màxim homenatge.**

12.3.2.3 Direct and indirect objects in the third person

In English, personal pronouns have the same form for direct and indirect object ('me', 'him', 'her', 'them'). In Catalan, in the first and second persons, the forms for the direct and indirect object are identical (**em**, etc., **et**, etc., **ens**, etc., **us**, etc.). Third-person masculine plural **els**, (**-los**, **'ls**) serve as both direct and indirect object, but otherwise the direct/indirect distinction is marked for the third person. This means that particular attention to appropriateness of form in relation to function must be paid when third-person objects are involved. The general point is best illustrated by referring to use of the third-person direct object shown above in **12.3.2.1** (and **25.3**) and then by reviewing the main patterns of use and details of meaning of indirect objects (see **25.4**).

Generally speaking if a verb has only one object, it is a direct object:

Les odia.
She hates them (*f.*).

La vam aguantar.
We endured it/her (*f.*).

No el puc descriure de cap altra forma.
I can't describe him in any other way.

As mentioned in **25.4**, a few verbs which have personal subjects take only an indirect object, but no direct object, at least in the standard variety, viz. **pegar** 'strike', **telefonar** 'telephone', **trucar** 'call', 'ring':

Els vaig trucar.	I rang them (*m.* or *f.*).
No li peguis.	Don't hit him/her.

Typical uses of indirect object **li/els**

The underlying principle is that the indirect object pronouns **li/els** represent the person (and sometimes the thing) interested in or by the meaning of the verb phrase, the 'interest' being broadly related either to 'gaining from' or to 'losing by' an action. English will often have 'to', 'for', or 'from' in corresponding phrases. The examples given below are all translated as referring to 'him/her/them', but in virtually every case the translation could be 'you' with the pronouns referring to **vostè(s)**.

In the first group of sentences below there is a direct object noun phrase (or noun clause/sentential complement) present as well as the dative/indirect object. (Only in exceptional circumstances can a Catalan clause have more than one direct object; it can never have more than one indirect object.)

Indirect object and direct object

(i)   Receiving or acquiring something:

Li vaig entregar el paquet.	I delivered the parcel to him.
Els ensenyarem com s'hi va.	We'll show them how to get there.
Digueu-li com es fa.	Tell her how it's done.
Qui els subministra combustible?	Who supplies them (with) fuel?
Algú li va atansar el plànol.	Someone handed him the street plan.
Li han hagut de posar una injecció.	They have had to give her an injection.
Li va merèixer moltes lloances.	It earned her a lot of praise.
El pare li havia encomanat la seva ambició.	His father had infected him with his ambition.
No se'ls ha acudit de denunciar-ho.	It didn't occur to them to report it.
Li he promès que ho faré.	I've promised him I'll do it.

(ii)   Loss or removal from:

Li han furtat la llibreta d'estalvis.
They've pinched her savings book.

Això li ha tret un gran pes del damunt.
This has taken a great weight from his shoulders.

Li vaig comprar una dotzena d'ous.
I bought a dozen eggs from her. (Note this could also mean 'I bought a dozen eggs *for* her'.)

Un veí va arrabassar-li la clau dels dits.
A neighbour snatched the key from his fingers.

(iii) Enquiring, requesting, requiring:

Pregunta-li si ho sap.
Ask her if she knows.

Els vam fer una sèrie de preguntes.
We put a series of questions to them.

Demanem-li aquest favor.
Let us ask this favour of him.

Aquest detall els deu haver cridat l'atenció.
This detail must have attracted their attention.

Era una feina que li exigia una concentració total.
It was a job that called for her total concentration.

(iv) Many set phrase involving **tenir** or **fer** plus a noun, expressing an emotion or reaction:

Per què li tens tanta enveja?	Why are you so jealous of her?
No li feia por.	It didn't frighten him.
No li fa res que pleguem d'hora.	She doesn't mind if we finish work early.

(v) Indicating persons affected by something done to a part of the body or to an intimate possession (see **7.4** and **25.4** on structural differences, including omission of the possessive adjective, between Catalan and English possessive constructions):

Afluixa-li el cinturó de seguretat.	Loosen her seat-belt.
Els degué costar un ronyó.	It must have cost them a packet.
Algú li trepitjava els peus.	Someone was treading on his feet.
L'excitació li entumia el membre.	The excitement made his member swell.
Se'ls havia espatllat el cotxe.	Their car had broken down.
Ja li cuidarem el gos.	We'll look after the/his dog for him.

(vi) Indicating a person's involvement in or being closely affected by a verbal action. This device is characteristic of colloquial and familiar contexts, when the speaker displays strong affective involvement in what they are talking about. The effect and nuances of this 'ethic dative' in Catalan (see **25.4**) are very often difficult to convey in English. The preposition 'on' ('on me', 'on you', 'on him', etc.) sometimes has the same force in colloquial English, but in translation the effect will usually be transposed to (or from) another part of the English sentence:

El nen se'ls estava posant molt fresc.
Their child was getting very cheeky with them.

El seu marit se li està quedant primíssim.
Her husband's getting terribly thin.

As in the examples above, this construction frequently involves combination of two (or more) pronoun clitics. The whole question of combination of pronouns is covered in **12.9**.

The second group of sentences, containing an indirect but no direct object, are perhaps more tricky for English speakers. In nearly every case the subject is inanimate or impersonal: such verbs are usually regarded as 'intransitive' (see **25.4**).

Indirect object but no direct object

(i)   Receiving or acquiring something:

A veure si li toca un premi.	Let's see if she gets a prize.
Els correspon la meitat dels beneficis.	They are entitled to half of the profits.
Li interessa saber-ho.	It's in his interest to know.
No li sembla que . . .?	Doesn't she think that . . .?
No els convenia que s'anunciés.	It didn't suit them for it to be announced.
El clima no li provava.	The climate didn't suit her.
Els sonava malament.	It sounded wrong to them.
Li és igual.	It's all the same to him.
Li consta que . . .	She knows for sure that . . .
Què li passa?	What's wrong with him?
No li agrada això?	Doesn't he like this?
Els va caure bé el guia.	The guide made a good impression on them.
I ara li sap molt de greu.	And now he is very sorry. (lit. It causes much regret to him.)
Els arribava una pudor d'oli barat.	A smell of cheap oil reached them.

(ii)   Loss or removal from:

Els queia la bava.	They were drooling.

(iii)   (In)sufficiency, lack, excess:

No els basta això?	Isn't that enough for them?
Li faltava un pulmó.	One of his lungs was missing.

Els pantalons li venien massa estrets.	Her trousers were too tight.
No els ha sobrat res del que els vam donar.	They have nothing over from what we gave them.

This multiplicity of meanings and nuances associated with the indirect object can give rise to various ambiguities:

Li van adquirir un cotxe nou.
They acquired a new car from him *or* for him.

No li penso comprar res.
I don't intend to buy anything from him *or* for him.

Algú li ha pispat un boli.
Someone has pinched a biro from him *or* for him.

Context nearly always clarifies what meaning is intended. Otherwise ambiguity can be resolved by recasting the sentence: **Va comprar el regal per a mi/ d'ella** 'He bought the present for me/from her'. Correspondingly, gender ambiguity in **li** or **els** can be resolved, where circumstance makes it necessary, by introducing **a ell, a ella, a ells, a elles** (or a fuller reference to the actual indirect object) as appropriate:

No cal explicar-li a ella que . . .
There's no need to explain to *her* that . . .

I tu creus que a ells els ha d'importar més que a elles?
And you think it's more important to the men than to the women?

(See **12.8** below on redundant pronouns.)

Unlike the direct object third-person pronouns, which can refer both to persons and to things, the use of **li** and **els** is restricted in some measure to personal indirect objects. The pronoun **hi**, discussed in **12.7**, covers many of the cases where an indirect object construction has an inanimate object, as in **La salsa era bona, però hi faltava un poc més de sal** 'The sauce was good, but it needed a bit more salt'; **A aquests diners s'hi ha d'afegir una nova aportació** 'A new contribution is to be added to this money'; **Acosta la cadira a en Joan** 'Move the chair closer to Joan' → **Acosta-li la cadira**, but **Acosta la cadira a la paret** 'Move the chair closer to the wall' → **Acosta-hi la cadira**. For further discussion, see **12.7ii**.

12.4   THIRD-PERSON REFLEXIVE CLITICS

Reflexive and pronominal verbs are discussed in detail in Chapter 23. For the purposes of the present chapter the point to be remarked on is that, while for the first two persons the reflexive pronoun is not distinct from the normal indirect object and direct object forms (**em**, etc., **et**, etc., **ens**, etc., **us/vos**), there is a separate form for the third-person reflexive pronoun. **Es** (**s'**, **-se**, **'s**) is used for both singular and plural (and is also the form corresponding to **vostè(s)**). It performs both the direct object and the indirect object functions.

Direct object

S'ha vestit ella sola.
She got dressed all by herself.

S'han rentat però encara no s'han pentinat.
They've got washed but they haven't combed their hair yet.

Indirect object

S'ha deixat una nota.	She has left herself a note.
S'han arrissat els cabells.	They have had their hair curled.
S'ha begut un got de llet.	He's drunk a glass of milk.

See Chapter 29 on **es** as impersonal subject.

As a single pronoun, **es** behaves, phonologically and orthographically, exactly like a normal pronominal clitic (on the pattern of **em** and **et**) in relation to the verb with which it stands: **Es posarà dret** 'He will stand up, **S'ha posat dret** 'He has stood up', **Posi's dret/Posin-se drets** 'Stand up' (**vostè(s)**).

Various combinations of weak pronouns involving **es** will be encountered in **12.9.3.7**.

12.5 THE NEUTER PRONOUN **ho**

This weak pronoun represents the direct object 'it' when the direct object complement cannot be identified as a specific noun. **Ho** thus refers to something actually or notionally represented by **això/allò** 'this'/'that', or it can stand for a whole idea or sentence. The use of neuter pronouns in general is discussed in **6.5**.

–Heu descobert quan arribarà l'avió? –No, encara no ho hem pogut saber.
'Have you discovered when the plane gets in?' 'No, we haven't found out yet.'

No volia dir-nos el que cercava i era impossible endevinar-ho.
He wouldn't tell us what he was looking for and it was impossible to guess.

In the last two cases the subordinate clauses **quan arribarà l'avió** and **el que cercava** could both be represented by **això/allò**: **Heu descobert això, No volia dir-nos allò**. The same examples also illustrate how the anaphora with **ho** is not always expressed in English:

Ho sento.
I'm sorry.

No ho sé.
I don't know.

Li hem explicat com s'ha de fer, però no sé si ho ha entès.
We've explained to him how it has to be done, but I don't know if he's understood.

Aquella és una heroïna, però mai no ho diries.
That woman is a heroine, but you'd never tell.

English 'it' is translated by **ho** in sentences like **Ho trobo increïble** 'I find it incredible', **Ho crèiem impossible** 'We thought it impossible', **Ho veig difícil** 'It looks hard to me' (lit. I see it hard), but not when 'it' anticipates a full complement clause following the main verb:

Considero intolerable que facin tal proposta.
I consider it intolerable that they should make such a proposal.

Trobàvem escandalós que no se'ls castigués.
We found it scandalous that they weren't punished.

The clitic **ho** is also used to represent the predicate (an indefinite noun phrase, an adjective phrase or an adverbial/prepositional phrase) of the verbs **ser** 'be', **estar** 'be', **semblar/parèixer** 'seem', 'look', **aparentar** 'show', 'look', **resultar** 'turn out', **esdevenir** 'become':

Indefinite noun phrases:

Voldria esser metge, però no ho seré.
I would like to be a doctor, but I won't be one.

Ja no ho som, de veïnes.
We aren't any more – neighbours, that is.

Adjective phrases:

Et pregunto si és llicenciada o no ho és.
I'm asking you whether she is a graduate or not.

Està malalta, però no ho aparenta.
She is ill, but she doesn't show it.

Adverbial/prepositional phrases:

–Aquelles flors són per al menjador? –Aquestes ho són.
'Are those flowers for the dining room?' 'These are' (sc. for the dining room).

Aquest xicot és d'Albaida, i aquell altre també ho és.
This lad is from Albaida, and that one is (sc. from Albaida) too.

–És prop? –Sí, però no ho sembla.
'Is it near?' 'Yes, but it doesn't seem like it.'

Avui se'ls veu molt afectats, però demà no ho estaran pas tant.
They appear very upset today, but tomorrow they won't be so badly affected.

(The predicate of **estar** is always expressed with **hi** in Balearic; see **12.7iv**.)

Where a noun attribute is definite rather than indefinite, use of **el/els** is preferred to **ho** in the normative standard language:

–Vostè no és el senyor Ribes. –I si el fos?
'You aren't Mr Ribas.' 'And (what) if I was (him)?'

Vull saber si és el cap de departament o no l'és.
I want to know if he is the head of department or not.

Té dinou anys pero no els aparenta.
She is nineteen but she doesn't look it.

Ho would be acceptable in these last examples (**Vull saber si és el cap de departament o no ho és**): see also **12.6vi** and **12.7iv** for **en** and **hi** in this attributive function.

12.6   THE ADVERBIAL PRONOUN en

This adverbial pronoun represents basically **de** + noun phrase in a variety of constructions:

(i)   **En** meaning 'from' or 'out of' in expressions of place:

Han entrat a classe a les nou i no n'han sortit fins gairebé la una.
They went into lessons at nine o'clock and didn't come out until nearly one.

Ell devia sortir cap a Palma justament quan jo en tornava.
He must have been setting out for Palma just as I was coming back (from there).

Si vas al pis de dalt, baixa'n les capses.
If you're going to the top floor bring down the boxes (from there).

(ii)   **En** meaning 'of'/'about' or 'from' in other contexts (including the complements of adjectives):

–T'ha explicat allò de la vaga? –No; és que no volia parlar-ne (i.e. de la vaga).

'Did he explain to you about the strike?' 'No, he didn't want to talk about it.'

La física no és el seu fort: no en té ni idea (i.e. de la física).

Physics isn't his strong point: he's got no idea about it.

–Ja estic fart d'aquesta feina. –Paciència, que tots n'estem farts (i.e. d'aquesta feina; fart de = 'tired of').

'I'm sick and tired of this job.' 'Have patience, we're all fed up with it.'

La iniciativa d'enganxar els cartells va ser un gran èxit; tot el barri n'era ple (ple de = 'full of').

The initiative of sticking up the posters was a great success; the whole neighbourhood was covered in them.

(iii) **En** in a possessive function relating to the complement of a direct object:

Hem vist els efectes de la reacció, però encara no n'hem descobert les causes.

We have seen the effects of the reaction, but still haven't discovered its causes.

Era un poble molt bonic, però ara no puc recordar-ne el nom.

It was a very attractive village, but I can't remember the name of it now.

(iv) **En** referring to the object of a verb that takes a prepositional object with **de**:

Has aconseguit una gran victòria i ara en presumeixes.

You have achieved a great victory and now you are boasting about it.

Si fem això crec que ens en penedirem ben aviat.

If we do that I think we'll very soon regret it.

As many such verbs are pronominal (formed with the reflexive pronoun) such constructions involve **en** in a two-pronoun group: see below **12.9.3.7**.

In popular speech the prepositional verb **recordar-se de** has the **en** encrusted on to the infinitive (forming non-standard **enrecordar-se de**), so that **en** is repeated to express the object: **No sé si se n'enrecordarà** (instead of . . . **se'n recordarà**) 'I don't know if she will remember'.

(v) **En** representing a noun phrase presented in a partitive sense (for example, the complement of a numeral or quantifier):

–Ha vingut algun client? –No, no n'ha vingut cap encara.

'Have any customers come?' 'No, none have come yet.'

–Prendreu cafè? –No, gràcies, ja n'he pres.
'Will you have coffee?' 'No thanks, I've had some already.'

De tots els convocats, només n'han assistit cinc.
Only five have turned up out of all those who were invited.

Tenia tres fills, però va morir-ne un en un accident de treball.
She used to have three sons, but one (of them) died in an accident at
work.

–Encara queden sol·licitants per entrevistar? –Ja no en queden gaires.
'Are there still some applicants to be interviewed?' 'There aren't many
left now.'

Ja són sis els morts . . . i en podrien ser més.
Six people are already dead . . . and there could be more.

When a noun is represented by partitive **en**, any adjectives referring to
that noun are preceded by **de** (often with no direct structural equivalence
in English):

D'aquests sobres, en vull deu de corrents i tres de grans.
I want ten normal-size and three big envelopes like these.

Tinc tres camises verdes però només en tinc una de blanca.
I've got three green shirts but only one white one.

Volíem comprar maduixes però no en trobàvem de fresques.
We wanted to buy some strawberries but couldn't find any fresh ones.

Similarly, a noun represented by partitive **en** is preceded by **de** if it is
repeated, either before or after the verb (left- or right-detached, see
Chapter 36):

De paciència no en té gens.
She has no patience at all.

Jo no en pronunciaria mai, de renecs així.
I would never utter curses like that.

De totes les cartes que he rebut encara no n'he contestades (or **contestat**)
més que dues o tres.
Of all the letters I have received I have still answered only two or three.

(On the optional agreement of the past participle with a clitic **en**, see
21.1.2iv.)
Partitive **en** occurs frequently as complement of **hi ha** 'there is' (in all
tenses) so that the combination **n'hi** (**en** + **hi**) is something of a fixed
idiom (see **12.7v**):

Compra pa, que no n'hi ha gens a casa.
Buy some bread because there's none at home.

Buscava una altra solució però em vaig adonar que no n'hi havia cap/que no podia haver-n'hi cap.
I was looking for another solution but realized there wasn't one/could not be one.

(vi) Attributive **en**:

The pronoun **ho** used to represent the complement of **ser, estar, semblar,** etc., as described in **12.5**, is colloquially replaced by **en**:

La recompensa important que s'havia esmentat, no en va resultar tant com ens havíem imaginat.
The significant reward that had been mentioned proved to be less so than we'd imagined.

In this example **no ho va resultar** would be preferred by normative grammar, but constructions with **en** do seem firmly rooted, and **ho** would be avoided by some in exclamations like **Que n'és, de valent!** 'How brave he is!' (see **27.2.2.2**).

(vii) **En** with verbs of motion:

Anar-se'n 'to go (away)' and **tornar-se'n** 'to return' have the pronouns (pronominal + **en**) idiomatically as an integral part. (On the position and spelling of pronouns in combination, see section **12.9**.)

Quan jo me n'anava tu ja te'n tornaves.
As I was leaving you were already coming back.

Other common verbs of motion (**venir, volar, pujar, baixar**) are also occasionally found in an analogous prepositional form: **venir-se'n** 'come back', 'come down', **(en)volar-se'n** 'fly away', **pujar-se'n** 'climb up', **baixar-se'n** 'go down' (see **23.6**):

Se'n ve la vaca tota sola. És cega. (Joan Maragall, *La vaca cega*)
The cow comes back this way all on her own. She is blind.

Els ocells se'n volaran si el xiquet se'n puja a l'arbre. (Solà, *Normativa*)
The birds will fly away if the boy climbs the tree.

Sortir-se'n (**eixir-se'n** in Valencia), from **sortir/eixir** 'go/come out', is used idiomatically to mean 'get by', 'manage', 'cope':

–Com va la feina? –Me'n vaig sortint.
'How's the job going?' 'I'm getting along nicely.'

La seva situació era difícil, però se'n va sortir molt bé.
Her situation was very difficult, but she coped very well.

(viii) **en** with **dir** 'call' and associated idioms:

En represents a complement of the verb **dir** in the sense of 'call', 'say (= name, designate)':

Per què li dius Mariana, si no se'n diu pas?
Why are you calling her Mariana if that's not her name?

Els valencians diuen *rabosa* de la guineu: com en diuen a les Balears?
The Valencians say *rabosa* for 'fox': what's it called in the Balearic Islands?

Likewise with **nomenar** 'appoint':

Podrà ser el nou secretari del partit, encara que ell no creu que l'en nomenin.
He could be the new party secretary, although he doesn't think he'll be appointed.

Note the idiomatic use of **dir-ne** in the conditional, meaning 'might call', 'might refer to' and so on; and similarly **diguem-ne** 'so to speak', 'as it were':

Em refereixo a allò que en diríem el seu tacte diplomàtic.
I am referring to what we might call his diplomatic tact.

en aquesta mena de relació diguem-ne platònica
in this type of, as it were, Platonic relationship

(ix)   Examples of other idioms involving **en**:

Es va fer comunista quan estudiava en la universitat, i la seva dona també se'n va fer per aquell temps.
He became a communist while at university, and his wife also became one around that time.

Quinze i vuit fan vint-i-tres, i en porto dos.
Fifteen and eight make twenty-three, so carry two.

haver-n'hi prou: Ja n'hi ha prou de xafardeig!
          That's enough gossip!

tenir-ne prou: Amb això en tinc prou.
          That's enough for me.

No n'hi ha per tant!
There's no need to make such a fuss!

See **25.2** for discussion of **en** corresponding to the subject of certain unaccusative verbs.

12.7   THE ADVERBIAL PRONOUN **hi**

Use of this pronoun can be described under seven main headings:

(i)   **Hi** standing for the combination of any preposition, other than **de**, with a noun phrase. Representing **a/en** + noun phrase, **hi** frequently corresponds to 'there' in expressions of place and movement:

Vaig buscar-te al bar, però no hi eres.
I looked for you in the bar but you weren't there.

Obre el calaix i posa-hi aquests papers.
Open the drawer and put these papers in (it).

Per molt que els altres critiquin la teva gestió, jo no hi veig cap deficiència.
However much the others criticize your procedure, I don't see any deficiency in it.

Ens havien parlat tant de Morella que al final vam decidir d'anar-hi.
We had heard so much about Morella that we finally decided to go there.

–Heu vingut a través del bosc? –No, avui no hi hem vingut.
'Did you come through the wood?' 'No we didn't come that way today.'

There are many cases where **a** or **en** does not refer to physical location or direction (see (ii) below):

No el conec ni sé si hi puc confiar. (hi = en ell)
I don't know him and don't know if I can trust him.

Si jo renunciava a tenir-ho, hi renunciaries tu també? (hi = a tenir-ho)
If I turned it down would you (do so) as well?

La situació és dura i li costarà d'acostumar-s'hi. (hi = a ella = a la situació)
The situation is hard and he'll find it difficult to get used to it.

Examples of other prepositions (+ noun phrase) represented by **hi**:

Avui juguem contra un equip que fa anys que no hi juguem.
Today we are playing a team that we haven't played against for years.

–Encara penses en la Carme? –No deixaré mai de pensar-hi.
'Are you still thinking about Carme?' 'I'll never stop thinking about her.'

Sortia amb en Terenci, però ja no hi surt.
She used to go out with Terenci but she doesn't (go out with him) any more.

El camí era tan estret que el camió no podia passar-hi.
The track was so narrow that the lorry couldn't get along it.

(ii) **Hi** standing for an inanimate indirect object:

En Nicolau dedicarà l'estiu a la redacció de la gramàtica.
Nicolau will devote the summer to writing the grammar.
→ **En Nicolau hi dedicarà l'estiu.**
  Nicolau will devote the summer to it.

Gemma donà colps a la taula.
lit. Gemma gave blows to the table.
→ **Gemma hi donà colps.**
  lit. Gemma gave blows to it.

El govern no concedia prou importància a les crítiques de l'oposició.
The government did not grant enough importance to opposition
  criticisms.
→ **El govern no hi concedia prou importància.**
  The government did not grant them enough importance.

A això, hi he dedicat molt de temps.
I have devoted a lot of time to this.

El problema sembla insoluble si no hi apliquem la ciència.
The problem seems insoluble if we don't apply science to it.

Use of **hi** instead of **li** (see **12.3.2.3**) for an inanimate indirect object
appears to be affected by various fine distinctions. There is clearly an
overlap between the locative/directional function of **a** (covered in (i)
above), as can be detected in some examples already given: **Acosta-hi (a
la paret) la cadira** 'Move the chair closer to it (the wall)', **La situació és
dura i li costarà d'acostumar-s'hi** 'The situation is hard and he'll find it
difficult to get used to it', **si no hi apliquem (al problema) la ciència** 'if we
don't apply science to it (the problem)'.

  The impersonal/personal distinction is readily observed in contrasting
sentences like:

En aquest edifici hi trobo un sol punt flac.
I find just one weak point in this building.

A en Pere li trobo un sol punt flac.
I find just one weak point in Pere.

Hi dedica la tarda (a la feina).
He devotes the afternoon to it (work).

Li dedica la tarda (a la seva filla).
He devotes the afternoon to her (his daughter).

Hi, on the other hand, would not be used in examples like the following:

(A la parròquia), el governador li ha regalat un orgue.
The governor has made a present of an organ to the parish.

(A la Universitat), li ha llegat el seu arxiu.
He has left his archive to the University.

(A l'Ajuntament), li han ofert un nou cotxe de bombers.
The Town Council has been offered a new fire engine.

Here it would seem that the human constituents of the impersonal indirect object (the parishioners, the members of the University, the Town Councillors, respectively) are understood. This may be seen as a sort of personification of the inanimate indirect object, a feature affecting the issue when **li** is used instead of **hi** in alternatives such as the following:

Aquest rellotge s'aturarà si no li/hi dónes corda.
This clock will stop if you don't wind it up.

Mirava el cartell i li/hi donava cops.
She was looking at the poster and hitting it.

(iii) **Hi** corresponding to an adverb or an adverbial (a prepositional phrase). Note that, unlike in (i) above, **hi** may represent an adverbial containing the preposition **de**.

Si els teus amics es porten sempre tan bé, perquè no t'hi saps portar tu?
If your friends always behave so well, why can't you?

Normalment comencen a les vuit, però avui no hi començaran pas.
They normally begin at eight o'clock but they won't today.

Diu que treballa de pressa, però veig que no hi treballa gens.
He says he works quickly but I can see that he doesn't at all.

(iv) **Hi** representing the predicate complement (adjective, adverb, or indefinite noun phrase) of verbs like **quedar(-se)**, **tornar-se**, **posar-se** 'become', **aparèixer**, **presentar-se** 'appear', **anar** 'go' (in the sense of 'become'), **resultar** 'turn out', **tenir** 'have', **trobar** 'find', **romandre** 'remain':

Digué que el ferro es tornaria or, però no s'hi va tornar.
He said the iron would turn into gold but it didn't.

–Té les cames molt llargues. –Sí que les hi té.
'He has very long legs.' 'He certainly has'.

Jo vaig quedar vermell, i ella s'hi va posar encara més.
I turned red, and she went even redder.

Abans aquesta recepta ens ha resultat molt bé, però sembla que aquesta vegada no hi resulti.
This recipe has worked well for us before, but this time it looks as though it won't.

–És gaire salat aquest arròs? –Sí que l'hi trobo.
'Is this risotto very salty?' 'I certainly find it is.'

Note, however, that the attribute of **ser**, **estar**, **semblar**, **esdevenir** and **aparentar** is expressed with **ho**, as explained at **12.5** above. Despite this, everyday language sometimes produces **hi** instead of **ho** with the verbs just mentioned, as, for example in:

Ell estarà content, però els altres no hi (for ho) **estarem gens.**
He'll be satisfied, but the rest of us won't be at all.

(On **en** instead of **hi** in this context, see **12.6vi**.)

(v)   **hi** standing with the verb **haver** in the impersonal expression 'there is/ there are', etc.

No pot haver-hi cap altra explicació.
There can be no other explanation.

Un quiosc que hi ha a la plaça.
A news-stand in the square.

Demà hi haurà pluges arreu del país.
Tomorrow there will be rain all over the country.

Informal colloquial usage sometimes makes **haver** agree with a plural 'subject', but sentences like **Hi han molts que s'ho creuen** 'There are many who believe it' or **Hi havien cues a totes les botigues** 'There were queues in all the shops' would be out of place in formal written styles.

As remarked in **12.6v**, partitive **en** frequently occurs with **hi ha**, etc. (in the combination **n'hi**), indicating the quantity of whatever the impersonal expression refers to. See the examples given in **12.6v** in line with:

Si vols una carpeta, en aquest calaix n'hi ha de totes les mides.
If you want a folder, there are some of every size in this drawer.

Només va haver-n'hi dos o tres, d'errors per corregir.
There were only two or three mistakes to correct.

(vi)   **Hi** accompanying verbs of seeing and hearing used intransitively, including figurative senses:

Pobre noia: no hi veu ni hi sent.
Poor girl: she can neither see nor hear.

Havien apagat els llums i no ens hi vèiem.
They had put the lights out and we couldn't see.

No s'hi veia de contenta.
She was absolutely thrilled. (lit. She could not see, so pleased was she.)

No hi veu més enllà del nas.
He can't see further than the end of his nose.

(vii) Examples of other idioms involving **hi**:

No hi fa res.
It doesn't matter.

No s'hi val que em facin això.
It's not right that they should do this to me.

Tothom pot dir-hi la seva.
Everyone can have their say.

Em sembla que el conec, però no hi caic.
I think I know him, but I can't place him.

Què hi farem?
What is to be done (about it)? (expressing resignation)

Per molt que s'hi miri, farà un bunyol.
However careful he is, he'll make a mess of it.

No et pot entendre, home: no veus que no hi és tot?
He can't understand you, you know: can't you see he's not all there?

L'oncle repapieja; ja no hi toca.
Uncle is now doddery; he's lost his marbles.

No hi entenc gens, en geografia.
I'm no good at geography.

Fent-ho així, no hi perds res.
By doing it this way you've nothing to lose.

On combinations of third-person object pronouns in which **hi** stands for indirect object **li**, see **12.9.3.3** below, and for non-standard uses of 'indirect object' **hi**, **12.3.2.2** above and **12.9.3.5**.

12.7.1   NON-USE OF en AND hi IN VALENCIAN DIALECTS

Ordinary Valencian Catalan displays only a restricted range of the uses of **en** and **hi** discussed in **12.6** and **12.7**. The following examples (taken mainly from Solà, *Sintaxi i normativa*) illustrate spontaneous Valencian usage:

Si vas al pis de dalt, baixa les capses/baixa d'allí les capses. (standard: . . . **baixa'n les capses.**)
If you're going to the flat upstairs, bring the boxes down (from there).

–Vas a Girona? –Justament jo ara vinc de Girona/ara vinc d'allí. (standard: ... jo ara en vinc.)
'Are you going to Girona?' 'I've just come from there.'

Vés al menjador: encara trobaràs (allà) el meu germà. (standard: ... encara hi trobaràs ...)
Go to the dining room; my brother will still be there.

No veu els seus amics, però manté contacte epistolar. (standard: ... hi manté ...)
He doesn't see his friends, but he is in touch (with them) by letter.

Em volien obligar a votar, però em vaig negar. (standard: ... m'hi vaig negar ...)
They wanted to make me vote but I refused.

Si aquests voten a favor del projecte, jo votaré en contra. (standard: ... hi votaré en contra ...)
If these people vote in favour of the plan I'll vote against.

Alguns troben que té els cabells massa llargs: jo no veig que els tinga. (standard: ... que els hi tinga.)
Some find his hair is too long: I don't find it so.

Tothom pot dir la seua. (standard ... dir-hi ...)
Everyone can have their say.

12.8 'REDUNDANT' CLITIC OBJECT PRONOUNS

Catalan makes frequent use of clitic object pronouns in situations where these are apparently superfluous, as the person or thing to which they refer is represented in the sentence either by a strong pronoun or by a noun: **No hi penso tornar mai més, a aquell lloc nefast** 'I don't intend to go back to that dreadful place ever again', **D'això en diem una ficada de pota** 'That's what we call putting your foot in it' (see **36.4–5**).

Some occurrences of these apparently redundant pronouns are structural, virtually obligatory in that without them the sentence would be ungrammatical. Others (**12.8.2**) are regarded as characteristic of uneducated speech and are discouraged by normative grammar.

12.8.1 STRUCTURALLY REDUNDANT CLITICS

Old Catalan **a mi pareix que** 'it seems to me that' has evolved to modern **a mi me/em pareix que**, so that this particular construction without 'redundant' reiteration of the personal pronoun object in the weak pronoun **me/em** would nowadays be completely ungrammatical. This structural redundancy is likewise illustrated in the Catalan equivalent of 'everything', where direct object **tot** cannot stand without **ho** (cf. 'it all'): **Ho comprèn tot** 'She understands everything/understands it all' (see **8.2**).

In modern Catalan when a sentence begins with a verbal argument – a direct or indirect object, or an adverbial complement – it is necessary to repeat reference to it in the form of the corresponding weak object pronoun.

A la mare li comprarem un rellotge.	We'll buy mother a watch.
De vosaltres en parlem sovint.	We are often talking about you.
A nosaltres no ens perdonaran mai.	They will never forgive us.
Això, ho hem de tenir sempre en compte.	We must always bear this in mind.

This construction effectively topicalizes the object by giving it priority in the sentence (see **36.4**), giving an emphasis that in English would be conveyed by intonation. The simple construction (different word order) which does not involve repetition carries the same semantic value, with neutral emphasis: **Comprarem un rellotge a la mare, Parlem sovint de vosaltres, Hem de tenir sempre en compte això.**

If the object is not placed first in the sentence, a distinction is observed in the behaviour of 'redundant' pronouns. Normative grammar allows (but does not impose) duplication of first- and second-person pronouns:

M'acusen a mi de ...   I am accused of ...
Us felicito a tots vosaltres.   I congratulate all of you.
No destruirem el planeta, però sí que podem destruir-nos a nosaltres mateixos. (*El Temps*)
We won't destroy the planet, but we may destroy ourselves.

With third-person objects (including **vostè(s)**), however, repetition of the weak pronoun is deemed acceptable only when, as illustrated above, the other specification of the object comes before the verb, not after it:

Felicito a tots vostès.	I congratulate all of you.
Hem d'entregar això al director.	We've got to deliver this to the director.
Dius a en Frederic que ...	You can tell Frederic that ...

In cases resembling these but with the object placed before the verb, structural redundancy is quite normal: **A en Frederic li dius que ...**, with emphasis now on Frederic.

12.8.2   NON-STANDARD CONSTRUCTIONS WITH REDUNDANT PRONOUNS

In **36.5** we discuss the phenomenon of right detachment, where an element of a sentence is placed at the end, as a kind of 'afterthought', separated from the main structure by a pause or a comma, as in:

T'hi acostumaràs aviat, a la nova feina.	You'll soon get used to it, your new job.

In this construction, the detached element is always represented explicitly in the main part of the sentence, that is, the following is ungrammatical:

***T'acostumaràs aviat, a la nova feina.**	You'll soon get used, to your new job.

(The same elements, without the pause or comma, are perfectly all right, of course:

T'acostumaràs aviat a la nova feina.	You'll soon get used to your new job.)

What is quite common in colloquial usage is a pattern which seems to combine the right-detached structure with the basic sentence pattern to give the following, with redundant pronoun, yet with no pause, or comma:

(non-standard) **T'hi acostumaràs aviat a la nova feina.**
You'll soon get used to your new job.

This pattern is never found with direct objects, so we do not find in any style:

***Ja l'he tancada la ràdio.**	
Ja he tancat la ràdio.	I've already turned the radio off.

But it is very common with indirect objects and adverbial/prepositional objects (represented by **en** or **hi**). Constructions on the lines of **Li dius a en Frederic . . .**, **Li hem d'entregar això al director** are commonly encountered in speech and even in writing (see **25.4** and **36.5**), but are considered to be non-standard. The following are colloquial:

(non-standard) **No vull posar-hi sucre al cafè.**
I don't want to put sugar in the coffee.

(non-standard) **No en saben res de l'accident.**
They know nothing about the accident.

A rather different kind of of structural redundancy is the appearance of **en** in the formulaic opening of folk tales and ballads (**Si n'eren tres tambors** 'There were these three drummers', **Si n'hi havia en Jan Bonhome** 'Once there was a person called Jan Bonhome (= Jack Goodman)').

Uneducated non-standard speech produces repetitions of pronominal **en** and **hi** themselves. Redundancy here is created by clitic raising without the corresponding suppression, as in:

(non-standard) **Te'n vaig parlar-ne ahir.**	I spoke to you about it yesterday.

(for **Vaig parlar-te'n ahir** or **Te'n vaig parlar ahir**.)

(non-standard) **A casa hi hauré d'anar-hi.**   I shall have to go home.
(for **A casa hauré d'anar-hi** or **A casa hi hauré d'anar.**)

Pleonastic clitics in relative clauses

The phenomenon (which is mentioned in **31.2.2**) whereby a weak pronoun in a relative clause syntactically complements a bare relative marker (**que**), tends to occur spontaneously and frequently in popular speech with other relative pronouns, in constructions where the pronoun is logically quite redundant. In the examples below the item shown in parentheses would not appear in writing (unless reproducing colloquial usage):

Són coses que ja (les) sabem de memòria.
They are things that we know off by heart.

**El nostre comportament, en què tots (hi) podeu veure una gran voluntat de
complaure-us.**
Our behaviour, in which you can all see a great concern to please you.

Aquell poble on (hi) vam passar una nit espantosa.
That village where we spent a dreadful night.

In the case of dative subject verbs (**25.4**), however, the pleonastic clitic cannot be omitted.

Coneixem moltes persones a les quals els agrada xafardejar.
We know a lot of people who like gossiping.

12.9 WEAK OBJECT PRONOUNS IN COMBINATION

12.9.1 GENERAL

Sections **12.1–12.8** have covered functions and forms of single pronouns (although combinations of two pronouns have appeared in some of the examples given). Normal usage frequently requires that two or three (occasionally even four) items in a sentence be represented in weak pronoun form: thus, **Dóna'm el llibre** 'Give me the book' → **Dóna-me'l** 'Give it to me', **Et duran els paquets a casa** 'They will take the parcels to your house for you' → **Te'ls duran a casa** (two-pronoun group) 'They will take them to your house for you' → **Te'ls hi duran** (three-pronoun group) 'They will take them there for you'.

The general rules for positioning of pronoun groups are as for single pronouns, described in **12.2** above, although some aspects of clitic mobility are affected by the presence of more than one weak pronoun in a sentence (**12.9.4**).

Displacement of stress to the final syllable of enclitic groups occurs in

Balearic dialects, as for single enclitics (**12.1.2vi**): **trobar-t'hi** [tɾobaɾˈti], **anar-se'n** [ənaɾˈsən].

The intricacies of spelling conforming to phonetic modifications of pronouns in contact with other pronouns and with the verb are covered in detail in **12.9.2** and **12.9.3**. In general, all enclitic pronoun groups are (like single enclitics) attached to the verb with either a hyphen (where no elision occurs) or an apostrophe (where there is elision): **Acompanya-m'hi** 'Go there with me', **Acompanya'ls-hi** 'Go there with them', **Has d'acompanyar-les-hi** 'You should go there with them'. Proclitic groups are internally 'punctuated' only with the apostrophe (showing elision).

12.9.2   ORDER OF CONSECUTIVE PRONOMINAL CLITICS

Some old-fashioned grammarians considered the functional sequence indirect object–direct object as the major determinant of the order of weak pronouns in combination. This analysis, however, is clearly inadequate as a global description, and is useful only as a rule of thumb for certain regularly occurring groups: e.g. **Envia-m'ho** 'Send it to me', **Ja te'ls portaré** 'I'll bring them to you', **Us la presentarem** 'We will introduce her to you', **Se l'ha menjat** 'He has eaten it up', etc. (See **12.9.3.2** for the special case of pronoun order in Balearic.)

The invariable order of pronominal clitics when two or more appear together is fully represented in the following diagram:

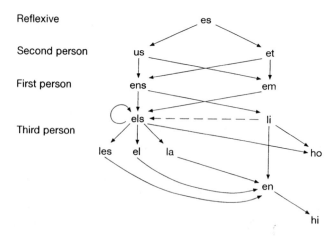

Figure 12.1 Order of weak pronouns in combination

Note 1: The forms given in the diagram are the reinforced ones **em**, **et**, etc. Spelling in particular groupings depends upon points of contact between pronouns and verb and between individual pronouns, as is laid out in detail in the table in **12.9.4** (and subsequently explained): **te n'has recordat**, **recorda-te'n**, **poseu-vos-els**, **posat-te'ls**, and so on.

Note 2: Arrows in the diagram indicate the only viable order: e.g. **me l'ha donada**, **n'hi havia cinc**, **ni me'n recordava**, **s'hi conformarà**, **se'ns els menjarà**, etc.

Note 3: Broken horizontal arrow **els** ←- - - - **li** relates to the Valencian solutions **li'ls**, **li les**, **li'l**, **li la** corresponding to **els hi**, **les hi**, **l'hi**, **la hi** prevalent in other dialects. See **12.9.3.3**.

The information in the diagram above can be reduced to five key points, each of which is inclusive of the subsequent one(s):

(i) **Ho, en,** and **hi** occupy the final place in any group where one of them appears: **Te n'has anat** 'You left', **Ens en faran** 'They will make some for us', **Han de trobar-s'hi** 'They are to meet there', **No us ho puc dir** 'I can't tell you'. Of these three pronouns, only **en** and **hi** can appear together, invariably in the order **en + hi**: **No n'hi ha** 'There isn't any', **Deuen haver-n'hi posat** 'They must have put some in'.

(ii) **Es** comes first in any group in which it appears: **S'ho ha empassat** 'She has swallowed it', **Volien emportar-se'ls** 'They wanted to take them away'.

(iii) A first- or second-person pronoun (**em, ens, et, us**) will precede any third-person pronoun in a group: **Tradueix-m'ho al català** 'Translate it into Catalan for me', **Hauríeu de guardar-vos-els** 'You ought to keep them', **No ens les vendran** 'They won't sell them to us', **Me li van presentar** 'They introduced me to him/her'.

(iv) A second-person pronoun will precede any first-person pronoun in a group: **Poseu-vos-em al davant** 'Stand in front of me', **No te'ns posis tan exigent** 'Don't be so demanding of us'.

(v) **Li** or **els** precede any other third-person pronoun with morphemic base [l]: **No cal dur-li'l** 'There's no need to take it to him' (Valencian), **Has de deixar-los-el llegir** 'You must let them read it', **Envia'ls-els** 'Send them to them'.

The spelling of pronouns in groups conforms to five basic points:

(i) Before or after the verb, the full forms **me, te** and **se** are used when these pronouns come first in any group, except when they precede **ho** or **hi**, in which case the elided forms **m', t',** and **s'** are used: **Me'l vendrà, Me l'ha venut, M'ho vendrà, Ven-me'l, Ven-me-la, Has de vendre-me'l, Has de vendre-me-la.**

(ii) Pronouns other than **me, te,** and **se** coming first in a group adopt the form they would have if they were single pronouns (**12.2.1**): **Ens la portaran, Us ho explicarem, Traduïu-nos-el, Compra'ns-en, Els ho demanaré.**

(iii) In a two-pronoun group standing before the verb, the second pronoun behaves as though it were standing alone (see again **12.2.1**) with the verb in question: **Me l'arreglarà, Ens els ha arreglat, Te l'enviaré, Els ho explicarem, Les hi posarem.**

(iv) In a two-pronoun group standing after the verb, the second pronoun takes the reduced form if it possesses one or keeps the hyphenated full form if it cannot be reduced: **Torna-me'l, Torna-me-la, Torna'ns-els, Torna-li'l, Torna-li-ho.**

(v) With proclitic groups, pronoun–verb elision (where possible) has priority over pronoun–pronoun elision: with enclitic groups, pronoun–pronoun elision has priority over verb–pronoun elision. In other words elision, if it is to occur, will be as far to the right as possible: **Me l'has tret, Has de treure-me'l, Se'n va, Se n'ha anat, Te'n recordes, Te n'has de recordar, Recorda-te'n.** The only exception to this is **l'en** (and this is justified on the grounds that *le'n would imply the existence of a form *le which does not otherwise occur).

The application of these general principles is fully illustrated in the table given on pp. 204–5.

12.9.3   TABLE OF TWO-PRONOUN GROUPS

The table given on pp. 204–5 (adapted from Badia, *Gramàtica*) shows the combination and spelling of all two-pronoun groups. The following observations will facilitate consultation.

First- and second-person pronouns (i.e. **em, et, ens, us**) are undifferentiated for direct object and indirect object functions; third-person forms (identical for **vostè(s)**) are differentiated according to function (e.g. **li**, indirect object singular *m.* and *f.*; **el**, direct object singular *m.*; **els**, direct object plural *m.*; **els**, indirect object plural *m.* and *f.*).

Each box contains the result of combining the head of each horizontal row with the head of each vertical column. Four combinations are given in each box, even when some are identical. The numbers 1–4 in each box correspond to the four situations affecting pronunciation and spelling according to whether the group stands:

1 after a verb ending in a consonant or semivowel **-u**
2 after a verb ending in a vowel (excluding semivowel **-u**)
3 before a verb beginning in a consonant
4 before a verb beginning in a vowel or **h-**

The forms presented in the table are those which are recognized as correct and universally applicable in the standard written language. The Valencian solution for **li** + another [l]-base third-person pronoun (row VII) has some currency in the literary language, alongside the more widespread solution shown in row VI a–d; see **12.9.3.3**. Informal written registers and colloquial usage diverge considerably from the pattern of the formal standard which is based on eastern dialects, particularly the language of Barcelona and environs. These deviations from the standard, already introduced in relation to single pronouns, are discussed in general terms in the sections following the table.

Note that the logical combination of direct object **ho** + adverbial **hi** is in fact realized **l'hi**: see **12.9.3.4iv**.

12.9.3.1 Formation of two-pronoun groups

The table on pp. 204–5 supplies the model for every combination of two pronominal clitics according to the point of contact with the verb and its pronunciation/spelling. It would be tiresome and redundant to provide an example of each single one of the more than three hundred instances laid out in the table. What follows below is a relatively full sample of cases involving first-person singular indirect objects (**em, ens**), in combination with various third-person direct objects.

The sentences **Em llegiràs l'anunci** 'You will read the notice to me' and **M'has llegit l'anunci** 'You have read the notice to me' correspond to **Me'l llegiràs** 'You will read it to me' and **Me l'has llegit** 'You have read it to me' when the direct object (**l'anunci**) is represented by a pronoun. Similarly **Llegeix-me l'anunci** and **Llegeixi'm** (vostè) **l'anunci** 'Read the notice to me' correspond to **Llegeix-me'l** and **Llegeixi-me'l**. Then, with feminine direct objects (singular **la proposta** 'the proposal', plural **les propostes**), we have:

Me la llegiràs.	**Me les llegiràs.**
Me l'has llegit/llegida.	**Me les has llegit/llegides.**
Llegeix-me-la.	**Llegeix-me-les.**
Llegeixi-me-la.	**Llegeixi-me-les.**

The same direct object pronouns combine in groups with **ens** as follows:

(l'anunci)	**(els anuncis)**
Ens el llegiràs.	**Ens els llegiràs.**
Ens l'has llegit.	**Ens els has llegit/llegits.**
Llegeix-nos-el.	**Llegeix-nos-els.**
Llegeixi'ns-el.	**Llegeixi'ns-els.**
(la proposta)	**(les propostes)**
Ens la llegiràs.	**Ens les llegiràs.**
Ens l'has llegit/llegida.	**Ens les has llegit/llegides.**
Llegeix-nos-la.	**Llegeix-nos-les.**
Llegeixi'ns-la.	**Llegeixi'ns-les.**

Further examples, showing two complements represented as pronouns:

Et concediran l'autorització.
They will grant you permission.
→ **Te la concediran.**

Table of combinations of two weak object pronouns

	a el DO	b la DO	c els DO	d les DO	e li IO	f els IO	g en	h hi	i ho	j em	k et	l ens	m us
I em	1-me'l 2-me'l 3 me'l 4 me l'	1-me-la 2-me-la 3 me la 4 me l'	1-me'ls 2-me'ls 3 me'ls 4 me'ls	1-me-les 2-me-les 3 me les 4 me les	1-me-li 2-me-li 3 me li 4 me li	1-me'ls 2-me'ls 3 me'ls 4 me'ls	1-me'n 2-me'n 3 me'n 4 me n'	1-m'hi 2-m'hi 3 m'hi 4 m'hi	1-m'ho 2-m'ho 3 m'ho 4 m'ho				
II et	1-te'l 2-te'l 3 te'l 4 te l'	1-te-la 2-te-la 3 te la 4 te l'	1-te'ls 2-te'ls 3 te'ls 4 te'ls	1-te-les 2-te-les 3 te les 4 te les	1-te-li 2-te-li 3 te li 4 te li	1-te'ls 2-te'ls 3 te'ls 4 te'ls	1-te'n 2-te'n 3 te'n 4 te n'	1-t'hi 2-t'hi 3 t'hi 4 t'hi	1-t'ho 2-t'ho 3 t'ho 4 t'ho	1-te'm 2-te'm 3 te'm 4 te m'		1-te'ns 2-te'ns 3 te'ns 4 te'ns	
III es	1-se'l 2-se'l 3 se'l 4 se l'	1-se-la 2-se-la 3 se la 4 se l'	1-se'ls 2-se'ls 3 se'ls 4 se'ls	1-se-les 2-se-les 3 se les 4 se les	1-se-li 2-se-li 3 se li 4 se li	1-se'ls 2-se'ls 3 se'ls 4 se'ls	1-se'n 2-se'n 3 se'n 4 se n'	1-s'hi 2-s'hi 3 s'hi 4 s'hi	1-s'ho 2-s'ho 3 s'ho 4 s'ho	1-se'm 2-se'm 3 se'm 4 se m'	1-se't 2-se't 3 se't 4 se t'	1-se'ns 2-se'ns 3 se'ns 4 se'ns	1-se-us 2-se-us 3 se us 4 se us
IV ens	1-nos-el 2-ns-el 3 ens el 4 ens l'	1-nos-la 2-ns-la 3 ens la 4 ens l'	1-nos-els 2-ns-els 3 ens els 4 ens els	1-nos-les 2-ns-les 3 ens les 4 ens les	1-nos-li 2-ns-li 3 ens li 4 ens li	1-nos-els 2-ns-els 3 ens els 4 ens els	1-nos-en 2-ns-en 3 ens en 4 ens n'	1-nos-hi 2-ns-hi 3 ens hi 4 ens hi	1-nos-ho 2-ns-ho 3 ens ho 4 ens ho				
V us	1-vos-el 2-us-el 3 us el 4 us l'	1-vos-la 2-us-la 3 us la 4 us l'	1-vos-els 2-us-els 3 us els 4 us els	1-vos-les 2-us-les 3 us les 4 us les	1-vos-li 2-us-li 3 us li 4 us li	1-vos-els 2-us-els 3 us els 4 us els	1-vos-en 2-us-en 3 us en 4 us n'	1-vos-hi 2-us-hi 3 us hi 4 us hi	1-vos-ho 2-us-ho 3 us ho 4 us ho	1-vos-em 2-us-em 3 us em 4 us m'		1-vos-ens 2-us-ens 3 us ens 4 us ens	
VI li IO gen.	1-l'hi 2-l'hi 3 l'hi 4 l'hi	1-la-hi 2-la-hi 3 la hi 4 la hi	1-los-hi 2-'ls-hi 3 els hi 4 els hi	1-les-hi 2-les-hi 3 les hi 4 les hi			1-li'n 2-li'n 3 li'n 4 li'n	1-li-hi 2-li-hi 3 li hi 4 li hi	1-li-ho 2-li-ho 3 li ho 4 li ho				
VII li IO Val.	1-li'l 2-li'l 3 li'l 4 li l'	1-li-la 2-li-la 3 li la 4 li l'	1-li'ls 2-li'ls 3 li'ls 4 li'ls	1-li-les 2-li-les 3 li les 4 li les			1-li'n 2-li'n 3 li'n 4 li n'	1-li-hi 2-li-hi 3 li hi 4 li hi	1-li-ho 2-li-ho 3 li ho 4 li ho				

	el (DO)	la (DO)	els (DO)	les (DO)	en	hi	ho
VIII els IO	1 -los-el 2 'ls-el 3 els el 4 els l'	1 -los-la 2 'ls-la 3 els la 4 els l'	1 -los-els 2 'ls-els 3 els els 4 els els	1 -los-les 2 'ls-les 3 els les 4 els les	1 -los-en 2 'ls-en 3 els en 4 els n'	1 -los-hi 2 'ls-hi 3 els hi 4 els hi	1 -los-ho 2 'ls-ho 3 els ho 4 els ho
IX el DO					1 -l'en 2 -l'en 3 l'en 4 el n'	1 -l'hi 2 -l'hi 3 l'hi 4 l'hi	
X els DO					1 -los-en 2 'ls-en 3 els en 4 els n'	1 -los-hi 2 'ls-hi 3 els hi 4 els hi	
XI la DO					1 -la'n 2 -la'n 3 la'n 4 la n'	1 -la-hi 2 -la-hi 3 la hi 4 la hi	
XII les DO					1 -les-en 2 -les-en 3 les en 4 les n'	1 -les-hi 2 -les-hi 3 les hi 4 les hi	
XIII en						1 -n'hi 2 -n'hi 3 n'hi 4 n'hi	

Note 1: In the table above, references are to row followed by column: thus Ib refers to row I column b, combinations of **em** with *f.* direct object **la**. More precise reference to rows is made by small arabic numerals 1–4.

Note 2: Ib 4, IIb 4, IIIb 4, IVb 4, Vb 4: before unstressed (h)i- or (h)u- the full form **la** is preferred to elided **l'**: e.g. **Me la informaran, Me la humilien.**

Note 3: IVg 1: for the first- and second-person plural imperative **-nos-** and **-us-** may be replaced in speech after imperatives by **'s** (pronounced [z]; see **12.1.3i**) even though this is not admitted as standard: e.g., **Anem's-en** for **Anem-nos-en**, **Felicitem's-en** for **Felicitem-nos-en**; **Aneu's-en** for **Aneu-vos-en**, **Feliciteu's-en** for **Feliciteu-vos-en.**

Note 4: Va–j 3–4 and VI 3–4: **vos** can replace **us** in all these groups, e.g., **Vos ho diré** for **Us ho diré, Vos en portarem** for **Us en portarem**.

Note 5: VIb–d, VIg–i: see below, sections **12.9.3.3–12.9.3.5** for full discussion of variant combinations and of non-standard forms involving third-person indirect objects.

Hauríem de queixar-nos del seu comportament.
We ought to complain about their behaviour.
→ **Hauríem de queixar-nos-en./Ens n'hauríem de queixar.**

Treu el cotxe del garatge.
Take the car out of the garage.
→ **Treu-l'en.**
    (cf. **Tregui'l (vostè) del garatge.**
      → **Tregui-l'en.**)

Us hem parlat sovint d'aquest problema.
We have often talked to you about this problem.
→ **Us n'hem parlat sovint.**
    (cf. **Hem de parlar-vos-en.**)

Ha desat els estris a l'armari.
He's put the utensils away in the cupboard.
→ **Els hi ha desat.**

No sé si queda gaire benzina al dipòsit.
I don't know if there's much petrol left in the tank.
→ **No sé si n'hi queda gaire.**

Poc es pensava que ho faríem.
Little did she think we'd do it.
→ **Poc s'ho pensava.**

Em vaig trobar/M'he trobat en Pere a la cantonada.
I met up with Pere on the corner.
→ **Me'l vaig trobar/Me l'he trobat a la cantonada.**

Fixa't en les seves paraules.
Take notice of her words.
→ **Fixa-t'hi.**

Us recordareu d'aquests detalls?
Will you remember these details?
→ **Us en recordareu?**
    (cf. **Us heu recordat d'aquests detalls.**
      → **Us n'heu recordat.**)

S'han rentat els peus/les mans.
They have washed their feet/hands.
→ **Se'ls/Se les han rentat.**

12.9.3.2 *Inversion of clitic order in Balearic dialects*

Balearic Catalan conserves the construction from the old language where
third-person non-reflexive direct objects (**el, els, la, les**) precede the indirect

object pronoun: thus, **Els m'ha llegit** for **Me'ls ha llegit** 'He has read them to me', **La't duré/La te duré** for **Te la duré** 'I'll bring it to you'. When pronouns follow the verb (e.g. **Posa-la't/Posa-la-te** for **Posa-te-la** 'Put it on') the stress shifts to the final syllable, as remarked in **12.1.2vi**. Balearic dialects also prefer weak pronouns before the third-person forms (**vostè(s)**) of the positive imperative: **Els me posi aquí** 'Put them here for me', as well as **Posi'ls-me aquí** (standard: **Posi-me'ls aquí**).

While deemed informal, these colloquial features are retained in written reproduction of local Balearic speech and in texts that adopt a popular tone.

12.9.3.3   Combinations of two third-person pronouns

Valencian dialects systematically combine indirect object **li** and **els** with direct object **el**, **els**, **la** and **les**, as shown in VII a–d and VIII a–d of the table on pp. 204–5.

> **Esta cadira és per a Roser; porta-li-la.**
> This chair is for Roser; take it over to her.

> **Si la pianista necessita algú que li gire els fulls, per què no li'ls gires tu?**
> If the pianist needs someone to turn the pages, why don't you turn them for her?

In normal usage, elsewhere, however, the substitution of **li** by **hi** is virtually ubiquitous, producing the combinations shown in VI a–d. (The behaviour of plural indirect object **els** is commented on below in this section and further in **12.9.3.5**.) Here the notional order of indirect object followed by direct object is inverted, with direct object **el**, **la**, **els**, and **les** preceding indirect object **hi**. (In fact, **hi** in this arrangement conforms to the rule, expressed in **12.9.2**, by which this pronoun comes last in any group where it occurs.)

> **Em va deixar el seu diccionari i encara no l'hi he tornat.**
> She lent me her dictionary and I still haven't given it back to her.

> **Sap quins llibres vol i diu que els hi enviem de seguida.**
> He knows which books he wants and tells us to send him them immediately.

> **Si s'ha oblidat de l'adreça, torna-la-hi a dir.**
> If she has forgotten the address tell her it again.

The **la + hi** combination shown in the last example is consistently pronounced as though it were **l'hi** and it is frequently found in this form in writing. Normative prescription, however, prefers the non-elided group shown above and below in:

Feia temps que reclamava aquesta concessió i finalment la hi han concedida.
She had been asking for this concession for some time and finally she has
  been granted it.

Similarly the combination **li** + **ho** is very frequently pronounced and sometimes reproduced in writing as **l'hi**, against even stronger prescriptivist
censure:

**Has explicat al pare com s'ha embolicat l'asssumpte? Si no, l'hi (= li ho)
hauries de dir ara mateix.**
Have you explained to father how complicated the matter has become? If
  not, you ought to tell him straightaway.

Li has confessat allò o no l'hi (= li ho) has confessat?
Did you confess that to him/her or did you not?

(For further discussion of the group **l'hi**, see **12.9.3.4**.)
  Expression of the indirect object by **hi** is accepted as standard only for the
singular, substituting **li**, but not for plural indirect object **els**. In combination
with any third-person direct object pronoun (**el, la, els, les, ho**) **els** forms the
groups shown in VIII a–d and VIII i of the table on pp. 204–5, thus:

Els ha pres la maleta i encara no els l'ha tornada.
He has taken their suitcase and still hasn't returned it to them.

Em demanen aquests informes, però no sé com els els podré fer arribar.
They're asking me for these reports, but I don't know how I'll be able to get
  them to them.

Most written styles observe this formal convention, but in spontaneous
speech the portmanteau **els hi** is pervasive for the combination of indirect
object **els** with any third-person direct object. See **12.9.3.5** below.

12.9.3.4 The groups l'hi and n'hi

In everyday spoken Catalan the groups **l'hi, la hi, li ho** and **li hi** are given a
pronunciation identical to that of the single pronoun **li**. In order to get the
spelling right, users need to keep in mind the syntactic and semantic functions that are being expressed.

(i) The group **l'hi** corresponds to two different sets of functional
     components:

   (a) Masculine singular direct object **el** combined with adverbial **hi**, as
        in **Posa el formatge a la nevera** 'Put the cheese in the fridge' → **Posa-
        l'hi.**

   (b) **Hi** standing for singular indirect object **li** (*m.* and *f.*) preceded by
        masculine singular direct object **el** (the alternative to the Valencian

solution **li'l** discussed in **12.9.3.3**), as in **Serveixi el segon plat a la meva senyora** 'Serve my wife her second course' → **Serveixi-l'hi** (Val. **Servisca-li'l**).

(ii) The group **la hi** corresponds to two different sets of functional components:

(a) Feminine singular direct object **la** combined with adverbial **hi**, as in **Fica la carta en aquest sobre** 'Put the letter in this envelope → **Fica-la-hi**.

(b) **Hi** standing for singular indirect object **li** (*m.* and *f.*) preceded by feminine singular direct object **la** (the alternative to the Valencian solution **li la** discussed in **12.9.3.3**), as in **Llegeix la carta a l'àvia** 'Read the letter to grandmother' → **Llegeix-la-hi** (Val. **Llig-li-la**).

(iii) The group **li ho** combines indirect object singular (*m.* and *f.*) **li** with neuter direct object **ho**, as in **Explicaré tot això al meu amic** 'I'll explain all this to my friend' → **Li ho explicaré**.

(iv) The group **li hi** combines indirect object singular (*m.* and *f.*) **li** with adverbial **hi**, as in **El pare vol que li dugui el paquet al despatx** 'Father wants me to take the parcel to his office for him' → **El pare vol que li hi dugui el paquet**.

L'hi occurs also as the solution for the combination **ho + hi** (see **12.9.3.9**), as in **Porta tot això a l'abocador** 'Take all this to the dump' → **Porta-l'hi**.

Against this background it is possible to differentiate in writing between the [li] syllable representing the single pronoun **li** or colloquial pronunciation of any of the combinations just analysed:

Ja li he contat el que va passar i no li ho penso tornar a repetir.
I have already told her what happened and I don't intend to repeat it (to her) again.

Escolti, li duc un paquet; on vol que l'hi posi?
Excuse me, I've brought you a parcel; where do you want me to put it for you?

The group **li'n** can also be analogously subjected to the **li** → **hi** substitution, producing **n'hi**. This form is less highly regarded than **li'n**, but it has wide currency in colloquial usage and does not appear out of place in informal written styles:

Si vostè vol sentir acudits, ja n'hi (= li n') explicaré un parell.
If you want to hear some jokes, I'll tell you a couple.

Here again functional analysis is useful to distinguish between this non-standard combination and the correct use of **n'hi**, when partitive **en** combines with adverbial (circumstantial complement) **hi: Posaran rètols a tots els pas-sadissos** 'They will put up signs in all the corridors' → **N'hi posaran**. See also above **12.6v** and **12.7v** on partitive **en** as complement of the verb **haver-hi: n'hi ha**, etc.

The exclamatory **Déu n'hi do** (lit. May God provide (some of it to him/ her)), expressing mild admiration at an expression of quantity or quality, shows popular fossilization of this **li'n** → **n'hi** transformation (though the form can also be justified on the grounds that **hi** does not correspond to any particular noun phrase; it could equally well be a vague locative).

12.9.3.5   The group els hi: colloquial versus normative usage

As remarked in **12.3.2.2**, the indirect object plural pronoun **els** (**-los**, **'ls**) is frequently pronounced with a support vowel [i], producing [əlzi] which, if represented in writing, appears as **els hi**. The function of **els hi = els**, a single pronoun, is seen in an instance like **He entregat el manuscrit als editors** 'I have delivered the manuscript to the publishers' → (non-standard) **Els hi he entregat el manuscrit**.

Correct standard combinations of indirect object **els** with any third-person direct object pronoun are shown in the table on pp. 204–5 (VIII a–d and VIII i), and are discussed at the end of section **12.9.3.3**. In colloquial practice, however, use of **els hi** is so prevalent that it operates as a kind of communicative and invariable 'free card' in any combination of a third-person direct object pronoun with indirect object **hi**, *when either of the complements (direct object or indirect object) is plural*. The following set, using **programa** (*m.*) 'programme' and **entrada** (*f.*) 'ticket' for the direct object, and **company** 'companion'/'friend' for the indirect object, provides illustration. The correct pronoun combination is given in the third column:

	non-standard	standard
He demanat el programa als companys.	**Els hi he demanat.**	**Els l'he demanat.**
He demanat els programes als companys.	**Els hi he demanat.**	**Els els he demanat.**
He demanat l'entrada als companys.	**Els hi he demanat.**	**Els l'he demanat.**
He demanat les entrades als companys.	**Els hi he demanat.**	**Els les he demanat.**
He demanat les entrades al company.	**Els hi he demanat.**	**Les hi (= li les) he demanat.**

The presence of locative **hi** can produce 'illogical' **els**:

	non-standard	standard
He demanat les entrades a l'oficina.	**Els hi he demanat.**	**Les hi he demanat.**

while **hi** itself is 'illogical' in analogous combinations of indirect object **els** with neuter **ho** and partitive **en**:

	non-standard	standard
He demanat tot això als companys.	Els hi he demanat.	Els ho he demanat.
He demanat entrades als companys.	Els hi he demanat.	Els n'he demanat.

The examples above are to be contrasted with other correct combinations of **els** with **hi**, where each component has its own grammatical function. As well as **He demanat els programes al company** → **Els hi he demanat** (els = programes, hi (=li) = al company), observe **hi** as locative in cases like the following: **Redactaran els fullets al despatx** 'They will write the leaflets in the office' → **Els hi redactaran**; **Enviaran els esborranys dels textos als col·laboradors/a les col·laboradores a la facultat** 'They will send the drafts of the texts to the contributors at the faculty' → **Els hi enviaran els esborranys dels textos.**

12.9.3.6   *First- and second-person pronouns in combination*

As shown in the diagram given in **12.9.2**, the only possible combination of first-person and second-person pronouns is one in which the second person precedes the first person. In these the first-person pronoun must be an indirect object (including ethic dative). Thus **No te m'enfadis** 'Don't get angry with me', **Te'ns pots adreçar en castellà si vols** 'You may address us in Castilian if you wish', **Ja us ens heu cruspit tots els cacauets?** 'Have you scoffed all the peanuts (that we put out or that we fancied eating)?' There is no possibility of forming a pronoun group in which a first-person pronoun (direct object or reflexive) precedes a second-person one. In order, then, to express the idea 'I shall come closer to you' (*sg.* and *pl.*) Catalan resorts to a strong pronoun for the indirect object 'to you': **M'acostaré a tu/a vosaltres**. Likewise, **Ens confessarem a tu/a vosaltres** 'We shall confess to you'. While there is perhaps no theoretical objection to ?**Me li acostaré** or ?**Me'ls acostaré**, ?**Ens li confessarem** or ?**Ens els confessarem**, with **li/els** (grammatically third person) standing for **vostè(s)** (semantically second person), in practice the strong pronoun construction invariably replaces the weak pronouns thus, **M'acostaré a vostè(s)** (or **M'hi acostaré** with **a vostè(s)** taken as a location rather than as an indirect object), **Ens confessarem a vostè(s)**.

12.9.3.7   *Pronominal verbs with clitic groups*

The regularity with which the ethic dative occurs in Catalan (see **12.3.2.3vi**, **23.1i** and **25.4**) together with the wide repertoire of pronominal verbs (Chapter 23 in general) means that many clitic groups are headed by a pronoun with one or other of these functions. Such combinations may involve an ethic dative or a reflexive element, a pronominal verb with an inanimate subject (as discussed in **23.4**) or impersonal **es** (see **29.2**):

Ethic dative:

No t'ho prenguis així.	Don't take it like that.
Ja ens en comprarem.	We'll (certainly) buy some (of them for ourselves).

Reflexive:

Sembla que se n'han rentat les mans.	It appears they've washed their hands of it.

Pronominal verbs:

Poc s'ho podia haver imaginat.	Little could he have imagined it.
S'hi han equivocat de mala manera.	They have got this badly wrong.
Abans no eres tan sorrut; t'hi has tornat amb els anys.	You used not to be so surly; you've become so over the years.
Te'ls pots endur si vols.	You can take them away with you if you wish.
No s'hi amoïni, senyora.	Don't worry about it, madam.
Se'ns ha embussat l'aigüera.	Our sink has got blocked.
Se m'ha acabat el tabac.	I've run out of tobacco.
No se'n deu haver recordat.	She can't have remembered.

Impersonal:

Se n'ha parlat molt.	There has been a lot of talk about it.
No s'hi pot aparcar.	There's no parking there.
No se'ls pot demanar més.	No more can be asked of them.

12.9.3.8   Phonetic contact in pronoun groups

Related to the defective forms of single pronouns discussed in **12.1.3** is the persistent appearance, in speech of all registers, of a transitional vowel sound [ə] separating two consonants in contact within a clitic group. This support vowel – an analogue of the initial vowel of the reinforced pronouns – is conventionally represented in deliberately non-standard writing by e standing between the affected pronouns. One frequently hears for example **Us e les portaré demà** 'I'll bring them to you tomorrow' (parallel with the reinforced masculine plural **els** in **Us els portaré demà**), **Els e n'hauries d'explicar més, d'acudits com aquest** 'You ought to tell them more jokes like that one', **Ens e l'ha posat al balcó** 'He's put it on the balcony for us'. The standard form of the above examples is: **Us les portaré, Els n'hauries, Ens l'ha posat**. The intercalated **e** appears in only those written texts which deliberately reproduce the colloquial pronunciation.

12.9.3.9 *Impossible combinations*

A sequence of two identical clitics is ungrammatical. Thus (see **29.2.1i**) impersonal use of **es** is incompatible with verbs that are themselves reflexive or pronominal. The multiplicity of functions of **en** and **hi** likewise means that other combinations of identical clitics are semantically interpretable but decisively avoided in practice. A sentence like **Traurem moltes conclusions del debat** 'We shall draw plenty of conclusions from the debate' could have either complement represented by **en: En traurem moltes conclusions** or **En traurem moltes (de conclusions) del debat.** It is not possible however for these to be reduced to ***en + en** in combination; the only solution is (ambiguous) **En traurem moltes.** Similarly for notional ***hi + hi: Anirem a Caldetes amb el cotxe, i els altres també hi aniran** 'We shall go to Caldetes by car and so will the others (go there in it)', not ***. . . hi hi aniran.**

Combinations of **ho** with either **en** or **hi** produce either the conversion of **ho** to **l'** (as mentioned in **12.9.3.4: Porta tota això a l'abocador → Porta-l'hi**) or use of a single clitic (suppressing or giving alternative expression to the other complement): **Treu això del calaix** 'Take that out of the drawer' **→ Treu-l'en/ Treu-ho del calaix/Treu-ne això.**

This phenomenon may be resolved differently when there is a 'lexically based' clitic component of the infinitive (e.g. **dur-se'n** 'take away', **passar- (s')ho bé** 'have a good time'). In such cases the lexically based pronouns may remain intact in contact with other clitics:

Això, pots dur-te-n'ho.   You can take that away with you.

12.9.4 MOBILITY AFFECTING PRONOUN GROUPS

Clitic mobility is discussed in **12.2.3.** The main principles set out there with regard to single pronouns apply also to pronoun groups, and transformations with two (or more) pronouns can readily be created for several of the examples given in the earlier section: e.g., **Ens l'estava arreglant/Estava arreglant-nos-el/-nos-la** 'She was mending it for us', **Penses explicar-li-ho aviat?/Li ho penses explicar aviat?** 'Do you intend to explain it to him/her soon?' (The popular tendency to attach clitics to both verbs, an aspect of redundancy (see **12.8**), is avoided in all careful speech, and in all writing: (non-standard: **T'ho vaig dir-t'ho ben clarament** for **T'ho vaig dir/Vaig dir-t'ho ben clarament** 'I told you quite clearly').)

A pronoun group which logically belongs together will not be split so that one item goes before the conjugated verb and the other is attached to the dependant infinitive or gerund.

Si ens els vinguessin a oferir a nosaltres. = Si vinguessin a oferir-nos-els a nosaltres.
*Si ens vinguessin a oferir-los.
If they were to come and offer them to us.

The only cases where weak pronouns are not combined within the same clause are when they are logically the complements of different verbs, and thus not a group:

Es van atrevir a insultar-lo.   They dared to insult him.
T'hauries d'afanyar a corregir-ho.   You should make haste to correct it.

Causative verbs (**25.5**) allow separation in this way or proclitic attachment of the group to the first verb, that is, they allow clitic raising (**12.2.3**):

Ens deixaran repassar-ho. =
Ens ho deixaran repassar.   They will let us revise it.

(But obviously not *****Deixaran repassar-nos-ho**, which would involve clitic lowering, much less *****Ho deixaran repassar-nos** which would involve both clitic lowering and illogical splitting.)

Fes-lo parlar-ne. = Fes-l'en parlar.   Make him talk about it.

Perception verbs governing an infinitival clause work in the same way:

Li sentiren dir-ho. = Li ho sentiren dir. They heard her say it.

12.9.5   GROUPS CONTAINING MORE THAN TWO PRONOUNS

Groups of three, and even four or more, pronouns do occur. In a sentence like **He d'enviar la carta als meus parents a Tarragona** 'I must send the letter to my relatives in Tarragona' all three complements can be represented in pronoun form as either **Els la hi he d'enviar** or **He d'enviar-los-la-hi**. The verb **anar-se'n** 'to go (away)' already has a lexically based two-pronoun group in the infinitive, and this group can readily be augmented with other complements:

Se me'n va anar el peu i vaig caure.   My foot slipped and I fell.

In another instance involving this verb a parent might ask in surprise to a young child who has gone to school on her own:

Te me n'hi has anat tota sola?   Did you go off there all alone?

As in the last example, these complex pronoun groups almost inevitably involve a pronominal verb or use of the ethic dative, present here in **me**, untranslatable in this case but expressing the speaker's moral interest in the situation.

The order of three or more pronouns in combination conforms to the diagram shown in **12.9.2**.

12.9.6   FORMS OF PRONOUNS IN COMPLEX GROUPS

The following observations describe effects on form and spelling when a two-pronoun group is augmented. A basic rule is that a group may have only one apostrophe, which goes as far to the right as possible:

(i)   Alterations to the second pronoun in the group:

   (a)   'm/em and 't/et become respectively m' and t' before hi or ho, me and te before any other pronoun:

No se'm sentia.	I couldn't be heard.
No se m'hi sentia.	I couldn't be heard there.
Se't quedarà l'original.	He'll keep the original (that belongs to you).
Se te'l quedarà.	He'll keep it.

   (b)   El/lo and 'l become l' before hi or en:

Feu-lo venir.	Make him come.
Feu-l'hi venir.	Make him come there.
Hem d'endur-nos-el d'aquest lloc.	We must take it/him from this place.
Hem d'endur-nos-l'en.	We must take it/him from here.

   (c)   En and 'n become n' before hi or ho:

Ens en portaran al despatx.	They'll bring us some to the office.
Ens n'hi portaran.	They'll bring us some there.
Has d'emportar-te'n tot això.	You must take all this away from there.
Has d'emportar-te-n'ho.	You must take it all away from there.

(ii)   Forms of the last pronoun in a group:

   (a)   Em, ens, et, el, els, en or 'm, 'ns, 't, 'l, 'ls, 'n occur according to whether the second pronoun ends, respectively, in a consonant or a vowel:

Se'ns en van servir unes racions enormes.
We were served enormous portions of it.

No se me'n podia deixar en aquell moment.
I couldn't be lent any at that time.

Se me'n reia.
He was making fun of me over it.

Se'ns en reia.
He was making fun of us over it.

(b)   **M', t', l', n'** occur if they precede a verb beginning in a vowel or **h** + vowel:

Se te l'ha quedat.	He's kept it (and it belonged to you).
(cf. **Se te'l quedarà.**	He'll keep it.)
Te'ns en menjaràs el tros més bo.	You'll eat the tastiest bit of it.
(cf. **Te'ns n'has menjat el tros més bo.**	You've eaten the tastiest bit of it.)

(In speech the pronoun group in both of the last two examples would sound like **te'ns en** because the second one would be affected by the phonetic feature described in **12.9.3.8**, with the intercalated support vowel producing *****te'ns e n'has . . .**)

Se me l'ha empassada.	He's gone and swallowed it.
(cf. **Se me la va empassar.**	He went and swallowed it.)

(c)   The **se'n** group (characteristic of verbs of motion) can admit a third intercalated pronoun or can precede adverbial **hi**, according to the consecutive order shown in the diagram at **12.9.2**, and as already illustrated by the last example given in **12.9.5** above. Further examples:

El gos aquest, si em distrec ni que sigui un segon, se me'n va al carrer.
If I turn my back for even a second, this dog (of mine) runs off into the street.

Em distrec un segon, i se me n'hi va.
I turn my back for a second and he's off out there.

Another common pattern of three-pronoun grouping is reflexive **es** (in the full form **se**) preceding the combinations **l'hi, la hi, els hi, les hi** (and adapted variants):

Tots els del grup es van enfurismar quan ell se'ls hi va ficar.
Everybody in the group got mad when he interfered (in what they were doing).

The incompatible pairs mentioned in **12.9.3.9** (*****en en**, *****hi hi**, *****ho en**, *****ho hi**) obviously cannot figure in any larger combination.

(d)   **Els n'hi** (pronounced **els e n'hi**) often occurs as a colloquial variant of **els en**. Functional analysis discloses that **hi** is redundant in (non-standard) **Els n'hi va distribuir** ← **El conferenciant va distribuir resums als assistents** 'The lecturer distributed summaries to those present', and that the correct combination is **els en** 'some to them'. There are instances, however, where **els n'hi** is a valid standard combination where each of the three components has its own grammatical function. **Ha posat paranys per als intrusos al bosc** 'He has set traps for intruders in the wood' could genuinely be reduced to **Els n'hi ha posat**.

The intricately exacting nature of the Catalan pronoun system endows the language with great agility and expressiveness, and careful attention to this important area of grammar can be highly rewarding. The linguist Joan Solà presents a progression that culminates in a combination of six weak pronouns (**Se te me li n'hi posarà tres**) as a reduction of the sentence **Aquell amic nostre** (→ **te me**) **és capaç de posar-se a casa** (→ **hi**) **tres parents** (→ **'n**) **del senyor Pere** (→ **li**) 'That friend of ours is able to give lodging in his house to three relatives of Senyor Pere'. Naturally, pronoun combinations such as this are far from common, but they are certainly not ruled out in principle. Combinations of two or three pronouns occur regularly in everyday speech.

PART II: ADVERBS, PREPOSITIONS, AND CONJUNCTIONS

13 ADVERBS AND ADVERBIALS

In Catalan the distinction between prepositions (which take complements) and adverbs (which do not) is not a fundamental one; as will become apparent, many common items appear in both syntactic roles. Traditionally, adverbs and adverbials qualify verbs, adjectives, predicates and whole clauses or sentences. (The name adverbials is given to phrases, often prepositional phrases or noun phrases in terms of their internal structure, which function in a similar manner to adverbs.) Adverbs which are themselves followed by prepositional phrase complements will be treated in **14.3**, as compound prepositions; those which are followed by **que** + a finite clause will be discussed in Chapter 33, as adverbial clauses. The regular comparatives, etc., of adverbs are formed in the same way as those of adjectives (see Chapter 5).

Many common adverbs are simple, underived words: **ara** 'now', **fora** 'out', **força** 'quite', **bé** 'well'. Some adjectives, particularly in fixed expressions, do duty as adverbs without change, for example, **aguantar ferm** 'hold tight', **jugar brut** 'play dirty'; see section **13.1.2**.

Some adverbs and adverbials can receive the diminutive suffix -**et**, for example, **llunyet** 'a bit far', **de presseta** 'in a bit of a hurry', **poc a poquet** 'rather slowly'/'gradually'; likewise the superlative affix -**íssim**, as in **llunyíssim** 'extremely far', **tardíssim** 'extremely late'.

A number of adverbs are formed by compounding, such as **enlaire** 'aloft' (from **en l'aire** 'in the air'), **només** 'only' (from **no** 'not' + **més** 'more'), **tothora** 'always' (from **tot** 'all' + **hora** 'hour'). Adverbs which are regularly derived from adjectives with the suffix -**ment** (see **13.1**) are, strictly speaking, compound words. Some adverbials are derived from adjectives or verbs using the suffix -**ons**, as in **de genollons** 'on one's knees' (from **genoll** 'knee'), **a reculons** 'backwards' (from **recular** 'retreat'). The structure of adverbials is in general quite varied; many of them superficially resemble prepositional phrases, but the noun they appear to contain may have no independent existence: thus **a dojo** 'abundantly', **de gairell** 'obliquely', **d'esquitllentes** 'stealthily'. Even when the noun involved occurs elsewhere, the adverbial may have an unpredictable sense, as in **amb prou feines** 'hardly' (lit. with enough tasks), **de puntetes** 'on tiptoe' (lit. on little tips). Only a selection of adverbials is included in the following sections.

The sentence position of adverbs and adverbials is discussed in **36.8**.

13.1   MORPHOLOGY OF ADVERBS

13.1.1   ADVERBS IN -ment

Adverbs are productively derived from adjectives by adding **-ment** to the feminine form. (If the adjective is invariable for gender, the feminine form is the same as the masculine, of course.) A written accent on the feminine adjective is retained, since adverbs in **-ment** are pronounced with two stresses, like compounds.

m. adj.	*f. adj.*	*adverb*	
viu	**viva**	**vivament**	in a lively way
exprés	**expressa**	**expressament**	expressly, on purpose
lliure	**lliure**	**lliurement**	freely
fàcil	**fàcil**	**fàcilment**	easily
automàtic	**automàtica**	**automàticament**	automatically

Consecutive adverbs in -ment

When two or more adverbs are conjoined, **-ment** may be omitted from all but the first, though it need not be: **humilment i devota** or **humilment i devotament** 'humbly and devoutly'.

13.1.2   ADJECTIVES UNCHANGED AS ADVERBS

A few adjectives are quite widely used adverbially without suffixation, especially **clar** 'clear(ly)', **ràpid** 'quick(ly)', **lent** 'slow(ly)', though the derived adverbs in **-ment** are equally current:

Ho va explicar bastant clar/clarament.	She explained it fairly clearly.
No ho van fer gaire ràpid/ràpidament.	They didn't do it very quickly.
Parlaven molt lent/lentament.	They spoke very slowly.

Just 'precisely'/'exactly'/'just' is probably more frequent than **justament** in this sense (**justament** also means 'justly', 'duly'):

S'ha presentat just quan tu te n'anaves.
She turned up just as you were leaving.

Hem calculat just el que gastarem.
We've calculated precisely what we shall spend.

Tenien el taulell just al mig de la botiga.
They had the counter right in the middle of the shop.

Otherwise, adjectives used adverbially tend to be confined to certain set expressions, where, often, the corresponding English expression also uses an adjective adverbially:

agafar fort	hold tight/grasp firmly	**mirar prim**	be fussy
		parlar baix	speak low
aguantar ferm	hold fast	**parlar mal**	speak ill
anar llarg	take a long time	**passar just**	just go through/just
anar llarg de	have too much		fit
costar car	cost dear	**saber greu**	regret (**Això em sap**
anar curt	be short (of money)		**greu** 'I am sorry
jugar brut	play dirty		about that')
jugar net	play clean	**saltar alt**	jump high
llaurar dret	plough straight	**treballar fi**	work skilfully
llaurar fondo	plough deep	**veure-hi clar**	see clearly
menjar dolç	eat sweet things	**viure tranquil**	live in peace
menjar salat	eat savoury food	etc.	

13.2.   ADVERBS/ADVERBIALS OF PLACE (INCLUDING DIRECTION)

on	where (interrogative and relative)
onsevol (onsevulla/onsevulga)	wherever
pertot, arreu, pertot arreu, a tot arreu	everywhere
enlloc	nowhere, anywhere (in negative, interrogative or conditional contexts)
Si els veus enlloc, m'ho dius, oi?	If you see them anywhere, you'll tell me, won't you?
en algun lloc, per alguna banda, etc.	somewhere

Note that there is no ready-made expression in Catalan for 'somewhere', though in the Balearics **a part o a banda** may have this sense (**No trob el paraigua; el dec haver deixat a part o a banda** 'I can't find my umbrella; I must have left it somewhere'). While **onsevol** is current in Valencian and **onsevulla** in Balearic, the terms for 'wherever' are elsewhere exclusively literary (and not very common). One is more likely to say **en qualsevol lloc** 'in whatever place', or to use some other expression, as in **on vulguis** 'where you wish', **a tot arreu on vagi** 'wherever she goes' (lit. to everywhere where she may go), **Els trobaré, on siguin** 'I'll find them wherever they are'.

Demonstrative adverbs of place

ací (Val.)	here
aquí	here, (there)
allí, allà	there
d'ací d'allà	from side to side
ençà	this side, nearer
d'aquell temps ençà/d'ençà d'aquell temps	since that time
enllà	that side, beyond
Fes-te enllà.	Go further off.

Allí and **allà** are synonymous; both are widely used. In Valencian, where a three-term demonstrative system is in use (**6.2**), **ací** 'here (near me)' corresponds to **este** 'this', **allí/allà** 'there'; 'yonder' corresponds to **aquell** 'that'; and, theoretically, **aquí** 'there (near you)' corresponds to **eixe** 'that (near you)'. Spontaneous Valencian uses **ahí** for 'there (near you)', but this form is avoided in writing.

Horizontal directions

dins, dintre	in, inside, within
endins	in (motion)
Poseu-lo més endins; que així caurà.	Put it further in; it'll fall off there.
mar endins	out to sea
terra endins	inland
fora, al defora	out, outside
enfora	out, outwards
Caminava pit enfora.	He walked with his chest out.
La casa d'ells és més enfora.	Their house is further away.
davant, al davant	in front
endavant, avant	forward(s), ahead
Endavant!	Come in! (said in response to a knock at the door)
darrere, al darrere, rere; detràs (non-standard)	behind
endarrere, enrere, arrere	backwards
Fes-te enrere!	Get back!
molts anys endarrere	many years ago, many years previously

(a la) dreta	(on the) right
Tombeu a la dreta.	Turn right.
(a l')esquerra	(on the) left
L'àrab s'escriu de dreta a esquerra.	Arabic is written from right to left.

Note that the locative adverb forms beginning with **en-** often (though not always) imply motion or direction and have a deictic sense, relating the movement (perhaps vaguely) to the location of the speaker or hearer.

The spellings **darrera**, **enrera**, etc., are still widely found, but the forms in **-e** are now regarded as correct by the Institut d'Estudis Catalans.

Vertical directions

sobre, dessobre (literary), **damunt, al damunt**	on top, above
Deixa-ho allà sobre.	Leave it on top there.
com damunt hem dit	as we have said above
sota, dessota, al dessota, davall	below, underneath
(**davall** is preferred in Valencia and the Balearics, the other forms elsewhere)	
L'un era sobre, l'altre sota.	One was on top, the other underneath.
amunt	up(wards)
Avui pujarem molt amunt.	Today we'll go quite far up.
avall	down(wards)
Es passejaven amunt i avall.	They were walking up and down.
alt	high
volar alt	fly high
baix	low
L'arquer ha tirat massa baix.	The archer aimed too low.
dalt	up above, upstairs, at the top
S'han reunit (a) dalt al despatx.	They are meeting upstairs in the office.
baix	down below, downstairs, at the bottom
tenir el cotxe a baix	keep the car downstairs (in the basement)
(a) dalt de tot	at/to the very top
de dalt a baix	from top to toe
daltabaix	down (from top to bottom)
Es va enfilar i va caure daltabaix de la teulada.	She climbed up and fell (all the way) down from the roof.
al capdamunt	at/to the top

al capdavall	at/to the bottom, (fig.) finally, after all
enlaire	aloft, up in the air
Mans enlaire!	Hands up!

Amunt and **avall** usually express movement, whereas (**a**) **dalt** and (**a**) **baix** denote locations, but note **com hem dit més amunt** 'as we said above', **com llegirem més avall** 'as we shall see below'; **dalt** and **baix** usually refer to the top and bottom of something continuous, whereas **sobre** and **sota** express the relative location of separate objects. Note expressions like **Rambla amunt** 'up the Rambla', **escales amunt** 'up the steps', **muntanya avall** 'down the mountain', **Les llàgrimes li queien galtes avall** 'Tears rolled down his cheeks'.

Proximity

prop	near(by)
lluny	far (away)
a la vora, a tocar	close
Ara ja hi som molt a la vora.	Now we are very close to it.
al costat	beside, alongside
devora (Bal.)	alongside
als afores	on the outskirts
en mig, al mig	in the middle, in the midst
entremig	in between, in the midst
Ell va sortir d'entremig.	He came out from among (them).
a l'entorn, al voltant	around, in the vicinity
L'hort té arbres tot al voltant.	The plot has trees all round.
a part, a banda	aside, on one side
Aquest el posarem a part.	We'll put this one on one side.

Notice that the simple adverbs, at least, can readily be preceded by a preposition, to indicate direction more precisely.

On és?	Where is he/she/it?
D'on és?	Where is he/she/it from?
On anem? or **A on anem?**	Where shall we go?
cap allà	in that direction (lit. towards there)
No les vèiem per enlloc.	We didn't see them anywhere about.
des d'aquí	from here
Ja són a fora.	They are (lit. at) outside now. = **Ja són fora.**

When **a** = 'at', the expressions with **a** are synonymous with those without **a**; the forms with **a** are less formal: **a on, a dins/a dintre, a davant, a darrere, a damunt, a sobre, a sota, a dalt, a baix, a prop.** Similarly **a lluny** is current in Valencian and Balearic, but is regarded as non-standard.

13.3 ADVERBS/ADVERBIALS OF TIME

As with the adverbs/adverbials of place, those of time which denote a point can be preceded by a preposition; so, for example, **des de quan** 'since when', **des d'aleshores** 'since then', **des de sempre** literally 'since always', **des d'abans** 'since before', **d'ara endavant** 'from now on', **a partir de llavors/de llavors ençà/ des de llavors** 'since then'.

quan	when
note **A quina hora?**	At what time (of day)? When?
ara	now
ara com ara, ara per ara, de moment	for the moment, at present
Ara com ara, no sabria dir-t'ho.	I couldn't tell you at present.
a hores d'ara	by now, by this time
A hores d'ara ja deu haver arribat a Nova York.	By now he must have arrived in New York.
actualment	currently, at present
llavors, aleshores (literary)	then
ja	already
Ja érem lluny de Tortosa.	We were already a long way from Tortosa.

The basic meaning of **ja** is 'already'; but its use in Catalan is somewhat different from the corresponding word in English. **Ja** corresponds to 'now', 'by now', when it emphasizes that any earlier stage is over and done with:

> **Tot això ja és molt diferent.** All this is very different now.

In negative and interrogative contexts **ja** may correspond to '(no) longer', 'yet':

> **Ja no tens dret a fer això.** You no longer have the right to do that.
>
> **Ja són aquí?** Are they here yet?
> (different from: **Encara són aquí?** Are they still here?)

Often it serves to reinforce a present-tense verb and may not be translated in English:

–Cambrer! –Ja vinc.	'Waiter!' 'I'm coming.'
Ja veig que era molt fàcil.	I can see that it was very easy.

With a future tense, **ja** indicates certainty on the part of the speaker, or relates the future time closely to the present:

Ja ho faran.	They will do it (I'm sure).
Ja veurem si és veritat o no.	We'll (soon) see whether it is true or not.

encara	still, yet (in negative contexts)
Encara treballes a l'ajuntament?	Are you still working for the council?
No l'he vista encara, la pel·lícula.	I haven't seen it yet, the film.

adés, suara (Bal.)	just now, in a moment
Adés s'hi negava.	Just now she refused to do it.
Espera-la, que suara tornarà.	Wait for her; she'll be back in a moment.

Adés is current in Valencian, and **suara** is current in the Balearics and Valencian; in Catalonia they are rather literary.

ara mateix	right now, this minute
abans de gaire	before long
aviat, prompte (Val.), **prest** (Val., Bal.)	soon
com més aviat millor	as soon as possible
de seguida, tot seguit, tot d'una (Bal.)	immediately
sempre, tothora (literary)	always
sovint	often
tot sovint, ben sovint	very often
freqüentment, espesses vegades (Bal.)	frequently
a vegades, de vegades, a voltes (esp. Val.)	sometimes
a la llarga, més tard o més d'hora	sooner or later
de tant en tant, ara i adés (literary), **adesiara** (literary, Bal.)	from time to time
rarament, rares vegades, poc sovint, de tard en tard	rarely
una vegada, un cop, una volta (Val.), **un pic** (Bal.)	once
d'hora, dejorn (Val., Bal.)	early
sopar d'hora	have dinner early

tard	late
mai, jamai (literary)	never, ever (see **26.1.5**)
mai més, pus mai (Bal.)	never again, ever again (see **26.1.9**)
No hi tornaré mai més.	I'll never go there again.
alhora, a la vegada	at the same time, at once
Hem arribat tots tres alhora.	We all three arrived at once.
a deshora, inoportunament	at the wrong time
abans	before
dos dies abans	two days before
per endavant	in advance
després	after(wards)
mentrestant, entretant, en l'endemig (literary), **mentrimentres** (Val.)	meanwhile
Tu, què feies mentrestant?	What were you doing in the meantime?

Temporal deictics

avui, hui (Val.)	today
ahir	yesterday
demà	tomorrow
aquest matí, avui (de)matí	this morning
aquest vespre, avui vespre	this evening
enguany	this year
l'endemà	the next day
anit	tonight, last night
On dormirem anit?	Where shall we sleep tonight?
Tota la família va venir anit.	All the family came last night.

Though current elsewhere, **anit** is usually replaced in Barcelona by **aquesta nit** 'this night', which can refer to the night at either end of today. Similarly **enguany** is replaced by **aquest any** in Barcelona.

anit passada	last night
abans-d'ahir, despús-ahir (Val., Bal., etc.)	the day before yesterday
demà passat, despús-demà (Val., etc.)	the day after tomorrow
demà passat l'altre	three days from now

(**L'altre** may be added to the other 'day before yesterday' and 'day after tomorrow' forms in the same way.)

To situate a state or event at a specific moment in time, a noun with some kind of modifying expression needs no preposition:

El veiem cada dia.	We see him every day.
El vam veure aquell cap de setmana.	We saw him that weekend.
l'any passat	last year
l'agost de l'any passat	in August last year
el dia trenta	on the 30th
aquest vespre, avui vespre	this evening
el 1958 (**any** understood)	in 1958
el quinze de gener	on January 15th
el mes vinent	next month
el segle passat (or **al segle passat**)	last century
Va arribar l'u de setembre.	She came on the first of September.
ahir vespre	yesterday evening
demà matí	tomorrow morning.

(Valencian and Balearic use **dia x** without article or preposition: **Una nota que es publicà dia 26 de febrer** 'A note which was published on 26 February'. On the general use of the article with days and dates, see **3.1.4.4**.)

There are alternative ways to express the year of some event: **J.S. Bach va néixer l'any 1685/va néixer el 1685/va néixer en 1685** 'J.S. Bach was born in 1685'.

The names of the days of the week are used alone indicating 'time at which': **Van arribar diumenge** 'They came on Sunday', but if preceded by an adjective there needs to be an article: **Dissabte passat hi hagué un robatori** 'Last Saturday there was a burglary' = **El passat dissabte hi hagué un robatori**. Note **Avui som dilluns** 'Today is Monday' (lit. Today we are Monday). The plural form of the weekdays, with definite article but no preposition, expresses weekly occurrences: **Els dimecres mengem arròs** 'On Wednesdays we eat paella'. (Some normative grammarians prefer the singular here: **El dimecres mengem arròs**, but the plural is used more spontaneously.)

Distributive expressions like 'five times a week' use the definite article in Catalan, with **el** generally preceded by **a** to give the form **al**; the forms **l'**, **la**, more often occur without **a**:

cobrar 15.000 pessetes al mes	get 15,000 pesetas a/per month
Guanya mil pessetes (a) l'hora.	She earns 1000 pesetas an hour.
Tinc lliçó dues vegades (a) la setmana.	I have a lesson twice a week.

To express 'ago' Catalan uses the verb **fer** 'make' (third-person singular only): thus **Ha sortit fa deu minuts** 'He went out ten minutes ago', **Hi treballa des de fa uns quants anys** 'She has been working here for several years' (lit. . . . since it makes several years, i.e. . . . since several years ago), **Deu fer uns deu anys d'ençà que va morir** 'It'll be about ten years ago that he died' = 'It'll be about ten years since he died', **Quant fa que vas canviar de feina?** 'How long ago did you change your job?', 'How long is it since you changed your job?', **Fa només un quart que han marxat** 'They left only a quarter of an hour ago'. Unlike 'ago' in English which is restricted to present tense contexts, the Catalan **fer** construction can shift to other tenses. Thus we can say **Feia només un quart que havien marxat** 'They had left only a quarter of an hour before/ previously'. On tense usage in such constructions see **17.2.2** and **32.2.24**.

Times of day

de dia, de dies	by day
de nit, de nits	by night
a punta de dia, a trenc d'alba	at daybreak
de matí, de bon matí	early in the morning
al matí	in the morning
a mig matí	mid-morning
a(l) migdia	at noon
a l'hora de dinar	at lunch time
havent dinat	after lunch
a la tarda, a la vesprada (Val.),	in the afternoon
(a) horabaixa/s'horabaixa (Bal.)	
a hora baixa	late afternoon
cap al tard, al capvespre, a entrada de	late afternoon, early evening, when
fosc	it gets dark
al vespre	in the evening
havent sopat	after dinner
a la nit	at night

13.4 ADVERBS/ADVERBIALS OF MANNER

There is an extensive, open, list of adverbs of manner and manner phrases, including the majority of the adverbs derived from adjectives by means of the suffix **-ment** (**13.1.1**). The simple ones are:

com	how, as (interrogative, exclamation, and relative)
Com t'ho has fet, això?	How did you (manage to) do that?
Fes-ho com et sembli.	Do it how you choose.
així	thus, in this way
ben, bé	well, very
mal, malament	badly

The forms **ben** and **mal** are used only preceding what they qualify, thus **ben fet** 'well done', **ben difícil** 'quite difficult', **ben a la vora** 'quite near'; 'very near', **mal adobat** 'badly repaired', **mal vist** 'disapproved of' (lit. badly seen). **Bé** and **malament** are used in other positions: **Ho fas molt bé** 'You're doing very well'.

To express the comparative and superlative ('better', 'best', 'worse', 'worst'), the regular **més** 'more' can precede all these forms (**més ben, més bé, més mal, més malament**); alternatively, the forms **millor** 'better', 'best', **pitjor** 'worse', 'worst' can be used (see **5.2.1**).

Avui va tot més malament/pitjor.
Today it's all going worse.

El finestró ha quedat més ben pintat que la porta.
The shutter has turned out better painted than the door.

Other simple manner adverbs

debades, endebades	in vain, (Val.) gratis
corrents	quickly, in a hurry
arreu	in succession
dempeus (literary)	standing

'Standing, on foot' is more commonly expressed with the adjective **dret**.

Posa't dreta!	Stand up straight!
exprés (= **expressament, a posta, a dretes**)	on purpose
ensems (literary)	together

'Together' is more commonly expressed by means of the plural adjectives **junts, plegats**, or with the temporal adverb **alhora** 'at the same time':

Ara estem junts.	Now we're together.
Sempre van plegats.	They're always together.
No podeu entrar tots alhora.	You can't all get in together.
igual	in the same way

Unlike English, Catalan readily puts a manner adverb between a verb and its direct object (particularly if the adverb is shorter; see also **36.8**):

Escriu-me corrents aqueixa carta.
Write me that letter quickly.

Va resoldre hàbilment la difícil situació.
He skilfully sorted out the difficult situation./He sorted out the difficult situation skilfully.

Note:

d'alguna manera/en alguna manera	somehow
d'altra manera	otherwise
M'han convidat; d'altra manera no hi aniria.	They invited me; I wouldn't go otherwise.

See **17.2.1.2** for the use of adverbs with compound tenses.

13.4.1   USAGE OF MANNER ADVERBS

Catalan uses derived manner adverbs in **-ment** rather less than English uses corresponding adverbs in '-ly'. Adverbial notions will often be expressed in prepositional phrases as below, or using an adjective, in apposition with the subject of the clause.

d'una manera honesta	honourably
d'una manera impacient	impatiently
amb sinceritat	sincerely
amb impaciència	impatiently
Va respondre irritat.	He replied irritably.

13.5   ADVERBS/ADVERBIALS OF QUALIFICATION AND INCLUSION

Traditionally these adverbs/adverbials are not identified as a separate semantic or pragmatic category; one finds them scattered among adverbs of manner, of degree, sentence adverbs, and elsewhere.

ben bé, exactament, precisament, just	exactly
No és ben bé el mateix.	It's not exactly the same/not quite the same.
És precisament el que volia.	It's just what I wanted.
just darrere la comissaria	right behind the police station
més aviat, més aïnes (Val.), **més tost** (Bal.)	rather
Sentia més aviat compassió que por.	I felt pity rather than fear.
El trobo més aviat dolç.	I find it on the sweet side.
sobretot, més que més	especially, above all
No hi volen anar, més que més anant-hi tu.	They don't want to go there, especially since you're going.
només, sols, solament, tan sols, únicament	only
fins, fins i tot, àdhuc (literary), **inclús** form not accepted by IEC)	even
L'aplaudiren tots, fins i tot els seus adversaris.	They all applauded him, even his opponents.
(non-standard) **Inclús arribarà a parlar català.**	She will even manage to speak Catalan.
ni, ni tan sols	not even (see **26.1.6**)

almenys, si més no, si altra cosa no, almanco (Bal.)	at least
Almenys voldria que em contestessin.	I wish at least they would answer.
Digueu-me, si més no, qui us ho ha dit.	Tell me, at least, who told you.
si fa no fa, més o menys, més o manco (Bal.), **aproximadament**	approximately, more or less
L'habitació feia si fa no fa sis metres de llarg.	The room was approximately six metres long.
amb prou feines, amb prou faena (Val.), **a penes**	hardly, no sooner
Eren tants, que amb prou feines els hem poguts comptar.	There were so many that we could hardly count them.
A penes havíem sortit de casa que es va posar a ploure.	No sooner had we gone out than it started to rain.
pel cap alt	at most
pel cap baix	at the least
també	also, as well
tampoc	either, neither (see **26.1.7**)
L'endemà tampoc no feia bon temps.	The weather wasn't good the next day either.
gairebé, quasi	almost, nearly
Gairebé no poguérem parlar.	We were hardly able to speak.
Quasi no me n'adonava.	I was hardly aware of it.
Aproven gairebé sempre.	They nearly always pass.

13.6   DEGREE ADVERBS/ADVERBIALS

Degree adjectives have been discussed at **8.2**; many degree adverbs have exactly the same form as the adjectives. These are exemplified first below. Degree adverbs and adverbials can modify verb phrases, adjectives, or other adverbs.

que, com . . . de (exclamative; see **27.2.2.2** and **27.2.3**)	how!
Que malament que canten!	How badly they're singing!
Com és de lleig!	How ugly it is!

In current Catalan there is no interrogative degree adverb corresponding to 'how . . . ?', hence no convenient way of expressing exactly, for example. 'How soon can you let us know?', 'How near are we to our destination?' For the former, one might say, **Quan ens ho faràs saber?** 'When will you let us know?' or **Ens ho faràs saber aviat?** 'Will you let us know soon?'; for the latter,

Falta gaire per arribar a la nostra destinació? (lit. Is there much missing for us to arrive at our destination?). Consider also **Passa gaire sovint?** 'How often does it happen?' (lit. Does it happen very often?), **Ens sorprenia que el camí fos tan curt** 'We were surprised at how short the distance was' (lit. . . . that the way was so short).

molt	very, a lot, much
Treballaven molt de pressa.	They worked very fast.
Treballaven molt.	They worked hard (i.e. a lot).
És molt menys acceptable.	It is much less acceptable.
gaire	(not) much, very (in negative, interrogative and conditional contexts)
Tardaràs gaire a eixir del bany?	Will you be very long in (lit. in coming out of) the bathroom?
una casa no gaire espaiosa	a not very spacious house
poc	not very, not much
Era poc divertit.	It was not very entertaining.
molt poc intel·ligent	very unintelligent (i.e. pretty stupid)
El blau m'agrada poc.	I don't like the blue one very much.

Poc (or the more emphatic **gens**) frequently negates an adjective where English prefers the prefixed negative form: **poc freqüent** 'infrequent', **poc sofisticat** 'unsophisticated', **poc acostumat** 'unaccustomed', **gens airós** 'most ungraceful'. (Note also **a poc (a) poc** 'slowly', 'gradually'.)

tan, tant	as, so (much) (**tan** is used when it precedes what is qualified)
No vagis tan de pressa.	Don't go so fast. (**tan** modifies **de pressa**)
M'agradava tant com l'altre.	I liked it as much as the other one. (**tant** modifies **m'agradava**)
El riu va tan ple que l'aigua frega el pont.	The river is so full that the water is touching the bridge.
més	more
Ho has deixat més enllà.	You've left it further away (over there).
Hauríem de viatjar més.	We ought to do more travelling.
d'allò més	extremely
Els va agradar d'allò més.	They were extremely fond of it. (lit. It pleased them extremely.)
menys, manco (esp. Bal.), **més poc**	less
Tens deu anys manco que jo.	You are ten years younger than I am. (lit. You have ten years less than I.)
Com més el necessito, menys el tinc.	The more I need him, the less I have him.

tot	all, quite
Vingueren tot sobtadament.	They came very suddenly.

There is unexpected agreement of the degree adverb **tot** with a following adjective in the following examples:

Les he deixades totes soles.	I have left them (*f.*) all alone.
La pobra noia estava tota avergonyida.	The poor girl was quite embarrassed.
Ho ha fet tota sola.	She has done it all on her own.

(Adverbial **tot** (invariable) occurs in some set expressions, before a noun used adjectivally:

Érem tot orelles/ulls.	We were all ears/eyes.)

The adverbial function of **tot** is also to be noted in common expressions like **tot sovint** 'very often', **tot recte/dret** 'straight on', **tot seguit** 'immediately afterwards', **tot d'una** 'all of a sudden' The use of **tot** introducing a gerund with the meaning of 'while', 'as' is discussed in **22.2.4.1**.

massa	too, too much
Anem massa a poc a poc.	We're going too slowly.
Estudia molt, potser massa.	She studies a lot, perhaps too much.
força	quite, very, quite a lot
Es fa força difícil.	It is becoming quite difficult.
Ens coneixem força.	We know each other pretty well.
prou	enough, quite, sufficiently
Ja ets prou gran.	You're old enough now.
Has menjat prou?	Have you eaten enough?
bastant	fairly, quite a lot (less than **prou**)
Ho fan bastant malament.	They do it fairly badly.
Va resultar bastant més delicat que no ens havíem imaginat.	It proved to be rather more delicate than we had imagined.
mig	half (see below)
Venien mig convençuts.	They came half persuaded.

With verbs, **mig** 'half' operates as an inseparable prefix: **Només la mig obrí** 'He only half-opened it'; **S'han mig adormit** 'They have nodded off' (lit. . . . half gone to sleep).

Degree adverbs which are not also adjectives

absolutament	absolutely, thoroughly
excepcionalment	exceptionally

extremament	extremely
extremadament, extraordinàriament	extraordinarily
del tot, completament	wholly, completely
Ho trobo del tot inacceptable que . . .	I find it wholly unacceptable that . . .
qui-sap-lo	greatly, a lot
M'interessa qui-sap-lo.	I'm greatly interested in it.
així de (+ adjective or adverb) (popular)	so
exacte de (+ adjective or adverb)	just as, exactly as
El meu rellotge marxa exacte de bé que el teu.	My watch works just as well as yours.
Aquesta sala és exacte de gran que aquella altra.	This room is exactly the same size/just as big as that other one.
igual de (+ adjective or adverb)	equally, just as (see **5.1**)
És igual de difícil trobar una plaça de pàrking.	It's just as difficult to find a garage space.
Aquesta màquina funciona igual de bé que aquella.	This machine works just as well as that one.
a bastament (following an adjective or adverb)	enough
una mica, un poc, un xic, quelcom (literary, and only preceding qualified item)	somewhat, a bit
Haurem de caminar una mica.	We'll have to walk a bit.
El trobàvem un poc millorat.	We found him a bit better.
Són quelcom distrets.	They are somewhat absent-minded.
(no) gens	any, (not) at all (in interrogative and negative contexts); stronger form: **gens ni mica**
Ha plogut gens?	Has it rained at all?
una gestió no gens fàcil	not at all an easy step

13.7 SENTENCE ADVERBS/ADVERBIALS

Sentence adverbs/adverbials are those which do not qualify any particular constituent of the sentence they appear in. Their function rather is to indicate to the receiver how the current sentence is to be connected to the discourse, or how the speaker reacts to the content of what is expressed. Many such items may occur at the beginning of a sentence, or, parenthetically, after the first phrase, or at the end.

certament	certainly
per cert	indeed, incidentally
en efecte, efectivament **La vostra teoria explica, en efecte, tots aquests fets.**	indeed Your theory does explain all these facts.
de fet	in fact
ben segur	assuredly

de veres, de debò, de veritat, sí que . . .
  De veres que vindrem./Sí que vindrem.
  M'he fet mal de debò.
	really, truly, seriously
	We will come, really.
	I've really hurt myself.

(Note that **de debò**, unlike the other expressions, favours final position.)

en realitat	in fact, actually

(Remember that **actualment** means 'at present, currently'.)
  En realitat, està bastant bé de preu.   In fact, it is quite cheap.

evidentment, és clar (que . . .)	evidently, plainly, clearly, of course, definitely
És clar que t'estima!	Clearly/Of course she loves you!
T'estima, és clar.	She loves you, clearly.
i tant que . . .	of course, and how!
I tant que pense dir-li el que opine d'això!	Indeed I do plan to tell him what I think of it!
òbviament	obviously
per descomptat, naturalment	naturally
sens dubte	undoubtedly (i.e. certainly), no doubt (i.e. probably)
no cal dir-ho, això sí **Els vostres, no cal dir-ho/això sí, són preferibles.**	naturally, of course Yours are preferable, I agree.

Possibility

potser, a la millor, tal vegada, tal volta (esp. Val.)	perhaps, maybe
Ni tan sols la va esmentar; a la millor l'ha oblidada.	She didn't even mention her; perhaps she has forgotten her.

si de cas, si per cas, si un cas (Bal.) — perhaps, possibly (making a suggestion)

Si de cas, per a avançar, el que podries fer és esperar-me a la cantonada. — Possibly, so as not to waste time, what you could do is wait for me at the corner.

per ventura — perhaps (used ironically (= surely not?))

Que ets ric, per ventura? Doncs per què li dónes tants diners? — Are you rich, perhaps? (evidently not) Then why are you giving her so much money?

(In the Balearics **per ventura** is used more generally as a synonym for **potser**.)

també, així mateix, igualment — also, as well, too
A part les raons dites hi ha, així mateix, altres motius. — Besides the reasons mentioned there are, as well, other causes.
Hi han assistit, igualment, tots els altres membres. — All the other members were present, too.

a més, a més a més, de més, de més a més, endemés, ultra això — in addition, moreover

semblantment — similarly

per altra part, d'altra banda — moreover

altrament — moreover, otherwise
Segur que vindran; altrament, no m'ho haurien dit. — I'm sure they'll come; otherwise, they wouldn't have said so.

així, doncs, per tant — therefore, thus, in that case, then
No ens vols ajudar? Doncs no ho farem! — Won't you help us? We won't do it, then!
Què seria, doncs, de tu si no era que ella t'ha ajudat tant? — Where would you be, in that case, if it weren't that she had helped you?

i doncs — so (then)
I doncs, que també veniu? — So, are you coming too?
(On **doncs** see **15.1.7**.)

per conseqüent, en conseqüència — consequently, therefore

. . . però — however, though
Ell t'ho cedirà tot, amb la condició, però, que li resti alguna cosa per a viure. — He will make it all over to you, on condition, however, that he has something left to live on.

tanmateix
  Tanmateix ha vingut; ja us ho deia
    que res li'n privaria.
  Tens els diners que vols i tanmateix
    no te'n serveixes.

yet, even so
She's come, even so; I told you
  nothing would stop her.
You've got all the money you want,
  and yet you don't use it.

per això (colloquial, not in initial
  position)
  Ha vingut, per això.

though (see **15.1.5.1**)

He came, though.

**malgrat això, a desgrat d'això, això
no obstant, no obstant això,
nogensmenys** (literary)

nevertheless, despite that

amb tot, tot i així, així i tot
  Té molta feina; amb tot, tractant-se de
    tu, ho farà.

even so
He is very busy; even so, seeing
  that it is you, he will do it.

**de tota manera, de totes maneres, sigui
  com vulgui**

anyway, be that as it may

**(al cap i) a la fi, al capdavall, comptat i
  debatut, fet i fet, en darrer terme**
  Al capdavall ets un idiota.

after all, all things considered,
  when all's said and done
After all, you're an idiot.

Note the difference between **a la fi** 'after all', 'in the end', **per fi** 'finally' and **en fi** 'well', 'then':

  A la fi he vist que no tenia raó.
  Em referiré, per fi, al problema de la
    llibertat.
  En fi, ja ho veurem.

In the end I saw I was wrong.
I shall mention, finally, the
  question of freedom
Well, then, we shall see.

en certa manera
  En certa manera, tenen raó.

up to a point, in a way
In a way, they're right.

**sobretot, principalment, majorment, per
  damunt de tot**

above all, principally

generalment, en general, per regla general   generally, mostly

normalment, habitualment   normally, usually

excepcionalment, per excepció   exceptionally

Some adverbs/adverbials of speaker reaction or evaluation are: **per sort, afortunadament** 'fortunately', **desgraciadament, dissortadament** 'unfortunately', 'regrettably', **senzillament** 'simply', **francament** 'frankly', **preferentment** 'preferably', **aparentment, en aparença** 'apparently', **fonamentalment** 'basically', **en teoria** 'theoretically', **seriosament** 'seriously'.

Catalan does not always use a sentence adverb where English does; a complex sentence is often more idiomatic. So, for example, 'allegedly': **segons diuen** (lit. according to (what) they say)), **es diu que** ... (lit. it is said that ...); 'understandably': **es comprèn que** ... (lit. it is understood that ...), 'undoubtedly': **no hi ha dubte que** ... (lit. there is no doubt that ...); 'apparently': **es veu que** ... (lit. it is seen that ...), or **pel que es veu** (lit. from what can be seen).

14 PREPOSITIONS

Prepositions in Catalan have complements which may be noun phrases (the typical case), adverbials (see **13.2**), prepositional phrases (see Compound prepositions below), non-finite verbs (see below), or clauses (see Chapter 33).

Phonologically and morphologically prepositions fall into three groups: atonic or unstressed prepositions like **de**, **en** (**14.1**), simple tonic prepositions (**14.2**), and compound tonic prepositions (**14.3**). Many of the tonic prepositions are closely related in sense and usage to adverbs.

14.1 ATONIC PREPOSITIONS

These are **a**, **amb**, **de**, **en**, **per** and the compound atonic preposition **per a**. They are very common, occurring in a wide range of grammatical (case-marking) and locational functions which only partially correspond to any particular English preposition. **A**, **de**, **per** and **per a** combine with following masculine definite articles **el**, **els** (and *salat* **es**), giving the following forms (see also **3.1.1**):

al (a + el), **als** (a + els), **as** (a + es)
del (de + el), **dels** (de + els), **des** (de + es)
pel (per + el), **pels** (per + els), **pes** (per + es)
per al (per a + el), **per als** (per a + els), **per as** (per a + es, but **per a** is virtually
   unused in the varieties and styles where the *article salat* is found)

The prevocalic forms **l'**, **s'** of the masculine article do not combine. See **3.1** for more details on the use of variants of the definite articles.

14.1.1 A AND en

These prepositions are taken together since, in some functions at least, their use overlaps. The area of meaning involved is broadly speaking that denoted in English by 'at', 'in', 'on', 'to'.

14.1.1.1 *A with the direct object of transitive verbs*

In standard Catalan, the direct object of a transitive verb is not generally introduced by a preposition. (Colloquial speech does often use **a**, or its variants **en/an**, [ənə], before definite animate direct objects.) Stressed personal pronouns, however, are preceded by **a**:

Jo el corregiré a ell, i ell em corregirà a mi.
I'll correct him and he'll correct me.

A vostè, l'esperem demà.
You, we are expecting tomorrow.

Tothom 'everyone', **tots** '(them) all', **ningú** 'no one', forms of the relative pronoun **el qual** 'who', and the relative/interrogative pronoun **qui** 'who' may also be preceded by **a** in direct object function, but need not be. An animate direct object which immediately follows a grammatical subject may also take **a**:

Ens miràvem l'un a l'altre.   We watched one another.

More generally, the use of **a** before a definite animate direct object is tolerated when its absence might suggest that the noun phrase involved was a subject.

T'estima com a la seva mare.
She loves you like (she loves) her mother.

A Núria, no crec que la pugues convèncer.
I don't think you can persuade *Núria*.

Als funcionaris no els satisfà la proposta de la jornada intensiva.
Civil servants are not satisfied by the proposal for continuous working.

In the last two examples, **a** makes clear that a noun phrase in initial position is not subject but direct object (see **25.3**). A is, in fact, generally used with direct objects which are left-dislocated: see **25.3** and **36.4**.

14.1.1.2 *A with indirect object*

The indirect object of a verb is marked by **a**:

Han atorgat un premi al millor llibre de contes.
They have awarded a prize to the best book of short stories.

A mi, no m'ho ha dit.
She hasn't told *me*.

Escriu a en Pere.
Write to Pere.

Colloquial speech often uses **en, amb**, or a variant of these, in such cases, but this is regarded as unacceptable in written language, and in formal styles.

14.1.1.3 *Expressions of place: a and en*

Depending on the context, both **a** and **en** may be found expressing place at which (location) and place to which (direction). In the standard language the distribution is as set out below. The tendency is for **a** to be used for both location and direction when physical location is at issue; **a** also tends to be preferred before the definite article in both location and direction functions, while, in contrast, **en** tends to be preferred, in both functions, before the indefinite article, and **algun** 'some', **aquest/aqueix** 'this' and **aquell** 'that'.

(i)   Physical location/direction

Firstly, for expressions of location and direction in physical, three-dimensional space, a basic pattern uses **en** for location and **a** for direction (to), when the following word is (a) a noun, (b) an adjective, (c) a numeral, (d) a quantifier/indefinite (except **un**, **algun**) or a degree adverb, or (e) a relative pronoun:

before	*location:* ***en***	*direction (to):* ***a***
(a) *noun*	**No trobaren allotjament ni en hotels, ni en pensions, ni en cases particulars.** They did not find accommodation in hotels, guest houses, or private houses.	**Anem a sales diferents.** We are going to different rooms.
(b) *adjective*	**Viuen en grans edificis.** They live in large buildings.	**Viatgem a llunyanes terres.** We are travelling to distant lands.
(c) *numeral*	**He estudiat en tres universitats.** I have been a student at three universities.	**Els enviem a tres universitats.** We are sending them to three universities.
(d) *quantifier/ indefinite (except* **un/algun***)*	**Això passa en molts llocs.** That happens in many places.	**Pujarem a quasi tots els pisos.** We'll go up to nearly all the apartments.
(e) *relative pronoun*	**el pis en el qual** (or **en què**) **vivia** the flat in which I lived	**la terrassa a la qual** (or **a què**) **hem pujat** the balcony to which we went up

The use of **a** instead of **en** to express location in all of these contexts is quite widespread in both speech and written sources, and is regarded as acceptable in case (d) particularly with everyday expressions; thus **Això passa a cada casa**

'That happens in every house', **Plou a tot Catalunya** 'It's raining in the whole of Catalonia'. The use of **en** for direction before **altres** is also acceptable: **Anirem aquí i en altres llocs** 'We'll go there and to other places'.

In addition to a certain degree of merger of the distinction between location and direction in cases (a) to (e) in the table, there is more firmly established neutralization in the following cases.

A for location = direction: place names

With place names, location as well as direction is expressed by means of **a**:

fabricat a Suïssa	made in Switzerland
La vam enviar a Suïssa.	We sent it to Switzerland.
una acampada al Pirineu	a camping holiday in the Pyrenees

(For location, Valencian prefers **en** with place names: **Ací en València ha plogut** 'Here in Valencia it has been raining'.) Place names with modifying adjectives are treated as cultural concepts rather than physical locations, hence retain **en** for location: **en la Catalunya actual** 'in present-day Catalonia', **en la Roma antiga** 'in ancient Rome'. (However, **a** may be found here too, probably due to the combined pressure of the adjacent definite article and the geographical name.) Names of periodicals or television/radio stations are often treated as proper names, so **he llegit a «Serra d'Or»** 'I read in *Serra d'Or*', **Publiquem l'article a «Caplletra»** 'We are publishing the article in *Caplletra*', **Ho he vist a TV3** 'I saw it on TV3'.

A for location = direction: idioms with a 'at'

A expresses location or direction in certain fixed phrases containing an unmodified noun without a determiner: **a casa** 'at home'/'home', **a palau** 'in/to the palace', **a taula** 'at/to (the) table', **a fira** 'at/to the fair', **a mercat** 'at/to market', **a missa** 'at/to Mass', **a classe/a escola** 'at/to school', **a muntanya** 'in/to the mountains', etc. **A terra** means 'on the ground'/'to the ground'; **en terra** means 'on land' (location or direction).

Què has fet a classe?	What did you do in/at school? (location)
Que no has anat a missa?	Have you not been to Mass? (direction)
A taula!	Lunch/Dinner/Supper is ready! (direction)

A for location = direction: definite article and quin

The use of **a** (= 'place where') instead of **en** is generally preferred before the definite article and before **quin** 'which?':

Els hem trobat al carrer.
We found them in the street. (location)

Els hem llençat al carrer.
We threw them into the street. (direction)

A quina cadira seies?
Which chair were you sitting in? (location)

Tinc mal a la cama.
I have a pain in my leg.

La inflamació es va estendre a la cama.
The inflammation spread to the leg. (direction)

Polèmica per la venda de llibres als centres docents.
Controversy concerning the sale of books in educational establishments.
(Note ambiguity: the phrase can also mean ' . . . the sale of books to
educational establishments')

Although, as under **(ii)** below, a distinction between **en** (location) and **a** (direction) is usually maintained for abstract places, the concept of physical places easily extends to situations and events which have physical extent: **al ball** 'at/to the dance', **a la festa** 'at/to the party', **a l'enterrament** 'at/to the funeral', **a la batalla de l'Ebre** 'in/to the Ebro battle'. But **en** is often found for location when the prepositional phrase precedes the verb, especially before **el**, **els** (which in the Eastern dialect group sound the same as **al**, **als**):

En els carrers, hi havia poca llum.   In the streets there was not much light.
En el meu sac, n'hi ha.   In my handbag there are some.

En for direction to = *location*

With physical places, and when the following word is **un** 'a', **algun** 'some', or one of the demonstratives **aquest** 'this', **aqueix** 'that' or **aquell** 'that', then **en**, as well as expressing location, is preferred to **a** for the expression of direction to, though **a** is also correct:

Desitjàvem que la festa se celebràs en una sala més gran.
We wanted the party to be held in a larger room. (location)

Van traslladar-nos en (or **a**) **una sala més gran.**
They moved us to a larger room. (direction)

Fugiren en (or **a**) **algun indret desconegut.**
They fled to some unknown location.

S'instal·laren en algun indret desconegut.
They settled in some unknown location.

In some varieties, particularly Balearic, **en** for **a** 'to' (direction) occurs with the definite article too:

Pugem en es poble.   Let's go up to the village.

(ii) Figurative place

When the location or direction is figurative rather than literal the distinction between **en** for location and **a** for direction is preferred before all types of word.

el desig expressat en l'assemblea	the wish expressed at the meeting
el desig expressat a l'assemblea	the wish expressed to the meeting
mots que apareixen en la llengua parlada	words which occur in the spoken language
problemes en l'ensenyament	problems in education

However, there is in the eastern dialect area quite a widespread tendency to use **a** for non-physical 'place in which' in constructions similar to those mentioned in (**i**) on p. 245 where '**a** for location = direction' is found:

Indicàvem al nostre comentari anterior. (. . . en el . . .)
We pointed out in our previous comment.

com diu Kissinger a les seves memòries. (. . . en les . . .)
as Kissinger says in his memoirs

In many everyday expressions it is hard to see why one would object to this: **Ho llegim al diari** 'We read it in the paper', **Coses que passen a la vida!** 'Things which happen in life' (i.e. 'just one of those things'). The distinction drawn by grammarians between physical place and figurative place cannot always be clearly made, and the difference in usage in these two contexts is more realistically thought of as a tendency or a preference.

14.1.1.4   Verbal complements with a, en

Certain verbs require prepositional phrase complements with **a** or **en**, determined in each case by the verb in question; the preposition is carried over to constructions with a noun derived from the verb.

Verbs with **a**:

accedir a	agree to	**contribuir a**	contribute to
acostumar a	accustom (someone) to	so **contribució a**	contribution to
		convertir a	convert (someone) to
arriscar-se a	take a risk in		
confiar a	entrust (someone / something) to	so **conversió a**	conversion to

dedicar a	dedicate (someone / something) to	**exposar a**	expose (someone / something) to
so **dedicació a**	dedication to	so **exposició a**	exposure to
excitar a	excite (someone) to	**procedir a**	proceed to

Verbs with **en**:

afanyar-se en	work hard at	**influir en**	have influence on
complaure's en	take pleasure in	so **influència en**	influence on
so **complaença en**	pleasure in	**insistir en**	insist on
confiar en	trust in	so **insistència en**	insistence on
so **confiança en**	trust in	**interessar en**	interest (someone) in
consistir en	consist of/in		
convertir en	convert/turn (something) into	so **interès en**	interest in
		obstinar-se en	persist in
creure en	believe in	**participar en**	participate in
so **creença en**	belief in	so **participació,**	participation,
delitar-se en	delight in	**participant en**	participant in
so **delit en**	delight in	(**participar a** is also found but is
entossudir-se en	obstinately persist in	judged incorrect)
so **tossuderia en**	obstinacy in	**pensar en**	think about, have (something) in one's thoughts
entretenir-se en	spend time in, amuse oneself at		
		tardar en, trigar en	delay in
equivocar-se en	be mistake in	so **tardança/**	
so **equivocació en**	mistake in	**trigança en**	delay in
exercitar-se en	train in/at, practise	**vacil·lar en**	hesitate in
		so **vacil·lació en**	hesitation in
implicar en	implicate (someone) in		

However, it is important to note that, when the complement of such a verb + preposition is an infinitive, **en** is replaced by **a** (**20.3.1.1**), thus:

Tot consisteix en això.
Everything consists in that.

Tot consisteix a fer això.
Everything consists in doing that.

Tarden molt en la resolució de l'afer.
They are taking a long time in the resolution of the matter.

Tarden molt a venir.
They are taking a long time in coming.

En followed by an infinitive occurs only in temporal adverbial expressions (see **20.4**).

The prepositions **en** and **a** are dropped before a complement clause introduced by **que** (**14.1.5** and **32.4.2**).

14.1.1.5 A and en in time expressions

Both **a** and **en** are used in time expressions; some examples containing **a** were given in **13.3**. **A** is the general preposition for 'time to which', and often for 'time at which' (especially before the definite article) as in the following:

arribar a final de mes	get to the end of the month
Dinarem a les dues.	We shall have lunch at 2 o'clock.
Hi anàvem a la tardor.	We used to go there in autumn.
Va viure al segle XIX.	She lived in the nineteenth century. (merely locates the period of her existence)

En may focus on an extent of time, and corresponds often to 'during' or 'within':

fer una cosa en quinze dies	do something in/within a fortnight
Ho vaig fer en un moment.	I did it in a very short time.
en els darrers mesos . . .	in recent months . . .
en les èpoques posteriors . . .	in subsequent periods . . .
En el segle XV es va desenvolupar molt la prosa catalana.	In/during the fifteenth century Catalan prose underwent great development.

However, before words other than the definite article, **en** may also express no more than a point in time:

En aquell temps Jesús digué.	At that time Jesus said.
En dies així tothom està content.	On days like this everyone is happy.
Us ho contaré en altres ocasions.	I'll tell you about it on other occasions.

Note expressions like **d'avui en quinze** 'a fortnight from today', **de dijous en vuit** 'a week on Thursday'.

The construction of temporal (and causal) infinitive clauses with the preposition **en** is favoured by normative grammars (see **20.4**):

En arribar als vint anys, entraven en quinta.
On reaching the age of twenty, they were called up.

The construction with **al** (**a l'**) is also found, though frowned upon by grammarians:

A l'arribar a la plaça, la legió s'escampà.
On arriving in the square, the legion spread out.

14.1.1.6 Idioms with *a* + infinitive

Verbs of perception, particularly **sentir** 'hear' and **veure** 'see', may take **a** before an infinitive complement, particularly in the expressions **sentir a dir** and **veure a venir**:

He sentit (a) dir que no vindrà.
I have heard that she won't come. (lit. . . . have heard (to) say that . . .)

L'hem vist (a) venir.
We saw him coming.

Pronominal quantifiers such as **res** 'anything'/'nothing', **alguna cosa/quelcom** 'something', **molt** 'much', **gaire** '(not) much', **poc** 'little' require **a** before an infinitive:

No hi ha res a fer.	There's nothing to be done.
Si tenien alguna cosa a perdre.	If they had anything to lose.
No tenien gaire a guanyar.	They hadn't much to gain.
Hi ha molt poc a dir sobre això.	There is very little to be said about that.

Note the expressions **tenir a veure amb** 'have to do with': **Què té a veure això amb el que he dit?** 'What has that got to do with what I said', and **és a dir** 'that is to say', 'I mean'.

14.1.1.7 Other constructions with *en*

En occurs in prepositional phrase adjuncts of manner, e.g.:

parlar en veu alta   speak out loud (lit. in high voice)

and in prepositional phrase complements of certain nouns and adjectives, such as:

doctor en ciències	Doctor of Science
un país ric en minerals	a country rich in minerals

14.1.2 Amb 'WITH'

The correspondence of Catalan **amb** with English 'with' is close, though naturally there are some differences. The following senses can be identified:

Company:

Cada dia surt amb la Joana.	He goes out with Joana every day.
Amb la Joana, sortim cada dia.	Joana and I go out every day.

Concurrence (verbal notions which involve more than one party as subject):

Es casa amb el seu cosí.	She is marrying her cousin.
S'ha barallat amb la seva millor amiga.	She has fallen out with her best friend.

Contact:

Una barca es tocava amb l'altra.	One boat touched the other.
Aquella teoria topa amb dificultats.	

That theory runs into difficulties. (**topar amb** 'bump into', 'collide with')

Instrument:

fregar les rajoles amb la baieta	mop the tiles with the cloth
demostrar amb proves	prove (lit. demonstrate with proofs)
viatjar amb tren/amb avió/amb autocar	travel by train/plane/coach (**en** may also be used; see **3.2.3iv**)

Manner:

escriure una paraula amb hac	spell a word with H
treballar amb agilitat	work with agility

Certain verbs (not many) require an **amb** phrase as one of their complements:

amenaçar (algú) amb	threaten (somebody) with
comptar amb	count on, rely on
conformar-se amb	content oneself with
somiar amb	dream about
trobar-se amb algú	meet/run into someone
haver-n'hi prou amb	be enough to
N'hi ha prou amb sentir-ho una vegada.	It's enough to hear it once.
tenir-ne prou amb	have enough with, suffice
En tenim prou amb els ingressos mensuals.	Our monthly income is sufficient.

Often, before an infinitive, **amb** is replaced by another preposition (see **20.3.1.1**): L'amenaçaven amb l'expulsió 'They threatened him with dismissal', but L'amenaçaven d'expulsar-lo 'They threatened to dismiss him'; Vés amb compte amb la brutícia 'Watch out for the muck', but Vés amb compte a no embrutar-te 'Take care not to get dirty'; N'hi ha prou amb la reproducció d'una part 'It is enough with the reproduction of part of it', but N'hi ha prou de/a/amb reproduir-ne una part 'It is enough to reproduce part of it'.

14.1.3   De 'OF', 'FROM', ETC.

De takes the form **d'** before a word beginning with a vowel (which may be preceded by a silent h). The letter i may be consonantal, so **exercicis de ioga** 'yoga exercises'. In Valencian, u may be consonantal also, thus **Este diari no és**

de hui 'This newspaper isn't today's' (= General Catalan: **Aquest diari no és d'avui**). **De** is not reduced to **d'** before the names of vowel letters: **Quan va seguida de a, de o i de u, s'escriu ç** 'When followed by a, o, or u, ç is written'; nor before the titles of books, newspapers, etc. which are enclosed in inverted commas: **els titulars de «El Temps»** 'the headlines in *El Temps*'. Some writers (esp. Valencian) prefer **de** to **d'** before words beginning with the negative prefix **a-**: **No veig res de anormal** 'I don't see anything unusual'.

For **de** in 'compound prepositions', see below; for **de** 'than' in certain comparative constructions, see **5.2** and **5.2.3**; for **de** with infinitive clauses see **20.2.1**.

14.1.3.1 De + noun phrase as complement or adjunct of a verb

A prepositional phrase with **de**, as the complement or adjunct of a verb, may express a wide range of concepts.

Origin:	**sortir de casa**	go out of the house
	El té de naixença.	He has had it from birth.
Separation:	**L'hem exclosa de la comissió.**	We have excluded her from the committee.
Cause, motive:	**morir de set**	die of thirst
	avergonyir-se de les seves accions	be ashamed of one's actions
Means:	**viure de renda**	live on investment income
Agent:	**estimat de tothom**	loved by everyone
	(see below under **per**, and **29.1.2**)	

A prepositional phrase with **de** may be the obligatory complement (including infinitive complement) of certain verbs (mostly pronominal, see Chapter 23), for example:

abstenir-se de	refrain from		**penedir-se de**	repent (of)
adonar-se de	realize		**queixar-se de**	complain of/about
burlar-se de	make fun of		**recordar-se de**	remember
doldre's de	complain of/about		**riure's de**	laugh at
dubtar de	doubt, have doubts about		**saber de**	know about, have knowledge of
gloriejar-se de	boast of/be proud of		**No saben de música.**	They have no knowledge of music.
oblidar-se de	forget/be forgetful of			
parlar de	speak of			

Temporal adjuncts with **de**:

Hi anem de nit.	We go there by night.
Qui de jove no treballa . . .	He who does not work when young . . .

14.1.3.2   *De* + noun phrase (or infinitive) complement of adjective or quantifier

Certain adjectives take a **de** complement, such as in:

ple de prejudicis	full of prejudice	**amic de les arts**	fond of the arts
curt de vista	short-sighted	**amic de discutir**	fond of arguing

Partitive complements (definite noun phrases), of numerals, quantifier adjectives, and adverbs, etc., are introduced with **de**:

tres de les seves companyes	three of her comrades
pocs dels quadres	few of the pictures

A dislocated noun phrase (left or right), specifying something already represented by the partitive clitic **en**, is expressed with **de** (cf. **12.6v**):

De llibres, en té molts, però no el que necessite.
Books, he has a lot of, but not the one I need.

En vols més, de sopa?
Do you want any more soup?

14.1.3.3   *De* + pronominal adjective

An important feature of Catalan grammar is the use of **de** + adjective in an indefinite noun phrase where the noun is understood from the context (**12.6v**). In many cases this use corresponds to the English pronoun 'one(s)':

No tinc cigarrets americans, però sí de francesos.
I haven't got American cigarettes, but I have got French ones.

Seria preferible convertir aquesta frase tan llarga en dues de curtes.
It would be preferable to change this very long sentence into two short ones.

En este corral hi ha dos vaques teues i cinc de meues.
In this yard there are two of your cows and five of mine.

Si són necessaris més arguments, encara en tinc de més convincents.
If more arguments are necessary, I (still) have some more convincing ones.

A similar construction is found with **res** 'anything'/'nothing':

La pel·lícula no té res d'especial.	The film hasn't got anything special.
Si saps res de nou, m'avises.	If you find out anything new, let me know.

14.1.3.4   De + noun phrase (or infinitive) as complement of noun phrase

The commonest way of using a noun phrase to modify another is with the preposition **de**; the range of semantic relations is very wide, corresponding not only to English 'of' and 'from'. Here are a few examples:

vins del Penedès	wines from the Penedès
una taula de marbre	a marble table
manual de química	chemistry textbook
dia de festa	holiday (lit. day of holiday)
el martell del lampista	the plumber's hammer
la llum del sol	the light of the sun
la ciutat de Lleida	the city of Lleida
el mes d'octubre	the month of October
la feina d'escriptor	the task of a writer
la feina d'escriure	the task of writing

14.1.4   Per AND per a

The correct use of these prepositions is a topic of major controversy in Catalan normative grammar. It may be useful to set out briefly the source of the controversy, and to identify the positions taken up. Broadly speaking the two prepositions cover the semantic field of English 'by', 'because of', and 'for'. In spoken Valencian **per** covers, roughly, the senses 'by' and 'because of' together with part of English 'for', with **per a** corresponding to the rest of 'for'; this Valencian usage matches that of Spanish *por* and *para* closely. In the spontaneous speech of the rest of the Catalan-speaking area, only **per** is used, covering the whole semantic field. The standard grammatical tradition established by Pompeu Fabra, and defended and elaborated in recent years by Josep Ruaix, recommends a distinction in which **per** has a somewhat greater role than in spoken Valencian. Many users, however, have found the proposed distinction difficult to apply, particularly in infinitival clauses. Joan Coromines, supported more recently by Joan Solà, recommended a modification in the direction of (non-Valencian) spontaneous usage, by which the distinction in function between **per** and **per a** would be maintained only before noun phrase complements, with **per** alone being used elsewhere. Most written Catalan adheres more or less consistently either to the Fabra-Ruaix model (still the more prestigious), or to the Coromines-Solà model, despite the artificiality of both of them. A more radical solution, adopted explicitly in the 1980s in the *Diari de Barcelona* and associated publications, copied the spoken non-Valencian usage, and ignored **per a** altogether; this also appears to have been the practice of the major novelist Mercè Rodoreda. In what follows, we attempt to set out correct usage according to the Fabra-Ruaix model. The practical recommendation, for the non-native speaker outside Valencia, is: if in doubt, use **per**.

14.1.4.1 *Per* and *per a* with noun phrase complements

(i) *Per expresses:*

(a) Locative 'through', 'via', 'by', 'over', 'about':

El tirà per la finestra.
She threw it out of (lit. through) the window.

de Barcelona a Lleida per Igualada
from Barcelona to Lleida via Igualada

Anava venent pels pobles.
He went around the villages selling. (lit. He went selling through the villages.)

Eren pels camps.
They were (around/about) in the fields.

(b) Temporal 'during', 'sometime in', 'for the length of':

Pel gener hi fa molt fred.	In January it is very cold there. (not necessarily throughout January)
Tornaran per la sega.	They will return at/around harvest time.
L'hi vaig llogar per un any.	I rented it to her for a year.

Note expressions like **per la tarda** '(sometime) in the afternoon', **per la nit** '(sometime) at night' are judged incorrect, **a la tarda**, **a la nit** being preferred.

(c) Instrument/manner/cause: 'by', 'through':

Ho han tramès per correu.	They sent it by post.
T'ho han dit per broma.	They said it to you as a joke.
vendre-ho per peces	to sell it by the piece
Per prudència no faria mai res.	Through caution he would never do anything.
El vaig agafar per les mans.	I took him by the hands.

(d) Agent, including generally the agent of passive constructions:

Li ho vaig fer dir per l'advocat.
I communicated it to her through the lawyer. (lit. I made it said to her by the lawyer.)

Ha estat mort pels seus mateixos partidaris.
He has been killed by his own supporters.

l'arbre abatut pel vent
the tree blown down by the wind

On **de** instead of **per** expressing the agent of a passive in certain cases, see **29.1.2**.

(e)   Distribution:

un paquet per viatger   one piece of luggage per passenger

(f)   Exchange, substitution:

Tu fes-li preguntes i jo contestaré per ell.
You ask him questions and I'll reply for him/on his behalf.

L'han venut per no-res.
They have sold it for next to nothing.

(g)   Predicative: 'as', 'for':

Em van prendre pel meu germà.	They took me for my brother.
Tothom el tenia per lladre.	Everyone took him as/to be a thief.
El van deixar per mort.	They left him for dead.

(h)   Favour/consideration: 'for', 'for the sake of':

S'ha interessat per tu.	He has taken an interest on your behalf.
per l'amor de Déu!	for God's sake/for the love of God
Per mi, ja te'n pots anar.	As far as I'm concerned, you may leave.
Jo estic per ell, i no per tu.	I am on his side, not on yours.
És molt alta per l'edat que té.	She is very tall for her age/considering her age.

(j)   Motive: 'because of', the motivating factor is in existence before the act that it motivates:

Tot ho fem per la pàtria.	We do it all for our country.
treballar per la justícia social	work for social justice

(ii)   Per a expresses:

(a)   Beneficiary:

Han fet una tribuna per als convidats.
They have made a platform for the guests.

un paquet per al veí de dalt
a parcel for the neighbour upstairs

(b)   Destination/goal/purpose (including temporal and locative 'destination'):

seients reservats per als invàlids   seats reserved for the disabled

(The distinction between **per** and **per a** suggested in this section allows a contrast between for example **un aparell dissenyat per a minusvàlids** 'a device designed for disabled people' and **un aparell dissenyat per minusvàlids** 'a device designed by disabled people'.)

No és bo per a res.	It isn't good for anything.
No tenim temps per a res.	We haven't got time for anything.
esperit de vi per a cremar	alcohol for burning
N'encarregarem un per a dijous.	We'll order one for Thursday.
Ho deixarem per a més endavant.	We'll leave it for later.
A les vuit surt un tren per a Madrid.	At 8 o'clock a train leaves for Madrid.
Per a mi va ser una sorpresa total.	It came as a complete surprise to me.

The complements of **molt** 'a lot', **massa** 'too (much)', and **prou** 'enough' probably belong here too:

Tenen prou exemplars per a tothom.
They have enough copies for everyone.

Són massa diners per a nosaltres.
It is too much money for us.

14.1.4.2 *Per/per a with infinitive complements*

When the complement of the preposition is an infinitive, in principle the same distinctions apply as in **14.1.4.1**. However, the distinction between 'motive' (= **per 14.1.4.1i(j)**) and 'destination/goal/purpose' (= **per a 14.1.4.1ii(b)**) is a subtle one, and it is this range of meaning that is involved in most of the infinitival clauses. The constructions we are dealing with here (**per** or **per a** + infinitive) are adjuncts of verbs or nominalized verbs. The numbering of functions corresponds to that in **14.1.4.1**. It is with infinitive complements that Coromines, followed by Solà, recommended the use of **per** to cover all the senses mentioned here.

(i) *Per*

(c) Expressing manner or instrument:

Començo per recordar que demà no hi haurà classe.
I begin by reminding (you) that there will be no class tomorrow.

per posar un exemple
to mention an example

Molts autors, per no dir la majoria, creuen que ...
Many authors, not to say the majority, believe ...

(c)   Expressing cause: 'because of', 'as a result of' (= **pel fet de**). (Coromines and Solà reject this construction, at least with simple infinitives, as being unauthentic, but Ruaix shows that it is widely used.)

Ho diu per haver-ho sentit.
She says it as a result of hearing it said.

imposar multes per aparcar malament
impose fines for improper parking

L'han tancat a la presó per robar un cotxe.
They have locked him up for stealing (i.e. having stolen) a car.

Those who find the above example unauthentic recommend the use of a compound infinitive, if the sense allows:

L'han tancat a la presó per haver robat un cotxe.

When the reason persists, rather than just preceding its effect, of course, the compound (perfect) infinitive does not work; here those who reject the **per** + infinitive pattern insist on **perquè** 'because' with a finite verb.

Odiava la competitivitat per creure que era la causa de tots els problemes socials.
Odiava la competitivtat perquè creia que era la causa de tots els problemes socials.
He hated competitiveness because he believed it was the cause of all social problems.

Sometimes the sense 'considering', 'despite' is apparent (resembling the example given above, **És molt alta per l'edat que té** 'She is very tall for her age'):

Per llegir tants llibres, poc saps.
Considering you read so many books, you don't know much.

Per ser parenta nostra, no es porta gaire bé.
Considering she's a relative of ours, she isn't behaving very well.

(j)   Expressing motive or intention (= **per tal de, a fi de, amb la intenció de**). The infinitive phrase is the adjunct of a verb or noun expressing voluntary action and the subject of the infinitive is understood to be the same as the subject of the main verb:

Treballa per guanyar-se la vida.
He works to earn a living.

Vinc per veure'l.
I've come to see him.

la nostra anada a Girona per visitar els parents
our journey to Girona to visit relatives

un esforç per superar les dificultats
an effort to overcome the difficulties

No vaig voler dir res per no haver de discutir.
I didn't want to say anything so as not to have to argue.

(See **33.3.2** for complement clauses whose subject is not that of the main verb.)

Per is required in the complement of certain verbs, adjectives and nouns, such as:

Verbs:

apostar per	bet on
decidir-se per	decide in favour of
(not = **decidir-se a**	decide to)
delir-se per	long to
estar per	pay attention to
Estigues per conduir.	Concentrate on driving.
frisar/frissar per	be impatient to, be in a hurry to
interessar-se per	take an interest in/on behalf of
and **interès per**	interest in
S'interessa per saber com va anar l'experiment.	She is interested to know how the experiment went.
maldar per	strive to/struggle to
optar per	opt to, choose to
and **opció per**	choice to
preocupar-se per	worry about
vetllar per	watch over/take care of/make sure to
Cal que els poders públics vetllin per facilitar l'ensenyament en totes dues llengües.	Public authorities must take care to facilitate teaching in both languages.
votar per	vote for

Adjectives:

àvid per	eager to
una societat àvida per modernitzar-se	a society eager to modernize
impacient per	impatient to

Nouns:

ambició per	ambition to
curiositat per	curiosity about
enveja per	desire to

gust per	taste for
obsessió per	obsession with
l'obsessió del govern per aplicar mesures antiinflacionistes	the government's obsession with applying anti-inflationary measures
pressa per	hurry to
pruïja per	urge to, itch to

Per introducing a 'future passive' infinitive construction dependent on a noun:

Vostè té moltes coses per explicar.	You have a lot of things to explain. (i.e. things to-be-explained)
El rei tenia tres filles per casar.	The king had three daughters as yet unmarried.
problemes per resoldre	problems to solve
Val més boig conegut que savi per conèixer.	Better the devil you know . . . (lit. A known madman is worth more than a to-be-known wise man.)

(ii) Per a

Per a + infinitive expresses destination or purpose, after an expression without a volitional component, or with different (implied) subjects for main clause and subordinate infinitive (= **de cara a** 'towards', **amb vista a** 'with a view to', **amb destinació a** 'directed to'):

Verbs of necessity, appropriateness, sufficiency, existence, insufficiency:

Calen arguments de pes per a convèncer-la.
Substantial arguments are necessary in order to persuade her.

Aquests diners són per a gastar-los durant les vacances.
This money is to spend (lit. it) during the holidays.

N'hi ha per a donar i per a vendre.
There is (enough) to give and to sell, i.e. there's more than enough.

L'experiència d'avui basta per a renunciar-hi.
Today's experience is sufficient to (make me) give it up.

Similarly depending on quantifier expressions:

És molt d'hora per a telefonar-li.	It is very early to phone him.
És prou boig per a intentar-ho.	He is mad enough to try it.

Verbs expressing use, preparation, etc.: in the case of verbs of 'preparation' one might say that the notion of destination overrides that of motive:

El telescopi serveix per a mirar objectes llunyans.
The telescope is used in order to look at distant objects.

Aprofito l'avinentesa per a expressar-li el meu sincer agraïment.
I take advantage of this opportunity to express to you my sincere gratitude.

Calders es preparà de jove per a ser narrador.
Calders prepared himself as a young man to be a writer of fiction.

estudiar per a ser metge
to study to be a doctor

Destination/purpose complements of non-verbal categories:

Tinc matèria per a ocupar-me'n llarga estona.	I have material to keep me busy (lit. to occupy myself with it) for a long while.
Em falta corda per a lligar-ho.	I am short of string to tie it with.
Aquesta fruita no és bona per a menjar.	This fruit is not good to eat.
un producte útil per a netejar	a product useful for cleaning (with)

Note:

Tinc una màquina per a pintar.	I have a machine for painting.
not = Tinc una màquina per pintar.	I have a machine to be painted.
Va empassar-se unes pastilles per a dormir.	She took some sleeping tablets.
not = Va empassar-se unes pastilles per dormir.	She took some tablets in order to sleep.

(In the first case per a dormir depends on pastilles, while in the second per dormir depends on va empassar-se (unes pastilles).)

Destination/purpose complements of impersonal, or passive verbs, or with vague subjects:

portatge: dret que es paga per a passar per certs llocs
portatge: a tax which is paid in order to pass through certain places

Per a estudiar tal punt, hem de distingir entre . . .
To investigate this point, we have to distinguish . . .

With infinitive subject not equivalent to main clause subject:

El govern de Filipines designa onze bisbes per a negociar amb la guerrilla comunista.
The Philippines government names eleven bishops to negotiate with the communist guerrillas.

Li va donar una carta per a tirar-la a la bústia.
He gave him a letter to put in the letter-box.

Per a to introduce verbal adjunct expressing posteriority (attenuated sense of destination):

Els cavalls varen reprendre el trot, per a guanyar, al cap d'una estona, el darrer repit de la costa.
The horses resumed their pace, to reach, after a short while, the last gradient on the coast. (i.e. resumed . . . and reached . . .)

14.1.5   WEAK PREPOSITIONS DROPPED BEFORE que (CONJUNCTION)

When a finite complement clause, beginning with **que** 'that', is the object of a weak preposition (including compound prepositions), the weak preposition is dropped. The question of 'preposition drop' is discussed in detail in **32.4–5**.

A has been dropped in, e.g.:

S'exposa que el negoci vagi malament.	He is taking the risk that the business will suffer.
gràcies que ella hi ha intervingut	thanks to her having intervened in it

Amb has been dropped in, e.g.:

Vés amb compte que no t'embrutis.	Take care that you don't get dirty.
N'hi ha prou que en reproduïm una part.	It is sufficient that we reproduce a part of it.

De has been dropped in, e.g.:

abans que es casessin	before they got married
M'he adonat que ella era present.	I have realized that she was present.
a causa que trigava tant	because of the fact that it took so long

En has been dropped in, e.g.:

Pensa que has de venir.	Take thought that you have to come.
Tinc interès que pugueu veure les pintures.	I am concerned that you should be able to see the paintings.
Confia que se'n sortirà.	She is confident she'll get out of it.

Retention of weak prepositions before **que** is characteristic of non-standard Catalan, being more or less universal in spontaneous styles.

14.2   SIMPLE TONIC PREPOSITIONS

The use of these prepositions is primarily a matter for the dictionary.

14.2.1   NON-DERIVED PREPOSITIONS

com	as
contra	against
entre	between, among
excepte	except
fins	up to, until
malgrat	despite
pro	in favour of, on behalf of
segons	according to
sense	without
ultra	beyond, over and above (literary)
vers/devers/envers	towards (motion) (literary) (= **cap a**: **14.3.1**)
vers/envers	in relation to/towards; facing towards (= **de cara a**)
vers/devers	approximately, about
envers	in comparison with (= **en vist**, **al costat de**)
en vist (literary)	compared to, in comparison with

14.2.2   SIMPLE PREPOSITIONS DERIVED FROM GERUNDS/ PARTICIPLES

durant	during
mitjançant (literary)	by means of, through
no obstant (literary)	despite (= **malgrat**)
salvant, salvat (literary)	except for, save, barring

14.2.3   PREPOSITIONS WHICH ARE USED EITHER AS SIMPLE, OR AS COMPOUND

Some prepositions have alternative simple and compound forms (the compounds nearly all with **de**). All of these are derived from other parts of speech: nouns, e.g. **vora (de)** 'near', 'beside' from **vora** 'edge'; from participles, e.g. **llevat (de)** 'except', from **llevar** 'take off'; or, in most cases from adverbs, such as **darrere** 'behind'. In Catalonia, spontaneous speech generally prefers the compound forms, and these are obligatory (i) when the complement is a personal pronoun, e.g. **davant d'ella** 'in front of her', (ii) when the preposition is separated from its complement, e.g. **darrere mateix de l'església** 'right behind the church'. Balearic speech, and the written language, especially in more formal styles, prefer the simple forms. When they are used as compound prepositions with **de**, and their complement is a personal pronoun, they more often take a form of the corresponding possessive adjective in place of the expected **de** + personal pronoun. For example, **davall nostre** 'below us', **sobre meu** 'on me', (see **7.5**).

Derived from nouns:

vora (de)	near, beside
a part (de)	apart from

Derived from gerunds/participles:

llevat (de)	except
tret (de)	except
tocant (a)	with respect to (**tocant a** is regularly compound in the sense 'right next to')

Derived from adverbs:

damunt (de)	on, over
darrere (de)	behind
davall (de) (Val., Bal.)	under
davant (de)	in front of
deçà (de)	this side of
dellà (de)	that side of, on the far side of
dejús (de) (North Catalonia)	under
dins (de), dedins (de), dintre (de)	inside, within
fins (a/en)	up to, until
sobre (de), dessobre (de)	on, above, over
sota (de), dessota (de)	under, beneath

Note also the prepositional expressions **a la vora de, al damunt de, al davant de, al darrere de, al defora de, al dessota de**, frequently used alternatives to **vora (de), damunt (de)**, etc.

Further information on *fins*

When **fins** is used in a temporal sense ('until'), it is generally followed by **a** only when the following time expression would have **a** on its own account, so **No arribaran fins dissabte** 'They won't arrive until Saturday' (compare **Arribaran dissabte** 'They will arrive on Saturday'), but **No arribaran fins a la tarda** 'They won't arrive until the afternoon' (compare **Arribaran a la tarda** 'They will arrive in the afternoon'), **Hi estic fins a les set** 'I am here until 7 o'clock'.

Similarly, in a locative sense, **fins** is followed by an expression for 'place at which', and these, as we have seen, often include **a** (sometimes **en**, though expected **en** is often omitted):

He llegit fins a la pàgina 50.	I've read up to page 50.
Fins (a) on aneu?	How far are you going? (lit. up to where . . .)
Vés fins (a) dalt.	Go up to the next floor.
Volem pujar fins (en) aquella ermita.	We want to climb as far as that hermitage.

In expressions other than those of time and place, and in counting expressions ('up to but not beyond'), **fins** is always followed by **a**:

fins al dia 30 inclusivament	up to and including the 30th
Te'n donaran fins a catorze.	They'll give you up to fourteen of them.
Ha insistit fins a aconseguir-ho.	She insisted until she obtained it.

14.3 COMPOUND PREPOSITIONS AND 'PREPOSITIONAL EXPRESSIONS'

Syntactically, compound prepositions consist of a noun, adverb, prepositional or other phrase, which is followed by a prepositional phrase complement introduced by **a** or, in the majority of cases, **de**. Unlike the prepositions mentioned in the previous section (**14.2.3**), here the **a** or **de** element is omissible only in very special circumstances (including generally before the complementizer **que** in the standard language as in **14.1.5**).

14.3.1 COMPOUND PREPOSITIONS DERIVED FROM NOUNS AND FROM WORDS OF MISCELLANEOUS CATEGORIES

cap a   towards, around/approximately

Before adverbs of place beginning with unstressed **a-** or **e-**, and before demonstratives beginning with **aqu-**, the form **cap** is used alone: **cap aquí** 'towards here', 'over here', **cap amunt** 'upwards', **cap avall** 'downwards', **cap enrere** 'backwards', etc.

Quan vagis cap a casa, avisa'm.	When you go home(wards), let me know.
Vindré cap a les nou.	I'll come about nine o'clock.

com a   as, as being, in one's role as

(Note difference from **com** 'as', 'like'.) However, if a definite or indefinite article, or a demonstrative adjective follows, **a** is omitted.

Va ser invitat com a president de l'associació.
He was invited as president of the association.

El bandegem com a indesitjable.
We exclude him as undesirable.

Com a comerciant no té cap garantia.
As a trader she has no guarantee.

Dóna-li mil pessetes com a paga i senyal.
Give him 1000 ptas as a deposit.

Se la van partir com a bons germans.
They divided it as good brothers. (i.e. being good brothers; **com bons germans** would mean 'like good brothers, as if they were good brothers')

Accepti això com la mostra més viva de gratitud.
Accept this as the most vivid expression of gratitude.

El miraven com aquell qui els havia de salvar.
They looked on him as the one who would save them.

The semantic distinction as above between **com** and **com a**, recommended by normative grammarians, is possible only before a noun not preceded by an article or a demonstrative. It is probably not found in spontaneous usage, where the distribution is merely formal: **com** is used before articles and demonstratives, **com a** elsewhere, covering the whole range of 'as', 'like', 'as being', 'in one's role as': **Discutien com a bojos** 'they were arguing like mad'.

des de   from, since (source)

Ens escrivim des de fa dos anys.
We have been writing to each other for two years. (lit. since two years ago)

enfront de	facing, opposite versus
entorn de	around
gràcies a	thanks to
quant a, pel que fa a, respecte a	with respect to, as regards

14.3.2 COMPOUND PREPOSITIONS DERIVED FROM ADVERBS

(a) prop de	near	**dret a**	towards, in the direction of
a través de	across, through		
a menys de	except	**enmig de**	among, amidst
abans de	before (time)	**fora de,**	
arran de	level with, immediately after	**defora de,** **enfora de**	outside, except
		lluny de	far from
després de	after	**més enllà de**	beyond, later than

14.3.3 'PREPOSITIONAL EXPRESSIONS' WHICH ARE LEXICALIZED PREPOSITIONAL PHRASES

Often, as in (i) below, the nouns in prepositional expressions lack expected determiners; in (ii) we have normally constructed prepositional phrases which take their own prepositional phrase complement. Both groups always have **de**. Only a selection of examples is given of each type.

(i)

a base de	based on, consisting in, by means of	**de/per por de**	for fear of
		en lloc de	instead of
a favor de	in favour of	**per mitjà de**	by means of
a pesar de	in spite of	**per culpa de**	as a (negative)
a partir de	from, as from, starting from		result of
		sense sabuda de	without the
a causa de	because of		knowledge of

(ii)

a la dreta de	on the right of	**al costat de**	beside, alongside
al cap de	at the end of, after	**al llarg de**	along
		al voltant de	around

Note also the unusually constructed **de . . . estant** 'from (source)' and **de . . . ençà** 'from (since)'. The more normally constructed **d'ençà de** is used in the same sense; all of these can approximately be replaced by **des de**:

D'aquí estant es veu la torre.
From here you can see the tower.

De la torre estant se sent la remor del mar.
From the tower you can hear the sound of the sea.

D'un quant temps ençà no es publica.
It hasn't been published for some while.

15 CONJUNCTIONS

This chapter deals with lexical items which link and establish a relationship between clauses or elements within a clause. The term 'conjunction' is applied rather loosely to this whole category, which includes words or phrases that might more appropriately be called adverbs or particles. Modern grammar distinguishes between conjunctions, complementizers, and subordinators in analysing their relevance to the functions of coordination and subordination in complex sentences. Here we describe individual items, retaining the broad division between coordinating conjunctions (**15.1**), and complementizers (**15.2–4**). Subordinating conjunctions are treated in the chapters on adverbial clauses (Chapter 33) and conditionals (Chapter 34).

15.1   COORDINATING CONJUNCTIONS

15.1.1   I 'AND'

I 'and' is used much the same as its English equivalent.

En Pere i la Sara arribaran demà.	Pere and Sara will be arriving tomorrow.
Van comprar peres i pomes.	They bought pears and apples.
Jo faré els paquets i tu els portaràs a correus.	I'll make the parcels and you'll post them.

Catalan surnames officially include the paternal followed by the maternal family name, usually linked by **i**: **Josep Pous i Pagès, Agnès Cotoner i Soley**. In practice, according to family custom or individual preference, either **i** or the second surname can be omitted from a person's usual signature: **Manuel Pérez Saldanya, Josep Pla, Clementina Arderiu**.

15.1.2   Ni 'NOR', 'AND NOT', 'NOT . . . EITHER', 'NEITHER'

Ni is the negative form for simple coordination; see also **26.1.2** for further details.

Ella no pot anar-hi, ni jo tampoc.
She can't go, and neither can I. (lit. nor I either)

The construction **ni . . . ni . . .** is used in distributive expressions (see **15.1.3**):

No ho comprenia ni ell ni el seu company.
Neither he nor his companion understood.

15.1.3 DISTRIBUTIVES

As with **ni . . . ni . . .**, distributives are terms that occur in pairs, syntactically expressing an alternative or balanced correlation. The principal cases are:

aquí . . . allí . . .	here . . . there . . . , in one place . . . in another . . .
mig . . . mig . . .	half . . . half . . .
ja . . . ja . . .	now . . . now . . . , sometimes . . . sometimes . . .
ara . . . ara . . .	now . . . now . . . , sometimes . . . sometimes . . .
(sometimes substituted by the more archaic **adés . . . adés . . .** or **ara . . . adés . . .**)	
sia . . . sia . . .	either . . . or, whether it be . . . or . . .
fos . . . fos . . .	either . . . or, whether it be . . . or . . .
entre (que) . . .	(variously rendered)
i (que) . . .	
que . . . que . . .	both . . . and . . .

Examples:

Hi hagué una aclamació fervorosa; aquí aplaudien, allí desplegaven banderes.
There was fervent acclaim, with some people applauding and others unfurling flags.

Ho han aconseguit, mig per instint mig a dretcient.
They've managed it, half by instinct, half deliberately.

Ja brilla el sol, ja els núvols cobreixen el cel.
One minute the sun is shining, the next the sky is covered in cloud.

Ara s'encenen els llums, ara s'apaguen.
The lights keep coming on and going out.

Sia estiu sia hivern, sempre surt a passeig.
Whether it be summer or winter she always takes a walk.

Tenia una paraula per a tots, fossin veïns seus fossin desconeguts.
She had something to say to everyone, whether they were neighbours or people she didn't know.

N'hi deuen cabre més de vint, entre asseguts i drets.
There'll be room for over twenty, between sitting and standing.

Entre que plovia i que em trobava malalt, al final no hi vaig anar.
With it raining and my being ill, in the end I didn't go.

Que vells que nous, n'hi devia haver ben bé un centenar.
Old ones and new ones together, there must have been a good hundred of
them.

Many other particular distributive expressions can be made with various
grammatical elements:

A fora feia fred, a dins calor.
Outside it was cold, inside (it was) warm.

**A un costat/A la dreta es van arrenglerar els militars, a l'altre/a l'esquerra els
civils.**
On one side/On the right the soldiers lined up, on the other/on the left the
civilians.

Per mi és un geni, per d'altres és un pallasso.
I think he's a genius, other people think he's a clown.

Vist des d'aquí sembla verd, vist d'allà té un color més aviat blavós.
Seen from here it looks green, while seen from over there it has a rather
bluish colour.

15.1.3.1   Translating 'both . . . and . . .'

Distributive **tant . . . com . . .** and **així . . . com . . .** cover many instances of
English 'both . . . and . . .':

Ha viatjat molt, tant pel seu país com a l'estranger.
She has travelled a lot, both in her own country and abroad.

Portaven armes, així ofensives com defensives.
They were carrying both offensive and defensive arms.

Tant en Miquel com la Sara van estudiar medicina.
Both Miquel and Sara studied medicine.

However, when the elements are joined not just in additive combination but
in a way that emphasizes or contrasts them, then 'both . . . and . . .' is rendered adverbially, by **a més a més** 'moreover' or by **al mateix temps, alhora** 'at
the same time':

Trobo que és impressionant i alhora grotesc.
I find it both impressive and grotesque.

Refresca i a més a més alimenta.
It both refreshes and nourishes.

Such constructions overlap with use of the adversative **no (solament) . . . sinó
(també)** 'not (only) . . . but (also)' (see **15.1.5.2**):

Has d'estimar no solament els amics sinó els enemics.
You must love both your friends and your enemies.

15.1.4 O 'OR'

O is the equivalent of 'or' in most contexts:

Deu tenir disset o divuit anys.   He must be seventeen or eighteen (years
                                       old).

Fes-ho ara mateix, o et castigaré.   Do it right now, or I'll punish you.

but note the obligatory use of **ni** in negative contexts:

Ho han fet sense queixes ni protestes.   They did it without complaint or
                                             protest.

Where a sharp alternative is being established **o** may be reinforced with **bé** or, more emphatically with **si no**:

Us telefonaré des de Perpinyà o bé des de la frontera.
I'll phone you from Perpignan or from the border.

Explica'ns-ho, o si no, et denunciarem a la policia.
Explain to us, otherwise we'll report you to the police.

(In either of these last two examples the reinforcing **bé** or **si no** could be omitted with only minimal change of force.)

Technical and commercial Catalan reproduces the formula 'and/or' as **i/o**; its use is becoming more widespread:

Cal parlar amb el director i/o el tresorer.
You must speak with the manager and/or the treasurer.

15.1.4.1   *O sia 'or (in other words)'*

O sia denotes equivalence. (Here **sia** is an old form of the present subjunctive of 'be'; parallel expressions with current verb forms are also used: **o sigui/o siga**.)

la pèrfida Albió, o sia Anglaterra
perfidious Albion, or (in other words) England

el protagonista, o sia el personatge principal de l'obra
the protagonist, that is, the main character in the play

15.1.4.2   *O . . . o . . . 'either . . . or'*

O . . . o . . . occurs regularly as a distributive expression, the equivalent of 'either . . . or . . .':

O no s'ha explicat bé, o jo sóc idiota.
Either he's not explained himself properly or I'm an idiot.

O serà a casa seva o se n'haurà anat a comprar.
She'll either be at home or be out shopping.

In this construction **bé** (but not **si no**) may again reinforce **o**, as explained in
15.1.4.

15.1.5   ADVERSATIVES: **Però, sinó**

While both **però** and **sinó** translate 'but', particular attention must be paid to
the distinctive functions of these two words.

15.1.5.1   Però 'but'

Però corresponds to 'but' establishing opposition between concepts or
coordinate clauses (affirmative or negative):

Ho han fet ràpidament però de mala gana.
They did it quickly but reluctantly.

Hem trucat diverses vegades, però no ha contestat ningú.
We have phoned several times, but there was no reply.

No m'agrada gaire, però encara el penso comprar.
I don't like it much, but I still plan to buy it.

When **però** is placed after one or more elements in the second of two clauses,
it has the concessive value of 'however', 'though':

**Us prestarem aquests diners, amb la condició, però, que no els malbarateu en
    frivolitats.**
We'll lend you this money, but only on condition that you don't waste it on
    frivolities.

A mi m'agrada molt la idea; en Carles, però, encara hi té els seus dubtes.
I like the idea a lot; Carles, though, still has doubts about it.

In speech, rather than **però** at the end of a sentence one often hears **per'xò**
(strictly a contraction of **per això**):

–Aquest davanter nou és molt jove. –Juga bé, però/per'xò.
'This new forward is very young.' 'He's a good player, though.'

A mi no m'has de convèncer, però.
You aren't going to convince me, though.

15.1.5.2 Sinó 'but'

Whereas **però** translates 'but' expressing restriction of, or opposition to, a preceding idea (which may be affirmative or negative), **sinó** has the special function of rendering 'but' when it *contradicts* a preceding (always negative) statement. Another way to describe this is to say that, while **però** sets up an idea in opposition to what has just been said, **sinó** establishes a modification or rectification within a single general (negative) assertion:

No penso en els fills sinó en els pares.
I'm not thinking of the children but of the parents.

Li ho comunicaré no solament a ell sinó a tots els seus companys.
I shall inform not just him but all his companions.

No hi puc dir res sinó que em sap molt de greu.
I can say nothing but that I am very sorry.

As in the last example above, **sinó** is supported by **que** if the following conjunct contains a finite verb:

No discuteixen, sinó que canvien parers.
They're not arguing but (they are) exchanging opinions.

(For stylistic reasons **que** (and even **sinó que**) may be suppressed in such constructions: **no discuteixen, (sinó (que)) canvien parers.**)
  While **sinó** will almost invariably follow a negative, 'but' after a negative is not always translated by this word. Compare:

No està malalta, però diu que se sent molt cansada.
She isn't ill, but she says she feels very tired.

with

No està malalta sinó molt cansada.
She isn't ill but very tired.

This difference between **sinó** and **però** is further highlighted when it is seen how **però** is sometimes reinforced by **sí (que)**:

No són germans sinó (que són) cosins.
They are not brothers but cousins.

No té germans, però sí (que té) un cosí que viu al Canadà.
He does not have any brothers but he does have a cousin living in Canada.

The first sentence makes a distinction within the general category ('relatives', implied), whereas the second opposes two separate categories ('brother' and 'other relatives').
  Like English 'but', **sinó** also has the value of 'except' after a negative:

No feien sinó queixar-se.
They did nothing but complain.

Ningú no ho ha vist sinó tu.
Nobody saw it but you.

En tres mesos no he menjat sinó pollastre.
For three months I have eaten nothing but chicken.

On the difference between **sinó** and **si no**, see **15.3i**.

15.1.6   ADDITIVE EXPRESSIONS

There is a type of conjunction that expresses continuity, succession, or accumulation in the linking of elements within or between sentences; the semantic relation is more elaborate than just 'and', or 'but'. The main ones are:

(i) encara	further, besides, as well	**ni res**	nor anything
com també	likewise	**encara més**	furthermore, moreover
ni (tan sols)	not even	**així mateix**	likewise, similarly
		ni solament	not even

A més and **de més** 'furthermore', 'besides' are frequently duplicated as **a més a més** and **de més a més**; **i fins i tot** 'and even' is frequently reduced to **. . . i tot**, placed after the item to which it refers.

Vostè pot entrevistar-la i encara pot fer-li una fotografia si vol.
You can interview her and can take a photo of her as well if you want.

Vam donar-li les gràcies i, a més, una bona propina.
We thanked him and gave him a good tip as well.

El van lligar i fins i tot li van tapar els ulls/ . . . i li van tapar els ulls i tot.
They tied him up and even blindfolded him.

Ens han cobrat l'allotjament com també/i així mateix part de les despeses del viatge.
They have charged us for board and lodging as well as for part of the travel costs.

No han concedit premis ni trofeus ni res.
They haven't awarded prizes, trophies or anything.

M'ha vist però ni (tan sols) m'ha dit hola.
She saw me but she didn't even say hello.

As in the last example above, **ni** alone can convey the meaning of 'not even' (**26.1.2**):

Ni ell mateix no se n'adona.   He doesn't even realize it himself.

15.1.7   Doncs AS A CONTINUATIVE

At the head of a sentence **doncs** 'well' occurs frequently to establish continuity or coherence between what follows and either a preceding utterance or the context itself.

Doncs, com t'explicava . . .	Well, as I was explaining to you . . .
Doncs jo sí que vull inscriure-m'hi.	Well I do want to sign up for it.
I doncs, que també veniu?	So then, you're coming too?

Doncs and other illatives

As well as being a response signal and initiator, **doncs** commonly has the illative function of presenting a consequence of or inference from what has just been said. It often corresponds to 'in that case', translated usually as 'well' or 'then', both in colloquial/informal registers and in more elevated language dealing with logical relationships. **Doncs** may occur at the beginning of a clause, or after it, separated by a comma.

Que no t'agrada? Doncs no t'ho mengis.
You don't like it? Well don't eat it./Don't eat it then.

No contesten? Ja deuen haver marxat, doncs.
They aren't replying? They must have left already, then.

Tot A és B; tot B és C; doncs tot A és C.
All A is B; all B is C; therefore all A is C.

Other nuances are observed in the use of **doncs**, which is among the most ubiquitous words in Catalan conversation.

Like English 'well', it may tone down the response to a question, adding perhaps a modest or tentative note. It also functions as a spontaneous 'silence filler' or as indication that the speaker has reflected before responding:

Com s'ha de resoldre això? Doncs, convé que procedim amb molta cautela.
How is this to be resolved? Well, we should proceed with great caution.

No està satisfet del resultat? Doncs, jo crec que n'hauria d'estar ben content.
Isn't he satisfied with the result? Well, I think he should be thoroughly pleased with it.

Preceded by **i** and used interrogatively, **doncs** stands elliptically for a vague question about consequence:

I doncs?   So, what's to be done?

Losing its illative force, **doncs** may convey a strong hint of contrast or contradiction:

Tu no ho saps fer? Doncs ell sí.   You can't do it? Well *he* can.

–**Aquests no volen saber-ne res** –**Doncs a mi m'han d'escoltar.**
'They don't want to hear about it.' 'Well they're going to have to listen to
me.'

(Use of **doncs** as a *causal* conjunction is common in speech, though
stigmatized.

(non-standard)	**No ho va fer, doncs estava malalta.**
(standard)	**No ho va fer perquè estava malalta.**
	She didn't do it as she was ill.

Causals are discussed in **33.3.1**.)
   Colloquial usage in the Balearic dialects has **idò** (a variant of **i doncs**)
instead of **doncs** in all the contexts described above.
   Other illative conjunctions are:

| **per tant** | therefore | **així, així és que** | so, thus |
| **per conseguent** | consequently | | |

15.2   Que 'THAT'

The use of **que**, and of the accented form **què**, as a relative pronoun is discussed in Chapter 31. The degree adverb **que** is discussed in **13.6** and **27.2.2.2**.
Here we deal with **que** as a subordinating conjunction or complementizer.

15.2.1   Que AS COMPLEMENTIZER

Que introduces clauses in a way comparable to English 'that' (see Chapter
32), although **que** is never omitted before the subordinate clause.

(i)   Subject clause:

És obvi que no vol venir.
It's obvious (that) he doesn't want to come.

No està bé que li ho diguis.
It's wrong for you to tell him/that you should tell him.

(ii)   Clause complement of copula:

| **La veritat és que no s'ho creuen.** | The truth is (that) they don't believe it. |
| **La nostra opinió és que t'equivoques.** | Our opinion is that you are mistaken. |

(iii) Direct object clause:

Han confirmat que assistiran a la cerimònia.
They have confirmed that they will be present at the ceremony.

Diu que ho farà aviat.
He says she will do it soon.

No volem que hi vagis sol.
We don't want you to go there alone.

(iv) Object complement clause, after prepositional verb or noun:

Insisteixen que es faci així.
They insist that it be done like this.

L'has d'acostumar que s'entreni cada dia.
You must get him used to training every day.

S'han recordat que els ho havíem promès?
Have they remembered that we'd promised them (it)?

Vénen amb la noció que ens podran estafar.
They've come with the notion that they can swindle us.

In this last group the preposition is dropped (as in English) before **que** (see **32.4–5** for details of this phenomenon).

(v) **Que** 'as far as', in frequently used formulae of the kind:

que jo sàpiga   as far as I know/for all I know

15.2.2   **Que** IN COMPOUND CONJUNCTIONS

Que is preceded by many words (adverbs, prepositions, and others) to form compound conjunctions, introducing adverbial clauses (Chapter 33). Some common examples are:

ja que	since (causal)	**tot seguit que**	as soon as
sols que	except that	**d'ençà que**	since (temporal)
encara que	although	**per més que**	however much

(It will be noticed that some elements combining with **que** are themselves compounds, as is the case with **tot seguit que**, **d'ençà que**, and **per més que**.)

With **puix** 'since' (confined like **car** 'since' to literary usage) the use of **que** is optional, as it is too with **com** 'as', 'since' (although the compound form is prevalent in the latter case):

Com que és tan tard, no els penso esperar.
As it's so late I don't intend to wait for them.

To the list of compound conjunctions can be added many like **a fi de** 'with the object of', **de por de** 'for fear of' which drop **de** before **que** opening a clause:

Ho repeteixo a fi que no t'hi equivoquis.
I'm repeating it so that you don't get it wrong.

15.2.3   **Que** AT THE HEAD OF A MAIN CLAUSE

Que may appear at the head of a main clause, especially in speech. Such constructions may be classified as follows:

(i)   Brief questions not introduced by an interrogative word (more details in **27.1.1.1**):

Que voleu prendre un cafè?   Would you like a coffee?
Que no em sents?   Can't you hear me?

(ii)   Other sentences where, rather as in (i) above, a verb like **dir** 'say' or **preguntar** 'ask' might well be understood to introduce the main verb:

Que si m'ha agradat?   (Did you ask) if I liked it?
Llavors jo que entro i els començo a   Then in I come and start to bawl
   escridassar.   at them.
Ell que sí, que s'hi vol apuntar.   He definitely wants to sign up.
Mira, que aquí hi ha un error.   Look, there's a mistake here.
Socorreu-me! Que m'ofego!   Help! I'm drowning!

The last two examples can be compared with group (iii) below.

(iii) Colloquially, as a general vague subordinator/coordinator: **que** is often inserted to connect one idea to another where English might use a more explicit link word, or perhaps imply the connection with just a pause (possibly represented in writing by a dash):

Corre, home! Que farem tard!
Get a move on, man! We're going to be late.

Parla més fluix, que ens escolten aquells.
Keep your voice down – that lot can hear us.

Escriu-ho en majúscules, que s'ha d'emfasitzar.
Write it in capital letters, as it has to be stressed.

Van arribar que jo encara no havia marxat.
They arrived before I had left.

Des de l'octubre que no ha fumat cap cigarret.
She hasn't smoked a cigarette since October.

The last two examples can be related to temporal expressions discussed in **33.2.2**.

(iv) Colloquially, expressing that 'the penny has dropped':

Ah! que vostè és aquell . . .
Ah! (so) you're that person who . . .

Mira, que s'ha d'introduir cap per avall.
Look, you've got to put it in upside down.

(v) With the subjunctive, expressing commands, exhortations, and wishes (more details in **19.6**):

Que vingui i ho veurà.	Just let him come and then he'll see.
Que no sigui res.	(I hope you can) just take it in your stride.

15.3   Si 'IF'

Like 'if' in English, **si** is used: (i) to express condition (Chapter 34) and (ii) to introduce indirect questions (**27.1.2**):

(i)   Conditions

Si vols venir amb nosaltres, t'hauràs d'afanyar.
If you want to come with us, you'll have to get a move on.

Si haguessis vingut abans, l'hauries vist.
If you'd come earlier you would have seen him.

See Chapter 34 for detailed discussion of conditional sentences.
As with English 'if', **si** alone can convey acknowledgement of a fact, sometimes with a mildly concessive implication (see **33.3.3**):

Si callen no és perquè no en sàpiguen res.
If they're not saying anything it's not because they don't know anything about it.

Compound **si bé** is concessive:

Si bé són parents, no s'assemblen gens.
Even though they are related, they don't look at all alike.

Si no 'if not' has the meaning of 'otherwise', standing for a full clause:

Embolica-ho ben embolicat; si no, es trencarà.
Wrap it up really well; otherwise it will get broken.

(**Si no** in this construction is to be distinguished from **sinó**; see **15.1.5.2**, and **26.1.4**. The appearance of **sinó** in place of **si no** is a common error even in well-edited texts.)

In a clause expressing a simple exclusive condition, with the meaning 'unless', **doncs** can support **si (no)** in formal contexts:

Serà multat per la seva absència, si doncs no té cap justificació.
He will be fined for his absence, unless he has some justification.

(ii)   Indirect questions (see 27.2.2.2)

Pregunta-li si en sap alguna cosa.
Ask her if she knows anything about it.

Ara tinc el dubte de si li vaig enviar el fax.
I'm now wondering if I ever sent him the fax.

15.4.   Com 'HOW'

As well as appearing in various modal expressions (see **33.2.3**), **com** 'how' may substitute **que** introducing clauses which are complements of verbs of perception, memory, or communication:

Has vist com ha saltat?
Did you see how he jumped?/Did you see him jump?

Et vull fer entendre com ha canviat tot.
I want to make you understand how everything has changed.

Em recordo de com reia quan ens veia.
I remember how she used to laugh when she saw us.

A distinction can be observed between:

Vaig veure que baixava de l'avió.   I saw him getting off the plane.

and

Vaig veure com baixava de l'avió.   I saw him getting off the plane.

Both sentences may have the same translation in English, but the second indicates that there was something significant or unusual about the action observed.

For **com** in exclamations, see **27.2.2**.

PART III: VERBS

16 MORPHOLOGY OF THE VERB

It is no doubt in the area of verb morphology that differences between the dialects of Catalan are most noticeable. In a written text, it is most likely to be the verb forms which reveal that the text is, for example, Valencian or Balearic. For this reason we give full attention in this section not only to the General variety of Catalan (based on the usage of the Central dialect of eastern Catalonia and Barcelona in particular) but also to the forms of other varieties which are accepted in writing and in formal styles of speaking.

It is very generally the case that compound verbs (containing prefixes such as **con-**, **de-**, **en-**, **ex-**, **sub-**, etc.) have the same inflections as the root verbs they are based on. We shall not attempt to mention all such compounds when dealing with irregular root verbs. Good dictionaries make clear which model a compound verb follows.

Since the focus of this chapter is on forms, and since the correspondence between Catalan and English verb forms is not straightforward, English glosses will not generally be given here. In this chapter, for convenience we use the following person/number abbreviations:

1*sg.*	first-person singular	1*pl.*	first-person plural
2*sg.*	second-person singular	2*pl.*	second-person plural
3*sg.*	third-person singular	3*pl.*	third-person plural

The usage of indicative forms is discussed in Chapter 17 and the use of the subjunctive is dealt with in Chapter 19. Non-finite forms are dealt with in Chapters 20–22.

16.1 QUESTIONS OF ORTHOGRAPHY

Some of the difficulties or irregularities of Catalan verb forms concern matters of orthography (see Chapter 37). We deal with these here first. Then, in the main part of this chapter, we shall not comment further on those alternations in form which are either purely orthographic, or which correspond to regular phonological alternations not specific to verb forms.

16.1.1 ORTHOGRAPHY: REGULAR PHONOLOGICAL ALTERNATIONS

In Catalan, the voiced consonants **b, d, g,** become voiceless (i.e. **p, t, c**) when in word-final position or before **s**. When a vowel precedes, this is regularly represented in the spelling. Thus from **rebre** we have 2*sg.* present indicative **reps,** 3*sg.* present indicative **rep;** from **poder, pots** and **pot;** corresponding to **cregut** we have 1*sg.* present indicative **crec.** When a consonant precedes, this change is not normally represented in spelling (thus we write **corb** 'crow', **tard** 'late', and **sang** 'blood'). The verb **perdre,** 2*sg.* present indicative **perds** 3*sg.* present indicative **perd** follows this rule; however, 1*sg.* present indicative is written with **-c** even when a consonant precedes; thus **resolc** beside **resolgui,** etc., **tinc** beside **tingui.**

The Balearic form of the 1*sg.* present indicative of Conjugation I (**-ar** verbs), which has no suffix after the stem, is also an exception to the general spelling rule. From **trobar** we have in Balearic **jo trob;** from **mudar, jo mud;** from **pagar, jo pag.** For the 1*sg.* present indicative of verbs from other conjugations (which also often have no suffix in other varieties than Balearic) the recommendations of the Institut d'Estudis Catalans are inconsistent; according to one recommendation, they do follow the general rule; thus from **penedir-se,** we have **jo em penet,** like **tu et penets, ell/ella es penet,** and this is the spelling usually found in Valencian: **jo cap, jo decep, jo put, jo rep.** The other recommendation, specifically in the context of Balearic first-person singulars, is for Conjugation II and III verbs to be spelt according to the same principle as Conjugation I, viz. **jo cab, jo deceb, jo pud, jo reb.**

Intervocalic **-v-** regularly corresponds with **-u-** in syllable codas; thus **escrivim, escrivint,** but **escriu, escriure,** etc., **devem, devia,** but **deus, deuria,** etc.

Word-medial (post-vocalic) **-j-** (**-g-** before **e** or **i**) regularly corresponds to **-ig** in final position (thus **boja** 'mad (*f.sg.*)' corresponds to **boig** 'mad (*m.sg.*)'). This is reflected in a few verb forms, such as 3*sg.* present indicative **fuig** from **fugir,** or, from **veure,** 1*sg.* present indicative **veig,** corresponding to 1*pl.* present subjunctive **vegem;** from **haver,** 1*sg.* present indicative **haig,** corresponding to 1*pl.* present subjunctive **hàgim.** (In Balearic the 1*sg.* present indicative of Conjugation I verbs with medial **-j-,** such as **envejar,** ends in **-ig,** according to this principle, so **jo enveig,** and also from **alleujar, jo alleuig,** from **assuaujar, jo assuauig,** etc.; but, after a consonant, from **menjar: jo menj,** from **forjar, jo forj,** and so forth. Outside verbs, medial **-tj-** normally corresponds likewise with final **-ig;** but here, in Balearic 1*sg.* present indicative verb forms, the medial spelling is retained, hence, e.g. **desig** 'desire (n)' but **jo desitj** 'I desire'.)

Other particularities to note in Balearic 1*sg.* indicatives are: **-l·l-** becomes **-l** in final position: **instil·lar: jo instil;** **-nn-** and **-ss-** become **-n-** and **-s-** respectively: **nannar, jo nan; passar, jo pas; -rr-** is retained: **xerrar, jo xerr.**

In all varieties, after a stem which ends in a consonant + **r** or **l,** the vowel **e** is added if no other vowel immediately follows, in order to make the sequence pronounceable. This affects the verb **córrer** (Conjugation II, stem **corr-**); hence 2*sg.* present indicative **corres**, 3*sg.* present indicative/2*sg.* imperative **corre**, and lies behind the preterite etc. stem **correg(u)-**: **corr-** + **-g-**. **Obrir** and **omplir** (Conjugation IIIb) are also affected: 2*sg.* present indicative **obres**, **omples**, 3*sg.* present indicative/2*sg.* imperative **obre**, **omple**. (Note in Balearic this rule never applies to 1*sg.* present indicative of any verb, so Balearic 1*sg.* present indicative **cobr** (from **cobrar**), **entr** (from **entrar**), **corr** (from **córrer**), **obr**, **umpl**; in the 2*sg.* present indicative and 3*sg.* present indicative/2*sg.* imperative in Balearic it is optional, so **obrs/obres/obris, obr/obre/obri**.)

16.1.2   REGULAR SPELLING ALTERNATIONS FOR CONSONANTS

The general orthographic rule described in **37.3.1** affects inflectional alternations in verbs as follows:

'Hard'   -c- is written -qu- before -e- or -i-.
'Hard'   -g- is written -gu- before -e- or -i-.
          -j- is written -g- before -e- or -i-.
          -tj- is written -tg- before -e- or -i-.
          -ç- is written -c- before -e- or -i-.

Thus: **pecar, pecava, pecat**, etc., but **pequem, pequin**, etc.;
      colgar, colgant, colgàrem, etc., but **colgues/colguis, colgueu**, etc.;
also **crec, crega, cregut**, but **creguem, creguis, cregué**, etc.;
      envejar, envejam, envejaria, etc., but **envegem, envegí, envegi**, etc.;
      trepitjar, trepitjau, trepitjàs, etc., but **trepitgeu, trepitgés, trepitgi**, etc.;
      alçar, alçaven, alçada, etc., but **alci, alce, alcéssiu**, etc.
also **venç, vença, vençut**, but **vèncer, vencem, vencia**, etc.

16.1.3   DIAERESIS (¨) AND RELATED ISSUES

The diaeresis is used over **i** when another vowel precedes, to indicate that the i is syllabic (and does not form a diphthong with the preceding vowel). Hence in Conjugation I verbs, we have, from **crear**, present subjunctive forms **creï**, **creïs, creïn**; so, from **canviar: canviï, canviïs, canviïn**; from **lloar: lloï, lloïs, lloïn**; from **evacuar: evacuï, evacuïs, evacuïn**. A -u- between vowels is consonantal, so does not provoke a diaeresis on a following -i: so from **creuar**: present subjunctive **creui, creuis**, etc.

Conjugation I verbs ending in -aiar, -eiar, -oiar, (with consonantal -i-) replace the expected present subjunctive *-aii, *-eii, *-oii with -aï, -eï, -oï, etc. Thus from **esglaiar: esglaï, esglaïs, esglaïn** and note also 1*sg.* preterite **esglaí**; similarly, from **remeiar: remeï, remeïs, remeïn** and 1*sg.* preterite **remeí**; and from **comboiar: acomboï, acomboïs, acomboïn** and 1*sg.* preterite **acomboí**.

In Conjugation III verbs whose stems end in a vowel, the diaeresis will appear over -i- in the ending. By general spelling rule, an acute accent to mark required stress overrides a diaeresis (37.5.1). By special convention, the diaeresis is omitted from Conjugation III verbs in the gerund, the infinitive, and the future and conditional (whose forms are based on the infinitive). These three points can be illustrated from the conjugation of **agrair** 'to thank': present indicative 1*pl.* **agraïm**, 2*pl.* **agraïu**; participle **agraït/agraïda/ agraïts/agraïdes**; imperfect **agraïa, agraïes, agraíem, agraíeu, agraïen**; preterite **agraí, agraïres, agraírem, agraíreu, agraïren**; but gerund **agraint**, future **agrairé**, conditional **agrairia**, etc. Specifically Valencian variants with the diaeresis are: present indicative **agraïx, agraïxes, agraïxen**; present subjunctive **agraïsca, agraïsques, agraïsquen**; past subjunctive **agraïra, agraïres, agraïren**.

The diaeresis is regularly used over -u- when -q- or -g- precedes to indicate that the -u- is not just a 'silent' graphic device. It thus appears regularly in verbs such as **adequar** with /kw/, and **enaiguar** with /gw/, whenever the stem is followed by -e- or -i-, hence **adeqüem, enaigües**, etc.

Exceptionally, and rather inconsistently, -ü- is used in two verbs, **argüir** and **aguar** to indicate that the -u- is syllabic. **Argüir** has -ü- throughout its paradigm (and as it is a Conjugation III verb with a vowel-final stem, we get a sequence of diaereses -üï- in several of its forms, such as **argüïa**). In **aguar** the -u- is written with an accent -ú- when it is stressed, otherwise with a diaeresis -ü- when it precedes -e- or -i-. Because the stressed vowel is marked, the unstressed -i- of the present subjunctive needs no diaeresis. (In fact the anomalous use of diacritics on this rare verb creates more problems than it solves.)

16.1.4   WRITTEN ACCENTS

On verbs, as on other words, the normal function of the acute or grave accent is to mark the position of word stress, coupled with the closed or open vowel quality in the case of -e- or -o-. In a few cases, the function of the written accent, on a word which would not require one by the normal spelling rules, is to distinguish homonyms (see 37.5.3). There are a few verb forms so marked. They are the following:

   from **anar**, 2*sg.* imperative **vés** (distinguished from **ves** 2*sg.* imperative of
      veure 'see');
   from **donar**, 2*sg.* present indicative **dónes** (not usually Val. 2*sg.* present
      subjunctive **dones**), 3*sg.* present indicative/2*sg.* imperative **dóna** (to dis-
      tinguish from *sg.* **dona**, *pl.* **dones** 'woman');
   from **fer**, 3*sg.* preterite **féu** (distinguished from 2*pl.* present indicative **feu**),
      and, in Balearic, 2*sg.* imperative **fé** (distinguished from **fe** 'faith');

from **moldre**, participle **mòlt, mòlta, mòlts, mòltes** (to distinguish from the quantifier adjective **molt** 'many'/'much');

from **saber**, 1*sg.* present indicative **sé** (to distinguish from the reflexive pronoun **se**);

from **ser/ésser**, 1*sg.* present indicative **sóc** (distinguished from **soc** 'tree-stump'), 1*sg.* present indicative **só** (distinguished from **so** 'sound'), 3*sg.* present indicative **és** (distinguished from reflexive pronoun **es**), 1*sg.*/3*sg.* past subjunctive/conditional **fóra** (distinguished from **fora** 'out');

from **tenir**, 3*sg.* present indicative and 2*sg.* imperative **té** (distinguished from 2*sg.* personal pronoun **te**);

from **venir**, 2*sg.* present indicative **véns**, 3*pl.* present indicative **vénen** (distinguished from the corresponding forms **vens, venen** from **vendre** 'sell'), and in Balearic, additionally **vénc** 1*sg.* present indicative, **véngui** 1*sg.*/3*sg.* present subjunctive, etc. (Here the corresponding forms in the General variety have stem vowel **i: vinc, vingui**, etc.);

from **veure**, 3*sg.* preterite **véu** (distinguished from 3*sg.* present indicative **veu**, and from **veu** 'voice').

Though in other respects compound verbs have the same form of the root as the simple verb they are based on, 'contrastive' accents are retained on compounds only to the extent that the contrast remains (or unless required by regular spelling rules). Thus **desfer** has 3*sg.* preterite **desféu** (distinguished from 2*pl.* present indicative **desfeu**); **contenir, retenir** have 3*sg.* present indicative **conté, reté** respectively, because the accent is now required to mark stress on the final syllable; **prevenir** has 2*sg.* present indicative **prevens** and 3*pl.* present indicative **prevenen**, but **revenir** has **revéns, revénen**, distinct from **revens, revenen** from **revendre** 'resell'; **preveure** has 3*sg.* preterite **prevéu** (distinguished from 3*sg.* present indicative **preveu**); **remoldre** 'regrind' has participle **remòlt, remòlta, remòlts, remòltes** for no very good reason.

On the other hand, regular spelling rules may require accents on compounds which are not required on simple verbs; thus from **desfer**, 2*sg.* present indicative **desfàs**, 3*sg.* present indicative **desfà**; from **prevenir** 3*sg.* present indicative **prevé** (but **venir** 3*sg.* present indicative **ve**); from **confondre** participle **confós** (*m.sg.*); from **descosir**, 3*sg.* present indicative **descús**; from **reprendre** 3*sg.* present indicative **reprèn**. In these cases the accent indicates final syllable stress on a word ending in a vowel or -**s** or -**n**.

Reflecting pronunciation, western dialects and Valencian in particular may have -é- in verb forms corresponding to -è- of other varieties. In Valencian this applies to all verb forms; so General **atènyer, empènyer, estrènyer, conèixer, aparèixer, crèiem, dèiem, fèiem, admès, atès, imprès**, etc., are in Valencian **atényer, empényer, estrényer, conéixer, aparéixer, créiem, déiem, féiem, admés, atés, imprés**, etc.

16.1.5   OTHER SPELLING POINTS

In the verbs **dur, lluir, pruir** there are optional alternative spellings for the 2*sg.* present indicative and 3*sg.* present indicative (= 2*sg.* imperative): **duus** or **dus, duu** or **du; lluus** or **llus, lluu** or **llu; pruus** or **prus, pruu** or **pru.**

As regularly, medial -ss- becomes -s in word-final position, so from **tossir** 3*sg.* present indicative **tus.**

16.2   CONJUGATION CLASSES

On the basis of their inflectional paradigms, Catalan verbs fall into three classes (with some subdivisions). Of the 4,500 or so verbs in the *Diccionari General de la Llengua Catalana*, some 3,500 are of Conjugation I, and about 700 of Conjugation IIIa, the remainder being divided between II and IIIb. Originally these classes were characterized by their thematic vowels (vowels appearing between root and inflection): -a- for class I, -e-/-u- or zero for class II, and -i- for class III. In the modern language, however, the thematic vowels of classes I and II in particular are no longer prominent. The classes are, moreover, not distinct in every tense/mood/aspect sub-paradigm; most notably the imperfect has the same endings in Conjugations II and III, and in the General variety, the present and past subjunctive have the same endings in I and II. There is only a handful of irregular verbs whose forms follow patterns of more than one conjugation (to be mentioned in **16.2.4**).

16.2.1   CONJUGATION I

Verbs of Conjugation I have their infinitive ending in -**ar**. The great majority of verbs are in this class, and all of them are regular except for **estar** and **anar**. (Among other irregularities, these two verbs have certain forms from other conjugations: **16.2.4**.) The characteristic -**a**- is present in the infinitive -**ar** (and the related future and conditional -**aré**, -**aria**, etc.), the gerund -**ant**, the participle -**at**, the preterite -**ares**, -**à**, etc., and, in Balearic and Valencian, in the past subjunctive -**às**/-**ara**, etc. (One special Balearic irregularity is **despert** as the participle of **despertar**.) In so far as forms of **dar** 'give' are still used, they are those of a regular Conjugation I verb with stem **d**-.

16.2.2   CONJUGATION II

Conjugation II contains most of the irregular verbs (**16.6**); many Conjugation II verbs in particular have irregular participles. The infinitives of Conjugation II are more varied in ending than its other inflections: there are four subtypes.

(i)   Infinitive in -**re**, as in **batre, perdre, estendre, beure**, etc. (Note that -**d**- is inserted before -re, and in the related future and conditional forms, after stems ending in -l- or -n-; thus **dolent: doldre, prenent: prendre**.)

(ii) Infinitive in unstressed -er. This ending rather than -re occurs after certain consonants, namely:

-x-: **créixer, merèixer, nàixer**, etc. (all irregular)

-m-: **témer, fúmer, prémer** (with its compounds in **es-, re-**), **trémer** (all regular)

-ny-: **atènyer, empènyer, fènyer, (e)strènyer** (with its compounds in **con-, de-, re-**), **plànyer** (with its compound in **com-**), **pertànyer** (largely regular)

-rr-: **córrer** (with its compounds in **a-, con-, de-, des-, dis-, en-, es-, in-, o-, re-, so-**) (irregular)

/-s-/: **tòrcer** (with its compound in **des-**), **vèncer** (with its compounds in **con-, re-**) (both regular), **ésser** (highly irregular)

(iii) Infinitive in -r, after vowel-final stem: **dir** (with its compounds in **a-, contra-, des-, inter-, mal-, pre-, re-**), **dur** (with its compound in **en-**), **fer** (with its compounds in **contra-, des-, estra-, per-, re-, satis-**); from one point of view **estar** could be said to belong here, with stressed -a- in the stem and epenthetic e- before initial **s** + a consonant.

(iv) Infinitive in stressed -er: a few verbs only, all of them irregular, many having alternative infinitive forms in -re. In all cases the -e- of the infinitive is deleted in the future and conditional. The verbs are: **cabre/caber, caldre/caler, doldre/doler, esser** (Bal. form of **ser/ésser**), **haver, poder, saber, soler, valer/valdre** (with its compounds in **equi-, pre-**), **voler**.

Conjugation II verbs have thematic -e- in the 1*pl.*/2*pl.* present indicative, the gerund, the preterite, and the past subjunctive, thematic -i- in the imperfect, and thematic -u- in the regular participle.

16.2.3   CONJUGATION III

Conjugation III verbs have infinitives in -ir. There are two major subgroups. Conjugation IIIa, also known, for historical reasons as 'inchoative', manifests stem alternation: an extended form of the stem occurs in the singular and the 3*pl.* of the present indicative and of the present subjunctive. In the General variety this extension is -eix-; in NW Catalan it is -ix-; in Balearic and formal Valencian it is -esc- in the 1*sg.* present indicative and in the present subjunctive, -eix- in the rest of the present indicative. In less formal Valencian it is -isc- in the 1*sg.* present indicative and in the present subjunctive, -ix- in the rest of the present indicative. There is a considerable number of verbs of this type. Apart from the stem alternation just mentioned they are regular, though a few have irregular participles.

Conjugation IIIb verbs lack the inchoative stem extension. There are relatively few of them, and most of these are irregular in some respect.

Some verbs, as indicated below, may be conjugated either as IIIa or as IIIb; the IIIb forms are more usual. There is a handful of verbs conjugated according to IIIb in Valencian and Balearic (as indicated below) which are IIIa in other varieties.

IIIb verbs:

acudir IIIa or IIIb (esp. IIIb as an impersonal pronominal verb 'occur'; IIIa in the sense 'turn up', 'be present')
afegir (Val. IIIb, elsewhere IIIa)
ajupir
arrupir-se IIIa or IIIb
brunzir IIIa or IIIb
bullir (with its compound in **re-**)
cenyir (Bal. IIIb or IIIa, elsewhere IIIa)
collir (with its compounds in **a-**, **es-**, **re-**)
consumir (with its compounds **resumir**, **presumir**) IIIa or IIIb
cosir (with its compounds in **des-**, **re-**)
cruixir (not **escruixir** which is IIIa)
dormir (with its compound in **a-**)
eixir (with its compounds in **des-**, **re-**, **sobre-**; mixed conjugation in Val.;
    16.6.3)
engolir (Val. IIIb, elsewhere IIIa)
escopir
esmunyir-se
ferir (Bal. IIIb, elsewhere IIIa)
fregir (Val. IIIb, elsewhere IIIa)
fugir (with its compounds in **de-**, **en-**)
grunyir
llegir (with its compound in **re-**) (Val., Minorcan IIIb, elsewhere IIIa)
lluir (with its compound in **re-**) (IIIb 'shine' literally (of lights, stars, etc.);
    in figurative senses 'display', 'shine': IIIa)
mentir (with its compound in **des-**) IIIa or IIIb
morir (with its compound in **pre-**)
munyir
obrir (with its compounds in **entre-**, **re-**)
oir (with its compounds in **des-**, **entre-**) IIIa or IIIb (IIIb in Valencian)
omplir (with its compound in **re-**)
penedir-se (Bal. IIIb, elsewhere IIIa)
percudir IIIa or IIIb
pruir
pudir
punyir

renyir (Val. IIIb, elsewhere IIIa)

retrunyir

sentir (with its compounds in con-, pres-, ress-, but not assentir, dissentir which are IIIa)

sortir (with its compounds in re-, sobre-)

teixir (Val. IIIb, elsewhere IIIa)

tenir (mixed II/IIIb, see 16.6.3)

tenyir (Val. IIIb, with its compound in des-, but retenyir IIIa or IIIb; elsewhere IIIa)

tossir (Bal. optionally IIIa)

venir (mixed II/IIIb, see 16.6.3)

vestir (Bal. IIIa or IIIb, Val. IIIb, with its compounds in des-, re-, but not envestir, investir IIIa; elsewhere IIIa)

16.2.4   VERBS OF MIXED CONJUGATION

A few irregular verbs have forms from more than one conjugation: anar, which is basically a Conjugation I verb, has some irregular present indicative and subjunctive forms from Conjugation II, on the stems vaj-, va-, and future and conditional forms from Conjugation III, on the future stem anir-. Estar, also mostly of Conjugation I ('star' with epenthetic e-), has Conjugation II forms in the present indicative on the stem sta-, and Conjugation II forms on the stem (e)stig- in the present subjunctive, preterite, and past subjunctive. Tenir, venir, escriure, and viure (with their compounds) have certain forms from each of Conjugations II and IIIb; eixir may have certain forms from II as well as IIIb. The conjugation of these verbs is set out in 16.6.3. In Balearic and Valencian prendre has, in certain styles, 1pl. and 2pl. present indicative from III, viz. prenim, preniu.

16.3   SYNCRETISMS

Not all of the verb inflections are formally distinct from each other; some forms display inflectional homonymy or syncretism, that is, they are ambiguous.

Except in a few verbs which have an irregular imperative, the 2sg. imperative has the same form as the 3sg. present indicative (e.g. compra, ven), and the 2pl. imperative has the same form as the 2pl. present indicative (e.g. compreu (Bal. comprau), veneu). The 3sg. and the 1pl. and 3pl. imperatives are always identical with the corresponding persons of the present subjunctive.

In North Catalan, in verbs of Conjugation I, the 1sg. present indicative has the same form as the 1sg./3sg. present subjunctive, e.g. compri.

In Valencian verbs of Conjugation I the present subjunctive is identical with the present indicative except in the 3sg.: 1sg. compre, 2sg. compres, 3sg.

present indicative **compra**, 3*sg.* present subjunctive **compre**, 1*pl.* **comprem**, 2*pl.* **compreu**, 3*pl.* **compren**.

In Valencian, where both the simple preterite and the past subjunctive in -r- are used, their forms for the 2*sg.* and all the plural are identical for all verbs, e.g. **comprares, compràrem, compràreu, compraren**.

In the General variety and Valencian, in regular verbs of Conjugations I and II, and nearly all verbs of Conjugation III, the 1*pl.* and 2*pl.* present subjunctive is identical with the present indicative, e.g. **comprem, compreu; trametem, trameteu; servim, serviu**. In Balearic, however, the 1*pl.* and 2*pl.* present indicative and present subjunctive are always distinct in Conjugations I and III and optional in Conjugation II. In the other varieties the distinction between present indicative and present subjunctive in 1–2*pl.* is found only in cases of stem alternation.

In the imperfect, conditional, and present and past subjunctive of all literary dialects the 1*sg.* is identical with the 3*sg.* (e.g. imperfect 1*sg.* = 3*sg.* **comprava**, conditional 1*sg.* = 3*sg.* **compraria**, present subjunctive 1*sg.* = 3*sg.* **compri** (Val. **compre**), past subjunctive 1*sg.* = 3*sg.* **comprés** (Bal./Val. **compràs**, Val. **comprara**).

16.4   IRREGULARITY IN VERBAL INFLECTION

We have mentioned so far in passing several irregular verbs or irregular forms; here we give an outline of what irregularity consists of. First, though, we should specify what a regular verb is; it is one whose stem is the same in all forms (setting aside regular alternations of phonology or spelling which affect all words in the appropriate conditions, see **16.1**). Its endings are those established for the majority of words of its class. (Stem alternation in Conjugation IIIa is not regarded as an irregularity since the alternation is always of the same kind, and affects the vast majority of verbs in Conjugation III.)

Most of the irregularity in Catalan verbs arises in the form of unpredictable stem alternation. (And no verb has irregular inflectional endings without having some stem alternation as well.) Most irregular verbs have two alternating stems, several have three, and only a few have more; **ésser**, the most irregular verb, has eleven stem alternants. Stem alternation will be explained fully in **16.6**.

Irregularity of inflectional endings is not widespread. We have already considered (**16.2**) alternation in the endings of the infinitive of Conjugation II. The gerund has no irregularities except concerning the pronunciation of -**ent** (see **16.5.2**). Irregularity in the participle (**16.5.3**) can perhaps best be seen as a matter of irregular stems, though some generalizations can be drawn. Stem alternation is also the source of nearly all the irregularity in the present indicative (**16.5.5**), though in Balearic some verbs have forms with an irregular 1*pl.* and 2*pl.* ending, e.g. **deim, deis** corresponding to General **diem, dieu,** from **dir,** while Valencian has special forms for **obrir** and **omplir** (IIIb). A small group of Conjugation II verbs have anomalous endings and stem variants in the imperative (**16.5.11**). Apart from the unusual present subjunctive of **cabre** and **saber** in the General variety, linked with unusual stem alternants, there are no irregularities in the endings of the present subjunctive (**16.5.9**) or the past subjunctive (**16.5.10**), though there are some important dialect differences. A few verbs of Conjugation II have an irregular imperfect (**16.5.6.1**), lacking the characteristic stressed -i- element, and therefore stressed on the stem. Three verbs only (**ser, fer,** and **veure**) have irregular endings in the preterite 1*sg.* and 3*sg.*, or more accurately, they have special stems with no endings (**16.5.6.2**). These irregularities in inflectional endings will be discussed in detail in the relevant subsections of **16.5.**

16.5   INFLECTIONAL CATEGORIES OF THE VERB

The non-finite verb categories are infinitive (**16.5.1**), gerund (**16.5.2**), and (past) participle (**16.5.3**); by definition these lack expression of person (agreement with subject of the verb). The (past) participle takes adjective-type inflections of number and gender (agreeing with the surface subject of a passive verb, and in certain contexts with the object of a verb in the perfect, see **21.1.2**). The use of the infinitive is discussed in Chapter 20, the use of the gerund in Chapter 22, and the use of the participle in Chapter 21. The so-called present participle is also dealt with in Chapter 21.

Finite verbs agree with the subject in person (1, 2, 3) and number (singular or plural) (**16.5.4**).

Tense categories are present, past, future. The expression of present and past overlaps with the expression of mood and aspect. (For usage, see Chapter 17.)

The mood categories are indicative, imperative, and subjunctive. The indicative combines with all tenses (present: **16.5.5**, past: **16.5.6**, future: **16.5.7**), but the imperative (**16.5.11**) is found only allied with present tense, and the subjunctive only with present (**16.5.9**) and past tense (**16.5.10**). (For the use of the subjunctive, see Chapter 19; for the use of the imperative, see Chapter 28.)

The aspect categories are perfective and imperfective; they are distinguished only in the past tense (**16.5.6**), and only marginally in the subjunctive mood (**16.5.10**). Preterite is the conventional name for the past perfective indicative, while imperfect is the conventional name for the past imperfective indicative. (For the use of the aspectually marked categories, see **17.1.3.1.**)

Perfect and conditional do not fit neatly into the framework of tense, aspect, and mood. Perfect in Catalan (**16.5.12**) is expressed periphrastically via the auxiliary verb **haver** (sometimes **ser** in North Catalan and **esser** in Balearic) with the participle of the verb in question. Perfect combines with all of the categories of tense, aspect, and mood (also with conditional) except that there is no perfect imperative. (For the use of the perfect, see **17.2.2.**) The conditional (**16.5.8**) is morphologically related to both the future and the (past) imperfect, and one of its uses is as a relative tense 'future in the past'. (For the use of the conditional, see **17.1.5** and Chapter 34.)

16.5.1   INFINITIVE

The forms of the infinitive have been illustrated above in the presentation of Conjugation classes (**16.2** and see **20.1**). The infinitive is the citation form of a verb in Catalan; for example it provides the heading for dictionary entries. This practice has one unfortunate consequence for the learner, as in nearly all cases (all of Conjugation I and III) the stem of a verb is unstressed in the infinitive form. Due to the reorganization of the vowel system in unstressed syllables (**38.1.2**), it is thus usually not possible to identify from a phonetic transcription of the dictionary entry of a verb (the infinitive), whether the quality of a stem -e- or -o- is open or closed. A few dictionaries, such as the *Diccionari català-francès francès-català* published by Enciclopèdia Catalana, SA, do provide this information.

Corresponding to Conjugation II infinitives in stressed -er (**16.2.2iv**), colloquial speech often uses variants in -**guer**, which are not admitted in writing, for example **volguer** (non-standard) corresponding to standard **voler**.

In varieties other than Valencian, the final -r of an infinitive is not pronounced except when a clitic pronoun is attached, as in e.g. **cobrar-ho, cobrar-les, cobrar-nos, cobrar-ne**. In the informal styles of some regions, the final -r of the unstressed -er ending of certain class II verbs is not pronounced even before clitic pronouns, and this is admitted in less formal writing. The clitic takes the form it would have after a -**re** infinitive (see **12.1.3**). Thus:

Formal	Informal
conèixer-me	coneixe'm
convèncer-te	convence't
convèncer-se	convence's
conèixer-la	coneixe-la
convèncer-lo	convence'l
conèixer-ho	coneixe-ho
convèncer-hi	convence-hi
conèixer-ne	coneixe'n
convèncer-nos	convence'ns
conèixer-vos	coneixe-us
conèixer-los	coneixe'ls

Similarly, then, **convence-te'n, coneixe-us-hi, convence'ls-en**, and so on. Note that, with suppression of the final **-r**, the written accent is no longer required on the infinitive.

16.5.2 GERUND

The form of the gerund is straightforward: following the stem, we have **-ant** for Conjugation I, **-ent** for Conjugation II, and **-int** for Conjugation III. In the case of irregular verbs, which have more than one stem, the stem of the gerund is that of the 1*pl.* and 2*pl.* present indicative, which is also generally that of the imperfect. In the case of those verbs that have a stem variant in /-g-/, colloquial speech often extends this stem to the gerund, to give non-standard **volguent, sapiguent, duguent**, etc. These forms are not accepted in writing (standard **volent, sabent, duent**, etc.). (For usage see Chapter 22.)

16.5.3 PARTICIPLE

The regular (past) participle consists of the addition of /+d/ after the stem + thematic vowel. The final /d/ by regular process becomes voiceless in final position or before **-s**, and is written **-t** (see **38.2.1iii**). All participles, regular and irregular, have regular inflection for number and gender. Thus we have, for example:

Conj I   :   from **pagar**, *m.sg.* **pagat**, *f.sg.* **pagada**, *m.pl.* **pagats**, *f.pl.* **pagades**
Conj II :   from **perdre**, *m.sg.* **perdut**, *f.sg.* **perduda**, *m.pl.* **perduts**, *f.pl.* **perdudes**
Conj III: from **llegir**, *m.sg.* **llegit**, *f.sg.* **llegida**, *m.pl.* **llegits**, *f.pl.* **llegides**

In addition to their strictly verbal use, participles also have the function of verbal adjectives, which are passive in meaning from transitive verbs, active from intransitive ones. (For usage of the participle, see Chapter 21.)

If an irregular Conjugation II verb has a regular participle, this will be formed on the stem variant that ends in **-g** or **-sc** if there is one: thus **creure, cregut; córrer, corregut; créixer, crescut; pertànyer, pertangut** (also **pertanyut**). But **vendre** more usually has as participle **venut** (though **vengut** is also acceptable).

A large proportion of Conjugation II verbs, and a very small number of Conjugation III verbs have irregular participles. Nearly all the verbs which have irregular participles are irregular in other ways also. Irregular participles are 'athematic', that is, they display no vowel after the verb stem. Irregular participles do not add /+d/, but rather one of three alternatives: /+st/ (**-st**), /+z/ (**-s**), or /+t/ (**-t**). Of these, **-st** is restricted to just three verbs, with their compounds (see below). Which of the remaining two occurs is largely (though not completely) predictable, depending on the final phoneme of the stem. A consonant other than **-l-** or **-r-** is deleted before these suffixes, and there is sometimes a change of the stem vowel also.

Participles in **-st**:

(i)   participles in **-st** occur for **pondre** and its compounds (**compondre, respondre, correspondre**, etc.): **post, posta, post(o)s, postes**;

(ii) for **veure** and its compounds (**entreveure, preveure, reveure**): **vist, vista, vist(o)s, vistes**;

(iii) and in Valencian for **riure** (and its compound **somriure**): **rist, rista, rist(o)s, ristes**. (Elsewhere **riure** has a regular participle **rigut**.)

Irregular participles in /+z/ (**-s**) occur for:

(i)   verb stems ending in **-n** (other than **pondre**, just mentioned): thus from **atendre: atès, atesa, atesos, ateses; defendre: defès, defesa, defesos, defeses**; and likewise for **dependre, despendre, encendre, entendre, estendre, fendre, ofendre, prendre** (with **aprendre, comprendre**, etc.), **pretendre, romandre, suspendre; fondre** (with **confondre, difondre**): **fos, fosa, fosos, foses**; likewise **tondre**. (**Fondre** also has an alternative irregular participle **fus**.);

(ii) verb stems ending in **-t**, all the examples being compounds of **-metre** (**admetre, cometre, emetre, ometre, permetre, prometre, trametre**, etc.): **admès, admesa, admesos, admeses**, etc.;

(iii) verb stems ending in **-m: imprimir** (sole example, and **imprimir** is otherwise regular IIIa): **imprès, impresa, impresos, impreses**;

(iv) two verbs only with alternating stems in vowel/[w]/[g]: **cloure** (with compounds **concloure, descloure, incloure**, etc.): **clos, closa, closos, closes; raure: ras, rasa, rasos, rases** (alongside regular participle **ragut**);

(v)   two only of the verb stems ending in **-ny: atènyer: atès, atesa, atesos, ateses; empènyer: empès, empesa, empesos, empeses**.

In the remaining cases, irregular participles have /+t/ (**-t**):

(vi) after vowel-final stems: **coure** (**co-/cou-/cog-**): **cuit, cuita, cuits, cuites** (also regular **cogut**); **fer: fet, feta**, etc.; **dir: dit, dita**, etc.; **dur: dut, duta**, etc. (in Bal. **duit, duita**, etc.); **traure/treure: tret, treta**, etc.;

(vii) after **-r** (all examples are from Conjugation III): if **-r** is preceded by a consonant (C), then **-Cr + t** becomes **-Cert**; otherwise **-t** follows the **-r** of the stem. Thus from **cobrir: cobert, coberta**, etc.; **obrir: obert, oberta**, etc.; **sofrir: sofert, soferta**, etc. (also regular **sofrit, sofrida** etc.); from **oferir: ofert, oferta**, etc. (also regular **oferit, oferida** etc.); **morir: mort, morta**, etc.;

(viii) after **-l**: if **-l** is preceded by a consonant, then **-Cl + t** becomes **-Clert** (all examples are from Conjugation III); otherwise **-t** follows the **-l** of the stem. Thus from **complir: complert, complerta,** etc.; **establir: establert, establerta,** etc.; **omplir: omplert, omplerta,** etc.; **reblir: reblert, reblerta,** etc.; **suplir: suplert, suplerta,** etc. (for all of these five verbs, regular participles in -**it**, -**ida** are also in use). From **resoldre** (likewise **absoldre, dissoldre,** etc.): **resolt, resolta,** etc.; **moldre: mòlt, mòlta,** etc.;

(ix)   stems in -**ny** in verbs not previously mentioned: **estrènyer** (similarly **constrènyer, restrènyer): estret, estreta,** etc.;

(x)   stems in -**v**: **escriure** (with compounds **inscriure, prescriure, transcriure,** etc.): **escrit, escrita,** etc.;

(xi)   stems in -**j**-: from **fregir** and **fugir** Balearic has participles **frit, frita,** and **fuit, fuita,** respectively. In other varieties these verbs have regular participles **fregit, fregida,** and **fugit, fugida.**

16.5.4   PERSON/NUMBER ENDINGS

The polite 2*sg.* pronoun **vostè** is always associated with 3*sg.* verb forms (likewise the 2*pl.* **vostès** with 3*pl.* verb forms). The polite 2*sg.* **vós** is associated with 2*pl.* forms (see **11.1–3**).

Person/number endings are always the last element of a verbal inflection. Except in the 2*sg.* imperative, the 2*sg.* is marked with -**s**; the 1*pl.* is always marked with -**m**, the 2*pl.* with consonantal -**u** (except for a small group of irregular verbs which, in Balearic only, have a form in -**is**), and the 3*pl.* with -**n**.

The 1*sg.* is marked in a variety of ways: by a distinct vowel, such as future -**é**, preterite -**í**, or present indicative -**o** (General variety); by the use, in the present indicative, of a stem variant (no suffix) which is otherwise characteristic of the present subjunctive, thus **dic** 'I say', **veig** 'I see', **traduesc** 'I translate'; or the 1*sg.* may not be distinctly marked at all (see **16.3**). The 3*sg.* rarely has a specific inflection, and is identified by the absence of other person/number inflections.

The 2*sg.* imperative is generally identical with the 3*sg.* present indicative; a number of verbs have an irregular 2*sg.* imperative (often an earlier subjunctive form) which does end in -**s**, such as **sigues** 'be', **vés** 'go'; see **16.5.11.**

16.5.5   PRESENT INDICATIVE

The present indicative is not strongly characterized, having little distinctive material other than the stem and person/number endings. However 1*pl.* and 2*pl.* always have between the stem and -**m**, -**u** a stressed vowel, which is one of the thematic vowels. The 3*pl.* ends in -**en** in all conjugations in all dialects. There are important differences between the dialects especially in Conjugation I.

In the present indicative stress falls on the last (or only) vowel of the stem in the singular and the 3*pl.*, but on the suffix in the 1*pl.* and 2*pl.*

In the following tables, regional forms which do not differ from the General model are put in ordinary type.

Conjugation I *posar* 'put'

	General	N. Catalan	Balearic	Valencian
1*sg.*	**poso**	**posi**	**pos**	**pose**
2*sg.*	**poses**	poses	poses	poses
3*sg.*	**posa**	posa	posa	posa
1*pl.*	**posem**	posem	**posam**	posem
2*pl.*	**poseu**	poseu	**posau**	poseu
3*pl.*	**posen**	posen	posen	posen

The Balearic form has no ending in the 1*sg.* after a consonant (including consonantal -i- and -u-). This is true even for verbs ending in consonant clusters, so we have for example, **jo entr, jo mescl, jo observ, jo localitz**, etc. When the stem ends in a vowel, Balearic adds consonantal -i after -e- or -i-, and consonantal -u after -o- or -u-. Thus from **crear: crei, crees, crea**, etc.; from **estudiar: estudii, estudies, estudia**, etc.; from **lloar: llou, lloes, lloa**, etc.; from **suar: suu, sues, sua**, etc. Verbs with stems ending in /-kw/ or /-gw/ add -o in Balearic as in the General variety (**adequo, enaiguo**, etc.).

Conjugation II (regular) *perdre* 'lose'

	General	N. Catalan	Balearic	Valencian
1*sg.*	**perdo**	**perdi**	**perd**	**perd**
2*sg.*	**perds**	perds	perds	perds
3*sg.*	**perd**	perd	perd	perd
1*pl.*	**perdem**	perdem	perdem	perdem
2*pl.*	**perdeu**	perdeu	perdeu	perdeu
3*pl.*	**perden**	perden	perden	perden

Note that in regular verbs of Conjugation II in Balearic and Valencian the 1*sg.* present indicative and the 3*sg.* present indicative are identical.

Conjugation II (irregular verb with two stem alternants) *vendre* 'sell'

	General
1*sg.*	**venc**
2*sg.*	**vens**
3*sg.*	**ven**
1*pl.*	**venem**
2*pl.*	**veneu**
3*pl.*	**venen**

These forms are current in all dialects.

Verbs with two or more stem alternants always distinguish 1*sg.* from 3*sg.*, as in the above example, by selecting different stems, and have no -o in 1*sg.* Dialect differences do arise, in the case of irregular verbs with more than two stems, as to which stem is chosen for 1*pl.* and 2*pl.* Verbs whose stems end in a sibilant (-ix-, -ç-, -s-) have, for phonological reasons, a 2*sg.* form in -es: thus **torces, vences, apareixes**, etc. (In Balearic, this is optional after -ix-: **coneixs/coneixes, creixs/creixes**.) For similar reasons (**16.1.1**) **córrer** has 2*sg.* **corres** and 3*sg.* **corre** (in Balearic also **corrs, corr**).

In Balearic, those verbs which as in other dialects have an irregular, stem-stressed imperfect, have in addition unusual stem-stressed forms in the 1*pl.* and 2*pl.* present indicative:

caure:	imperfect **queia**:	Bal. 1*pl.* **queim**, 2*pl.* **queis**
creure:	imperfect **creia**:	Bal. 1*pl.* **creim**, 2*pl.* **creis**
dir:	imperfect **deia**:	Bal. 1*pl.* **deim**, 2*pl.* **deis**
dur:	imperfect **duia**:	Bal. 1*pl.* **duim**, 2*pl.* **duis**
fer:	imperfect **feia**:	Bal. 1*pl.* **feim**, 2*pl.* **feis**
jeure:	imperfect **jeia**:	Bal. 1*pl.* **jeim**, 2*pl.* **jeis**
riure:	imperfect **reia**:	Bal. 1*pl.* **reim**, 2*pl.* **reis**
seure:	imperfect **seia**:	Bal. 1*pl.* **seim**, 2*pl.* **seis**
treure:	imperfect **treia**:	Bal. 1*pl.* **treim**, 2*pl.* **treis**
veure:	imperfect **veia**:	Bal. 1*pl.* **veim**, 2*pl.* **veis**

Conjugation IIIa (with stem extension) **patir** *'suffer'*

	General	NW Cat.	N. Cat.	Balearic	Valencian
1*sg.*	**pateixo**	**patixo**	**pateixi**	**patesc**	**patisc**
2*sg.*	**pateixes**	**patixes**	pateixes	**pateixes/pateixs**	**patixes**
3*sg.*	**pateix**	**patix**	pateix	pateix	**patix**
1*pl.*	**patim**	patim	patim	patim	patim
2*pl.*	**patiu**	patiu	patiu	patiu	patiu
3*pl.*	**pateixen**	**patixen**	pateixen	pateixen	**patixen**

In Conjugation IIIa the stem extension (-**eix**-, -**ix**-, -**esc**-, -**isc**-) is found only when stress would otherwise fall on the verb stem, that is, in the singular and 3*pl.* of the present (indicative, subjunctive, imperative). The stem extension has -e- in the eastern dialect group (E. Catalonia, N. Catalonia, Balearic) and -i- in the western group (NW Catalan, Valencian). In formal written Valencian the Balearic variants (but not **pateixs**) are often used, even though spoken Valencian always uses the forms with -i-. In Valencian the 1*sg.* is often spelt -**ixc** (and present subjunctive -**ixca**, etc.). The spelling -**isc** is now recommended by the IEC for Valencian.

*Conjugation IIIb **dormir** 'sleep'*

	General	N. Catalan	Balearic	Valencian
1*sg.*	**dormo**	**dormi**	**dorm**	**dorm**
2*sg.*	**dorms**	dorms	dorms	dorms
3*sg.*	**dorm**	dorm	dorm	dorm
1*pl.*	**dormim**	dormim	dormim	dormim
2*pl.*	**dormiu**	dormiu	dormiu	dormiu
3*pl.*	**dormen**	dormen	dormen	dormen

In Conjugation III, as in II, verbs whose stems end in a sibilant (-**ix**-, -**g**-, -**ç**-, -**ss**-, -**s**-, -**z**-) have, for phonological reasons, a 2*sg.* form in -**es**: **ixes, fuges, tusses, cuses, brunzes**. Balearic optionally does not use this variant after -**ix** or -**ig**: **pareixes/pareixs, fuges/fuigs**. In Conjugation IIIb, as in regular verbs of Conjugation II, 1*sg.* = 3*sg.* in Balearic and Valencian.

16.5.6   PAST TENSES

16.5.6.1   *(Past) imperfect*

There are only two regular models for the imperfect; Conjugations II and III follow exactly the same pattern. Only ten verbs have an irregular imperfect.

	Conj. I **posar**	Conj. II (= III) **perdre**
1*sg.*	**posava**	**perdia**
2*sg.*	**posaves**	**perdies**
3*sg.*	**posava**	**perdia**
1*pl.*	**posàvem**	**perdíem**
2*pl.*	**posàveu**	**perdíeu**
3*pl.*	**posaven**	**perdien**

The irregular imperfects are found in those ten verbs (of Conjugation II) one of whose alternant stems ends in consonantal -**i**. Stress falls on the stem throughout the paradigm.

Conjugation II irregular imperfect

	caure	**creure**	**dur**
1*sg.*	**queia**	**creia**	**duia**
2*sg.*	**queies**	**creies**	**duies**
3*sg.*	**queia**	**creia**	**duia**
1*pl.*	**quèiem**	**crèiem**	**dúiem**
2*pl.*	**quèieu**	**crèieu**	**dúieu**
3*pl.*	**queien**	**creien**	**duien**

The other verbs with an irregular imperfect are **dir** (**deia**, etc.), **fer** (**feia**, etc.), **jeure/jaure** (**jeia**, etc.), **riure** (**reia**, etc.), **seure** (**seia**, etc.), **treure/traure** (**treia**, etc.), **veure** (**veia**, etc.). (As mentioned previously, Valencian prefers -é- to -è- in all verb forms, so Valencian **quéiem**, **créieu**, etc.)

16.5.6.2 Preterite (past perfective indicative)

There are two general patterns of preterite formation, a synthetic one, and an analytic or periphrastic one. The periphrastic one uses an auxiliary verb with stem **va-**, together with the infinitive. An affix -**re**- is characteristic of the 2*sg.* and all the plural forms of the synthetic preterite, and this is found attached to the auxiliary **va-** also, in one of its optional paradigms. The 1*sg.* inflection of the synthetic preterite in all conjugations is -**i**; the other inflections display a thematic vowel depending on the conjugation.

Synthetic preterite

	Conj. I **posar**	Conj. II **perdre**	Conj. III **dormir**
1*sg.*	**posí**	**perdí**	**dormí**
2*sg.*	**posares**	**perderes**	**dormires**
3*sg.*	**posà**	**perdé**	**dormí**
1*pl.*	**posàrem**	**perdérem**	**dormírem**
2*pl.*	**posàreu**	**perdéreu**	**dormíreu**
3*pl.*	**posaren**	**perderen**	**dormiren**

Most irregular verbs of Conjugation II add the regular endings above to one of their stem variants, the one that ends in /g/ or /sk/ if there is one; thus, from **creure**: **creguí, cregueres, cregué**, etc.; from **viure**: **visquí, visqueres, visqué**, etc.

Three verbs only have strong (i.e. stem-stressed) forms in the synthetic preterite, and then only in the 1*sg.* and 3*sg.* They are **fer**, which has **fiu, feres, féu, férem, féreu, feren**; **ser/ésser/esser**, which has **fui** (Val. **fon**), **fores, fou, fórem, fóreu, foren**; and **veure**, which has **viu, veres/veieres, véu** (Val. also **viu**), **vérem/veiérem, véreu/veiéreu, veren/veieren**. **Veure** also uses a weak 3*sg.* **veié**.

The analytic preterite uses an auxiliary **va-** element followed by the infinitive of the verb in question. The paradigm of the preterite auxiliary is:

Analytic preterite auxiliary

1*sg.*	**vaig**	
2*sg.*	**vas**	or **vares**
3*sg.*	**va**	
1*pl.*	**vam**	or **vàrem**
2*pl.*	**vau**	or **vàreu**
3*pl.*	**van**	or **varen**

Of the alternative forms, those in the first column are preferred by normative grammar. (1*sg.* **vàreig**, 1*pl.* **vem**, 2*pl.* **veu** are used additionally in speech but are 'not recommended'.) Thus the analytic alternatives, for example, to the synthetic paradigms above, are: **vaig posar, vas/vares posar, va posar, vam/vàrem posar, vau/vàreu posar, van/varen posar; vaig perdre**, etc.; **vaig dormir**, etc.

Except for the synthetic preterite forms of **deure: deguí, degueres**, etc., which are generally current, in spontaneous speech the synthetic preterite is current only in central Valencian, and to some extent in the Balearics; the analytic preterite is used in all regions. In written Catalan both synthetic and analytic forms are widely used, with the exception of the synthetic 1*sg.* (**posí, perdí, dormí**, etc.) which is common only in Valencian and in Ibiza.

16.5.7   FUTURE

The future tense is constructed on the pattern: infinitive (minus final -e if there is one) + the endings **-é, -às, -à, -em, -eu, -an**, all of which are stressed. Thus:

	Conj. I **posar**	Conj. II **perdre**	Conj. III **dormir**
1*sg.*	posaré	perdré	dormiré
2*sg.*	posaràs	perdràs	dormiràs
3*sg.*	posarà	perdrà	dormirà
1*pl.*	posarem	perdrem	dormirem
2*pl.*	posareu	perdreu	dormireu
3*pl.*	posaran	perdran	dormiran

Conjugation II verbs with an infinitive in stressed -er use a different, more regular, base to construct the future (and conditional) on. Thus from **saber: sabré, sabràs, sabrà**, etc.; **poder: podré; voler: voldré; valer/valdre: valdré; haver: hauré**, etc. **Tenir** and **venir**, which have alternative infinitive forms **tindre** and **vindre**, use only the latter as the base for the future: **tindré, vindré**, etc. (**tendré, vendré**, etc. in Majorcan). **Anar** exceptionally has future **aniré**, etc.

A few Conjugation II irregular verbs which have -e- in the stem of the infinitive, have -a- in the future/conditional stem. They are firstly **fer**: future **faré**, etc., conditional **faria**, etc.; and also those verbs which more generally have -e- in the stem when it is stressed but -a- when it is not, namely, **heure, jeure, treure, néixer**, and **péixer**: future: **hauré, jauré, trauré, naixeré, paixeré**, etc.; conditional: **hauria, jauria, trauria, naixeria, paixeria**, etc.

16.5.8   CONDITIONAL

The conditional is always built on exactly the same base as the future, using endings which are the same as those of the imperfect of Conjugations II and III.

	Conj. I posar	Conj. II perdre	Conj. III dormir
1sg.	posaria	perdria	dormiria
2sg.	posaries	perdries	dormiries
3sg.	posaria	perdria	dormiria
1pl.	posaríem	perdríem	dormiríem
2pl.	posaríeu	perdríeu	dormiríeu
3pl.	posarien	perdrien	dormirien

The verbs **ser/ésser/esser** and **haver** have alternative conditionals to their regular ones, **seria, hauria**, etc. (The alternative paradigms are in fact those of the **-r-** past subjunctive which is current in Valencian; see **16.5.10.1**.)

*Second conditional of **ser, haver***

	ser	haver
1sg.	fóra	haguera
2sg.	fores	hagueres
3sg.	fóra	haguera
1pl.	fórem	haguérem
2pl.	fóreu	haguéreu
3pl.	foren	hagueren

See **34.6.1** for the usage of these forms.

16.5.9 PRESENT SUBJUNCTIVE

The eastern dialect group (N. Catalonia, E. Catalonia, Balearics) has developed a characteristic subjunctive marker **-i-** for the unstressed endings (singular and *3pl.*) of all conjugations. These forms have entirely replaced the older forms in North Catalonia and the central dialect (E. Catalonia), and very largely in Balearic also; they are increasingly used in the Northwestern area, but not at all in Valencian. A characteristic of Balearic is to employ distinct forms for present indicative and present subjunctive in *1pl.* and *2pl.* In other regions the inflectional endings for these are identical, and the distinction is maintained only where there is stem alternation.

*Conjugation I **posar** 'put'*

	General/Balearic	NW and Valencian
1sg.	posi	pose
2sg.	posis	poses
3sg.	posi	pose
1pl.	posem	posem
2pl.	poseu	poseu
3pl.	posin	posen

Note that the NW and Valencian forms differ from the Valencian present indicative only in the 3*sg.*

Early Catalan had forms of the present subjunctive singular of Conjugation I with no vowel in the ending. A very few of these forms survive as relics in expressions such as: **Déu vos guard** (a greeting: lit. May God protect you), **Déu me'n guard!** 'God forbid!', **Déu ajut quan . . .** 'God knows when . . . ' (lit. May God assist when . . .), **Déu n'hi do!** 'What a lot!' (lit. May God give of it there! (**do** is an old 3*sg.* present subjunctive of **donar**)), **Déu t'ho pac** 'May God reward you for it' (**pac = pagui**), **Llamp te mat** 'May lightning kill you'.

*Conjugation II (regular) present indicative **perdre** 'lose'*

	General	Balearic	NW and Valencian
1*sg.*	**perdi**	perdi	**perda**
2*sg.*	**perdis**	perdis	**perdes**
3*sg.*	**perdi**	perdi	**perda**
1*pl.*	**perdem**	**perdiguem**/perdem	perdem
2*pl.*	**perdeu**	**perdigueu**/perdeu	perdeu
3*pl.*	**perdin**	perdin	**perden**

The NW and Valencian forms differ from the present indicative only in the singular. Note Balearic introduces an element **-igu-** into regular verbs of Conjugation II and all Conjugation III, to distinguish present subjunctive from present indicative in 1–2*pl.*

*Conjugation II (irregular verb with two stem alternants) **vendre** 'sell'*

	General/Balearic	NW and Valencian
1*sg.*	**vengui**	**venga**
2*sg.*	**venguis**	**vengues**
3*sg.*	**vengui**	**venga**
1*pl.*	**venguem**	venguem
2*pl.*	**vengueu**	vengueu
3*pl.*	**venguin**	**venguen**

In the present subjunctive, Conjugation II verbs with two or more stem alternants use the alternant in /-g/, if they have one. Colloquial Valencian varieties make use of some older forms of 1*pl.* and 2*pl.* present subjunctive, especially for common verbs, **dir: digam, digau; ser: sigam, sigau; venir: vingam, vingau,** etc.

The earlier type without inflectional **-i-**, which is retained in NW and Valencian, is found in the General and Balearic varieties in two verbs only: **saber** and **cabre**. In these particular verbs Valencian uses forms without **-g-**:

*Conjugation II (irregular verbs **saber, cabre**)*

	General/Balearic		Valencian	
1*sg.*	sàpiga	càpiga	sàpia	càpia
2*sg.*	sàpigues	càpigues	sàpies	càpies
3*sg.*	sàpiga	càpiga	sàpia	càpia
1*pl.*	sapiguem	capiguem	sapiem	capiem
2*pl.*	sapigueu	capigueu	sapieu	capieu
3*pl.*	sàpiguen	càpiguen	sàpien	càpien

Colloquial (non-standard) speech in Palma (Majorca) displays a strong tendency to extend the special system of endings of **saber** and **cabre** to all verbs, regular and irregular, of all conjugations: **càntiga** etc., **rèbiga** etc., **dòrmiga** etc., **servèsquiga**, etc.

*Conjugation IIIa **patir** 'suffer'*

	General	Balearic	Alternative Bal./ formal Val.	NW and Valencian
1*sg.*	pateixi	patesqui	patesca	patisca
2*sg.*	pateixis	patesquis	patesques	patisques
3*sg.*	pateixi	patesqui	patesca	patisca
1*pl.*	patim	patiguem	patim	patim
2*pl.*	patiu	patigueu	patiu	patiu
3*pl.*	pateixin	patesquin	patesquen	patisquen

The third column contains traditional forms, still used to some in extent in Balearic, and in formal written Valencian. In Valencian the spelling **-ixca**, **-ixques**, etc., is often found; the forms above are those recommended by the IEC.

*Conjugation IIIb **dormir** 'sleep'*

	General	Balearic	NW and Valencian
1*sg.*	dormi	dormi	dorma
2*sg.*	dormis	dormis	dormes
3*sg.*	dormi	dormi	dorma
1*pl.*	dormim	dormiguem	dormim
2*pl.*	dormiu	dormigueu	dormiu
3*pl.*	dormin	dormin	dormen

The NW and Valencian forms differ from the present indicative only in the singular.

In the General variety and Balearic a few older forms of the present subjunctive of Conjugation II/III are used in certain expressions, such as **o sia** (or **o sigui**) 'that is to say' (lit. or let it be), **adéu-siau** 'good-bye', **vaja** 'well' (interjection), **Vejam** 'Let's see', **Vinga!** 'Come on!', **Visca!** 'Long live . . . !'.

16.5.10   PAST SUBJUNCTIVE

16.5.10.1   Synthetic past subjunctive

The synthetic past subjunctive is always based on the same stem as (the plural of) the preterite. There are two basic models, with some variation in detail between the dialects. One model uses forms with -ss- in the suffix; the other uses -r-. The -r- model is exclusively Valencian; written Valencian also makes substantial use of the most traditional form of the -ss- past subjunctive, which avoids -i- in the unstressed final syllable, namely, for example (2sg.) -asses, -esses, -isses. These traditional forms are also used in Balearic, alongside the forms listed below. In the General variety and in NW the endings for Conjugations I and II are the same. In other varieties the thematic conjugation vowels occur before -ss- or -r-.

Conjugation I *posar*

	General	Balearic	NW and literary Val.	Val. (literary)	Val. -r-
1sg.	posés	posàs	posés	posàs	posara
2sg.	posessis	posassis	posesses	posasses	posares
3sg.	posés	posàs	posés	posàs	posara
1pl.	poséssim	posàssim	poséssem	posàssem	posàrem
2pl.	poséssiu	posàssiu	posésseu	posàsseu	posàreu
3pl.	posessin	posassin	posessen	posassen	posaren

Conjugation II *perdre*

	General/Balearic	NW and literary Val.	Val. -r-
1sg.	perdés	perdés	perdera
2sg.	perdessis	perdesses	perderes
3sg.	perdés	perdés	perdera
1pl.	perdéssim	perdéssem	perdérem
2pl.	perdéssiu	perdésseu	perdéreu
3pl.	perdessin	perdessen	perderen

Conjugation III *patir*

	General/Balearic	Valencian (literary)	Valencian -r-
1sg.	patís	patís	patira
2sg.	patissis	patisses	patires
3sg.	patís	patís	patira
1pl.	patíssim	patíssem	patírem
2pl.	patíssiu	patísseu	patíreu
3pl.	patissin	patissen	patiren

16.5.10.2   Past perfective subjunctive

Although the past subjunctive (**16.5.10.1**) may be used for both perfective and imperfective aspect (corresponding to both the preterite and the imperfect indicative), there is a distinct, analytic past perfective subjunctive, constructed on the basis of subjunctive forms of the auxiliary **va-**, followed by the infinitive of the verb in question, which is used in certain constructions (**19.2.4iii–iv**). The auxiliary has the following forms:

	General	NW and Valencian
1*sg.*	vagi	vaja
2*sg.*	vagis	vages
3*sg.*	vagi	vaja
1*pl.*	vàgim	vàgem
2*pl.*	vàgiu	vàgeu
3*pl.*	vagin	vagen

Note that the forms of the 1*pl.* and 2*pl.* of the auxiliary are stressed on the stem, a pattern not found elsewhere in present-type paradigms in words of more than one syllable, except in the perfect auxiliary **haver**. Thus the past perfective subjunctive of **posar**: **vagi posar**, etc.; of **perdre**: **vagi perdre**, etc.; of **patir**: **vagi patir**, etc.

16.5.11   IMPERATIVE

There are few distinct imperative forms. The regular pattern, demonstrating syncretism (**16.3**), is:

2*sg.* imperative = 3*sg.* present indicative
2*pl.* imperative = 2*pl.* present indicative
other persons: imperative = present subjunctive

In most cases, the 1*pl.* imperative = 1*pl.* present subjunctive is also the same form as the 1*pl.* present indicative: **cantem** 'we sing'/'that we sing'/'let us sing', **agraïm** 'we thank'/'that we thank'/'let us thank', etc. For this reason, and also because the 2*pl.* imperative has the same form as the 2*pl.* indicative, it is quite common, even in those verbs where 1*pl.* present subjunctive is not = 1*pl.* present indicative, to use in the 1*pl.* imperative the form of the 1*pl.* indicative. J. Ruaix has recommended that this usage be regarded as standard, thus **concloem** 'let us conclude' (for **concloguem**), **mengem i bevem** 'let us eat and drink' (for **beguem**), **entenem-nos** 'let us understand each other', 'let us be clear' (for **entenguem-nos**), **seiem-hi a contemplar** 'let us sit down and look' (for **seguem-hi**).

Dialect variants of present indicative and present subjunctive carry over to the corresponding forms of the imperative (whence it is clear that the syncretism is not just fortuitous).

Thus:

from **posar**: 2*sg.* posa, 3*sg.* posi/pose, 1*pl.* posem, 2*pl.* poseu/posau, 3*pl.*
   posin/posen;

from **perdre**: perd, perdi/perda, perdem/perdiguem, perdeu, perdin/perden;

from **patir**: pateix/patix, pateixi/patesqui/patesca/patisca, patim/patiguem,
   patiu, pateixin/patesquin/patesquen/patisquen;

from **dormir**: dorm, dormi/dorma, dormim/dormiguem, dormiu, dormin/
   dormen.

In negative constructions the present subjunctive is used in all persons: **no
posis, no pateixis, no vingueu**, etc. (See Chapter 28.)

The 2*sg.* imperative of most Conjugation II and III verbs ends in a consonant. In the spoken language (and informal written), alternative forms are used
when such an imperative is followed by a clitic pronoun. These alternative
forms resemble the 3*pl.* present indicative without the final -n. (For IIIa verbs
spoken Balearic uses the stem with -i instead of the stem with -eix.) The clitic
pronoun then assumes its postvocalic form.

Written	Spoken	
mor-te	**more't**	cf. 3*pl.* present indicative **moren**
fuig-hi	**fuge-hi**	cf. 3*pl.* present indicative **fugen**
rep-ho	**rebe-ho**	cf. 3*pl.* present indicative **reben**
venç-la	**vence-la**	cf. 3*pl.* present indicative **vencen**
cull-les	**culle-les**	cf. 3*pl.* present indicative **cullen**
plany-me	**planye'm**	cf. 3*pl.* present indicative **planyen**
vesteix-te	**vesteixe't**	cf. 3*pl.* present indicative **vesteixen**
	(Bal. **vesti't**)	

A few verbs have irregular imperative forms in both the 2*sg.* and the 2*pl.* One
pattern repeated in several verbs is the use of forms identical to the old
(= current Valencian and NW) present subjunctive. Thus:

dir: 2*sg.* **digues**, 2*pl.* **digueu** (Bal. **digau**)

estar: 2*sg.* **estigues**, 2*pl.* **estigueu** (Bal. **estigau**); for **estar**, Balearic and
   Valencian also use regular forms: Bal. **està, estau**, and Val. **està, esteu**.

poder: 2*sg.* **pugues**, 2*pl.* **pugueu**

saber: 2*sg.* **sàpigues**, 2*pl.* **sapigueu** (Bal. **sapigau**) (Val. **sàpies, sapieu**)

ser: 2*sg.* **sigues**, 2*pl.* **sigueu** (Bal. **sigau, siau**)

tenir: 2*sg.* **tingues**, 2*pl.* **tingueu** (alongside regular and other forms)

veure: 2*sg.* **veges**, 2*pl.* **vegeu** (alongside regular and other forms)

voler: 2*sg.* **vulgues**, 2*pl.* **vulgueu**

Riure has such an irregular imperative in 2*pl.* only (**rigueu** (but Bal. **reis** = 2*pl.*
present indicative), 2*sg.* **riu**).

In the spoken language, and in informal writing, the -s of these 2*sg.* forms is omitted before a suffixed clitic pronoun, which then adopts its postvocalic form, for example:

Formal	Informal
digues-li	**digue-li**
estigues-te	**estigue't**
sigues-nos	**sigue'ns**

The remaining irregular forms are (with 2*pl.* as above, or regular = 2*pl.* present indicative):

anar: 2*sg.* **vés**
fer: 2*sg.* **fes** (Bal. **fé**)
dir: Val. 2*sg.* **dis**
dur: Val. 2*sg.* **dus** (informal, as well as expected **duu/du**)
morir: Val. 2*sg.* **muir** (as well as expected **mor**)
prevenir: 2*sg.* **prevén** (Val. also **previn**, and likewise for **avenir**, **desavenir**, **intervenir** and **reconvenir**); other compounds of **venir** use 2*sg.* **-vén**, 2*pl.* **-veniu**, even in Valencian
tenir: 2*sg.* **ten** (Val. **tin**), also reg. **té** (= 3*sg.* present indicative) as well as **tingues** (see above). Compounds of **tenir** use 2*sg.* **-tén** (Val. **-tín**) or **-tingues**, 2*pl.* **-teniu** or **-tingueu**
venir: 2*sg.* **vine**
veure: 2*sg.* **ves** (as well as expected 2*sg.* **veu**, 2*pl.* **veieu**, and the forms mentioned above)

16.5.12   PERFECT (ANTERIOR)

The periphrastic perfect forms are also referred to as compound tenses; see **17.2**. Perfect is expressed by a form of the auxiliary verb **haver** (**esser** with certain verbs in Balearic and N. Catalan) followed by the participle of the verb in question. Perfect combines with all the other finite and non-finite verb categories except imperative (i.e. there is no ***haveu posat!**).

The forms of the auxiliary **haver** are:

Infinitive: **haver**, thus **haver posat** 'to have put', **haver perdut**, **haver dormit**
Gerund: **havent**, thus **havent posat** 'having put', **havent perdut**, **havent dormit**
Participle: **hagut**

Present indicative:

1*sg.*   **he** (Note that in the construction **haver de** + infinitive 'have to', the form **haig** is also used)
2*sg.*   **has**

3sg.   **ha**
1pl.   **hem** (also **havem**)
2pl.   **heu** (also **haveu**)
3pl.   **han**
   thus: **he posat** 'I have put', **he perdut, he dormit**, etc.

Imperfect:

1sg.   **havia**
2sg.   **havies**
3sg.   **havia**
1pl.   **havíem**
2pl.   **havíeu**
3pl.   **havien**
   thus: **havia posat** 'I had put', **havia perdut, havia dormit**, etc.

Preterite:

1sg.	**haguí**	or	**vaig haver**
2sg.	**hagueres**	or	**vas/vares haver**
3sg.	**hagué**	or	**va haver**
1pl.	**haguérem**	or	**vam/vàrem haver**
2pl.	**haguéreu**	or	**vau/vàreu haver**
3pl.	**hagueren**	or	**van/varen haver**

   thus: **haguí posat** or **vaig haver posat** 'I had put', **haguí perdut** or **vaig haver perdut, haguí dormit** or **vaig haver dormit**, etc.

Future:

1sg.   **hauré**
2sg.   **hauràs**
3sg.   **haurà**
1pl.   **haurem**
2pl.   **haureu**
3pl.   **hauran**
   thus: **hauré posat** 'I will have put', **hauré perdut, hauré dormit**, etc.

Conditional:

1sg.	**hauria**	or	**haguera**
2sg.	**hauries**	or	**hagueres**
3sg.	**hauria**	or	**haguera**
1pl.	**hauríem**	or	**haguérem**
2pl.	**hauríeu**	or	**haguéreu**
3pl.	**haurien**	or	**hagueren**

   thus: **hauria posat** 'I would have put', **hauria perdut, hauria dormit**, etc.

Present subjunctive:

	General	NW and Valencian
1sg.	hagi	haja
2sg.	hagis	hages
3sg.	hagi	haja
1pl.	hàgim	hàgem
2pl.	hàgiu	hàgeu
3pl.	hagin	hagen

thus: **hagi/haja posat, hagi/haja perdut, hagi/haja dormit**, etc.

Past subjunctive:

	General	NW and Valencian	Valencian
1sg.	hagués	hagués	haguera
2sg.	haguessis	haguesses	hagueres
3sg.	hagués	hagués	haguera
1pl.	haguéssim	haguéssem	haguérem
2pl.	haguéssiu	haguésseu	haguéreu
3pl.	haguessin	haguessen	hagueren

thus: **hagués/haguera posat, hagués/haguera perdut, hagués/haguera dormit**, etc.

Past perfective subjunctive:

	General	NW and Valencian
1sg.	vagi haver	vaja haver
2sg.	vagis haver	vages haver
3sg.	vagi haver	vaja haver
1pl.	vàgim haver	vàgem haver
2pl.	vàgiu haver	vàgeu haver
3pl.	vagin haver	vagen haver

thus: **vagi/vaja haver posat, vagi/vaja haver perdut, vagi/vaja haver dormit**, etc.

As mentioned above, in Balearic, the perfect/anterior of certain verbs may be formed with the auxiliary **esser** 'be'. In this respect, Balearic usage is quite similar to that found in French or Italian. The verbs involved are:

(i)   pronominal and reflexive verbs, e.g. **se són retirats/se són retirades** 'they have withdrawn', **me som sorprès/me som sorpresa** 'I have surprised myself';

(ii) **anar, tornar, venir, esser, estar, néixer, quedar, romandre**, and other verbs similar in sense, thus **som anat/anada** 'I have gone', **ets vengut/venguda** 'you have come', **érem estats/estades** 'we had been', etc.

When the perfect is constructed with **esser**, the participle always agrees in number and gender with the subject.

16.6 IRREGULAR VERBS (STEM ALTERNATION)

Apart from relatively few irregularities in inflectional endings, which have been detailed in **16.5**, irregularity in Catalan verbs consists in stem variation. Most irregular verbs have two or three stems, which are distributed across the various inflectional categories in comparable ways. In what follows we draw attention specifically to the system or pattern in the irregularities. Most Catalan dictionaries and grammars provide tables or lists of forms for irregular as well as regular verbs. Irregular verbs of Conjugation II are treated in **16.6.1**; those of Conjugation III are treated in **16.6.2**. In **16.6.3** we deal with those few irregular verbs which are of mixed conjugation, namely, **anar**, **eixir**, **escriure**, **estar**, **tenir**, **venir**, and **viure**.

16.6.1 IRREGULAR VERBS OF CONJUGATION II

The majority of Conjugation II verbs are irregular. Those that are regular, with no stem variation, are as follows:

Regular verbs of Conjugation II

(i)   Most stems ending in a labial stop: **-b-**: **rebre**, **concebre**, **decebre**, **percebre** (but **cabre/caber** and **saber** are irregular); **-p-**: **rompre**; **-m-**: **fúmer**, **prémer**, **témer**, **trémer**.

(ii)   Most stems ending in a dental/alveolar obstruent: **-d-**: **perdre** (but **poder** is irregular); **-t-**: **batre**, **botre**, **fotre**, **retre** (though compounds of **-metre** have an irregular participle); **tòrcer**, **vèncer** (but **ser/ésser/esser** is highly irregular).

(iii) Some stems in **-ny-** are regular in the General variety but may be irregular elsewhere: **fènyer**, **pertànyer**, **plànyer**.

(iv)   The rare verb **cerndre** may be regular or irregular.

The most general pattern of irregularity in Conjugation II, found in two-stem verbs like **doldre**, is for the stems to be distributed on the following pattern:

stem 1 (**dol-**):
   infinitive: **doldre**
   (+ future, conditional): **doldré**, **doldria**, etc.
   imperfect: **dolia**, etc.
   present indicative (except 1*sg.*): 2*sg.* **dols**, 3*sg.* **dol**, etc.
   gerund: **dolent**

stem 2 (**dolg-**):
   1*sg.* present indicative: **dolc**
   present subjunctive: **dolgui** (or **dolga**), etc.

past subjunctive: **dolgués** (or **dolguera**), etc.
preterite (synthetic): **dolguí**, etc.
participle: **dolgut**

Verbs with more than two stems use the third stem for a subset of either set
1 or set 2 above; for example, they may have another stem for the irregular
(strong) participle. Thus **encendre** has participle **encès**, otherwise stem 1 **encen-**,
stem 2 **enceng-**; or **beure**, which has stem 1 **bev-**, stem 2 **beg-**, and in addition
stem 1B **beu-** in the infinitive/future stem, and the 2–3*sg.* and 3*pl.* present
indicative; thus with stem 1, imperfect **bevia**, etc., present indicative 1*pl.*
bevem, present indicative 2*pl.* **beveu**, gerund **bevent**; with stem 1B, infinitive
beure, future **beuré**, etc., conditional **beuria**, etc. Very few verbs have more
than three stems, making further sub-divisions. The pattern of distribution of
variant verb stems can be illustrated by the following diagram:

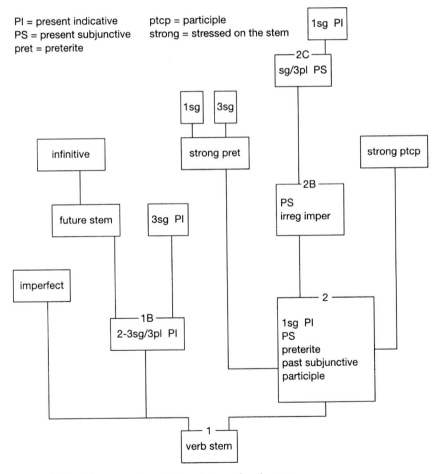

Figure 16.1   Diagram of possible variation of verb stems

If a verb carries a specification for a morphological category, this overrides any specification below for that category on the path back to verb stem (1). Thus, if a verb has just a stem 2 as well as a stem 1, stem 2 is used in the 1*sg.* present indicative, the present subjunctive, the preterite, the past subjunctive, and the participle, and stem 1 elsewhere. If it has stem 2B as well as a stem 2 (e.g. **poder**), stem 2B (**pug-**) is used in the present subjunctive, in the 1*sg.* present indicative and in the irregular imperative, stem 2 (**pog-**) in the preterite, the past subjunctive and the participle, and stem 1 (**pod-**) elsewhere. (From this perspective, a regular verb is, of course, one which has no stem specification more specific than verb stem 1.)

The main branches in the diagram are not entirely independent; thus no verb (except **anar**) has a stem 1B without also having a stem 2.

There are five verbs: **néixer**, **péixer**, **heure**, **jeure**, and **treure**, which in the eastern dialect group alternate the vowel in the stem (in addition to other irregularities). The vowel -e- appears when the stem is stressed, the vowel -a- otherwise. In western varieties -a- appears throughout the paradigm except the (irregular) imperfect of **jaure** (**jeia**, etc.) and **traure** (**treia**, etc.), the western infinitives being **nàixer**, **pàixer**, **haure**, **jaure**, and **traure**.

Conjugation II irregular verbs

Conjugation II irregular verbs are arranged below in alphabetical order of the infinitive.

absoldre (likewise resoldre, dissoldre)

> strong participle: **absolt**, **absolta**, etc.
> otherwise like **doldre**: stem 1: **absol**, stem 2: **absolg-**

admetre

> strong participle: **admès**, **admesa**, etc.
> otherwise: regular

atendre

> strong participle: **atès**, **atesa**, etc.
> stem 1: **aten-**
>> infinitive: **atendre**
>> future: **atendré**, etc., conditional: **atendria**, etc.
>> present indicative: 2*sg.*–3*pl.* **atens**, **atèn**, **atenem**, **ateneu**, **atenen**
>> imperfect: **atenia**, etc.
>> gerund: **atenent**
> stem 2: **ateng-**
>> 1*sg.* present indicative: **atenc**

present subjunctive: **atengui, atenguis, atengui, atenguem, atengueu, atenguin**; Val./NW **atenga, atengues, atenga**, atenguem, atengueu, **atenguen**
preterite: **atenguí**, etc.
past subjunctive: **atengués**, etc.; Val. **atenguera**, etc.

atènyer

strong participle: **atès, atesa**, etc.
otherwise regular

beure

stem 1: **bev-**
  present indicative: 1*pl.* **bevem**, 2*pl.* **beveu**
  imperfect: **bevia**, etc.
  gerund: **bevent**
stem 1B: **beu-**
  infinitive: **beure**
  future: **beuré**, etc.; conditional: **beuria**, etc.
  present indicative: 2*sg.* **beus**, 3*sg.* **beu**, 3*pl.* **beuen**
stem 2: **beg-**
  1*sg.* present indicative: **bec**
  present subjunctive: **begui, beguis, begui, beguem, begueu, beguin**; Val./
  NW **bega, begues, bega**, beguem, begueu, **beguen**
  preterite: **beguí**, etc.
  past subjunctive: **begués**, etc.; Val. **beguera**, etc.
  participle: **begut, beguda**, etc.

cabre (or **caber**)

present subjunctive stem: **capig-**
  present subjunctive: **càpiga, càpigues, càpiga, capiguem, capigueu, càpiguen**
  (Val. present subjunctive stem: **capi-**
  Val. present subjunctive: **càpia, càpies, càpia, capiem, capieu, càpien**)
otherwise regular:
  infinitive: **cabre (caber)**
  future: **cabré**, etc.; conditional: **cabria**, etc.
  present indicative: **cabo** (Bal./Val. **cap**), **caps, cap, cabem, cabeu, caben**
  imperfect: **cabia**, etc.
  gerund: **cabent**
  preterite: **cabí**, etc.
  past subjunctive: **cabés**, etc.; Val. **cabera**, etc.
  participle: **cabut, cabuda**, etc.

caldre (or **caler**) 3*sg.* and 3*pl.* only

like **valer**: stem 1: **cal-**, stem 2: **calg-**

caure

Irregular imperfect: **queia, queies, queia, quèiem, quèieu, queien**
Bal. irregular present indicative: 1*pl.* **queim**, 2*pl.* **queis**
stem 1: **cai-**
  present indicative: 1*pl.* **caiem**, 2*pl.* **caieu**
  gerund: **caient**
(Val. stem 1: **ca-**
  Val. present indicative: 1*pl.* **caem**, 2*pl.* **caeu**
  Val. gerund: **caent**)
stem 1B: **cau-**
  infinitive: **caure**
  future: **cauré**, etc.; conditional: **cauria**, etc.
  present indicative: 2*sg.* **caus**, 3*sg.* **cau**, 3*pl.* **cauen**
stem 2: **caig-**
  1*sg.* present indicative: **caic**
  present subjunctive: **caigui, caiguis, caigui, caiguem, caigueu, caiguin**;
  Val./NW **caiga, caigues, caiga**, caiguem, caigueu, **caiguen**
  preterite: **caiguí**, etc.
  past subjunctive: **caigués**, etc.; Val. **caiguera**, etc.
  participle: **caigut, caiguda**, etc.

cerndre

like **vendre**: stem 1: **cern-**, stem 2: **cerng-**
(*or* regular: stem **cern-**)

cloure

strong participle: **clos, closa**, etc.
otherwise like **plaure**: stem 1: **clo-**, stem 1B: **clou-**, stem 2: **clog-**

conèixer

stem 1: **coneix-**
  infinitive: **conèixer**
  future: **coneixeré**, etc.; conditional: **coneixeria**, etc.
  present indicative: 2*sg.*–3*pl.* **coneixes** (Bal. also **coneixs**), **coneix,
  coneixem, coneixeu, coneixen**
  imperfect: **coneixia**, etc.
  gerund: **coneixent**
stem 2: **coneg-**
  1*sg.* present indicative: **conec**
  present subjunctive: **conegui, coneguis, conegui, coneguem, conegueu,
  coneguin**; Val./NW **conega, conegues, conega**, coneguem, conegueu,
  coneguen
  preterite: **coneguí**, etc.

past subjunctive: **conegués**, etc.; Val. **coneguera**, etc.
participle: **conegut, coneguda**, etc.

córrer

stem 1: **corr-**
  infinitive: **córrer**
  future: **correré**, etc.; conditional: **correria**, etc.
  present indicative: 1*sg.* **corro** (Bal. **corr**; for Val., see stem 2), 2*sg.* **corres**
  (Bal. also **corrs**), 3*sg.* **corre** (Bal. also **corr**), *pl.* **correm, correu, corren**
  imperfect: **corria**, etc.
  present subjunctive: **corri, corris, corri, correm, correu, corrin** (for Val.
  see stem 2) (or: stem 2B **correg-**: present subjunctive: 1*pl.* **correguem**,
  2*pl.* **corregueu**)
  gerund: **corrent**
stem 2: **correg-**
  Val. 1*sg.* present indicative: **córrec**
  Val. present subjunctive: **córrega, córregues, córrega, correguem, corregueu, córreguen** (alternative General present subjunctive forms:
  1*pl.* **correguem**, 2*pl.* **corregueu**)
  preterite: **correguí**, etc.
  past subjunctive: **corregués**, etc.; Val. **correguera**, etc.
  participle: **corregut, correguda**, etc.

coure

strong participle: **cuit, cuita**, etc. meaning 'cook', regular **cogut, coguda**,
  etc. meaning 'smart'
otherwise like **plaure**: stem 1: **co-**, stem 1B: **cou-**, stem 2: **cog-**

créixer

participle: **crescut, crescuda**, etc. (In the most common usage of Catalonia
  this is the only form based on the stem **cresc-**.)
stem 1: **creix-**
  infinitive: **créixer**
  future: **creixeré**, etc.; conditional: **creixeria**, etc.
  imperfect: **creixia**, etc.
  present indicative: 2*sg.*–3*pl.* **creixes** (Bal. also **creixs**), **creix, creixem,
  creixeu, creixen**
  gerund: **creixent**
In Catalonia the rest of the verb is built on the same stem **creix-** (= stem 1).
  1*sg.* present indicative: **creixo**
  present subjunctive: **creixi, creixis, creixi, creixem, creixeu, creixin** (NW
  also **creixa, creixes, creixa,** creixem, creixeu, **creixen**)
  preterite: **creixí**, etc.
  past subjunctive: **creixés**, etc.

stem 2: **cresc-** (preferred in Bal., Val.)
  1*sg.* present indicative: **cresc**
  present subjunctive: Bal. **cresqui, cresquis, cresqui, cresquem, cres-queu, cresquin**; Val. **cresca, cresques, cresca,** cresquem, cresqueu, **cresquen**
  preterite: **cresquí,** etc.
  past subjunctive: **cresqués,** etc.; Val. **cresquera,** etc.

creure

  irregular imperfect: **creia, creies, creia, crèiem, crèieu, creien**
  Bal. irregular present indicative: 1*pl.* **creim,** 2*pl.* **creis**
  stem 1: **crei-**
    present indicative: 1*pl.* **creiem,** 2*pl.* **creieu**
    gerund: **creient**
  (Val. stem 1: **cre-**
    present indicative: 1*pl.* **creem,** 2*pl.* **creeu**
    gerund: **creent**)
  stem 1B: **creu-**
    infinitive: **creure**
    future: **creuré,** etc., conditional: **creuria,** etc.
    present indicative: 2*sg.* **creus,** 3*sg.* **creu,** 3*pl.* **creuen**
  stem 2: **creg-**
    1*sg.* present indicative: **crec**
    present subjunctive: **cregui, creguis, cregui, creguem, cregueu, creguin;** Val./NW **crega, cregues, crega,** creguem, cregueu, **creguen**
    preterite: **creguí,** etc.
    past subjunctive: **cregués,** etc.; Val. **creguera,** etc.
    participle: **cregut, creguda,** etc.

defendre

  strong participle: **defès, defesa,** etc.
  otherwise like **atendre**: stem 1: **defen-,** stem 2: **defeng-**

dependre

  strong participle: **depès, depesa,** etc.
  otherwise like **atendre**: stem 1: **depen-,** stem 2: **depeng-**

despendre

  strong participle: **despès, despesa,** etc.
  otherwise like **atendre**: stem 1: **despen-,** stem 2: **despeng-**

deure

  like **beure**: stem 1: **dev-,** stem 1B: **deu-,** stem 2: **deg-**

dir

irregular imperative: Val. 2*sg.* **dis** (and see stem 2)
strong participle: **dit, dita,** etc.
infinitive: **dir**
future: **diré,** etc.; conditional: **diria,** etc.
irregular imperfect: **deia, deies, deia, dèiem, dèieu, deien**
Bal. irregular present indicative: 1*pl.* **deim,** 2*pl.* **deis**
stem 1: **di-**
  present indicative: 1*pl.* **diem,** 2*pl.* **dieu**
  gerund: **dient**
stem 1B: **diu-**
  present indicative: 2*sg.* **dius,** 3*sg.* **diu,** 3*pl.* **diuen**
stem 2: **dig-**
  1*sg.* present indicative: **dic**
  present subjunctive: **digui, diguis, digui, diguem, digueu, diguin;** Val./NW
  diga, digues, diga, diguem, digueu, **diguen**
  irregular imperative: 2*sg.* **digues,** 2*pl.* **digueu** (Bal. **digau**)
  preterite: **diguí,** etc.
  past subjunctive: **digués,** etc.; Val. **diguera,** etc.

dissoldre

like **absoldre**

distendre

strong participle: **distès, distesa,** etc.
otherwise like **atendre:** stem 1: **disten-,** stem 2: **disteng-**

doldre

stem 1: **dol-**
  infinitive: **doldre**
  future: **doldré,** etc.; conditional: **doldria,** etc.
  present indicative: 2*sg.*–3*pl.* **dols, dol, dolem, doleu, dolen**
  imperfect **dolia,** etc.
  gerund: **dolent**
stem 2: **dolg-**
  1*sg.* present indicative: **dolc**
  present subjunctive: **dolgui, dolguis, dolgui, dolguem, dolgueu, dolguin;**
  Val./NW **dolga, dolgues, dolga,** dolguem, dolgueu, **dolguen**
  preterite: **dolguí,** etc.
  past subjunctive: **dolgués,** etc.; Val. **dolguera,** etc.
  participle: **dolgut, dolguda,** etc.

dur

Val. irregular imperative: 2*sg.* **dus**
strong participle: **dut, duta,** etc.; Bal. **duit, duita,** etc.
irregular imperfect: **duia, duies, duia, dúiem, dúieu, duien**
Bal. irregular present indicative: 1*pl.* **duim,** 2*pl.* **duis**
infinitive: **dur**
future: **duré,** etc.; conditional **duria,** etc.
stem 1: **du-**
   present indicative: 1*pl.* **duem,** 2*pl.* **dueu**
   gerund: **duent**
stem 1B: **du(u)-**
   present indicative: 2*sg.* **duus/dus,** 3*sg.* **duu/du,** 3*pl.* **duen**
stem 2: **dug-**
   1*sg.* present indicative: **duc**
   present subjunctive: **dugui, duguis, dugui, duguem, dugueu, duguin;** Val./
   NW **duga, dugues, duga,** duguem, dugueu, **duguen**
   preterite: **duguí,** etc.
   past subjunctive: **dugués,** etc.; Val. **duguera,** etc.

empènyer

strong participle: **empès, empesa,** etc.
otherwise: regular

encendre

strong participle: **encès, encesa,** etc.
otherwise like **atendre:** stem 1: **encen-,** stem 2: **enceng-**

entendre

strong participle: **entès, entesa,** etc.
otherwise like **atendre**

escriure (verb of mixed conjugation, see **16.6.3**)

estendre

strong participle: **estès, estesa,** etc.
otherwise like **atendre:** stem 1: **esten-,** stem 2: **esteng-**

estrènyer

strong participle: **estret, estreta,** etc.
(Bal. stem 2: **estreng-**
   1*sg.* present indicative: **estrenc**
   present subjunctive: **estrengui, estrenguis, estrengui, estrenguem, estren-
   gueu, estrenguin**

preterite: **estrenguí**, etc.
past subjunctive: **estrengués**, etc.)
otherwise regular (stem 2 = stem 1): **estreny-**

fènyer

like **pertànyer**
either regular (stem 2 = stem 1)
or stem 1: **feny-**, stem 2: **feng-**

fer

infinitive: **fer**
future stem: **far-**: **faré, faràs**, etc.; conditional: **faria, faries**, etc.
irregular imperfect: **feia, feies, feia, fèiem, fèieu, feien**
Bal. irregular present indicative: 1*pl.* **feim**, 2*pl.* **feis**
1*sg.* present indicative: **faig**
irregular imperative: 2*sg.* **fés**, Bal. **fé**
strong participle: **fet, feta**, etc.
strong preterite: 1*sg.* **fiu**, 3*sg.* **féu**
stem 1: **f-** (= stem 2)
  present indicative: 1*pl.* **fem**, 2*pl.* **feu**
  gerund: **fent**
stem 1B: **fa-**
  present indicative: 2*sg.* **fas**, 3*sg.* **fa**, 3*pl.* **fan**
stem 2 (present subjunctive not taken by stem 2C, remainder of preterite,
  past subjunctive): **f-** (= stem 1)
  present subjunctive: 1*pl.* **fem**, 2*pl.* **feu**
  preterite: 2*sg.* **feres**, *pl.* **férem, féreu, feren**
  past subjunctive: **fes, fessis** (Val./NW **fesses**), etc.
stem 2C: **faç-**
  Bal. optional 1*sg.* present indicative: **faç**
  present subjunctive: *sg.*/3*pl.*: **faci, facis, faci, facin**; Val./NW/optionally
  Bal. **faça, faces, faça, facen**; also Bal. 1*pl.* **facem**, 2*pl.* **faceu**

fondre

strong participle: **fos, fosa**, etc.
otherwise like **atendre**: stem 1: **fon-** (3*sg.* present indicative: **fon**), stem 2:
  fong-

haure (*or* **haver**; Val. and NW variant of **heure**)

stem 1: **hav-**
  infinitive: **haver** (also stem 1B **haure**, see below)
  present indicative: 1*pl.* **havem**, 2*pl.* **haveu**
  imperfect: **havia**, etc.
  gerund: **havent**

stem 1B: **hau-**
　　infinitive: **haure**
　　future: **hauré**, etc.; conditional: **hauria**, etc.
　　present indicative: 2*sg.* **haus**, 3*sg.* **hau**, 3*pl.* **hauen**
　stem 2: **hag-**
　　1*sg.* present indicative: **hac**
　　present subjunctive: **hagui, haguis, hagui, haguem, hagueu, haguin**; Val.
　　haga, hagues, haga, haguem, hagueu, **haguen**
　　preterite: **haguí,** etc.
　　past subjunctive: **hagués,** etc.; Val. **haguera,** etc.
　　participle: **hagut, haguda,** etc.

haver (auxiliary) see **16.15.12**

heure (or **haver**; Val. and NW use the variant **haure** q.v.)

　future stem: **haur-**, future: **hauré**, etc.; conditional: **hauria**, etc.
　stem 1: **hav-**
　　infinitive: **haver** (also stem 1B **heure**, see below)
　　present indicative: 1*pl.* **havem**, 2*pl.* **haveu**
　　imperfect: **havia**, etc.
　　gerund: **havent**
　stem 1B: **heu-**
　　infinitive: **heure**
　　present indicative: 2*sg.* **heus**, 3*sg.* **heu**, 3*pl.* **heuen**
　stem 2: **hag-**
　　present subjunctive: 1*pl.* **haguem**, 2*pl.* **hagueu**
　　preterite: **haguí,** etc.
　　past subjunctive: **hagués,** etc.
　　participle: **hagut, haguda,** etc.
　stem 2C: **heg-**
　　1*sg.* present indicative: **hec**
　　present subjunctive: 1*sg.* **hegui**, 2*sg.* **heguis**, 3*sg.* **hegui**, 3*pl.* **heguin**

jaure (Val. and NW variant of **jeure**)

　irregular imperfect: **jeia, jeies, jeia, jèiem, jèieu, jeien**
　stem 1: **jai-** (Val. **ja-**)
　　present indicative: 1*pl.* **jaiem**, 2*pl.* **jaieu** (Val. **jaem, jaeu**)
　　gerund: **jaient** (Val. **jaent**)
　stem 1B: **jau-**
　　infinitive: **jaure**
　　future: **jauré,** etc.; conditional: **jauria**, etc.
　　present indicative: 2*sg.* **jaus**, 3*sg.* **jau**, 3*pl.* **jauen**
　stem 2: **jag-**
　　1*sg.* present indicative: **jac**

present subjunctive: **jagui, jaguis, jagui, jaguem, jagueu, jaguin**; Val./NW
jaga, jagues, jaga, jaguem, jagueu, **jaguen**
preterite: **jaguí**, etc.
past subjunctive: **jagués**, etc.; Val. **jaguera**, etc.
participle: **jagut, jaguda**, etc.

jeure (Val. and NW use the variant **jaure** q.v.)

future stem: **jaur-**, future: **jauré**, etc.; conditional: **jauria**, etc.
irregular imperfect: **jeia, jeies, jeia, jèiem, jèieu, jeien**
Bal. irregular present indicative: 1*pl.* **jeim**, 2*pl.* **jeis**
stem 1: **jai-**
  present indicative: 1*pl.* **jaiem**, 2*pl.* **jaieu**
  gerund: **jaient**
stem 1B: **jeu-**
  infinitive: **jeure**
  present indicative: 2*sg.* **jeus**, 3*sg.* **jeu**, 3*pl.* **jeuen**
stem 2: **jag-**
  present subjunctive: 1*pl.* **jaguem**, 2*pl.* **jagueu**
  preterite: **jaguí**, etc.
  past subjunctive: **jagués**, etc.
  participle: **jagut, jaguda**, etc.
stem 2C: **jeg-**
  1*sg.* present indicative: **jec**
  present subjunctive: 1*sg.* **jegui**, 2*sg.* **jeguis**, 3*sg.* **jegui**, 3*pl.* **jeguin**

lleure

like **beure** (3*sg.* only): stem 1: **llev-**, stem 1B: **lleu-**, stem 2: **lleg-**

merèixer

like **créixer**:
  participle: **merescut, merescuda**, etc.; stem 1: **mereix-**, stem 2 (Bal. Val.):
  meresc-, elsewhere stem 2 = stem 1: **mereix-**

-metre

see **admetre**

moldre

strong participle: **mòlt, mòlta**, etc.
otherwise like **doldre**: stem 1: **mol-**, stem 2: **molg-**

moure

like **beure**: stem 1: **mov-**, stem 1B: **mou-**, stem 2: **mog-**

nàixer (Val. and NW variant of **néixer**)

stem 1: **naix-**
infinitive: **nàixer**
future: **naixeré**, etc.; conditional: **naixeria**, etc.
present indicative: 2*sg.*–3*pl.* **naixes, naix, naixem, naixeu, naixen**
imperfect: **naixia**, etc.
gerund: **naixent**
(NW stem 2B: **naix-** = stem 1
NW 1*sg.* present indicative: **naixo**
NW present subjunctive: **naixi, naixis, naixi, naixem, naixeu, naixin** (also
naixa, naixes, naixa, naixem, naixeu, **naixen**))
stem 2: **nasc-**
Val. 1*sg.* present indicative: **nasc**
Val. present subjunctive: **nasca, nasques, nasca, nasquem, nasqueu,
nasquen**
preterite: **nasquí**, etc.
past subjunctive: **nasqués**, etc.; Val. **nasquera**, etc.
participle: **nascut, nascuda**, etc.

néixer (Val. and NW use the variant **nàixer** q.v.)

participle: **nascut, nascuda**, etc.
future stem: **naixer-**, future: **naixeré**, etc.; conditional: **naixeria**, etc.
stem 1: **naix-**
imperfect: **naixia**, etc.
present indicative: 1*pl.* **naixem**, 2*pl.* **naixeu**
gerund: **naixent**
stem 1B: **neix-**
infinitive: **néixer**
present indicative: 2*sg.* **neixes**, 3*sg.* **neix**, 3*pl.* **neixen**
either
stem 2 (= stem 1): **naix-**
present subjunctive: 1*pl.* **naixem**, 2*pl.* **naixeu**
preterite: **naixí**, etc.
past subjunctive: **naixés**, etc.
stem 2C (= stem 1B): **neix-**
1*sg.* present indicative: **neixo**, Bal. **neix**
present subjunctive: 1*sg.* **neixi**, 2*sg.* **neixis**, 3*sg.* **neixi**, 3*pl.* **neixin**
or
stem 2: **nasc-**
present subjunctive: 1*pl.* **nasquem**, 2*pl.* **nasqueu**
preterite: **nasquí**, etc.
past subjunctive: **nasqués**, etc.

Bal. stem 2C: **nesc-**
  Bal. 1*sg.* present indicative: **nesc**
  Bal. present subjunctive: 1*sg.* **nesqui**, 2*sg.* **nesquis**, 3*sg.* **nesqui**, 3*pl.*
  nesquin

noure

  like **plaure**: stem 1: **no-**, stem 1B: **nou-**, stem 2: **nog-** or **noug-**

ofendre

  strong participle: **ofès, ofesa**, etc.
  otherwise like **atendre**: stem 1: **ofen-**, stem 2: **ofeng-**

pàixer (Val. and NW variant of **péixer**)

  like **nàixer**: stem 1: **paix-**, stem 2: **pasc-**

parèixer

  Bal. weak participle **parescut, parescuda**, etc.
  otherwise like **conèixer**: stem 1: **pareix-**, stem: 2: **pareg-**
  Also Bal. stem 2B: **paresc-**
    Bal. 1*sg.* present indicative: **paresc**
    Bal. present subjunctive: **paresqui, paresquis, paresqui, paresquem, pares-**
    queu, paresquin

péixer (Val. and NW use the variant **pàixer** q.v.)

  like **néixer**:
  infinitive: **péixer**; future stem: **paixer-**, future: **paixeré**, etc.; conditional:
  paixeria, etc.; stem 1: **paix-**, stem 1B: **peix-**
    either stem 2 = stem 1: **paix-**, stem 2C = stem 1B: **peix-**
    or stem 2: **pasc-**, Bal. stem 2C: **pesc-**

pertànyer

  participle: **pertangut, pertanguda**, etc.
  otherwise
  either
    regular (stem 2 = stem 1)
  or
    stem 1: **pertany-**
    stem 2: **pertang-**
      1*sg.* present indicative: **pertanc**
      present subjunctive: **pertangui, pertanguis, pertangui, pertanguem,**
      pertangueu, pertanguin
      preterite: **pertanguí**, etc.
      past subjunctive: **pertangués**, etc.
      participle: **pertangut, pertanguda**, etc.

plànyer

> *either*
>> regular (stem 2 = stem 1)
>
> *or*
>> stem 1: **plany-**, stem 2: **plang-**

plaure

> stem 1: **pla-**
>> present indicative: 1*pl.* **plaem**, 2*pl.* **plaeu**
>> imperfect: **plaïa, plaïes**, etc.
>> gerund: **plaent**
>
> stem 1B: **plau-**
>> infinitive: **plaure**
>> future: **plauré**, etc.; conditional: **plauria**, etc.
>> present indicative: 2*sg.* **plaus**, 3*sg.* **plau**, 3*pl.* **plauen**
>
> stem 2: **plag-**
>> 1*sg.* present indicative: **plac**
>> present subjunctive: **plagui, plaguis, plagui, plaguem, plagueu, plaguin**;
>> Val./NW **plaga, plagues, plaga**, plaguem, plagueu, **plaguen**
>> preterite: **plaguí**, etc.
>> past subjunctive: **plagués**, etc.; Val. **plaguera**, etc.
>> participle: **plagut, plaguda**, etc.

ploure

> like **beure**: stem 1: **plov-**, stem 1B: **plou-**, stem 2: **plog-**

poder

Note the vowel alternation -**u**-/-**o**- has the same distribution in **poder** and **voler**.

> infinitive: **poder**
> stem 1: **pod-**
>> future stem: **podr-**; future: **podré**, etc.; conditional: **podria**, etc.
>> present indicative: 2*sg.*–3*pl.* **pots, pot, podem, podeu, poden**
>> imperfect: **podia**, etc.
>> gerund: **podent**
>
> stem 2: **pog-**
>> preterite: **poguí**, etc.
>> past subjunctive: **pogués**, etc.; Val. **poguera**, etc.
>> participle: **pogut, poguda**, etc.
>
> stem 2B: **pug-**
>> 1*sg.* present indicative: **puc**
>> present subjunctive: **pugui, puguis, pugui, puguem, pugueu, puguin**; Val./
>> NW/optionally Bal. **puga, pugues, puga**, puguem, pugueu, **puguen**
>> irregular imperative: **pugues, pugueu**

pondre

strong participle: **post, posta**, etc.
otherwise like **atendre**: stem 1: **pon-** (*3sg.* present indicative: **pon**), stem 2:
  pong-

prendre

strong participle: **pres, presa**, etc.
otherwise like **atendre**: stem 1: **pren-** (*3sg.* present indicative: **pren**), stem 2:
  preng-

pretendre

strong participle: **pretès, pretesa**, etc.
otherwise like **atendre**: stem 1: **preten-**, stem 2: **preteng-**

raure

Val. strong participle **ras, rasa**, etc. (elsewhere regular **ragut**)
otherwise like **plaure**: stem 1: **ra-**, stem 1B: **rau-**, stem 2: **rag-**

resoldre

like **absoldre**

respondre

like **pondre**

riure

Val. strong participle: **rist, rista**, etc. (elsewhere regular **rigut**)
irregular imperfect: **reia, reies, reia, rèiem, rèieu, reien**
Bal. irregular present indicative: 1*pl.* **reim**, 2*pl.* **reis**
stem 1: **ri-**
  present indicative: 1*pl.* **riem**, 2*pl.* **rieu**
  gerund: **rient**
stem 1B: **riu-**
  infinitive: **riure**
  future: **riuré**, etc.; conditional: **riuria**, etc.
  present indicative: 2*sg.* **rius**, 3*sg.* **riu**, 3*pl.* **riuen**
stem 2: **rig-**
  1*sg.* present indicative: **ric**
  present subjunctive: **rigui, riguis, rigui, riguem, rigueu, riguin**; Val./NW
  riga, rigues, riga, riguem, rigueu, riguen
  irregular imperative: 2*pl.* only **rigueu** (but Bal. **reis** = 2*pl.* present indicative); 2*sg.* regular: **riu**
  preterite: **riguí**, etc.
  past subjunctive: **rigués**, etc.; Val. **riguera**, etc.
  participle: **rigut, riguda**, etc.

romandre

> strong participle: **romàs, romasa**, etc.
> otherwise like **atendre**: stem 1: **roman-** (3*sg.* present indicative: **roman**), stem 2: **romang-**

saber

> 1*sg.* present indicative: **sé**
> irregular imperative: **sàpigues, sapigueu** (Bal. **sapigau**), Val. **sàpies, sapieu**
> otherwise like **cabre**: present subjunctive stem: **sapig-** (Val. **sapi-**), stem 1/2: **sab-**

ser/ésser/esser

> participle (weak): **estat, estada**, etc., or in less formal styles, **sigut**
> strong preterite: 1*sg.* **fui**, 3*sg.* **fou**
> infinitive: **ser, ésser** (more formal), Bal. **esser**
> future stem: **ser-**, future: **seré, seràs**, etc.; conditional: **seria, series**, etc.
> irregular imperfect: **er-**: **era, eres, era, érem, éreu, eren**
> gerund: **sent** or **essent**
> 1*sg.* present indicative: **sóc/só** (Bal. **som**)
> 2*sg.* present indicative: **ets**; Val. informal **eres**
> 3*sg.* present indicative: **és**
> stem 1B: **so-**
>> present indicative *pl.*: **som, sou, són**
> stem 2 (remainder of preterite, past subjunctive, also 2nd conditional): **fo-**, i.e.:
>> preterite: 2*sg.* **fores**, *pl.* **fórem, fóreu, foren**
>> past subjunctive: **fos, fossis** (Val./NW **fosses**), etc.
>> or (Val.): **fóra, fores**, (these forms also 2nd conditional)
> stem 2B (present subjunctive and irregular imperative): **sig-**
>> present subjunctive: **sigui, siguis, sigui, siguem, sigueu, siguin**; Val./NW/ optionally Bal. **siga, sigues, siga**, siguem, sigueu, **siguen**
>> irregular imperative: **sigues, sigueu** (Bal. **sigau, siau**)

seure

> like **creure**:
> irregular imperfect: **seia, seies, seia, sèiem, sèieu, seien**; Bal. irregular present indicative: 1*pl.* **seim**, 2*pl.* **seis**; stem 1: **sei-** (Val. **se-**), stem 1B: **seu-**, stem 2: **seg-**

soler

> like **doldre**: stem 1: **sol-**, stem 2: **solg-**

suspendre

strong participle: **suspès**, **suspesa**, etc.
otherwise like **atendre**: stem 1: **suspen-**, stem 2: **suspeng-**

toldre

strong participle: **tolt**, **tolta**, etc.
otherwise like **doldre**: stem 1: **tol-**, stem 2: **tolg-**

tondre

strong participle: **tos**, **tosa**, etc.
otherwise like **atendre**: stem 1: **ton-** (3*sg.* present indicative: **ton**), stem 2: **tong-**

traure (Val. and NW variant of **treure**)

participle **tret**, **treta**, etc.
otherwise like **jaure**: irregular imperfect: **treia**, **treies**, **treia**, **trèiem**, **trèieu**, **treien**
stem 1: **trai-** (Val. **tra-**), stem 1B: **trau-**, stem 2: **trag-**

treure
(Val. and NW use the variant **traure** q.v.)

participle **tret**, **treta**, etc.
otherwise like **jeure**: future stem: **traur-**, future: **trauré**, etc.; conditional: **trauria**, etc.; irregular imperfect: **treia**, **treies**, **treia**, **trèiem**, **trèieu**, **treien**; Bal. irregular present indicative: 1*pl.* **treim**, 2*pl.* **treis**; stem 1: **trai-**; stem 1B: **treu-**, infinitive: **treure**; stem 2: **trag-**, stem 2C: **treg-**

valer

infinitive: **valer** or **valdre**
future stem: **valdr-**; future: **valdré**, conditional: **valdria**
otherwise like **doldre**: stem 1: **val-**, stem 2: **valg-**

vendre

weak participle **venut**, **venuda**, etc.
otherwise like **atendre**: stem 1: **ven-** (3*sg.* present indicative: **ven**), stem 2: **veng-**

veure

strong participle: **vist**, **vista**, etc.
strong preterite: 1*sg.* **viu**, 3*sg.* **véu** (Val. **viu**) (or 3*sg.* weak **veié**)
irregular imperfect: **veia**, **veies**, **veia**, **vèiem**, **vèieu**, **veien**
Bal. irregular present indicative: 1*pl.* **veim**, 2*pl.* **veis**

stem 1: **vei-**
    present indicative: 1*pl.* **veiem**, 2*pl.* **veieu**
    gerund: **veient**
(Val. stem 1: **ve-**
    Val. present indicative: 1*pl.* **veem**, 2*pl.* **veeu**
    Val. gerund: **veent**)
stem 2: **vei-** (or **v-**)
    remainder of preterite: **veieres**, **veiérem**, **veié**, **veiéreu**, **veieren** (or esp. Val. **veres**, **vérem**, **véreu**, **veren**)
    past subjunctive: **veiés**, etc., Bal. **ves**, **vessis**, **ves**, **véssim**, **véssiu**, **vessin**; Val. **vera**, **veres**, etc.
stem 1B: **veu-**
    infinitive: **veure**
    future: **veuré**, etc.; conditional: **veuria**, etc.
    (colloquial Valencian infinitive **vore**, future: **voré**, conditional: **voria**)
    present indicative: 2*sg.* **veus**, 3*sg.* **veu**, 3*pl.* **veuen**
stem 2B: **vej-**
    1*sg.* present indicative: **veig**
    present subjunctive: **vegi**, **vegis**, **vegi**, **vegem**, **vegeu**, **vegin**; Val./NW/ optionally Bal. **veja**, **veges**, **veja**, vegem, vegeu, **vegen**
    irregular imperative (alongside regular forms **veu**, **veieu**): **veges** (also **ves**), **vegeu**

viure
(verb of mixed conjugation, see **16.6.3**)

voler

    1*sg.* present indicative: **vull**
    infinitive: **voler**
stem 1: **vol-**
    future stem: **voldr-**; future: **voldré**, etc.; conditional: **voldria**, etc.
    present indicative: 2*sg.*–3*pl.* **vols**, **vol**, **volem**, **voleu**, **volen**
    imperfect: **volia**, etc.
    gerund: **volent**
stem 2: **volg-**
    preterite: **volguí**, etc.
    past subjunctive: **volgués**, etc.; Val. **volguera**, etc.
    participle: **volgut**, **volguda**, etc.
stem 2B: **vulg-**
    present subjunctive: **vulgui**, **vulguis**, **vulgui**, **vulguem**, **vulgueu**, **vulguin**; Val./NW/optionally Bal. **vulga**, **vulgues**, **vulga**, vulguem, vulgueu, **vulguen**
    irregular imperative: **vulgues**, **vulgueu**

16.6.2   IRREGULAR VERBS OF CONJUGATION III

Two types of irregularity are found among Conjugation III verbs; a dozen or so verbs have an irregular participle, though some of these have an optional regular form which is preferred in Valencian. The other type involves stem alternation in the present indicative and present subjunctive (and of course the identical imperative forms); fourteen or so verbs of Conjugation IIIb are affected.

The 'strong IIIb' stem is found in the singular and *3pl.* of the present indicative and present subjunctive.

The weak IIIb stem is found elsewhere.

Note that the strong IIIb stem occurs in exactly the same inflectional categories in which Conjugation IIIa verbs use the extended stem form in **-eix-**/**-esc-**, etc.

In addition, **obrir** has a special paradigm in Valencian and Balearic, and **omplir** also in Valencian, involving an unusual **-i-** element in the 2–3*sg.* and *3pl.* present indicative, and a stem variant in **-g-** in the contexts where stem 2B occurs in Conjugation II: the 1*sg.* present indicative and the present subjunctive.

afegir

> Val. strong IIIb stem: **afig-**
>> present indicative *sg.*/*3pl.*: **afig, afiges, afig, afigen**
>> present subjunctive *sg.*/*3pl.*: **afija, afiges, afija, afigen**
> Val. weak IIIb stem: **afeg-**
> elsewhere regular IIIa

cobrir

> participle: **cobert, coberta**, etc.
> otherwise regular IIIa

collir

> strong IIIb stem: **cull-**
>> present indicative *sg.*/*3pl.*: **cullo** (Bal./Val. **cull**), **culls, cull, cullen**
>> present subjunctive *sg.*/*3pl.*: **culli, cullis, culli, cullin**; Val./NW **culla, culles, culla, cullen**
> weak IIIb stem: **coll-**

complir

> participle **complert, complerta**, etc. (or regular **complit, complida**, etc.)
> otherwise regular IIIa

cosir

> strong IIIb stem: **cus-**
>> present indicative *sg.*/*3pl.*: **cuso** (Bal./Val. **cus**), **cuses, cus, cusen**

present subjunctive *sg./3pl.*: **cusi, cusis, cusi, cusin**; Val./NW **cusa, cuses, cusa, cusen**
weak IIIb stem: **cos-**

eixir (verb of mixed conjugation, see **16.6.3**)

engolir

> Val. strong IIIb stem: **engul-**
> present indicative *sg./3pl.*: **engul, enguls, engul, engulen**
> present subjunctive *sg./3pl.*: **engula, engules, engula, engulen**
> Val. weak IIIb stem: **engol-**
> elsewhere regular IIIa

escopir

> strong IIIb stem: **escup-**
> present indicative *sg./3pl.*: **escupo** (Bal./Val. **escup**), **escups, escup, escupen**
> present subjunctive *sg./3pl.*: **escupi, escupis, escupi, escupin**; Val./NW **escupa, escupes, escupa, escupen**
> weak IIIb stem: **escop-**

establir

> participle: **establert, establerta**, etc. (or regular **establit, establida**, etc.)
> otherwise regular IIIa

fugir

> Bal. participle **fuit, fuita**, etc.
> otherwise regular IIIb stem: **fuj-**
> > present indicative: **fujo** (Bal./Val. **fuig**), **fuges** (Bal. **fuigs**), **fuig, fugim, fugiu, fugen**
> > present subjunctive: **fugi, fugis, fugi, fugim** (Bal. **fugiguem**), **fugiu** (Bal. **fugigueu**), **fugin**; Val./NW. **fuja, fuges, fuja**, fugim, fugiu, **fugen**

imprimir

> participle **imprès, impresa**, etc.
> otherwise regular IIIa

llegir

> Val. strong IIIb stem: **llig-**
> present indicative *sg./3pl.*: **llig, lliges, llig, lligen**
> present subjunctive *sg./3pl.*: **llija, lliges, llija, lligen**
> Val. weak IIIb stem: **lleg-**
> elsewhere regular IIIa

lluir

The following Conjugation IIIb forms seem to be standard:

present indicative: **lluus, lluu, lluïm, lluïu, lluen**
present subjunctive: **lluï, lluïs, lluï, lluïm, lluïu, lluïn**
regular imperative: **lluu, lluïm, lluïu**
otherwise regular IIIa

morir

participle **mort, morta**, etc.
Val. stem 2C **muir-** (optionally Bal. also)
  1*sg.* present indicative: **muir**
  present subjunctive: 1*sg.* **muiri**, 2*sg.* **muiris**, 3*sg.* **muiri**, 3*pl.* **muirin**; Val.
  muira, muires, muira, muiren
elsewhere IIIb stem **mor-**

obrir

participle **obert, oberta**, etc.
Val. stem 2B: **obrig-**
  1*sg.* present indicative: **òbric**
  present subjunctive: **òbriga, òbrigues, òbriga, obriguem, obrigueu, òbriguen**
elsewhere IIIb stem: **obr-**
  General present indicative: **obro, obres, obre, obrim, obriu, obren**
  Val. present indicative 2–3*sg.*, *pl.*: **obris, obri**, obrim, obriu, **obrin**
  Bal. present indicative: **obr, obris/obrs, obri/obr**, obrim, obriu, **obrin**
otherwise regular IIIb stem: **obr-**

oferir

participle **ofert, oferta**, etc. (or regular **oferit, oferida**, etc.)
otherwise regular IIIa

oir

infinitive: **oir**
future: **oiré**, etc., conditional: **oiria**, etc.
Val. stem 1B: **ou-**
  present indicative: 2*sg.* **ous**, 3*sg.* **ou**, 3*pl.* **ouen**
Val. stem 2B: **oj-**
  1*sg.* present indicative: **oig**
  present subjunctive: **oja, oges, oja, ogem, ogeu, ogen**
elsewhere/otherwise regular IIIa stem: **o-**

omplir

participle **omplert, omplerta**, etc. (or regular **omplit, omplida**, etc.)
Val. stem 2B: **omplig-**
  1*sg.* present indicative: **òmplic**

present subjunctive: **òmpliga, òmpligues, òmpliga, ompliguem, ompligueu, òmpliguen**

Bal. strong IIIb stem: **umpl-**

> Bal. present indicative *sg./3pl.*: **umpl, umpls, umpl, umplen**
> Bal. present subjunctive *sg./3pl.*: **umpli, umplis, umpli, umplin**

elsewhere IIIb stem: **ompl-**

> General present indicative: **omplo, omples, omple, omplim, ompliu, omplen**
> Val. present indicative 2–3*sg.*, *pl.*: **omplis, ompli**, omplim, ompliu, **omplin**

otherwise regular IIIb stem: **ompl-**

pruir

Only the following IIIb forms are standard:

> present indicative: 2*sg.* **pruus**, 3*sg.* **pruu**
> otherwise regular IIIa

reblir

> participle **reblert, reblerta**, etc. (or regular **reblit, reblida**, etc.)
> otherwise regular IIIa

renyir

> Val. like **tenyir**: strong IIIb stem: **riny-**; weak IIIb stem: **reny-** elsewhere
> regular IIIa

soferir

> participle **sofert, soferta**, etc. (or regular **soferit, soferida**, etc.)
> otherwise regular IIIa

sortir

> strong IIIb stem: **surt-**
> > present indicative *sg./3pl.*: **surto** (Bal./Val. **surt**), **surts, surt, surten**
> > present subjunctive *sg./3pl.*: **surti, surtis, surti, surtin**; Val./NW **surta, surtes, surta, surten**
> weak IIIb stem: **sort-**

suplir

> participle **suplert, suplerta**, etc. (or regular **suplit, suplida**, etc.)
> otherwise regular IIIa

teixir

> Val. strong IIIb stem: **tix-**
> > present indicative *sg./3pl.*: **tix, tixes, tix, tixen**
> > present subjunctive *sg./3pl.*: **tixa, tixes, tixa, tixen**
> Val. weak IIIb stem: **teix-**
> elsewhere regular IIIa

tenir (verb of mixed conjugation, see **16.6.3**)

tenyir

> Val. strong IIIb stem: **tiny-**
> > present indicative *sg./3pl.*: **tiny, tinys, tiny, tinyen**
> > present subjunctive *sg./3pl.*: **tinya, tinyes, tinya, tinyen**
> Val. weak IIIb stem: **teny-**
> elsewhere regular IIIa

tossir

> strong IIIb stem: **tuss-**
> > present indicative *sg./3pl.*: **tusso** (Bal./Val. **tus**), **tusses, tus, tussen**
> > present subjunctive *sg./3pl.*: **tussi, tussis, tussi, tussin**; Val./NW **tussa, tusses, tussa, tussen**
> weak IIIb stem: **toss-**
> Bal. optionally IIIa

venir (verb of mixed conjugation, see **16.6.3**)

vestir

> Val. strong IIIb stem: **vist-**
> > present indicative *sg./3pl.*: **vist, vistes, vist, visten**
> > present subjunctive *sg./3pl.*: **vista, vistes, vista, visten**
> Val. weak IIIb stem: **vest-**
> (Bal. optionally IIIb stem: **vest-**
> > present indicative: **vest, vests, vest, vestim, vestiu, vesten**
> > present subjunctive: **vesti, vestis, vesti, vestim/vestiguem, vestiu/vestigueu, vestin**)
> elsewhere regular IIIa

16.6.3   IRREGULAR VERBS OF MIXED CONJUGATION

anar

> infinitive: **anar** (**an-** Conjugation I)
> future stem: **anir-** (**an-** Conjugation III): future: **aniré, aniràs**, etc.; conditional: **aniria**, etc.
> stem 1: **an-** (regular Conjugation I)
> > present indicative: 1*pl.* **anem, aneu**, Bal. **anam, anau**
> > imperfect: **anava**, etc.
> > gerund: **anant**
> > present subjunctive: 1*pl.* **anem**, 2*pl.* **aneu**
> > preterite: **aní, anares**, etc.
> > past subjunctive: **anés**, Bal. etc. **anàs**, Val. **anara**, etc.
> > participle (weak): **anat, anada**, etc.

stem 1B: **va-**
   present indicative: 2*sg.* **vas**, 3*sg.* **va**, 3*pl.* **van**
irregular imperative: 2*sg.* **vés**
stem 2C: **vaj-**
   1*sg.* present indicative: **vaig**
   sg./3pl. present subjunctive: **vagi, vagis, vagi, vagin**; Val./NW **vaja, vages, vaja, vagen**

eixir (verb of mixed conjugation, at least in Valencian)

regular (weak) participle: **eixit, eixida**, etc.
strong Conjugation IIIb stem: **ix-**
   2–3*sg./3pl.* present indicative: **ixes, ix, ixen**
weak Conjugation IIIb stem: **eix-**
   infinitive: **eixir**
   future: **eixiré**, etc.; conditional: **eixiria**, etc.
   1–2*pl.* present indicative: **eixim, eixiu**
   imperfect: **eixia**, etc.
   gerund: **eixint**
then
either
   stem 2: **isc-** (Conjugation II) (Valencian preference)
      1*sg.* present indicative: **isc**
      present subjunctive: **isca, isques, isca, isquem, isqueu, isquen**
      preterite: **isquí**, etc.
      past subjunctive: **isqués**, etc.; Val. **isquera**, etc.
or
   strong Conjugation IIIb stem: **ix-**
      1*sg.* present indicative: **ixo**
      present subjunctive: **ixi, ixis, ixi, ixin**
   weak Conjugation IIIb stem: **eix-**
      preterite: **eixí**, etc.
      past subjunctive: **eixís**, etc.

escriure

strong participle: **escrit, escrita**, etc.
stem 1: **escriv-** (Conjugation III)
   present indicative: 1*pl.* **escrivim**, 2*pl.* **escriviu**
   imperfect: **escrivia**, etc.
   gerund: **escrivint**
(major variant) preterite/past subjunctive stem = stem 1: **escriv-** (Conjugation III)
   preterite: **escriví, escrivires**, etc.
   past subjunctive: **escrivís**, etc.

stem 1B: **escriu-** (Conjugation II)
  infinitive: **escriure**
  future: **escriuré**, etc.; conditional: **escriuria**, etc.
  present indicative: 2*sg.* **escrius**, 3*sg.* **escriu**, 3*pl.* **escriuen**
stem 2 (1*sg.* present indicative, present subjunctive, and alternative for preterite, past subjunctive): **escrig-** (Conjugation II)
  1*sg.* present indicative: **escric**
  present subjunctive: **escrigui, escriguis, escrigui, escriguem, escrigueu, escriguin**; Val./NW **escriga, escrigues, escriga, escriguem, escrigueu, escriguen**
  (alternative) preterite: **escriguí**, etc.
  (alternative) past subjunctive: **escrigués**, etc.; Val. **escriguera**, etc.

estar

stem 1: **est-** (Conjugation I)
  infinitive: **estar**
  future: **estaré**, etc.; conditional: **estaria**, etc.
  present indicative: 1*pl.* **estem**, 2*pl.* **esteu**, Bal. **estam, estau**
  imperfect: **estava**, etc.
  gerund: **estant**
participle: regular (weak) **estat, estada**, etc.
stem 1B: **(e)sta-**
  present indicative: 2*sg.* **estàs**, 3*sg.* **està**, 3*pl.* **estan**
  imperative: Bal. 2*sg.* **està**, 2*pl.* **estau**; Val. 2*sg.* **està**, 2*pl.* **esteu**
stem 2: **estig-** (Conjugation II)
  1*sg.* present indicative: **estic**
  present subjunctive: **estigui, estiguis, estigui, estiguem, estigueu, estiguin**; Val./NW **estiga, estigues, estiga, estiguem, estigueu, estiguen**
  irregular imperative: 2*sg.* **estigues**, 2*pl.* **estigueu** (Bal. **estigau**)
  preterite: **estiguí**, etc.
  past subjunctive: **estigués**, etc.; Val. **estiguera**, etc.

tenir
Note the close parallel between **venir** and **tenir**, in all except their imperatives.

infinitive: **tenir** (less formal **tindre**)
future stem: **tindr-** (Bal. **tendr-**): future: **tindré**, etc.; conditional: **tindria**, etc.
  (Bal. **tendré, tendria**, etc.)
3*sg.* present indicative: **té**
irregular imperative: 2*sg.* in compounds only: **-tén**
stem 1: **ten-** (Conjugation IIIb)
  present indicative: 2*sg.* **tens**, 1*pl.* **tenim**, 2*pl.* **teniu**, 3*pl.* **tenen**
  imperfect: **tenia**, etc.
  gerund: **tenint**

stem 2: **ting-** (Conjugation II)
 1*sg.* present indicative: **tinc**
 present subjunctive: **tingui, tinguis, tingui, tinguem, tingueu, tinguin**; Val./
 NW **tinga, tingues, tinga,** tinguem, tingueu, **tinguen**
 irregular imperative: **tingues, tingueu** (alongside regular **té, teniu;** Val.
 also 2*sg.* **tin**)
 preterite: **tinguí,** etc.
 past subjunctive: **tingués,** etc.; Val. **tinguera,** etc.
 participle: **tingut, tinguda,** etc.
(Bal.: stem 2: **teng-** (Conjugation II)
 1*sg.* present indicative: **tenc**
 present subjunctive: **tengui, tenguis, tengui, tenguem, tengueu, tenguen**
 preterite: **tenguí,** etc.
 past subjunctive: **tengués,** etc.
 participle: **tengut, tenguda,** etc.)

venir

Note the close parallel between **venir** and **tenir,** in all except their imperatives.

irregular imperative: 2*sg.* **vine** (in compounds: **-vén**)
 infinitive: **venir** (less formal **vindre**)
 future stem: **vindr-** (Bal. **vendr-**): future: **vindré,** etc.; conditional: **vindria,**
  etc.; (Bal. **vendré, vendria,** etc.)
 3*sg.* present indicative: **ve**
 stem 1: **ven-** (Conjugation IIIb)
 present indicative: 2*sg.* **véns,** 1*pl.* **venim,** 2*pl.* **veniu,** 3*pl.* **vénen**
 imperfect: **venia,** etc.
 gerund: **venint**
 stem 2: **ving-** (Conjugation II)
 1*sg.* present indicative: **vinc**
 present subjunctive: **vingui, vinguis, vingui, vinguem, vingueu, vinguin;**
 Val./NW **vinga, vingues, vinga,** vinguem, vingueu, **vinguen**
 preterite: **vinguí,** etc.
 past subjunctive: **vingués,** etc.; Val. **vinguera,** etc.
 participle: **vingut, vinguda,** etc.
(Bal. stem 2: **veng-** (Conjugation II)
 1*sg.* present indicative: **vénc**
 present subjunctive: **véngui, vénguis, véngui, venguem, vengueu, vénguen**
 preterite: **venguí,** etc.
 past subjunctive: **vengués,** etc.
 participle: **vengut, venguda,** etc.)

viure

stem 1: **viv-** (Conjugation III)
 present indicative: 1*pl.* **vivim,** 2*pl.* **viviu**

imperfect: **vivia**, etc.

gerund: **vivint**

stem 1B: **viu-** (Conjugation II)

    infinitive: **viure**

    future: **viuré**, etc.; conditional: **viuria**, etc.

    present indicative: 2*sg.* **vius**, 3*sg.* **viu**, 3*pl.* **viuen**

stem 2: **visc-** (Conjugation II)

    1*sg.* present indicative: **visc**

    present subjunctive: **visqui, visquis, visqui, visquem, visqueu, visquin**; Val./ NW/optionally Bal. **visca, visques, visca**, visquem, visqueu, **visquen**

    preterite: **visquí**, etc.

    past subjunctive: **visqués**, etc.; Val. **visquera**, etc.

    participle: **viscut, viscuda**, etc.

17 USE OF INDICATIVE (NON-CONTINUOUS) VERB FORMS

In this chapter we look at the use of the most fundamental finite verb forms. The forms themselves have been presented in Chapter 16. The use of compound or periphrastic 'progressive forms' is covered in Chapter 18, and the use of the subjunctive forms is covered in Chapter 19. The sets of verb forms here combine in various ways the categories of tense and aspect. The category of tense relates the time of the event or state presented by the verb either to the time of the speech event (with values past, present, and future), or to some other time mentioned in the discourse or inferred from the context (anteriority or relative tense, for example pluperfect, future perfect). Aspect in Catalan involves two systems: perfective versus imperfective, a distinction which is made only within the past tense, and the perfect, which, strictly speaking, occurs only within present tense; see **17.2** on perfect and other compound forms.

17.1 SIMPLE FORMS

17.1.1 PRESENT INDICATIVE

The forms of the present indicative are discussed at **16.5.5**; what follows is to be read in conjunction with discussion of the Catalan progressive (continuous) forms in **18.1** and **18.2**. The most regular use of the present tense is to refer to situations in progress at the time of speaking. Although this does not include all the uses of the present tense, as will be seen below, it reflects uses like simultaneous, actual, habitual or general present. This tense corresponds to three patterns in English: **parlo** 'I speak' (simple), 'I do speak' (compound with auxiliary 'do'), and 'I am speaking' (progressive: 'be' + gerund).

Canta com un àngel.
She is singing/sings like an angel. (i.e. is singing now)

En aquest moment la teva amiga torna del mercat.
At this moment your friend is coming back from the market.

Ara li llegeixen el veredicte.
They are now reading out the verdict to him.

Sí que ho entenc.
I do understand.

The Catalan simple present itself may have a progressive value, so that it often appears (as above) where English uses the progressive form. In many contexts the distinction between the two available forms in Catalan is very slight:

Plou?/Està plovent? Doncs no surto.   Is it raining? I'm not going out then.

Escriu/Està escrivint les seves memòries.   He's writing his memoirs.

The simple present in Catalan otherwise can be described as denoting:

(i)   Current states:

Sembla trista.   She looks sad.
Fa sol.   It's sunny.

(ii)   Events seen as belonging to an actual, habitual or general present:

Encara viuen en aquest carrer.
They still live in this street.

Els teus amics no creuen en aquestes coses.
Your friends don't believe in these things.

Tothom pensa que cal fer alguna cosa.
Everybody thinks that something must be done.

Cada dilluns vaig al cinema.
I go to the cinema every Monday.

The present can also be used to give orders, especially in illative sentences or in coordinations (see Chapter 28):

Així, doncs, demà em compres el diari.
So, then, you'll buy me the newspaper tomorrow.

Te'n vas a la botiga de la cantonada i em portes dues llaunes de cervesa.
Off you go to the shop on the corner and fetch me two cans of beer.

Strict coincidence between present time and present tense is not always maintained. In fact, the present tense can refer both to the past and to the future. For example, the present tense ('historic present') may be used to narrate facts that occurred in the past. This device is favoured as a way of enlivening narrative or historical writing, and it occurs also in speech more frequently than the equivalent in English (e.g. 'Then he gets on his high horse and tries to tell us how to do it'). The historic present assumes awareness in the reader/ listener that the events referred to belong in the past.

El Tractat dels Pirineus de 1659 separa Catalunya Nord de la resta del territori.
The Treaty of the Pyrenees in 1659 separated North Catalonia from the rest of the territory.

–Seu aquí– em diu –i treu-te aquestes sabatotes brutes.
'Sit down here,' she said to me, 'and take off those horrible dirty shoes.'

Future events or intentions can also be expressed with the present tense. Again, the listener will be aware of the time through other clues, like adverbs or coherence with the rest of the text:

Demà em present al banc i em queix al director.
Tomorrow I'm going to the bank and complaining to the manager.

Jo li explico la situació ara mateix.
I'll explain the situation to her right now.

Què faig amb això?
What shall I do with this?

Conditional clauses can refer to a possible future event. In these cases the choice of tense depends not on the time but on the possibilities of the hypothesis becoming a reality; for full discussion of conditional sentences see Chapter 34.

Si mai m'ho torna a dir, el denuncio/el denunciaré.
If he ever says that to me again I'll report him.

Si vas a aquell restaurant, ja veuràs com hi tornes/hi tornaràs.
If you try that restaurant you see how you'll go back there again.

As mentioned above, present time is also expressed through the present tense of the progressive (or continuous) periphrasis **estar** + gerund (**18.1**). The choice between the simple present and the progressive is similar in certain respects to the corresponding pattern in English – there are contexts in which, for example, **diuen** equals 'they say', and **estan dient** equals 'they are saying'. But this parallelism can also be misleading; whatever else may also be appropriate, the Catalan simple present is always appropriate when describing a situation contemporaneous with the speech time, whereas, for English, with activity verbs, only the progressive is appropriate. Thus, for example, **Què diuen?** 'What are they saying?' This contrast is discussed more fully in Chapter 18.

17.1.2 PRETERITE

The preterite (past perfective) has two equivalent forms in Catalan: the simple (or synthetic): **arribaren** 'they arrived', and the periphrastic (or analytic):

van arribar 'they arrived' (see **16.5.6.2**). The first-person singular form of the synthetic preterite, e.g. **aní** 'I went', is virtually obsolete, occurring only in Valencia and Ibiza and in some poetry.

Both ways of conjugating this tense are equivalent and do not produce differences in meaning. The standard written language alternates freely (and evenly) between the simple and the periphrastic preterite, and it is normal to find both forms present in the same sentence:

> **S'acostà a la porta i va trucar-hi dos cops. = Es va acostar a la porta i hi trucà dos cops.**
> He went up to the door and knocked twice.

In any given piece of writing, prevalence of the periphrastic preterite will be associated with an informal tone, while prevalence of the simple form will produce an effect of formality. This phenomenon reflects the fact that in speech the simple preterite is only very occasionally used except in the Balearic and Valencian dialects (where it is natural and very much alive, alongside the periphrastic form).

17.1.2.1 *Use of the preterite*

The preterite combines past time with perfective aspect; in expressing perfective aspect, the preterite contrasts with the imperfect (below **17.1.3**). Perfective aspect locates a situation in the past without focusing on its extent in time, its internal subdivisions (if any), or its relation to another situation. The preterite is used when the event or state represented by the verb occurred in a time which is past and finished *except when today is involved*. The past time referred to by this tense is thus a period that does not include 'today', or is a time not regarded as being connected to the present (for which the present perfect is appropriate). The comparative illustrations given below draw attention to this distinction.

> **L'any passat varen tenir un fill. = L'any passat tingueren un fill.**
> Last year they had a son.

> ***Enguany varen tenir un fill./*Enguany tingueren un fill.**
> This year they had a son. (The preterite is unacceptable in Catalan because **enguany** 'this year' includes the present moment: here the present perfect is required: **Enguany han tingut un fill.**)

> **No vares veure el teu germà ahir?/No veieres el teu germà ahir?**
> Didn't you see your brother yesterday? (*No vares veure el teu germà avui de matí?** or *No vares veure el teu germà avui de matí?** is impossible for 'Didn't you see your brother this morning?' which can only be **No has vist el teu germà avui de matí?**)

English speakers need to be particularly careful over how Catalan distinguishes in this way between two degrees of remoteness in the past. Use of the preterite very clearly marks reference to a past that is cut off from the present. It is thus quite ungrammatical to use this tense for events that occurred in the same unit of time as the moment of utterance, i.e. a period including 'today', or a period referred to with the demonstrative **aquest** 'this'. We return to this matter in discussion of the present perfect in **17.2.2**.

The above discussion highlights the perfective aspect of the preterite tense which presents events as over and complete, cut off in a past time, with the idea of completeness (ending but also sometimes beginning) to the fore. Understanding the relation of the preterite to the imperfect tense is essential for correct translation of the English simple past, and the rest of this section should be read in conjunction with **17.1.3** (especially **17.1.3.1**) below.

Main areas of use of the preterite:

(i)   Single completed events/situations (or, in the negative, non-events):

Es van treure els abrics abans d'entrar a l'auditori.
They took off their coats before going into the auditorium.

Va ser una bestiesa no aprofitar aquella ocasió.
It was stupid not to take that opportunity.

No van haver de repetir-m'ho dues vegades.
They didn't have to tell me twice.

(ii) Events or situations occurring in a specific, finite period of time:

Va estar un any a la presó.
He was in prison for a year.

Durant tot aquell temps no vàrem parlar de cap altra cosa.
During all that time we spoke of nothing else.

Per un segon vaig pensar que em volien matar.
For a second I thought that they wanted to kill me.

Va estar resant durant ben bé una hora.
He spent a good hour praying. (See **18.1.1iii** on past progressive.)

If, as above, the period of time that saw completion of the event is mentioned, the preterite must be used. Sometimes the actual period of time is implicit rather than explicit, and it may be force of the preterite itself which conveys the idea that the event took place in a finite time-span now seen as completed.

Va ser el millor cap de secció que hem tingut mai.
He was (during his period of office) the best section head we have ever
   had.

Que jo sàpiga, mai no visqueren aquí.
As far as I know, they never lived here.

If the event is repeated but discontinuous within a specified period, the preterite may be used (instead of the more frequent option of the imperfect):

Aquell estiu vam anar cada matí a la platja.
That summer we went to the beach every morning.

(iii) Indicating the beginning of a state or event:

Així que vaig poder li vaig tornar la quantitat que li devia.
As soon as I could I paid him back the amount I owed him.

Un somriure irònic es va dibuixar en els seus llavis.
An ironic smile began to form on his lips.

(iv) Other nuances:

The meaning of certain verbs can be modified in line with the perfective aspect of the preterite. Thus, in this tense, **poder** 'be able to' can acquire the sense of 'manage to', 'succeed in':

No van poder visitar-nos aquell dia.
They didn't get/manage to see us that day.

Saber in the preterite can mean 'find out', 'realize':

Ho vaig saber preguntant pel bar.
I found out by asking around in the bar.

Quan saberen que havien aprovat . . .
When they found out they had passed . . .

The preterite of **tenir** 'have' and **voler** 'want', 'be willing' emphasizes the idea of a single event:

Vaig tenir la impressió que . . .
I had the impression that . . . /I was struck by the idea that . . .

No van voler entrar-hi.
They did not want to go in. (i.e. they made the decision or declared that they would not go in)

Volgueren convèncer-nos que era veritat.
They tried to convince us that it was true.

Conèixer in the preterite means 'get to know'/'meet' or 'be introduced to':

Ens vam conèixer a la universitat.	We met at university.
Quan dius que la vas conèixer?	When do you say you got to know her?

The clearly perfective force of the sentences given above contrasts with the much more general, descriptive aspect conveyed when these verbs are used in the imperfect tense: e.g., **Tenia la impressió que . . .** , **No volien entrar-hi** express not single events but states of mind, in line with further discussion provided in **17.1.3.1**.

17.1.3 IMPERFECT

The imperfect indicative is defined by two features: the past-ness and the extension over time of the event or state referred to. Expressing imperfective aspect, it refers to events or states seen as having temporal extent, either in themselves, or at least relative to some other state or event which interrupts them. Thus, it is the tense used for habitual events or states in the past.

The English simple past 'I went there' may be perfective or imperfective, and can only be translated into Catalan when it is known which aspect is meant. This will depend on actual clues (usually adverbials) in the sentence or from implications of context: thus, 'I went there yesterday' is perfective and accordingly preterite in Catalan: **Hi vaig anar ahir**, while 'I went there often when I was young' is (typically, though not necessarily) imperfective and accordingly imperfect in Catalan: **Hi anava sovint quan era jove**.

English constructions like 'I used to go', 'I was going', and 'I would (habitually) go' will almost always correspond to the Catalan imperfect. Further discussion is provided at **17.1.3.1**.

Examples of the imperfect in use:

Quan érem més joves anàvem a ballar cada dissabte.
When we were younger we used to go dancing every Saturday.

En temps dels meus avis la gent era més galant.
In my grandparents' day people were more courteous.

Els antics creien que el sol s'encenia cada matí.
The ancients used to believe that the sun was lit every morning.

Quan vaig arribar-hi, en Miquel ja tocava.
When I got there Miquel was already playing.

Brillava el sol i vaig decidir de fer un tomb.
The sun was shining and I decided to take a stroll.

The last two examples, where the preterite and the imperfect operate together in one sentence, illustrate how (especially in narration) the imperfect is the form used for description and for supplying 'background' to other (usually preterite) events/states. This includes reference to a situation which is seen as having already begun at the time of another completed event occurring:

Jo me n'anava quan va sonar el timbre.
I was just leaving when the phone bell rang.

Hi passaven dos anys 'They spent two years there' (imperfect) is appropriate when the speaker is going on to mention some event which happened during that period, or perhaps has already mentioned an event which gave rise to the state of their spending two years. **Hi passaren dos anys** 'They spent two years there' (preterite) is appropriate when the speaker states a historical fact, without relating it explicitly to other events or states.

Other functions of the imperfect tense:

(i) Dramatization:

In literary and journalistic styles the imperfect can acquire a perfective value, i.e. it can be used instead of the preterite. The effect of this device (which is always deployed sparingly) is to dramatize the action, presenting it as though it were unfolding in the narrative past. This can only be done when the time in which the event occurs is mentioned explicitly:

Vint anys després es declarava la guerra.
Twenty years later war was being declared/was declared.

El 1833 s'iniciava la Renaixença a Catalunya.
The Catalan *Renaixença* began in 1833.

(ii) Courtesy:

Together with the conditional (see **17.1.5**), the imperfect is also the tense of politeness in making requests:

Volia saber el preu del vestit verd.
I (just) wanted to know how much the green suit is.

Venia per la feina que ofereixen a l'anunci.
I've come about the job announced in the advert.

(iii) Intention or imminence:

Que bé que hagis trucat: ara mateix veníem a veure't.
How lucky you should phone: we were just coming to see you.

L'autobús ja partia, però he pogut aturar-lo.
The bus was just leaving but I managed to stop it.

In a related context, the imperfect can point towards the future:

Quina llàstima que estigui malalt: demà havíem d'anar d'excursió.
What a pity he's ill: we were going hiking tomorrow.

Ha dit que no vindria, justament avui que teníem partit a la tarda.
He said he wouldn't come, today of all days when we've got a match this
  afternoon.

(iv) Condition:

Si venies a veure'm et convidaria a dinar.
If you came to see me I'd invite you to lunch.

In the following example (colloquial style) the imperfect indicative is
used in both clauses of an unreal (counterfactual) condition.

Si m'ho tornava a dir, et juro que el matava.
If he'd said it to me again, I swear I'd have killed him.

For more on conditional sentences generally and use of the imperfect
indicative/subjunctive in these constructions, see **34.1–6**.

(v) Alternation with the imperfect progressive:

Unless imminence is implied (**Ens n'anàvem aquella tarda** 'We were leaving that afternoon', a quasi-future as covered in (iii) above), the progressive and simple imperfect forms are virtually interchangeable:

Jo mirava/estava mirant les notícies quan vaig sentir un xiscle.
I was watching the news when I heard a scream.

Of these alternatives, the simple imperfect is perhaps the more traditional usage, while the progressive is increasingly common.

17.1.3.1 *Preterite versus imperfect: translation issues*

In the examples used and discussed in this section all instances of the preterite tense would be substituted by the perfect – e.g. **he vist** for **vaig veure** – if
the event referred to took place in a time period including 'today' or in a past
time still seen as connected to the present, as explained in **17.1.2.1** and **17.2.2**.
  As already illustrated, the question of aspect (perfective or imperfective) is
fundamental in differentiating between use of the preterite or the imperfect
tense in Catalan. The aspectual distinction is elusive for English speakers,
mainly because the English simple past-tense form ('I went', 'I gave', etc.) can
cover both. The presence of adverbial clues in the sentence may give an
indication of which aspect is being expressed, thereby facilitating translation:
compare **Ho fèiem molt sovint** 'We did it very often' with **Ho vam fer per
primera vegada** 'We did it for the first time'. Note however that the presence
of an additional time adverbial may override this: **Durant aquell curs ho férem
molt sovint** 'We did it very often that year', **Ho fèiem per primera vegada quan
va sonar el telèfon** 'We were doing it for the first time when the phone rang'.
These examples illustrate nicely the fact that aspectual choice is not directly

determined by the nature of situations, but rather by how the speaker wishes to present them in relation to other situations. Where no such clues are provided, the tense used in Catalan will be determined by (and itself convey) the aspect in which the speaker considers the event referred to: **Ho va pagar tot amb xecs de viatge** 'He paid for everything in travellers' cheques' expresses a single, completed event, while **Ho pagava tot amb xecs de viatge**, still translatable as 'He paid for everything in travellers' cheques', nonetheless expresses that the paying was extended in time – in relation to something or other – inviting typically the inference that the event was repeated.

Clarification of this matter can be gained by considering some particular cases where the use of one form or the other presents nuances of meaning very closely tied to questions of aspect. The comments on the following pairs explain the implications of aspectual choice:

Era impossible convence'l.
It was impossible to convince him. (description of the other's attitude)

Va ser impossible convence'l.
It was impossible to convince him. (We tried but failed.)

Havia de consultar el metge.
I needed to see the doctor. (no information implied about whether the consultation took place)

Vaig haver de consultar el metge.
I had to (and did) consult the doctor.

No volíem entrar-hi.
We didn't want to go in.

No vam voler entrar-hi.
We didn't want to go in (and we didn't).

Estaven mirant les estrelles.
They were looking at the stars. (descriptive)

Van estar mirant les estrelles.
They stood (stayed) looking at the stars. (for a finite period of time: a perfective demarcation given to a state marked as inherently extended by the progressive periphrasis)

The last pair above illustrates how use of the preterite can imply a finite time-span for the event, presenting duration as a single completed event. This idea may be associated with a lifetime, as in:

Visqueren sempre junts i s'estimaren fins al final.
They lived together always and loved one another until the end.

Repeated or habitual events will typically be in the imperfect, but the preterite is alternatively found when the period in which repetition occurs is itself specified. So, **Anava cada matí a la platja** 'He went to the beach every morning' is distinctly imperfective in aspect, but addition of a qualifying phrase like **durant aquella setmana** 'during that week' allows the perfective aspect of each repeated event to be optionally foregrounded: **Durant aquella setmana anava/va anar cada matí a la platja.** Similarly:

> **Aquell any només treballàvem/vam treballar dos dies a la setmana.**
> That year we only worked two days a week.

Uncertainty can often be resolved by attempting the paraphrase of an English simple past as either of these alternative imperfects, or by testing aspect through introducing a notional adverbial. Thus 'made' will be **feia** if 'was making' or 'used to make' can be substituted without disruption: **La màquina** *feia* **molt de soroll** 'The engine made/used to make/was making a lot of noise' (cf. **La màquina** *va fer* **molt de soroll quan la vam engegar** 'The engine made a lot of noise when we started it up'). Similarly, out of context, there is no way of telling whether 'He gave me good advice' means **Em va donar bons consells** or **Em donava bons consells.** If the context would allow 'on that occasion', for example, the preterite is appropriate; or if the context suggests 'usually' then the imperfect will be appropriate.

17.1.4   FUTURE

The future tense in Catalan behaves in many respects like the 'shall/will' English counterpart:

> **Demà es declararà el veredicte.**
> Tomorrow the verdict will be declared.

> **Avui tancarem a les dues.**
> We'll close at two o'clock today.

> **Estic segur que vendrem tot el gènere.**
> I'm sure we shall sell all the stock.

> **Si no em dius res, et passaré a recollir sobre les vuit.**
> If you don't let me know differently, I'll pick you up around eight o'clock.

> **Ens ha promès que no ho tornarà a fer.**
> He has promised us not to do it again.

Informal replacement of the future by the present indicative is common (see above **17.1.1**), extending slightly further than the corresponding substitution in English:

Demà anem a Ciutadella.	We're going to Ciutadella tomorrow.
On posem les maletes?	Where shall we put the cases?

Other uses of the future tense involve pragmatic connotations of probability, surprise, or concession.

(i) Future of probability

With the presence of the adverb **potser** 'perhaps', or a synonym like **tal vegada, tal volta, per ventura**, etc., the future can express probability or doubt. Note the rendering by 'may' in the following examples:

Potser els teus pares canviaran d'opinió.
Perhaps your parents may change their minds.

El govern per ventura l'indultarà.
The government may perhaps give him a reprieve.

Spoken Catalan also uses the future to express that something is inferred to be the case. This use is regarded by normative grammarians as a Spanish interference phenomenon. The 'authentic' inferential construction, which is also perfectly normal in speech, uses the periphrasis **deure** + infinitive (see **18.2.1**):

(non-standard) **No sé si els altres pensaran això (en aquest moment).**
No sé si els altres deuen pensar això.
I don't know if the others will think so.

(non-standard) **En aquests moments m'estaran esperant a l'aeroport.**
En aquests moments em deuen estar esperant a l'aeroport.
At this very moment they'll be (= they must be) waiting for me at the airport.

(ii) Future of surprise

No em diràs que el vares insultar d'aquesta manera!
Don't tell me that you insulted him like that!

N'arribaràs a dir, de beneitures!
You really do come out with some stupid things!

The examples above can be said to refer figuratively to a future event, but the stress is placed here on the surprise effect, as the following equivalents show:

Vols dir que el vares insultar d'aquesta manera?
Did you really insult him like that?

Mira que n'arribes a dir, de beneitures!
Just look what stupid things you come out with!

(iii) Future of concession

Two clauses with verbs in the future and coordinated by an adversative conjunction can be the equivalent of a concessive construction. In such cases the future in the first clause has identical value to the verb in the present subjunctive governed by a concessive conjunction (see **33.3.3** and **19.4.2**).

Anirà a cent classes de conducció, però no n'aprendrà mai. = Encara que vagi a cent classes de conducció no n'aprendrà mai.
He could take a hundred driving lessons but will still never learn to drive.

Direu el que voldreu, però aquest llibre és bo.
You can say what you like but this book is good.

17.1.4.1   The future tense in subordinate clauses

The future is an alternative to the present subjunctive in temporal clauses referring to a future event and in relative clauses with an indefinite antecedent (see **19.3** and **19.4.7**).

(i) Future in temporal clauses

T'ho diré quan n'estaré segur del tot. = T'ho diré quan n'estigui segur del tot.
I'll tell you when I'm quite certain about it.

Quan ton pare ho sabrà s'enfadarà molt. = Quan ton pare ho sàpiga s'enfadarà molt.
When your father finds out he'll be really angry.

(ii) Future in relative clauses

Qui no entregarà el treball abans del trenta de juny suspendrà. = Qui no entregui el treball abans del trenta de juny suspendrà.
Anybody not handing in the work by June 30 will fail.

Els productes que passaran de les cinquanta mil pessetes s'abaixaran un deu per cent. = Els productes que passin de les cinquanta mil pessetes s'abaixaran un deu per cent.
Goods priced at over 50,000 pesetas will reduced by ten per cent.

In the modern language there is a strong tendency for the present subjunctive to be preferred to the future in both these types of clause. Use of the future, however, does have an advantage and is recommended for the first and second persons plural of regular verbs (where present indicative and present subjunctive are identical in form). The sentence **Els qui us queixareu no anireu a la llista** 'Those of you who complain will not go on the list' avoids ambiguity with **Els qui us queixeu no anireu a la llista**, which can refer either to those who are complaining at present or to those who may complain in the future.

17.1.5   CONDITIONAL

The conditional is used in the consequence clause of a conditional construction when the verb in the condition clause ('if' clause) is not in the present tense. (For discussion of conditional constructions, See Chapter 34.)

Si encara fes sol podríem continuar jugant.
If the sun stayed out we could keep on playing.

Si venies et mostraria la biblioteca.
If you came I'd show you our library.

(On the alternation of imperfect indicative/subjunctive in the 'if'-clause see **34.4** and **34.5**.)

The conditional also expresses implied conditions, as the corresponding 'would'/'should' forms do in English:

Això seria fantàstic!
That would be fantastic!

Podríem ajornar la reunió fins demà.
We could postpone the meeting until tomorrow.

Com m'agadaria d'haver-ho vist!
How I would like to have seen it!

In addition, the conditional expresses 'future in the past', that is, future with respect to a past reference point. The conditional can likewise express probability from a past perspective, in the contexts in which the future can have this sense (**17.1.4i**). For the purpose of sequence of tenses the conditional counts as a past tense. So the subjunctive in a subordinate clause governed by a conditional will normally go in the past tense: compare **Serà millor que no en sàpiguen res** 'It will be better that they know nothing about it' with **Seria millor que no en sabessin res** 'It would be better that they knew nothing about it'.

The function of the conditional in expressing a future event from a perspective placed in the past can be seen in the following adaptations of some examples used in section **17.1.4** above:

(i) Conditional as 'future in the past'

Digueren que l'endemà es declararia el veredicte.
They said the verdict would be declared the next day.

Decidírem que aquell dia tancaríem a les dues.
We decided we would close at two o'clock that day.

Estava segur que vendríem tot el gènere.
I was sure we would sell all the stock.

No et vaig dir que, si no em deies res, et passaria a recollir sobre les vuit?
Didn't I tell you that unless you let me know differently, I'd pick you up around eight o'clock?

Ens havia promès que no ho tornaria a fer.
He had promised us not to do it again.

(ii) Conditional of probability (compare 17.1.4i)

Pensaves que potser els teus pares canviarien d'opinió.
You thought that perhaps your parents would change their mind.

Tothom deia que el govern per ventura l'indultaria.
Everybody said that the government would perhaps give him a reprieve.

As with the future, the use of the conditional alone to express probability by inference is regarded as a Castilianism. The periphrasis **deure** (in a past tense) + infinitive is both current and authentic:

(non-standard) **No sabia si els altres pensarien això.**
No sabia si els altres devien pensar això.
I didn't know if the others would think so/would have thought so.

(non-standard) **En aquells moments m'estarien esperant a l'aeroport.**
En aquells moments em devien estar esperant a l'aeroport.
At that very moment they would (= must) have been waiting for me at the airport.

The conditional can be used instead of the imperfect to make polite requests (17.1.3ii) and to tone down expressions of wishing or wanting:

Que em podries dir on és la farmàcia?
Could you tell me where the chemist's is?

Voldria confessar-te una cosa molt delicada.
I'd like to confess something very delicate to you.

Podrien ser una mica més amables.
They could be a bit friendlier.

El que hauríeu de fer és . . .
What you ought to do is . . .

Rhetorical questions are often framed in the conditional:

Qui gosaria contradir-me?   Who would dare to contradict me?
On sentiries una música semblant? Where would you hear such music?

17.2 COMPOUND TENSES

17.2.1.1 Meanings of compound tenses

The compound tenses of Catalan are similar in many respects to the comparable English ones using 'have' and the past participle; they have two related functions. One, found largely in the present perfect, is to express perfect aspect, that is, roughly speaking 'past with present relevance'; thus **l'he vist** 'I have seen it' contrasts with **el vaig veure** 'I saw it' much as the English translations do. See **17.1.2.1**, and **17.2.2**. The other value of the compound tenses (especially the past perfect or pluperfect, the future perfect and the non-finite forms) is to express anteriority in relative time: **Ens va recomanar una pel·lícula que *havíem vist* vàries vegades** 'She recommended to us a film that we *had seen* several times'.

Li he regalat les joies de la meva àvia.
I have made her a present of my grandmother's jewels.

Aquest matí no he tingut temps d'afaitar-me.
I didn't have time for a shave this morning.

Em semblava que ja t'ho havia dit.
I thought I had already told you.

En tornar tu ja haurem acabat d'arreglar l'horari.
When you come back we will have finished arranging the timetable.

Ara ja hauríem enllestit aquesta feina, si tu ens hi haguessis ajudat més.
We would have had this job finished by now, if you had given us more help with it.

17.2.1.2 Compound tenses: auxiliary verbs and complements

The compound tenses (present perfect, pluperfect, future perfect and conditional perfect) are formed in Catalan by the participle preceded by the present, imperfect, future or conditional form respectively of the auxiliary verb **haver** (with 1*pl.* **hem** and 2*pl.* **heu** more usual than **havem**, **haveu**, which appear especially in formal speech; see **16.5.12** for details of the forms). In certain regions it is also possible to use as auxiliary the verb **ésser** 'be'. This is the normal solution in North Catalonia and a possible one in the Balearic Islands, especially (but not only), in this second case, with pronominal and movement verbs: **És partida** (= **Ha partit**) **fa poc** 'She left a short time ago', **No fa pas gaire que se n'és anat** (= **se n'ha anat**) 'It's not very long since he went away'.

Catalan cannot omit the participle in the way that English does in responses: 'Have you turned off the gas?' 'Yes, I have', must be **–Que has tancat el gas? –Sí** or **–Sí que l'he tancat.**

Compound tenses act as a unit when taking weak pronouns, adverbs or other complements. As a general rule other words will not come between the auxiliary and the past participle: object pronouns, where present, always precede the inflected finite forms of **haver** (but not the infinitive itself, or the gerund **havent**; see below):

Li ho he dit moltes vegades.
***He li ho dit moltes vegades.**
***Li ho he moltes vegades dit.**
I've told her many times.

However, a few adverbs of manner, especially **mal** and **ben**, can be placed between the auxiliary and the participle for emphasis in cases like:

Ho hem fet i ho hem ben fet.
We have done it and we have done it well.

Que si ha cantat? Ha mal cantat tota l'ària.
You want to know if he sang? He sang the entire aria and ruined it!

The compound infinitive is formed by the infinitive **haver** with the appropriate past participle:

Ara no em sap gens de greu d'haver vingut.
Now I'm not at all sorry to have come.

Where object pronouns are associated with the perfect infinitive they are attached enclitically to **haver**:

Aviat et penediràs d'haver-li-ho dit.
You'll soon regret having told him.

17.2.1.3   Agreement of participle in compound tenses

The past participle in a compound tense is invariable except when a direct object is one of these weak pronouns: **els**, **la**, **les** or **en**; here agreement is optional, though recommended by normative grammars. The point is discussed in detail at **21.1.2**.

17.2.1.4   Coordination of compound tenses

If there is no change of subject, it is not necessary to repeat the auxiliary in coordinations of two or more equivalent compound tenses. However, it is preferable to repeat the auxiliary when complements or parenthetical elements separate the different verbs:

Hem menjat un entrepà i begut una cervesa.
We have eaten a sandwich and drunk a beer.

Hem menjat un entrepà de tonyina i lletuga i hem begut una cervesa.
We have eaten a tuna and lettuce sandwich and drunk a beer.

Havíem dit i repetit que aquell era un lloc perillós.
We had said and repeated that that was a dangerous place.

Havíem dit ben clarament a tothom i havíem repetit que aquell era un lloc perillós.
We had said quite clearly to everybody and had repeated that that was a dangerous place.

When a pronominal verb is followed by a non-pronominal one it is safest to repeat the auxiliary: otherwise **S'han assegut a taula i menjat** could perhaps be taken for **S'han assegut a taula i s'han menjat**, not 'They sat down and ate' but 'They sat down and ate one another'. For this reason **S'han assegut a taula i han menjat** is preferable. Repetition of the auxiliary is obligatory when the pronominal verb comes second: **He entrat i m'he assegut a la primera cadira que he trobat** 'I went in and sat down in the first chair I found'.

17.2.2 PRESENT PERFECT

The present perfect is used for an event or state located in the past when there is a time adverbial whose sense includes the present moment: 'today', 'this morning', 'this week', 'this year', 'this century', 'this millennium', and so on:

Avui hem vist el teu germà.
We have seen/We saw your brother today.

Enguany he anat dues vegades al futbol.
I have been to two football matches this year.

El nostre segle ha vist dues guerres mundials.
Our century has seen two world wars.

and also for an event or state located by a time adverbial which does not include the present moment but is part of 'today':

Avui de matí he anat a comprar el pa. (even if we are in the afternoon)
This morning I went to buy the bread.

Aquesta tarda ha plogut molt. (even if we are in the evening)
This afternoon it rained a lot.

The actual or implied presence of deictic **aquest** (= this; **avui** = **aquest dia**) can be considered to determine use of the present perfect in Catalan, as illustrated in:

Aquesta nit no he dormit gens bé.
I didn't sleep at all well last night. ('last night' felt to be continuous with 'today')

Anit passada no vaig dormir gens bé.

I didn't sleep at all well last night. ('last night' felt as belonging to 'yesterday')

The present perfect is also used to refer to a situation started (or even completed) in the past but which is still connected to the present in some way or whose consequences are still felt. If the situation is not felt any more as connected to the present time, the preterite will be preferred:

Jo he nascut en aquesta terra i hi vull morir.

I was born in this land and here I wish to die. (but **Jo vaig néixer en aquesta terra** if we refer to the fact of being born and do not want to stress its consequences)

Ha estat sempre molt bona persona amb mi.

She has always been good to me. (but **Va ser sempre molt bona persona amb mi** if she is already dead or is not a **bona persona** any more)

La guerra civil ha deixat molt mals records als Països Catalans.

The Civil War has left very bad memories in the *Països Catalans*. (but **La guerra civil va deixar molt mals records als Països Catalans** if we consider that those 'bad memories' are now over)

Jesucrist ha vingut al món a salvar els pecadors.

Jesus came into the world to save sinners. (likely to be uttered by a Christian who feels personally affected by the remote event)

Jesucrist va venir al món a salvar els pecadors.

(the same statement made more objectively, expressing less personal involvement)

Catalan does not use the present perfect to refer to an event or state which started in the past and is still valid at the present time, where English does use its corresponding perfect (or perfect progressive), along with a temporal expression like 'for x (amount of time)', or 'since . . . '. Thus:

Treballo aquí (des de fa) vuit mesos.

I have worked here for eight months./I have been working here for eight months.

Se celebra a Londres des del 1895.

It has been held in London since 1895.

Quant temps fa que estàs jubilat?

How long have you been retired?

Fa estona que espera?

Have you been waiting long?

The same point applies to past tense forms:

Treballava allà (des de feia) vuit mesos quan va arribar el nou director.
I had worked/been working there for eight months when the new boss arrived.

Feia estona que esperava?
Had you been waiting long?

The present perfect progressive (**18.1.3v**) is sometimes found, combining the senses of perfect aspect with progressive aspect. This pattern is regarded by some as a calque of the corresponding English construction 'have' + 'been' + 'x-ing'.

He estat calculant les despeses que això suposa.
I have spent some time calculating the expense entailed. (*or* I have been calculating . . .)

17.2.3 PLUPERFECT

The pluperfect is used to indicate a state or event occurring before some other (more recent) past moment expressed by a different verb (or implied in the context):

El dia que va morir havia dit a la seva dona que no tornaria gaire tard a casa.
The day he died he had told his wife he would not be back home late.

Abans de les eleccions ja havien dit que no abaixarien els imposts.
Before the elections they had already said they wouldn't bring taxes down.

Encara que s'havia entrenat molt va jugar un partit molt dolent.
Although he had done a lot of training he played a very bad game.

Rules of sequence allow the pluperfect to refer, in the frame of conditional sentences with an imperfect, to events or states to be completed in the future:

Va recordar-nos que si en el futur ell continuava essent el nostre cap seria perquè havia (or hauria) actuat amb dignitat.
He reminded us that if in the future he continued to be in charge of us it would be because he had behaved with dignity.

17.2.4 PAST ANTERIOR

The past anterior is formed with the preterite of **haver** (either the simple preterite **haguí**, **hagueres**, etc., or the periphrastic **vaig haver**, **vas haver**, etc.) together with the participle. This tense refers to an event completed immediately before another one in the past.

Després que hagué dit això alçà la copa i brindà.
After he had said that he raised his glass and proposed a toast.

Encara no hagueres partit que ell ja et dejectava.
No sooner had you left than he was maligning you.

Quan vaig haver pagat les multes em tornaren el cotxe.
When I had paid the fines they gave me my car back

However, if the immediately preceding event is a habitual one, the pluperfect is preferred. Notice that in this context there is a remnant of the aspectual distinction – perfective **vaig haver** versus imperfective **havia** – not otherwise found in the compound tenses:

Sempre que havia plogut sortia a cercar caragols.
Whenever it had rained he went out looking for snails.

Quan ja havia sortit de la feina sempre es recordava que no havia desconnectat l'ordinador.
When he had left work he would always remember that he hadn't switched off the computer.

The past anterior is used only in temporal adverbial clauses, after **quan** 'when', **després que** 'after', **així que** 'as soon as', **de seguida que** 'immediately', **a penes** 'scarcely', and so on. This tense is confined to rather formal written contexts, and its use appears to be diminishing, being replaced by either the pluperfect or (especially after **després que**) the preterite. There is virtually no distinction in meaning between **Després que hagué entrat el president cantaren l'himne nacional** 'After the president had entered they sang the national anthem' and **Després que va entrar el president cantaren l'himne nacional** 'After the president entered they sang the national anthem'; see **33.2.2.6**.

17.2.5 FUTURE PERFECT

The future perfect is the tense of future events or states completed before another future one:

Abans de gaire ja ens haurem oblidat de tots aquests patiments.
Before long we shall have forgotten all this suffering.

L'any que ve haurem viscut vint anys en aquesta casa.
Next year we shall have lived twenty years in his house.

This compound future also appears in temporal and relative clauses, as an alternative to the construction with the subjunctive (see above **17.1.4.1**). English tends to be less precise in this particular, not using the future perfect in cases like the following:

Quan haureu (= Quan hàgiu) llegit el llibre sabreu més coses que abans.
When you have read the book you will know more than you did before.

Els qui m'hauran (= Els qui m'hagin) escoltat bé s'adonaran de la importància d'aquesta qüestió.
Those who have listened to me properly will understand the importance of this matter.

As with the simple future tense, expressions of inference (see **17.1.4**) referred to past situations are preferably made with the periphrasis **deure** + infinitive:

(non-standard) **No l'hauràs insultat d'aquesta manera!**
No el deus haver insultat d'aquesta manera!
You can't have insulted him like that!

(non-standard) **Què haurà fet el Barça?**
Què deu haver fet el Barça?
I wonder how Barcelona Football Club will have got on.

17.2.6   CONDITIONAL PERFECT

The conditional perfect occurs in the main clause of counterfactual conditional sentences where the 'if'-clause may take the pluperfect indicative or subjunctive (see **34.4** and **34.5**), as in:

Si m'haguessis fet cas no t'hauries equivocat.
If you had taken notice of me you wouldn't have got it wrong.

Avui hauríem anat d'excursió si no hagués plogut.
Today we would have gone on an outing if it hadn't rained.

See **34.6** for the alternative conditional conjugation of **haver** (**haguera** = **hauria**) and for more detailed discussion of conditional constructions.
    Like its English counterpart, the conditional perfect in Catalan also expresses 'future perfect in the past', that is it says the event in question, A, occurred before another, B, which was subsequent to a third past event, C.

Ajornar la decisió fins l'endemà hauria significat un risc considerable.
Putting off the decision until the next day would have meant a considerable risk.

Tothom creia que abans de fi d'any hauria caigut el govern.
Everybody believed that the government would have fallen before the end of the year.

In many such contexts, especially colloquially, the imperfect or conditional forms occur instead of the conditional perfect: so, for the examples above, we would have **ajornar la decisió . . . significava/significaria . . .** and **. . . cauria el govern.**

Other functions of the simple conditional are matched in the compound form, including implied condition (**No m'ho hauria cregut mai** 'I never would have believed it') and polite toning down:

Ja me n'hauríeu pogut informar abans.
You might have informed me earlier.

Hauria volgut parlar-ne amb tu.
I would have liked to talk to you about it.

Expressions of inference using the conditional perfect are deemed non-standard, the construction with **deure** (here in the imperfect tense) being preferred:

(non-standard) **Algú hauria obert la porta la nit abans.**
Algú devia haver obert la porta la nit abans.
Someone must have opened the door the night before.

18 PROGRESSIVE CONSTRUCTIONS AND OTHER VERBAL PERIPHRASES

18.1 PROGRESSIVE VERB FORMS: GENERAL

A full range of progressive (or 'continuous') verb forms is constructed from the appropriate forms of **estar** as auxiliary and the gerund of the verb in question (see Chapter 22): **estic descansant, van estar xerrant, estarem treballant**, etc. These resemble English 'I'm resting', 'they were chatting', 'we shall be working', etc., but some very specific distinctions and restrictions apply. We cover similar constructions involving **anar, venir**, or **seguir** as auxiliary verb in **18.1.2**.

18.1.1 Estar + GERUND

Estar + gerund is the principal progressive form; it is used in the following contexts:

(i)   To express that an event or state is, was, or will be actually in progress at the time:

Ara no l'hi puc passar, que està parlant per l'altra línia.
I can't put you through to him now, as he's on the other line.

Ens deuen estar observant de darrere les cortines.
They must be watching us from behind the curtains.

El pare Bauçà no vindrà perquè estarà dient missa.
Father Bauçà won't be coming as he'll be saying Mass.

One can contrast the Catalan non-progressive and progressive tenses in the last examples. In none of these instances (. . . **està parlant** . . . , . . . **estar observant** . . . , . . . **estarà dient** . . .) would the non-progressive form sound natural, unless possibly there were also an explicit time adverbial:
. . . **en aquest moment parla** . . . , . . . **ara ens deuen observar** . . .
Compare the examples above with the main-clause tenses in:

L'any que ve ens envien a Eivissa.
Next year they're sending us to Ibiza. (future)

Si ho tornes a fer, me'n vaig.
If you do it again, I'm leaving. (future)

Sempre fiquen el nas allà on no els demanen.
They're always interfering where they aren't wanted. (habitual present)

Ja sabíeu que ens n'anàvem l'endemà.
You knew we were leaving the next day. (future in the past)

    The restriction concerning simultaneity is consistently adhered to. **Ajudeu-me, que caic** 'Help me, I'm falling' would be heard from someone slipping from a branch, say, but . . . , **que estic caient** would make sense only if the speaker were already in mid-air. Thus, similarly, **Vinc** means 'I'm coming', when the speaker is probably not yet in motion. 'I'm drowning' really means 'I'm about to drown', so Catalan-speakers shout **Ai, que m'ofego!**, and **Que et mareges?** means 'Are you feeling sick?'

(ii) Always subject to the primary condition of simultaneity, to imply that an event is temporary or unexpected:

Actualment estem vivint a Sabadell.	At present we're living in Sabadell.
S'estaven posant molt nerviosos.	They were getting very nervous.

Mild protest or lively interest may also be conveyed:

Però, què t'estàs empatollant ara?	But what are you going on about now?

(iii) To express duration of an event over a period of time:

Van estar escodrinyant les proves durant un mes llarg.
They were scrutinizing the evidence for a month or more.

Vam haver d'estar esperant al carrer fins que va acabar el partit.
We had to wait outside in the street until the match ended.

Estaran marcant el pas mentre no els donin llum verda.
They'll be marking time until they get the go-ahead.

This use of the progressive makes it possible to give 'perfective' demarcation to an extended event or state (see **17.1.2.1** and **17.1.3.1**), and the very particular force of the preterite progressive, with this function, is to be observed. English has no equivalent.

(iv) Occasionally to express accumulation or repetition:

Últimament s'està queixant molt.
She has been complaining a lot recently.

M'estava bevent una ampolla diària de ginebra quan el metge m'ho va prohibir.
I was drinking a bottle of gin a day when the doctor told me to stop.

The Catalan progressive refines or expands, without substantially modifying, the meaning of the non-progressive form. Thus, in many contexts, the progressive and non-progressive forms are interchangeable:

Mediten./Estan meditant.
They are meditating.

Jo parlava amb l'Enric./Jo estava parlant amb l'Enric.
I was talking to Enric.

Where the verb itself denotes a continuous event, **estar** + gerund serves to stress duration or continuity:

–Què feien? –Preparaven el sopar./Estaven preparant el sopar.
'What were they doing?' 'They were preparing dinner.'

Some commentators detect an Anglicism here, imported via the influence of Castilian Spanish, and advise against overuse of the progressive. Nevertheless one observes marked consistency in the following conversational pattern: question non-progressive, followed by response in the progressive form: **–Què fas? –Estic** + gerund. Only occasionally, and in particular circumstances where continuity/duration is emphasized, will the stimulus question be in the progressive form:

–Però, què m'estàs dient ara? –Estic intentant explicar-te que . . ./Intento explicar-te que . . .
'But what are you telling me now?' 'I'm trying to explain . . .'

18.1.2   OTHER PROGRESSIVE FORMS WITH THE GERUND

anar + gerund

This construction is found, as a more expressive alternative to **estar** + gerund, where the idea of cumulative progression or actual motion is prominent:

Cada dia noto que em vaig fent més vell.
I'm aware of getting older by the day.

El cel s'anava ennuvolant.
The sky was clouding over.

Anava saludant els convidats un per un.
She went round greeting the guests one by one.

The colloquialisms **anar fent** and **anar tirant** are in common use to express the idea of 'be coping', 'be getting on reasonably well', 'be keeping at it':

No hem aconseguit progressos espectaculars, però anem fent.
We haven't made spectacular progress, but we're still plugging away.

Ha superat la crisi, i ara va tirant.
He has got over the crisis and is now doing all right.

venir + gerund

Use of **venir** 'come' with the gerund is restricted firstly to contexts where the idea of coming towards the speaker is prominent:

I ara han vingut queixant-se que res no funciona.
And now they've come complaining that nothing works.

En David sempre ve xiulant.
David is always whistling (when he comes this way).

Venir + gerund also has a temporal sense, approximately 'have been doing', as in:

Fa anys que vénen reivindicant una línia de ferrocarril.
For years now they have been demanding a railway line.

continuar/seguir + gerund

Continuar 'continue' combines with a gerund to convey 'go on . . . -ing'. Very often English 'still' is an appropriate translation:

Continuen insistint en això?
Are they still insisting on this?

Han mantingut i continuen mantenint bones relacions amb els seus rivals.
They have maintained good relations with their competitors, and still do.

Seguir with the gerund is also found with the same meaning of 'go on . . . -ing', although this construction is regarded as less genuine than the one with **continuar**:

Segueixen treballant a l'ajuntament.
They are still working at the town hall.

18.1.3   RESTRICTIONS ON USE OF PROGRESSIVE FORMS

Progressive forms are not normally used in the following contexts:

(i)   With verbs which express emotion (e.g., **odiar/avorrir** 'hate', **enyorar** 'miss', **estimar** 'love') nor with **saber** 'know' or **conèixer** 'be acquainted with'. Here Catalan usage coincides with English in avoiding the progressive with 'mental state' verbs.

With **fer mal** 'hurt' the progressive form would be most unusual:

Ara em fa mal de debò.   It's really hurting now.

(ii) With verbs that refer to states rather than activities (where English does allow the progressive):

Aquell dia no portava corbata.	That day he wasn't wearing a tie.
Sembla molt emocionada.	She's looking very excited.
Els núvols tapaven la lluna.	The clouds were hiding the moon.
El que fa falta és . . .	What's lacking is . . .

For verbs of physical posture or position, the Catalan progressive refers only to the event, not to the state. English 'he's sitting (e.g., on a bench)' will be **està assegut** or **seu**; the actual action of 'sitting down' is what is conveyed by **està seient** or **està asseient-se**. Likewise **estaven estirats a la sorra** describes people 'lying on the sand', while **s'estaven estirant a la sorra** denotes the action itself of 'lying down'; and so too **estava agenollada** 'she was kneeling' i.e. 'in a kneeling posture', but **s'estava agenollant** 'she was (in the act of) kneeling down'.

(iii) With main verb **estar** or with verbs of motion (**anar, venir, tornar,** etc.):

Estàs molt elegant avui.
You're looking very elegant today.

A on vas?
Where are you going?

–D'on ve tota aquesta gent? –Tornen del concert.
'Where are all these people coming from?' 'They're coming back from the concert.'

(iv) Generally with **ser/ésser**, although certain cases are encountered, often regarded as blatant anglicisms:

El debat està sent controlat pels organismes del partit.
Discussion is being controlled by the party organizations.

Unless the passive with **ser** must be used for other reasons, it seems prudent to avoid sentences like **La façana està sent restaurada** 'The facade is being restored', in favour of **S'està/Estan restaurant la façana.**

(v) It used to be said that Catalan did not combine compound tenses (with **haver**) with progressive forms. However, examples like the following are increasingly found. To say these are calqued on English models would perhaps be an oversimplification.

Durant cinc anys he estat donant classes a estudiants de primer de carrera.
For five years I have been teaching first-year undergraduates.

18.2   OTHER VERBAL PERIPHRASES: GENERAL

Verbal periphrasis occurs in other constructions where a modal and a principal verb are combined to express a single verbal notion. The range considered here is divided according to whether the periphrasis operates with the infinitive (**18.2.1**) or the past participle (**18.2.2**) of the principal verb.

18.2.1   MODAL + INFINITIVE

Included here among the modal periphrases are the major verbal functions of reiteration (**tornar a** + infinitive), obligation (**haver de** + infinitive), probability (**deure** + infinitive; see **17.1.4i**), ability/possibility (**poder** + infinitive), desire/willingness (**voler** + infinitive). Examples:

No ho torneu a fer.
Don't do it again.

No sé quan ens tornarem a veure.
I don't know when we shall see one another again.

Hem de marxar avui.
We must leave today.

Hauries d'haver-ho fet abans.
You ought to have done it earlier.

Deu haver-hi una manera d'arreglar-ho.
There must be a way to sort it out.

Deuran arribar amb el tren de les cinc.
They must be arriving on the 5 o'clock train.

No puc dir-t'ho sense mirar l'agenda.
I can't tell you without looking at my diary.

Les coses podrien haver resultat d'una altra manera.
Things could have turned out differently.

Vols venir amb mi?
Do you want to come with me?

Ells, però, no volien saber-ne res.
They didn't want to know anything about it, though.

(The obligatory sense of **haver de** is sometimes very dilute, and this periphrasis can thus express an emphatic future meaning:

Demà se n'han d'anar a Brussel·les.   Tomorrow they'll be off to Brussels.)

Saber + infinitive 'know how (to do something)' belongs to this category of periphrasis, sometimes translating 'be able'/'can'. It is differentiated from **poder** + infinitive in that it denotes mental/intellectual capacity or a skill, rather than physical ability. The distinction can be seen in the following pair of sentences:

No puc nedar.
I can't swim (e.g., because I've got a broken leg).

No sé nedar, perquè de petit no me'n van ensenyar.
I can't swim, because I wasn't taught to when I was little.

Other periphrases add specific nuances to the basic meaning of a main verb:

Rompre a (near-synonym of **començar/posar-se/arrencar a**) + infinitive means 'begin suddenly', 'break into':

De sobte rompé a plorar.	She suddenly burst into tears/burst out crying.
Llavors van rompre a cantar.	Then they broke into song.

Estar a punt de + infinitive means 'be about to', 'be nearly':

L'aigua deu estar a punt de bullir.	The water must be nearly boiling.

Estàvem a punt de sortir quan va sonar el telèfon.
We were about to go out when the phone rang.

Estar per + infinitive expresses an event that still remains to be done (so that the meaning may come close to **estar a punt de**), with various idiomatic equivalents in English:

Les patates encara estan per pelar.
The potatoes haven't been peeled yet/still haven't been peeled.

Estic per dir-li-ho.
I'm ready to tell him.

L'autocar de Perpinyà està per arribar.
The Perpignan coach hasn't come in yet/is due now.

Anar a + infinitive serves mainly to express imminent or intended action in the past:

Anava a dir que . . .   I was going to say that . . .

Use of the periphrastic **anar a** + infinitive 'be going to' is nothing like as extensive or as natural as it is in English or in the other Romance languages. This is in part because of the vigour of the periphrastic preterite (see **16.5.6.2**) whose auxiliary derives from forms of **anar** and coincides with them in several parts. Best advice is to stay with the simple future, except for the instances considered below. So:

Ara us diré el que penso fer. (not *Ara us vaig a dir . . .)
I'm now going to tell you what I intend to do.

La comissió es reunirà d'aquí a pocs dies. (not *La comissió va a reunir-se . . .)
The committee is going to meet in a few days' time.

For the reasons just explained, and as remarked above, **haver de** + infinitive can perform as a (stressed) periphrastic future:

Què n'han de pensar els veïns?
What are the neighbours (going) to think?

Ha de ser molt dura la seva resposta.
Their response is going to be very tough.

Otherwise **anar a** + infinitive can be used to express a future event when an idea of actual physical motion (or the imminence thereof) is involved:

Anava a treure el cotxe, però de sobte se'm va acudir de cridar un taxi.
I was going to get the car out, but it suddenly occurred to me to call a taxi.

Semblava que anés a caure.
It looked as though she was going to fall.

Note that in these examples, as in **Anava a dir que** . . . above, **anar a** + infinitive is mostly used in the past imperfect, and often carries the implication 'was going to (but didn't)'.

Venir a + infinitive translates 'add up to', 'amount to', 'turn out to':

La conclusió, doncs, ve a ser la mateixa.
The conclusion, then, turns out to be the same.

Tot plegat et vindrà a costar un dineral.
All told it will cost you a packet.

Pensar + infinitive is very commonly used for 'intend to':

No penso fer-ho fins demà.
I don't intend doing it until tomorrow.

Quan penses enllestir aquest capítol?
When do you intend to finish this chapter?

Arribar a + infinitive covers a range of idioms associated with the idea of 'reach the point of':

Això encara no arriba a ser una solució satisfactòria.
That still doesn't amount to a satisfactory solution.

La seva actitud m'arribava a irritar.
Their attitude was coming to irritate me.

Que n'arriba a ser, de talòs!
How dim he is!/How dim can you get?

No ho arribo a entendre.
I can't understand it.

'Become' can be translated by **arribar a ser** (see **30.6vi(b)**).

Acabar de + infinitive (occurring only in the present and imperfect tenses) has the meaning of 'have just + past participle':

S'acaba de declarar el resultat.	The result has just been declared.
Acabaven de treure el pa del forn.	They had just taken the bread out of the oven.

This construction should not be confused with use of **no acabar de** + infinitive, which qualifies the main verb with the idea of 'not quite', 'not fully':

No ho acabo d'entendre.
I still don't understand it./I just don't understand it.

No els acabava d'agradar.
They didn't really like it.

Fer + infinitive means 'make or have (something) done', 'something' being the situation of the infinitive. See **25.5**:

No em facis plorar.	Don't make me cry.
Han fet pintar el menjador.	They have had the dining room painted.

(Note how the infinitive can acquire passive meaning in periphrases involving **acabar de** and **fer**: **pa acabat de fer** 'freshly baked bread', **fer netejar la sala** 'have the room cleaned', **fer-se fer un suèter de punt** 'have a sweater knitted'.)

18.2.1.1 Weak object pronouns in verbal periphrases

Verbal periphrasis involving auxiliary or modal + gerund and auxiliary or modal + infinitive allows optional mobility of any associated pronominal clitics. These can be positioned either proclitically (before the conjugated auxiliary) or enclitically (attached to the gerund or infinitive), as is described in **12.2.3** and **12.9.4**. In general enclitic forms appear more formal; however, many subtle factors appear to affect choice of position, without any discernible alteration of meaning or emphasis. Balearic varieties strongly prefer the proclitic alternative, and this is the tendency in spontaneous speech more generally:

Ens estan prenent el pèl. = Estan prenent-nos el pèl.
They're pulling our leg.

Hi acaba d'arribar. = Acaba d'arribar-hi.
He has just arrived (there).

The position of pronominal clitics in periphrases with the past participle, discussed in **18.2.2**, is always proclitic.

18.2.2   AUXILIARY + (PAST) PARTICIPLE

This class includes the compound past tenses with **haver** (also dialectally **ésser**, sometimes **tenir: 16.5.12, 17.2** and **21.1.2**).

The verbs **deixar** 'leave', **quedar** 'stay', and **restar** 'stay' introduce the participle in periphrases which focus a past event in terms of consequence:

Les seves paraules em van deixar parat.
Her words left me bewildered.

Les negociacions han quedat interrompudes.
The negotiations have been interrupted.

La pedra rodolà muntanya avall fins a restar clavada entre dos arbres.
The stone rolled down the mountain until it wedged itself between two
    trees.

The passive voice (**ser** + past participle: see **29.1.1–4**) and the associated construction with **estar** + past participle (**30.5**) can also be thought of as belonging to this group of verbal periphrases.

19 THE SUBJUNCTIVE

19.1 GENERAL

The forms of the subjunctive mood are widely used in Catalan, and the principles governing their use are not always easy to grasp, at least for speakers of English which has nothing really comparable. Various areas and instances of use of the subjunctive are covered elsewhere in relation to particular grammatical features (such as Chapter 15, conjunctions; Chapter 17, contrasts with the indicative mood; Chapter 26, negation; Chapter 28, negative imperatives; Chapter 31, relative clauses; Chapter 32, complement clauses; Chapter 33, adverbial clauses; Chapter 34, conditional sentences). This central chapter is thus to be read in conjunction with the other chapters or sections referred to.

As the name implies, the subjunctive is mostly found in subordinate clauses (19.2–5). Use of the subjunctive in main clauses is discussed in section 19.6.

Much ink has been spilt in the attempt to identify a 'core meaning' of the subjunctive mood in Catalan and related languages. What we say here necessarily oversimplifies, but is intended as a frame of reference to guide the user. The subjunctive has been described as the mood of non-assertion or of inactuality. A speaker may use the subjunctive when he or she is not committed to the truth of the proposition in question in the current context of discourse. This non-commitment to truth may arise from several sources. The speaker may doubt the truth of the proposition, may entertain it as a wish to be fulfilled in the future, may be unable to ascertain the truth of the proposition, may be mentioning it only to recall another speaker's statement, may hold the proposition as hypothetical. Part of the difficulty arises from the fact that none of these circumstances necessarily of itself requires the use of the subjunctive, or excludes the use of the indicative. In some cases the selection of the subjunctive or of the indicative corresponds primarily to grammatical convention. In the following sections we shall devote most attention to those grammatical contexts where there is a choice.

19.2 THE SUBJUNCTIVE IN COMPLEMENT CLAUSES

A complement clause (32.1) is introduced by the complementizer **que** 'that'; it may be the subject or object of a main verb, or in apposition to a noun phrase, as in **la idea que** . . . 'the idea that . . .', **el fet que** . . . 'the fact that'. It is likely to take the subjunctive when the speaker is not committed to asserting that the content of the **que** clause is factual, that it actually is the case in the speaker's current mental model.

19.2.1 'THEMATIC' SUBJUNCTIVE

The subjunctive is generally used in complement clauses which precede the main verb:

Que en Xavier festegi amb la Núria no vol dir res.
The fact that Xavier is going out with Núria doesn't mean anything.
or Xavier's going out with Núria doesn't mean anything.

Que trobés a faltar Anna era una cosa, i passar sense cap dona n'era una altra.
That I missed Anna was one thing, but doing without a woman at all was another.

Que el secret no s'hagi divulgat és la millor prova que és, en suma, un secret.
The fact that the secret hasn't been spread is the best proof that it is, in fact, a secret.

In these examples the speaker in fact presupposes the truth of the **que** clause; but asserting the truth of it is not the point of the utterance. Rather the focus is on the *significance* of 'Xavier's going out with Núria', 'my missing Anna', 'the lack of diffusion of the secret'. (Notice that a similar effect is often produced in English by using a gerund or a nominalizing noun phrase rather than a clause.) The **que** clause reminds the hearer of something they already know in order to make some comment on it. In superficially similar contexts the indicative may appear:

Que ella coneixia els maneigs de l'Agustí disposant de la seva fortuna ... ja fa temps que se sabia.
That she was aware of Agustí's manoeuvres disposing of her fortune had been known for some time.

Que les coses han de canviar en l'àmbit autonòmic ho admeten fins i tot els presidents socialistes.
That things have to change in the autonomy sphere is admitted even by socialist prime ministers.

Here the function of the indicative in the **que** clause is either to present information which is in fact new to the hearer, or to confirm by repetition.

The same considerations affect choice of mood in clauses in apposition to **el fet, la idea**, whether they precede or follow the main verb. The subjunctive backgrounds the information in the **que** clause:

Potser el fet que no s'haguessin presentat, que cap dels dos no coneguès el nom de l'altre, la tallava.
Perhaps the fact that they hadn't been introduced, that neither of them knew the other's name, inhibited her. (the main point is her inhibition)

No m'avenia al fet que em derrotès un detall tan insignificant.
I couldn't get over the fact that I should have been beaten by such an insignificant detail.
or I couldn't come to terms with my being beaten . . .

The indicative, in contrast, foregrounds the **que** clause, presenting it as new information:

El que sorprèn modernament és el fet que la comunitat femenina es dividia en tres grups diferents.
What surprises us nowadays is the fact that the female community was divided into three different groups. (the main point is the division of the community into three groups, a fact which is, in addition, surprising)

El fet que el cos fou trobat flotant vora la Barrière, no prova pas el lloc on fou llançat a l'aigua.
The fact that the body was found floating off la Barrière does not indicate the place where it was thrown into the water.

19.2.2 SUBJUNCTIVE IN EMOTIVE CONTEXTS

In **que** clauses dependent on verbs (or other expressions) of emotion or evaluation the subjunctive is very common. Such verbs are **alegrar-se** 'be glad', **convenir** 'be appropriate', **doldre** 'sadden', **empipar** 'annoy', **emprenyar** 'annoy', **estranyar** 'surprise', **molestar** 'bother', **saber greu** 'regret', **sentir** 'regret', **sorprendre** 'surprise'; other expressions include **ser llàstima** 'be a pity', **ser interessant** 'be interesting', **ser significatiu** 'be significant', **estar content** 'be pleased'. As in earlier examples, the content of the **que** clause is presupposed to be true, but is presented to the hearer/reader as the cause of the emotive or evaluative reaction:

Em molesta que vulgui justificar la política mantinguda pels Estats Units a Amèrica Central.
I am annoyed that he tries to justify the policy of the United States in Central America.

Li sap greu que en Carles no hagi assistit al concert.
She is sorry that Carles wasn't at the concert.

No li sap greu que en Carles no hagi assistit al concert.
She isn't sorry that Carles wasn't at the concert.

Li sap greu que en Carles no hagi assistit al concert?
Is she sorry that Carles wasn't at the concert?

L'estrany és que no el canonitzessin.
The surprising thing is that they did not canonize him.

M'esgarrifo de pensar que algú pugui arribar a pertorbar la pau d'una casa.
I'm horrified to think that anyone could manage to disrupt the tranquillity of a household.

Less commonly, the indicative is found. As before, its use asserts new information, alongside the emotional or evaluative comment:

És sorprenent que avui, de sobte, en plena boutique londinenca de Chelsea en retrobo l'atmosfera.
It is surprising that today, suddenly, right in the middle of a Chelsea boutique, I recognize that atmosphere. (I recognize that atmosphere, and it is surprising)

Estic contenta que almenys hi ha un professor que l'aprecia.
I am glad there's at least one teacher who values him. (there's one teacher who values him, and I'm glad)

With **sort que** 'fortunately', the indicative is normal:

Sort que no hi havia el Pare Rodés.
Fortunately Father Rodés wasn't there.

19.2.3 OPTATIVE SUBJUNCTIVE

The subjunctive is normal in a **que** clause which expresses the content of a wish, desire, intention or request. (The content of a wish is necessarily not a fact.) The time of the situation expressed in the **que** clause may not precede that of the main clause:

Vol que acabis la tesi a corre-cuita.
She wants you to finish the thesis hurriedly.

La seva intenció era que no la fessis esperar més.
Her intention was that you shouldn't make her wait any longer.

Els aconsellarem que no s'hi fiquin.
We'll advise them not to get involved in it.

The use of the subjunctive after expressions denoting cause or achievement is similar. Such expressions are **aconseguir** 'achieve', **causar** 'cause', **deixar** 'let', **evitar** 'avoid', **fer** 'make', 'cause', **forçar** 'force', **impossibilitar** 'make impossible', **manar** 'order', **motivar** 'motivate', 'incline', **obligar** 'oblige', **permetre** 'allow', **persuadir** 'persuade':

Què fa que siguis tan llest?
What makes you (be) so clever?

Li impediren que em digués la veritat.
They prevented him from telling me the truth.

Aconseguiren que la Marta anés amb ells.
They managed to get Marta to go with them.

No permeté que vinguessin els periodistes a l'acte.
He did not allow the journalists to come to the session.

Verbs of saying or telling, like **aconsellar** 'advise', **advertir** 'warn', **contestar** 'reply', **cridar** 'call', 'shout', **dir** 'say', **insinuar** 'hint', **repetir** 'repeat', **telefonar** 'telephone', **xiuxiuejar** 'whisper', take the subjunctive in a subordinate clause which denotes the substance of a request, but the indicative (other things being equal) in a subordinate clause which expresses a statement:

Va repetir que calléssim.
He repeated that we should be quiet.
vs.
Va repetir que no s'havia aprovat el conveni.
He repeated that the agreement had not been ratified.

El Paco Huertas havia trucat dient que era l'encarregat del cas i que l'esperessin.
Paco Huertas had rung to say that he was (indicative) in charge of the case and that they should wait (subjunctive) for him.

Li vaig cridar que no entrés.
I shouted to her not to go in.

19.2.4   POTENTIAL SUBJUNCTIVE

The subjunctive is very frequently used in complement clauses dependent on expressions of (i) necessity, (ii) probability or possibility, (iii) appearance, (iv) doubt or denial. As in the cases already mentioned, the essential reason for using the subjunctive is that the speaker is not in a position, or does not wish, to assert that such-and-such is the case. Expressions of 'hope' and 'fear' often take the subjunctive; this pattern perhaps belongs here too (v).

(i) Among expressions of necessity are: **caldre que** 'be necessary that', **ser necessari que** 'be necessary that', **necessitar que** 'need that', **la necessitat que** 'necessity/need that', **ser essencial que** 'be essential that', **ser impossible que** 'be impossible that' (i.e. 'necessary that not'), **no poder ser que** 'cannot be that':

Cal que ho prenguis més seriosament.
You must take it more seriously.

No pot ser que s'hagi espatllat.
It's impossible for it to have broken down.

(ii) Expressions of probability and possibility are those like: **ser probable que** 'be likely that', **No hi ha dubte que** 'There is no doubt that', **ser possible que** 'be possible that', **poder ser que** 'may be that', **la possibilitat que** 'the possibility that':

Et sembla probable que rebaixin la factura?
Do you think it's likely that they'll reduce the bill?

Pot ser que s'ho creguin.
It may be that they (will) believe it.

És versemblant que per aquesta raó es vagi donar a la ribera el nom de la població.
It is plausible that for this reason the river was given the name of the settlement.

(iii) Expressions of appearance more often than not take the indicative; this is especially true in the case of **semblar** or **parèixer** 'seem' or **fer l'efecte** 'look', 'appear' used with an indirect object. These expressions function like 'believe' or 'think' and present a proposition as *actual*, at least within the speaker's mental model. Without an indirect object expressed, however, it is as if one were to say 'it seems (to someone, but I don't vouch for it)'; hence subjunctive:

Indicative:

Em sembla que la clau, la té l'Emili.
I think it's Emili who has the key.

Li semblava que el veia allí, plantat, mirant-la fixament.
It seemed to her that she could see him standing there, staring at her.

Subjunctive:

Sembla que vulgui entrar.
It seems as if she wants to get in.

Expressions of supposition or imagination work in a similar way, with the indicative when a qualified assertion is at issue, but with the subjunctive when no one is presented as currently holding the view, for example, when the expression of supposition or imagination is not itself an indicative verb:

Indicative:

M'he imaginat que el prior em reprenia per no cantar amb els altres monjos.
I imagined that the prior was reproving me for not singing with the other
   monks.

Admeto que ho vaig fer jo.
I admit that I did it.

Accepto que ho vaig fer jo.
I accept that I did it.

Suposo que ho vaig fer jo.
I suppose that I did it.

Sospito que ha passat per ací.
I suspect it has gone through here.

Subjunctive:

Imaginem-nos per un moment que ho hagi dit ella/que ho vagi dir ella.
Let us imagine for a moment that she said it.

Suposem per un moment que ho hagi dit ella/que ho vagi dir ella.
Let us suppose for a moment that she said it.

Acceptem per un moment que ho hagi dit ella/que ho vagi dir ella.
Let us accept for a moment that she said it.

Admetem per un moment que ho hagi dit ella/que ho vagi dir ella.
Let us admit for a moment that she said it.

**imaginant-nos/suposant/acceptant/admetent que ho hagi dit ella/que ho vagi
   dir ella**
imagining/supposing/accepting/admitting that she (may have) said it

la hipòtesi/la suposició que ho hagi dit ella/que ho vagi dir ella
the hypothesis/the supposition that she said it

In the examples immediately above the alternative **que ho vagi dir ella** illustrates the use of the past perfective subjunctive (**16.5.10.2**) which is further
illustrated in (iv) below.

   (iv) Expressions of doubt and denial typically provoke the subjunctive in a
complement clause, except when the speaker explicitly presents as true that
which someone else doubts or denies. Included here are expressions of saying,
believing, etc., which are negated, such as **no dir que** 'not say that', **no pensar
que** 'not think that', **no creure que** 'not believe that', **no adonar-se que** 'not
realize that', **sense que** 'without' (**26.1.3**), etc. 'Doubt' includes also rhetorical
questions which bear the connotation 'surely not':

Subjunctive:

Dubtava que tornés mai més.
She doubted that he would ever return.

No és que jo me'n queixi.
It's not that I'm complaining.

sense que jo me'n queixés
without my complaining

No creus que se'n recordin?
Don't you think they (will) remember it?

L'Arnau negà que l'Anna hagués acudit a la manifestació.
Arnau denied that Anna had joined in the demonstration.

L'Arnau negà que l'Anna acudís/vagi acudir a la manifestació.
Arnau denied that Anna joined in the demonstration.

Qui et diu que no haja estat Emili l'autor d'aquesta trencadissa?
What makes you think Emili wasn't responsible for this smash-up?

No sabia que fos escriptora.
I didn't know she was a writer.

Em resulta difícil de creure que entre els esclaus hi hagi qualitats tan uniformes.
It's hard to believe that among the slaves there should be such uniform characteristics.

Creu realment que puguin acusar Felip dels dos assassinats?
Do you really think they could accuse Felip of the two murders?

Indicative:

Poc s'ho pensaven uns minuts abans que tot els sortiria tan rodó.
They little thought a few minutes earlier that it would all turn out so well for them (which it did).

No s'ho creurà ningú que demà us executen.
No one will believe that you are to be executed tomorrow (which you are).

La Carme no es va adonar que en Pere hi era.
Carme didn't realize Pere was there (which he was).

No sabia que era escriptora.
She was a writer, which I didn't know.

It is predominantly in this doubt/denial context that the past perfective subjunctive (**16.5.10.2**) may occur. In all other contexts of subjunctive use the aspectual distinction conveyed by the contrast between the imperfect and the preterite indicative is not maintained. Here, at least for some speakers, an explicitly perfective meaning may be expressed in a subjunctive clause.

És impossible que ho vagi escriure ella.
It's impossible that *she* wrote it. (perhaps because the speaker knows that someone else wrote it)

Vostè creu que el president ho vagi permetre?
Do you believe the chairman allowed it?

Despite this possibility, the ordinary past subjunctive does not, by contrast, imply specifically imperfective aspect. The past perfective subjunctive is purely optional, and it would be quite correct to express the sense of the above examples with the past subjunctive:

És impossible que ho escrivís ella.
Vostè creu que el president ho permetés?

(v) Expressions of fear and hope give rise to particular problems. In the case of fear there is a gap, recognized by normative grammarians, between the traditional pattern of construction, with expletive **no**, and the pattern of spontaneous use. (In the traditional norm a complement clause after an expression denoting fear contains an element **no** which is labelled 'expletive' because no logical negation is expressed.) With the fear examples, when the main clause is positive, both indicative (future/conditional) and subjunctive are found. With 'hope' the problem is that the verb **esperar** covers a wider range of meaning than English 'hope', and not all senses of **esperar** induce the same construction.

(a)   Positive main clause, positive complement (traditional expletive **no** when subjunctive is used):

Tinc por que els veïns no ho contin tot./Tinc por que els veïns ho contaran tot. (more spontaneous) **Tinc por que els veïns ho contin tot.**
I'm afraid the neighbours will tell all.

(b)   Positive main clause, negative complement:

Tinc por que els veïns no ho contaran tot. (more spontaneous) **Tinc por que els veïns no ho contin tot.**
I'm afraid the neighbours won't tell all.

Note the ambiguity whereby the first form in (a) is identical to the 'more spontaneous' version in (b) but with opposite meaning. With a negative main clause, there are no alternatives (subjunctive is obligatory) and no ambiguity; **no**, if used in the subordinate clause, has its regular negative sense.

(c)   Negative main clause, positive complement:

No tinc por que els veïns ho contin tot.
I'm not afraid the neighbours will tell all.

(d)   Negative main clause, negative complement:

No tinc por que els veïns no ho contin tot.
I'm not afraid the neighbours won't tell all.

Expressions of hope, such as **esperar que** 'hope that', **confiar que** 'trust/expect that', **l'esperança que** 'the hope that', are normally followed by the indicative. However, in the sense 'wait for', 'wait until', **esperar** is followed by the subjunctive (optative sense; 19.2.3).

Confie que em concediran la beca que vaig demanar.
I expect that I'll be granted the scholarship I applied for.

Esperem que tot et va bé
We hope all is well with you.

Estaven esperant que el seu gendre els ajudés.
They were waiting for their son-in-law to help them.

Espero que pari de ploure.
I'm waiting till it stops raining.

19.3   SUBJUNCTIVE IN RELATIVE CLAUSES

The indicative is very frequently used in relative clauses (Chapter 31). This corresponds to the presumption of existence of the referent in the world of discourse (not necessarily the real world). However, when the speaker does not know of, or does not wish to be committed to, the existence of the referent, or denies its existence, or when a specific referent among a group cannot be identified, the subjunctive is used.

Vol pescar un peix que segons ell pesa cinc quilos. (indicative)
He wants to catch a fish which, according to him, weighs five kilos. (he believes such a fish exists and wants to catch it)

En Manel busca un llibre on s'analitza el mode en les clàusules relatives. (indicative)
Manel is looking for a book (a specific book which he believes exists) which contains an analysis of mood in relative clauses.

En Manel busca un llibre on s'analitzi el mode. (subjunctive)
Manel is looking for a book (any book, if there is one) which contains an analysis of mood.

No trobàvem ningú que ens aconsellés.
We couldn't find anyone to advise us.

Cada vegada que visitis el poble te n'enamoraràs més.
Each time you visit the village you will fall more in love with it. (no specific times can be identified)

D'aquests quadres, et regalaré el que més t'agradi.
Of these pictures, I'll give you whichever one you like best.

No n'hi ha cap d'aquests remeis que sigui eficaç.
There is not one of these treatments that works.

A similar pattern is found with free relatives (= substantival relatives, those without a head noun).

Qui no vol pols, que no vagi a l'era.
(proverb, lit. Whoever does not want dust, let him not go to the threshing floor, approx. = If you don't like the heat, stay out of the kitchen.)

El qui hagi acabat l'examen pot anar-se'n.
Anyone who has finished the exam may leave. (perhaps nobody has)

Traditionally, and still to some extent in colloquial Valencian and Balearic, the future/conditional may be used in indefinite free relative clauses, in place of the subjunctive, which is generally more frequent nowadays (see **17.1.4.1**):

Els que hauran treballat seran recompensats.
Those who work will be rewarded.

Els que es mourien/moguessin serien afusellats.
Those who moved would be shot.

A small number of constructions allow, optionally, the subjunctive in a relative clause which is clearly referential, that is, where the speaker plausibly believes that what the relative clause denotes does actually exist. The choice here is parallel to that of the 'thematic' subjunctive in complement clauses (**19.2.1**). The contexts in which this choice is available are: after **poc** 'few', 'little', **només**, **solament**, **únic**, **sol** 'only', and in superlative constructions (including **primer** 'first', and **darrer/últim** 'last'):

Té pocs alumnes que saben/sàpiguen parlar i escriure correctament en català.
He has few pupils who can speak and write Catalan correctly.

Només conec una persona que pot/pugui ajudar-te.
I know only one person who can help you.

És el llibre més interessant que han/hagin llegit.
It is the most interesting book they have read.

With the indicative, these sentences assert the characteristic ('can speak and write Catalan correctly', 'can help you', 'they have read') and mention the quantity ('few', 'only one', 'most (interesting)'). With the subjunctive they assert the quantity, and mention the characteristic. The indicative is more often found in these constructions, though the subjunctive is likely to be induced by the presence in the relative clause of **poder**, of the perfect (**haver**), or of **mai** 'ever'.

A relative clause which depends on a noun which itself occurs in a clause with an emotive (**19.2.2**) or optative (**19.2.3**) subjunctive may use a subjunctive even if the noun phrase has definite reference; again in these contexts the use of the indicative corresponds to the speaker asserting the characteristic, the subjunctive to mentioning it in passing:

Em sorprèn que hagi trobat una persona que el suporta.
There's a person who puts up with him, and I'm surprised he's found such a person.

Em sorprèn que hagi trobat una persona que el suporti.
I'm surprised he's found a person to put up with him.

Note again here the Catalan subjunctive corresponding to a non-finite verb in English.

19.3.1   SUBJUNCTIVE IN OPTATIVE RELATIVE CLAUSES

An important type of subjunctive relative clause is one that expresses the desired or intended qualities of the referent: 'X such that it might/could . . .', 'X intended to . . .'. Because of this intentional element, the time reference of the relative clause must be subsequent to that of the main clause. (The phrase **una persona que el suporti** 'someone to put up with him' in the previous example can be interpreted in this way.)

Ens ha semblat oportú de publicar uns quants llibres senzills que ajudin a fer conèixer la vida i el missatge dels monjos.
It seemed a good opportunity to publish a few straightforward books to help make known the life and message of the monks.

Busco una minyona que em netegi la casa.
I am looking for a maid to clean my house.

Em va començar a dir paraules que encara em posessin més calent.
He began to say things to me which would make/such as to make me even more angry.

19.4   THE SUBJUNCTIVE IN ADVERBIAL CLAUSES

In adverbial clauses (cause, concession, condition, purpose, manner, time, etc., see Chapters 33–34) the subjunctive is used when the situation is hypothetical, not yet realized, unspecific within a set, contrary to fact, and so on. But in some cases the selection of indicative or subjunctive is rather more conventional.

19.4.1   SUBJUNCTIVE IN CAUSAL CLAUSES

Generally speaking, real causes are expressed with the indicative; possible causes which the speaker rejects or is suspicious of are expressed with the subjunctive:

Indicative:

No vam anar d'acampada perquè feia molt mal oratge.
We didn't go camping because it was very windy.

No vau anar d'acampada perquè feia molt mal oratge?
Did you not go camping because it was very windy? (which it was)

Subjunctive:

No ha eixit a passejar perquè li abellís.
He didn't go out for a walk because he wanted to (but for some other reason).

Ha eixit a passejar perquè li abellís?
Did he go out for a walk because he wanted to? (sc. I expect not for that reason.)

Occasionally, when the 'cause' clause precedes the main clause, and especially if the compound conjunction **com sigui que** is involved, a 'real' cause may appear in the subjunctive; compare thematic subjunctive (**19.2.1**):

A tots cinc els vaig sentir usar el mot; com sigui que em fingís ignorant, me'n donaren més detalls.
I heard all five of them use the word; as I feigned ignorance, they gave me more details.

19.4.2   SUBJUNCTIVE IN CONCESSIVE CLAUSES

The thematic subjunctive (corresponding to a factual situation which is nonetheless backgrounded, **19.2.1**) is common in the case of concessive constructions. In fact, one need not assume that a distinction between foreground (assertion) and background (mention) is always intended; that is, the choice of indicative or subjunctive in 'real' concession clauses may be arbitrary. The subjunctive is still the norm in hypothetical contexts, of course. Concessive clauses in general are discussed in more detail at **33.3.3**.

Indicative:

Encara que feia mal oratge, vam anar d'acampada.
Even though it was very windy, we went camping.

Per més que el renyo no en fa cas.
However much I scold him he takes no notice.

Subjunctive:

Encara que siguis mon pare no tens dret a parlar-me com ho fas.
Even though you are my father you have no right to speak to me like that. (real)

Ni que tronés, no deixarien de venir.
Not even if it thundered would they fail to come. (hypothetical)

Mal que et sàpiga, hi anirem.
Even though you (may) regret it, we'll go. (future/hypothetical)

Mentre sigui veritat el que diu, no hi ha cap problema.
Provided what she says is true, there is no problem. (hypothetical)

Per més que el renyis no en farà cas.
However much you (might) scold him, he'll take no notice.

19.4.3   SUBJUNCTIVE IN CONDITIONAL CLAUSES

The use of moods and tenses in conditional clauses with **si** 'if', and so on, is given separate treatment in Chapter 34.

19.4.4   SUBJUNCTIVE IN PURPOSE CLAUSES

As in the case of optative complement clauses (**19.2.3**) expressing wishes or intentions, the subjunctive is required also in purpose clauses. Note that **perquè** with the indicative corresponds to 'because' (cause, **19.4.1**), but with the subjunctive it corresponds to 'in order that' (purpose, when the time reference is subsequent to that of the main clause). See **33.3.2** for more general discussion of purpose clauses.

En Joan em telefonà per tal que li expliqués com utilitzar l'ordenador.
Joan phoned me so that I could explain to him how to use the computer.

Hem tancat el conill en una gàbia perquè no se'ns escapi.
We have shut the rabbit up in a cage so that it doesn't escape.

19.4.5 SUBJUNCTIVE IN RESULT CLAUSES

One might expect that consequences which the speaker admits to be factual would always require the indicative. And this is indeed the case with expressions such as **tant . . . que** 'so much/many . . . that', **de tal manera que** 'in such a way that', **de manera que** 'so that'. There are a few constructions, though, which deviate from this: **d'aquí que** 'hence' *may* use a 'thematic' subjunctive (**19.2.1**), and **prou . . . perquè** 'sufficient(ly) . . . that' seems normally to take the subjunctive. (See **33.3.4** for result clauses in general.)

D'aquí que don Joan . . . admirés en la burgesia un ferment de vida exaltada.
Hence Don Joan admired in the bourgeoisie a ferment of intense life.

D'aquí que el nostre objectiu aporti un punt de connexió.
Hence our objective brings in a connecting point.

Provava d'imitar la bella veu de Franklin, i hi reeixia prou perquè llur cosí fes una rialleta.
He tried to imitate the fine voice of Franklin, and succeeded well enough for their cousin to smile.

19.4.6 SUBJUNCTIVE IN MANNER CLAUSES

The use of the indicative and subjunctive moods after conjunctions like **com** 'as', **segons (que)** 'according as' again reflects the general principles mentioned in **19.4**. **Com si** 'as if' requires the subjunctive (past or pluperfect), inasmuch as it expresses an unreal hypothesis. (See **33.2.3** for general discussion of manner clauses.)

Hem d'anar tirant com puguem.
We must get along as best we can.

Ara sembla blau, ara gris, segons com te'l miris.
Sometimes it looks blue, sometimes grey, according to how you look at it.
  (subjunctive because each act of looking is an unspecified one from a set)

Tu, fes com si no en sabessis res.
Just act as if you knew nothing about it.

19.4.7 SUBJUNCTIVE IN TIME CLAUSES

Temporal clauses (with **quan** 'when', **així que** 'as soon as', **mentre** 'while', **sempre que** 'whenever', **fins que (no)** 'until', **després que** 'after', etc.) are generally constructed according to the principles mentioned in **19.4**. However, future or unspecified time reference may be expressed with the future or conditional tenses, instead of with the subjunctive. The former pattern is generally regarded as more 'literary', but it is also current in some spoken varieties. See **33.2.2** on temporal clauses in general.

Va dubtar de la seva mort fins que va veure'n els certificats. (indicative)
He doubted her death until he saw the death certificates.

Dubtaré de la seva mort fins que (no) en vegi els certificats. (subjunctive)
I shall doubt her death until I see the death certificates.

Li vaig dir que cada vegada que passés per Lleida aniria a veure'ls.
I told her that whenever I was in Lleida I'd go to see them.

Així que el veuré/veja, pense dir-li'n una de fresca.
As soon as I see him I intend to give him a piece of my mind.

Després que hauràs/hages llegit l'extracte, parlarem de l'assumpte.
After you have read the extract, we'll talk about the matter.

Abans que 'before' is always followed by the subjunctive, even when the clause denotes an admitted fact:

Va apagar el cigarro abans que vingués el professor.
He put out the cigar before the teacher arrived.

Often, as in this example, the subjunctive might be justified in terms of fear (**19.2.4**) or wish (that not) (**19.2.3**), but this is not always so:

Tots els líders eren morts abans que s'acabés la guerra.
All the leaders were dead before the war ended.

Perhaps by analogy with this pattern, it is increasingly common for **després que** 'after' to be followed by the subjunctive also, even when an admitted fact is expressed:

Tot just després que abandonés/va abandonar el meu despatx em vaig posar en contacte amb Washington.
Immediately after she left my office I contacted Washington.

19.5   TENSE USAGE IN SUBJUNCTIVE CLAUSES

Because fewer tense distinctions are made in the subjunctive (and because there is no conditional subjunctive) we need to give some attention to how tense usage in subjunctive subordinate clauses corresponds with the tenses in the main clauses they depend on. As there is no future subjunctive the present subjunctive is used corresponding to future time. With that proviso, generally speaking the tense in the subordinate clause is straightforwardly determined by the sense. Observe, though, that as in English, after a past tense main clause, a subordinate clause will normally also have a past tense, unless the speaker specifically intends to shift time perspective. Note that the conditional counts as a past tense in this respect. The examples below illustrate typical patterns and are not meant to be exclusive.

(i)   Main clause in present indicative:

M'agrada que xiuli. (present subjunctive)
I like him to whistle./I like it that he whistles. (habitual)

Volen que deixis de fumar. (present subjunctive)
They want you to stop smoking. (future)

Estic contenta que hagis vingut. ((present) perfect subjunctive)
I am glad you have come.

No és possible que ho diguessin (past subjunctive)/ . . . **que ho vagin dir.** (past perfective subjunctive)
It is impossible that they said it/that they should have said it. (present comment on past situation)

Dubto que hi haguessin estat d'acord. (pluperfect subjunctive)
I doubt whether/that they would have agreed.

(ii) Main clause in future:

Bastarà que acabin a finals de mes. (present subjunctive)
It will be enough if they finish by the end of the month.

Insistireu que ja hagin aprobat abans de formalitzar la matrícula? ((present) perfect subjunctive)
Will you insist that they have already passed before completing registration?

(iii) Main clause in (present) perfect:

T'he dit que estiguis quieta. (present subjunctive)
I told you to be still. (present/future)

Li hem demanat que ens deixi 50.000 pessetes. (present subjunctive)
We have asked her to lend us 50,000 pesetas. (future)

Ha estat un miracle que no t'hagin reconegut. ((present) perfect subjunctive)
It is a miracle they didn't recognize/haven't recognized you. (in a situation where the speaker might say **No t'han reconegut** 'They didn't recognize/haven't recognized you')

Ha estat un miracle que no et reconeguessin. (past subjunctive)
It is/was a miracle they didn't recognize you. (in a situation where the speaker might say **No et van reconèixer** or **No et reconeixien** 'They didn't recognize you')

(iv) Main clause in past tense (imperfect, preterite, or pluperfect):

La idea era que cobressin cada mes. (past subjunctive)
The idea was for them to be paid every month.

Ens va sorprendre que estigués tan gras. (past subjunctive)
We were surprised he was so fat.

Va ser un miracle que no et reconeguessin/vagin reconèixer. (past/past perfective subjunctive)
It was a miracle they didn't recognize you.

M'estranyava que no haguessis protestat. (pluperfect subjunctive)
I was surprised you hadn't objected.

Déu va decretar que les serps no tinguin potes. (present subjunctive)
God decreed that snakes have no legs. (decree for all time, including present and future; deliberate shift of time perspective)

Déu va decretar que les serps no tinguessin potes. (past subjunctive)
God decreed that snakes should have no legs. (neutral about time-scale of decree)

Què vas fer ahir perquè avui estiguis tan baldat? (present subjunctive)
What did you do yesterday to make you so worn out today?

Li havíem demanat que ens deixés 50.000 pessetes. (past subjunctive)
We had asked her to lend us 50,000 pesetas. (future-in-the-past/conditional)

(v) Main clause in conditional or conditional perfect:

En tindríem prou que se'ns en disculpessin. (past subjunctive)
We would be satisfied with their offering us an apology./It would be enough if they offered us an apology.

Li hauríem demanat que ens deixés 50.000 pessetes. (past subjunctive)
We would have asked her to lend us 50,000 pesetas. (future-in-the-past/conditional)

Hauria preferit que s'hagués enterrat allà on va morir. (pluperfect subjunctive)
She would have preferred him to have been buried where he died./She would have preferred it if he had been buried where he died. (counter-factual conditional)

(vi) Main clause imperative:

Digui'ls que s'afanyin. (present subjunctive)   Tell them to hurry up.

19.6   SUBJUNCTIVE IN MAIN CLAUSES

An important use of the subjunctive in main clauses is to express wishes (**27.2.4**), most often using the present subjunctive after **que**. **Tant de bo** 'I wish'/'if only' is followed by present or past subjunctive, and expresses a vaguer hope. **Així** + subjunctive is restricted to a few expressions; likewise **Déu** + subjunctive (without **que**) 'May God . . .'.

Que se'n vagi!	Let him go away!
Que tinguis sort!	Good luck!
Tant de bo me'n parlessin.	I hope they talk to me about it.
Tant de bo que hagués guanyat el premi.	If only I had won the prize.
Així rebentares, canalla.	I hope you burst, swine.
Déu l'hi pagui.	May God reward you.
Déu nos en guard de . . .	God forbid that we should . . .

The past perfect subjunctive (without **que**, and especially second person) is a way of expressing 'if only . . .' + 'you should have . . .' (see also **34.8**):

Haguessis telefonat i ara ho sabries.
You should have phoned/if only you had phoned, now you'd know.

Ho haguessis dit.
You should have said./If only you had said (we could have done something about it).

Que + subjunctive in main clauses may express shock alongside regret:

Però que ara es valguin d'aquestes trampes amb el menjar, i a costa de la salut de tots!
To think that now they should use these tricks with food, at the risk of everyone's health!

I que això hagi de passar en la nostra família; que siguis tu la meva germana.
To think that this should occur in our family; that you should be my sister.

Note also the use of main clause subjunctive in expressions like: **Costi el que costi** 'Whatever it costs'/'However much it costs' (lit. Let it cost what it may cost), **Sigui quan sigui** 'Whenever it may be', **Sigui com sigui** 'However it may be'; and to express 'whether or not', for example: **Plogui o no, anirem d'excursió** 'Whether or not it rains, we'll go out', **Sigui perquè es trobava malament, sigui perquè no li abellia . . .** 'Whether it was because she wasn't well, or because it didn't appeal to her . . .'.

Finally, a main verb following (but not preceding) an expression like **potser**, **tal volta**, **possiblement** 'perhaps' is quite often in the subjunctive in normal usage (cf. **19.2.4ii**), though this is regarded as non-standard:

Potser hagi/ha vingut i no ens n'hem assabentat.
Perhaps he has arrived and we haven't realized.

Tal vegada fos/seria millor . . .
Perhaps it would be better . . .

20 THE INFINITIVE

20.1 MORPHOLOGY OF THE INFINITIVE

The infinitive suffix basically consists of an **-r** added to the verb stem, some-times with a 'thematic' vowel intervening: **menjar** 'eat', stem **menj-**; **rebre** 'receive', stem **reb-**; **córrer** 'run', stem **corr-**; **dormir** 'sleep', stem **dorm-**. The forms are discussed in detail at **16.2, 16.5.1**. The compound infinitive is formed with the infinitive of the auxiliary verb **haver** and the (past) parti-ciple: **haver menjat** 'have eaten', **haver rebut** 'have received', etc.

20.2 INFINITIVE PHRASES AS VERBAL CONSTRUCTIONS

In the majority of uses an infinitive phrase is predominantly verbal: the infini-tive may retain the verb's usual complements, and may be modified by an adverb or adverbial adjunct:

[**Dir aquestes coses d'aquesta manera**] **no t'ajudarà.**
Saying those things this way will not help you.

No vull [**repetir-te tantes vegades la mateixa història**].
I don't want to tell you the same story over and over again.

It is important to notice that in this function the Catalan infinitive sometimes corresponds to an English gerund and sometimes to an English infinitive, depending on the kind of relation between the infinitive and the main verb. It is equally important to observe that in Catalan it is the infinitive, not the gerund (see Chapter 22, especially **22.3.2**), that functions as a verbal noun.

Infinitive phrases may display explicit marking of the passive voice, e.g **Tots aquests arbres hauran de ser tallats** 'All these trees must be cut down', though this is not always the case (any more than it is in English): **El seu comporta-ment és difícil d'entendre** 'Their behaviour is difficult to understand'. Tense in infinitive phrases is restricted to the marking of relative anteriority by means of the compound infinitive as in **Els sabrà greu d'haver comprat el pis** 'They will regret having bought the flat'; imperfective aspect can be marked only through the progressive periphrasis with **estar** + gerund: **Després d'estar mirant-les una llarga estona, finalment va decidir comprar-ne una** 'After look-ing at them for a long while, he finally decided to buy one'.

A certain number of infinitives have become fully nominal (taking determiners, adjective modification, and so on, such as **un dinar lleuger** 'a light lunch', **un deure moral** 'a moral duty'). These are discussed in **20.5**.

20.2.1   De INTRODUCING THE INFINITIVE

As can be seen in the examples already given, in some cases, but not in all, an infinitive is introduced by **de**. In fact, there are cases (i) where **de** is obligatory, (ii) where **de** is optional, its presence on the whole connoting a more formal (some would say 'more authentic') style, and (iii) where **de** is ungrammatical.

(i) Obligatory de before infinitive

Certain verbs are constructed with a prepositional object phrase. When the preposition is **de** this is also retained before an infinitive object. The following verbs, for example, take objects with **de**: **abstenir-se de** 'refrain from', **oblidar-se de** 'forget', **parlar de** 'talk about', 'discuss', **recordar-se de** 'remember', **saber de** 'be good at' (distinct from **saber** 'know how to'). **Haver de** 'have to', which does not take nominal objects, has **de** as a fixed element.

> **M'he oblidat d'escriure-li la carta que li vaig prometre.**
> I forgot to write her the letter I promised.

> **Tots saben de cantar.**
> They are all good at singing. (cf. **Tots saben cantar** 'They all know how to sing')

> **Hem de comprar pa.**   *Hem comprar pa.**
> We have to buy some bread.

The following verbs of requesting or commanding are constructed either with an indirect object followed by **de** (obligatory) and an infinitive, or with a complement clause with **que** (+ subjunctive). The construction with **de** + infinitive is more formal. The verbs are: **aconsellar** 'advise', **demanar** 'request', 'ask', **dir** 'tell', **ordenar** 'order', **pregar** 'ask', **proposar** 'suggest', **suplicar** 'beg'.

> **Els vaig aconsellar d'enviar les sol·licituds de seguida.** (= **Els vaig aconsellar que enviessin les sol·licituds de seguida.**)
> I advised them to send their applications straightaway.

> **Els proposàrem d'encarregar-se'n ells mateixos.** (= **Els proposàrem que se n'encarreguessin ells mateixos.**)
> We suggested to them that they should deal with it themselves.

Note that **de** obligatorily introduces a 'passive' infinitive complement of an adjective, as in **difícil d'entendre** 'hard to understand'; **Fou una contradicció no gens senzilla de resoldre** 'It was a contradiction not at all easy to resolve'.

(ii) Optional *de* before infinitive

Traditionally **de** introduces an infinitive phrase which occurs after the main verb and is (a) its subject or predicate, or (b) the direct object of verbs such as **acordar** 'agree', **cercar** 'try', **convenir** 'agree', **deliberar** 'decide', **desitjar** 'wish', **esperar** 'hope', 'expect', **jurar** 'swear', **oferir** 'offer', **pensar** 'intend', **pretendre** 'attempt', 'aim', **procurar** 'attempt', **proposar** 'intend', 'propose', **prometre** 'promise', **provar** 'try', **refusar** 'refuse', **resoldre** 'decide'. The use of **de** in this context is strongly preferred in more formal styles, but its absence is in no way non-standard. Examples of the presence and absence of this 'optional' **de** will be found throughout this chapter.

(a)   **T'agradarà (de) saber-ho.**
      You will be pleased to know it.

      Ens ha resultat molt difícil (de) recollir les dades.
      It has proved very hard for us to collect the data.

      No us convé gens (de) fer aquestes coses.
      It's not at all right for you to do these things.

      Prohibit (d')afixar cartells.
      Bill-posting is prohibited.

      L'objectiu serà (de) lluitar contra la fam.
      The aim will be to fight hunger.

(Note that some grammarians regard **de** before a *predicate* infinitive, as in this last example, as a hypercorrection. In this view also **de** is not appropriate when an infinitive phrase is the postposed subject in a *wh*-question:

      De què t'aprofita afavorir el ric?   ? . . . **d'afavorir el ric?**
      What advantage is it to you to favour the rich?)

(b)   **Sempre pretenia (d')assegurar-me que no passaria res.**
      He always attempted to assure me that it would be all right.

      Vàrem acordar (de) vendre la casa.
      We agreed to sell the house.

      M'han proposat (de) fer de conductor
      They've proposed that I should be the driver.

This optional **de** introducing infinitives has only a superficial resemblance to the true preposition **de**. Note in particular that an infinitival direct object (with or without **de**) can be substituted only by the pronoun **ho** and never by the pronoun **en**; see **12.5** and **12.6vi**.

      Ho vàrem acordar.   ***En vàrem acordar.**   We agreed it.
      M'ho han proposat.   ***Me n'han proposat.**   They have suggested it to me.

(iii)   No de before infinitive

After certain modal-type verbs which establish a very close relation with a following infinitive **de** cannot be used. Such verbs are: **caldre** 'be necessary', **deure** 'must', **gosar** 'dare', **necessitar** 'need', **poder** 'can', 'may', **saber** 'know how to', **soler** 'be accustomed to', **voler** 'want'. We may add here the basic causative verbs **deixar** 'let' (not = **deixar de** 'fail' with obligatory **de**), and **fer** 'make'; and the perception verbs **escoltar** 'listen to', **mirar** 'look at', **oir** 'hear', **sentir** 'hear', **veure** 'see' (but **veure de** 'try' has obligatory **de**). Note that clitic raising (**12.2.3**) takes place with these verbs. There are probably other verbs which never, or rarely, take **de** before a following infinitive, but we have not found a source which attempts to offer a complete list.

> **Vull veure el director.**   ***Vull de veure ...**
> I want to see the manager.

> **La pregunta, per òbvia, no necessita gairebé ser formulada.**
> ***no necessita ... de ser ...**
> The question, being so obvious, hardly needs to be asked.

> **Els hem deixat anar al cinema.**   ***Els hem deixat d'anar ...**
> We have let them go to the cinema.

20.2.2   SUBJECTS OF INFINITIVE PHRASES

Like all non-finite forms, the infinitive does not explicitly express the person/number category of its subject. In most cases the identity of the subject is inferred from the construction, though in some cases the subject of the infinitive can be made explicit within the phrase (iv).

(i) Open interpretation of infinitive subject

The infinitive may have a generic or unspecified subject:

> **Està prohibit (de) fumar.**
> Smoking prohibited.

> **Resistir és vèncer.**
> To resist is to overcome.

> **Menjar greix fa que augmenti el colesterol.**
> Eating fat makes the cholesterol level go up.

> **Convenia abandonar ràpidament el país.**
> It was time to get out of the country quickly.

This pattern is common when the infinitive phrase is subject of its own clause as in the above examples, or when the infinitive depends on a main clause element which typically takes an indirect object, such as **aconsellar** 'advise', **ordenar** 'order', **prohibir** 'forbid', **suggerir** 'suggest', **permetre** 'allow', and **convenir** 'be suitable', **fàcil** 'easy', **agradable** 'pleasant', **impossible** 'impossible':

No permeten regirar els papers.
They don't let you/anyone rummage through the papers.

Va resultar impossible de trobar allotjament.
It proved impossible to find accommodation.

When an indirect object is explicitly mentioned in the main clause, of course, that determines the identity of the subject of the infinitive:

Treballar amb ell és fàcil per a mi.
It is easy for me to work with him.

No ens permeten regirar els papers.
They don't let us rummage through the papers.

(ii) Infinitive subject = main clause object

The subject of the infinitive is coreferential with a direct object or indirect object of the verb of the main clause when there is one.

Direct object: **obligar** 'oblige', **autoritzar** 'authorize', **acusar** 'accuse', **invitar** 'invite', **encantar** 'delight', etc.

Hem invitat els teus companys a prendre cafè.
We have invited your friends for coffee. (lit. 'to take coffee'; understood '(for them) to take coffee')

La va acusar d'haver robat la seva bossa.
She accused her of having stolen her bag.

M'encanta tocar el clavecí.
I love playing the harpsichord. (i.e. 'for me to play' not 'for anyone to play')

(Note **M'encanta que toquis el clavecí** 'I love you to play the harpsichord'; here an infinitive phrase would not be possible in Catalan.)

Indirect object: see list above (i), and e.g. **impedir** 'prevent', **ensenyar (a)** 'teach', 'show how', **proposar** 'suggest', **exigir** 'require', **dir** 'tell':

Els hem dit de seguir-nos.   We have told them to follow us.

(iii) Infinitive subject = main clause subject

Here the subject of the infinitive is coreferential with the subject of the main clause. This is the most frequent case, with verbs that do not take an object (other than the infinitive phrase itself). There is a large number of verbs here, such as those of propositional attitude: **creure** 'believe', **admetre** 'admit', **desitjar** 'wish', **confiar** 'trust', **pensar** 'intend', **esperar** 'hope', **refusar** 'refuse', and all the modal-type verbs mentioned in **18.2.1** (verbal periphrases): **voler** 'want', **poder** 'can', **acabar de** 'have just', etc. and for example, **intentar** 'try', **cercar** 'try'.

> **La Maria Josep creu saber qui ho ha dit.**
> Maria Josep believes she knows who said it.

> **Els treballadors acaben de convocar la vaga general.**
> The workers have just called a general strike.

> **Els actors van a començar la funció.**
> The actors are going to open the show.

> **Els enemics han arribat a dir totes aquestes mentides.**
> The enemy has gone as far as to tell all these lies.

> **El petroli ha començat a brollar.**
> The oil has started flowing.

> **Amb la calor, les gallines han deixat de pondre.**
> With the heat the hens have stopped laying.

> **Els jugadors no estan per donar suport al president.**
> The players are not in favour of supporting the chairman.

> **La tortuga no pot arribar mai abans que la llebre.**
> The tortoise will never be able to get there quicker than the hare.

> **Quan van sentir els trons, els nens van rompre a plorar.**
> When they heard the thunder the children burst into tears.

Note that there are (as with the corresponding English versions) a few verbs which while taking an indirect object do not give the indirect object control over a following infinitive but rather retain control with their own subject; these are verbs of promising, offering, swearing – verbs of commitment:

> **Li vaig oferir d'acompanyar-la.**
> I offered (to her) to accompany her.

> **Ens han promès de tornar-nos els diners abans de finals d'any.**
> They have promised to return us the money before the end of the year.

It seems that with **proposar** 'propose', 'suggest', at least, interpretation of an infinitive's subject is ambiguous:

> **Em va proposar de fer de conductor.**
> He suggested his/my acting as driver.

The same pattern – with main clause subject interpreted as subject of the infinitive – is common in adverbial expressions introduced by prepositions (see **20.3.4.2**).

(iv) The subject of the infinitive is expressed

Rentar-se ell la roba era l'únic que podia fer.
Doing the laundry himself was the only option.

Va ser arribar ell i posar-se tots a riure.
He turned up and they all burst out laughing.

Menjar ara nosaltres no seria mala idea.
For us to eat now wouldn't be a bad idea.

These examples show explicit subjects, but this is only possible in an infinitive phrase acting as subject in the main sentence, in an adverbial phrase introduced by a preposition (see **20.4** below) and in an independent exclamative question:

Venir jo a veure't?! Mai de la vida!
Me come and see you?! Not on your life!

In all of these cases the explicit subject must follow the infinitive.

20.3   INFINITIVE PHRASES INTEGRATED AS ELEMENTS OF FINITE CLAUSES

Most often, a verbal infinitive phrase appears as an argument of a clause (that is, as subject, predicate, complement, direct object, prepositional object; **20.3.1.1**), in a prepositional adjunct of a clause, or as complement of a noun or adjective. Infinitive phrases used absolutely will be discussed in **20.4**.
    We have already seen various examples of infinitive phrases as subject.

Anar-me'n d'aquí no em sap cap greu.   I'm not at all sorry to leave here.
Treballar amb ell és fàcil per a mi.   It is easy for me to work with him.

As mentioned in **20.2.1ii**, when an infinitive phrase is placed after the verb, the infinitive can be introduced by **de**.
    Examples of infinitive phrases as direct objects introduced by optional **de** have been discussed at **20.2.1ii(b)**. As mentioned in **20.2.1iii** modal-type verbs and verbs of perception do not take **de** before a following infinitive. **Sentir** and **veure** may take **a** before an infinitive, though this construction is perhaps somewhat old-fashioned.

Mai no havia sentit (a) tocar tan bé la trompeta.
I had never heard the trumpet played so well.

Et veig (a) venir.
I can see you coming.

20.3.1 INFINITIVE PHRASE AS PREPOSITIONAL OBJECT

An infinitive phrase may be the object of a subcategorized preposition (that is, the specified preposition + its object is a complement, **20.3.1.1**), or it may be the object of a preposition functioning as an (optional) adverbial adjunct (**20.3.1.2**).

20.3.1.1 Infinitive phrase as subcategorized prepositional object

Very many verbs, nouns, and adjectives take a prepositional phrase complement with a specified preposition. Generally speaking the required preposition appears before an infinitive phrase as it does before a noun phrase. thus, for example, with **a**:

invitar algú a una recepció	invite someone to a reception
invitar algú a fer alguna cosa	invite someone to do something
una invitació a una recepció	an invitation to a reception
una invitació a fer alguna cosa	an invitation to do something

with **de**:

descuidar-se d'alguna cosa	forget something
descuidar-se de fer alguna cosa	forget to do something

(Note that with real **de**, as here, unlike the optional **de** discussed in **20.2.1ii(b)**, the **de** phrase can be pronominalized with **en**: **Me n'he descuidat** 'I forgot it'.)

un projecte de desenvolupament	a project for development/a development project
un projecte de desenvolupar una cosa	a project to develop something

Note that complements of nouns are normally introduced by **de**.

However when the preposition is **en** 'in', 'to', **per a** 'for', or **amb** 'with', the matter is not quite so straightforward. As mentioned in **14.1.1.4**, **en** is replaced by **a** before an infinitive in standard Catalan, so **Tot consisteix en això** 'Everything consists in that', but **Tot consisteix a fer això** 'Everything consists in doing that'; **vacil·lar en una decisió** 'hesitate in a decision', **vacil·lar a prendre una decisió** 'hesitate to make a decision'. And as discussed in detail in **14.1.4.2**, both usage and normative recommendation vary with respect to the distinction between **per** and **per a**, and in particular whether the distinction is maintained before an infinitive, so: **bastar per a algú** 'be sufficient for someone', **bastar per a fer alguna cosa** or **bastar per fer alguna cosa** 'be sufficient to do something'. There seems also to be a certain reluctance to retain **amb** before an infinitive, though not such that we could say there is a rule in the matter. Note the following:

L'amenaçaven amb l'expulsió.	They threatened him with expulsion.
L'amenaçaven d'expulsar-lo.	They threatened to expel him.
(? . . . amb expulsar-lo)	
Estic d'acord amb la teva sortida.	I agree with your leaving.
Estic d'acord a sortir/de sortir.	I agree to leave.
Alerta amb el gos!	Watch out for the dog!
Alerta a relliscar!	Watch out not to slip!

Other contexts where this is noted:

acontentar-se amb alguna cosa	content oneself with something
acontentar-se de/a fer alguna cosa	content oneself with doing something
haver-n'hi prou amb + noun phrase	be enough with
haver-n'hi prou de/a + infinitive	be enough to
tenir prou amb + noun phrase	have enough with
tenir prou de/a + infinitive	have enough with doing something
estar content amb + noun phrase	be happy with
estar content de + infinitive	be happy to

A few verbs take a preposition + infinitive object with the preposition being optionally either **a** or **de**. In all cases the use of **de** is formal, while **a** is appropriate at any level. The verbs are **acostumar a/de** 'accustom (someone/something) to', 'be accustomed to', **aprendre a/de** 'learn to', **atrevir-se a/de** 'dare to', **començar a/de** 'begin to', **forçar a/de** 'force to', **obligar a/de** 'oblige to'.

Acostumen a/de venir a les vuit.	They usually come at eight.
Aprenia a/de llegir.	She was learning to read.
S'atreviran a/de negar-s'hi una altra vegada?	Will they dare to refuse again?
L'havien obligat a/de fer-ho.	They had obliged him to do it.
Varen forçar-lo a/de declarar la seva inenció.	They forced him to declare his intention.

20.3.1.2 *Infinitive phrase object of preposition as adverbial adjunct*

An infinitive phrase may be the object of a preposition as an adverbial adjunct. A wide range of prepositions can occur, and there is little remarkable about the construction. The subject of the infinitive is inferred to be whatever is appropriate to the context.

N'han anat venent exemplars fins a exhaurir l'edició.
They went on selling copies until the edition went out of print. (lit. until exhausting the edition)

Ho va afirmar malgrat estar convençuda del contrari.
She asserted it despite being convinced of the opposite.

Al cap de passar dos dies a la presó, frisava per poder tornar a córrer.
After spending two days in prison, he was anxious to be able to go running again.

En lloc d'insistir tant, ens valdria més buscar una solució de compromís.
Instead of insisting, it would be better for us to seek a compromise solution.

A base de triar totes les assignatures més lingüístiques, em vaig muntar una llicenciatura de lingüística general abans que una tal cosa existís.
Through choosing all the most linguistic courses, I constructed for myself a degree in general linguistics before such a thing existed.

A certain number of prepositions function to form an adverbial adjunct either with an infinitive or with **que** and a finite clause. Here is a list of the most common ones that admit both constructions:

a fi de	a fi que	so as to/so that
a menys de	a menys que	unless
abans de	abans que	before
amb	amb que	provided (that)
d'ençà de	d'ençà que	since
des de	des que	since
després de	després que	after
fins (a)	fins que	until
fora de	fora que	apart from/except for
malgrat	malgrat que	despite
per/de por de	per/de por que	for fear of
per	perquè	because (of) (see **14.1.4.2**)
per a	perquè	in order to/in order that (see **14.1.4.2**)
sense	sense que	without
per tal de	per tal que	so as to/so that

Where both constructions are available, the general preference is to use the infinitive construction when the subjects of the main clause and the adverbial are understood to be the same, and to use the finite adverbial clause otherwise.

Recullen llenya de la platja, per tal de fer-ne una foguera.
They collect firewood from the beach, in order to make a bonfire.

Fins tenir-ne els resultats, ens estimem més no fer comentaris.
Until we get the results, we prefer not to comment.

Fins que tinguem els resultats, no seria lícit de fer comenatris.
Until we get the results, it would not be appropriate to comment.

**Malgrat haver aprovat el disseny del projecte, el municipi encara no ha ator-
gat el permís de construir.**
Despite having approved the project design, the council has not yet granted
planning permission.

**Malgrat que s'hagi aprovat el disseny del projecte, el municipi encara no ha
atorgat el permís de construir.**
Despite the project design having been approved, the council has not yet
granted planning permission.

When the subjects are different, it is also possible to use an infinitive phrase
with the subject expressed (after the infinitive: see **20.2.2iv**). More investigation is needed of the constraints on these infinitive + subject constructions,
and on the contexts in which they may be preferred.

Després d'anar-te'n tu, vindrà en Joan.
After you have gone, Joan will come.

Abans de venir en Joan, tu te n'havies anat.
Before Joan came, you had gone.

**Malgrat haver-se aprovat el disseny del projecte, el municipi encara no ha
atorgat el permís de construir.**
Despite the project design having been approved, the council has not yet
granted planning permission.

20.3.1.3   *Infinitive in indefinite relative clauses and indirect questions*

An infinitive may be used in an indefinite (non-specific) relative clause rather
as it can in English (see **31.10ii**); the subject of the infinitive is understood to
be the subject (or indirect object) of the main clause.

No té ningú amb qui parlar.
She hasn't anyone to talk to.

Necessito algú amb qui discutir alguns aspectes del projecte.
I need someone to discuss certain aspects of the proposal with.

Pregunta si hi ha cap prestatge on posar-lo.
Ask if there's a shelf to put it on.

Likewise with indefinite free relatives (which overlap with indirect questions):

No trobava amb qui casar-se.   She couldn't find anybody to marry her.
No tenien a qui escriure.   They didn't have anyone to write to.

With indirect questions, **com** 'how' + infinitive seems normal in a variety of contexts:

No sé com anar a Olot.   I don't know how to get to Olot.
Vaig demanar com anar a Olot.   I asked how to get to Olot.
Em van explicar com anar a Olot. They told me how to get to Olot.

With other question words, the infinitive is acceptable when the main verb is **saber** 'know' (or more specifically **no saber** 'not know'):

No sabia amb qui fer l'article.
I didn't know who to write the article with.

No sabem si anar demà a la biblioteca.
We don't know whether to go to the library tomorrow.

No saps a quin diccionari buscar-lo?
Don't you know which dictionary to look for it in?

No sap què fer/quan fer-ho.
She doesn't know what to do/when to do it.

However, it is clear that many of the infinitive questions of English do not work when translated literally into Catalan: 'She asked me when to arrive' *Em va preguntar quan arribar → Em va preguntar quan calia arribar; 'I showed him what to do' *Li vaig ensenyar què fer → Li vaig ensenyar què havia de fer.

The whole matter of infinitives in relative clauses and questions in Catalan needs further investigation.

20.4   En + INFINITIVE IN TEMPORAL ADVERBIAL PHRASES

The construction **en** + infinitive is equivalent in meaning to **quan** + inflected verb (literally most like English 'on' + gerund, but more frequently used). The construction is rather literary; an alternative with **al** + infinitive (which is regarded as non-standard) is somewhat more spontaneous, but could hardly be said to be popular or frequent in speech.

En estar malalt, el millor és cridar el metge. (= Quan algú està malalt, el millor és cridar el metge.)
When (some)one is ill the best thing is to call the doctor.

S'alegrà molt en veure el seu professor.
She was very cheered to see/when she saw her teacher.

The compound infinitive (**haver** + past participle) may be used to make explicit that the situation in the infinitive phrase precedes that of the main clause, but this sense is also compatible with the simple infinitive.

En haver tornat la família de la platja trucarem als nostres amics.
En tornar la família de la platja ...
When the family have come back from the beach we'll phone our friends.

In the standard language, these temporal phrases are the only cases where an infinitive can be preceded by preposition **en** (see **20.3.1.1** and **14.1.1.4**).

20.4.1   Tot i + INFINITIVE IN CONCESSIVE PHRASES

In addition to the more common use of the gerund to make non-finite concessive phrases (**22.2.4.1**), the infinitive is also found in this function, introduced by the concessive **tot i**.

tot i haver captat el vots dels immigrants
despite having chased the immigrants' votes

Tot i dir aquelles animalades va plantejar la qüestió prou sòlidament.
Despite saying those daft things he outlined the topic in a very sound way.

20.5   NOMINALIZED INFINITIVES

Some infinitives have become nouns in their own right: they admit a determiner, adjectives, and, in some cases, plural inflection. The subject or object of the infinitive, if present, is expressed in a **de** phrase. There are some forty or so of these completely nominalized infinitives. Their meaning is often specialized beyond a mere substantivization of their verbal notion.

aquells parlars de França
those dialects of France (from **parlar** 'speak')

en un obrir i tancar d'ulls
in an instant (lit. in an opening and closing of eyes)

Vam fer un bon esmorzar.
We had a good breakfast. (from **esmorzar** 'eat breakfast'; similarly **dinar** 'lunch', **berenar** 'tea', 'snack', **sopar** 'dinner')

Teníem massa deures professionals. (from **deure** 'ought'/'must', 'owe')
We had too many professional duties.

L'ésser humà necessita un mínim d'intimitat. (from **ésser** 'be')
Human beings need a minimum of privacy.

Li va donar les gràcies amb un somriure. (from **somriure** 'smile')
He thanked her with a smile.

al meu entendre (from **entendre** 'understand')
in my opinion

It is not unusual in both writing and speech for other infinitives to be nominalized with a singular masculine definite article (or occasionally another determiner), though normative grammarians recommend avoiding this construction if at all possible.

a cada sortida de la mestressa, a cada trucar a la porta . . .
at each appearance of the lady of the house, at each knock at the door . . .

Els calderers atabalen el veïnat amb el seu picar.
The boilermakers annoy the neighbourhood with their hammering.

per evitar que hom m'engavanyi el fruir tranquil del dia de demà
to prevent anyone's constraining me from peaceful enjoyment of tomorrow

This last example where **fruir** has an adjective and a direct object in a **de** phrase is syntactically very similar to the fully lexicalized nominal infinitives mentioned above. We can say that nominalization of infinitives is an ongoing grammatical process in Catalan, but it should not be assumed that one can freely take any infinitive and turn it into a noun. In very many cases a noun derivationally related to the verb already exists and will be used in preference; the last example could well have said **la fruïció tranquil·la del dia de demà**.

In many such cases (though not all as the above examples show) the nominalized infinitive refers to the manner of doing something, rather than, or in addition to, the fact of it.

Aquell lluitar seu tan vigorós (= **Aquella manera seva de lluitar tan vigorosa**)
li proporcionà la victòria.
That vigorous way he has of fighting earned victory for him.

No he vist mai un conduir tan perillós (= **una manera de conduir tan perillosa**).
I've never seen such a dangerous way of driving.

Unlike those seen at the beginning of this section, these nominalized infinitives do not accept plural formation (*Tenen uns conduirs molt perillosos) nor the postposition of their logical subject (*Aquell lluitar ell . . .). They must be differentiated from infinitives acting as subjects of main clauses, which are never introduced by an article or demonstrative:

Dir aquestes coses no t'ajudarà.	*El dir aquestes coses no t'ajudarà.
Saying these things won't help you.	
No m'agrada jugar a cartes.	*No m'agrada el jugar a cartes.
I don't like card games.	
Fer això no convé a cap preu.	*El fer això no convé a cap preu.
To do this is quite the wrong thing.	

21 PARTICIPLES

This chapter covers the (past) participle and the so-called present participle in -ant, -ent.

21.1 (PAST) PARTICIPLE: GENERAL

For the morphology of the participle see **16.5.3**; there are some additional observations in **21.1.1**. The (past) participle is a form of the verb which, in some of its functions at least, is strongly adjectival. Catalan 'past' participles have two main functions:

(i) In combination with auxiliary **haver**, and more rarely **tenir** or **ser**, to form the perfect and other compound tenses. The compound tenses of all verbs are formed with **haver**: the participle appears in its masculine singular form except for the particular cases mentioned in **21.1.2iv**. In the less common perfect-tense formations with **tenir** or **ser** (**21.1.2ii** and **iii**) agreement of the past participle does occur. For detailed discussion of the compound tenses in general see **17.2**.

(ii) The participle may function adjectivally, in which case it will agree in number and gender like any adjective: **una solució atrevida** 'a bold solution', **arguments improvisats** 'improvised arguments', **benvolguts amics/ benvolgudes amigues** 'dear friends', **una desesperada temptativa** 'a desperate attempt', and so on. The past participle of a transitive verb is passive, that is, when used adjectivally it modifies a noun which is the direct object of the verb in question, for example, **uns temes molt debatuts** 'some much debated topics'.

As an adjective, a participle may in appropriate circumstances stand before a noun (see **4.2.1**): **els meus estimats amics** 'my beloved friends', **la controvertida decisió** 'the controversial decision', **una molt arriscada (però decidida) acció** 'a very risky (but resolute) action'. Further instances of participles which may also stand as true adjectives are:

abandonat	abandoned/deserted	**elevat**	elevated
alarmat	alarmed	**emocionat**	excited/moved
allunyat	remote	**justificat**	justified
conegut	(well) known	**marcat**	marked
dedicat	dedicated	**resignat**	resigned
degut	due	**suposat**	alleged/supposed

and many others. The meaning of many participles, however, ensures that they retain their verbal force so that they may not precede a noun:

una cama trencada	a broken leg
una reunió ajornada	a postponed meeting
papers llençats	discarded papers
un document imprès	a printed document
una nena pentinada	a little girl whose hair has been combed

The participial adjectives, or adjectival participles, have the property that they may appear with **ser** without creating a passive sentence, thus: **La teva reacció era exagerada** 'Your reaction was exaggerated', **El to era elevat** 'The tone was elevated', **La seva cara m'era desconeguda** 'Her face was unknown to me'. Note **L'orquestra era dirigida per X** 'The orchestra was conducted by X' (passive) compared with the ungrammatical *L'orquestra era dirigida; **dirigit** is a non-adjectival (verbal) participle. The participles of some verbs may either be adjectival or form part of a true passive construction: only in context is it possible to determine whether **oberta** in **La porta era oberta** 'The door was open(ed)' is a descriptive adjective ('open') or a non-adjectival verbal participle 'opened'. The passive voice is discussed in detail in **29.1** while subtleties of adjectives used with the verbs **ser** and **estar** are dealt with in **30.5**.

Adjectival participles may, like other adjectives, become nouns when they are introduced by an article or demonstrative: **un exiliat** 'an exile', **un mort** 'a dead body', **(aquests) impresos** '(these) printed papers', **els afectats d'aquest afer** 'those (who are) affected by this matter'. As in the last instance, such nominalizations often correspond to an English relative clause.

There is a considerable number of adjectives that resemble participles but which are not derived (directly) from verbs: **desgraciat** 'unhappy', **indefinit** 'indefinite', **desmesurat** 'disproportionate', **indiscriminat** 'indiscriminate', and so on.

21.1.1   OBSERVATIONS ON (PAST) PARTICIPLE FORMS

The formation of regular and irregular participles is covered in **16.5.3**. There follow two points of special note.

Estar and ser (ésser)

The participle of **estar** is regular **estat**. Although, as the participle of **ésser** (ser), in some dialects, the form **sigut** is common, the form **estat** (which is also the participle of **estar**) is preferred in formal contexts and registers. Preference for **estat** has the additional practical advantage for foreign learners, in that it circumvents, in the compound tenses, uncertainty over the choice between **ser** and **estar**. See Chapter 30.

Què ha sigut/estat això?
What was that?

Aquesta ha estat una empresa molt perillosa.
This has been a very dangerous undertaking.

Morir and *matar*

Although **matat** 'killed' exists as the regular participle of **matar** 'to kill', **mort** (from **morir** 'to die') replaces it in most contexts, so that **Brutus ha mort Cèsar** 'Brutus has killed Caesar' would be the usual perfect tense form corresponding to the preterite **Brutus matà Cèsar** 'Brutus killed Caesar'. **Matat** is used, however, when the idea of killing is stressed (especially, in the reflexive form, for suicides) or when the emphasis is on death caused by violent accident:

Obsedida pels remordiments, s'ha matat.
Obsessed by remorse, she killed herself.

Tres persones s'han matat avui per l'autopista.
Three people have been killed today on the motorway.

21.1.2 SYNTAX OF PARTICIPLES: AGREEMENT

In addition to when the participle acts as a true adjective (**21.1ii**), agreement occurs in passive constructions, in compound tenses using auxiliary **tenir** or **ser**, and in compound tenses with **haver** when third-person direct-object clitic pronouns are involved.

(i)   The passive voice (see Chapter 29). When a transitive verb is used passively the participle agrees in number and gender with the subject of the passive construction (which can be represented as the object of the corresponding active version of the same sentence):

La ciutat ha estat presa per l'enemic.
The city has been taken by the enemy.

(cf. **L'enemic ha pres la ciutat.**
The enemy have taken the city.)

Les seves ironies eren enteses per tothom.
Her ironies were understood by everyone.

(cf. **Tothom entenia les seves ironies.**
Everyone understood her ironies.)

(ii) **Tenir** sometimes substitutes **haver** before the past participle, in the idiom **Tinc entès que ...** 'I gather/understand that ... ', and in some other contexts involving transitive verbs, to add connotations of decisiveness or to emphasize the idea of possession, or responsibility of the agent, the adjectival function of the participle is prominent. Here the participle agrees in number and gender with the object:

Tinc estudiada una solució.	I have thought out a solution.
(cf. **He estudiat una solució.**)	
No tenies demanada la nova edició?	Hadn't you ordered the new
(cf. **No havies demanat la nova edició?**)	edition?
Teníem resolt d'acomiadar-los.	We had resolved to dismiss them.
Ja tenia preparada una contestació.	She had already prepared an answer, *or* She already had an answer ready.

This type of construction with **tenir** can facilitate a more flexible word order, giving even more prominence to the adjectival force of the participle, and with the idea of possession frequently highlighted:

Ja tenim la taula parada.
We have laid the table already.
(cf. **Ja tenim parada la taula./Ja hem parat la taula.**)

Hem de tenir la taula parada abans de les nou.
We must have the table laid before nine o'clock.

Tinc estalviades gairebé cinquanta mil lliures.
I have saved up almost fifty thousand pounds.

(iii) The use of **ser/ésser/esser** as an auxiliary verb in compound (perfect) tenses survives only in North Catalonia and in Balearic dialects, principally with reflexives and with verbs expressing movement (**17.2.1.2**). Agreement of the past participle with the subject of the verb occurs in all cases:

Ells són venguts/Elles són vengudes (= **han vingut**) **de lluny.**
They have come from far away.

Ells se són asseguts./Elles se són assegudes. (= **s'han assegut**)
They have sat down.

(iv) Agreement of the participle with **haver.** Past participles forming compound tenses with the auxiliary **haver** may agree in gender and number with any of the pronouns **el, la, els, les, en,** in any of their contextual forms. That is, agreement occurs when one of these third-person pronouns precedes the participle:

He portat el diari → L'he portat.
I've brought the newspaper → it.

He portat la revista → L'he portada.
I've brought the magazine → it.

He portat els diaris → **Els he portats.**
I've brought the newspapers → them.

He portat les revistes → **Les he portades.**
I've brought the magazines → them.

–Has dut pa? –Sí que n'he dut.
'Have you brought any bread?' 'Yes (I have brought some).'

–Has dut farina?–Sí que n'he duta.
'Have you brought any flour?' 'Yes (I have brought some).'

–Han dut ous? –Sí que n'han duts.
'Have they brought any eggs?' 'Yes (they have brought some).'

–Heu dut olives? –Sí que n'hem dutes.
'Have you brought any olives?' 'Yes (we have brought some).'

Em sabia greu d'haver-la portada.
I regretted having brought it.

In modern usage there is a strong tendency for the participle to remain invariable in these cases, although agreement is retained more frequently with **la** than with the other third-person pronouns or **en**.

–Les claus, que les has portat/portades? –Sí que les he portat/portades.
'Did you bring the keys?' 'Yes I did bring them.'

Thus **l'he rebuda** 'I have received it' with participle agreement would probably be as common as or more common than the alternative **l'he rebut** (where **l'** = **la carta** 'the letter'), whereas **els he rebuts**, with a third-person masculine plural object (e.g. **els paquets** 'the parcels'), would be less common than **els he rebut**. Likewise with **en**:

D'aquestes opcions, només n'hem considerat/considerades dues o tres.
We have considered only two or three of these options.

When the conjugated verb is **voler** 'want', **poder** 'be able', **saber** 'know how to', **fer** 'have (something) done', **gosar** 'dare' or **haver de** 'have to', prescription commends the still widespread practice of making the participle agree (when, as is optional, the object pronoun precedes the conjugated verb, even though the direct object clearly belongs logically to the dependent infinitive), as in:

Les peres eren podrides i les hem hagudes de llençar. (= . . . hem hagut de llençar-les.)
The pears were rotten and we have had to throw them away.

La seva resposta, no l'he sabuda interpretar. (= . . . no he sabut interpretar-la.)
I haven't been able to interpret their reply.

Note, by the way, that though the conventional presentation in Catalan grammar speaks of agreement of past participles with preceding third-person direct object clitics, **se** is always excluded. Agreement with indirect object clitics **li/els/hi** certainly never takes place. But whereas agreement with the clitics of the series **el/la/els/les** relates to these only in a direct object function, some examples of **en**, with agreement, correspond to subjects (**25.2**), or to complements of noun phrases:

–Han vingut moltes dependentes? –N'ha vinguda una.
'Have many assistants come?' 'One has.'

De peticions, se n'han presentades moltes.
As for petitions, a lot have been presented.

As agreement of the participle with a preceding clitic pronoun is always optional, and as the evolution of the language can be seen to be towards non-agreement as the norm, foreign students of Catalan can be guided by the principle of 'if in doubt, keep the past participle invariable'.

21.1.3   SYNTAX OF PARTICIPLES: PARTICIPLE PHRASES

Participle phrases are common in Catalan. Such structures are often the same as in English:

Me'n vaig anar, convençut que ningú no en diria res.
I left, convinced that nobody would say anything.

Decidides a resoldre el misteri . . .
Determined to resolve the mystery . . .

Van emprendre la campanya electoral encoratjats per les enquestes.
They embarked on the electoral campaign heartened by the opinion polls.

Sometimes English will have a present participle/gerund in the corresponding expression:

Ajagut damunt el sofà no feia més que mirar la televisió.
Lying on the sofa he was just watching the television.

Va fer tota la carrera allotjada a casa d'una tia seva.
She did her whole university course lodging with an aunt.

English does however have other structures which can be rendered in Catalan by a participle phrase as in:

Ho rebutjà irritada.
She turned it down irritably.

–Però què fas? va preguntar alarmada.
'But what are you doing?' she asked in alarm.

el seu germà, nascut el 1938 i mort el 1991
his brother, who was born in 1938 and died in 1991

Particularly to be noted is the order participle + subject in constructions where the participle and its subject form a subordinate (usually temporal) absolute adverbial phrase:

Investigats tots els detalls, aviat formularem una conclusió.
Now that all the details have been investigated we shall soon formulate a conclusion.

Ateses les nostres dificultats . . .
Given our difficulties . . .

Arribada la núvia, va començar la festa.
Once the bride had arrived the party began.

(**Arribar** appears to be the only verb of motion allowing this construction. One would not hear *****Partida la comitiva, sobrevingué un llarg silenci** for 'When the delegation had left a long pause followed'. The equivalent would be a full clause: **Quan hagué partit la comitiva . . .**).

Participial constructions often have a conditional or concessive sense:

Portat així el fulard, té un no sé què de distingit.
If you wear the scarf like this, it looks rather distinguished.

Posats a criticar, el plat principal era massa salat pel meu gust.
If we're being critical, the main course was a bit too salty for my taste.

Girada la pedra cap per avall, les inscripcions es llegeixen més clarament.
If the stone is turned upside down, the inscriptions can be read more clearly.

When the participle has an agent expressed, the agent can be introduced by the preposition **per** or, perhaps as frequently, by the compound **per part de**:

Acabada la introducció pel/per part del president, s'inicià el debat.
When the introduction by the chairman was finished, the discussion began.

These absolute participle phrases are favoured in literary and formal written styles, but they are not alien to the everyday language and they figure in a number of idioms (adverbial) and popular sayings:

Fet i fet, tampoc no sóc tan ase.	Come to that, I'm not so daft.
tot comptat i debatut	when all is said and done.
Ben mirat, potser ens vam equivocar.	On reflection, perhaps we were wrong.
Feta la llei feta la trampa. (proverb)	Laws are made to be broken.
Morta la cuca, mort el verí. (proverb)	You've got to kill the insect to get rid of the poison.

21.2 PRESENT PARTICIPLE

Many (but not all) verbs present an adjectival present participle, formed by addition of the following endings to the lexical stem:

Conjugation I	**cant(-ar)**	-ant
Conjugation II	**tém(-er)**	-ent
	reb(-re)	-ent
Conjugation III	**dorm(-ir)**	-ent
	(serv(-ir)	-ent)

To be observed is the coincidence in form between the present participle and gerund of both first and second conjugation verbs. But in the third conjugation -**ent** (present participle) contrasts with -**int** (gerund). (A notable oddity is the mixed-conjugation **escriure** 'write' which has the participle **escrivent** but gerund **escrivint**.) This distinction between participle and gerund can be seen in pairs like:

Porta aigua bullent.	Bring boiling water. (adjectival participle)
L'aigua està bullint.	The water is boiling. (gerund)
Arribaran el mes vinent.	They will arrive next month.
els convidats que aniran venint	the guests who will be turning up
la Bella Dorment	Sleeping Beauty
Si estan dormint, no els molesteu.	If they are sleeping, don't disturb them.

Present participles agree in number with the noun they modify, but no gender distinction is made in either singular or plural forms:

m.sg. and *f.sg.*	*m.pl.* and *f. pl.*	
semblant	**semblants**	similar
atraient	**atraients**	attractive

Some present participles have become established as nouns, and these cases do have specific feminine forms:

l'aprenent	**l'aprenenta**	apprentice	**el president**	**la presidenta**	president
l'assistent	**l'assistenta**	assistant	**el servent**	**la serventa**	servant
l'estudiant	**l'estudianta**	student			

Compare with the above, however, other nominalized present participles without gender agreement: **el/la cantant** 'singer', **el/la combatent** 'combatant', **el/la suplent** 'substitute', **el/la comerciant** 'trader', **el/la contrincant** 'opponent', etc. (more details in **1.1.5**).

21.2.1   SYNTAX OF PRESENT PARTICIPLE

The present participle is basically an adjective, and it is thus to be carefully distinguished from the gerund (see above **bullent** *vs.* **bullint, vinent** *vs.* **venint**, and also **22.1.2** and **22.2.4.2**) whose function is fundamentally verbal. The present participle, then, is used to qualify a noun (and, like other adjectives, can itself be used, 'pronominally', as, for example, **els creients** 'believers'). The point is reinforced by considering the adjectival value of **suplent** ('substitute', 'deputy', present participle of transitive **suplir** 'substitute', 'stand in') contrasted with the verbal function of gerund **suplint** (taking its own direct object) in the following pair:

Hem tingut un professor suplent.
We've had a stand-in teacher.

Hem tingut un professor nou suplint el nostre.
We've had a new teacher standing in for our usual one.

In the first case the adjectival **suplent** is tied closely in position after its noun, whereas the **suplint** clause has mobility within the sentence:

Suplint el nostre hem tingut un professor nou.
Hem tingut, suplint el nostre, un professor nou.

Many words in **-nt** are not strictly speaking participles but rather non-verbal adjectives: **aparent, corrent, brillant, bastant,** etc. While new **-nt** present participles are constantly being formed and becoming established, for example, **canviant,** 'changing', **relaxant** 'relaxing', they cannot be coined from any verb at will. English speakers must thus avoid the temptation to invent equivalents of English adjectival present participles in '-ing' along the lines of **movent. (Note **peces mòbils** 'moving parts', **un discurs commovedor** 'a moving speech'.) This can be seen in common instances like **plegable** 'folding', **aigua potable** 'drinking water', **plantes enfiladisses** 'climbing plants'. In other cases, a Catalan (past) participle corresponds to English words in '-ing':

ajagut	lying	**divertit**	amusing
assegut	sitting	**dormit**	sleeping, asleep
atrevit	daring	**entretingut**	entertaining
avorrit/ensopit	boring	**pesat**	boring, irritating
cansat	tiring	**suat**	sweating, hot

English speakers should also avoid the temptation to introduce the present participle (or gerund) in constructions where English '-ing' corresponds to a relative clause in Catalan (see **22.1.2, 22.3.1,** and **31.10i**).

22 THE GERUND

22.1 THE GERUND: INTRODUCTION

22.1.1 ASPECT AND TENSE

The inflection of the gerund is dealt with at **16.5.2**. The simple gerund itself is 'tenseless'; the tense reference it conveys is always determined by the main verb which it accompanies, and with whose action it is simultaneous. As a verbal modifier, however, a gerund does have an aspectual connotation deriving from the simultaneity just mentioned, which can be considered either durative or progressive:

En Miquel estava meditant.	Miquel was meditating. (durative)
En Miquel anava meditant.	Miquel went on meditating. (progressive)

The aspectual element, nevertheless, is determined not by the gerund alone but by the verbs on which it depends in this kind of periphrasis (see **18.1.1** and **18.1.2**). The compound gerund of any verb is obtained by adding the (past) participle to the gerund of **haver**: **havent dinat** 'having lunched', **havent pres** 'having taken', **havent dormit** 'having slept', **havent sabut** 'having known', etc. These forms express anteriority, that is, denote a time that precedes that of the main verb. There are some examples of the use of the compound gerund in **22.2.4.1**.

22.1.2 INFLECTION: THE GERUND AS VERBAL MODIFIER

Unlike the participles, the gerund presents no nominal inflection for gender and number. This is another feature opposing gerund and present participle (see **21.2.1**).

The important point is that the Catalan gerund is basically a non-finite verbal form whose primary function is adverbial, and it can thus correctly modify only verbs (present in the sentence or implied) except in the special circumstances described in **22.2.4.2**. 'An appendix supplying more documentation' should not be translated with the gerund (***un apèndix fornint més documentació**) but rather with a relative clause: **un apèndix que forneix/fornia més documentació**. Only in captions does the gerund exceptionally appear without an accompanying finite verb (**les meves germanes sortint del parc** 'my sisters coming out of the park', beneath a photograph, for example). Otherwise, as indicated, English speakers need to take particular care not to misuse the gerund as a participle, and to use the relative construction as the most natural solution in Catalan for frequently occurring cases like:

Se'm va acostar un tipus que portava una gavardina bruta.
I was approached by a character wearing a dirty raincoat.

A recepció es pot obtenir un plànol que mostra tots els llocs d'interès turístic.
A map showing all the sites of interest to tourists can be obtained in reception.

These characteristics of the gerund will be further illustrated in discussion of various features of related syntax given in the following sections.

22.2   SYNTAX OF THE GERUND

22.2.1   WEAK PRONOUN POSITION

Typically, any weak pronoun complements will be attached enclitically to the gerund:

Fent-ho així acabaràs aviat.
(By) doing it like this you will finish quickly.

Escrivien contant-me coses de la seva feina.
They used to write telling me things about their work.

(North Catalan, though, behaves like French and consistently places the pronoun before the gerund.)

When the gerund is governed by a finite verb (that is, in durative or progressive periphrases) a weak pronoun can either precede the main verb or follow the gerund. See **12.2.3**.

Ens anirem coneixent a poc a poc. = Anirem coneixent-nos a poc a poc.
We shall gradually get to know one another.

22.2.2   AMBIGUITY IN GERUND SUBJECTS

The adverbial function of the gerund and the mobility of adverbial components within a sentence mean that there may be ambiguity in the interpretation of the subject of the gerund in **L'Enric trobà la Maria cantant**. Here the meaning could be either 'Enric came across Maria (who was) singing' or 'When he was singing Enric came across Maria'. Such cases of ambiguity (see **22.2.4.3**) can always be resolved in this way:

Els vaig veure quan baixaven de l'avió.
I saw them as they were getting off the plane.

Els vaig veure quan baixava de l'avió.
I saw them as I was getting off the plane.

Either of the options above would clarify, if context were insufficient, the possible ambiguity (perhaps stronger in Catalan than in the English equivalent) of:

Els vaig veure baixant de l'avió.   I saw them getting off the plane.

22.2.3   GERUND IN ABSOLUTE PHRASES

The gerund, with its (logical) subject, object, and other complements, can be the nucleus of an absolute gerund phrase (e.g. **Sabent-ho tu ja ho sap tothom** 'With you knowing it everybody now knows it'). The adverbial functions (conditional, causal, concessive, temporal, etc.) performed by such absolute gerund phrases coincide with part of the range available when the gerund and the main verb have the same subject (see **22.2.4.1**). English translation of this type of absolute clause often involves a conjugated verb:

Dient això ella tampoc no ho creurem. (concessive)
Although she might say that we still won't believe it.

Pagant l'empresa, els dinars sempre cauen bé. (temporal)
When the firm is paying, lunches are always a pleasure.

Aportant ells aquesta quantitat el premi serà més substancial. (means or condition)
By their contributing this sum/If they contribute this sum the prize will be more substantial.

Tractant-se d'una emergència el metge us atendrà de seguida. (causal)
As it's an emergency the doctor will see you immediately.

Observe that these absolute gerund phrases show the virtually obligatory order, in non-finite constructions, of the subject following the verb, as in the examples above.

22.2.4   SYNTACTIC FUNCTIONS OF THE GERUND

22.2.4.1   *Adverbial functions*

The main area of use of the gerund, including absolute phrases discussed in **22.2.3**, is the modification of the main verb phrase in a sentence. Structurally the gerund clause in **Dient aquestes coses no tindràs mai amics** 'If you say these things you'll never have any friends' has the same function as the simple adverb **així** when the sentence is recast as **Així no tindràs mai amics** 'You'll never have any friends (if you behave) like this'. Likewise, a gerund phrase can be seen to be the equivalent of a full subordinate clause with a finite verb, as in **Jugant per la plaça es va rompre un braç = Quan jugava per la plaça es va rompre un braç** '(When he was) playing in the square he broke his arm', and in examples shown at **22.2.3**.

Following from what is said about tense in **22.1.1**, the situation denoted by the gerund will be simultaneous or virtually simultaneous with that of the main verb, as is seen in:

Van marxar remugant.
They went off muttering.

Vam pujar l'escala saltant de dos en dos els esglaons.
We skipped up the stairs two at a time.

Fent-me l'ullet féu veure que havia entès l'al·lusió.
Winking at me he let on that he had understood the allusion.

Normative grammarians insist that the action expressed by the gerund must always be simultaneous to that expressed by the main verb. Modern journalism in particular is frequently charged with abuse of the gerund in producing sentences like the following:

(non-standard) **Van fugir de pressa, detenint-los la policia pocs dies després.**
(recommended) **Van fugir de pressa, però la policia els va detenir pocs dies després.**
They fled quickly, being arrested by the police a few days later.

(non-standard) **Actuà a París i a Roma, esdevenint una celebritat mundial abans de complir vint anys.**
(recommended) **Actuà a París i a Roma, i esdevingué una celebritat mundial abans de complir vint anys.**
She performed in Paris and Rome, becoming a world-wide celebrity before the age of twenty.

Note, though, that there is no infraction when the action of the gerund occurs immediately before that of the main verb, as in **Es va fer famosa publicant les seves confessions** 'She became famous by publishing her confessions', or in **Agafant el micròfon començà a cantar** 'Taking the microphone she began to sing'.

The main information conveyed by the gerund phrase may itself be temporal, as is the case when **ser** or **estar** is involved:

Estant a Roma podrem visitar el Coliseu.
While staying in Rome we'll be able to visit the Colosseum.

Essent ella a la presó, un parent seu va portar el negoci familiar.
When/While she was in prison, one of her relatives ran the family business.

But the basic temporal reference (simultaneity) is very commonly complemented by another (or more than one other) connotation, typically of manner, means, condition, concession, cause or purpose. Overlapping can easily be seen between the divisions of adverbial function given below:

(i) Manner:

Em va saludar somrient.
She greeted me with a smile.

(ii) Means or method (overlapping with conditional function, as in the examples given in (iii) below):

Podeu obtenir més informació escrivint-nos o trucant-nos per telèfon.
You can obtain more information by writing to us or phoning us.

Repartint diaris pel veïnat ha après les adreces de tots els veïns.
From delivering newspapers around the neighbourhood he has learnt the addresses of everyone who lives there.

(iii) Condition:

Explicant-los-ho tu, és més probable que s'ho creguin.
If you explain it to them it's more likely they'll believe it.

Sent tan importants, no voldran pas seure amb nosaltres.
Being/If they are so important they won't want to sit with us.

(iv) Concession:

Havent estat un dels nostres col·laboradors més fidels, aquesta vegada ens ha fallat.
Despite having been one of our most faithful contributors, this time he has let us down.

Tot suprimint aquest paràgraf, el text encara ens resultarà massa llarg.
Even if we knock out this paragraph, we'll still find the text is too long.

(In its concessive function the gerund is frequently accompanied by the adjunct **tot**, as here, or **tot i**, see below.)

(v) Cause:

Adonant-se de la meva presència, va adoptar un to més suau.
Becoming aware of my presence, she adopted a softer tone.

Havent pintat les parets, ara convé que canviem les cortines.
Having painted the walls we now need to change the curtains.

(vi) Purpose (invariably with verbs of communication):

Ens han escrit expressant (= per expressar) el seu condol.
They have written to express their condolences.

Ens va trucar ahir demanant (= per demanar) més aclariments.
She phoned us yesterday asking for more clarifications.

These clauses with the gerund (especially temporal and concessive) sometimes occur introduced by **tot (i)** or **bo i**, stressing the idea of simultaneity or opposition:

Tot/Bo i dinant establirem els termes del contracte.
Over lunch we will fix the terms of the contract.

Els de la Creu Roja, tot i acudint amb rapidesa, no hi van ser a temps per reanimar-la.
The Red Cross people, although responding quickly, were not in time to revive her.

This reinforcement with **tot (i)/bo i** is optional, a matter of idiolectal or stylistic preference in all registers.

22.2.4.2   *Adjectival behaviour of the gerund*

In certain cases the gerund (with its complements) appears to modify a noun and thus to have an adjectival function:

L'avi, explicant tot el que havia viscut, entretenia els néts hores i hores.
Grandfather, recounting everything he had lived through, kept his grandchildren amused for hours on end.

La coral, seleccionant un repertori tan variat, pretenia satisfer tot l'auditori.
The choir, selecting such a varied repertoire, aimed to satisfy the whole audience.

Els metges, receptant tranquil·litzants a dojo, contribueixen a les drogoaddiccions.
Doctors prescribing handfuls of tranquillizers are making drug addiction worse.

That the role of each of these gerund clauses is adjectival is shown by the way that they readily convert into relative (i.e. adjectival) clauses: **l'avi, el qual explicava, . . . , la coral, que havia seleccionat . . . , els metges, els quals recepten . . .** It is to be observed that gerunds used in this way can be converted into explicative or non-restrictive clauses (see **31.1.2**) but not into restrictive ones. These considerations are relevant for the foreign learner because of their bearing on the contrast between the Catalan gerund and the English '-ing' form (where French can also produce interference). The point is returned to in **22.3.1**.

The subject of this adjectival gerund may coincide with either the subject of the main verb (as in the examples given immediately above) or with its object, as in:

He vist en Joan fent cua per pagar la contribució.
I saw Joan queuing to pay his (local) tax.

Trobaren el seu germà corrent per les muntanyes.
They met her brother running in the mountains.

A restriction operating here is that the gerund in such constructions can be only of verbs of perceivable action:

*He menjat unes pomes essent agres.
He menjat unes pomes (que eren) agres.
I ate some bitter-tasting apples.

*Ens van explicar unes coses semblant increïbles.
Ens van explicar unes coses que semblaven increïbles.
They told us some incredible-sounding things.

*He hagut d'aclucar els ulls per mirar aquells llums brillant tant.
He hagut d'aclucar els ulls per mirar aquells llums que brillen tant.
I had to close my eyes to look at those lights shining so brightly.

22.2.4.3   *The gerund modifying a direct object*

As already seen, the gerund is used (like the English '-ing' form) to refer to actions being performed by persons who are the objects of certain types of verb.

(i)   Verbs of 'encountering', like **agafar** 'catch', **sorprendre** 'surprise', **pillar/ enxampar** (colloquial) 'nab', 'catch', **detenir/arrestar** 'arrest', **trobar** 'find', 'meet', and others, also **deixar** 'leave':

No hi ha cap examen on no enxampin algú copiant.
There is no exam where they don't catch somebody copying.

El deixaren dormint la mona.
They left him sleeping off his hangover.

(ii)   Verbs of representation, like **dibuixar** 'draw', **descriure** 'describe', **retratar** 'portray', **fotogafiar** 'photograph', **mostrar** 'show', **representar** 'represent', **imaginar(-se)** 'imagine', etc.:

És una vella fotografia que mostra el meu avi embarcant-se cap a Cuba.
It's a an old photograph which shows my grandfather embarking for Cuba.

Te'ls has d'imaginar arribant al cim.
You must imagine them reaching the summit.

Captions of illustrations, photographs, etc., belong to this category. As mentioned (in **22.1.2**) this is virtually the only context in which the gerund appears correctly without any accompanying verb:

La guàrdia d'honor formant a la porta del palau
The guard of honour lining up at the palace gate

Un petroler iranià salpant del port
An Iranian oil-tanker steaming out of the port

(iii) Verbs of perception: after **veure** 'see' (and synonyms), **sentir** 'hear', and other less common verbs of perception the gerund may qualify the object of the main verb. In this function the infinitive or a subordinate adverbial clause often occurs instead of the gerund. The infinitive is preferred to the gerund to denote perfective aspect, that is, a completed action, while the gerund (imperfective in aspect) shows the action going on as it is being perceived:

Els vam veure parar la tenda.
We saw them pitch the tent.

Els vam mirar parant la tenda.
We saw them pitch (= as they were pitching) the tent./We saw them
 pitching the tent.

The construction with a finite subordinate clause is preferred when ambiguity concerning the subject of the gerund might otherwise arise (**22.2.2**):

La vaig veure estenent la roba./La vaig veure que estenia la roba.
I saw her hanging out the washing.

22.3   TRANSLATING THE ENGLISH '-ING' FORM

Sections **22.3.1–5** describe cases where the English '-ing' form will not be translated by the Catalan gerund.

22.3.1   EQUIVALENTS OF RESTRICTIVE RELATIVE CLAUSES

The restrictive/non-restrictive distinction is established in **22.2.4.2**: the examples given there of gerunds standing for non-restrictive adjectival clauses should be contrasted with the following restrictive cases, where the relative clause is the only option in Catalan.

   *****La família vivint al segon pis són molt bona gent.**
   La família que viu al segon pis són molt bona gent.
   The family living on the second floor are very nice people.

*Digues-ho a la primera persona sortint de l'ascensor.
Digues-ho a la primera persona que surti de l'ascensor.
Tell the first person coming out of the lift.

(On relative clauses in general, see Chapter 31.)

22.3.2 VERBAL NOUNS

It is the Catalan infinitive alone and not the gerund which performs the function of the verbal noun (see **20.2**), whether as subject or object of a main verb:

Subject:

Nedar és bo per a la teva salut.
Swimming is good for your health.

M'agrada sortir amb tu.
I like going out with you.

Serà difícil controlar-los.
Keeping a check on them will be difficult./It will be difficult to keep a check on them.

Object:

Detesto haver de fer cua.
I hate having to queue.

Ha procurat persuadir-me, però només ha aconseguit irritar-me.
She has tried persuading me but has managed only to annoy me.

S'estimaven més morir que trair la causa.
They preferred dying to betraying the cause.

Sometimes a specific Catalan noun is available for such contexts: **La natació és bona per a la salut** 'Swimming is good for one's health', **El ciclisme/La pesca és un passatemps molt sa** 'Cycling/Fishing is a healthy pastime'.

When the English main verb and gerund do not have the same subject, in Catalan a subordinate clause with the subjunctive must be used, as described in **19.2**. (Observe how many of the examples in **19.2** have an English gerund in the translation.)

No m'agrada que tornin a aquestes hores de la nit.
I don't like them coming back at this time of night.

Proposo que se li imposi una multa.
I propose fining him.

Et molesta que fumi?
Do you mind my smoking/if I smoke?

22.3.3   PREPOSITIONAL OBJECTS

Here again the Catalan infinitive or subordinate clause corresponds to '-ing' in the function of a verbal noun:

Teníem moltes ganes de tornar-hi.
We were looking forward to going back there.

Se n'han anat sense acomiadar-se de ningú.
They have left without saying goodbye to anybody.

Li han posat una multa per haver aparcat en una zona prohibida.
They have fined him for parking (having parked) in a prohibited zone.

És una manera d'evitar que et vinguin a empipar amb nicieses.
It's a way of avoiding them coming and annoying you with silly things.

22.3.4   PASSIVE USES OF '-ING'

English '-ing' frequently substitutes a passive infinitive (e.g. 'This needs repairing' = 'This needs to be repaired'). A Catalan passive may be the equivalent (**Això ha de ser rectificat** 'This needs rectifying'), but the solution is usually an impersonal construction with an infinitive or a subordinate clause:

Cal estudiar-ho a fons.
It needs studying in depth.

Convé redactar de bell nou el paràgraf sencer.
The whole paragraph needs rewriting.

No fa falta que li ho repetim.
She doesn't need it repeating (to her by us).

22.3.5   ENGLISH GERUND MODIFYING A NOUN

English '-ing' + noun phrases usually correspond to Catalan noun + **de** + infinitive when the '-ing' word is itself a noun: **botes de muntar** 'riding boots', **carnet de conduir** 'driving licence', **canya de pescar** 'fishing rod' (but **un vaixell pescador** 'a fishing boat'), **màquina de cosir** 'sewing machine', etc. Sometimes a Catalan noun provides the qualification, as in **saló de lectura** 'reading room', **lliçons de cant i de ball** 'singing and dancing lessons', **embarcació de vela** 'sailing boat'.

If '-ing' is a participial adjective, Catalan will have a relative clause, unless a specific participle in -**ant** or -**ent** exists (see **21.2.1**): **notícies preocupants** 'worrying news', **objecte volant no identificat**, 'unidentified flying object', **líquid bullent** 'boiling liquid', **gràfica ascendent** 'rising curve', **raons convincents** 'convincing reasons', etc., but **una nina que plora** 'a crying doll'.

The above solutions, however, do not apply to every case. Other instances will be covered by:

(i)   Specific nouns: **falç** 'reaping hook', **volant** 'steering wheel', **bata** 'dressing gown', **menjador** 'dining room', etc.

(ii) Specific qualifying adjectives: **una notícia dolorosa** 'distressing news', **una resposta decebedora** 'a disappointing reply', **la pressió intensificadora** 'intensifying pressure', **un dependent atent/servicial/obsequiós** 'an obliging shop assistant', **la línia divisòria** 'dividing line', **la companyia naviliera** 'shipping company', **l'agent marítim** 'shipping agent', **un home extraordinari** 'an amazing man', etc.

(iii) Analytical formulae or idiomatic equivalents: **un llibre que val la pena de llegir** 'a rewarding book', **uns fets que causen perplexitat** 'perplexing facts', **l'edat de tenir fills** 'child-bearing age', **avions en vol** 'flying aircraft', **l'esperit de lluita** 'fighting spirit', **la dona de la neteja** 'cleaning lady', **el Mur de les Lamentacions** 'the Wailing Wall', **sala d'espera** 'waiting room'.

23 PRONOMINAL VERBS

23.1 GENERAL

Pronominal verbs are those which appear with an object pronoun (i.e. **em, et, es, ens, us, es,** in the appropriate form) of the same person as the subject of the verb: **M'he llevat** 'I got up', **Pentina't** 'Comb your hair', **Aneu-vos-en** 'Go away'. Verbs in the third person, including **vostè(s)**, take the reflexive pronoun **es** (**s', -se, 's**) for both singular and plural. When standing alone or as a verbal noun, the infinitive takes enclitic **-se** or **'s** (**identificar-se** 'identify oneself', **renovar-se o morir** 'be renewed or die', **moure's** 'move' (intransitive)), which is how pronominal verbs are given in word lists, dictionaries, etc.

Many Catalan verbs can be used in this way, and there is an important group (see **23.5ii**) which exist only in the pronominal form. Older grammars refer to all such cases as 'reflexive verbs', but this is misleading. A true reflexive verb is a transitive one whose direct or indirect object, expressed as a pronoun, is one and the same as its subject, i.e. a verb expressing an action done by a subject to or for him/herself: **M'afaito** 'I have a shave', **Talla't les ungles** 'Cut your nails'. However only a small percentage of pronominal verbs have this truly reflexive sense (**23.2**). Reciprocity is also expressed by this pronominal construction (**23.3**):

> **Ens estimem de debò.**
> We really love each other.

> **Es van repartir els caramels entre ells.**
> They shared out the sweets among themselves.

Beyond these two cases (reflexivity and reciprocity) the behaviour of Catalan pronominal verbs cannot be neatly described by reference to English structures.

The subtleties of the Catalan weak-object-pronoun system (discussed in Chapter 12) and the passive or impersonal uses of **es** (covered in Chapter 29) affect the complexity of this phenomenon, as do several other contrasts between Catalan and English. The following points affecting translation are to be borne in mind:

(i)   Nuances of the ethic dative (**12.3.2.3** and **25.4**):

> **Me'ls vaig trobar al supermercat.**
> I came across them in the supermarket.

Te l'hauries de vendre.
You ought to sell it.

Here pronominalization of the verb expresses the subject's close involvement or interest in the event. In other similar cases the ethic dative stresses totality of an event:

Me l'he llegit d'una tirada.
I read it at one go.

Es va cruspir un plat de canelons.
He scoffed down a plateful of cannelloni.

(See **23.8.**)

(ii) Transitivity and intransitivity:
Pronominalization through the 'reflexive passive' (discussed in **23.4** below; see also **29.2**) may make a transitive verb intransitive:

Es va obrir la porta.   The door opened.
S'ha embussat l'aigüera.   The drain is blocked.

Many transitive verbs have pronominal intransitive counterparts, where the pronominalized form acquires one or more additional senses. **Enfilar** 'thread (a needle)' has the pronominal counterpart **enfilar-se**, an intransitive verb of motion meaning 'go up', 'climb' (presumably via the notion of 'thread one's way'), which can take an adverbial or prepositional complement:

S'enfilava penya amunt xiulant, com si no li costés gens.
She was going up the hill whistling, as though there were nothing to it.

Els nens s'han enfilat a l'arbre més alt.
The children have climbed the highest tree.

While the logic in this kind of process is clear, there is no simple pattern of equivalence in English to match all cases. Sometimes a single English verb, used both transitively and intransitively, corresponds to non-pronominal and pronominal forms in Catalan (as with **obrir/obrir-se** in **Es va obrir la porta**, above):

Para el motor!   Stop the engine!
S'ha parat el motor.   The engine has stopped.

In other cases, a single verb in Catalan is differentiated through pronominalization where two different verbs are used in English:

llevar	lift off, lift up	**llevar-se**	get up
acostar	bring near(er)	**acostar-se**	approach
portar	carry	**portar-se**	behave

More details and examples are given in **23.5**.

(iii) 'Become':
The single English verb 'become' is rendered by a range of Catalan verbs, many of them pronominal: **fer-se, posar-se, tornar-se, convertir-se (en), transformar-se (en)**. Examples are given and translation issues discussed in **30.6**.

(iv) Exclusively pronominal verbs **(23.5ii)**, pronominal verbs that take prepositional objects **(23.5 and 23.7)**, and verbs whose pronominal form has a specialized meaning **(23.6 and 23.9)**.

23.2 PRONOMINAL VERBS WITH REFLEXIVE FUNCTION

This use – not, it should be stressed, the commonest incidence of the pronominal form – expresses an action done by someone to themself. Three characteristic features of this reflexive construction are that:

(i) The verb is always transitive.

(ii) The subject is usually animate (contrasting with the so-called 'reflexive passive': **Es va obrir la porta** 'The door opened', **Es lloguen cotxes** 'Cars for hire', see **23.4** and **29.2**).

(iii) The pronoun may represent either the direct or the indirect object: **Ens hem rentat** 'We've had a wash', **Ens hem rentat les mans** 'We've washed our hands'.

Examples of reflexive constructions:

S'estan dutxant.	They're having a shower.
Tregui's l'americana.	Take your jacket off.
Compte, que t'esquitxaràs!	Watch out, you'll get splashed!
S'ha trencat una cama.	He's broken a leg.
Em vaig tallar amb un tros de vidre.	I cut myself on a piece of glass.
No s'han preparat per a la cursa.	They haven't prepared (themselves) for the race.

Other observations on true reflexives:

(iv) The subject in these reflexive constructions may be emphasized by use of the subject pronoun, frequently reinforced by the appropriate form of **sol** 'alone' or **mateix** '-self':

La nena ja es vesteix (ella) sola.
The little girl now dresses herself.

Ens hem de felicitar nosaltres mateixos.
We must congratulate ourselves (lit. We ourselves must congratulate us.
  See (vii) below.)

Si vols estar ben servit, fes-te tu mateix el llit. (proverb)
If you want a job done properly, do it yourself. (lit. If you want to be well
  served, make your bed yourself.)

(v)   The reflexive object may be emphasized by use of the appropriate strong
      pronoun reinforced by **mateix**, introduced by **a** for both direct and
      indirect objects:

Us heu delatat a vosaltres mateixos.   You have betrayed yourselves.
T'has de conèixer a tu mateix(a).   You have to know yourself.

The third-person (singular and plural) strong reflexive pronoun **si** may
appear in formal style:

S'odia a si mateix.   He hates himself.
S'hauran defraudat a si mateixos. The will have cheated themselves.

But except when it corresponds to 'oneself', this use of **si** tends to be
avoided in favour of **ell/ella, ells/elles** (**11.4.2**):

S'ha estafat a ell mateix.
He has swindled himself.

Es concediren a ells mateixos un augment de sou.
They gave themselves a pay increase.

(vi) Prepositions other than **a** may introduce the strong (object) pronoun to
      modify the subject/object of a reflexive action:

T'ho hauries de mirar per tu mateix.
You ought to take a look at it for yourself.

S'han repartit els beneficis entre elles mateixes.
They have shared the profits out among themselves.

(vii) Verbs expressing harm or hurt may use **mateix** reinforcing either the
      prepositional strong pronoun (emphasizing the reflexive object) or the
      subject pronoun:

Jo mateix em complico la vida./Em complico la vida a mi mateix.
I make life difficult for myself.

Us perjudiqueu (a) vosaltres mateixos.
You make things worse for yourselves.

(viii) With certain common verbs the reflexive form can mean 'get/have something done (for oneself)' as well as the true reflexive 'do something to/for oneself':

S'han construït una torre a la costa.
They have built themselves a chalet/had a chalet built (to their specifications) on the coast.

M'he de tallar els cabells.
I must cut my hair./I must have a haircut.

In many such cases there is no ambiguity, as the action is not likely to be performed by the subject:

S'ha hagut d'operar d'una apendicitis.
He has had to have an operation for appendicitis.

Si et fa mal aquest queixal, treu-te'l.
If that tooth hurts, have it taken out.

Where ambiguity might occur it may be avoided either by use of **fer** or **deixar**, or by use of the personal pronoun with **sol** or **mateix**:

M'he fet tallar els cabells.
I have had my hair cut.

No us heu de deixar operar, llevat de casos d'extrema urgència.
You must not have an operation, except in cases of extreme urgency.

Et pots fer la manicura tu mateixa a casa.
You can give yourself a manicure at home.

23.3   PRONOMINAL VERBS WITH RECIPROCAL MEANING

The reciprocal sense, logically, involves only plural verbs. A pronominal verb in the plural may express reciprocity of event, that is, an activity done 'to/for one another'.

'Ajudem-nos' ha de ser la nostra consigna.
'Help one another' must be our watchword.

Es van conèixer a Palamós.
They met in Palamós.

S'abraçaven i es donaven cops a l'esquena.
They were embracing and patting each other on the back.

L'un a l'altre/els uns als altres may clarify or reinforce the reciprocal meaning, an effect which can also be achieved by the adverbs **mútuament** or

recíprocament. Thus **S'irriten** could mean 'They get irritated', but **S'irriten l'un a l'altre** or **S'irriten mútuament** makes it clear that 'They irritate each other'.

Where the plural subject includes both male and female, masculine pronouns are always used:

En Francesc i la Marta s'elogien sovint l'un a l'altre.
Francesc and Marta often sing each other's praises.

Els homes i les dones s'han de respectar tots els uns als altres.
Men and women must all respect one another.

(cf. **Les joves i les velles es miraven amb recel les unes a les altres.**
The old women and the young ones were looking suspiciously at one another.)

23.4   PRONOMINAL VERBS WITH INANIMATE SUBJECTS

The construction, known as the reflexive passive, is semantically equivalent to a passive, but has the apparent form of a transitive construction. The underlying direct object appears as subject while the direct-object position is occupied by a (third-person) reflexive pronoun: **Els seus llibres es van editar a València** 'His books were published in Valencia'. Detailed discussion is provided in **29.2** of this complex grammatical construction. Here attention is paid to one function in which it is frequently found, that corresponding to an English intransitive (or detransitivized) form – **El tren es va parar** 'The train stopped' – or to the colloquial passive construction with 'got' – **Aquí s'ha esborrat una línia** 'A line has got deleted here'. From the point of view of English, it appears to involve the featuring of inanimate (invariably third-person) subjects in reflexive actions:

Les coses s'han embolicat de mala manera.
Things have got into an almighty mess.

La vaixella s'haurà de tornar a l'armari.
The crockery will have to be put back in the cupboard.

S'ha enfonsat el vaixell.
The ship has sunk.

La grip no es cura amb aspirines.
Flu isn't cured with aspirins.

An indirect object pronoun (**em, et, li, ens, us, els**, in the appropriate form) can combine with **es** to indicate ownership or interest of the person(s) affected by the situation:

Se'ns acaba d'espatllar el vídeo.
Our video has just gone wrong.

Se m'han barrejat els papers i ara no trobo la carta que buscava.
My papers have got mixed up and now I can't find the letter I was looking for.

el premi que se li ha concedit
the prize she has been awarded

Se'ns perfila una conclusió alternativa.
An alternative conclusion is becoming visible (to us).

As with passive and impersonal constructions generally, the effect may be to distance the speaker or to disclaim responsibility for the event concerned:

si no se m'hagués trencat la corda
if the rope hadn't gone and broken

La cosa se'ns ha anat embullant, i ara no sabem com sortir-nos-en.
The matter has got more and more involved and now we can't find a way out.

23.5 PRONOMINALIZATION: VARIANT PATTERNS IN TRANSLATION

Seeking word-for-word or structural equivalences between English and Catalan is an insecure basis for working with the Catalan system of pronominalization described thus far. Certain patterns are discernible, however, in the divergences between the two languages, if we focus our analysis on questions of transitivity and intransitivity. The following broad lines of contrast can be established:

(i)   Catalan transitive verbs with pronominal forms correspond to a single verb in English (used both transitively and intransitively):

Arreglaré els documents ara mateix.	I'll get the documents ready right away.
M'arreglaré ara mateix.	I'll get ready right away.
Això no em preocupa gens.	This doesn't worry me at all.
No us preocupeu: tot anirà bé.	Don't worry: everything will be fine.

Similarly: **amoïnar(-se)** 'bother', **aturar(-se)/parar(-se)** 'stop', **moure('s)** 'move', **concentrar(-se)** 'concentrate', **despertar(-se)** 'awaken'/'wake (up)', **doblegar(-se)** 'bend', **asseure('s)** 'sit', **afaitar(-se)** 'shave', **entrenar (-se)** 'train', **buidar(-se)** 'empty', **ofegar(-se)** 'drown', **ennuegar(-se)** 'choke', **traslladar(-se)** 'move', **mudar(-se)** 'change', **entortolligar(-se)** 'twist', **escalfar(-se)** 'warm up', etc. From the Catalan point of view many of these examples may be truly reflexive (e.g. **afaitar-se**), although English does not always use a reflexive verb (though even English may do so, with 'shave (oneself)', 'worry (oneself)', 'train (oneself)', 'move (oneself)', 'bother (oneself)', and so on).

(ii) Verbs which exist only in the pronominal form. This set can be divided into:

(a) Intransitive:

esblaimar-se	turn pale	**enrojolar-se**	blush
afarrossar-se	gorge (oneself)	**enrogallar-se**	become hoarse

(b) Transitive:

descuidar-se	forget (something)	**emportar-se**	take away
empassar-se	swallow	**endur-se**	take away
empatollar-se	go on (about something)	**quedar-se**	keep

(c) Verbs taking a prepositional complement, most commonly with **a** or **de** but also other prepositions:

assemblar-se a	resemble	**penedir-se de**	repent of
atrevir-se a	dare to	**queixar-se de**	complain about
abstenir-se de	abstain/refrain from	**rebel·lar-se contra**	rebel against
adonar-se de	realize		
descuidar-se de	forget to	**esforçar-se en**	try hard to/at
desempallegar-se de	escape from		

(iii) There is a clear relationship between the transitive and the intransitive (pronominal) sense, though a different verb or construction may be required in English:

aclarir	clarify, clear	**aclarir-se**	become brighter (weather)
admirar	admire	**admirar-se (de)**	be surprised, marvel (at)
alegrar	cheer (up), gladden	**alegrar-se**	be glad/happy, rejoice
divertir	amuse	**divertir-se**	have fun, enjoy oneself
esgarriar	mislead	**esgarriar-se**	straggle, go wrong
interessar	interest	**interessar-se en/per**	have/take an interest in
preocupar	worry	**preocupar-se de/per**	worry about
obsessionar	obsess	**obsessionar-se per**	be obsessed with
fixar	fix	**fixar-se en**	notice
etc.			

Under this heading is an important group of change-of-state verbs whose pronominal form corresponds to an English expression with 'become', 'grow', 'turn' or to an English passive with 'be', 'get'. Included here are verbs expressing change of colour: **engroguir** 'make yellow', **engroguir-se** 'turn yellow'; **enrogir** 'redden'/'make red', **enrogir-se** 'turn red'; **ennegrir** 'blacken', **ennegrir-se**, 'turn black'; **emblanquir** 'whiten', **emblanquir-se** 'turn white'; **enverdir** 'colour green', **enverdir-se** 'turn green'. Then:

avorrir	bore	**avorrir-se**	get bored
aprimar	make thin(ner)	**aprimar-se**	get thinner, slim
divorciar	divorce	**divorciar-se**	get divorced
espantar	frighten	**espantar-se**	be(come) frightened
(also near-synonyms **esfereir** and **esverar**: **esfereir-se/esverar-se**)			
endurir	harden	**endurir-se**	grow hard
empantanegar	bog down	**empantanegar-se**	get bogged down
embolicar	entangle	**embolicar-se**	get entangled
enfadar/enutjar	annoy	**enfadar-se/enut- jar-se**	get angry
engreixar	fatten	**engreixar-se**	get fat
ensopir	bore	**ensopir-se**	be(come)/get bored
ensordir	deafen	**ensordir-se**	grow/become deaf
entristir	sadden	**entristir-se**	grow sad
emprenyar	irritate intensely	**emprenyar-se**	be pissed off
estranyar	puzzle	**estranyar-se**	be puzzled
fastiguejar	annoy	**fastiguejar-se**	get annoyed
molestar	bother	**molestar-se**	be bothered
etc.			

The pronominal form of the majority of such verbs which can take a complement will introduce it with **de** or **amb**, whereas English deploys a wider range of prepositions:

M'alegro molt d'aquesta notícia.
I'm delighted by/with/at this bit of news.

S'ha divorciat del segon marit.
She has (got) divorced (from) her second husband.

Ja ens n'hem avorrit.
We've got bored with it.

Some verbs like **avorrir-se** 'get bored (with)', **ensopir-se** 'get sent to sleep (by)', **divertir-se** 'have fun (with)', **embolicar-se** 'get involved (with/in)', take **en** or **amb** depending on context:

Es van divertir molt amb tantes facècies.
They were greatly amused by/with/at such jesting.

M'he embolicat en una qüestió molt espinosa.
I have got mixed up in a very thorny business.

Ton germà s'ha embolicat amb uns personatges poc recomanables.
Your brother has got involved with some undesirable characters.

The above group can be contrasted with non-pronominal intransitive verbs
that denote changes of state:

agonitzar	be dying	**emmudir**	become silent,
augmentar	increase		lose one's voice
clarejar	become light(er)/	**empal·lidir**	become pale/
	brighter (esp.		pallid
	day, weather)	**néixer**	be born, come
créixer	grow		into being
disminuir	diminish	**ressuscitar**	come back to life

Millorar 'improve' and **empitjorar** 'get worse' both exist side by side with
millorar-se and **empitjorar-se**. **Envellir** can mean 'live a long time' as well
as 'grow old', but **envellir-se** is more usual in the latter sense, analogous
with **rejovenir-se** 'become younger'.

(iv) Two quite different English verbs translate the non-pronominal and
pronominal forms of a single Catalan verb. The most obvious cases are
dir 'say', 'tell' and **dir-se** 'be called'; **portar** 'carry', 'wear' and **portar-se**
'behave'. Similarly:

acomiadar	dismiss, see off	**acomiadar-se**	say good-bye
acostar	bring near(er)	**acostar-se**	approach
afanyar	press, bother	**afanyar-se**	toil, strive hard, hurry
aixecar	raise, lift up	**aixecar-se**	rise, get/stand up
alçar	raise	**alçar-se**	rise (up)
aprimar	make thin(ner)	**aprimar-se**	slim
avorrir	hate	**avorrir-se**	be bored, get bored
enamorar	captivate	**enamorar-se**	fall in love
engrossir	fatten	**engrossir-se**	put on weight
entrebancar	obstruct, hamper	**entrebancar-se**	stumble
llevar	lift off/up	**llevar-se**	get up

23.6   PRONOMINAL VERBS OF MOTION

The idiomatic usage of some pronominal verbs of motion requires special
attention.

23.6.1   Anar-se'n 'LEAVE', 'GO AWAY'

The simple verb 'go' is rendered in Catalan by **anar**. When used in the simple
non-pronominal form it frequently requires the pronominal clitic complement **hi** 'there' (see **12.7**), not always translated in English:

Si vas a l'espectacle, digues-m'ho, que també hi penso anar. Oi que podríem anar-hi plegats?
If you're going to the show, tell me as I plan to go as well. We could go together, couldn't we?

'Go away' can be translated by **marxar** (never pronominalized): **Què, que ja marxeu?** 'What, are you leaving already?' The commonest way of saying 'go away', 'leave', however, is with **anar-se'n** (cf. French *aller/s'en aller*), which appears also in other idioms.

Me'n vaig./Me n'he d'anar.
I'm leaving./I must leave.

Vés-te'n.
Go away.

Te n'has anat massa d'hora.
You left too early.

No podeu anar-vos-en sense acomiadar-vos.
You can't leave without saying goodbye.

In English equivalents 'away' does not always appear, as **anar-se'n** means 'go (somewhere else)' from where the subject is now:

Demà se'n va a Tortosa.
She's off to/going to/leaving for Tortosa tomorrow.

Ja no puc més; me'n vaig.
I can't stand any more; I'm going.

Other idioms with **anar-se'n**:

(i)   Meaning 'leak', of something held in a recipient:

L'aigua del càntir se n'anava per una esquerda.
The water in the pitcher was leaking (out) through a crack.

(ii)   In a physical movement or operation, referring to a part of the body, **anar-se'n** means 'slip':

Se li'n va anar la mà i em va vessar la salsa al damunt.
His hand slipped and he spilt the sauce all over me.

Se me n'ha anat el peu i he caigut de morros a terra.
My foot slipped and I fell flat on my face.

(iii) **Anar-se'n** is also used figuratively of an event or effort that comes to nothing, or of an item that is falling to pieces:

Els volia apallissar, però tot se'n va anar en crits i amenaces.
He wanted to thrash them, but it just ended up in a lot of shouting and
threatening.

Aquest projecte se'ns n'ha anat en orris.
This plan has gone awry.

Duia un vestit que se n'anava a trossos.
He was wearing a tattered suit.

23.6.2   OTHER PRONOMINAL VERBS OF MOTION

(i) **venir-se'n**
Formed by analogy with **anar-se'n**, this pronominal form emphasizes
subjective awareness of movement towards where the speaker is situated:

Topant de cap en una i altra soca // se'n ve la vaca tota sola; és cega.
(J. Maragall)
Knocking her head against a trunk here and a trunk there/the cow comes
onwards all alone; she is blind.

Venir-se'n (a baix) is used of a roof or ceiling collapsing, synonymous
with **enfonsar-se:**

Si no reparem aquesta esquerda, se'ns en vindrà a baix tot el sostre.
If we don't repair that crack, the whole ceiling will come down.

(ii) **tornar-se'n**
This verb is an emphatic form of **tornar** 'return', 'go back':

Van arribar a les set, i a les vuit ja se'n tornaven.
They arrived at seven o'clock and by eight they were already on their way
back.

In popular speech **tornar** is sometimes reinforced as **entornar** without
dropping the clitic **en:**

Se n'han entornat sense dir-nos res.
They've gone back without saying anything to us.

A similar phenomenon is also observed with **enretirar-se** 'return', 'back
off', which can acquire a redundant **en:**

No t'enretiris/No te n'enretiris; acosta-t'hi més.
Don't back away; move closer.

(iii) Similar analogies with **anar-se'n** produce colloquial forms like **pujar-se'n**
'go up', **baixar-se'n** 'go/come down', **llevar-se'n** 'get up'.

23.7   PRONOMINAL VERBS OF REMEMBERING AND FORGETTING

'Remember' (something in the past) is translated by **recordar** and 'forget' by **oblidar**:

Recordes aquella cançó?	Do you remember that song?
Sabia la data però l'he oblidada.	I used to know the date, but I've forgotten it.

The basic function of remembering is frequently expressed by **recordar-se de** with a noun complement and **recordar-se que/com** introducing a clause (matched in 'forgetting' by **oblidar-se de** or **oblidar-se que**):

Us recordeu de les seves paraules?
Do you remember their words?

Li ho hem dit, però es veu que no se n'ha recordat.
We told him, but he obviously hasn't remembered.

No t'oblidis que ens ho havies promès.
Don't forget you had promised us.

The pronominal form **recordar-se** is favoured when 'remember' implies not forgetting something or to do something:

Ens vas assegurar que ho faries; te'n recordes?
You assured us you would do it; do you remember?

Us heu de recordar de demanar taula.
You must remember/not forget to book a table.

In this sort of context the antonym of **recordar-se** is **descuidar-se** 'forget', 'neglect' (two verbs which become interchangeable through use of the negative: **descuidar-se = no recordar-se** and vice versa). **Descuidar-se** likewise introduces an infinitive with **de** and a clause with **que**:

No ens descuidem de trucar al lampista.
We'd better not forget to phone the plumber.

M'havia descuidat que demà és el seu aniversari.
I'd forgotten that tomorrow is his birthday.

However, this verb, unlike **recordar-se**, behaves transitively when introducing a noun phrase complement (without the preposition **de**):

M'havia descuidat el paraigua en el cotxe.
I'd left my umbrella in the car./I'd forgotten to bring my umbrella from the car.

Constructions with both **recordar-se** and **descuidar-se** frequently entail the use of **en** standing for the complement. There is a tendency for this to be automatic, even when redundant, and in everyday speech sentences like the following are common:

> **Recorda-te'n que demà has d'anar al dentista.**
> Remember you have to go to the dentist's tomorrow.

> **Te n'has descuidat que havies de comprar-li un regal?**
> Have you forgotten you had to buy him a present?

(See **12.8** and **36.4–5** for discussion of redundant pronouns in general.)

23.8   PRONOMINAL VERBS OF CONSUMPTION

Some transitive verbs in this semantic range can be pronominalized to emphasize decisiveness or completeness of the event. This can be illustrated by contrasting non-pronominal and pronominal uses of the same verb in specific contexts:

Sempre bevem vi.	We always drink wine.
S'ha begut mitja ampolla de vi.	She has drunk half a bottle of wine.
Prenc somnífers per dormir.	I'm taking sleeping pills to sleep.
Vinga, pren-te una d'aquestes pastilles.	Come on, take one of these tablets.

23.9   PRONOMINAL VERBS OF KNOWLEDGE AND PERCEPTION

Pronominalization occurs frequently with verbs in this category. The issue is best addressed in terms of practice and usage with individual verbs rather than through attempting to generalize about nuances of meaning.

(i)   **creure('s)** 'believe'
This verb also translates 'think' in most contexts where **pensar-se** (see below, ii) could also to be used. The pronominal form **creure's** is common, virtually interchangeable with both **creure** and **pensar(-se)** introducing a clause:

> **(Et) creus que m'equivoco, doncs?**   Do you think I'm wrong, then?
> **(Em) creia que arribarien més d'hora.**   I thought they would be arriving earlier.

(ii)   **pensar-se** 'think'
Non-pronominal **pensar** rarely introduces a clause with **que**, except when the literal meaning of 'think'/'be thinking' is prominent. Otherwise

pronominal **pensar-se** is preferred, synonymous with **creure('s)** in the sense of 'think'/'believe':

Qui et penses que ets? Who do you think you are?
Em penso que són bojos. I think they're mad.

No et pensis occurs frequently as an interjection meaning something like 'bet your life', 'to be sure', reinforcing an affirmation:

Ho faran perquè són tossuts, no et pensis.
They'll do it, because they're stubborn, you'll see.

(iii) **imaginar-se** 'imagine'
The pronominal form of transitive **imaginar** is used in the sense of 'suppose', 'think' (a meaning not available in standard Catalan to the simple **imaginar**):

M'imaginava que resultaria més fàcil.
*Imaginava que resultaria més fàcil.
I thought it would prove to be easier.

(iv) **adonar-se** 'realize' (Bal. **témer-se**)
This verb takes a prepositional object with **de**:

No s'adona gens de la importància d'això.
She doesn't realize at all how important this is.

És la fi d'una era: que no te n'adones?
It's the end of an era: don't you realize?

Or it can introduce a clause with **que**:

Ara m'adono que tenies raó tu. I realize now that you were right.
No ens adonàvem que fos tan tard. We didn't realize it was so late.

(v) **saber(-se)** 'know'
Although regarded as a non-standard construction, for the sake of emphasis this verb is occasionally used pronominally with a direct object:

Tot això, m'ho sé de memòria ja. I already know all this off by heart.

(vi) **entendre('s)** 'understand'
In addition to the normal behaviour of a transitive verb which can be pronominalized with particular effects (**Això no s'entén** 'This can't be understood', **Són dos que s'entenen** 'They're two people who get on well together'), three specific idioms with this verb are to be noted. One is with the pronominal form **entendre's amb** 'have/come to an understanding with', which can be ambiguous, with implications of striking up a relationship:

Em vaig entendre amb la seva secretària.
I came to an understanding with her secretary.

S'entenia molt bé amb aquell grup d'alumnes.
She got on very well with that group of students.

The second is **entendre's de** 'be good at', 'know all about', usually appearing with clitic **en** and the actual complement preceding the verb or following the phrase:

De motos, no me n'entenc gens ni mica.
I don't know anything about motorbikes.

Ell no se n'entén, d'aquestes qüestions.
He's no good at this kind of thing.

The third is the intransitive use of the verb with a prepositional object, **entendre en** 'be good at', 'know all about' something:

Hi entenen moltíssim en matemàtiques.
They are very good at mathematics.

No li parlis d'art, que no hi entén.
Don't talk to her about art; she knows nothing about it.

When no object is specified, **entendre** is pronominalized in this context:

No m'hi entenc gens.   I can't work any of this out.

23.10   PRONOMINAL VERBS WITH SPECIALIZED USES AND MEANINGS

Distinct differences of nuance can be observed between non-pronominal and pronominal uses of certain verbs in different contexts:

(i)   **morir(-se)** 'die'
The pronominal form **morir-se** tends to be used when the cause of death is not specified, and in figurative senses. Accidental or deliberately caused death is expressed by **morir**, the non-pronominal form generally being preferred in formal contexts.

Ha mort el fundador.	The founder has died.
(Es) van morir de fam/en un accident de cotxe.	They died of hunger/in a car crash.
Ha mort cremat.	He was burnt to death.
Aquests arbres es moren tots.	All these trees are dying.
Ens moríem de riure.	We were dying with laughter.

(ii) **trobar(-se)** 'find', 'meet'
Transitive **trobar** means both 'find' and 'meet (by accident)':

He trobat la peça que faltava.	I have found the missing piece.
Saps qui he trobat pel carrer?	Do you know who I met in the street?

Used reciprocally **trobar-se** translates 'meet (by accident or by design)':

Es van trobar tot passejant per la Rambla.
They bumped into each other as they were strolling in the Rambla.

Ens hem de trobar a tres quarts de deu.
We are to meet at 9.45.

Trobar-se amb is an alternative to **trobar** in the sense of 'meet (by accident)', 'come across':

Saps amb qui m'he trobat pel carrer?
Do you know who I met in the street?

Trobar-se can (like French *se trouver*) translate 'be', either expressing location or introducing an adjective:

Jo aleshores em trobava a Lourdes.	At that time I was in Lourdes.
Avui em trobo millor.	I'm better today.

(iii) **veure's** 'be'
Like **trobar-se** with an adjective, this verb can translate 'be':

S'hi ha vist ben confós.	He was quite confused by it.

(iv) **guanyar(-se)** 'earn', 'win'
Guanyar generally translates both 'earn' and 'win':

No guanyen més de 100.000 pessetes la setmana.
They don't earn more than 100,000 pesetas a week.

Ha guanyat el primer premi.
She has won first prize.

Guanyar-se is used metaphorically and in contexts where the object is being emphasized:

S'han guanyat el respecte de tothom.
They have earned everybody's respect.

En aquesta operació, s'hi pensa guanyar una fortuna.
He intends to make a fortune in this operation.

(v) **riure('s)** 'laugh'
This verb is pronominalized only when the sense is that of 'laugh at', 'mock':

Tothom reia.	Everybody was laughing.
Tothom es reia d'ell.	Everybody was making fun of him.

The transitive use of **riure** meaning 'laugh at (something amusing)' is highly regarded (**Tothom reia els seus acudits** 'Everyone laughed at their jokes'), but popular usage resorts to **riure's de** with this meaning.

(vi) **estar(-se)** (variations on) 'be'
On the function of **estar** translating 'be', see Chapter 30. The pronominal form of this verb is (notionally) optional in virtually all sentences where the meaning is 'be/stay (for a given period of time)'. Pronominalization often gives force to the idea of 'staying':

M'estic en una pensió a la Plaça Major.
I'm staying in a *pension* in the Plaça Major.

Aviat serem a Reus: no ens hi estarem, però, més de dues hores.
We'll soon be in Reus: we shan't be staying there for more than two hours, though.

In some dialects this sense of 'stay' extends to that of 'live'/'reside':

Actualment (s')està al carrer Nàpols.
He lives at present in Nàpols Street.

Note that **estar-se de**, followed by an infinitive, means 'refrain from':

El metge m'ha dit que m'estigui de fumar.
The doctor has told me to stop smoking.

Per mi no us estigueu.
Don't mind me./Don't hesitate on my account.

(vii) Idioms with **prendre's** and **passar-se**:
Prendre 'take' is always pronominalized when it is used in expressions with the sense of 'adopt an attitude':

No t'ho prenguis tan seriosament.	Don't take it so seriously.
Prengui-s'ho amb calma.	Take it easy.

Pronominal **passar-se** always occurs with **bé**, **malament**, and certain other adverbs in idioms referring to 'enjoyment'. Basically **passar-s'ho bé** means 'have a good time', 'enjoy oneself' and **passar-s'ho malament** means the opposite:

M'ho vaig passar molt bé, en aquella excursió.
I had a really good time on that walk.

Entre tot plegat, ens ho vam passar malament.
With one thing and another, we didn't enjoy ourselves.

(viii) **Asseure's, ajeure's,** and **adormir-se** are the action verbs (with punctual meaning 'sit down', 'lie down', 'go to sleep') corresponding to the stative verbs **seure** 'sit'/'be seated', **jeure** 'lie', **dormir** 'sleep'/'be asleep'.

S'ha assegut a la cadira.
She sat (down) in the chair.

Ha segut a la cadira tot el matí.
She sat in the chair all morning.

S'ajeien damunt l'arena cada cop que es trobaven cansats.
They lay down on the sand whenever they felt tired.

Jeien damunt l'arena cada matí.
They lay on the sand every morning./They used to lie . . .

S'ha adormit a la cadira.
She fell asleep in the chair.

Ha dormit a la cadira tot el matí.
She slept in the chair all morning.

PART IV: SENTENCE TYPES: SIMPLE AND COMPLEX

24 INTERJECTIONS AND IDEOPHONES

24.1 INTERJECTIONS

This field being one of the most unstable parts of the grammar due to continuous creation and change, we cannot offer more than a selection of the most common expressions in Catalan. (It is observed that interjections very frequently occur in conjunction with exclamations, which are covered in **27.2**.) When one of these expressions seems to be limited to a given area we indicate Central, Val(encia) or Bal(earic Islands) after it. Translations, where we supply them, are approximate. In many cases communicative equivalents, from within the semantic area indicated by the heading, will be determined by the context.

Admiration, surprise

Ai, ai!, **Ui!**, **Bufa!**	Cor!
Ai!	Oh dear!/Whoops!
Carai!/Caram!/Caratsus!	Gosh!/Blimey!
Hala!, **Mira!**, **Mi-te'l!** (Central)	
(or **Mi-te'ls!**, **Mi-te-la!**, etc.), **I ara!**	Never!
Oh!, **Ah!**, **Apa!** (Central)	Go on!
Renoi! (Central)	Crikey!
Vaja!/Què dius ara?	Get away!
Ves que tal! (Bal.), **Xe!** (Val.), **Uep!** (Bal.),	
Déu meu!/Déu mevet!/Mare de Déu!	Goodness me!/Heavens above!

After another person's deserved punishment or bother

Elis, elis! (children's taunt)	
Més te'n mereixes/més te'n mereix!	Serves you/him right!
T'ho has ben cercat!, **Ja t'està bé!**, **fort!** (Bal.)	

Answering the telephone

Digui?, **Digueu?**, **Digau?** (Bal.)	Hello.

Apology

Perdó.	Sorry.
Perdona./Perdoni./Perdoneu.	I'm sorry.
Disculpa./Disculpi./Disculpeu.	I'm sorry.
Ho sento molt.	I'm very sorry.

Calling attention

Ei!, Ep!, Alto!	Hold it, Stop.
Auxili!, Socors!, Ajuda!, Adjutori!	Help!

Confirmation (emphatic)

Això mateix!	Quite right./Exactly.
Ja ho crec!	Of course.
I tant!	Indeed.
Déu n'hi do!	(see **24.1.1**).

Disapproval, dissent

Ca!, Bah!, Fora!, Fuig!, De cap manera!	No way!
I ara!	Never!/Get away with you!
Ni de bon tros!	Not likely!
Per aquestes!, Ni així!, Ca barret!, Bon vent (i barca nova)!	On your bike!

Encouragement

Ànim!, Apa!, Força!, (Au) vinga/vénga!, Som-hi! (see **24.1.1**), **Amunt!, Au idò!** (Bal.)

(**Vinga!** is used as a farewell greeting in Girona; **au idò!** (Bal.) is also a farewell greeting.)

Enough

Prou!, Ja està bé!, Ja n'hi ha!	Enough.

Good wishes

Enhorabona!/Felicitats!	Congratulations!
(Per) molts (d')anys!	Happy birthday!/Many happy returns!
Salut (i força)!	Cheers! (in toasts), Good health!

Bon Nadal i any nou!	Merry Christmas and a Happy New Year.
Records!/Memòries! (Bal.)	Regards, Best wishes.

The usual answer to **records** or **memòries** is **de part teva/seva/vostra**.

Happiness ('Yippee!')

Oidà! (Central), **Hurra!**, **Visca!**

Incredulity

Ca!, **Apa!**, **Bah!**, **Hala vés!**, **No serà tant!**, **Vols dir?**	Really?
No fotis!	Come off it!

Oaths and curses ('damn!', etc.)

Vatua!, **Vatua el món!**, **Hòstia!**, **Putes!** (vulgar), **Punyeta!** (familiar), **Mal llamp! Rellamp!**, **(Me) cago en . . . !**, **Dimoni!**, **Diantre!**

Hòstia! is vulgar. It is often substituted by the euphemisms **Ostres!**, **Òstima!**, **O estimada meva!** **(Me) cago en . . . . !** is also vulgar. It can be replaced by the euphemism **(Me) caso en . . . !**

Pain ('ouch!')

Ai!, **Oi oi!**, **Ui!**

Oi-oi is also a children's word for 'pain'.

Please

per favor, si vols/vol/volen	if you would (be so kind)
si et/li/us plau	(if you) please (see **28.4**)

Putting at ease

No t'amoïnis./No s'amoïni./No us amoïneu.	Don't trouble.
No et preocupis./No es preocupi./No us preocupeu.	Don't worry.
Tranquil./Tranquil·la.	Take it easy! (with gender corresponding to the person addressed)
No pateixis./No pateixi./No patiu! **Fora nirvis!** (Bal.)	Don't worry!/Never mind!
Tu mateix(a)./Vostè mateix(a)./Vosaltres mateixos/-es.	Help yourself/yourselves./Go ahead.

Resignation

Què hi farem? (lit. What are we to do about it?)

Revulsion

Ecs!	Ugh!/Yuck!
Quin fàstic!, Quin oi! (Bal.)	How disgusting!/How revolting!

Salutations

Two systems of greetings exist in Catalan, the continental and the Balearic:

Continental: **bon dia** 'good morning', **bona tarda** (Central)/**bona vesprada** (Val.) 'good afternoon', **bona nit** 'good evening', 'good night'.

Balearic: **bon dia** 'good day' i.e. 'good morning' or 'good afternoon', **bon vespre** 'good evening' as opening greeting; **bona nit** 'good night', or as a greeting exchanged when passing someone without stopping.

General greetings used all day are **hola** 'hello', **adéu** or **adéu-siau** 'goodbye'. **Uep!** is also used in Balearic instead of **hola**. **Com està/estàs/esteu/estan?, Com va?**, or **Com anam?** (Bal.), are equivalents of 'How are you?' (**Com va?** is conjugated in Northern Catalonia, i.e., **Com vas?/Com aneu?**)

Silence

Pst!, Silenci!, Calla!/Calleu!

Sympathy

Quina llàstima!
What a pity!/How sad! (for general purposes)

Us/T'/L'acompanyo en el sentiment.
You have my sympathy/condolences.

Que en el cel el/la vegem./Que pugueu pregar molts d'anys per ell/ella. (at funerals)
May we see him/her in heaven./May you be able to pray for him/her for many years.

Talking to large animals

Arri!	Gee up!
Oixque!	Go to the left
Ollaó!	Go to the right

Xo!	Whoa!
Ou!	Stop! (Bal.)
Arruix!	Go away! (for any kind of animal, Bal.)

Thanks

Gràcies./Mercès.	Thank you.
Moltes gràcies.	Many thanks.
De res.	You're welcome.
No hi ha per a tant.	Don't mention it.
No s'ho val. (less common)	Don't mention it.

Thanks are expressed less commonly and less elaborately in Catalan than in English.

Threats

| **Ja veuràs!** | You'll see! |
| **Sols que m'entenguis!** | Understand! (used in Balearic after an explicit threat) |

Warnings

| **Ves amb compte!** | Be careful! |
| **Atenció!**, **Compte!**, **Alerta!**, (non-standard) **Cuidado!** | Careful!, Look out! |

Alertar can be conjugated as an intransitive verb in this use in Bal.; thus, you say **alerta!** for the 2nd person singular and **alertau!** for the 2nd person plural.

Wishes and curses

Tant de bo + complement clause (verb in subjunctive, see **19.6**):

| **Tant de bo que plogui aviat.** | It would be nice if it rained soon. |

If the wish is hostile, then **mal** + curse (verb in subjunctive):

| **Mal et pegués un llamp a sobre!** | May you be struck by lightning! |

24.1.1 SOME SPECIAL INTERJECTIONS

Certain interjections are characteristic of specific conversational contexts, and, being very typical of colloquial Catalan, merit separate comment here.

I tant! and **I tant que . . . !** communicate emphatic affirmation, agreement with or confirmation of an idea just expressed:

–T'han agradat els regals? –I tant (que m'han agradat)!
'Did you like the presents?' 'I certainly did!'

Si m'ho torna a dir, m'enfadaré de debò. I tant que m'enfadaré!
If he says that to me again I'll get really cross. I sure will!

Home! literally 'man!' appears frequently in exclamations of encouragement or surprise, or simply as a means of reinforcing what is being said (repetition often being the English equivalent):

Corre, home!, que farem tard!	Get a move on, man! We're going to be late.
Sí, home!, sí!	Yes, of course!
Home, podria haver estat molt pitjor.	It really could have been a lot worse.

The interjection **home!** may be addressed to a woman, but **dona!** is also available as alternative in this case:

No t'hi amoïnis, dona!	Don't let it bother you, dear!
Sí, dona!, sí.	Yes, of course!

The emphatic affirmation **sí, senyor(a)!** 'yes, yes'/'yes, of course!' is also worth observing in this context.

Déu n'hi do! is used to stress, with moderation, both quantity or quality:

–Tens gana? –Home, Déu n'hi do!
'Are you hungry?' 'Well, yes I am quite.'

–És gaire lluny? –Déu n'hi do! No hi seran pas abans de mitjanit.
'Is it far?' 'It's a good way off. They won't be there before midnight.'

This expression may be bound syntactically into a sentence by use of **que**:

El xaval aquell juga que Déu n'hi do!
That lad is a pretty good player.

Hi fan uns plats que Déu n'hi do!
They cook some rather good dishes there.

A diminutive form **Déu n'hi doret!** is also heard:

Déu n'hi doret com canatava aquella!	That woman really could sing!

Xe! is stereotypically Valencian, being in that dialect the equivalent of **home!** (see above) in communicating a wide range of responses or emphases: surprise, enthusiasm, pleasure, anger, etc.

Xe! Quina alegria!	How very pleased I am!

Ves (per on)! (from **veure** 'see') expresses true or feigned surprise:

Vaig regirar tots els calaixos buscant la clau i, ves per on, la tenia a la butxaca.
I turned the drawers inside out looking for the key and, would you believe it, it was in my pocket.

Rai (Central; in Val. and Bal. **res** takes the place of **rai**) is used to deny or play down the importance of something just said. For example:

–Ha perdut la feina. –La feina rai, mentre tingui salut.
'She has lost her job.' 'The job doesn't matter, as long as her health is good.'

–Enguany no guanyarem la Copa d'Europa. –La Copa d'Europa rai, hem de concentrar-nos en la lliga.
'We shan't win the European Cup this year.' 'Never mind the European Cup; we need to concentrate on the league.'

The second-person subject pronoun **tu!** often occurs as an interjection in colloquial expressions of admiration or surprise:

Va ser genial, tu!
It was really brilliant!

Han vingut molts més dels que ens esperàvem: una invasió, tu!
Many more have turned up than we expected: we've been over-run!

Mare meva! and **Mare de Déu!** (the latter slightly blasphemous) can be independent interjections or can support other exclamatory utterances:

I tant, Mare de Déu!, i tant!
Not half, Good Heavens! Not half!/You can say that again!

Som-hi? 'ready?' is used to ask, generally in an encouraging way, if someone is ready to take action; the positive response is **(Sí) som-hi!** 'OK'/'Ready when you are'/'Let's go'/'Let's do it then'. **Som-hi!** alone expresses willingness to act or encouragement to others to act.

24.2 IDEOPHONES

Ideophones constitute a differentiated class of words which typically express either distinctive sounds (basically onomatopoeic) or visually distinctive types of action. Ideophones often exhibit peculiar phonological features, such as segments not occurring in any other word formation. Reduplication and vowel alternation are characteristics of such items. Catalan has a particularly rich repertoire of ideophones, as illustrated in the following sample:

(i)   Basically onomatopoeic ideophones:

bum-bum	represents boom or a booming sound.
catric-catrac	represents clatter or rattle (of machinery).
cloc-cloc	represents clucking (of hen) or clucking sound.
fru-fru	represents rustle (of fabrics) or similar rustling sound.
nyic-nyic	represents an irritatingly persistent (and high-pitched) sound.
nyigo-nyigo	represents the sound of an out-of-tune or badly played stringed instrument.
nyac/nyaca	represents the impact of two things colliding.
ning-nang	represents the sound of a (large) bell.
ning-ning	represents the sound of a (small) bell.
tiro-liro	represents squeak of a wind instrument.
xerric-xerrac	represents a harshly grating sound.
xiu-xiu	represents indistinct whispering or muttering sounds.
xup-xup	represents a gentle bubbling sound.

All of the above can function as nouns, while many can be adverbial, for example:

el xiu-xiu del ventijol
the whispering of the breeze

Tot el sant dia estan xiu-xiu i segur que maquinen alguna cosa.
All day long they talk secretively among themselves and they're obviously plotting something.

(ii) Noun ideophones:

un(a) baliga-balaga	an irresponsible person
fer cofis-i-mofis	get up to no good/sly tricks (two or more people)
tenir cori-mori	have heartburn/pain in the chest
un farrigo-farraga	a bad mix-up
fer la gara-gara	flatter/butter up
un pengim-penjam	an untidily dressed person
(also adverbial:	
caminar pengim-penjam	shamble awkwardly)
un poti-poti	confusion/confused situation/untidy mess
el rau-rau	nagging conscience (from onomatopoeia of rubbing or grating)
Sentia un rau-rau al cor.	He felt a nagging regret in his heart.
un tol·le-tol·le	(collective expression of protest or indignation)
fer la viu-viu	get by as best one can

(iii) Adverbial ideophones:

banzim-banzam	tottering, moving unsteadily from side to side
(pagar) bitllo-bitllo	(pay) in cash, on the nail
leri-leri	very near (to)
El cor encara li bat però està leri-leri de morir.	His heart is still beating but he is very close to death.
de nyigui-nyogui	badly or carelessly constructed
nyic-i-nyac	in constant and niggling disagreement
tau-tau	moderately well
La cosa ha anat tau-tau.	It's gone OK.
xano-xano/xino-xano	at a deliberately steady or slow (walking) pace

25 SIMPLE SENTENCES AND GRAMMATICAL RELATIONS

25.1 SIMPLE SENTENCES

Typical simple sentences consist of a verb and one or more arguments, that is, phrases that must be present for the sentence to be grammatical. Intransitive verbs are constructed with just one argument: the subject noun phrase, as in **Ha arribat el tren?** 'Has the train arrived?' A few intransitive verbs (weather verbs) normally have not even a subject, e.g. **Nevava** 'It snowed'. Transitive verbs (using this term in a broad sense) are those that are constructed with more than one argument, for example, with a subject and a direct object noun phrase, as in **El tren portava les bigues** 'The train brought the girders'; with a subject and an indirect object phrase, as in **Li agraden els pastissos** 'He likes cakes' (lit. 'Cakes please to him') with a subject noun phrase and a locative phrase, as in **Nosaltres vam anar a Grècia** 'We went to Greece'; with a subject, a direct, and an indirect object, as in **L'Enric va oferir una rosa a la Rosa** 'Enric offered Rosa a rose'; with a subject, a direct object, and a locative phrase, as in **Fuster va posar les mans a la taula** 'Fuster put his hands on the table'. Less often, verbs take other types of arguments, for example, a prepositional phrase with a specified preposition, as in **fiar-se de** 'trust' (lit. 'trust oneself of '): **El nostre fill no es fia dels seus amics** 'Our son does not trust his friends'; or a verb may take as complement a manner adverbial, as with **portar-se** 'behave': **Es portaven molt malament** 'They behaved very badly'; or a nominal complement, as in **Els catalans el van elegir president** 'The Catalans elected him president' (where **el** is the direct object and **president** is the nominal complement). Copular verbs (Chapter 30) fall outside the major transitive/intransitive dichotomy.

In addition to a verb and its arguments (which either must be present or may only be absent in narrowly specified circumstances), sentences may contain adverbial or prepositional phrase adjuncts, specifying place, time, manner, etc., as in:

> *Ahir* no vaig poder llegir *gaire bé* el diari *a casa d'en Miquel.*
> Yesterday I couldn't read the paper very well at Miquel's house.

25.2 SUBJECTS

25.2.1 PERSONAL AND IMPERSONAL SUBJECTS

The subject pronouns (**11.1**) are not required to be present, since finite verbs largely indicate what the subject is by means of inflections (see **11.5.1**). Even where a verb form would in itself be ambiguous (as **Sentia** 'I/he/she/you (*sg.* polite) heard'), subject pronouns are used only to avoid real ambiguity. The subject pronouns are used when there is an explicit or implied contrast:

Jo he demanat peix, tu has demanat arròs, i ells han demanat bistecs.
I asked for fish, you asked for paella, and they asked for steaks.

Among intransitive verbs there are some whose subjects share some features with the objects of transitive verbs. In particular, indefinite or quantified noun phrases can be pronominalized with **en** (**12.6v**). These intransitive verbs are called 'unaccusative'; the subjects of other intransitive verbs, or of transitive verbs, cannot be represented by **en**.

N'arribaven tres, de vaques.   Three cows arrived.

Observe that **En menjaven tres, de vaques** cannot mean 'Three cows were eating' (but only 'Cows, they were eating three of them'). It is only with such unaccusative constructions that, in the perfect tense with **haver**, the participle may agree in number and gender with the clitic pronoun **en** representing the subject (**21.1.2**):

Van arribar tres vaques, i ara n'han arribades moltes més.
Three cows arrived, and now many more have arrived.

An unspecified or generic (impersonal) subject is usually expressed with the reflexive pronoun **es** and a third-person verb. See Chapter 29 for detailed discussion of impersonal **es** and related constructions.

Es creu que no en vindran gaires.
It is thought not many will come.

No es podia trobar una biblioteca adequada.
You/One couldn't find an adequate library.

In literary varieties the impersonal subject pronoun **hom** is also used:

Ací hom treballa molt.   Here one works hard.

In impersonal constructions with **es**, when the verb is transitive and the object is plural, the verb agrees in number with the object. Historically the semantic object became the grammatical subject (whence number agreement) and the reflexive pronoun **es** bore the role of the grammatical direct object. However, it is debatable whether such an analysis is realistic for the contemporary language.

A Catalunya, s'hi mengen bones patates.
In Catalonia people eat good potatoes./Good potatoes can be eaten. (orig.
Good potatoes eat themselves.)

No es troben raons suficients.
You/One can't find adequate reasons.

25.2.2   SUBJECTLESS IMPERSONAL VERBS

The verbs **haver** and **ser** present particular uses in their third-person singular
forms. Such constructions have no grammatical subject or, in logic, a subject
which is so indefinite as to be indeterminate.

Translating relevant tenses of 'there is', **haver** always takes the adverbial
clitic **hi**, so that in this context the infinitive is considered to be **haver-hi** (see
30.1). The words accompanying **hi ha**, etc., stand formally as direct object of
the verb:

Hi ha tres possibilitats.
There are three possibilities.

No hi podia haver hagut cap altra manera d'aconseguir-ho.
There could not have been any other way of achieving it.

In standard Catalan this impersonal construction with **haver-hi** admits only
the singular form (**Hi ha tres possibilitats**). In most dialects, however, including those of the major cities, the tendency to make the verb agree with
a plural complement is quite deeply rooted, even in educated speech (a phenomenon not dissimilar from English 'there's' + plural noun, and comparably
tolerable):

Hi havien molts errors. (standard **Hi havia . . .**)
There were a lot of mistakes.

Poden haver-hi circumstàncies atenuants. (standard **Pot haver-hi . . .**)
There may be attenuating circumstances.

Haver appears without **hi** in the archaic temporal expression **temps ha** 'some
time ago', although temporal expressions meaning 'ago' (see **33.2.2**) are usually made with subjectless **fer** standing before the elapsed time referred to: **fa
molt de temps/tres mesos** 'a long time/three months ago'.

The principal cases for observing the impersonal use of **ser** are expressions
like:

És aviat/tard.   It's early/late.
Ja era de nit.   It was already night(time).

Impersonal constructions involving **ser** with a noun, adjective, or infinitive
complement, or **ser** followed by a clause, conform to a similar logic by which
the notional subject can be understood to be an indeterminate 'it'.

És curiós; fa un moment ho deia jo.
It's odd; I was saying it just a moment ago.

Subjectless impersonal expressions of weather conditions

While there are some verbs denoting specific weather conditions or phenomena (and their metaphorical application) – **ploure** 'rain' (**Plou molt al Pirineu**
'It rains a lot in the Pyrenees'), **nevar** 'snow', **tronar** 'thunder' – **fer** 'do',
'make' is used in general descriptions of the weather: **Fa bo** 'It's nice weather',
Fa sol 'It's sunny', **Fa núvol**, 'It's cloudy', **Fa un dia lleig/esplèndid** 'It's an
awful/splendid day'. (The subject of these expressions is understood to be 'the
weather', and thus agreement is not generally found with a plural complement: **Fa dies bons** 'It's been nice these last few days'. Agreement does occur,
though, when verbs of weather are used figuratively:

Plovien elogis de totes bandes.   Praises rained down from all directions.

Fer is also used pronominally to express changes in the weather or in atmospheric conditions: **S'ha fet fosc** 'It's gone/turned dark', **S'ha fet clar** 'It has
become daylight'. Cloudy conditions are also expressed by **ennuvolar-se**
'become cloudy', 'cloud over' or **estar núvol** 'be cloudy'.

Other subjectless impersonal expressions: *caldre*, *diu*

The impersonal verb **caldre** 'be necessary' exists only (all tenses) in the third
person. It can be followed by a noun, by an infinitive, or by a clause (with the
verb always in the subjunctive).

Cal una eina per descargolar.	What's needed is a tool for unscrewing.
Calia temps i molta paciència.	Time and a lot of patience were necessary.
No cal patir.	There's no need to be upset.
Ens ha calgut enllestir-ho avui.	We have had to finish it today.
Cal que ens ho diguis aviat.	You must tell us soon.

With a plural noun complement either the singular or the plural form of
caldre is equally acceptable in sentences like:

Calia/Calien molts diners.	A lot of money was necessary.
Cal/Calen més cadires.	More chairs are needed.

(This contrasts with uncertainty over the acceptability of plural agreement
with **haver-hi**, discussed above.) The impersonal verbal phrase **fer falta** is
synonymous with **caldre**.

Reporting of fact or opinion can be prefaced by **Diu que** 'It is said that . . ./
The saying goes . . . ', favoured in colloquial usage over **Diuen que** or **Es diu que**:

Diu que demà hi haurà vaga.
The word is that there'll be a strike tomorrow.

25.3   DIRECT OBJECTS

Personal pronouns have unstressed (clitic) direct object forms distinct from subject forms (Chapter 12). Other noun phrases generally take no special form as direct objects, but the preposition **a** is used before direct object noun phrases in certain limited contexts. See **14.1.1.1** for details. To the cases mentioned there we may add that dislocated (Chapter 36) direct object phrases which denote people require the preposition **a**:

A Kristeva i als seus seguidors, els preocupaven més les implicacions semiòtiques.
Kristeva and her followers were more concerned with the semiotic implications.

–Satisfà que hi hagi un comitè de direcció? –A molts escriptors, no.
'Is it enough that there should be a management committee?' 'For many writers, it isn't.' (lit. Does it satisfy . . . ? (To) many writers, no.)

Ja sé com l'hai d'amoixar, a Na Rosó. (J. Ruyra)
Now I know how to flatter her, (that is,) Rosó.

In Balearic this usage extends to inanimate direct objects which are left-dislocated:

A ses tovalloles, posa-les dins es calaix.   Put the napkins in the drawer.

A personal pronoun direct object must always be represented by a clitic pronoun, even if a stressed personal pronoun is also present:

El veurem a ell avui, i et veurem a tu demà.
We shall see him today, and we shall see you tomorrow.
(Not ***Veurem a ell . . .**)

No ens han informat a nosaltres de les beques que vam sol·licitar.
They haven't informed *us* about the scholarships we applied for.
(**No ens han informat de les beques . . .** is normal, though less emphatic; ***No han informat a nosaltres . . .** is ungrammatical.)

In Catalan, much more usually than in English, a generic or impersonal direct object ('people', 'you', 'one') may be totally absent, as in the second example in this section, **Satisfà que hi hagi . . . ?**

Aquella proposta no convenç.
That suggestion is unconvincing. (lit. does not persuade)

El soroll no deixa dormir.
The noise doesn't let you/people sleep.

La situació a Bòsnia preocupa molt.
The Bosnian situation is very worrying.

25.4   INDIRECT OBJECTS

Except in the third person, the indirect object unstressed (clitic) personal pronouns are the same as the direct object ones (**12.3.2.3**). The third-person indirect object clitics are **li** (*sg.*) and **els/los** (*pl.*, both genders). Stressed indirect object pronouns, and other types of indirect object noun phrases, are marked with the preposition **a**.

El govern no concedeix prou importància als petits empresaris.
The government does not grant enough importance to small businessmen.

El govern no els concedeix prou importància.
The government does not grant them enough importance.

As with direct objects, a personal pronoun indirect object must always be represented by a clitic pronoun, even if a stressed personal pronoun is also present:

No li han ensenyat a vostè les cartes que Foix em va escriure?
Have they not shown you the letters Foix wrote me?

Després us ho explicarem a vosaltres.
Afterwards we'll explain it to *you*.

In certain cases, though not all, – the constraints are not yet well understood – an indirect object which is inanimate can be represented by the 'locative' clitic **hi**. This usage is illustrated in **12.7ii**.

When an indirect object phrase is placed before the verb, in a dislocation construction, it is usual to 'double' it with a clitic pronoun.

A l'home(,) l'experiència li ha ensenyat . . .
Man has learnt by experience. (lit. To man, experience has taught him . . .)

Als meus germans, això no els importa gaire.
My brothers and sisters are not very worried about that. (lit. To my brothers, that does not matter much to them.)

In informal styles, this pattern of clitic doubling occurs also in relative clauses and *wh*-questions, and even when the phrasal indirect object is in its normal post-verbal position. Some grammarians regard this not just as informal, but as non-standard.

?A qui li enviarem la llista de preus.	Who shall we send the price list to?
?els clients a qui els vam enviar la llista	the customers we sent the list to
?L'Enric li va donar una rosa a la Rosa.	Enric gave a rose to Rosa.
?Li ho direm al teu germà.	We will tell your brother. (lit. We will tell him it to your brother.)

There are a few so-called dative subject verbs which have an indirect object but no direct object. Their grammatical subject is typically inanimate and their grammatical indirect object is normally animate. These verbs require an indirect object clitic to be present, wherever the indirect object phrase happens to be placed. (The clitic can only be omitted if the understood indirect object is generic/impersonal.) Examples of such verbs are **plaure** 'please', **agradar** 'please'/'like', **convenir** 'suit', 'be appropriate', **escaure** 'suit', 'fit', 'become', **faltar** 'be lacking', **mancar** 'be lacking', **sobrar** 'be in excess', **semblar** 'seem', **parèixer** 'seem', **passar** 'happen', **acudir-se** 'occur':

> **Les persones a qui no els agrada l'aigua mineral amb gas n'hauran de beure de l'aixeta.**
> People who don't like fizzy mineral water will have to drink tap water.

> **la Júlia, a qui no li faltava coratge . . .**
> Julia, who did not lack courage . . .

> **A en Jaume no li sobraven recursos.**
> Jaume hadn't an excess of resources.

> **No li sobraven recursos(,) a en Jaume.**
> Jaume hadn't an excess of resources.

> **Al cotxe li faltava una roda.**
> The car had a wheel missing.

> **Mira a veure què els sembla als de producció aquesta foto.**
> Look and see what those in production think of this photo. (lit. . . . what seems to them to those of production . . .)

> **No falten propostes.**
> There is no shortage of suggestions. (omitted indirect object generic/impersonal)

As well as indicating the recipient of a verbal action (**Envia'm els documents** 'Send *me* the documents', **Us donaré un consell** 'I'll give *you* a piece of advice'), the indirect object pronoun can also indicate different ways in which a person is affected by what a verb phrase expresses. The actual way in which the person is affected is deduced from the meaning of the verb, from context or by common sense. Translation into English (not always comfortably possible) may involve a variety of prepositions according to detail of meaning or implication. The range of such nuances is exemplified in the following examples:

Us han deixat una fortuna.	They have left a fortune *to* you.
Em reservaran una habitació.	They will book a room *for* me.
Em van treure quatre bales.	They took four bullets *out of* me.
M'ha robat el cor.	She has stolen my heart *away.*

No us haurien de tenir enveja.	They ought not to be jealous *of* you.
Va tirar-me un objecte contundent.	He threw a sharp object *at* me.
Em provocà una reacció forta.	It produced a strong reaction *in* me.
Em van trobar un carnet de partit.	They found a party card *on* me.
Em van tirar una flassada al damunt.	They threw a blanket *over* me.
Per què no et compres un d'aquests?	Why don't you buy *yourself* one of these?
Sempre han de posar-nos entrebancs.	They always have to put obstacles *in our* way.

In Catalan, when a direct object is possessed by a person, it is normal to express the possessor as an indirect object of the verb in question; when the possession is inalienable this is the only idiomatic way to construct the sentence (see **7.4.1**):

Van pintar la casa de blau a aquest senyor.	They painted this man's house blue.
El dentista va treure una dent a la Núria.	The dentist removed one of Nuria's teeth.
Es va posar les mans al cap.	She put her hands on her head. (lit. She put to herself the hands on the head.)
No ens tocaran els llibres.	They won't touch our books.
No m'haurà vist la cara.	She won't have seen my face.
M'han trencat el braç.	They have broken my arm.

Similarly with possessed subjects of intransitive verbs:

Em cauen els cabells.	My hair is falling out.
Li rodava el cap.	His head was swimming.
Se'ns ha mort el lloro.	Our parrot has died (on us).

The foreign learner will need to appreciate that the Catalan indirect object has a range of functions far wider and more nuanced than that of the simple dative (**Ens ha parlat en francès** 'He spoke to us in French'), in order to be able to generate naturally expressions like **M'han robat la cartera** 'They have stolen my wallet' and others as illustrated above.

A further function of the grammatical indirect object is the so-called ethic dative (a pronominal clitic referring to a person involved in or affected by a situation, see **23.1**), which itself has multiple nuances.

El gos no em menja.
The dog won't eat.

Les plantes em creixien tortes.
My plants grew twisted./The plants grew twisted, in my case.

Aquella al·lota em camina d'una manera provocadora.
That girl walks in a provocative way (I find/it seems to me/in my experience).

25.4.1   PROBLEMATIC OR DISPUTED INDIRECT OBJECT CONSTRUCTIONS

There are several verbs for which the choice between direct and indirect object is not obvious, or is a matter of variation, or of dispute between grammarians. Some verbs which may in standard Catalan be constructed with either a direct or an indirect object, often with some difference in meaning, are: **advertir** 'warn (somebody of something)', 'point out (something to somebody)', **al·ludir** 'allude to', **contestar** 'contest'/'reject'/'protest against', 'answer'/'reply to', **cridar** 'call', 'call (out) to'/'shout to', **manar** 'order (someone to do something)', 'be in charge of'/'rule over', **obeir** 'obey', **pagar** 'pay', **pregar** 'request'/'ask', **renunciar** 'renounce', 'relinquish', **resistir** 'resist', 'bear', **robar** 'steal', **succeir** 'succeed'. The construction of these verbs needs to be consulted in a dictionary.

For the construction of verbs of permitting and prohibiting, see **25.5** below.

Three verbs which are transitive in meaning: **pegar** 'strike', **telefonar** 'telephone', and **trucar** 'call' are constructed with indirect objects in the standard language: **Li pegues** 'You strike him/her', **Li telefones** 'You telephone him/her', **Li truques** 'You call him/her'. Construction of these verbs with direct objects is common in informal styles.

No li (la) peguis.
Don't hit her.

Són les seves filles i no els (les) hauria de pegar.
They're his daughters and he ought not to beat them.

Li he (l'he) de trucar avui.
I've got to phone her today.

Note that, whereas most verbs denoting vocal activity – speaking, shouting, singing, and so on – take the hearer as an indirect object, **xiular** 'whistle (at)', 'call by whistling' takes only a direct object:

Si no el xiules, no et veurà.	If you don't whistle (at him), he won't see you.
Com les han xiulades, les actrius!	How they whistled at the actresses!

Several verbs of 'mental affect' have inanimate subjects and an indirect object of the person affected: **agradar** 'please', **coure** 'hurt', **doldre** 'grieve', **plaure** 'please', **remordir** 'cause remorse', **repugnar** 'revolt', **saber greu** 'cause regret' and **xocar** 'shock'. Many others, similar in meaning to these, in standard

Catalan have the person affected as direct object, but in non-standard usage may be found with indirect objects by analogy with the verbs mentioned above. The following are the ones that take only direct objects in standard Catalan:

afectar	affect	**estranyar**	surprise	**meravellar**	astonish
amoïnar	upset	**fascinar**	fascinate	**molestar**	bother
apassionar	thrill	**fastiguejar**	sicken,	**neguitejar**	worry
complaure	gratify		weary	**preocupar**	worry
concernir	concern	**horroritzar**	horrify	**rebentar**	rile
disgustar	disgust	**impressionar**	impress	**satisfer**	satisfy
emprenyar	annoy	**incomodar**	inconvenience	**sorprendre**	surprise
	(vulgar)	**indignar**	anger		

The verbs **encantar** 'charm', 'delight' and **interessar** 'interest' also take direct objects, but some authoritative dictionaries allow indirect objects as an alternative.

L'òpera les/els encantava.	They were very fond of opera.
Li encanta/L'encanta (de) passejar.	She loves strolling.
Això ja no li/?la interessa.	She isn't interested in this any more.
A qui l'interessa/li interessa visitar el palau?	Who is interested in visiting the palace?

25.5   VALENCY

In Catalan there are several means of reducing or increasing the number of arguments of a verb. The passive is a well-known way of reducing the number of arguments of a transitive verb, by removing the subject (Chapter 29). The impersonal with **es** has a similar function (Chapter 29). Or a transitive verb may become intransitive by being used pronominally (**23.1**). In some cases, many fewer than in English, the same verb can be used transitively and intransitively, with the transitive object becoming the intransitive subject, for example, **bullir** 'boil', **coure** 'cook', **penjar** 'hang'.

Bullim oli.	We are boiling oil.
L'oli bull.	The oil is boiling.
Hem penjat les claus a la paret.	We hung the keys on the wall.
Les claus pengen de la paret.	The keys are hanging on the wall.

Also as in English, some transitive verbs can become 'intransitive' by leaving the direct object unspecified. Examples are **beure** 'drink', **conduir** 'conduct', 'drive', lead', **estudiar** 'study', **llaurar** 'plough', **menjar** 'eat'.

The causative construction is the major way of increasing valency. In Catalan, two verbs are used in this pattern: **fer** 'make', 'get' and **deixar** 'allow', 'let'. The two verbs make use of the same construction which varies depending on whether the caused situation is expressed by an intransitive or by a transitive verb (which appears in the infinitive form).

With intransitive verbs, the original subject of the intransitive verb becomes the direct object of **fer/deixar**; if it is a full noun phrase, its regular position is after the infinitive. If the intransitive verb is normally reflexive, the reflexive pronoun is omitted:

El seu pare deixa treballar l'Emili els dissabtes.
His father lets Emili work on Saturdays.

Les va fer seure davant seu.
He made them (*f.pl.*) sit before him.

Deixarem sortir el camió.
We'll let the lorry come out.

Fes-lo parlar de Granada.
Get him to talk about Granada.

No em diguis això, que em faràs matar.
Don't tell me that, or you'll kill me. (= **Faràs que em mati.**)

El fan agenollar, i després estirar-se a terra.
They make him kneel, and then lie on the ground. (**agenollar-se** 'kneel')

With transitive verbs, the original subject becomes an indirect object; if it is a full noun phrase, its regular position is after the original object(s):

Faré pintar la paret a en Pere.
I'll get Pere to paint the wall.

El capellà li va fer donar diners als pobres.
The priest made him give money to the poor.

Arió va demanar que li deixessin tocar la cítara abans de llançar-lo al mar.
Arion requested that they should allow him to play the cithara before throwing him into the sea.

Essentially what is happening in these constructions with **deixar** and **fer** is that something resembling a compound verb is constructed, the parts of which are kept as close together as possible, and which can have not more than one direct object (though it may have two apparent indirect objects, as in the above example **El capellà li va fer donar diners als pobres**).

The construction of other verbs, sometimes of similar meaning to the above (such as **obligar** 'oblige' and **permetre** 'allow'), which take infinitive complements is rather different. Two patterns can be distinguished. With one group of verbs the infinitive itself (optionally preceded by **de**) acts as the direct object, while the logical subject of the infinitive becomes an indirect object. These verbs are also found constructed with other types of non-infinitive direct object. Examples of verbs of this group are: **aconsellar** 'advise', **demanar** 'request', **impedir** 'prevent', **ordenar** 'order', **permetre** 'allow', **proposar** 'suggest', **suplicar** 'beg':

Li han impedit (d')acostar-s'hi.
They stopped him coming near.

És un art que permet a les dones (d')atènyer la categoria de sublims.
It is a skill which allows women to attain the category of the sublime.

Als compradors, els aconsellem d'estudiar bé les instruccions per al maneig.
We advise purchasers to study the instructions carefully.

Because the logical subject of the infinitive is a surface indirect object, it cannot be directly passivized, hence, for example:

És prohibit als menors de 16 anys de comprar tabac.
not ***Els menors de 16 anys són prohibits de comprar tabac.**
People under 16 years of age are forbidden to buy tobacco. (lit. It is forbidden to those under 16 years to buy tobacco.)

The second group of verbs makes the logical subject of the infinitive into a direct object; the infinitive (like an indirect object) is preceded by **a**. A literal translation of the English passive is possible. Examples of verbs of this type are: **acostumar** 'accustom', **animar** 'encourage', **arrossegar** 'drag', **autoritzar** 'authorize', **avesar** 'accustom', **condemnar** 'condemn', **incitar** 'incite', **invitar** 'invite', **forçar** 'force', **habituar** 'accustom', **predisposar** 'predispose':

Hem d'incitar-les a treballar més bé.	We must stimulate them to work harder.
El va forçar a vestir-se de negre.	She forced him to wear black.
Fou forçat a vestir-se de negre.	He was forced to wear black.

Two verbs, **ajudar** 'help' and **obligar** 'oblige', show a mixed pattern, which recalls that of **deixar/fer**. (Note that in each case the infinitive is preceded by **a**.) If the subordinate verb is intransitive (or reflexive), its subject becomes a direct object of **ajudar/obligar**:

La va obligar a callar.	He made her be silent.
La va ajudar a sortir.	He helped her go out.
El va obligar a retractar-se.	She obliged him to retract.

However, if the subordinate verb is transitive, its subject may become either a direct or an indirect object of **ajudar/obligar**:

Li/La va ajudar a acabar la redacció.	He helped her to finish writing.
Li/La va obligar a firmar el contracte.	He obliged her to sign the contract.

Something similar appears also in constructions with **veure** 'see' and **sentir** 'hear' followed by an infinitive phrase:

El vaig veure entrar.	I saw him go in.
Li vaig veure llençar el rebut.	I saw him throw the receipt away.
La sentiren resar.	They heard her praying.
Li sentiren dir l'oració.	They heard her say the prayer.

This shift into the indirect object is associated with the status of the infinitive complement as the primary or more active object. A certain fluidity about which object is more active, together with the general vacillation between direct and indirect objects seen above, accounts for the frequency with which this norm is infringed, as in sentences like the following:

El mirà amb una estranya lluïssor als ulls sentint-*lo* refusar el sobre.
She watched him with a strange glint in her eyes as she heard him refuse to take the envelope.

Cal dir que mai no *l*'he sentit desqualificar ningú.
It has to be said that I have never heard him exclude anybody.

Ensenyar 'teach' can be followed by either **a** or **de** + infinitive, the logical subject of which may be either the direct or the indirect object of **ensenyar**.

Li ensenyen de caminar de pressa
They are teaching her to walk fast.

Li van ensenyar a ser astuta.
They taught her to be cunning.

Un manual ensenyarà els candidats del PP a explicar el seu programa.
A handbook will teach the PP candidates to explain their programme.

In all these cases, just as mentioned in **25.3**, if the subject of the subordinate verb is generic/indefinite, it can be omitted altogether (see **20.2.2i**):

Un llibre ajuda a triomfar.
A book helps (you) to succeed.

Permet d'atènyer la categoria de sublims.
It allows (you/people) to attain the category of the sublime.

La vam deixar fer.
We allowed it (*f.*) to be done. (lit. We allowed to do it.)

25.6   OTHER ARGUMENTS

As we have already mentioned, a few verbs take as an argument a nominal or adjectival complement which is not an object. The most important of these, the copular verbs **ésser/ser** and **estar**, are treated in Chapter 30. Others are, for example, **aparèixer** 'appear', **continuar** 'continue', **creure's** 'believe oneself', **esdevenir** 'become', **fer-se** 'become', **manifestar-se** 'show oneself', **mostrar-se** 'show oneself', **parèixer** 'seem', **posar-se** + adjective 'become', **quedar(-se)** 'remain', **restar** 'remain', **romandre** 'remain', **seguir** 'continue', **semblar** 'seem', 'look', **tornar-se** 'become'.

> **La maniobra apareixia clara.**
> The manoeuvre appeared clear.

> **Tots ells continuen/segueixen decidits a fer-ho.**
> All of them continue to be determined to do so.

> **Et creus l'àrbitre?**
> Do you think you're the referee? (lit. Do you believe yourself the referee?)

> **En dos anys es va fer advocat.**
> In two years he became a lawyer. (lit. . . . made himself . . .)

The representation of nominal and adjectival complements by clitic pronouns is a complex matter, with considerable variation between native speakers about which pronoun to choose (see **12.5–12.7**).

A few verbs, such as **anar** 'go', **venir** 'come', **posar** 'put', **ficar** 'put in', **treure/traure** 'take out/off', **afegir** 'add', are normally used with a locative complement. When this denotes a source or 'place from which' the clitic pronoun used is **en**; otherwise the locative phrase is represented by **hi**.

No et fiquis els dits a la boca.	Don't put your fingers in your mouth.
N'han tret tots els préssecs.	They have taken all the peaches out.
Anem-hi?	Shall we go (there)?

Many verbs require prepositional phrase complements. As with comparable verbs in English, the required preposition has to be specified lexically. Some examples are **atenir-se a** 'abide by', 'keep to', **fiar-se de** 'trust', **pensar en** 'think about', 'keep in mind', **recordar-se de** 'remember', **casar-se amb** 'marry'. The clitic **en** corresponds to prepositional complements with the preposition **de**; the clitic **hi** corresponds to all other types of prepositional complement:

> **No me'n fio.**
> I don't trust him/her/it/them/you.

> **Se'n recordaran?**
> Will they remember him/her/it/them/me/us/you?

> **Va dir que hi pensaria.**
> He said he would think about him/her/it/them/me/us/you.

Van prometre que s'atindrien a les vostres instruccions, i s'hi van atenir.
They promised they would abide by your instructions, and they did abide by them.

25.7   ADJUNCTS

Adverbial or prepositional phrase adjuncts, expressing place, time, manner, cause, etc., can be part of sentences of any type. Since, by definition, adjuncts are not required elements, and they do not have a special place in the sentence order (though there are more or less normal positions, see Chapter 36), their surface absence from a sentence does not need to be marked by a clitic element. Some types may be represented anaphorically by clitic pronouns, though. Commonly locative expressions are represented in this way (**hi** for situation or movement towards 'there'/'thither', 'here'/'hither', **en** for source 'thence'/'hence', **12.6–12.7**). Sometimes manner expressions are represented by **hi** 'thus'; occasionally time expressions are represented by **hi** 'then'; other adjuncts cannot be represented by a clitic pronoun:

Locative

També hem pujat al castell de Begur . . . S'hi veu tot el Baix Empordà . . . També hi hem vist magnífiques nuvolades.
We have also been up to Begur castle . . . You can see (there) all of the Baix Empordà . . . We have also seen wonderful cloudscapes there.

Va voler pujar al terrat. Hi passava aire i es veien molts terrats.
She wanted to go up to the roof. There was a breeze there and you could see a lot of roofs.

Voltà totes les festes majors per recordar-hi una mica les diades de la seva adolescència, per menjar-hi xocolata i truites . . ., per beure-hi sidra, per fer juguesques als partits de pilota, per contemplar com la gent ballava.
He went round all the fairs to remind him a little (at them) of the days of his adolescence, to eat chocolate and omelettes (there) . . ., to drink cider (there), to place bets on the ball games, to observe how people danced.

Manner

On vas, amb aquesta cara tan pintada? Que hi vas sempre?
Where are you going, with your face all painted? (Or) is that how you always go?

Time

Vine sempre abans de dinar; però vine-hi sempre, eh!
Always come before lunch; always come (before) then!

Ahir vam comprar les sabates, però no vam comprar el jersei.
Yesterday we bought the shoes, but we didn't buy the sweater (then).

Others

Em van regalar una bicicleta per l'èxit dels exàmens; jo volia que em rega-lessin uns esquís.
They gave me a bicycle for my exam results; I wanted them to give me skis (for the results).

Hi ha fenòmens no documentats; què cal fer?
There are unrecorded phenomena; what should be done (about them)?

26 NEGATION

26.1 FORMS OF NEGATION

26.1.1 No 'NOT'

The way to negate a positive sentence in Catalan is with the particle **no**. **No** must precede the verb or the pronominal clitics placed immediately before the verb:

La noia baixa les escales. → **La noia no baixa les escales.**
The girl is coming down the stairs. → The girl is not coming down the stairs.

Li han regalat un cotxe vermell. → **No li han regalat un cotxe vermell.**
They have given her a red car. → They have not given her a red car.

Observe that no auxiliary verb (corresponding to English 'do') is needed in Catalan when turning a positive sentence into a negative one:

M'agrada el futbol, però el tenis no em diu res.
I like football, but tennis does not do anything for me.

26.1.2 Ni 'NOT . . . EITHER/OR'/'NEITHER/NOR'

A construction similar to English ones involving 'not . . . (either) . . . or' occurs in Catalan using **ni** as a copulative conjunction placed between two elements under negation (**15.1.2**). This function is explained by the fact that **ni** is a compound of **no + i**:

Aquell dia no vaig dinar ni sopar.
That day I didn't have lunch or dinner.

No m'has instruït ni m'has convençut.
You have not taught me anything, nor have you convinced me.

Ni . . . ni . . . corresponds to English 'neither . . . nor . . . ' and links both phrases and clauses:

Ni has escrit ni has telefonat.
You neither wrote nor telephoned.

No cal que vinguin ni demà ni mai.
There's no need for them to come either tomorrow or ever.

Ni ho he fet jo ni hi ha qui s'ho pugui creure.
Neither did I do it nor is there anyone who could think that I did.

Note how **ni** replaces **no** in this construction before the first verb. However, when the element introduced by **ni** is a sentence (even if elliptical as in the second example below), it is possible to reinforce the negation in formal speech by adding **no**:

Tu no has vingut ni ells no m'han telefonat.
(or: **Ni has vingut tu ni ells m'han telefonat.**)
You did not come nor did they phone me, either.

Ni la mare ni el pare no se n'havien adonat.
(or: **Ni la mare ni el pare se n'havien adonat.**)
Neither mother nor father had realized.

There is an important restriction to this formal use: **ni** cannot directly precede **no**:

Ni he llegit aquell llibre ni m'interessa.
*Ni he llegit aquell llibre ni no m'interessa.
I have neither read that book nor am I interested in it.

For **ni** and **ni tan sols** 'not even', see **15.1.6** and **26.1.6**.

26.1.3   Sense 'WITHOUT'

Like English 'without', **sense** is the only other particle which can give a (subordinate) clause a negative meaning:

Ho farem sense dir res a ningú. (= **Ho farem i no direm res a ningú.**)
We'll do it without saying anything to anybody. (= We'll do it and will not say anything to anybody.)

Va comprar el cotxe sense demanar quant consumia. (= **Va comprar el cotxe i no va demanar quant consumia.**)
She bought the car without asking about its fuel consumption. (= She bought the car and did not ask about its fuel consumption.)

Observe that in the examples above **sense** is followed by an infinitive whose subject is that of the main clause. To introduce a negative subordinate clause with a different subject, **sense** is followed by **que** (see Chapter 19 for the use of subjunctive):

Ho farem sense que ningú se n'adoni.
We'll do it without anyone realizing.

Van comprar el cotxe sense que els diguessin quant consumia.
They bought the car without being told what the fuel consumption was.

Sense is an adverb as well as a preposition and conjunction; see **11.5.2iii**, **14.2.1**. **Sense** gives negative force to negative polarity words like **res, gens, ningú, mai, enlloc, cap** (see **26.1.5**).

T'escric sense cap motiu especial.
I am writing to you for no (lit. = without any) special reason.

Sense ningú que guardi la porta és fàcil d'esmunyir-s'hi.
Without anybody guarding the gate it's easy to slip through.

Sense haver vingut mai a Catalunya, parla molt bé el català.
Without ever having come to Catalonia, she speaks Catalan very well.

Van fer el viatge sense aturar-se enlloc.
They did the journey without stopping anywhere.

Sense conveys the opposite meaning of **amb**. In informal speech it is possible to hear the curious **amb sense** as the equivalent of **sense**:

Vols aigua amb gas o sense?
(informal) **Vols aigua amb gas o amb sense?**
Do you want sparkling or still mineral water?

26.1.4   Sinó 'BUT'

Sinó is an adversative conjunction 'but' (for fuller discussion see **15.1.5.2**) which is only used after a negative, 'not A . . . *but* B':

No han triat pernil, sinó formatge.
They didn't choose ham but cheese.

The contrast between **sinó** 'but' and **si no** 'if not' is discussed at **15.3i**.

26.1.5   NEGATIVE POLARITY ITEMS

The central framework of the system of negation in Catalan is more complex and nuanced than, say, Spanish or French. This complexity derives principally from the function of the elements called negative polarity items and their interaction with **no**. These items are: **cap** 'any one'/'not one'/'no', **enlloc** 'anywhere'/'nowhere', **gaire** '(not) much/many', **gens** '(not) any (at all)', **mai** 'ever'/'never', **ningú** 'anybody'/'nobody', **ningun(a)** 'any'/'no' (Val.), **pus** (used in the Balearic Islands only) 'any more'/'no more', **res** 'anything'/'nothing'. (The use of several of these is covered in Chapter 8 and in **13.6**.) The negative sense of these items can be seen in elliptical sentences like the answers in the following question–answer pairs:

–Quants de cotxes tens? –Cap.
'How many cars have you got?' 'None'.

–A on t'agradaria anar de viatge enguany? –Enlloc.
'Where would you like to go travelling this year?' 'Nowhere.'

–T'agraden gaire les ostres? –Gens.
'Do you like oysters?' 'Not at all.'

–Quants de cops has anat a Nova York? –Mai.
'How many times have you been to New York?' 'Never.'

–Qui ha vingut a veure't avui? –Ningú.
'Who has been to see you today?' 'Nobody.'

–Què regalaràs al teu amic per a Nadal? –Res.
'What will you give your friend for Christmas?' 'Nothing.'

Conventionally the expression **en ma/ta/sa vida** 'never in my/your/his/her/
their life' is included in this set:

–Tu has insultat alguna vegada en Joan? –En ma vida.
'Have you ever insulted Joan?' 'Never (in my whole life).'

However, in questions, conditional sentences, and in the standard of comparisons all these items produce a non-negative meaning (just as the generally
corresponding English 'any' and 'ever' do):

M'has comprat cap regal?
Have you bought me any presents?

Que et molesto gens, si fumo?
Do you mind at all if I smoke?

No sé si mai havia vist res de comparable.
I don't know if I had ever seen anything comparable.

Que ha vingut ningú a demanar per mi?
Has anybody come asking for me?

Volia res?
Were you wanting something? (= Was there anything I can do for you?)

No sé si li agrada gaire la sopa.
I don't know if he likes the soup (very) much.

Si tens gens de paciència . . .
If you have any patience at all . . .

Demana-li si en vol pus, d'aquest pastís.
Ask her if she wants any more of this pie.

M'agradaria de saber si en sa vida ha llegit cap llibre.
I'd like to know if she has (ever) read a (single) book in her life.

Aquells dies patien més fred que mai.
Those days they suffered the cold worse than ever.

Estava més ben preparada que ningú.
She was better qualified than anyone (else).

For the most part, then, these items only have a negative sense when the sentence is negated by other means (**no, ni,** or **sense** or a word with an inherently negative sense like **dubtar** 'doubt', **negar** 'deny').

The simple pattern of negation involving negative polarity items can be described as **no (ni, sense)** + verb + polarity item:

No he vist cap de les seves pel·lícules.
I haven't seen any film by her.

Ell i jo no havíem coincidit enlloc abans.
He and I had never met anywhere before.

No ens queda gens de pa.
We've no bread left at all.

La teva mare no ha vingut mai a veure't.
Your mother has never come to see you.

No m'agrada res del que diuen.
I don't like anything of what they say.

Ni ha mirat això ni s'ha pensat veure-ho en sa vida.
He hasn't looked at that nor does he intend to look at it for as long as he
   lives.

Van entrar a la sala sense fer gaire soroll.
They went into the room without making much noise.

El nin no vol pus sopa.
The lad doesn't want any more soup.

Dubto que ens hagin vist junts enlloc.
I doubt whether they have seen us anywhere together.

Observe that more than one negative particle may follow **no:**

No deien mai res a ningú.
They never said anything to anyone.

Jo encara no he revelat enlloc cap d'aquells secrets.
I still haven't revealed any of those secrets anywhere.

When the negative polarity item precedes the verb, some vacillation is observed over whether **no** appears or not. In this context, Catalan has two systems of negation applying: a formal system in which the presence of a complementary **no** in the sentence is obligatory, and a less formal system in which the preverbal negative polarity item suffices to negate the whole sentence:

Formal system:

> **Mai no hauria dit que t'agradés un menjar tan picant.**
> I would never have said that you would like such spicy food.

> **Enlloc del món no trobaríeu una terra tan fèrtil com aquesta.**
> Nowhere on earth would you find soil as fertile as this.

> **Ningú no diu beneitures d'aquest calibre.**
> Nobody comes out with idiotic things of that calibre.

> **Cap idea teva no m'agrada.**
> None of your ideas appeals to me.

Non-formal system:

> **Mai hauria dit que t'agradés un menjar tan picant.**
> **Enlloc del món trobaríeu una terra tan fèrtil com aquesta.**
> **Ningú diu beneitures d'aquest calibre.**
> **Cap idea teva m'agrada.**

Although normative authorities maintain preference for the first system, everyday usage in most dialects favours the second.

The situation can be related to the optional presence of **no** in elliptical utterances like:

> –Què t'ha dit? –(No) res.   'What did she say to you?' 'Nothing.'
> –T'ha agradat? –(No) gens.   'Did you like it?' 'Not at all.'

26.1.6 OTHER OBSERVATIONS ON NEGATIVE CONSTRUCTIONS

Poc

Poc 'little' forms an informal negative, used alone in initial position:

> **Poc es pensava que . . .**   Little did she think that . . .
> **Poc ho sé.**   I don't know./How should I know?
> **Poc t'ho dirà.**   She'll never tell you.

'Never'

Note that 'never' does not always appear as **mai** in Catalan negative equivalents:

No n'he vist cap com aquest.
I've never seen one like this.

No m'ha dit ni una sola vegada que m'estima.
She has never once told me she loves me.

No hi tornaré pus. (Bal.)
I'll never go back there.

'Not even', 'not by a long way', 'not at all'

'Not even' may be expressed by **ni** alone, or by **ni tan sols**:

Ni (tan sols) m'han conegut.   They didn't even recognize me.

Ni de lluny and **ni de bon tros** correspond to 'not by a long way':

No han complert, ni de bon tros/ni de lluny, els requisits de la convocatòria.
They haven't met, by a long way, the requirements of the application
procedure.

Adverbial **no . . . gens** 'not at all' can be reinforced with **ni mica**:

No m'has convençut gens ni mica.
You haven't convinced me in the slightest./You haven't begun to convince
me.

No . . . gota 'not . . . a drop' and **no . . . mica** 'not . . . a bit' are idiomatic
informal equivalents of **no . . . gens**:

No s'hi van lluir gota.
They didn't do at all well at it./They didn't make much of a good showing.

No era mica agradable.
It wasn't a bit nice.

En absolut is another expression for '(not) at all':

No ho faré en absolut.   I won't do it at all.
–Et fa res que vingui? –En absolut.   'Do you mind if I come?' 'Not at all.'

26.1.7 Tampoc 'NEITHER'

Tampoc 'neither', 'not . . . either', 'nor' (the negative of **també** 'also') functions rather like a negative polarity item. In elliptical constructions it can
stand alone or can be anticipated by **ni**.

No t'ha agradat? A mi tampoc.
Didn't you like it? Neither did I.

No han arribat els jugadors, ni l'àrbitre tampoc.
The players haven't arrived, nor has the referee/and the referee hasn't either.

The system **no/ni/sense** + verb + **tampoc** exists side by side with **tampoc** (+ **no**) + verb, in a similar way to the other negative polarity items (**26.1.5**).

No podem oblidar tampoc que . . . /Tampoc (no) podem oblidar que . . .
Nor should we forget that . . . /We shouldn't forget either that . . .

Els altres no s'hi sabien avenir tampoc./Els altres tampoc (no) s'hi sabien avenir.
The others couldn't agree to it either.

No ens van xiular però no ens aplaudiren tampoc./No ens van xiular però tampoc (no) ens aplaudiren.
We did not get booed (lit. whistled) but we did not get clapped either.

26.1.8 Pas

Pas is used in negative sentences in central Catalan in quite a different way from French *pas*. Catalan **pas**, in negative constructions, has a special communicative function of negating possible implications of what is being said (that is: 'despite appearances'/'despite what one might suppose', 'after all'):

Dir que està núvol no vol dir pas que hagi de ploure.
Saying it's cloudy doesn't mean it's going to rain.

No, senyor: no sóc pas l'home que vostè busca.
No, sir: I am not the man you are looking for.

No vindràs pas demà de matí? Jo que t'hauria esperat.
You won't be coming tomorrow morning (after all)? And I would have been waiting in for you.

Some questions are formulated with **no . . . pas** when implications might be attached to a likely answer:

No has vist pas en Joan?
You haven't (by any chance) seen Joan? (Because if you had . . .)

Pas can be also used in prohibitions (see **28.2**), telling someone not to do something they were about to do, or might be expected to do:

Això no ho féssiu pas, que és molt perillós.
I wouldn't do that; it's very dangerous.

No aturis pas l'autobús, que no portem diners.
Don't stop the bus, because we haven't got any money on us.

No obris pas una altra ampolla, que ja en tindrem prou amb aquesta.
Don't open another bottle; we'll have enough with this one.

Pas can also appear in elliptical negative sentences:

–**Heu comprat moltes joguines? –No pas cap per a tu.**
'Have you bought a lot of toys?' '(Yes but) not for you.'

–**Portes una vida ordenada? –Sí, però no pas per voluntat pròpia.**
'Do you lead an orderly life?' 'Yes, but not from choice.'

Pas can avoid contiguous repetition of **no** when the second term of a comparison is a negative clause, and the construction contains an 'expletive **no**' (see **5.2.2**).

És més barat anar de vacances a certs països que no pas no anar-hi.
It's cheaper to go on holiday in certain countries than not to go there.

Contrary to what occurs in French, the Catalan **pas** can be followed by negative polarity items. Because of the special meaning of Catalan **pas** this does not result in a double negation:

No he vist pas ningú.	I haven't seen anyone.
No pensem anar-hi pas mai.	We don't intend to go there ever.

Note that **pas** is exceptional in being able to occur between **haver** and the participle in compound (perfect) tenses, and likewise between the auxiliary element **va-** and the infinitive in the preterite. Unlike other negative items, though, it cannot precede the inflected verb form.

No he dit pas això./No he pas dit això.	* **Pas (no) he dit això.**
I didn't say that./I haven't said that.	
No he dit res./Res no he dit.	* **No he res dit.**
I haven't said anything.	
No ho van consentir pas./No ho van pas consentir.	* **Pas (no) ho van consentir.**
They didn't accept it.	

In North Catalan, **pas** can be the only element in a negative sentence; that is, in this variety it has taken on the role of the simple marker of negation (as in Occitan and in popular French):

Cantis pas aquesta cançó.	Don't sing that song.
Els mainatges diuen pas aquestes coses.	Young children don't say those things.

26.1.9   EXPRESSING 'NO MORE'/'NOT . . . ANY MORE'/'NO LONGER'

No . . . més (Bal. no . . . pus) and ja no are used to express that a situation no longer obtains.

No n'he sentit a parlar més.
I have heard nothing more (said) about it.

Ja no construeixen cases com aquestes.
They don't build houses like that any more.

Abans em semblava simpàtica, però ja no la hi trobo.
I used to think she was nice, but I don't any longer.

26.2   FURTHER POINTS ON NEGATION

26.2.1   THE SCOPE OF NEGATION

The category of general negation concerns cases in which a whole sentence is negated, as in:

M'agraden les novel·les policíaques.	I like detective novels.
No m'agraden les novel·les policíaques.	I don't like detective novels.
Ho enllestirà avui.	He will finish it today.
No ho enllestirà avui.	He will not finish it today.

In some apparent cases of general negation the negative attached to a main verb logically belongs with a subordinate verb in a complement clause. These cases of negative raising are discussed in **26.2.1.2.**

Negation need not apply to the whole of a sentence, however, and it is possible to negate a particular element within an affirmative construction.

He enllestit el pròleg, però no la conclusió.
I have finished the preface but not the conclusion.

Some types of particular negation are discussed below in **26.2.1.1.**

26.2.1.1   Particular negation

(i)   Negating nouns, adjectives, adverbs and quantifiers

In addition to the pattern of morphological negation of nouns, adjectives, and so on, with prefixes like **a-**, **des-**, **in-**, it is possible to negate individual lexical items by placing **no** before them. In such instances **no** introduces the idea of opposition rather than of absence, and, consequently, only abstract concepts: ideas, opinions or descriptions, not material things (***el no-vi** 'non-wine') can be 'negated' by this means): **la no-intervenció** 'non-intervention', **un pacte de no-agressió** 'a non-aggression pact', **una beguda no alcohòlica** 'a nonalcoholic drink', **una cosa no estranya per a ell** 'something not strange to him', **no gaire bé** 'not very well', **no sempre** 'not always', **no tothom** 'not everybody', **no gaires persones** 'not many people'.

> **No gaires persones tenen les idees tan clares, i no sempre raonen amb tanta contundència.**
> Not many people have such clear ideas, and not always do they argue with such vigour.

Notice the hyphen in the element **no-** used with a noun; see **37.6iv**.

(ii)   Negating participles, gerunds and infinitives

Participles, gerunds, and infinitives behave as verbs (although non-finite) with respect to negation, so negating one of these elements implies the general negation of the non-finite clause it appears in:

> **Els llibres no llegits no aprofiten a ningú.**
> Books not read are of no benefit to anyone.

> **Els fills no desitjats sempre pateixen.**
> Unwanted children always suffer.

> **No dient aquestes coses seran condemnats.**
> Through not saying these things they will be condemned.

> **No vivint a la casa va perdre els seus drets de llogater.**
> By not living in the house she lost her tenant's rights.

> **És un delicte no aturar-se en veure un accident.**
> It is an offence not to stop upon witnessing an accident.

> **Han telefonat per no haver d'anar-hi.**
> They have phoned so as not to have to go there.

26.2.1.2   Negative raising

When the verb in the main clause is **creure** 'think'/'believe', **desitjar/voler** 'want', **pensar** 'think'/'intend', **semblar** 'seem', **trobar** 'find', and others of similar meaning, there is no difference in force whether negation is applied to the verb in the main or the subordinate clause, though often the negation might more 'logically' be attached to the subordinate verb. Catalan and English are similar in this respect. (On the use of the subjunctive in the subordinate clause after a negative, see **19.2.4iv**.)

> **Creu que no li diran res. = No creu que li diguin res.**
> He thinks they won't say anything to him. = He doesn't think they will say anything to him.

Desitgen no veure'l mai més. = No desitgen veure'l mai més.
They want never to see him again. = They don't want to see him ever again.

Pensen no fer-li cap regal. = No pensen fer-li cap regal.
They intend not to give her a present. = They do not intend to give her a present.

Em sembla que no està bé. = No em sembla que estigui bé.
I think it's not right. = I don't think it's right.

Trobem que això no és raonable. = No trobem que això sigui raonable.
We find that this is not reasonable. = We don't find this is reasonable.

However with the majority of verbs a clear distinction of meaning is made according to whether **no** stands with the main verb or the subordinate:

Jo no he escollit tornar a aquesta feina.
I have not chosen to come back to this job.

cf. **Jo he escollit no tornar a aquesta feina.**
I have chosen not to come back to this job.

No esperen que compris el cotxe.
They aren't expecting you to buy the car.

cf. **Esperen que no compris el cotxe.**
They are expecting you not to buy the car.

No va prometre venir.
She didn't promise to come.

cf. **Va prometre no venir.**
She promised not to come.

27 INTERROGATION AND EXCLAMATION

27.1 INTERROGATION

27.1.1 DIRECT YES/NO QUESTIONS

The basic word-order scheme of Catalan is explained in Chapter 36. The formulation of yes/no questions in Catalan does not entail change of word order between an affirmative and a corresponding interrogative sentence. Thus, just as the statement 'Pere has come' could be expressed as either (a) **Ha vingut en Pere** or (b) **En Pere ha vingut**, so the question 'Has Pere come?' can be formed as either (a) **Ha vingut en Pere?** or (b) **En Pere ha vingut?**

The variations in word order in these examples do not depend on the difference between question and statement but on which part of the sentence is in focus, this being **en Pere** in (a) and **ha vingut** in (b). What gives a sentence an interrogative sense, then, marking the difference between **T'estimo** 'I love you' and **T'estimo?** 'Do I love you?', is not word order but intonation. (The usual description is that questions lack the final fall in pitch that statements present.)

Use of the inverted question mark ¿, employed to indicate either the beginning of a whole question or the part of a sentence that contains the interrogative element, has recently been proscribed by the Institut d'Estudis Catalans (see **37.7**). However it still appears in many texts particularly (a) to show that a sentence – usually a long one – which does not begin with an interrogative word is to be read as a question, or (b) to mark off the interrogative part of a sentence which contains a topicalized phrase, or a subordinate clause preceding the question:

> **¿No és idèntica llur política actual a la que seguien en la legislatura anterior?**
> Isn't their present policy identical to the one they pursued in the previous parliament?

> **Les conclusions que hem tret d'aquest debat i que tots subscrivim, ¿realment justifiquen que mantinguem aquesta postura?**
> Can our maintenance of this position really be justified by the conclusions which we have drawn from this debate and to which we all subscribe?

27.1.1.1 Introductory *que*

In the spoken language, short questions are generally introduced by an expletive unstressed **que** (not to be confused with **què**):

Hi ha ningú a la casa? = Que hi ha ningú a la casa?
Is there anybody in?

Has pagat la factura del gas? = Que has pagat la factura del gas?
Have you paid the gas bill?

No voleu venir-hi? = Que no voleu venir-hi?
Don't you want to come?

The **que** (see **15.2.3**) in these short questions is optional (although its use is very strongly favoured in spoken eastern central Catalan) and it does not convey any nuance of meaning or emphasis.

Another use of **que** is to introduce echo-questions (where its function is evidently related to an ellipsis of an underlying clause like **Dius que . . . ?**):

–Vas al bar? –Que si vaig al bar? I tant que hi vaig!
'Are you going to the bar?' 'Going to the bar? I sure am!'

–A on vas? –Que a on vaig? Vaig a can Pep.
'Where are you going?' 'Where am I going? I'm going to Pep's house.'

27.1.1.2 Tag questions

Direct yes/no questions can be reinforced adding **no?** or **oi?** (and, colloquially, **eh?**) at the end. This device covers the whole set of tag questions in English:

Som amics, oi? = Som amics, no?
We're friends, aren't we?

Trucaràs a les deu, oi? = Trucaràs a les deu, no?
You'll phone at 10 o'clock, won't you?

It is to be observed, though, that **no?** cannot follow a negative question:

No és pas tan dolent, oi?   It's not so bad, is it?
* No és pas tan dolent, no?

Another reinforcing construction involves introducing a question with **oi que**:

Oi que t'agrada?   You do like it, don't you?
Oi que no ho tornaran a fer?   They won't do it again, will they?

27.1.2 INDIRECT YES/NO QUESTIONS

An indirect yes/no question is introduced by **si** 'if'/'whether' (see **15.3**) and normally depends on verbs expressing knowledge or enquiry:

No sé si ho faran.
I don't know whether/if they'll do it.

No sé si plou o no.
I don't know whether or not it's raining.

Ignorava si el seu cognom era de procedència russa.
I did not know if her surname was of Russian origin.

Els preguntaré si volen venir a la festa.
I'll ask them if they want to come to the party.

Digues-li si pot guardar-nos els nens avui vespre.
Check whether he can baby-sit for us tonight.

27.1.3 *WH*-QUESTIONS (PARTIAL QUESTIONS)

27.1.3.1 *Qui?* 'who?' *què?* 'what?'

Qui? 'who?' is the interrogative pronoun referring to persons and **què?** 'what?' is its counterpart referring to things:

Qui vol venir a fer una volta?	Who wants to come for a stroll?
Qui va dir què?	Who said what?
Què passa al carrer?	What's going on in the street?
Què llegeixes?	What are you reading?

Observe that **qui** and **què** are pronouns and never adjectives. For this reason **què?** translates English 'what?' only when no noun follows. Adjectival 'what?' involves a construction with **quin** (see **27.1.3.4**):

De quin color és la teva jaqueta ?	What colour is your jacket?
***De què color és la teva jaqueta?**	
A quina edat vas acabar els estudis?	At what age did you complete your education?

27.1.3.2 *Adverbial interrogatives*

The adverbial interrogative words in Catalan are **quan?** 'when?', **on?** 'where?' (frequently reinforced with **a** 'to' or **de** 'from': **a on?** 'where?'/'whither?', **d'on?** 'where?'/'whence?'), **com?** 'how?' and **per què?** 'why?':

Quan has arribat?	When did you arrive?
On és en Miquel?	Where is Miquel?
D'on venim i a on anem?	Where have we come from and where are we going?
Com pot ser això?	How can this be?
Per què la gent s'avorreix tant?	Why do people get so bored?

Per què? 'why?' must not be confused with **perquè** 'because':

–Per què has vingut? –Perquè volia veure't.
'Why did you come?' 'Because I wanted to see you.'

27.1.3.3 Quant?

Quantitative **quant?** can function as an interrogative adjective, pronoun, or adverb. In the former case agreement with the noun covers the English distinction between count and non-count nouns 'how much?'/'how many?'; as an adverb it is invariable:

Quants (de) socis han vingut?	How many members have turned up?
Quanta (d')aigua hi ha dins l'aljub?	How much water is there in the cistern?
Quant (de) formatge ens resta?	How much cheese do we have left?
Quant han treballat avui?	How much have they worked today?

(On optional **de** with **quant** as an adjective, see **8.2.1**.)

Quant is frequently a pronoun (invariable) in questions like:

Quant val?/Quant costa?	What does it cost?/How much is it?
Quant fa que m'esperes?	How long have you been waiting for me for?
Quant hi ha d'aquí a Manresa?	How far is it from here to Manresa?

(Note that **què** can also be used with this meaning; thus, as alternatives to the preceding three examples: **Què val?**, **Què fa que m'esperes?**, **Què hi ha d'aquí a Manresa?**) If the noun governed by **quant** is known and unexpressed, it can be referred to by pronominal **en** (see **12.6v**) in a partitive function. When this occurs **quant** remains an adjective and, thus, agrees in gender and number with the underlying noun:

Quants (de) pans hi ha?	→ **Quants n'hi ha?**
How many loaves are there?	How many are there?
Quanta (de) ginebra has begut?	→ **Quanta n'has beguda?**
How much gin did you drink?	How much did you drink?

27.1.3.4   *Quin?* 'which?' and 'what?'

The adjective **quin** has the basic meaning of 'which?' or 'which one(s)?' It translates both 'which?' and the adjectival uses of 'what?', with gender and number agreement always necessary:

Quin col·lega t'ha dit això?	Which colleague told you that?
Quins colors t'agraden més?	Which colours do you like best?
Quina impressió t'ha fet?	What impression did it make on you?
Quins són els passos que ara hauríem de prendre?	What are the steps we ought to take now?

As in the last example, **quin** may be separated from the noun to which it refers; it may refer to a noun already present in the speaker's/hearer's mind:

De tots els llibres que has llegit, quin em recomanaries?
Of all the books you have read, which would you recommend to me?

Té: quina vols? (e.g. **d'aquestes flors**)
Here you are: which one (e.g. of these flowers) do you want?

Té: quin vols? (e.g. **d'aquests gelats**)
Here you are: which one (e.g. of these ice creams) do you want?

Note how 'what time?' is translated in **Quina hora és?** 'What time is it?' (lit. Which hour is it?). For 'What is your name?' and 'What date is it?' **Quin és el teu nom?** and **Quina data és?** are possible, but the colloquial preference is for **Com et dius?** and **A quants som?** respectively. Observe also the behaviour of **quin?** 'what?' = 'which of a set?' and **què?** 'what (is the nature of)?' contrasted in **Quin és el teu problema?** 'What's your problem?' and **Què és aquesta vida?** 'What is this life?'

27.1.3.5   *Prepositions with* wh-*words*

The introductory question words covered in **27.1.3.1–4** above can be preceded by a preposition to form an an interrogative prepositional phrase. English equivalents of such constructions frequently involve positioning the preposition at the end of the clause (an important aspect of word order in questions like that covered in **27.1.1**). In Catalan a preposition and the *wh*-word it governs can never be separated in this way.

A favor de qui penses votar?	Who do you intend to vote for?
A quina plana et refereixes?	Which page are you referring to?
Amb què l'hauríem d'adobar?	What ought we to mend it with?
Contra quanta gent us heu barallat?	How many people have you fallen out with?
Damunt què s'aguanten les columnes?	What do the columns stand upon?
De què tracta aquest programa?	What is this programme about?

De qui parles?	Who are you talking about?
De quantes persones estem parlant?	How many people are we talking about?
De quina mida és aquesta camisa?	What size is this shirt?
Des de quan saps conduir?	How long have you been able to drive? (lit. Since when do you know how to drive?)
Des d'on vénen els corredors?	Where are the runners coming from? (i.e. Where did they set out from?)
Fins on arriba el tren de les dotze?	How far does the 12 o'clock train go? (lit. Up to where . . . ?)
Per quant m'ho vens?	How much will you sell it me for?
Per a quan espera el nen?	When is she expecting her baby?

Observe that **per què?** 'why' (already a prepositional phrase) is never preceded by a preposition, nor is **com?** 'how', except in the (non-standard) phrase **A com va?** 'What price is it (by weight)?': **A com va el peix?** = **A quant va el peix?** 'How much (by weight) is the fish?'

27.1.3.6 *Word order in* wh-*questions*

In *wh-* (partial) questions the *wh*-phrase is always placed before the verb. Except when the *wh*-phrase is itself the subject of the sentence (**qui** or a noun phrase beginning with **quin** or **quant**), the subject has to come after the verb phrase (see Chapter 36). That is, in *wh*-questions, the word order template is *wh*-word + Verb + (Object) + (Subject).

Quan ha vingut en Pere? *Quan en Pere ha vingut?	When did Pere come?
Com ha fet la paret el paleta? *Com el paleta ha fet la paret?	How did the bricklayer build the wall?
On ha anat la mare? *On la mare ha anat?	Where has mother gone?

(In these cases the subject is often separated from the rest of the sentence by a comma: **Quan ha vingut, en Pere?** etc.) But compare the following where the *wh*-phrase is the sentence subject:

Qui ha vingut avui? *Ha vingut qui avui?	Who has come today?

(The inversion **Ha vingut qui?** is possible in an echo question, when the question echoes directly a previous sentence; in the above example, this would have the sense of 'Who did you say has come?' In this case the comma seems to be compulsory: **Ha vingut qui, avui?**)

Quin equip ha jugat més partits? *Ha jugat més partits quin equip?
Which team has played more games?

Quants policies han calgut per arrestar-lo? *Han calgut quants policies per Arrestar-lo?
How many policemen did it take to arrest him?

(**Han calgut quants policies per arrestar-lo?** is quite all right, of course, as an echo question: 'How many policemen did you say it took to arrest him?')

In a left-detachment construction (**36.4**), naturally, a phrase, including a subject, may appear to the left of a *wh*-word.

En Pere i la Maria fa temps que no vénen. En Pere, quan va venir per darrera vegada?
Pere and Maria haven't been here for a while. When was the last time Pere came?

Note that, as in English, if there is more than one *wh*-word in the same sentence, only one appears before the verb:

Qui va dir què?   Who said what?

27.1.3.7   *Emphasis in questions*

Equivalent to English 'who the devil/hell . . . ?', 'what the devil/hell . . . ?' is Catalan use of **diables** and **diantre** in similar contexts:

Què diantre passa aquí?   What the devil is going on here?
Qui diables ha escrit això?   Who the hell has written this?

At a more vulgar level altogether is the reinforcement of *wh*-question words by impolite or taboo words like **collons**, **cony**, **punyetes**, **putes**, all of which have English approximate equivalents in the ripest swearwords:

Què punyetes mires?   What the flaming hell are you looking at?
On putes és en Miquel?   Where the fuck is Miquel?
Per què collons això sempre em   Why does this always happen to me, for
  passa a mi?   fuck's sake?
Com cony ha passat l'accident?   How the bloody hell did the accident happen?

27.1.3.8   *Indirect wh- (partial) questions*

Indirect *wh*-questions display the same structure as the corresponding direct questions, with the introductory question word linking the subordinate clause to the main one. Some examples below show in parentheses the notionally related direct question.

No sabia qui havia vingut. (cf. **Qui ha vingut?**)
I didn't know who had come.

Pregunta-li què passa. (cf. **Què passa?**)
Ask her what is going on.

Digues quin dia em vindràs a veure. (cf. **Quin dia em vindràs a veure?**)
Say which day you will come to see me.

El cartell posava a quant anaven els productes diversos. (cf. **A quant anaven els productes diversos?**)
The poster showed the selling prices of the various products.

Ens hauries d'explicar com s'arregla i per a quan ha d'estar arreglat.
You ought to tell us how it can be sorted out and when it is to be sorted out by.

No et dirà pas de què es queixa.
He won't tell you what he is complaining about.

Saps amb quines eines treballaven?
Do you know what tools they used to work with?

Que + interrogative word

After the verbs **dir** 'say', 'tell' and **preguntar/demanar** 'ask', a question word may optionally (and informally) be preceded by **que**:

I llavors li vaig dir (que) què es pensava.	And then I asked him what the idea was.
M'han preguntat (que) si ho farem.	They've asked me if we'll do it.

The presence of **que** is required when the indirect question is given as a discrete unit referring back to something previously said:

–Què t'ha dit aquell? –Doncs, que si li faríem un descompte.
'What did that man say to you?' (He asked) 'Whether we would give him a discount.'

I vinga empipar-me amb preguntes estúpides: que en quin idioma s'havia de redactar el treball, que si s'havia d'escriure a màquina, que quan s'havia d'entregar.
And then he came out with all these stupid questions: what language did the essay have to be written in, did it have to be typed, when did it have to be handed in.

M'intrigava la pregunta que m'havia fet, que si coneixia un tal Gutiérrez.
I was intrigued by the question she had asked me, (about) whether I knew a certain Gutiérrez.

27.1.3.9 *Pseudo-relatives as indirect questions*

Other formulations of indirect questions involve pseudo-relative constructions (**31.10iii**). In cases like the following where there is not literally an
indirect question, that is, no speech act of questioning is reported, Catalan
prefers the pseudo-relative:

No creuràs els maldecaps que (= quants maldecaps) això ens ha provocat.
You won't believe the headaches this has caused us./ . . . how many headaches . . .

A veure si pots descobrir el dia que (= quin dia) va passar.
I wonder if you can discover on which day it happened.

Et faré una llista dels llibres que (= de quins llibres) has de consultar.
I'll make you a list of which books you need to consult.

Relative clauses with the neuter article **el** as antecedent (see **9.2.2**) are common in this type of construction:

Volia saber el que deia (= què deia).
I wanted to know what she was saying.

No recordo el que (= què) em van dir.
I don't remember what they told me.

Imagina't el que (= si, com) deu patir.
Just imagine how much she must be suffering.

Vejam si endevines el que (= quant) val.
Let's see if you can guess what it's worth.

**Poc et penses el que estaran contents (= com estaran de contents) els seus
pares.**
You just don't know how pleased her parents will be.

(See below on **com . . . de** and **27.2.3** on the intensifying article.)
   The same pattern is, in fact, found very widely when an indirect question is
literally involved. So one might say that idiomatic Catalan tends to avoid *wh-*
words in indirect questions as far as possible, and to seek an alternative
construction involving a relative clause. The Catalan alternatives have typically only a single idiomatic English equivalent:

**Digue'm quina part de la història trobes menys versemblant. = Digue'm la
part de la història que trobes menys versemblant.**
Tell me which part of the story you find least plausible.

The structure with **que** is not a true relative, but rather a particular type of
clause which is the outcome of an intensifying use of the article, conveying
now one of the functions of the interrogative adjective:

Pregunta'ls quins llibres han llegit. = **Pregunta'ls els llibres que han llegit.**
Ask them which books they have read.

Ignor a quines ciutats d'Europa tenen agències. = **Ignor les ciutats d'Europa en què tenen agències.**
I don't know which European cities they have agencies in.

Sempre contava quanta de fam va passar durant la guerra. = **Sempre contava la fam que va passar durant la guerra.**
She always used to relate how hungry she was during the war.

When the interrogative adjective is introduced by a preposition, this pre-position will go before the relative pronoun in the idiomatic alternative structure.

Ignoro per quines raons va absentar-se de la reunió. = **Ignoro les raons per les quals va absentar-se de la reunió.**
I don't know the reasons why she failed to attend the meeting.

Confessa de quants companys has abusat. = **Confessa els companys dels quals has abusat.**
Own up to how many friends you have abused.

In less careful expression, however, this formally correct order is not respected:

(non-standard) **Confessa dels companys que has abusat.**

Com . . . de

Indirect questions involving 'how?' as a degree modifier clearly show the relationship between interrogative and exclamative constructions (see **27.2.2**). An alternative to **com (de)** introducing an adjective is the periphrasis **fins a quin punt** (or **fins on**) 'to what extent':

Ningú no sap com és (de) malèvola aquella dona.
Nobody knows how malicious that woman is.

Cal reconèixer fins a quin punt és delicada la situació.
It must be recognised how delicate the situation is.

Colloquially the neuter article **el** (non-standard **lo**, see **9.2**) occurs directly before the adjective in this construction (non-standard **Poc et penses el/lo complicat que és aquest tema** 'You don't appreciate how complicated this matter is'), but normative grammarians prefer a construction with **com . . . de**.

Ningú no comprèn com és de perillosa aquella ruta.
Nobody understands how dangerous that route is.

27.2   EXCLAMATION

27.2.1   EXCLAMATORY INTONATION

The simplest form of exclamation is through intonation, where use of the exclamation mark indicates this oral feature and expressive function:

Els nostres han guanyat el partit! Our side has won the game!
Demà no hi ha escola! There's no school tomorrow!

As with the inverted question mark (see **27.1.1.1**), the Institut d'Estudis Catalans also repudiates use of inverted ¡ to mark the beginning of an exclamation. This punctuation mark is still found with some frequency in printed texts.

27.2.2   EXCLAMATIONS USING *WH*-WORDS

27.2.2.1   *Whole sentence exclamations*

Exclamations can be introduced by an interrogative word (especially **que, com,** and **quant**):

Com m'agraden els canelons!
How I love cannelloni!

Quantes paredetes (que) hi ha avui al mercat!
What a lot of stalls there are in the market today!

Que bé (que) cantes!
How well you sing!

Note the optional use of **que** to introduce the second part of this type of exclamation.

27.2.2.2   *Exclamatory phrases*

(i)   *Quantity*

For these exclamations, where no main verb is present, **que** and **quant** are used, the latter followed optionally by **de**:

Que flors! = Quantes (de) flors! What a lot of flowers!
Que gent! = Quanta (de) gent! What a lot of people!

Another exclamatory expression with the same sense is **quina (mà) de**:

Quants (d') espectadors! = Quina (mà) d'espectadors!
What a lot of spectators!

Quanta pluja! = Quina (mà) de pluja!
How it's raining!/How it rained!

(ii) Quality

Objects or persons

Exclamations stressing the quality of objects or persons are introduced by
quin. The quality emphasized follows **més** or **tan**:

Quin home més fort! = Quin home tan fort!	What a strong man!
Quina casa més neta! = Quina casa tan neta!	What a clean house!

Quality exclamations are possible, as in English, with no mention of the
stressed quality: **Quin home!** 'What a man!', **Quines flors!** 'What flowers!',
Quina casa! 'What a house!' Where a main verb follows it is optionally introduced by **que**:

Quines flors més boniques (que) han trobat! = Quines flors tan boniques (que)
   han trobat!
What pretty flowers they have found!

Adverbs and adjectives

The object of exclamation may be not a thing or a person but the quality or
state expressed by an adjective or adverb: **Que interessant!** 'How interesting!'
As with nouns **que** optionally introduces a following main clause when
present.

Adjectives:

Que blanca (que) t'ha quedat la roba!
How white your washing has turned out!

Que malalt (que) em trobo!
How ill I feel!

Adverbs:

Que barroerament (que) parla aquell!	How coarsely that man talks!
Que lluny (que) ha arribat la notícia!	How far the news has travelled!

Observe that in all these sentences the subject, when it appears, is placed after
the verb and never before it:

*Que lluny (que) la notícia ha arribat!

Note an alternative structure for an adjective, with 'be':

Que n'era, de dolent!	How bad it was!/It was awful, wasn't it?
Que n'és, de pesat, aquest!	What a bore that guy is!
Que en som, de llestos!	How clever we are!

Another way to stress qualities is with **com ... de** 'so', still using examples from the set above:

Que blanca (que) t'ha quedat la roba! = **Com t'ha quedat de blanca la roba!**
= **Com t'ha quedat la roba de blanca!**
Que malalt (que) em trobo! = **Com em trobo de malalt!**
Que barroerament (que) parla! = **Com parla de barroerament!**

Notice, though, that in this new structure word order is different: now it is verb + **de** + adverb/adjective + subject. Note also that the **com de** construction (but not **que**) can be used to form an indirect exclamation (see **27.1.3.8** above):

T'admiraràs com és d'interessant aquest llibre.
You'll be amazed how interesting this book is.

Fixa't com és d'espavilat aquest noi.
Just see how clever this boy is.

27.2.3   'INTENSIFYING' ARTICLE IN EXCLAMATIONS

The same intensifying use of the definite article used in the idiomatic alternative to indirect *wh*-questions (**27.1.3.9**) can be found in exclamative sentences completed with a relative clause. English allows a similar alternative in many instances, but the Catalan alternative without the *wh*-word is more frequent and more idiomatic than the English equivalent.

Quanta (de) llum que hi ha aquí dins! = **La llum que hi ha aquí dins!**
How bright it is in here!

Quin pànic que va causar! = **El pànic que va causar!**
What panic it caused! = The panic it caused!

Quina cara que feia! = **La cara que feia!**
What a face she put on! = The face she put on!

Són d'admirar les vegades que ha superat una derrota.
What's remarkable is the (number of) times she has overcome a setback.

Ningú no creu els dies que ha estat treballant en això.
No one can believe how many days he has been working on this.

Use of the neuter article **el** before an adjective or adverb in similar exclamations is, however, a different matter. Colloquial usage resorts to an intensifying use of (non-standard) **lo** in utterances like:

(non-standard) **M'admira lo grosses que són aquestes flors.**
I'm amazed at how big these flowers are.

(non-standard) **Amb lo petita que és i ja parla dues llengües!**
So young and yet she already speaks two languages!

(non-standard) **Lo bé que anava el nostre primer cotxe!**
How well our first car used to go!

The only standard means of achieving this intensification of an adjective/ adverb is with the formula **com** + verb + **de** + adjective/adverb:

M'admira com són de grosses aquestes flors.
Com és de petita i ja parla dues llengües!
Com anava de bé el nostre primer cotxe!

27.2.4 DESIDERATIVE SENTENCES

(i) Expressing positive wishes

Tant de bo que is used to express wishes in exclamatory form. The verb will be in the present subjunctive if the wish can be achieved and in the imperfect subjunctive if the wish is completely impossible (see **19.6**):

Tant de bo que vinguis a dinar demà.
How nice it would be if you could come to lunch tomorrow.

Tant de bo que la primavera durés tot l'any.
I wish springtime lasted all year.

To express not a wish but satisfaction for something that has already come about, **(tanta) sort que**, or **gràcies a Déu que**, forms the exclamation (with the verb in the indicative):

(Tanta) sort que m'ho vares dir.   It's a good job you told me!
Gràcies a Déu que no us heu fet mal!   What a relief that you weren't injured!

(ii) Expressing negative wishes (curses)

Expressions of negative wish have the verb in the subjunctive, with the tense (as for **tant de bo . . .** above) also depending on the possibilities of realization. The structure here is with **mal** directly introducing a clause without **que**:

Mal trobis el càstig de les teves accions.   You ought to get your just desserts.
Mal estiguéssiu tan malament com jo.   You ought to suffer like I do.

27.2.5 OTHER RELATED AND MISCELLANEOUS EXCLAMATIONS

Ja t'està bé!	It serves you right!
S'ho ha ben buscat!	It serves him right! (He had it coming to him.)
Ja els està bé per ser tan golafres!	It serves them right for being so greedy!
Ja me la pagaràs, aquesta!	I'll get you for that!
Ja me les pagaràs!	I'll get you for that!

Exclamations, naturally, are frequently associated with interjections (see Chapter 24):

Home! Quina sorpresa!	Gosh! What a surprise!
Carai, tu! Que pesat que t'estàs posant!	Christ! How annoying you're getting!

Exclamations may take the form of set expressions or popular sayings:

Hem begut oli!
We've done it now! (said when a difficult situation becomes worse)

Embolica que fa fort!
Would you believe it! (said when yet another complication is added to an already seemingly impossible situation)

28 IMPERATIVE UTTERANCES

This chapter deals with the expression, in main clauses, of instructions, offers, and requests, addressed to the hearer/recipient. That is, we are essentially concerned here with second-person requests. However, not only morphological second-person verb forms are involved. The first-person plural may include the hearer also, as in **Vegem-ho** 'Let's see'. And as mentioned in **11.3**, the polite second-person pronouns **vostè** 'you (*sg.*)' and **vostès** 'you (*pl.*)' are always associated with morphologically third-person verb forms. In a sense, imperative utterances can be seen as a special case of wishes; these are covered in **19.6**.

28.1 POSITIVE IMPERATIVE

For direct utterances, only the second-person singular (**tu**), positive imperative, has a special form (for details of the forms, see **16.5.11**). All other imperative forms (first-person plural, and **vostè(s)** third-person singular and third-person plural), and all negative imperatives, make use of the corresponding present subjunctive verb form.

Vine demà i ho veuràs.
Come (second-person singular) tomorrow and you'll see.

Fica les més antigues al calaix de baix.
Put (second-person singular) the older/oldest ones in the bottom drawer.

Calleu!
Be quiet! (second-person plural)

Mantinguem aquesta distinció.
Let us retain this distinction.

Fes-te cap allà.
Go (second-person singular) over there.

Enviïn-nos-el de seguida.
Send (third-person plural **vostès**) us it straightaway.

Deixem-ho córrer.
Let's leave it be.

The imperative of polite **vós** (**11.3** and **29.2.1i(c)**) appears in formal contexts and in instructions:

Consulteu l'índex.   Refer to the index.
Empenyeu.   Push. (on door)

28.2   NEGATIVE IMPERATIVE

Negative imperative constructions are always built with the subjunctive rather than the imperative form. Observe the following pairs:

Fes aquest exercici.
Do this exercise.

No facis aquest exercici.
Don't do this exercise.

Digues què t'ha passat.
Say what has happened to you.

No diguis què t'ha passat.
Don't say what has happened to you.

Pensa les conseqüències dels teus actes.
Think about the consequences of your actions.

No pensis les conseqüències dels teus actes.
Don't think about the consequences of your actions.

For some verbs the forms of the second-person plural imperative and subjunctive coincide:

Pagueu el que deveu.   Pay what you owe.
No pagueu el que deveu.   Don't pay what you owe.
Aneu a saludar aquella senyora. Go and say hello to that lady.
No aneu a saludar aquella senyora. Don't go and say hello to that lady.

The underlying modal difference in these cases is made clear in Balearic Catalan, where, for example, Conjugation I produces distinct imperative (= indicative) second-person plurals in -au:

Pagau el que deveu.   Pay what you owe.
No pagueu el que deveu. Don't pay what you owe.

On **pas** in negative imperatives, see **26.1.8**.

28.3 PRONOUN POSITION

Clitic pronouns follow positive imperative verb forms of all types (**12.2.2**), but precede verb forms in the negative.

Fes-li un petó.	Give her a kiss.
Intentem-ho.	Let's try it.
Diguin-los-ho de seguida.	Tell them (it) straightaway.
No li facis un petó.	Don't give her a kiss.
No ho intentem.	Let's not try it.
No els ho diguin de seguida.	Don't tell them (it) straightaway.

Subject pronouns, if present, normally follow a positive imperative verb form with its complements:

Carrega les cerveses tu.	You load the beers.
Les cartes, escrigui-les vostè.	As for the letters, you write them.

In some varieties, such as Balearic, and in the region of Girona, clitic pronouns precede morphologically third-person imperatives, as follows:

Els ho diguin de seguida.	Tell them (it) straightaway.
Ses cartes, les escrigui vostè.	As for the letters, you write them.
Els me faci vostè.	(You) make them for me.

28.4 OTHER EXPRESSIONS FOR ORDERS AND REQUESTS

A positive request may be expressed by **a** followed by an infinitive; the phrase **A veure** 'Let's see' is extremely common (as is **Veiam** – an archaic subjunctive form – with the same meaning).

Tots vosaltres, a recollir la taula.	You all clear the table.
A jeure.	Time for bed. (lit. to lie)

A polite request is often constructed as a question in the present tense (see **17.1.1**):

Em deixes un boli?	Will you lend me a biro?
Ens porta un cendrer, si us plau?	Will you bring an ashtray, please?

This present tense question is generally the commonest form of request which expresses politeness without self-abasement. One may also use a conditional form in a question, but this is nothing like so common as the English version:

Em deixaries un boli?	Would you lend me a biro?

On toned-down requests using **que** + subjunctive, see **19.6** and **32.2**. A yet more deferential request may include a phrase such as **fer el favor de** 'do the favour of'/'be kind enough to' or **tenir la bondat de** 'have the goodness to':

Em faries el favor de deixar la porta oberta?
Would you be kind enough to leave the door open?

Voleu fer el favor de deixar de fumar?
Would you please stop smoking?

Tingues la bondat de tirar la cortina.
Be so good as to draw the curtain.

However, the use of an imperative verb form in the expression **fer el favor** itself has the connotation of sarcastic politeness, suggesting irritation:

Fes el favor de callar!   Will you shut up?

A request can always be softened by 'please': **si us plau** (lit. if it pleases you) or **per favor**. **Si us plau** is often pronounced **sisplau**; some writers prefer to write **sisplau** on the grounds that, lacking the original **us** element, it is more fitting when neither **vós** nor **vosaltres** is being used. One may also hear **si et plau** for second-person singular **tu** address. These 'please' phrases are used somewhat less than their English counterpart. A Catalan request without 'please' is not regarded as rude.

29 PASSIVE AND IMPERSONAL SENTENCES

A passive construction is one in which a transitive verb is made to function so that its underlying (logical) object appears as its surface subject, its underlying subject being either absent – in the short passive: **La proposta fou rebutjada** 'The proposal was rejected' – or expressed as the agent of the action – in the long passive: **La proposta fou rebutjada per les autoritats** 'The proposal was rejected by the authorities'. Compare the active form: **Les autoritats rebutjaren la proposta** 'The authorities rejected the proposal'.

Impersonal utterances are those in which the identity of the agent is indeterminate or irrelevant. The short passive has this impersonal function in Catalan as it does in English: **Ha estat identificat un dels responsables** 'One of those responsible has been identified'. Then there are various other types of impersonal constructions in Catalan analogous with English: '*They* say that music soothes the soul', '*One* has to admit that . . . ', '*You* don't get much change out of a pound', as described in **29.3** below. In addition the Catalan reflexive passive or impersonal **es** (introduced in **23.4**) makes impersonal constructions where an English passive would probably be used (**No s'ha concedit l'autorització** 'Permission has not been granted') or, less frequently, where English resorts to some other construction (**Es lloguen barques** 'Rowing boats for hire').

Catalan can be considered, then, to have two options, more or less synonymous and equally valid in principle, for conveying a passive meaning:

> **Aquesta estàtua fou inaugurada l'any 1900.**
> approx. = **Aquesta estàtua es va inaugurar l'any 1900.**
> This statue was unveiled in 1900.

In practice, both in the written and in the spoken language, there is a tendency for the construction with impersonal **es** to be preferred, and this accounts in large measure for the simple observation that the passive with 'be' occurs in Catalan with considerably less frequency than it does in English. From the perspective of the foreign learner, the phenomenon can be treated as 'avoidance of the passive', stratagems for which are explained in **29.1.4**.

29.1   PASSIVE WITH ser/ésser 'BE'

29.1.1   PASSIVE MORPHOLOGY

The passive is formed from the appropriate tense and person of ser/ésser 'be' and the past participle, which agrees in number and gender with the subject of ser:

Active	Passive
Van firmar els comprovants.	**Els comprovants van ser firmats.**
They signed the receipts.	The receipts were signed.
El secretari ha convocat una elecció.	**Una elecció ha estat convocada pel secretari.**
The secretary has called an election.	An election has been called by the secretary.

29.1.2   THE PASSIVE AGENT

As in examples given so far, the passive agent is introduced by **per** 'by': **Fou educada per les monges** 'She was brought up by the nuns', etc. Verbs of acquaintance, affective attitude, and accompaniment, however, together with **fer** 'do', 'make' and other verbs denoting literal 'making' allow optional introduction of the agent by **de**:

És conegut de tothom.
He is known to/by everybody.

Era respectada i estimada de tots nosaltres.
She was respected and loved by all of us.

Vindrà acompanyada del marit.
She will be accompanied by her husband.

De + a third-person pronoun (e.g. **fet d'ell**) can optionally be fused as possessive **seu**, etc. (see **7.5**).

Això és fet d'ells/fet seu.	This was done by them.
No sé si és pintat d'ella/pintat seu.	I don't know if it was painted by her.

With first- and second-person agents in this context, the possessive is preferred:

Sí, senyor: és pintat meu.	Yes, indeed: it was painted by me.

The use of **de** to introduce passive agents may be extended to almost any verb in Balearic.

Aquest diari és llegit de molta de gent.
This newspaper is read by many people.

The phrase **per part de** 'on the part of' (note: not **de part de** 'on behalf of') can indicate the agent in impersonal constructions and is occasionally found with the passive:

l'ús que avui es fa per part de molts d'aquest mot
the use made by many people nowadays of this word

Aquesta mesura ha estat durament criticada per part del rector.
This measure has been strongly criticized by/on the part of the vice-chancellor.

29.1.3 USE OF THE PASSIVE

Some general observations provide the basis for good practice:

(i) English allows great latitude in use of the passive voice, to the extent that an indirect object or a prepositional object can appear as the subject of a passive construction: 'I was lent another copy', 'They have been brought good news', 'We'll soon be told the answer', 'It is not to be wondered at', 'They could be caught sight of '. Word-for-word translation into Catalan of this kind of sentence produces grotesquely alien results. The examples just given might be translated respectively as **Em van deixar un altre exemplar, Han rebut una bona notícia, Aviat se'ns dirà la solució, No se n'ha d'estranyar, S'albiraven.**

(ii) The passive with **ser** is, in general, more characteristic of (and more appropriate to) formal language. In ordinary speech and in informal written styles passive avoidance (see **29.1.4**) tends to operate. The following pairs of sentences are virtually equivalent in meaning, but recourse to either the impersonal **es** or impersonal 'they' is generally more spontaneous.

Moltes fàbriques han estat tancades. = S'han tancat moltes fàbriques.
Many factories have been closed down.

El veredicte serà anunciat abans de mitjanit. = Anunciaran el veredicte abans de mitjanit.
The verdict will be announced before midnight.

(iii) A general reluctance to 'think passive' is a feature of Catalan as it is of other Romance languages. However, this is not to say that the passive voice lacks vitality in the modern language. Indeed a certain increase in its use may be detected. This could be due, in part, to the successful influence, through Catalan-language education, of the old-school prescriptivists who have promoted the passive, at the expense of impersonal **es**, in order to enrich the expressive possibilities of Catalan, and also, it must be said, to mark the distance between it and Spanish. The phenomenon has been particularly observable in the language of journalism, where imitation of

English-language sources and models may be influential. This tendency has perhaps been more recently accentuated by insensitive calquing in dubbed versions of English-language film and television materials. Catalans are perhaps more likely to come out with **Serà renyat pel seu pare** than **El seu pare el renyarà** if they have in view or in mind the example of 'He'll be told off by his father'. Similarly with:

> **Ha estat operada per un metge de Barcelona.**
> = **Un metge de Barcelona li ha fet l'operació.**
> She was operated on by a Barcelona doctor.

By grammatical criteria, the alternatives considered so far in this section are all perfectly acceptable in standard Catalan. The question becomes one of how frequently the passive would be spontaneously generated by an educated user, and in which contexts. The general answer is clearly: less frequently than the passive would be used by an English-speaking counterpart, and in a more restricted range of contexts.

(iv) The long passive with the agent expressed does perform a specific function for which alternatives are relatively less practicable:

> **La bandera era portada per un desconegut.**
> The flag was carried by a stranger.

> **Sempre que els pobles han estat ferits pel llamp de la guerra, vencedors i vençuts han hagut de travessar períodes calamitosos.**
> Whenever communities have been struck by the thunderbolt of war, both victors and vanquished have had to live through calamitous times.

Introduction of the agent with **per** in an impersonal **es** construction is also encountered, but it tends to be disapproved of by normative grammarians.

> **Aquesta versió s'ha difós per certs periodistes.**
> This version has been spread by some journalists.
> (cf. **Aquesta versió ha estat difosa per certs periodistes.**)

The short passive, however, does give a lot of ground to impersonal **es**:

> **la possibilitat que forces alemanyes es despleguen a Bòsnia** (*El Temps*)
> **la possibilitat que forces alemanyes siguen desplegades a Bòsnia**
> the possibility of German forces being deployed in Bosnia

There is certainly a case for recommending use of the passive rather than impersonal **es** in cases (including the last one above) where ambiguity might arise because a true reflexive meaning might be construed, for example:

> **Les dues rodes dentades han estat separades/s'han separat.**
> The two cogs have been disengaged/have disengaged themselves.

(v) The passive operates much more comfortably with the preterite, future, perfect, and pluperfect tenses and with the infinitive than with the present, imperfect, and continuous tenses (that is, the forms that characteristically express imperfective aspect).

Van ser/Seran detinguts per la policia.
They were/will be arrested by the police.

The options above are appropriate in a wide range of contexts whereas **Eren/ Són detinguts** would require special contextual conditions. Similarly:

El monument serà restaurat/ha de ser restaurat per l'ajuntament.
The monument will be/is to be restored by the municipal authorities.

Most informants, however, feel that **El monument està sent restaurat** . . . '. . . is being restored' sounds unnatural, preferring for this and other imperfective senses to use impersonal **es**, or, where the agent is mentioned, an active sentence, either **L'ajuntament està restaurant el monument**, or, with topicalization, **El monument, l'està restaurant l'ajuntament (36.4)**.

The loose distinction between verbs which are themselves inherently 'perfective' (punctual, events) and those which are inherently 'imperfective' or durational (states) in meaning also affects this issue. Subject to the tense constraints just mentioned, the passive is more likely with the former than with the latter. Thus **Llurs paraules són escoltades** 'Their words are listened to' is more acceptable than **Llurs paraules són sentides** 'Their words are heard'. Verbs like **abandonar** 'abandon', **aprovar** 'approve (of)', **formar** 'form', **reservar** 'reserve', **atribuir** 'attribute', etc., occupy an area where the event/ state distinction is blurred, so that the nuance of aspect is what is prominent in the following alternatives :

Una quarta part del pressupost fou/era atribuïda al nou departament.
A quarter of the budget was allocated to the new department.

La instrucció va ser/era aprovada pel ministre.
The instruction was approved by the minister.

An important treatise on this subject, basically defining the limitations on the use of the passive, provocatively begins:

És ben sabut que . . . (J. Solà)   It is well known that . . .

(vi) The relationship between the true passive (**El poble va ser abandonat pels habitants** 'The town was abandoned by its inhabitants') and adjectival past participle constructions with **ser** and **estar** (**El poble era/estava abandonat** 'The town was deserted') is discussed at **21.1** and **30.5.1–2**.

29.1.4   CONSTRAINTS ON THE PASSIVE, ALTERNATIVE STRATAGEMS, THEMATIZATION

Rather than to attempt an inventory of verbs and contexts which do not admit passivization with **ser**, it is preferable to establish some guidelines for authentic use in the light of the preceding sections. The guidelines can be related to (i) frequency, and (ii) focus.

(i) English latitude with the passive accounts for the greater frequency of this form in any substantial text or utterance in English compared with the natural equivalent text or utterance in Catalan. (The frequency principle applies inversely, of course, in translation from Catalan to English, where one would expect to find the passive rendering various non-passive constructions in the Catalan original.) The point can be well illustrated by taking a sentence from George Orwell's *Homage to Catalonia*: 'The place was raided and Thompson was arrested, flung into jail, and kept for eight days in a cell so full of people that nobody had room to lie down.' The stringing together of four passives (' . . . raided, . . . arrested, . . . flung, . . . kept') and the elliptical subordination of the last two participles to the 'was' of 'was arrested' are perfectly natural and unobtrusive in English. The same sequence of actions would almost certainly be cast quite differently by a Catalan speaker, especially as 'the place' referred to is described in the preceding sentence as 'a hotel in a part of the town controlled by the Civil Guards'. Thus the opening clause would best be rendered as **Van assaltar el local** . . . (where the subject could be construed as either impersonal 'they' or 'the Civil Guards'). Then, if the passive **fou detingut** were employed for the central 'was arrested', as is feasible, the elliptical additions 'flung' and 'kept' might be expressed in an alternative construction, probably reverting to impersonal 'they', with the punctuation and the connective appropriately modified: **Van assaltar el local i Thompson fou detingut; el ficaren a la presó on el van tenir tancat durant vuit dies en una cel·la tan plena de presos** . . .

In other contexts, the constraints on the Catalan passive may be grammatical in nature. **Fou insultada pel seu marit** is feasible for 'She was insulted by her husband' (although not more so than the active **El seu marit la va insultar**, or indeed **La va insultar el seu marit**), while an active form, **El seu marit la insultava** or **La insultava el seu marit**, would invariably be preferred to *****Era insultada pel seu marit**. 'She was beaten by her husband' will be active, both in the preterite and the imperfect, **Li va pegar/Li pegava el seu marit**, because **pegar** takes an indirect object. Elsewhere, such constraints may often appear quite arbitrary. One can say **L'edifici fou enderrocat per una bomba** 'The building was demolished by a bomb', but more rarely **La finestra fou trencada per una pedra**, which would probably be turned into a sentence like **Van trencar la finestra d'una pedrada** 'The window was broken by a stone(throw)'. The passive may prove unacceptable with a personal pronoun, but acceptable with other types of agent: **Era envejada per tothom** 'She was envied by everyone', but not ?**Era envejada per mi** 'She was envied by me' (**Jo l'envejava**). The following are sentences of a type where the passive is the readiest option in English but most unlikely (or incorrect) in Catalan:

Aquest gos m'ha mossegat.	I've been bitten by this dog.
No t'irrita la seva actitud?	Aren't you irritated by their attitude?
La instrueix un professional.	She is coached by a professional.

(ii) One function of the passive is to 'thematize' or focus attention on the object of the verbal action by situating it at the beginning of the clause (see Chapter 36, especially **36.3–4**). English word order is restricted in its possibilities to achieve this effect other than via the passive. Catalan, on the other hand, has various alternative ways of achieving this thematization of the transitive object. The constructions described in (a)–(f) below can thus be considered as stratagems for passive avoidance (although this notion corresponds to the perspective of the foreign learner and not to the instincts of the native speaker).

(a) The simplest of these is to keep the sentence in the active form (as in the last examples given above), with postposing of the subject as appropriate. This construction can entail representation of the underlying object in the form of a clitic pronoun.

Vaig trucar a la porta. La va obrir un noi d'uns dotze anys.
I knocked at the door. It was opened by a boy of about twelve.

(b) The same effect can be obtained when a noun object is present. Catalan norms of word order (see **36.4**) allow the object to stand first in the sentence (left detachment), preceding the verb, in which case the object will be doubled by a redundant clitic object pronoun:

Aquests paquets, els haurem de portar demà a correus.
These parcels will have to be posted (by us) tomorrow.

Tot això, ja els ho havien explicat abans.
They had already been told all that before.

(c) The last examples in (i) above and those just given in (ii (a)) and (ii (b)) illustrate a recurrent feature which is readily converted into a guideline for good practice. That is, simply to 'think active'. Very many spontaneous passive constructions in English are equally as spontaneous in the Catalan active form. Again the possibilities of verb–subject inversion in Catalan (see **36.2**) facilitate matters:

Ho va descobrir un investigador belga.
It was discovered by a Belgian researcher.

Un mocador li cobria les espatlles.
Her shoulders were covered by a shawl.

(d) As already illustrated at several points above, use of impersonal 'they' in Catalan often corresponds to an English passive:

Li van denegar l'autorització.   He was refused permission.
T'han estafat.   You've been swindled.

(e) A pseudo-passive with **veure's**, **trobar-se**, or **quedar** will often replace **ser** with the participle:

Tot el país s'ha vist sacsejat per vents fortíssims. (*El Temps*)
The whole country has been buffeted by extremely strong winds.

El debat parlamentari ha quedat superat pel debat al carrer. (*El Temps*)
Parliamentary debate has given way to debate on the streets.

Es troba empantanegada en falsos problemes.
She's got bogged down in false problems.

(f) Notwithstanding the naturalness and frequency of the constructions covered in (a–e) above, the passive with impersonal **es** is the most consistently deployed alternative to the passive with **ser**:

No se li pot demanar més.
He can't be asked for more.

Això s'ha descrit com la seva proesa més heroica.
This has been described as his most heroic feat.

29.2   IMPERSONAL USES OF es

The impersonal use of **es** is also referred to, for historical reasons, as the reflexive passive. The **es** in question is the third-person reflexive clitic (whose spelling, **es**, **s'**, **-se**, **'s**, is affected by the position and spelling of the verb, as described in **12.1.2**).

The reflexive passive has been introduced in **23.4**, in relation to reflexivity, and its relationship with the true passive (**ser** + participle) is focused on above at several points. The basic observation that a sentence like **Es van plantejar moltes qüestions** is bound by common sense to mean 'Many questions were raised', rather than 'Many questions raised themselves', is a good point from which to complete description of this phenomenon.

Catalan, like Spanish, has gone further than French in allowing impersonal **es** constructions with intransitive verbs. Sentences like **S'hi està bé, aquí** 'One feels fine here/It's nice here' or **S'és major d'edat als 18 anys** 'One attains the age of majority at 18' obviously cannot be directly rendered by the passive (any more than by a literally reflexive construction). Natives tend to perceive the construction in **S'hi està bé, aquí** as basically different from that in **Es van plantejar moltes qüestions**, and they may reserve the term 'impersonal es' for the former and 'passive **es**' or 'reflexive passive' for the latter. The distinction, however, is less important to the foreign learner of Catalan than the observation that in either construction **es** *appears* to behave (because of its position – tending to begin the sentence – and because of its function in the cognitive meaning of the sentence) as the subject of the verb. This is relevant to: general structural behaviour, questions of overlap with other constructions (other equivalents of 'one' as subject, see **29.3**), and questions of agreement in number (**S'ha construït molts xalets** *vs.* **S'han construït molts xalets**; see **29.2.2**).

Further examples of impersonal uses of **es**:

Es veu que no vindran.
It looks as if they won't be coming.

El pollastre tallat a quarts . . . , se sala i es posa a fregir amb una mica d'oli.
(from cookery book by E. Millà)
The chicken, which has been cut into quarters . . . is seasoned and then fried in a little oil.

Es reparen rellotges.
Watches repaired.

Se sentia un soroll estrany.
A strange sound could be heard.

Es van produir més de cent avaries elèctriques en poques hores.
Over a hundred breakdowns in electricity supply occurred in a few hours.

On word order with impersonal constructions, see **36.2**.

29.2.1   IMPERSONAL es AND ALTERNATIVE CONSTRUCTIONS

Listening to any Catalan speech or perusal of any substantial written text will attest the frequency of impersonal **es**. Some constraints on its use are nevertheless to be observed. These correspond to (i) grammatical and (ii) stylistic considerations. In both areas one may detect influence of (or contrasts with) Spanish whose speakers are, on the whole, more elastic in using its equivalent and have gone further in seeing *se* as a subject pronoun.

(i) Grammatical constraints

(a)   Impersonal **es** is incompatible with verbs that are themselves reflexive or pronominal (Chapter 23); it can neither coexist with nor supplant pronominal **es**. Thus we can say **S'hi dorm molt bé en aquest llit** 'One sleeps very well in this bed'/'This is a very comfortable bed', but not (with **llevar-se** 'get up') ***Es lleva d'hora** nor ***Es es lleva d'hora** for 'One gets up early' (**Es lleva d'hora** can mean only 'She/He gets up early').

Impersonal expressions with reflexive or pronominal verbs have to be formed with **un/-a, (un) hom**, as described in **29.3**.

(b)   One does encounter sentences like:

Aquesta política s'ha aprovat per la majoria dels votants.
This policy has been approved by the majority of those voting.

Here there is a real agent, introduced by **per**, complementing the reflexive passive meaning of the construction (as in **Aquesta versió s'ha difós per certs periodistes**, commented on in **29.1.3iv** above). In normal usage, however, this type of sentence tends to be avoided, and there is a preference for either the long passive (**Aquesta política ha estat aprovada per la majoria dels votants**) or an active construction (**La majoria dels votants han aprovat aquesta política/Aquesta política, l'han aprovada la majoria dels votants**).

(c)   With imperatives (where **es** as 'subject' is attached enclitically to the verb) the language of bureaucracy does supply frequent examples of expressions like:

Vegi's la pàgina 123.   See page 123.
Demanin-se prospectes al nostre agent.   Ask our agent for a prospectus.

Use of the polite **vós** form of the imperative (**11.3**) is generally regarded as more genuine in this function (**Vegeu la pàgina 123; Demaneu prospectes al nostre agent**).

(d)   There is no reason why impersonal **es** should not combine with another pronominal clitic, and instances abound in all levels of language:

Anem a Can Pep, que s'hi menja força bé.
Let's go to Can Pep; the food's good there.

Se'ns comunica que demà hi haurà vaga.
We've been notified that there will be a strike tomorrow.

However, the basis of the impersonal **es** construction, as described so far, is that the original object of a transitive verb becomes the surface subject (**Se sentia un soroll**), or there is no direct object at all (**S'hi menja bé**). A more recent development is the pattern in which a transitive verb is used impersonally with **es** while its original direct object remains a surface direct object:

Els metges demanen que no se'ls critiqui i se'ls deixi treballar amb tran-quil·litat. (R. Solsona)
The doctors are asking not to be criticized and to be left to get on with their work.

A casa se la rep sempre amb els braços oberts.
At our house she is always welcomed with open arms.

Many authorities object to this construction, on the grounds that it reflects an encroachment of the Spanish pattern of making the reflexive pronoun function as a subject in transitive clauses. This said, alternatives to **Els metges demanen que no se'ls critiqui . . .** could only involve use of **un (hom)** or **hom** (see **29.3**), or the passive with **ser**, which are open to stylistic objections (essentially that they are felt to be too formal). The other example above, though, could well be recast in various ways, all natural and, according to several commentators, more authentic:

A casa la rebem sempre. (active construction preferred to both passive and impersonal **es**)
At our house we always welcome her.

Likewise, recasting the sentence **A Felipe González se l'acusa d'haver tolerat la** *guerra bruta* **contra ETA** as passive **Felipe González és/ha estat acusat d'haver tolerat . . .** 'Felipe González is accused of having tolerated the *dirty war* against ETA' (*Avui*), would avoid the pleonasm of the clitic object pronoun (**l'**). The impersonal use of a third-person plural verb is a natural alternative: **Acusen Felipe González d'haver tolerat . . . .** In a formal context **Hom acusa Felipe González . . .** would be another possibility; see **29.2.2** and **29.3**.

It is evident that, apart from instances like those in (a) above, grammatical considerations in this matter shade into the considerations of style that are discussed in the next section.

(ii)   Stylistic constraints on impersonal *es*

Overuse of any communicative or rhetorical feature tends to become monotonous. This principle validates the advice that good style in Catalan will not overwork impersonal **es** and will deploy equivalent resources possessed by the language, as appropriate to the context and the tone. By way of recapitulation, the main options are as follows:

Passive voice *versus* impersonal **es**:

Des d'avui es podrà detenir els conductors que beguin massa.
= **Des d'avui els conductors que beguin massa podran ser detinguts.**
From today drivers who drink too much may be arrested.

Impersonal 'they' *versus* impersonal **es**:

Se m'ha confirmat que el termini acaba demà.
= **M'han confirmat que el termini acaba demà.**
I have had confirmation that the deadline expires tomorrow.

Active forms *versus* impersonal **es** or passive:

D'aquesta manera es motiven els clients perquè comprin més.
In this way clients are motivated to buy more.

D'aquesta manera motivem (motiveu/motiven) els clients perquè comprin més.
In this way we (you/they) motivate clients to buy more.

Impersonal 'one' *versus* impersonal **es** or passive:

S'ha demostrat/Ha estat demostrat que . . .
Hom ha demostrat que . . .
It has been demonstrated that . . . (see **29.3.**)

29.2.2   AGREEMENT OF THE VERB WITH IMPERSONAL es

In theory, and in most dialects of Catalan, a verb used with impersonal **es** and a plural noun (surface subject) will be in the plural form. In other words, there is no evident formal distinction between impersonal **es** and other uses of this clitic.

S'han dutxat aquest matí. (reflexive)
They had a shower this morning.

No es poden veure. (reciprocal)
They can't stand the sight of one another.

Ja no es queixen pas tant. (pronominal)
They don't complain so much now.

Se serveixen immediatament, o bé es poden menjar freds. (i.e. **els calamars:**
E. Millà) (impersonal)
They are served immediately, or they can be eaten cold.

There is little or no vacillation over this agreement when impersonal **es** relates to a determinate subject standing before the verb:

Les maletes s'han de facturar.   The luggage must be checked in.

However, when dislocation, extraction, or relativization of the subject occurs in this construction, there is the possibility of the verb going in the singular (presumably because **es** now seems more like the subject of the verb). This usage is characteristic of northwestern dialects, and many grammarians regard it as non-standard.

Quants paquets dius que s'ha de facturar?
(recommended) **s'han de facturar . . .**
How many packets do you say have to be invoiced?

D'alguns anys ençà no s'ha vist gaires turistes per aquí.
(recommended) **s'han vist . . .**
In the last few years not many tourists have been seen round here.

Agreement of the verb with a plural subject is always the safe option.

There is no number agreement when an impersonal verb with **es** governs an infinitive clause (with its own plural object):

Aquí només es tracta de corregir errors.
Here it's just a matter of correcting mistakes.

An indirect question (which happens to begin with a plural noun phrase) is the subject in:

S'ignora encara quines mesures prendran.
It is still not known what measures they will take.

However, the link between modal **poder** 'can'/'may', **haver de** 'have to'/'must', **voler** 'want' and **acabar de** 'have just' and a dependent infinitive is tighter, so that we generally find agreement in number in impersonal **es** constructions involving these verbs (whether the underlying object precedes or goes after the verb). Notice that the plural noun phrase may be the subject of the finite verb + non-finite passive verb construction in the English versions:

S'han hagut de llençar els números endarrerits.
The back numbers have had to be thrown out.

Els impostos es poden pagar a finals d'any.
The taxes can be paid at the year end.

With **veure** 'see' and **sentir** 'hear' there is more variation:

S'havien/S'havia vist caure les fulles.
One had seen the leaves falling./The leaves had been seen to fall.

No s'havien sentit repetir les instruccions.
No one had heard the instructions repeated./?The instructions had not been heard to be repeated.

29.3 OTHER IMPERSONAL CONSTRUCTIONS

The foregoing sections disclose a grey area in which passive and impersonal functions are hard to differentiate syntactically or in theory. Grammarians are exercised by matters of topicalization and the identification of true and underlying subjects in such constructions. Does **Així no es resol res** equate to passive **Així res no és resolt** 'Nothing is solved this way', with 'nothing' as the subject, or is the idea of an impersonal subject 'Nobody solves anything this way' uppermost? These considerations can be subtly affected by whether the subject/underlying object stands before or after the verb: **Els candidats es distribueixen segons el lloc de naixement** might be felt to correspond closely to the passive **Els candidats són distribuïts ...** 'Candidates are distributed according to their place of birth' (with 'the candidates' as animate subject of an intransitive verb), whereas **Es distribueix(en) els candidats segons el lloc de naixement** could foreground the idea of 'somebody' distributing the candidates as 'object' of the verb. (This question is independent of more specific ambiguities which might arise from use of impersonal **es**, as mentioned at **29.1.3iv** above.)

Some of the constructions described below occur only rarely in the spoken language and may sound stilted; their availability nevertheless enriches the expressive repertoire with genuine forms appropriate to formal and literary discourse.

Although use of the reflexive **es** (see **29.2**) is by far the commonest and most natural way of rendering impersonal constructions in Catalan, there are occasional cases where recourse to **hom** (**un hom** or **un**) is more appropriate. It may avoid ambiguity, as in **Hom va felicitar el guanyador** 'The winner was congratulated', where **Es va felicitar . . .** could mean that the winner congratulated himself. And when the verb involved is itself reflexive then impersonal **es** cannot be used in any circumstances (**29.2.1i(a)**).

> **Hom/Un hom/Un/Una es pregunta com acabarà tot això.**
> One wonders how all this will end.

> **Hom etc. s'hi ha de presentar abans de les nou del matí.**
> One has to turn up/It is necessary to be there before 9 a.m.

(i) Hom

Old Catalan had the indefinite subject pronoun **hom** (related to **home** 'man'; cf. German *man*, French *on* 'one'). Modern prescriptive grammar has favoured its revival, with some degree of success, and this pronoun can be used, without sounding pretentious, in formal contexts and cultivated oral or written styles. Its effect can be considered roughly equivalent to ceremonious use of 'one' in English, although it overlaps also with impersonal expressions:

> **En aquestes circumstàncies hom prefereix sempre la solució més pragmàtica.**
> In these circumstances one always prefers the most pragmatic solution/the most pragmatic solution is always to be preferred.

> **Hom distribueix els candidats segons el lloc de naixement.**
> = **Es distribueixen els candidats segons el lloc de naixement.**
> Candidates are distributed according to their place of birth.

> **Hom no parla anglès aquí. = No es parla anglès aquí.**
> English is not spoken here.

Hom also appears as the subject of pronominal verbs used impersonally (see **29.2.1i**):

Hom es reserva el dret de contestar.	One reserves the right to reply.
Hom, llavors, es pregunta com concloure.	One wonders, then, how to conclude.

Prescriptive grammar traditionally assigns this last function to **un hom** (see (ii) below), but usage consistently defies the prescription, as in the examples.

(ii)   Un hom

In normative theory **un hom** is limited to the function of impersonal subject of pronominal verbs:

Mentre un hom se'n surti!	As long as one can get away with it!
Un hom no s'atreveix a parlar tan clar.	One dare not be so outspoken.

In practice **hom** and **un hom** are interchangeable as impersonal subject. Thus the examples given in (**i**) above could all be written with **un hom**, while the last two instances with **un hom** could be written with **hom**. Likewise,

Són casos en què (un) hom no sap què fer.
They are cases where one doesn't know what to do.

Quan (un) hom s'aixeca d'hora, ha d'esmorzar fort.
When one gets up early one needs a good breakfast.

With **un hom** there is perhaps the slight difference that the user has himself more clearly in mind as the subject than if **hom** alone is used:

Quan un hom està malalt . . .	When one is ill . . .

(iii)   Un/una

These functions of (**un**) **hom** are covered, in rather more spontaneous usage, by the indefinite article **un** as subject pronoun. This also enables gender distinction to be expressed; thus a female speaker might say **Una no sap mai què pot passar** 'One never knows what might happen' or **En casos així una s'estima més callar** 'In cases like this one prefers to remain silent', whereas the same ideas would be expressed by a male as **Un no sap mai . . .** and **. . . Un s'estima més . . .** It is clear from this, moreover, that the speaker has him/herself in mind despite resorting to the formal distancing of the impersonal pronoun. (The logic here is completed by conversational use of the second-person singular **tu** for this function – **No saps mai . . .**, **. . . t'estimes més . . .**, in these examples – as is described in (v) below.)

Un sempre es pregunta . . .	One always wonders . . .
Si un et demanava un favor . . .	If one were to ask you a favour . . .

When a female is making the utterance with self-reference intended:

Una se sent molt ofesa.
One feels very offended.

Una no pot sinó admirar un tal comportament.
One cannot but admire such behaviour.

(iv) La gent

It is common to find **la gent** 'people' used colloquially when the speaker conceives (and thus needs to construct) an impersonal sentence as having an identifiable, albeit indefinite/impersonal, subject:

La gent els va aplaudir, però sense gaire convicció.
They were applauded/People applauded them but without much conviction.

(v) Tu

Catalan has its equivalent of impersonal 'you' which is the conversational equivalent of formal **(un) hom**:

Puges per aquesta vorera i agafes el primer trencant a mà dreta.
You go up this side of the street and you take the first turn on the right.

Per molt que protestis, ningú no et fa cas.
However much you protest, nobody takes any notice.

Vostè(s) is heard in more formal circumstances, but then the person listening usually feels him/herself to be addressed directly: **Vostè puja per aquesta vorera i agafa el primer trencant a mà dreta; Per molt que vostè protesti . . .** The speaker may achieve the impersonal effect by resorting to es: **Es puja per aquesta vorera i s'agafa el primer trencant a mà dreta; Per molt que es protesti . . .**

(vi) Third-person plural

Frequent use is also made of third-person plural verb forms (with unspecified subjects) as mentioned above **29.1.4i** and **29.2.1ii**.

Em van presentar el nou director.   I was introduced to the new manager.

30 COPULAR SENTENCES (ser, estar, etc.)

This chapter is in essence concerned with constructions which in English involve the verb 'be'. There are two kinds of difficulties the user may experience. The first is that in Catalan more than one verb corresponds to English 'be': these are primarily **ser** (or **ésser**) and **estar**, but **haver-hi** also needs to be mentioned. The second is that in some contexts the preference for **ser** or **estar** differs according to dialect; and in some contexts non-standard usage favours **estar** where normative grammar recommends **ser**. Below we distinguish several syntactic or semantic contexts. The problematic contexts are discussed in **30.3** (location) and **30.5** (adjective/participle complements). The remainder are largely straightforward. The related concept 'become' is treated in **30.6**.

30.1 EXISTENCE AND COPULAR VERBS WITHOUT COMPLEMENTS

Corresponding to English 'there is', 'there are', etc., to state that something exists, Catalan uses **haver-hi**. In the standard language **haver-hi** is used only in the singular, but informal usage widely makes **haver-hi** agree in number with its noun phrase argument (see also **25.2.2**).

> **Al diari, hi ha anunciat un pis de lloguer que potser et convindrà.**
> In the paper there is a flat advertised to let that might suit you.

> **Allà baix hi havia els documents del cotxe.**
> Down there there were the car documents. (non-standard **hi havien els documents.**)

Haver-hi may often be made explicit in Catalan where English expresses location using a reduced relative clause (**31.10i**):

> **les eines que hi ha al calaix**   the tools in the drawer

Note the use of **haver-hi** to enquire whether someone is in:

> **Que hi ha en Pere?**   Is Pere in?

In positive statements and in questions **haver-hi** can be used with a definite noun phrase following (**els documents, en Pere**, in examples above). However, **haver-hi** cannot appear in a negative statement with a noun phrase in the preceding position, or with an understood or dislocated definite noun phrase; it is replaced by **ser-hi**, agreeing in number with the noun phrase in question.

No, no hi és, en Pere.	No, Pere's not in.
En Pere hi és.	Pere is there./There is Pere./Pere is in.
Vaig buscar les maletes però no hi eren.	I looked for the cases but they weren't there.
Els documents? Sí que hi són.	The documents? Yes, they are there.

Ser-hi must also be used with first- and second-person pronouns:

Aquí, només hi som nosaltres.	There is only us here.

Ser can be used alone without any complement in the sense 'be so', 'be the case' (see **25.2.2**):

No pot ser.	It can't be so.
No és que jo ho dubti.	It's not (the case) that I doubt it.

Estar can be used alone in the sense 'stop' (usually imperative), or 'be ready' (usually present); note also **estar-se de** + infinitive 'refrain from':

Per nosaltres no estigueu.	Don't mind us./Don't stop on our account.
Ja estàs?	Are you ready?/Have you finished?
No s'estan mai de dir-nos-ho.	They never stop telling us.
No em sé estar de dir . . .	I just have to say . . . /I can't help saying . . .

30.2   COPULA PREDICATES: IDENTITY, SET MEMBERSHIP

To express identity or set membership when the complement is a noun phrase (or infinitive), or a prepositional phrase with **de** indicating origin, possession, membership, material, etc., **ser** is used. Note that noun phrase complements indicating profession have no article in Catalan (indefinite article in English, see **3.2.3**).

Això és la mort per a ell.	That is death to him.
L'única solució era fer-la fora.	The only solution was to sack her.
El seu oncle és el metge del poble.	Her uncle is the village doctor.
La Marta era mestra d'escola.	Marta was a primary-school teacher (by profession).
Aquestes bicicletes són dels veïns.	These bicycles belong to the neighbours.
Són de Catalunya Nord.	They are from North Catalonia.
Jo no era de la colla.	I wasn't (one) of the group.
El teixit és de llana.	The fabric is of wool.

30.3 COPULA PREDICATES: LOCATION, TIME

Valencian speakers spontaneously use **estar** in any location/time expression; this usage is also increasingly common elsewhere but is regarded as non-standard. The standard language reflects the usage of more conservative speakers in maintaining a distinction between mere location (**ser**) and location explicitly extended over time (**estar**). This is illustrated in the following examples, where **estar** might also be translated as 'stay':

Les vaques eren a l'establa.
The cows were in the cowshed.

Reus és prop de Tarragona.
Reus is near Tarragona.

On són les claus?
Where are the keys?

La reunió serà a les deu en punt.
The meeting will be at 10 o'clock prompt.

Aviat serem a Girona; hi estarem tres hores.
We shall soon be in Girona; we shall stay there for three hours.

Tota aquella tarda estigueren a la piscina.
All that afternoon they were at the pool.

Estigues a la plaça fins que jo hi sigui i et rellevi.
Stay in the square until I am there to (lit. and) relieve you.

With animate subjects **estar**, or more often **estar-se**, is used in the sense of 'reside', and also 'work':

En Pere ara (s')està al carrer de Provença.
Now Pere lives on the *carrer de Provença*.

Quan vaig a París sempre (m')estic a l'hotel «Georges V».
When I go to Paris I always stay in the 'Georges V'.

La Joana (s')està a la Renault.
Joana works at/for Renault.

30.4 ADVERBIAL COMPLEMENTS OF 'BE'

When the complement of 'be' is an adverb, or a prepositional phrase which does not denote a location (and is not one of the **de** phrases mentioned in **30.2**), then the copular verb used is **estar**.

–Com estàs? –Estic molt bé.	'How are you?' 'I'm very well.'
Aquesta suma no està bé.	This sum isn't right.
Avui el bacallà no està a l'abast de tothom.	Nowadays cod is not within everybody's reach.
El segon volum ja està a la venda.	Volume two is now available/on sale.
En Ramon està en coma a la Delfos.	Ramon is in a coma at the Delfos clinic.
Jo hi estic en contra.	I'm against it.

In colloquial usage **estar bé** frequently is the equivalent of **ser bo** 'be good'.

> **Ha fet unes caricatures que estan molt bé. (= unes caricatures (que són) molt bones)**
> She's done some caricatures which are very good.

30.5 COPULA WITH ADJECTIVAL OR PARTICIPIAL COMPLEMENTS

We have discussed in **29.1** the passive construction involving **ser/ésser** 'be' + the participle of a transitive verb. In **21.1** we touched on the pattern in which **ser** occurs with a participle used adjectivally (stative sense), as in **La seva cara m'era desconeguda** 'Her face was unknown to me'. It is uses like the latter which we discuss more fully here, along with the predicative use of adjectives: **La seva cara era/estava blanca** 'Her face was white'.

With adjectival or participial complements both **ser** and **estar** are used; often (but not always) with an important difference of meaning where there is a choice. We need to start by distinguishing between animate subjects (**30.5.1**) and inanimate ones (**30.5.2**).

30.5.1 ANIMATE SUBJECTS WITH ADJECTIVAL OR PARTICIPIAL COMPLEMENTS

With an animate subject and an adjective or participle complement, **estar** is used to indicate that a quality is contingent, temporary, the result of some change, and so on. **Ser** indicates essential, defining, or (relatively) permanent qualities.

Estaven contents del nou horari.	They were pleased with the new timetable.
Estarem asseguts durant el discurs.	We shall be sitting down (i.e. seated) during the speech.
Estem morts de gana.	We are starving (hungry).
Després de la malaltia l'àvia estava dèbil i nerviosa.	After her illness grandmother was weak and nervous.

El poeta era dèbil i nerviós.	The poet was weak and nervous by nature).
En Tomeu és alt, ros, i fort de cames.	Tomeu is tall, fair, and strong-legged.
Tu ets més madur que jo.	You are older than I am.

Other adjectives, like **dèbil** and **nerviós** in the examples above, where a distinction of meaning accompanies the choice between **ser** and **estar**, are: **alegre** 'cheerful', **feliç** 'happy'/'fortunate', **trist** 'sad', **tranquil** 'calm', **quiet** 'placid', **elegant** 'smart', **prim** 'thin'/'slim', and so on.

The adjectives **viu** 'alive' and **mort** 'dead' (in their literal senses), **jove** 'young', **vell** 'old', **casat** 'married', **solter** 'unmarried', **vidu/viudo** 'widowed', **calb** 'bald', **coix** 'lame', and other adjectives denoting physical defects/ disabilities, were traditionally constructed with **ser** (regarding these qualities as essentially permanent or definitional), but in contemporary usage they are also often found with **estar**.

The following adjectives, which inherently denote temporary or changeable states, are normally used with **estar**: **animat** 'lively', **refredat** (estar refredat = 'have a cold'), **capacitat** 'trained', 'prepared', **exempt** 'exempt', **satisfet** 'satisfied', **gras** 'fat', **bo** 'well' (ser bo = 'be good'), **sa** 'well', 'healthy', **malalt** 'ill'. (Observe the difference between **Na Miquela està sana** 'Miquela is well' and **Caminar és sa** 'Walking is healthy'.)

The choice between **estar** and **ser** does not always reflect the semantic distinction mentioned between contingent and essential properties, but may be determined by specific lexical items. So note it is always **ser conscient** 'be conscious', 'realize', and usually **ser present** 'be present'. With **estar** the adjective **llest** means 'ready', 'prepared'; with **ser** it means 'intelligent', 'quick-witted':

Si en Jaume està llest, engegaré el motor.	If Jaume is ready, I'll start the engine.
En Jaume és llest i pràctic.	Jaume is clever and practical.

30.5.2 INANIMATE SUBJECTS WITH ADJECTIVAL OR PARTICIPIAL COMPLEMENTS

In the case of an inanimate subject and an adjective or participle complement, the traditional norm was to use **ser**, without regard to the distinction between contingent and essential, mentioned above (**30.5.1**).

L'aigua és bruta.	The water is dirty.
La sopa és freda.	The soup is cold.
El raïm ja és madur.	The grapes are ripe now.

Estar could also be used, either with participles, especially where the use of **ser** might suggest a passive construction, or in the sense 'stay', especially when a length of time is specified or suggested.

Participles:

> **El gerro està/és trencat.**
> The jug is broken.

> **Les cases estaven abandonades.**
> The houses were abandoned/were in an abandoned state.

(Compare: **Les cases eren abandonades** 'The houses were abandoned/were being abandoned', see **21.1**.)

Length of time:

> **La casa està bruta, perquè no la netegen mai.**
> The house is dirty, because it is never cleaned.

> **La seva imatge estava sempre present en la seva ànima.**
> His image was always present in her mind.

Participle/length of time:

> **El restaurant estarà tancat tot el mes d'agost.**
> The restaurant will be closed throughout August.

> **Durant una setmana la circulació per carretera estigué interrompuda.**
> For a week communication by road was cut.

Contemporary usage, however, tends in the direction of applying the same contingent/essential distinction with inanimate subjects as with animate ones, permitting contrasts such as the following to be made:

> **Aquests gelats són molt bons.**
> These ice creams are very good (i.e. a good type, a good brand, a good quality product).

> **Aquests gelats estan molt bons.**
> These ice creams are very good (i.e. are tasty, as shown by immediate experience).

> **El pal de llum és tort.**
> The lamp stand is (of a) twisted (design).

> **El pal de llum està tort.**
> The lamp stand is twisted (sc. as a result of damage).

According to this pattern the first three examples of **30.5.2** would be **L'aigua està bruta, La sopa està freda, El raïm ja està madur**. However, some grammarians who are generally disposed to tolerate **estar** with inanimate subjects still reject its use with adjectives such as **fred** 'cold', **calent** 'hot' when their appropriateness depends on sensory experience.

Other writers defend as genuine (and thus standard) the use of **estar** with inanimate subjects, contrasting with **ser,** in contexts where the quality attributed is produced deliberately:

El safareig és ple.
The sink is full. (just happens to be so)

El safareig ja està ple.
The sink is now full. (Someone has been filling it and their intention is now achieved.)

L'hotel serà buit aquest estiu.
The hotel will be empty this summer. (mere prediction)

L'hotel estarà buit aquest estiu.
The hotel will be empty this summer. (on purpose)

It would be unwise, though, to assume such a distinction is intended, in the absence of other supporting evidence.

30.6   VERBS TRANSLATING 'BECOME'

There is no single Catalan verb that translates English 'become'. Apart from the lexical intransitive verbs which have an inchoative component (such as **enrogallar-se** 'become hoarse', **aclarir-se** 'become brighter', see **23.5**), the following verbs (most, but not all of them pronominal) correspond to various aspects and nuances of the single English verb:

(i) Esdevenir

Esdevenir 'become' can take either a noun or an adjective as complement:

L'aneguet lleig esdevingué cigne.
The ugly duckling became a swan.

Molts pobres esdevindran immensament rics.
Many poor people will become immensely rich.

(In its pronominal form, **esdevenir-se** means 'happen', 'take place':

Això s'esdevingué fa més de vint anys.
This happened over twenty years ago.)

(ii) Posar-se

Used only with adjective complements, **posar-se** indicates change of mood, physical condition, disposition or appearance. The changes expressed by

posar-se tend to be relatively abrupt or short-lived. A distinction is observable between **S'ha posat molt irascible** 'He's become very irritable' and **(S')ha tornat molt irascible** (see below **(iii)**), the latter denoting a change more in character than in mood. **Posar-se** can be used with both animate and inanimate subjects:

Quan ho va saber, es va posar ben moixa.
When she found out she became really gloomy.

Si continues així, et posaràs malalt.
If you go on like this you'll become ill.

A l'aigua es posa blau.
In water it turns blue.

El to de la polèmica s'està posant crispat.
The tone of the dispute is becoming heated.

El dia se'ns posa núvol.
The day is turning cloudy.

Colloquially **posar-se** often refers to a person's appearance or how they are 'got up':

Em posaré d'estar per casa.   I'll put on some comfortable clothes.
Que elegant que t'has posat!   How smart you now look!

(iii) Tornar(-se)

Applied to animate subjects **tornar(-se)** usually implies involuntary mental or psychological change:

(S')han tornat molt mandrosos.
They have become very lazy.

Com és que (s')hagi tornat tan primmirada?
How is it that she has become so fussy?

With an inanimate physical subject the idea can be that of 'turn':

Aquestes peres (s')han tornat toves.
These pears have gone/turned soft.

Amb el canvi de temperatura el vi (es) tornarà agre.
With the change in temperature the wine will turn sour.

Occasionally also in this sense of 'turn' applied to a person:

Quan (es) va tornar vostè socialista?   When did you turn socialist?

The same verb can also be used with abstract inanimate nouns:

La intolerància (es) **torna cada dia més oberta.**
Intolerance is becoming more open by the day.

La seva actitud (es) **tornarà aviat menys agressiva.**
Their attitude will soon become less aggressive.

(iv) Fer-se

Used with both noun and adjective complements, **fer-se** generally implies voluntary change. It is also used for a change of role in professional and other circumstances:

S'ha fet polític/policia.
He has become a politician/a policeman.

Amb aquesta cançó es va fer famosa/rica.
With this song she became famous/rich.

There is little difference between (S')**està tornant cada vegada més gandul** and S'**està fent cada vegada més gandul** 'He's getting more and more idle', except that more wilfulness is implied in the latter.

Change or development in a person's life cycle may be expressed with **fer-se** or **tornar(-se)**: S'**ha fet gran/(S')ha tornat gran** 'He has grown up', S'**han fet molt vells/(S')han tornat molt vells** 'They have grown very old'. It is often applied to children to remark how they have changed:

Que gran que s'ha fet/(s')ha tornat aquest nen!
How this little chap has grown (up)!

Other idioms with **fer-se**:

Se'ns fa tard.	It's getting late.
Com s'ha fet aquella mossa!	Just look what that girl turned out like!
Em faig molt amb ells.	I get on very well with them.
Els cosins no es fan.	The cousins don't get on well together.

(v) Quedar(-se)

Although several authorities repudiate use of **quedar-se** in the context discussed here, its basic meaning of 'stay', 'be left', in both simple and pronominal forms would seem to validate it as translating nuances of 'become', especially when an idea of loss is implicit in that of change: **Que prim que t'has quedat!** 'How slim you have become!' sounds more plausible than **Que gras que t'has quedat!** 'How fat . . . !'

Després de l'accident, va quedar cega/muda/coixa/impedida.
The accident left her blind/dumb/lame/disabled.

Vaig quedar sorprès en sentir aquesta resposta.
I was surprised when I heard that reply.

Es van quedar sense un duro.
They were left penniless.

The verbs **restar** and **romandre** 'stay' cannot easily substitute **quedar(-se)** in cases like the above, as they denote 'state' or permanence rather than change:

Es van barallar, però van restar amics.
They had an argument, but they stayed friends.

Ha romàs vídua a 34 anys.
She's been left a widow at 34.

Note that **quedar-se** (not **quedar**) is used transitively meaning 'keep':

Com que ningú ho reclamava, m'ho vaig quedar.
As nobody claimed it, I kept it.

Quedi's el canvi.
Keep the change.

(vi) Other ways of translating 'become'

As illustrated in sections (i–v) above, Catalan tends to particularize the idea of 'becoming'. This tendency is even more pronounced in other common equivalents:

(a) **Convertir-se en** 'change into' introduces only noun or noun-phrase complements:

El turisme s'ha convertit en la font principal d'ingressos de la regió.
Tourism has become the region's principal source of income.

El sofà es converteix fàcilment en llit secundari.
The sofa easily becomes a spare bed.

Stronger connotations of 'transformation' are conveyed by **transformar-se en**:

Ja veuràs com la granota es transformarà en príncep.
Just watch how the frog turns into a prince.

(b) **Arribar a ser** 'come to be' expresses the result of a gradual process, often with the idea of 'manage to become' or 'become eventually':

No arribaràs mai a (ser) mestre d'obres.
You'll never become foreman.

Tan ase que semblava, i encara ha arribat a ser president.
Dim as he seemed, he's still become president.

(c) 'Become' meaning 'be appointed' is usually translated by means of **no-menar** 'designate' or simply **fer**, with the English subject becoming the object of a verb in the impersonal third person (**29.3vi**):

L'han nomenat/fet Director General.   He has become Director General.

31 RELATIVE CLAUSES

31.1 RELATIVE PRONOUNS

Catalan has four relative pronouns. (Unstressed) **que** and (stressed) **qui** and **què** are invariable; the compound **el qual** (**la qual**, **els quals**, **les quals**) agrees in number and in gender with the head noun or antecedent to which it refers, conforming also with its function as relative adjective (see **31.9**). Use of these pronouns is not differentiated in the same way as English 'who', 'whom', 'which', 'that'.

The functions and syntax of the various relative pronouns are described in **31.2–7**.

Adverbial **on** 'where', **quan** 'when' and, less frequently, **com** 'how' may introduce relative clauses, as in **És el carrer on vivia en Carles** 'It's the street where Carles used to live', see **31.8**.

Use of the indicative or subjunctive mood in relative clauses, illustrated in the examples throughout this chapter, is the subject of discussion in **17.1.4.1ii** and **19.3**.

31.1.1 THE ANTECEDENT OF A RELATIVE CLAUSE

The antecedent is the item in the main clause to which a relative pronoun refers, introducing a subordinate adjectival clause, according to the following basic pattern:

Tinc un gos. El meu gos es diu Tom.   I have a dog. My dog is called Tom.
→ **Tinc un gos que es diu Tom.**   → I have a dog (which is) called Tom.

The antecedent may be a full noun phrase or a pronoun or pronominal adjective:

Els clients que paguin per endavant rebran un descompte.
Customers paying in advance will receive a discount.

Aquests que ara t'envio són els documents que havies demanat.
These which I am now sending you are the documents you had asked for.

Representa un anar amunt i avall que cansa molt.
It means a to-ing and fro-ing which is very tiring.

For further discussion of antecedents, see **31.6**.

31.1.2 CHOICE OF RELATIVE PRONOUNS: RESTRICTIVE AND NON-RESTRICTIVE CLAUSES

Which Catalan relative pronoun is used is determined by the following factors (often in combination): whether the pronoun is subject or object in the relative clause, whether it follows a preposition, whether the antecedent is human or non-human, and whether the relative clause is restrictive or non-restrictive.

A restrictive relative clause specifies and limits the scope of its antecedent so that the listener can identify what is intended; the function of a non-restrictive clause is descriptive, giving additional information about an antecedent that is already identified in the discourse. Thus there is a difference between **Tenen tres fills que són arquitectes** 'They have three children who are architects' and **Tenen tres fills, que són arquitectes**. The first is restrictive: it indicates how many of the children (of whom there are implied to be more than three) are architects. The second is non-restrictive, giving information about all three children. Similarly for the following pair of sentences:

Els inquilins que se sentien perjudicats van protestar.
The tenants who felt aggrieved protested.

Els inquilins, que se sentien perjudicats, van protestar.
The tenants, who felt aggrieved, protested.

In the first the relative limits the antecedent 'tenants', identifying which sub-group of them protested. In the second the relative clause supplies additional information about the antecedent already conceived as a whole group.

In writing, a non-restrictive clause is typically separated by commas, corresponding to brief pauses in spoken delivery. Catalan allows the optional use of the compound relative pronoun (in the second example above, **els quals** for **que**, see **31.4**) to indicate clearly that a clause is non-restrictive, whereas English relies only on the pause or comma to make the distinction. (Note that the important pause is the one before the relative pronoun. Catalan punctuation conventions admit, and even prefer, a comma between a long restrictive clause and a following main verb; so, in **Els deixebles que escoltaren i aplaudiren fervorosament aquella conferència, no l'oblidaran mai** 'The pupils who heard and fervently applauded that lecture will never forget it', the relative clause is obviously restrictive.)

A relative clause referring to the whole of a unique entity is ipso facto non-restrictive:

El camp del Barça, que/el qual acull cada setmana més de 100.000 espectadors, és un dels llocs sagrats del futbol mundial.
Barcelona FC's ground, which every week welcomes over 100,000 spectators, is one of the shrines of world football.

31.1.3 THE POSITION OF RELATIVE PRONOUNS: GENERAL

Catalan, unlike English, never omits the relative pronoun:

les persones que més admirem	the people (who(m)) we most admire
les coses que feien	the things (that) they used to do
el dia que va morir Marilyn	the day (that) Marilyn died

(On verb + subject word order in relative clauses, see **36.6**.) In common with the other Romance languages, Catalan does not allow a preposition to be separated from the relative pronoun that it governs: **la pel·lícula de la qual parlaven** 'the film they were talking about/about which they were talking', **un tema damunt del qual s'ha estès un vel de silenci** 'a subject that a veil of silence has been spread over/over which a veil of silence has been spread'.

Less obvious is the fact that Catalan does not allow the relative pronoun to be separated from its antecedent by a verb phrase. The type of sentence sometimes heard in English 'Those hitch-hikers were Swedish that we picked up yesterday' can only go into Catalan as **Aquelles autoestopistes que vam recollir ahir eren sueques** or **Eren sueques aquelles autoestopistes que vam recollir ahir**. Only an adjectival phrase, standing in apposition to the head noun, can come between that antecedent and a relative clause:

> **els informes, alguns d'ells negatius però la gran majoria favorables, que s'han rebut sobre l'esdeveniment**
> the reports, some of them negative but in the majority favourable, that have come in on the event

When a Catalan relative clause refers to the subject of a preceding main clause whose order is verb–subject, it can have a contrastive force which English tends to make explicit:

> **Van arribar poc després els bombers, que tampoc no van poder apagar aquell infern.**
> The firefighters arrived shortly afterwards, but they could not quench that inferno either.

Whether or not this effect is present, the pattern of a main clause verb + subject followed by a relative clause (restrictive or non-restrictive) is very typical:

> **Han demanat la paraula 3 o 4 diputats que no havien intervingut fins llavors.**
> Three or four MPs who had not intervened until then asked for permission to speak.

> **Els seguien els holandesos, que duien el vestit nacional.**
> They were followed by the Dutch, who were wearing their national costume.

31.2   THE UNSTRESSED RELATIVE PRONOUN que

This is the most frequently used of the Catalan relative pronouns. **Que** can refer to both human and non-human antecedents; it can function as either subject or object inside the relative clause, which itself may be restrictive or non-restrictive (**31.1.2**). It can be exemplified, then, under four main headings:

(i)   **Que** as relative subject in a restrictive clause:

els especuladors que s'hi van cremar els dits
the speculators who got their fingers burnt

el torn que comença a les nou del vespre
the shift that begins at 9.00 p.m.

(ii)   **Que** as relative object in a restrictive clause:

els especuladors que ha interpel·lat el fiscal
the speculators who have been questioned by the public prosecutor

l'autobús que vam agafar ahir
the bus we caught yesterday

el xicot que acompanyava la Núria
the guy that Núria had with her

(In this context, as in (iv) below, referring to human direct objects, **a qui** is frequently heard for **que** – **el xicot a qui acompanyava la Núria** – but **que** is also frequent and correct, even when there is ambiguity: **el xicot que acompanyava la Núria** could mean either 'the guy that Núria had with her' or 'the guy that had Núria with him'.)

(iii)   **Que** as relative subject in a non-restrictive clause:

la música, que apaivaga l'esperit més atribolat, . . .
music, which soothes the most troubled spirit, . . .

Penso en la Maria, que se les sap totes.
I'm thinking about Maria, who never misses a trick.

(iv)   **Que** as relative object in a non-restrictive clause:

la cançó que cantà a París, i que després va gravar en el seu primer elapé
the song he sang in Paris, and which he later recorded on his first LP.
(Here only the second of the two relative clauses is non-restrictive.)

els principiants, que posarem en un grup a part
the beginners, whom we shall put in a separate group

On the use of compound **el qual** in non-restrictive clauses, see **31.4**.

31.2.1 Que IN RELATIVE CLAUSES OF TIME

Que is used in restrictive relative clauses of time where the antecedent is a nominal time expression:

l'any que ens vam conèixer	the year that we met
Ho faré el dia que vindràs.	I'll do it (on) the day you come.
la setmana/el mes/l'any que ve	next week/month/year

Non-restrictive relative clauses of time are formed with **quan** 'when', see **31.8**.

La notícia va esclatar per aquelles dates, quan tothom feia vacances.
The news broke around that time, when everybody was on holiday.

When the antecedent is introduced by an indefinite article, a construction with **en** + stressed **què** or **en** + compound **el qual** is used:

Eren uns anys en què/en els quals tots vam patir fam.
They were years in which we all went hungry.

Thus a distinction is generally observed between **el moment que m'ho diguis** 'the moment you tell me' and **un moment en què ell badava** 'a moment when he was not paying attention'.

Many temporal adverbial clauses are literally constructed on the basis of an adverb or noun phrase plus a relative clause:

ara que vostès han vingut   now that you have come

Likewise with **així que** 'as soon as', **sempre que** 'whenever', **cada vegada que** 'every time that', **a mesura que** 'as', and so on; see **33.2.2**.

31.2.2 NON-STANDARD/COLLOQUIAL CONSTRUCTIONS WITH que

In colloquial usage a bare **que** is used to head a relative clause which in more formal style would follow stricter conventions involving combination of prepositions and relative pronouns. A grasp of these patterns is important in order to understand everyday spoken Catalan. The basic mechanism of these simplified non-standard constructions involves the support of **que** by the presence of a weak pronoun that supplies required information about the role of the antecedent within the relative clause, as is seen in:

la noia que li vaig donar les claus (non-standard)
la noia a qui vaig donar les claus (standard)
the girl that I gave the keys to (lit. the girl that I gave her the keys)

and in

És una dona que la veiem cada dia. (non-standard)
És una dona que veiem cada dia. (standard)
She is a woman that we see every day.

Són coses que sempre les hauríem de tenir presents. (non-standard)
Són coses que sempre hauríem de tenir presents. (standard)
They are things which we should always bear in mind.

In these last two examples the weak pronoun – strictly redundant (see **12.8**) –
picks up the simple direct object function of **que** (see **33.3.4.1**). The pattern is
least common when, as here, the relative pronoun is a direct object. The
phenomenon may sometimes be found in writing, particularly if several
words separate the relative pronoun from the verb which affects it:

Ara et faré una confessió que mai abans no m'havia atrevit a fer-*la* a ningú.
(non-standard)
Ara et faré una confessió que mai abans no m'havia atrevit a fer a ningú.
(standard)
I'll now make to you a confession that I never dared make to anyone
before.

Els gramàtics aconsellen moltes construccions que en la llengua viva la gent
no *les* usa. (non-standard)
Els gramàtics aconsellen moltes construccions que en la llengua viva la gent
no usa. (standard)
Grammarians recommend many constructions that people do not use in
the living language.

With other roles than direct object within the relative clause, the pattern is
common in spontaneous casual speech, but, again, is avoided in writing.

un jugador de rugby que li han operat el fèmur (non-standard)
un jugador de rugby a qui/al qual han operat el fèmur (standard)
a rugby-player who has had a thigh operation

una tela que se'n fan cortines (non-standard)
una tela de què/de la qual es fan cortines (standard)
a material which curtains are made from

un home que mai no li surten bé les coses (non-standard)
un home a qui/al qual mai no li surten bé les coses (standard)
a man who things never turn out right for

When the relative pronoun has the role of possessor (object of the preposition **de**) the non-standard construction with expanded **que** is frequently
found (sometimes with the possessive adjective introducing the object of
possession):

un poble que totes les cases són d'una sola planta (non-standard)
a town whose/where the houses are all single-storeyed

el matrimoni vell que el fill major estudia a Lleida (non-standard)
the old couple whose eldest son is studying in Lleida

Són amics de tota la vida que coneixem massa bé les seves debilitats. (non-standard)
They're lifelong friends whose weaknesses we know only too well.

The last group displays avoidance of the possessive relative formed with **de** + compound **el qual** (see **31.5**), with which construction the standard versions would be: **un poble totes les cases del qual . . ., el matrimoni vell el fill major del qual . . ., . . . amics de tota la vida les debilitats dels quals . . .**

In informal style **que** can stand for a preposition + relative pronoun, provided its antecedent is governed by the same preposition:

Amb els amics que sortia abans, vaig arribar a avorrir-m'hi molt.
I got very bored *with* the friends I used to go around *with*.

Dels projectes que et vam parlar, més val que ens n'oblidem.
We might as well forget *about* the plans we talked to you *about*.

Als llocs que ja has anat, no val la pena de tornar-hi.
There's no point in going back *to* places you've been *to* already.

This construction is not conventionally included in the non-standard set discussed above (though some grammarians might feel it belongs there). On relative pronouns governed by prepositions, see **31.3** and **31.4.2**.

31.3 THE STRESSED RELATIVE PRONOUNS què AND qui

These forms are invariable and appear only after a preposition, **què** referring to things or (non-human) concepts and **qui** to persons.

Examples with **què**:

Aquestes són les fotos de què et parlava.
These are the photos I was telling you about.

l'assumpte a què ens referíem
the matter we were referring to

No trobo cap llibre amb què distreure'm.
I can't find any book to entertain myself with.

el motiu per què s'ha presentat
the reason why he turned up

Examples with **qui**:

Els amics en qui confiava m'han traït.
The friends I used to trust have betrayed me.

aquell amb qui sortia la Rosa
that guy Rosa used to go out with

l'artista de qui avui es parla tant
the artist that is so talked about nowadays

la persona a qui vaig entregar el paquet
the person I gave the parcel to

aquests companys nostres, a qui menyspreen els teus pares/que menyspreen . . .
those friends of ours, whom your parents despise

These stressed relative pronouns combine most readily with the unstressed prepositions (**a, de, per, en, amb**). Other prepositions, stressed and compound, tend to introduce the compound relative **el qual**, etc. (**31.4.2**; see **31.4.3** for non-standard use of **el/la/els/les que** in these cases).

On **qui** after pronoun or article antecedents, see **31.6.1** and **31.6.2**; on **qui** as headless relative, see **31.7**.

31.4 THE COMPOUND RELATIVE **el qual**, ETC.

As remarked, **qui**, **que**, and **què** are all invariable. The compound relative **el qual**, **la qual**, **els quals**, **les quals** agrees in number and gender with its antecedent. Strictly speaking **qual** is an adjective (see **31.9**) which, like other adjectives, can be used pronominally. **El qual** may substitute **que**, **qui**, and **què** as described in **31.4.1–3**. Where the alternative does exist, preference for the compound **el qual** is more characteristic of the written than of the spoken language.

31.4.1 COMPOUND RELATIVE INSTEAD OF **que**

El qual can be used instead of **que** in a non-restrictive function, both as subject and as object of the relative clause:

Els inquilins, que/els quals se sentien perjudicats, van protestar.
The tenants, who felt aggrieved, protested.

(Compare **Els inquilins que se sentien . . .**, restrictive function in which only **que** is used.)

En aquesta edició antiga, que/la qual vaig descobrir l'altre dia, hi ha menys errors.

In this old edition, which I discovered the other day, there are fewer errors.

(Compare restrictive **En l'edició que vaig descobrir l'altre dia . . .**)

This use of **el qual** instead of **que** is recommended when the relative clause is separated from its antecedent (and where English might resort to a different construction):

Un bidell va pujar al despatx amb un sobre gros, quan ja era l'hora de plegar, el qual portava l'etiqueta «Urgent».

A porter came up to the office with a large envelope, when it was already time for home, and this envelope had an 'Urgent' sticker on it.

Era una amistat de mena estranya, feta en temps difícils, interrompuda per llargues separacions, la qual és curiós que hagi durat tants anys.

It was a strange sort of friendship, struck up in difficult times, interrupted by long separations, and it is odd that it should have lasted for so many years.

31.4.2   COMPOUND RELATIVE AFTER A PREPOSITION, ETC.

El qual, etc. can be used as an alternative to **què** or **qui** after any preposition (including the unstressed ones illustrated in **31.3**): **la qüestió a què al·ludia** = **la qüestió a la qual al·ludia** 'the matter I was alluding to', **les eines amb què treballen** = **les eines amb les quals treballen** 'the tools they work with', **la noia de qui s'ha enamorat** = **la noia de la qual s'ha enamorat** 'the girl he has fallen in love with'. In the case of an unstressed preposition preference for the compound form corresponds to a higher or more formal register, but not very markedly so unless this option is insistently resorted to.

On the other hand, after stressed and compound prepositions, the compound relatives are more usually found, and they are exclusively used after a gerund or an infinitive:

Són abusos contra els quals hem de protestar.
They are abuses we must protest against.

Seguí un període durant el qual l'empresa va prosperar.
There followed a period during which the business prospered.

l'estàtua al voltant de la qual havien plantat tota mena de flors
the statue around which all kinds of flowers had been planted

L'epidèmia, combatent la qual els metges havien esmerçat esforços enormes, acabà arrasant el país.
The epidemic, in combatting which the doctors had invested enormous efforts, in the end devastated the country.

Perderen uns privilegis per obtenir els quals havien treballat tota la vida.
They lost privileges which they had worked all their lives to obtain.

As is illustrated in the examples above, the contexts in which compound relatives occur after a preposition tend to be of an elevated level of language, and this is more obviously so when they combine with an infinitive or gerund. More colloquial styles will tend to resort to simpler, analytical constructions (for example, **Són abusos i hem de protestar**) or to the relative pronoun groups discussed in **31.4.3**.

31.4.3   THE GROUPS el/la/els/les que

The combination **el que**, etc. is frequently heard after a preposition (instead of stressed **què/qui** or compound **el qual**, etc.), but is condemned as non-standard, in particular, as a Castilianism. Sentences like the following have wide currency in all dialects:

Les dades amb les que treballa són falses. (non-standard)
The data he's working with are false.

Han enderrocat els pilars sobre els que s'aguantava el pont. (non-standard)
They have demolished the pillars on which the bridge was supported.

Els artistes dels que parla són molt populars. (non-standard)
The artists she's talking about are very popular.

Les companyes en les que confiava l'han abandonada. (non-standard)
The companions in whom she trusted have abandoned her.

For each such case the alternative with stressed **què/qui** is generally more acceptable in any level of language: **Les dades amb què ...**; **Els pilars sobre què (els quals) ...**, **Els artistes de qui ...**, **Les companyes en qui ...** As remarked in **31.4.2**, use of compound **el qual**, etc. (for which the **el que**, etc. group are viewed as alien substitutes), introduced by stressed or compound prepositions, is characteristic of more formal language.

See **31.6.2** below for treatment of **el/la/els/les que** in a quite distinct construction, and **9.2.2** for **el que** as the neuter relative.

31.4.4   AMBIGUITY IN RELATIVE CLAUSES

Use of compound **el qual** is particularly convenient when ambiguity might otherwise occur over reference to an antecedent made in a non-restrictive relative clause. In the sentence **Van conèixer les filles del gerent, a qui ja havien escrit sobre la qüestió** 'They met the daughters of the administrator, to whom they had already written on the subject', **a qui** could refer either to 'the administrator' or to 'the daughters'. Either **al qual** (for the administrator) or **a les quals** (for the daughters) would clarify which referent is intended. Similarly:

Alguns títols d'aquesta sèrie, dels quals s'ha creat una demanda notable, seran reeditats aviat en una nova col·lecció de butxaca.

Some titles in this series, for which a significant demand has arisen, will be republished soon in a new paperback collection.

Here **dels quals** refers clearly to **títols**, whereas **de la qual** would refer to **sèrie**, and **de què** would be ambiguous.

31.5   THE POSSESSIVE RELATIVE

We deal here with constructions corresponding to 'whose', 'of which', in English. Standard Catalan here is less agile than some other Romance languages (compare Spanish *cuyo*, French *dont*). In possessive relative constructions the object of possession + **de** is combined with the appropriate form of compound **el/la/els/les qual(s)**, the latter agreeing in number and gender with the possessor. Thus:

un amic	**el nom** **l'adreça** **els cognoms** **les característiques**	**del qual**

a friend (*m.*) whose first name/address/surname/characteristics

una amiga	**el nom** **l'adreça** **els cognoms** **les característiques**	**de la qual**

a friend (*f.*) whose first name/address/surname/characteristics

uns amics	**el nom** **l'adreça** **els cognoms** **les característiques**	**dels quals**

friends (*m.*) whose first name/address/surname/characteristics

unes amigues	**el nom** **l'adreça** **els cognoms** **les característiques**	**de les quals**

friends (*f.*) whose first name/address/surname/characteristics

The order preferred is, as above, with the object of possession preceding the relative, but inversion is occasionally found as in **És un col·laborador del qual he comprovat la fidelitat** 'He is a collaborator whose faithfulness has been demonstrated to me', equivalent of **... la fidelitat del qual he comprovat**.

This somewhat tortuous construction tends to be replaced in colloquial use by the simplified pattern involving **que** with possessive adjective introducing the object of possession (see **31.2.2**) or with possession indicated by the clitic **en**:

> **una família que conec els seus secrets** (non-standard)
> **una família que en conec els secrets** (non-standard)
> a family whose secrets I know

Only the following models, with the preposition **de** preceding the relative pronoun, are regarded as acceptable in writing or in formal speech:

> **una família de la qual conec els secrets**
> **una família de què conec els secrets**

An even more complex construction occurs when the relative noun phrase is the complement of a noun which is itself the object of a preposition:

> **Era un informe sobre la veracitat del qual tenia els meus dubtes.**
> It was a report about whose veracity I had my doubts.

> **Introdueixen un nou model dels avantatges del qual tothom parla.**
> They are introducing a new model the advantages of which everybody is talking about.

31.6 OTHER ANTECEDENTS OF THE RELATIVE PRONOUNS

31.6.1 PRONOUNS AS ANTECEDENTS

As well as nouns or nominalized elements, pronouns may stand as antecedents of non-restrictive relative clauses:

> **M'acusen a mi, que no en sé res.**   They're accusing me, and I know nothing about it.

> **aquells, que tant de mal van fer**   those people, who did so much harm

A demonstrative or indefinite pronoun may head a relative clause introduced by unstressed **que**, forming a restrictive clause. In the case of the demonstratives the meaning is 'that/those/the one(s) who/which':

> **Aquells que han fet això seran castigats.**   Those who did this will be punished.

> **Van interrogar a tothom que ho va veure.**   Everyone who saw it was interrogated.

> **Menyspreen tot allò que no entenen.**   They scorn all that they do not understand.

(Neuter relatives like the last example are discussed in **9.2.2.**)

Qui may also be found in this context, referring to humans which are subjects of their relative clause: thus, **aquells qui** and **tothom qui** could occur in the first two of the preceding examples. More often, though, the distinction between human and non-human is eliminated in the undifferentiated use of **que** for all cases. In the further examples given below the possibility of optional **qui** is indicated:

No conec ningú que/qui ho entengui.	I don't know anybody who under-stands it.
No van esmentar ningú que coneguéssim.	They didn't mention anybody we knew.
Saludaven a tothom que veien.	They greeted everyone they saw.
Jo admiro aquells que/qui parlen clar.	I admire those who speak their mind.

The idiomatic expression **com aquell que/qui no fa res** (lit. 'like the person who does nothing') belongs to this set. It conveys the idea of an action being done without difficulty or complication:

Recità el soliloqui de Hamlet com aquell que/qui no fa res.
He recited Hamlet's soliloquy without giving it a second thought/with the greatest of ease.

31.6.2   ARTICLES AS ANTECEDENTS

A definite article may also be the antecedent of unstressed **que** (or **qui**, in line with the explanation given in **31.6.1**), forming the groups **el/la/els/les que** and translating 'the one(s) which'; further discussion is given at **35.1.1**. (This construction is not to be confused with **el que**, etc., coming after a prep-osition, as described in **31.4.3**.) The use and function of the definite article antecedent are similar to, and overlap with, the construction with the demonstrative: **els que estimo** = **aquells que estimo** 'the ones I love'. The definite article is used more than the demonstrative when the referent is non-human:

Pots venir amb el tren del migdia o amb el que surt a les 5 de la tarda.
You can come on the midday train or on the one which leaves at 5 p.m.

la camisa que porto i les que tinc a la maleta
the shirt I am wearing and the ones I have in my suitcase

(Here **aquestes que tinc a la maleta** would only be heard if the shirts could be pointed to.)

Els que/qui ho van veure no se n'oblidaran mai.
Those who saw it will never forget it.

Els que vam trobar eren tots estrangers.
The ones we found were all foreign/foreigners.

Va ser ella la que/qui em va ajudar més.
It was she who helped me most.

Els que surten perquè n'estan tips i els que entren perquè no tenen ganes de treballar, ni es fixen en els qui passen. (Jaume Fuster)
The ones coming out because they are fed up and the ones going in because they don't feel like working don't even notice the people going by.

An indefinite article may be the antecedent of this type of relative clause:

N'he vist unes que eren més grosses.	I've seen some which were bigger.
Aquí n'hi ha un que he preparat abans.	Here is one I prepared earlier.

(See also **31.7**, for examples of **hi ha** in headless relative constructions.)

As observed in **9.2.2**, to form the equivalent of an inanimate free (headless) relative clause, the definite article **el** is used as the dummy antecedent of an inanimate relative clause (**el que** 'what', 'that which'). (Non-standard but frequent colloquial usage has **lo que** rather than **el que** in this construction.) The neuter demonstratives **això** and **allò** can alternate with **el** in this function of nominalizing an adjectival clause:

Va passar el que havia de passar.
That which/What had to happen did happen.

Això que dius és una vertadera beneitura.
What you are saying is really silly.

Allò que a tu et convindria és que demà plogués.
What would suit you would be for it to rain tomorrow.

Observe that what we have here is the nominalization of a clause, rather than the omission of an understood noun. No supposed noun is suppressed in the examples given above. There are, however, near equivalents in which a noun appears as antecedent of the relative:

Va passar el fet que havia de passar.
The event that had to happen did happen.

Aquestes coses que dius són una vertadera beneitura.
These things you are saying are really silly.

La cosa que a tu et convdria és que demà plogués.
The thing that would suit you would be for it to rain tomorrow.

A nominalized clause as the standard of a comparison may be introduced by **del que** (see **5.2.3**):

> **És menys important del que et penses.**   It is less important than you think.
> **Corre més del que corria.**   She runs more than she used to.

El que etc., may only have the role of subject or object in the relative clause. When any other role is involved, either the antecedent will be repeated or it will be represented by demonstrative **aquest/aquell**:

> **És un model nou, successor digne d'aquell al qual tanta gent s'havia afeccionat.** (not *del al que)
> It's a new model, a worthy successor to the one that so many people had become fond of.

> **El nostre pis d'ara és més espaiós que aquell on vivíem abans.** (not *que el on)
> Our present flat is more spacious than the one we used to live in.

> **Porti'm una altra copa; que no m'agrada beure en les copes (= en aquestes) en què ja han begut altres persones.**
> Bring me another glass; I don't like drinking out of ones which other people have drunk out of.
> (Not *en les en les que . . . or *en les en què . . .; colloquial language would use here . . . **beure en les que ja hi han begut altres persones**; see **31.2.2.**)

31.7 HEADLESS RELATIVES

Headless relative clauses are also known as free or nominal relative clauses. **Qui** without an antecedent is an alternative to article + relative (**el/la que/qui** 'the one who') or demonstrative/indefinite + relative (**aquell(a) que/qui, tothom que/qui**) in many contexts where a human referent is involved:

> **Qui ha dit això no en sap res.**
> The person who/Whoever said this knows nothing about it.

> **Pots demanar-ho a qui vulguis.**
> You can ask whoever you want (= anyone).

> **Jo escric a qui bé em sembla.**
> I write to whoever I see fit.

> **A qui arribi primer, li donaran aquest trofeu.**
> The first person to finish will receive this trophy.

This use of **qui** is characteristic of proverbs and similar expressions: **Qui mal no pensa, mal no fa** 'He who thinks no evil does no evil', **Qui paga, mana** 'He who pays the piper calls the tune', **Qui dia passa, any empeny** 'We get a little older each day'. Other than in proverbs it is rather formal. **El que**, etc., (**31.6.2**) is the more everyday alternative, so corresponding to the first two above we might find **El que ha dit això . . .**, **Pots demanar-ho al que vulguis.**

The antecedent of a relative may be implicit in the construction **(n')hi ha** 'there are some (of them)':

Hi ha qui creu que això és inviable.	There are those who think this is unviable.
N'hi havia que no eren tan bons.	There were some which weren't as good.

The presence of an article or a demonstrative is compulsory when **qui** is plural, that is, when it agrees with a plural verb:

*Qui vindran seran benvinguts.
Els qui vindran seran benvinguts./Aquells qui vindran seran benvinguts.
Those who come/Whoever comes will be welcome.

Adverbial question words (**on** 'where', **quan** 'when' and **com** 'how', see **31.8**) can also function as headless relatives:

Ho posarem on tu diguis.	We'll put it wherever you say.
Quan tu vols és massa tard per a mi.	The time/When you say is too late for me.
És millor com ho fa ella.	The way she does it is best.

Note that, unlike English 'what', Catalan **què** cannot be used in a headless relative construction; **el que** or **allò que** must be used (further examples and discussion at **9.2.2**):

El que més m'agrada és escoltar música.	What I like best is to listen to music.

31.8 'ADVERBIAL' RELATIVES

The question-words (**on, quan, com**) can function as relative pronouns, as their English counterparts can, after suitable antecedents denoting places, times, or manners.

On 'where'/'in which'/'on which'/'at which' is generally equivalent to **en què, a què** (or **en el qual, al qual**, etc.):

la sala on ens reunim	the room where/in which we meet
l'obstacle on tots ensopeguem	the obstacle we all stumble over
la porta per on entraven les autoritats	the door the authorities went in through

Quan 'when' occurs only in non-restrictive clauses. See **31.2.1**.

fins i tot en aquell temps, quan la vida era molt més dura
even at that time, when life was much harder

Com 'how' may stand as a relative pronoun with a manner antecedent, or alone as a headless relative representing **la manera en què** or **la manera com** 'the way that/in which':

T'has de fixar (en la manera) com ho fa.
You must notice the way she does it.

No m'agrada com em mira la gent.
I don't like the way (that) people are looking at me.

31.9   RELATIVE ADJECTIVES

The compound **el qual**, etc., discussed in **31.4**, has in origin an adjectival function, which is seen in the following example:

Han imposat unes normes noves, les quals normes implicaran diversos canvis de procediment.
They have imposed some new regulations, which (regulations) will entail several changes in procedure.

Invertiren tres milions de dòlars, a la qual suma es va afegir la subvenció estatal.
They invested three million dollars, to which amount the state subsidy was added.

This relative adjective, however, is very sparingly used, even in formal writing, being characteristic of legal language. Alternative constructions are made by using **el qual** without a following noun, by repeating the antecedent (or a synonym) before a **que** clause in apposition, or by expressing the idea through a linked clause headed by a demonstrative:

Han imposat unes normes noves, les quals implicaran . . .
They have imposed some new rules, which imply . . .

Els posaren una multa de vint mil pessetes, quantitat que van haver d'entregar a l'acte.
They were fined 20,000 pesetas, which they had to pay on the spot.

Demanen una declaració oficial, i aquesta declaració s'ha de presentar per triplicat.
They require an official statement, and this has to be supplied in triplicate.

31.10   MISCELLANEOUS ASPECTS OF RELATIVE CONSTRUCTIONS

(i)   Catalan relative clauses occur in several contexts where English may use a different construction, such as a present participle, a passive participle, a prepositional phrase complement:

les tasses que hi ha a l'armari
the cups in the cupboard

els estris que tinc a la bossa
the tools in my bag

Hi havia una cua que s'estenia fins a la cantonada.
There was a queue stretching to the end of the block.

Les botigues que hi havia a la plaça feien més goig que les de l'avinguda.
The shops in the square looked more attractive than those in the avenue.

el panorama magnífic que és la badia vista des d'allí dalt
the magnificent vista of the bay seen from up there

(ii)   A relative clause may contain an infinitive rather than a finite verb (see **20.3.1.3**). Here Catalan mirrors English quite well.

No hi he vist res de què queixar-nos.
I saw nothing (for us) to complain about.

No troba amb qui casar-se.
He can't find anybody to marry.

Busco un llibre amb el qual distreure'm.
I'm looking for a book to entertain myself with.

(iii)   Pseudo-relatives. These are constructions which overlap with indirect questions, dependent on verbs of physical or mental perception; see **27.1.3.9** for further discussion.

No t'imagines la gent que hi havia! = No t'imagines quanta gent hi havia! = No t'imagines quina gentada hi havia!
You can't imagine how many people there were!

No sabien el que havíem fet. = No sabien què havíem fet.
They didn't know what we had done.

Pregunta el tren amb què hem de marxar. = Pregunta amb quin tren hem de marxar.
Ask what train we have to leave on.

(iv)   On the subjunctive used in relative clauses with a negative or indefinite antecedent, see **17.1.4.1**, **19.3**, and **19.3.1**. On the relative clause structure of cleft sentences, see **35.1**.

32 COMPLEMENT CLAUSES

Complement clauses, or noun clauses – introduced by **que** 'that', **com** 'how', **si** 'if', and so on – occupy the place typical of a noun phrase in a sentence. Such a clause may be the object of a verb, the subject of another clause, or the complement of a noun or adjective. Unlike English, Catalan never drops the complementizer (conjunction) **que** 'that' introducing a complement clause: **M'han dit que tornaran** 'They've told me (that) they'll come back'. Other divergences between English and Catalan syntax, including contexts where the subjunctive appears in complement clauses (see **19.2.1**), are discussed under separate headings in **32.1–3**. Other functions are described in **32.4–5**.

32.1 SUBJECT COMPLEMENT CLAUSES

Headed by **que** (except when forming an indirect question: see **27.1.2** and **27.1.3.8**), a subject complement clause may precede or follow the main verb.

> **Que és capaç de fer-ho ha estat prou demostrat; que vulgui fer-ho és una altra qüestió.**
> That she is able to do it has been well demonstrated; her wanting to do it is another matter.

> **M'irrita que seguin tan a la vora.**
> I'm irritated (by the fact) that they sit so close (to me).

> **Que sigui tan gelosa no ens hauria de sorprendre.**
> We shouldn't be surprised that she is so jealous.

> **M'agrada que m'expliquis aquestes coses.**
> I like you to tell me these things.

> **Ens consta que els altres ja han cobrat.**
> We know for sure that the others have already been paid.

Some differences in syntactic pattern between English and Catalan will be observed in these examples: in **M'agrada que ...** the finite clause in Catalan corresponds to an English infinitive clause; in **Ens consta que ...** the Catalan subject clause corresponds to the object clause in English. Also to be noted is the fact that many such subject clauses go with verbs that generally take the subjunctive (see **19.2.1** and **19.2.2**):

Em sap greu/Em sorprèn que t'ho prenguis així.
I'm sorry/surprised you are taking it like this.

No et va intrigar que portés aquell anell?
Weren't you intrigued (by the fact) that he was wearing that ring?

In colloquial speech **el** may be placed before a subject complement clause introduced by que: **M'irrita el que seguin tan a la vora** 'I'm irritated by the fact that they sit so close'. This construction is regarded as a Castilianism and is non-standard.

Impersonal expressions (except those stating a fact or certainty: **és veritat que** 'it's true that', **és segur que** 'it's certain that') always have the subjunctive in the complement clause predicated by 'it':

Era urgent que algú ho revisés.
It was urgent that someone checked it.

Sembla mentida que triguin tant.
It's incredible that they're taking so long.

Convé que s'enllesteixi aviat.
It's appropriate that it be finished off soon./It needs to be finished off soon.

32.2   OBJECT COMPLEMENT CLAUSES

An object complement clause usually follows the main verb:

Han confirmat que arribaran demà.
They have confirmed they'll be arriving tomorrow.

Havia observat que sempre entraven per la porta de darrere.
I had observed that they always went in by the back door.

Indirect commands (with the subordinate verb always in the subjunctive; see **19.2.3**) come into this category:

M'han suggerit que en faci una còpia.	They have suggested I make a copy of it.
Volem que te'n vagis.	We want you to go away.
Li he dit que no pateixi.	I told him not to get upset.

When the main verb is suppressed, **que** + subjunctive becomes the main clause, a toned-down imperative, as described in **19.6**:

(Vull) que se'n vagin ara mateix.	They'd better go away right now.
Que et diverteixis.	Enjoy yourself.
Que no sigui res.	The best of luck!

32.3   COMPLEMENT CLAUSE AS COMPLEMENT OF A NOUN OR ADJECTIVE

(i)   Complement of a noun:

El fet que els aplaudim els anima molt.
The fact that we applaud them spurs them on.

No qüestionem la idea que la nova política afavoreix els pobres.
We are not questioning the idea that the new policy favours the poor.

D'on treuen la noció que això ens ha d'agradar?
Where do they get the notion that we are going to like this?

Either the indicative (as in the last two examples) or the subjunctive mood may be appropriate in cases like these. Use of the subjunctive (**la idea que ...** *afavoreixi*, **la noció que això ens** *hagi* **d'agradar**) backgrounds information supplied in the complement clause, as explained in **19.2.1**, or it may convey an element of doubt or uncertainty on the part of the speaker.

(ii)   Complement of an adjective:

Estic molt satisfet que te n'hagis recordat.
I am very glad you have remembered.

No estàveu orgullosos que ens haguessin premiat?
Weren't you proud that we had won a prize?

Estic segur que tindran èxit.
I am sure they'll be successful.

In both (i) and (ii) above the **de** that governs a noun complement is dropped before the complement clause (**el fet d'aplaudir**, but **el fet que aplaudim**). In the spoken language there is a strong tendency for this **de** to be retained before the clause: e.g. **Vet aquí la prova (de) que no ens ha entès** 'Here's the proof that he hasn't understood us'. This feature is part of the more complex issue of preposition drop/non-drop as discussed in **14.1.5**, and in more detail in **32.4–5**.

32.4   COMPLEMENT CLAUSES AS OBJECTS OF PREPOSITIONS

32.4.1   TONIC PREPOSITIONS AND COMPLEMENT CLAUSES

Tonic prepositions like **excepte** 'except', **malgrat** 'despite', **segons** 'according to', and **sense** 'without' can introduce a **que** clause. Or, to put it another way, prepositions can combine with **que** to make complex conjunctions introducing adverbial clauses (Chapter 33).

Malgrat que parlava bé l'anglès, no va entendre el conferenciant.
Despite the fact that she spoke English well, she did not understand the lecturer.

Segons que ho vagin explicant, els posarem notes bones o dolentes.
According to how they explain it, we'll give them good or bad marks.

32.4.2 ATONIC PREPOSITIONS AND COMPLEMENT CLAUSES

The dropping of the preposition **de** is the normal pattern when a complement clause depends on either a noun or an adjective, as illustrated in **32.3**. The same process operates with verbs and verbal phrases that introduce their complement with one of the atonic prepositions **a** and **en** and **amb**. Thus the general rule is that an atonic preposition (**a, de, en, amb**) will drop before a complement clause; infraction of the rule is frequent in spontaneous usage, as described in **32.5**.

La demostració que no en sap res és que . . .
The proof that he knows nothing about it is that . . .

Comentaven la notícia que l'ambaixador havia tornat.
They were commenting on the news that the ambassador had come back.

Estem contents que hagis vingut.
We are pleased that you have come.

S'observa la tendència que els raigs convergeixin.
One observes the tendency for the rays to converge.

Compare, **la demostració _d'_això . . .** 'the proof of that', **la notícia _del_ retorn de l'ambaixador** 'the news of the ambassador's return', **contents _de_ la teva vinguda** 'pleased at your coming', **la tendència _a_ convergir** 'the tendency to converge'. Examples of complement clauses depending on verb + preposition constructions:

Els hem d'acostumar que no hi vagin.	We must get them used to not going there.
cf. **S'ha acostumat _a_ no anar-hi.**	They have got used to not going there.
S'adonarà aviat que s'ha equivocat.	He'll soon realize that he was wrong.
cf. **S'adonà aviat _del_ seu error.**	He soon realized his mistake.
M'havia oblidat que li ho havia de dir.	I had forgotten that I had to tell him.
cf. **M'he oblidat _de_ dir-li-ho.**	I have forgotten to tell him.

Té por que el denunciïn.	He is frightened of being reported.
cf. **Té por *de* denunciar-los.**	He is frightened to report them.
No m'havia fixat que ja eres aquí.	I hadn't noticed you were here.
cf. **T'has fixat *en* aquests detalls?**	Have you noticed these details?

The phenomenon of weak preposition drop is also observed when the compound prepositions, such as **abans de** 'before', **des de** 'since', **després de** 'after', **fins (a)** 'until', **per tal de** 'in order to', introduce a clause:

abans que ho facis	before you do it
cf. **abans *de* fer-ho**	before doing it
des que ho va saber	since he found out
cf. **des *d'*aquell dia**	from that day
fins que parteixin	until they depart
cf. **fins (*a*) la seva partida**	until their departure
per tal que no els eixordem	so that we don't deafen them
cf. **per tal *de* no eixordar-los**	so as not to deafen them

Usage in respect of the atonic preposition **amb** 'with' is more complicated. In the compound conditional conjunction **amb que** 'provided that', 'if only', **amb** is always retained.

Vindria tot seguit amb que li proporcionessin un vehicle.
He would come straightaway if only he were supplied with a vehicle.

When **amb** is itself the complement of an adjective, quantifier, etc., normative grammar recommends the general preposition-drop rule, but many speakers find this excessively unnatural.

N'hi ha prou que en reproduïm una part./N'hi ha prou amb que . . .
It is enough that we reproduce a part of it.

cf. **N'hi ha prou *amb* la reproducció d'una part.**
There is enough with the reproduction of part of it.

32.5   RESISTANCE TO PREPOSITION DROP

There are many constructions analogous to those covered in **32.4** which are less stable and where native speech habits display especial reluctance to drop the preposition before **que**. The presence of the preposition is deemed nonstandard but its absence is felt by speakers to be confusing or bizarre. Standard solutions to this dilemma are mentioned in (i)–(iv) below. Typical instances are:

gràcies (a) que hi vau intervenir a temps
thanks to your intervening in time

No aspiràvem **(a) que ens donessin el premi.**
We didn't aspire to being awarded the prize.

S'arrisquen (a) que tot els surti malament.
They're running the risk of it all turning out badly for them.

Uns resultats tan contradictoris deriven (de) que l'experiència ha estat incompleta.
Such contradictory results derive from the experiment being incomplete.

N'hi haurà prou (amb) que firmin el primer full.
It'll be sufficient if they just sign the first page.

En el que no estaven d'acord era (en) que . . .
What they didn't agree about was that . . .

L'havien amenaçat (amb) que el denunciarien.
They had threatened him with being reported.

Written representation of this construction sometimes replaces **que** by **què**, presumably by analogy with **per** → **per què** and with stressed relative **què** after a preposition:

Se sent satisfet amb què hagin aprovat (= **que hagin aprovat**) **l'examen.**
(Badia 1995: 356)
He feels satisfied (with the fact) that they have passed the exam.

Han d'estar esperançats en què la hipòtesi de pacte PSM-UM arribi a concretar-se. (*El Temps*, 18 September 1995)
They should be hopeful that the hypothetical PSM-UM pact can come about.

On this tricky point of usage and grammar the most reliable authorities coincide in remarking that Catalan has alternative natural resources which produce more authentic solutions for the preposition + **que** construction:

(i)   Preposition plus infinitive clause:

L'has d'acostumar a vestir-se ella sola.	You must get her used to dressing herself.

instead of **L'has d'acostumar (a) que es vesteixi sola.**

Ajuden a fer que la casa sigui més bonica.	They help to make it that the house is more attractive.

instead of **Ajuden (a) que la casa sigui més bonica.**

en (el) cas de venir-hi ella	in the event of her coming

instead of **en cas (de) que vingui ella**

Amenacen amb multar-lo.	They are threatening to fine him.

instead of **Amenacen (amb) que/què el multaran.**

(ii)   Use of an empty noun phrase before the clause:

Common expressions like **el fet que** 'the fact that', **la idea que** 'the idea that', **la possibilitat que** 'the possibility that', etc., are stable in that they more easily resist retention of **de** before **que**.

No podem acostumar-nos a la idea que . . .   (rather than **a que**)
We can't get used to the idea that . . .

gràcies al fet que estàvem ben preparats   (rather than **a que**)
thanks to our being well prepared

L'error prové del fet que s'han confós.   (rather than **de que**)
The mistake arises from the fact that they have been confused.

(iii) Corresponding noun instead of complement clause:

Veig la necessitat de la renegociació del contracte.
I can see the need for the renegotiation of the contract.

instead of:

Veig la necessitat que el contracte es renegociï.
I can see the need for the contract to be renegotiated.

El fracàs és degut a llur equivocació.
The failure is due to their mistake.

instead of:

El fracàs és degut que s'han equivocat.
The failure is due to their making a mistake.

(iv)   Other constructions:

A clause may be made to pick up its meaning as already represented in the sentence by **això** or **allò**:

Aquesta actitud seva té relació amb això: que s'havia deixat enganyar.
Aquesta actitud seva té relació amb allò d'haver-se deixat enganyar.
This attitude of his is related to his having let himself be deceived.

Either of these alternatives is regarded as preferable in standard Catalan to resorting to **té relació amb que/què**.

33 ADVERBIAL CLAUSES

33.1 GENERAL

Two distinct types of adverbial clause can be recognized: first, those acting like adverbs of place, time, or manner; and, second, those which limit the meaning conveyed in the main clause by means of a condition, a cause, a consequence, a purpose, a concession, or a comparison. In the following pages we shall discuss the full range of these adverbial clauses, except for conditionals which are studied separately in Chapter 34, and comparative clauses, which are covered in Chapter 5. The range of adverbial conjunctions is treated more fully in Chapter 15.

In this chapter we are concerned primarily with clauses introduced by a subordinating conjunction and containing a finite verb. Much of our discussion is also relevant to constructions involving a preposition + an infinitive (**20.3.1.2**). This is because of the large degree of lexical overlap, in the Catalan case, between adverbs (such as **sense** 'without', **abans** 'beforehand', **després** 'afterwards', see Chapter 13), prepositions (such as **sense** 'without', or compound prepositions such as **abans de** 'before', **després de** 'after', see Chapter 14), and adverbial conjunctions (such as **sense que** 'without that', **abans que** 'before', **després que** 'after', see Chapter 15).

33.2 ADVERBIAL CLAUSES OF PLACE, TIME AND MANNER

33.2.1 PLACE CLAUSES WITH **on** 'WHERE'

Vaig trobar el teu pare on tu em digueres.
I found your father where you told me (he'd be).

Et posaré la taula on tu vulguis.
I'll put the table where you want.

The linking function can be emphasized by using a locative demonstrative adverb (or a prepositional phrase with a general 'place' noun) as an antecedent in the main clause.

Vaig trobar el teu pare *allà* on tu em digueres.
Et posaré la taula *al lloc* on tu vulguis.

When the antecedent in the main clause is nominal, the conversion of the adverbial clause into a relative one is easy:

Vaig trobar el teu pare en aquell bar que tu em digueres. (not *. . . allà que tu em digueres)
I met your father in that bar you said.
Et posaré la taula al lloc que tu vulguis.

On can be preceded by a preposition to specify location more precisely:

Aquest és el camí per on arriben a la finca.
This is the track along which they get to the farm.

Et seguiré a on tu vagis.
I'll follow you to wherever you go.

La paret anava des d'on tu ets fins (a) on jo sóc.
The wall used to go from where you are to where I am now.

L'avió triga més quan vola cap (a) on bufa el vent.
The plane takes longer when it is heading into the wind.

33.2.2 ADVERBIAL CLAUSES OF TIME

On mood in temporal clauses see **19.4.7**.

33.2.2.1 *Time clauses with* **quan** *'when'*

A temporal clause gives some time specificity to the situation denoted in the clause it depends on. The most usual introductory word here is **quan** 'when'. As in English, the temporal frame expressed may be either that of simultaneity (or temporal overlap) or that of relating the situation in the main clause to another previously completed situation ('when' = 'after', see **33.2.2.6**). This distinction may be made explicit by verbal aspect.

Quan aquella parella ballava tothom mirava.
When (i.e. every time) that couple danced everybody watched.

Quan aquella parella balla tothom mira.
When (i.e. every time) that couple dances everybody watches.

Va ofegar una exclamació quan els va veure.
She let out a stifled exclamation when she saw them (i.e. after she saw them).

Also as in English, **quan** can give a causal cast to a temporal construction in sentences of the kind:

Quan dius les coses amb tanta de seguretat, vol dir que en tens proves.
When you speak with such certainty it means that you have proof.

Quan la candelera riu (vol dir que) lluny és l'estiu.
When Candlemas smiles, summer is a long way off. (popular saying)

33.2.2.2 *Duration: clauses with* **mentre** *'while',* **alhora que** *'at the same time as', and so on*

Temporal clauses expressing coincidence over a period are introduced by **mentre** 'while'. Normative grammar recommends a distinction between **mentre** 'while' and **mentre que** 'whereas', 'as long as', 'while'. That is, **mentre** on its own is strictly for cases of temporal overlap, while **mentre que** expresses a conditional or concessive nuance, or a relationship of contrast (as in this very sentence) where there may be no literal temporal relation. In many situations both senses are combined and either form is appropriate.

He filmat la costa mentre el sol es ponia.
I filmed the coastline while the sun was going down.

Jo estudiava mentre (que) el meu marit treballava.
I studied while/whereas my husband worked.

In translating 'as', care must be taken to distinguish between a specific point in time (**quan**) and duration (**mentre**):

Quan entris, mira el quadre que hi ha a la paret.
As you go in look at the picture on the wall.

Mentre ens passejàvem, comentàvem la collita.
As we strolled along, we talked about the harvest.

Alhora que introduces an action simultaneous with another one. In this sense it is equivalent to **mentre**. However, it seems that **alhora que** can only replace **mentre** when the two simultaneous actions are performed by the same subject.

Reia alhora que es queixava dels seus mals.
He was laughing (at the same time) as he was complaining about his troubles.

Estudiava alhora que escoltava música.
She was studying and listening to music at the same time.

D'aquesta manera ens vengem alhora que fem un servei a la societat.
In this way we get our revenge while doing something positive for society.

With different subjects, rather than ?**Ell es dutxava alhora que la seva germana prenia un bany** the preferred solution is to use the analytical phrase **al mateix temps que** 'at the same time as', which covers both **mentre** and **alhora que**:

Ell es dutxava al mateix temps que la seva germana prenia un bany.
He was taking a shower at the same time as his sister was having a bath.

Complirà un deure amb la societat al mateix temps que alliberarà la consciència.
She'll be discharging a duty to society at the same time as clearing her conscience.

A mesura que is used for *changes* of state which are related and simultaneous:

A mesura que perdia pes, el globus s'anava enlairant.
As it lost weight, the balloon rose through the air.

33.2.2.3   Repetition: clauses with **sempre que, cada vegada que**

Sempre que, cada vegada (cop/pic/volta) que 'whenever', 'every time that' introduce a repeated situation.

Sempre que necessita res em truca a la porta.
Whenever she needs anything she knocks on my door.

Cada vegada (cop/pic/volta) que ens veiem m'explica una xafarderia.
Every time we meet, he tells me a bit of gossip.

Sempre que with the subjunctive can have a conditional sense 'as long as':

Pots mirar-ho si vols, sempre que no ho toquis.
You can look at it if you like, as long as you don't touch it.

33.2.2.4   Duration over a period

Significant differences between English and Catalan verbal syntax are associated with temporal clauses referring to (i) something begun from a specified point of origin ('since X') and lasting up to the situation of the main verb, and (ii) a situation expressed by the main verb lasting up to ('before' or 'until') a point specified by the subordinate clause.

(i)   Duration from a starting point: clauses with **des que, d'ençà que** 'since'

Des de/d'ençà de (prepositions) and **des que/d'ençà que** (conjunctions), meaning 'since', measure time up to the beginning of the main verb situation:

El cel ja no és tan net d'ençà que han instal·lat aquesta fàbrica de ciment.
The sky has been less clear ever since they built this cement works.

Es comportava així des que havia perdut el seu pare.
She had been behaving like that (ever) since she had lost her father.

D'ençà que prens aquesta medicina tens més gana.
Since you've been taking this medicine you've had a better appetite.

It is important to notice the differences between English and Catalan tense usage in the main verbs of this kind of sentence. The difference can be explained by the notion that English measures forwards from the point in the past when the main verb situation began, whereas Catalan measures backwards from the standpoint of an ongoing action. Thus the English perfect 'I have been here for a while', or pluperfect 'I had been there for ages', correspond to a Catalan present and imperfect respectively. The use of **des de/des que, d'ençà de/d'ençà que** for expressing the span of time in the subordinate temporal clause is complemented by an impersonal use of the verb **fer (fa, feia** 'for', 'ago'; see **13.3**), the two patterns of construction often working hand in hand:

> **–Quant fa que estudies l'anglès? –L'estudio des que vaig tornar de Londres, ara fa dos anys.**
> 'How long have you been studying English (for)?' 'I've been studying it since I came back from London, two years ago.'

> **Des de quan dius que era l'amo? No en feia més de vint anys?**
> How long do you say he'd been the boss? Wasn't it (for) more than twenty years?

> **D'ençà que era fora no llegia cap diari.**
> Since she'd been away she hadn't read a newspaper.

Convergence with the English type of tense structure is visible, however, when the main situation is viewed as being completed rather than ongoing. Some view this combination of perfect (**haver** + participle) and progressive (**estar** + gerund) as a recent Anglicism, with the second version below being more authentic.

> **T'he estat esperant des de fa més d'una hora, i ara et truco a veure què passa.**
> **T'estic esperant des de fa més d'una hora . . .**
> I've been waiting for you for over an hour, and now I'm phoning to see what's going on.

(ii) Duration up to a finishing point: **fins que** 'until'

The preposition **fins (a)** 'until' and the conjunction **fins que** 'until' introduce expressions of the temporal endpoint of the situation in the main clause.

> **Va tocar la guitarra fins que van fer-li mal els dits.**
> She played the guitar until her fingers hurt.

When a temporal clause refers to a future situation the verb will be either in the subjunctive or in the future indicative (see **19.4.7**):

> **Fins que hagis/hauràs signat el contracte no et creuré.**
> Until you have signed the contract I won't believe you.

Fins que can be followed by an expletive **no** (see **19.2.4v** and **33.2.2.5**).

> **Fins que no hagis/hauràs signat el contracte no et creuré.**

33.2.2.5 Anteriority: *abans (que)* 'before'

An **abans** clause specifies a reference point which the main clause situation precedes.

> **Abans que es van desxifrar, molts especialistes dubtaven que les inscripcions jeroglífiques maies representessin textos.**
> Before they were deciphered, many specialists doubted that the Mayan hieroglyphic inscriptions contained texts.

If the reference point of the temporal clause is imagined (non-actual), its verb will be in the subjunctive (**19.2** and **19.4**).

> **Abans que poguessin criticar-me, jo ja els havia demanat perdó.**
> Before they could criticize me I'd already said sorry.

Unlike **fins que**, mentioned just above, a temporal clause with **abans que** referring to a future situation will always have the verb in the subjunctive, and never in the future indicative (see **19.4.7**):

> **Abans que diguis res vull explicar-te què m'ha passat.** (* **Abans que diràs** . . .)
> Before you say anything I want to explain what has happened to me.

> **Deixa'm obrir la finestra abans que encenguis el gas.** (* **abans que encendràs** . . .)
> Let me open the window before you light the gas.

Like **fins que**, however, **abans que** can be followed by an expletive **no**. In this respect the construction is connected to that with verbs of fearing (**19.2.4v**); that is, the source of the **no** seems to be the hope that something will *not* happen. In this case **abans que** can be reduced to **abans no**. The **abans no** version without **que** is more informal.

> **Abans (que) no diguis res vull explicar-te què m'ha passat.**
> Before you say anything I want to explain what has happened to me.

33.2.2.6 Posteriority: *després que* 'after', *quan* 'when' (= 'after')

Després que 'after' can be used with any appropriate tense or aspect form; **quan** 'when' carries the sense of 'after' when it is used with an appropriate perfective or compound (anterior) verb form (including the past anterior, see **17.2.4**).

> **Després que van veure un poc de món ella tornà a casa.**
> After they saw a bit of the world she came back home.

Després que hagueren vist un poc de món ella tornà a casa.
After they had seen a bit of the world she came back home.

Quan han vist el pati interior, jo els ensenyo les golfes.
When they have seen the courtyard, I show them the attics.

As mentioned in **19.4.7**, after **després que**, the subjunctive may also be used even though the clause refers to a real situation. To refer to a future situation preceding that of the main clause, a clause introduced by **quan** or **després que** may be followed either by a compound future (future perfect, see **17.2.5**) or a perfect subjunctive:

Quan hauràs picat pedra com jo sabràs què és la vida.
When you've been hewing stone for as long as I have you'll know what life
   is all about.

Després que hauran vist un poc de món ella tornarà a casa.
When they have seen a bit of the world she will come back home.

Quan els hàgiu aconseguit ens podreu retreure els vostres èxits.
You can't go on to us about your successes until you have achieved them.

See **17.1.4.1** and **19.4.7** for remarks on the alternation between future indicative and present subjunctive in subordinate clauses like the ones above and those referring to the future in the examples below.

A clause expressing immediate posteriority can be introduced by **així que**, **de seguida que**, **tan aviat com**, **tan bon punt**, **tot seguit que**, equivalents of 'as soon as', 'no sooner . . . than':

Així que arribi a casa digues-li que em truqui.
As soon as he gets home tell him to ring me.

De seguida que arribarà l'ambulància partirem cap a l'hospital.
As soon as the ambulance arrives we'll leave for the hospital.

cf. for a past situation:

De seguida que va arribar l'ambulància vam partir cap a l'hospital.
As soon as the ambulance arrived we left for the hospital.

Tan aviat com en sabrem el sexe decidirem el nom de la criatura.
As soon as we know what sex it is we'll decide on the child's name.

Tot seguit que em digué allò vaig començar a riure.
As soon as she said that I burst out laughing.

A penes 'scarcely', 'no sooner' can refer to past situations only:

A penes havíem sortit de casa que va començar a tronar.
No sooner had we left home than it started to thunder.

In informal style **només . . . que** can have this temporal sense too:

Només la va reconèixer que ella va pegar un xiscle.
He had only just recognized her when . . . /No sooner had he recognized her than she let out a scream.

Note the use of **que** meaning 'when' in this construction and in other informal patterns (**15.2.3iii**) like:

Va arribar a casa que el seu pare ja havia mort.
She got home when her father was already dead. (or, more idiomatically: She got home to find her father already dead.)

33.2.3   ADVERBIAL CLAUSES OF MANNER

Manner clauses can be introduced by a simple conjunction: **com** 'as', **segons** 'according to', or a compound one: **sense que** 'without', **igual que** 'like', 'just as', **en quant que/en tant que** 'in so far as'/'inasmuch as': **segons que, segons com** 'according as'. In these cases there may be a correlative element present in the main clause, an adverb like **així** 'so', **talment** 'so', **tal** 'such', or a noun relating to the idea of manner (**manera, forma**). Adverbial clauses of manner are also constructed with a non-finite verb without a conjunction, where the gerund or past participle is the verbal nucleus of the subordinate clause. These constructions are discussed in **21.4** (participle) and **22.2.3–4** (gerunds). See also **19.4.6** on mood in manner clauses.

Fes això com t'han ensenyat de fer-ho.
Do this as you have been taught to do it.

Entrarem a la fàbrica sense que ens vegin.
We'll go into the factory without anyone seeing us.

Esta dona canta igual que la meua professora de música.
This woman sings just like my music teacher.

Aquesta versió, en tant/quant que va ser revisada per l'autor mateix, s'ha de considerar la més autèntica.
This version, inasmuch as it was revised by the author himself, must be considered the most authentic.

Varen fer el codicil segons (que) els va dir l'advocat.
They made the codicil in accordance with what the lawyer told them.

Segons com bufi el vent salparem cap a un costat o cap a l'altre.
According to which way the wind is blowing we'll set sail in one direction or the other.

Segons com appears to be half way between a modal and a conditional link, so that the last example can be interpreted as: **Si el vent bufa d'una manera**

salparem cap a un costat i si el vent bufa d'una altra manera salparem cap a l'altre. This conditional content of **segons com** is even strengthened in **segons si**:

Em posaré el vestit verd o el negre segons si els convidats són molts o pocs.
I'll wear the green suit or the black one according to whether there are a lot of guests or just a few.

(i) Manner antecedent in the main clause

The presence of an adverb like **així, tal, talment, igual** or a noun meaning 'manner' like **manera, forma** underlines the 'manner' relationship between main and subordinate clause and makes the function of the adverbial manner clause similar to that of a relative clause:

Li agradava molt així com ballaves.
She really liked the way you danced.

Vivien tal com havien viscut els seus avantpassats.
They lived just as their forbears had lived.

Va ocórrer talment com t'ho he contat.
It happened just how I told you.

Ho he fet tal com tu m'ho has manat.
I did it just as you ordered.

Era un autor que escrivia igual com parlava.
He was an author who wrote just like he spoke.

Escriu la teva opinió així com la diries a un amic.
Write down your opinion just as you would tell it to a friend.

Cuina de la manera com en va aprendre de jove.
She cooks in the way that she learnt when she was young.

La forma com s'ha acomiadat m'ha semblat molt grollera.
The way she said goodbye seemed very rude to me.

Parles dels teus amics de la forma com jo parlo dels meus enemics.
You talk about your friends in the way that I talk about my enemies.

The connection between these constructions and relatives is especially obvious when the antecedent is a noun. In fact, a proper relative (preceded by preposition **en**) can appear in the place of **com**:

Cuina de la manera en la qual en va aprendre de jove.
La forma en què s'ha acomiadat m'ha semblat molt grollera.
Parlava dels seus amics en la forma en la qual jo parlo dels meus enemics.

(ii)   Manner clauses and comparison

Since **com** appears as an introductory element both of manner clauses and of the second term of a comparison of equality, there is a natural overlap between the two types of clause (see **5.1**). The coincidence is especially strong when the manner clause repeats the verb of the main clause:

> **El teu amic menja com mengen els porcs.**
> Your friend eats like pigs eat.

> **Hem dormit com dormen els óssos a l'hivern.**
> We have slept like bears sleep in winter (i.e. like logs).

The repeated verb is most often omitted:

> **El teu amic menja com els porcs.**
> **Hem dormit com els óssos a l'hivern.**

> **Parla tal com son pare.**
> He speaks just like his father.

Notice that **talment com** may be reduced to **talment** when no verb follows; here **talment** functions as a conjunction.

> **Menja talment un porc.**   He eats just like a pig.
> **S'amagava talment un lladre.**   He was hiding away just like a thief.

33.3   OTHER ADVERBIAL CLAUSES

33.3.1   CAUSAL CLAUSES

An initial classification can be established distinguishing causal clauses which introduce (i) a cause as new information: **perquè, que, per tal com, car, puix (que)** all rendering 'because', 'as', 'since', and (ii) a cause as already known: **vist que, atès que, com que, ja que** 'because', 'on account of the fact that'.

(i)   A cause explained as new information

A natural tendency is observed for such clauses to be placed after the main clause:

> **Varen atracar l'oficina aquell dia perquè sabien que hi havia diners.**
> They held up the branch that day because they knew there was money there.

> **Corre, corre, que farem tard.**
> Get a move on or we'll be late.

> **Viuran en l'opulència per tal com els seus negocis comencen a rutllar.**
> They will be living in opulence as their business is starting to boom.

Elevem en la nit un cant a crits car les paraules vessen de sentit. (S. Espriu)
Let us shout up a song into the night since our words are overflowing with
   meaning.

Caldrà fer-ho puix (que) ella ho ha manat.
It will have to be done for she has given the order.

Per tal com, car, puix (que) and **com sigui que,** belong to an elevated style,
being virtually unknown in colloquial registers. In all registers and styles
perquè is the commonest way of saying 'because' and synonymous 'as',
'since'. As illustrated in **15.2.3iii, que** frequently heads a causal clause
in familiar and colloquial speech. It is just the general complementizer 'that'
used vaguely. Its causal sense is derived purely from pragmatic inference. Causal clauses introduced by **car** and **que** can never precede the main
clause.

(ii)   Clauses introducing an already known cause

Atès que, com (que), donat que, ja que, vist que introduce a cause as being one
already known to both speaker and listener ('as' = 'on account of the fact
that', 'bearing in mind that'). Following a general tendency for word order to
be affected by 'informational weight', the normal position of such clauses is
before the main clause, obligatorily for those introduced by **com (que).** Other
compound causal conjunctions like **tenint esguard que** 'in view of the fact
that', **considerant que** 'considering that', **a causa que** 'because', **per raó que** 'for
the reason that', etc., are used in formal contexts.

Atès que tothom en ţé ganes avui anirem d'excursió.
As everybody is feeling like it we shall go on a trip out today.

Com (que) ara plou m'estimo més quedar a casa.
As it's raining now I prefer to stay in.

**Donat que la lliga s'ha posat tan difícil tots els equips hauran de fer fitxatges
   milionaris.**
With the league becoming so tight every team will have to make big-money
   signings.

Ja que ens donen facilitats haurem d'acabar la feina puntualment.
As facilities are provided we'll have to finish the job on time.

Vist que l'atur augmenta tant el govern haurà de prendre mesures.
Seeing that unemployment is increasing so much the government will have
   to take measures.

Since **atès, donat,** and **vist** are past participles they can be used in absolute
clauses with a causal meaning (**21.1.3**). In this case gender and number
agreement must be observed:

Ateses les ganes que tothom té d'anar d'excursió, avui hi anirem.
Seeing how keen everybody is take a trip out, we'll go today.

Donada la dificultat que ha assolit la lliga, tots els equips hauran de fer fitxatges milionaris.
Given the tightness in the league positions every team will have to make big-money signings.

Vistes les xifres a què ateny l'atur, el govern haurà de prendre mesures.
In view of the figures that unemployment is reaching . . .

33.3.1.1   Causal clauses and coordination

Observe how causal relationships (referring both to new information and to already known causes, as described above) can be expressed by coordination rather than subordination:

(Varen atracar l'oficina aquell dia perquè sabien que hi havia diners. →)
Sabien que hi havia diners i (per això) varen atracar l'oficina.
They knew there was money there and (because of this) they held up the branch.

(Atès que tothom en té ganes, avui anirem d'excursió. →)
Tothom té ganes d'anar d'excursió i (per això) hi anirem avui.
Everybody is keen to take a trip out and (on account of this) we'll go today.

This type of conversion is only possible with core causal clauses; peripheral causal clauses, namely, those introducing the (metalinguistic) cause of the utterance and not the cause of the facts, do not admit this process:

El vaixell ha tingut problemes perquè no ha arribat a port. (= (Crec que) el vaixell ha tingut problemes perquè no ha arribat a port.)
The ship has been in difficulties because it has not arrived in port.

cannot become * **El vaixell no ha arribat a port i (per això) ha tingut problemes.**

33.3.2   PURPOSE CLAUSES

This type of subordination overlaps with some expressions of 'result' as discussed in **33.3.4**, so that the following distinction can be observed:

(i) so that = 'in order that'	(ii) so that = 'in such a way that'
(purpose)	
perquè	**de manera que**
a fi que	**de forma que**
per tal que	**talment que**

Inasmuch as purpose is something 'unfulfilled' (or to be interpreted as a wish) in relation to the main situation, the verb in a subordinate clause after any of the above will appear in the subjunctive. **De manera que** and **de forma que**, when they express result (33.3.4), will be followed by the indicative. **A fi que** and **per tal que** are synonymous with **perquè** 'in order that', but they are characteristic of formal written language rather than spoken language.

T'ho explico perquè no fiquis la pota.
I'm telling you so that you don't go and put your foot in it.

Proposem aquesta solució perquè/a fi que/per tal que la qüestió quedi defini-tivament tancada.
We are proposing this solution so that the question can be definitively closed.

Es van disfressar de manera que ningú no els pogués reconèixer.
They put on disguises so that nobody would be able to recognize them.

Li ho van explicar talment que ho aprengués de seguida.
They explained it to her so that she would learn it straightaway.

No sigui que/no fos que (also **no fos cosa que, no fos cas que**) are slightly archaic forms, expressing negative purpose, which have nevertheless rather wider currency than English 'lest':

Hi vaig haver d'entrar de puntetes, no fos que despertés els nens.
I had to go in on tiptoe, lest I woke the children.

Fes-ho ara mateix, no sigui que te'n descuidis.
Do it right away, so as you don't forget.

It is the verbal mood that distinguishes in some cases between purpose and causal or between purpose and result meaning.

Surt al programa perquè la gent conegui la seva obra. (purpose)
He's appearing on the programme so that people will know his work.

Surt al programa perquè la gent coneix la seva obra. (causal)
He's appearing on the programme because people know his work.

S'amagaren a les golfes de manera que ningú no els descobrís. (purpose)
They hid in the attic so nobody discovered them. (= so that nobody should discover them)

S'amagaren a les golfes de manera que ningú no els va descobrir. (result)
They hid in the attic so nobody discovered them. (= with the result that nobody discovered them)

33.3.2.1 'Enough for', 'too much for'

With **prou** or **bastant** 'enough' and **massa** 'too much', 'too many', the standard of evaluation in a following clause is introduced by **perquè**:

S'hi van presentar massa candidats perquè els poguessin entrevistar a tots.
Too many candidates applied for them all to be interviewed.

Ja és prou gran perquè no l'hàgim de sermonejar.
He is old enough for us not to have to preach to him.

33.3.3 CONCESSIVE CLAUSES: **encara que** 'ALTHOUGH' AND EQUIVALENTS

Encara que 'although', 'even though' is the most common concessive conjunction. **(Per) bé que, malgrat que, si bé, (amb) tot i que, ni que** (the latter always negative) are near-equivalents also quite widely used. Concession is another category associated with the thematic function of the subjunctive mood; see **19.4.2**. **Mal que** and **i això que** 'even though' are also used in concessive clauses. **Baldament** and **jatsia que** 'although' are characteristic of literary or formal language (although **baldament**, popularly **maldament**, is common in Balearic dialects). **Baldament** and **mal que** are always followed by the subjunctive, and **i això que** always by the indicative (see below).

Encara que hagués de fer el camí a peu vindria a visitar-te.
Although I might have to come all the way on foot I'd come to see you.

Encara que n'abaixin el preu aquest producte no es vendrà.
Even if they bring the price down this product won't sell.

(Per) bé que en aquells terrenys hi ha molta d'aigua, la terra no és bona.
Although there is plenty of water in those lands, the soil is not good.

Malgrat que sigui petita, és prou valenta.
Despite being small, she's pretty dogged.

Va créixer sense pare, si bé la seva mare en va suplir l'afecte.
He grew up fatherless, although his mother filled the emotional gap.

Tot i que no hi era el secretari, van començar la reunió.
Even though the secretary wasn't there, they began the meeting.

No ho consentiria, ni que li ho demanessis mil vegades.
She wouldn't agree to it, (not) even if you asked her a thousand times.

No ho faria mal que el cel es besés amb la terra.
He wouldn't do it in a month of Sundays. (lit. even if the sky were to kiss the earth)

I això que meaning 'although', 'even though' occurs with some frequency in the spoken language and in more relaxed written styles. It is followed only by the indicative as it refers to events, actions, or ideas presented as realities. It can be understood to mean 'despite the fact that'. Clauses introduced by **i això que** invariably follow the main clause.

Ningú no va tastar l'arròs, i això que feia tan bona pinta.
Nobody tasted the rice, even though it looked so appetizing.

33.3.3.1 *Other concessive constructions*

Per + (més/molt) + noun, adjective or adverb **+ que** is a concessive formula expressing 'however much/many':

Per (més/molt) rica que sigui hi ha luxes que no es pot permetre.
However rich she may be there are certain luxuries she can't afford.

Per molts avantatges que els ofereixis encara te'n demanaran més.
However many advantages you offer them they'll still ask for more.

Per molt que is used as an independent adverbial subordinator:

Per molt que el renyis, encara continuarà fent el burro.
However much you scold him he'll still go on acting the goat.

Other principal conditional subordinators are the compound conjunctions:

amb que	provided that	**a condició que**	on condition that
sols que	just provided that, as long as	**sempre que**	as long as
		només que	if only, if . . . just
posat que	supposing that	**en cas que**	in case
mentre que	as long as, while		

All these require use of the subjunctive:

Vindria tot seguit amb que li proporcionessin un vehicle.
He would come straight away, provided he were supplied with a vehicle.

Posat que n'hi hagi, us en donarem a tots.
Provided there is any, we'll give you all some.

No em sap greu que et diverteixis, mentre que no abandonis els estudis.
I don't mind you having fun, as long as you don't give up studying.

Que facin el que vulguin, sols que/només que em deixin en pau.
Let them do as they please, as long as they don't bother me.

Absolute constructions with a gerund, especially if preceded by **(fins) i tot, tot i** 'even', or followed by **i tot**, can convey a concessive meaning, as discussed more fully at **22.2.4.1**:

Captant els vots dels immigrants no va poder guanyar les eleccions.
Even by chasing the immigrants' votes she still was not able to win the elections.

Tot essent parent nostre, sempre ens posa traves.
Although he's a relative of ours, he's always creating difficulties for us.

(For **tot i** + infinitive, see **20.4.1**.)

Other concessive expressions

Concessive expressions are also formed with:

(i) **Però**, and colloquially **per'xò** (see **15.1.5.1**), at the end of an independent clause:

    No ho farà pas, però.   He won't do it, even so.
    Canta bé, per'xò.   He's a good singer, though.

(ii) Additive **fins i tot**, and **ni (tan sols)**, translating 'even':

    M'agraden les prunes, fins i tot quan són verdes.
    I like plums, even when they're unripe.

    No compleix mai, ni tan sols si el renyen.
    He never does as he is told, (not) even if they scold him.

(iii) **Tanmateix** 'still', 'even so', 'however' is an adverb used with the sense of a whole (implicit) concessive clause:

    Hem tingut molts de problemes. Tanmateix, hem reeixit.
    We have had many problems. Even so, we have succeeded.

    (cf. **Encara que hem tingut molts de problemes, hem reeixit.**
        Although we've had many problems we have succeeded)

    Tens els diners que vols i tanmateix no te'n serveixes.
    You've all the money you want and still you don't use it.

33.3.3.2 *Position of concessive clauses*

A concessive clause is normally placed before the main clause. When it follows the main clause it is generally with the verb in the indicative, where concession overlaps with an adversative function.

No s'engreixen gaire, encara que mengen prou.
They aren't putting much weight on, even though they eat plenty.

(cf. **No s'engreixen gaire, però mengen prou.**)

Se n'havia anat a viure tot sol, encara que dinava a casa dels pares cada dia.
He'd gone away to live on his own, although he still lunched every day at his parents'.

(cf. Se n'havia anat a viure tot sol, però dinava a casa dels pares cada dia.)

33.3.4   RESULT CLAUSES

Subordinate clauses of manner can denote either intention (purpose and aim) or result; there is some discussion in **33.3.2**. It is use of the indicative after **de manera que** and **de forma que** (also occasionally **així que**) 'so that' = 'in such a way that' that establishes the meaning of result.

Es va commoure de tal manera/fins a tal punt que tots el vam compadir.
He was so moved that we all felt sorry for him.

Result or consecutive clauses introduce the result of a highlighted element in the main clause: 'so . . . . that', 'such . . . that'. The highlighting expressions in the main clause are those of degree, like **tant** (adjective and adverb), **tan** 'so', 'so much'/'so many', or of manner, like **tal** 'such'. Even **un, una** can act as an intensifier:

Hi havia tants de cotxes que era impossible aparcar.
There were *so many* cars it was impossible to park.

Va vestir-se de tal manera que ningú no el va reconèixer.
He dressed in *such* a way that nobody recognized him.

Treballa tant que algun dia tindrà un atac de cor.
He works so hard that one day he'll have a heart attack.

Té la cara tan blanca que sembla que estigui malalta.
Her face is so white that it looks as though she's ill.

Condueixes tan imprudentment que ningú no vol pujar al teu cotxe.
You drive so carelessly that no one wants to get in the car with you.

M'ha fet una tal resposta (una resposta tal) que no mereix que el torni a saludar.
His reply to me was such that I'll quite rightly ignore him from now on.

Estudia de (tal) forma que és impossible que no aprovi l'examen.
She is studying in such a way that she is bound to pass the exam.

Corren unes xafarderies que basten per fer malbé la seva reputació.
There is (such) gossip going around that could ruin his reputation.

33.3.4.1   *Que* as subordinator in result clauses

The complementizer **que** may even carry consecutive force on its own, that is, in the absence of an intensifier. This usage is rather informal, in that the precise relationship of the clauses linked by **que** is left to be inferred, as in these versions of examples given in **33.3.4**:

Té la cara blanca que sembla que estigui malalta.
Condueixes que ningú no vol pujar al teu cotxe.
Estudia que és impossible que no aprovi l'examen.
Corren xafarderies que basten per fer malbé la seva reputació.

While structurally **que basten . . .** in the last example might be interpreted as an adjectival relative clause ('which are sufficient to . . .', with **que** as relative pronoun rather than conjunction), other related instances show that **que** here is in fact the subordinating conjunction. Compare:

Ha rebut uns cops que és un miracle que no s'hagi mort.
He received such blows it is a miracle he didn't die. (result clause)

and

Ha rebut uns cops que l'han deixat mig mort.
He received some blows that left him half dead. (relative clause, see **31.1.2**, etc.)

Compare also:

És una feina que la faig amb els ulls tancats.
It's a job I can do with my eyes closed/such that I (can) do it . . . /It's the kind of job that I can do . . .

with the purely relative:

És una feina que faig amb els ulls tancats.
It's a job I do with my eyes closed.

The first example of this pair might also be seen as an example illustrating a pleonastic object clitic in a relative clause (**12.8**).

34 CONDITIONAL SENTENCES

34.1 GENERAL

34.1.1 TYPES OF CONDITIONAL SENTENCE

Si 'if', discussed in **15.3**, forms the compounds **si de cas, si per cas, per si**, all of which convey the idea of 'in case' or 'if by chance', and **si (doncs) no** 'unless' (**34.1.2**). Among conditional sentences in Catalan there is a loose basic division according to whether the verb in the 'if'-clause (condition) is in the indicative (i) or in the (past) subjunctive (ii). This is determined by the nature of the condition expressed in the condition clause, according to a general pattern described as follows:

(i)   Indicative verb in the condition clause:
open conditions (**34.2**)
fulfilled conditions (**34.3**)

(ii) Subjunctive verb in the condition clause:
unfulfilled conditions (counterfactual, **34.4**)
hypothetical conditions (counterfactual, **34.5**)

34.1.2 EXCEPTION (NEGATIVE CONDITION)

'Unless', 'if not' is most frequently rendered by **si no**:

No ho farem pas, si no ens hi obligues.
We won't do it unless you oblige us to.

Si doncs no is much more formal:

Serà indultat, si doncs no s'addueix cap altra prova de la seva culpabilitat.
He will be reprieved, unless further evidence of his guilt is adduced.

Other translations of 'unless' are taken up in **34.8**.

34.2 OPEN CONDITIONS

Clauses in this category express the idea that either fulfilment or non-fulfilment of a condition is equally possible. The subjunctive is not used for open conditions of this kind. The tense pattern is similar to that in English, the main combinations being:

(i)   **Si** + present + (consequence clause) present:

Si el burxes, sempre respon.
If you prod him he always responds.

Es veu molt més bé si es mira des d'aquí.
You can see it much better if you look from here.

(ii)   **Si** + present + (consequence clause) future or present with future sense:

Si no en diem res, aquells no se n'assabentaran.
If we don't say anything, they won't find out.

Si empenyeu així, s'obre de seguida.
If you push like this it'll open straight away.

(iii) **Si** + past + (consequence clause) past:

Si treballaven de nits, cobraven un plus.
If they worked nights they got a bonus.

Si van cometre aquest error, devia ser per culpa d'una distracció momentània.
If they made this mistake, it must have been because of a momentary distraction.

This last example might be seen as a case of a fulfilled condition, as described in **34.3**. As an open condition, the idea is that the speaker is not certain about whether the mistake was made or not.

(iv)   **Si** + past (including present perfect) + (consequence clause) present or future:

In this context the speaker of the main clause verb is not sure about facts referred to in the 'if'-clause.

Si encara no us heu decidit, ho deixarem córrer.
If you still haven't made your minds up, we'll give it a miss.

A nosaltres ens deurà quedar poc per fer, si ells ja van complir tot el que havien promès.
There can't be much left for us to do, if they carried out everything they said they would.

(v)   **Si** + present + (consequence clause) imperative:

Si voleu veure un autèntic espectacle, veniu amb mi.
If you want to see a real sight, come with me.

Si crema, no t'ho mengis.
If it's hot, don't eat it.

When open conditions are communicated in reported speech referring to the past, the imperfect or pluperfect indicative appears in the condition clause, with the conditional (or colloquially the imperfect indicative) in the consequence clause:

Va dir que podíem plegar d'hora si havíem enllestit aquella comanda.
He said we could finish work early if we had got that order ready.

I la conclusió va ser que l'haurien d'operar, si efectivament tenia el fetge tan destrossat.
And the conclusion was that they would have to operate, if indeed her liver was in such a terrible state.

This type of construction is to be understood as essentially an open condition in past tense frame, and is not to be confused with optional use of the imperfect indicative after **si** (+ main clause conditional or conditional perfect) in expressing hypothetical or remote conditions (see **34.5**).

34.3   FULFILLED CONDITIONS

Fulfilled conditions are not the statement of true 'conditions' but rather an indirect (often rhetorical) way of expressing ideas like 'the reason why', 'just because', 'whenever', and so forth. In such constructions the subjunctive is never used in the condition clause:

Si ens han estafat, és perquè hem badat.
If they've swindled us it's because we weren't paying attention.

Si han tingut sort, també s'ho han merescut.
They may have been lucky, but they deserved it too.

Si s'afanyaven, evitaven els embussos de l'hora punta.
If they got a move on they used to miss the rush-hour traffic jams.

This last example could also be categorized as an open condition of the kind shown in **34.2iii**.

34.4   UNFULFILLED CONDITIONS

Here the condition clause refers to a condition in the past which was not fulfilled and is not now fulfillable (past counterfactual). The commonest tense/mood pattern in such cases is **si** + pluperfect subjunctive (condition clause) with the conditional perfect in the consequence clause:

Si ho haguéssim sabut a temps, us hauríem avisat.
If we had found out in time we would have let you know.

Si no hagués estat per tu, no ho hauríem pogut resoldre mai.
If it hadn't been for you, we should never have been able to resolve it.

(Here the main clause could alternatively be constructed as **No podríem haver-ho resolt mai** 'We could never have resolved it'; see **34.6.5**.)

This type of condition can be expressed with the past subjunctive after **si** followed by the conditional in the main clause, when the facts referred to are immediately focused from the present moment:

Si no fos pel cinturó de seguretat, ja seria morta.
If it weren't for her safety belt she'd be dead now.

The majority of Catalan speakers nowadays instinctively and consistently use the subjunctive (imperfect or pluperfect) after **si** in these failed condition clauses. Normative grammar, however, does admit the pluperfect indicative in the condition clause of this kind of sentence, as in:

Si havien (= haguessin) invertit més diners en aquesta operació, n'haurien tret més beneficis.
If they'd invested more money in this operation, they'd have derived more profit from it.

The use of **havien** for **haguessin** here sounded 'strange' but not 'incorrect' to informants, and the failed condition meaning remains quite clear. It would just not be the construction formed spontaneously by most speakers in the great majority of contexts. There appears to be more doubt about the viability of this alternative when the condition clause has the verb in the negative:

?Si no havien contestat ràpidament, les coses s'haurien complicat.
If they hadn't replied quickly things would have become complicated.

On alternative forms of the conditional in sentences of this type, see **34.6**.

34.5   HYPOTHETICAL AND REMOTE CONDITIONS

The general pattern of construction for hypothetical and remote conditions is **si** + past subjunctive, with conditional in the consequence clause. (The imperfect indicative option in the consequence clause is shown at various points in what follows and summarized in **34.6.4**.)

A distinction can be observed between hypothetical conditions and those which are presented as remote or contrary to fact. The two types are illustrated in English by contrasting 'If you went to the first session you'd be sure to get a seat' and 'If I knew I'd tell you'. The first expresses a fulfillable condition, presented as a more hypothetical variant of the equivalent open condition 'If you go to the first session you'll be sure to get a seat'. With this type of condition, the alternative use of the imperfect indicative instead of the past subjunctive is commonly resorted to. Catalan, then, can express different degrees of hypothesis or likeliness in the condition:

(i) **Si véns d'hora, et podrem atendre.**
     If you come early we can deal with your enquiry.

(ii) **Si venies d'hora, et podríem atendre.**
     If you came early we could deal with your enquiry.

(iii) **Si vinguessis d'hora, et podríem atendre.**
     If you were to come early, we could deal with your enquiry.

The underlying meaning of all three sentences is virtually the same. Sentences (ii) and (iii), however, are explicitly more hypothetical than the open condition (i), hence the conditional of their main clause verb. The subjunctive after **si** in (iii) expresses, at least notionally, more uncertainty about fulfilment of the condition than the indicative (**venies**) in (ii) does.

On the other hand, there are sentences in which the condition, though achievable in principle, is contrary to fact (as in 'If I knew (but I don't), I'd tell you', unlike past counterfactuals as in **34.4**). Here the prevalent construction is with the past subjunctive in the condition clause:

Ho farien d'una altra manera si tinguessin a mà totes les eines que necessiten.
They would do it differently if they had to hand all the tools they need.

Si ho sabés, et juro que t'ho diria/deia.
If I knew, I swear I'd tell you.

Si donés una explicació clara, el perdonaríem/perdonàvem.
If he were to give a clear explanation we would forgive him.

There is obviously an overlap between hypothetical and remote conditions, as is seen in the last example above: the formulation with the past subjunctive implies that the condition is unlikely to be fulfilled or contrary to fact ('If he gave a clear explanation (but he probably won't/but he hasn't so far) . . .'), but it is only a short step to adapt it back (via **Si donava . . .**) to **Si dóna una explicació clara, el perdonarem** 'If he gives a clear explanation we will forgive him', as in the sentences (i)–(iii) discussed above. Thus the use of the imperfect indicative instead of the past subjunctive is still possible in these remote condition 'if'-clauses:

No els resultaria tan difícil si tenien (for tinguessin) a mà les eines que necessiten.
It wouldn't prove so difficult for them if they had available the tools they need.

Si no cridaves (for **cridessis**) **tant, et sentiríem més bé.**
If you didn't shout so loud we would hear you better.

And even a close alternation between the past subjunctive and the imperfect indicative in this context does not sound unusual:

Si jo parlés, si jo us deia tot el que em ronda pel cap, si jo obrís les comportes de la meva consciència, veuríeu baixar tota la porqueria que tinc acumulada. (R. Solsona)
If I were to speak out, if I told you everything that's going round in my head, if I were to open the floodgates of my conscience, you'd see all the accumulated filth dropping out.

A particular nuance is sometimes conveyed by use of the imperfect indicative in the 'if'-clause. A fine distinction may be drawn between **Si descobria que m'enganyava, no m'hi casaria** 'If I discovered he was deceiving me I wouldn't marry him' and **Si descobrís . . .** The first can be interpreted as an open condition in the past 'If I discovered that . . . ' rather than, with the subjunctive, the hypothetical 'If I were to discover that . . . '

English speakers, (especially those familiar with French: cf. *si j'étais riche* 'if I were rich') may be tempted to make life easier by resorting always to the imperfect indicative in expressing both remote and unfulfilled conditions. The temptation should be avoided, nevertheless, in favour of the more authentic alternation between this tense and the past subjunctive (with the latter prevalent), with attention to some of the nuances involved.

Alternative verb forms for the conditional in the consequence clause are discussed in **34.6**.

34.6 ALTERNATIVE CONDITIONAL VERB FORMS

34.6.1 Ser AND haver

Ser and **haver** have alternative forms for the conditional tense: **fóra**, etc., and **haguera**, etc., respectively (see **16.5.8**). While more widely encountered in the written language, these forms can replace the normal conditional (**seria**, etc., **hauria**, etc.) in any context. The **ser** forms are a good deal more often encountered than the **haver** ones:

Fóra/Seria millor no parlar-ne.
It would be better not to talk about it.

Si no m'ho haguessin demostrat amb proves, no ho haguera/hauria sospitat mai.
If I hadn't been given evidence, I never would have suspected it.

34.6.2   Fóra AND haguera AS PAST SUBJUNCTIVES

Valencian varieties have the **-ra** form for the past subjunctive of all verbs (see **16.5.10.1**). In these dialects **fóra**, etc., and **haguera**, etc., are the usual past subjunctive forms for **ser** and **haver** (instead of **fos**, etc., and **hagués**, etc.,) and they do not substitute for the conditional (**seria** and **hauria** being preferred). Valencian Catalan accordingly uses **haguera**, etc., in the 'if'-clause of the types of sentence described in **34.4** and **34.5**, with the conditional or conditional perfect in the main clause taking the **hauria** form:

'**Si m'haguera embolcallat amb la senyera, hauria fet impossible el projecte de la RTVV.**' (Amadeu Fabregat, reported in *Avui*)
'If I'd wrapped myself in the Catalan flag, it would have made the RTVV (autonomous Valencian broadcasting body) project impossible.'

Es barallaven com si foren xiquets petits.
They were falling out as though they were young kids.

34.6.3   PLUPERFECT SUBJUNCTIVE REPLACING CONDITIONAL PERFECT IN THE CONSEQUENCE CLAUSE

Some dialects consistently replace the conditional perfect (**hauria** or **haguera** + past participle) with the pluperfect subjunctive in the consequence clause of an unfulfilled (counterfactual) condition:

Si hagués fet mal temps, no haguessis (= hauries/hagueres) pogut sortir.
If the weather had been bad you wouldn't have been able to go out.

Si m'haguéssiu avisat a temps, ho hagués (= hauria/haguera) pogut arreglar.
If you'd let me know in time I could have sorted it out.

The tendency to use **hagués**, etc., instead of the conditional perfect in main clauses seems to be very strongly rooted and even to be coming more widespread (possibly under the influence of Spanish) though grammarians generally recommend the conditional perfect.

34.6.4   IMPERFECT INDICATIVE FOR CONDITIONAL

Speakers of central Catalan often resort to the imperfect indicative instead of the conditional in a consequence clause. This usage raises no objections for relaxed conversational contexts, but it is viewed as out of place in formal styles:

És clar: si pogués jo també em comprava (= compraria) un xalet així.
Obviously, if I could afford it I'd buy myself a villa like that.

Si no ho posessin tan difícil, molts més se n'hi inscrivien (= inscriurien).
If they didn't make it so difficult, many more of them would sign up.

34.6.5   CONDITIONAL PERFECT: VERB WITH INFINITIVE

When the conditional perfect category is applied to a construction involving a modal verb (**poder, voler, deure, haver de,** and so on) plus an infinitive, two alternative patterns are available, somewhat as in English 'would have been able to do it'/'could have done it'. In Catalan the alternatives are:

(i)   Conditional of modal + infinitive **haver** + past participle: **podria haver-ho fet.**

(ii)   Conditional perfect of modal (= conditional of **haver** + past participle of modal) + infinitive: **hauria pogut fer-ho.**

> **Si no haguéssiu insistit tant, no haurien volgut accedir-hi/no voldrien haver-hi accedit.**
> If you had not insisted so strongly, they would not have wanted to agree to it.

> **Si ell hagués caigut malalt, haurien hagut d'ajornar/haurien d'haver ajornat la sessió.**
> If he had fallen ill, they would have had to adjourn/would have to have adjourned the session.

The normal rules for the positioning of pronominal clitics also apply in such constructions. Clitics (see **12.2**) can precede the modal (conditional or conditional perfect) or they can be attached to the infinitive (simple or perfect), giving four possible alternatives:

> **Ho podria haver fet.**
> **Podria haver-ho fet.**
> **Hauria pogut fer-ho.**
> **Ho hauria pogut fer.**
> He would have been able to do it/could have done it.

34.7   FURTHER REMARKS ON si

34.7.1   Si 'IF': GENERAL

Even though a clause introduced by **si** will present a hypothesis rather than a fact or a reality, the subjunctive mood is used only in the conditions described in **34.4** and **34.5**. The present subjunctive *never* appears after **si**, and this, from the foreign learner's point of view, may be seen as a major exception to some primary considerations about the use of the subjunctive. Syntactic convention alone can account for the contrast between: **Si ve, ja li cantaré les veritats** 'If he comes, I'll give him a piece of my mind', and **Quan vingui, ja li cantaré les veritats** 'When he comes, I'll give him a piece of my mind'.

See, however, **34.8** for examples of the present subjunctive after some other conditional conjunctions.

English speakers should also avoid the temptation to use a future indicative after **si** in conditional clauses (corresponding to 'if . . . will + infinitive' in English):

Si mires les proves, hauràs de concloure . . .
***Si miraràs les proves, hauràs de concloure . . .**
If you will look at the evidence, you will have to conclude . . .

The verb **ser** 'be' cannot be omitted after **si**:

M'hi conformaré, si és absolutament necessari.
I'll agree to it, if absolutely necessary.

Vine abans, si és possible.
Come earlier, if possible.

On the other hand, **si** itself can sometimes be dropped before a past subjunctive expressing a wish or a regret, ('if only . . .', **19.6**), with the consequence clause itself often suppressed in this construction:

Ho haguessis vist . . .   If only you'd seen it . . .

It is quite common in colloquial speech to find **si** used without conditional force and with a merely emphatic function (often coming after **però** 'but'):

Però si jo no havia dit res.   But I hadn't said anything.
Però si . . .   But, but . . .

34.7.2 Com si 'AS IF'

Clauses introduced by **com si** 'as if' express unfulfilled or hypothetical/remote conditions, with the verb always in the pluperfect or past subjunctive:

Van arribar tots alhora, com si s'ho haguessin proposat.
They all arrived together, as though they had planned it.

Fes com si no en sabessis res.
Behave as though you knew nothing about it.

34.8 OTHER CONDITIONAL CONSTRUCTIONS

Other conjunctions that introduce conditional clauses, including those conveying ideas of 'if by chance', 'just in case' are **en cas que** 'in case', **per si (de cas)** '(just) in case', **a condició que** 'on condition that', **només que** 'if . . . just', **mentre que** 'while' and others like **just que, amb que** 'if only' which overlap with concessive senses (see **33.3.3**).

Agafa el xandall, en cas que vulguis/per si vols anar a córrer.
Take your tracksuit, in case you feel like going for a run.

Comprarem un parell d'ampolles més, per si de cas.
We'll buy a couple more bottles, just in case.

Acceptem aquest encàrrec, a condició que se'ns pagui al preu convingut.
We'll take this job on, provided we are paid at the agreed price.

Només que li posis quatre ratlles, la faràs contenta.
If you just drop her a line or two you'll make her happy.

Mentre que això sigui així, pots comptar amb mi.
As long as/While that's the case, you can count on me.

Just que/amb que ens donin la subvenció, ho podrem tirar endavant.
Provided/If only we get the grant, we'll be able to go ahead.

Further expressions corresponding to negative 'unless', are:

(i)   **Llevat que, fora que, tret que**; these may also be followed by **de** + an infinitive construction:

No enllestirem aquesta feina, fora que ens hi vinguin a ajudar.
We won't finish this job unless they come and help us.

És impossible, tret que es faci així.
It's impossible, unless you do it like this.

Fora de parlar amb els de la teua edat, res no vares aprendre a escola.
(Raimon)
Except for talking with your schoolmates, you learnt nothing at school.

Llevat de matar, ja has fet de tot.
Except murder, there's nothing you haven't done.

(ii) **Que no** 'without':

No l'escolto que no m'esclati de riure.
I can't listen to him without bursting out laughing.

(iii) **Sense que** 'without', 'unless':

No prendrà cap iniciativa sense que algú l'hi inciti.
He won't take any initiative unless someone incites him to/without someone prompting him to.

It is to be noted how these other conjunctions admit the present subjunctive, which never appears after **si** 'if'.

34.8.1   NON-STANDARD CONDITIONAL CONSTRUCTIONS

(i)   *Com* instead of *si*

Although proscribed by normative standards, colloquial habit allows the occasional use of **com** followed by the present or past subjunctive instead of **si** with the indicative. This occurs only with open conditions, usually in voicing a threat or a warning:

Com no callis, et mato.
If you don't shut up I'll kill you.

I li va dir que com es tornés a portar així, en pagaria les conseqüències.
And he told him that if he behaved like that again, he'd pay for it.

(ii)   *Preposition + infinitive replacing 'if'-clause*

Where the verbs in the condition clause and in the consequence clause have the same subject, some dialects (and non-standard speech generally) allow replacement of **si** + conjugated verb by **de** plus the infinitive:

De no haver-ho sabut a temps, hauríem ficat la pota.
If we hadn't found out in time, we'd have put our foot in it.

This structure is also possible with different subjects if the infinitive shows its subject explicitly:

De no haver-ho sabut ells a temps, hauríem ficat la pota.
If they hadn't found out in time, we'd have put our foot in it.

The preferred alternative to both of these constructions is the normal conditional clause with **si**: **Si no calles . . .; . . . si es tornava/tornés a portar . . .; Si no ho haguéssim sabut . . .; Si no ho haguessin sabut . . .**
On the other hand, in a certain range of idioms, **a** + infinitive is recognized as genuine in a conditional function:

A jutjar pel que diuen . . .
To judge/If we go by what they say . . .

No hem rebut la seva quota, a no ser que l'hagi pagada per transferència bancària.
We haven't received his subscription, unless he's paid it by banker's order.

34.8.2   SYNTACTIC STRATEGIES AVAILABLE TO INTRODUCE A CONDITION OTHER THAN WITH si

Both (i) the gerund (see **22.2.4.1**) and (ii) the past participle (see **21.1.3**) can stand in absolute constructions (i.e. not governed by a conjunction) that are alternatives to **si** clauses. As well as with the range of constructions described so far in this section, there are yet other syntactic strategies for conveying conditional meaning. The commonest of these involve the simple copulative conjunctions **i** 'and' and **o** 'or':

> **Només em mira amb aquells ulls i jo em desmaio.**
> If she just looks at me with those eyes, I swoon.

> **Fas això i t'escanyo.**
> Do that and I'll throttle you./If you do that I'll throttle you.

> **O em retornen els diners o els denuncio a la policia.**
> If they don't return my money I'll report them to the police.

Obviously, in these cases, the conditional meaning is equally implicit in the more literal English translation: 'She just looks at me . . . and . . .', 'You do that and . . .', 'Either they give me . . . or I . . .'.

A related construction is one in which the condition clause is formed without **si**. There is generally dislocation of the object, doubled by a clitic, with the main clause, equivalent to the condition clause, being introduced by **i** 'and':

> **Les declarés en públic, aquestes coses, i l'empaperaven.**
> Were he to say these things in public he'd be prosecuted.

> **Ho digués jo, això, i no em creurien pas.**
> If *I* were to say that, I wouldn't be believed.

34.9   TRANSLATING 'IF I WERE YOU . . .'

'If I were you' and the like are most economically done by using **de**, without any verb:

> **Jo de tu, callaria/callava.**
> If I were you I'd keep quiet.

> **Jo d'ella, hi hauria quedat a veure com acabava allò.**
> If I'd been her/in her place, I'd have stayed to see how it ended.

Otherwise a full conditional clause is required:

> **Si ens trobéssim/trobàvem en el seu cas/en aquesta circumstància, etc.**
> If we were in their position/in this circumstance, etc.

34.10 MISCELLANEOUS EXAMPLES OF CONDITIONAL SENTENCES

Catalan, like English, has a flexible and nuanced system for constructing conditional sentences. Structurally the two systems overlap up to a point, but expression in or translation into Catalan will frequently involve recasting English patterns, following the conventions of usage and the grammatical principles outlined in the preceding sections. The point is illustrated by the following examples (adapted from standard studies on English grammar):

Had they been here, they would have cried too.
Si haguessin estat aquí, també haurien/hagueren plorat.

Were it not so, we'd have to think again.
Si no fos així, ens ho hauríem de replantejar.

Were it to depend on me, there'd be no problem.
Si de mi depengués, no hi hauria problema.

I won't compromise, even if he offers/offered/were to offer me a fortune.
No transigeixo, ni que m'ofereixi/m'oferís una fortuna.
No transigeixo, ni tan sols si m'ofereix/m'oferís/m'oferia una fortuna.

I can't think of an alternative, unless it's to change the engine.
No se m'acut cap alternativa, si no és canviar el motor/(non-standard) a no ser que canviem el motor.

Unless I'm mistaken, tomorrow is her birthday.
Si no m'equivoco, demà fa anys.

Provided we're not interrupted we'll finish it today.
Sempre que no ens interrompin/si no ens interrompen, ho enllestirem avui.

Should you write to them, send them my regards.
Si els escrius, envia'ls records de part meva.

PART V: INFORMATION STRUCTURE AND WORD ORDER

35 CLEFT SENTENCES

35.1 CLEFT AND PSEUDO-CLEFT SENTENCES

Cleft and pseudo-cleft sentences have similar characteristics and functions in Catalan to those they have in English. The unmarked structure **En Vicenç va sortir ahir amb la Núria** 'Vicenç went out with Núria yesterday' could, for specific emphasis, become one of the following cleft sentences:

Va ser amb la Núria amb qui va sortir ahir en Vicenç.
It was Núria that Vicenç went out with yesterday./Núria is the one that . . .

Va ser en Vicenç qui va sortir ahir amb la Núria.
It was Vicenç that went out with Núria yesterday./Vicenç is the one who . . .

Va ser ahir que en Vicenç va sortir amb la Núria.
It was yesterday that Vicenç went out with Núria./Yesterday is when . . .

or (pseudo-cleft):

El qui va sortir ahir amb la Núria va ser en Vicenç.
(The one) who went out with Núria yesterday was Vicenç.

Amb qui va sortir ahir en Vicenç va ser amb la Núria.
(The one) whom Vicenç went out with yesterday was Núria.

Quan va sortir en Vicenç amb la Núria va ser ahir.
When Vicenç went out with Núria was yesterday.

In each case both languages achieve similar effects of focus by these procedures. We deal separately below with the two types (cleft and pseudo-cleft) paying particular attention to some distinctive structural features of Catalan. The alternative translations given above 'Núria is the one who . . . ' correspond more literally to the 'reverse pseudo-cleft' pattern of **35.1.2ii**.

35.1.1 CLEFT SENTENCES

Cleft sentences conform to the basic pattern of copular verb (**ser** 'be') + focused phrase + (nominalized) relative clause. (Logically, cleft sentences are equational sentences of the form noun phrase = noun phrase.) When the unmarked sentence **En Miquel ha telefonat** 'Miquel phoned' is transformed in this way into **És en Miquel el qui ha telefonat** 'It is Miquel who phoned', focus is placed on **Miquel**, in relation to a previous assertion, question, or supposition about the agent of the action. The implication would then be something like 'It is Miquel who phoned' (and not Glòria, for example). Similar effects can be observed in the following examples:

Són aquests pantalons els que hauries de dur (i no aquells altres).
It's these trousers you ought to wear (and not those other ones).

És al meu poble on fan bons torrons (i no al teu).
It's my village that they make good *torrons* in (and not yours).

És caminar aviat el que ens cal fer (i no quedar aquí asseguts).
Getting a move on soon is what we must do (and not stay sitting here).

In cleft structures the relative clause functions as a noun phrase complement, not as an (attributive) adjective and this explains why these cleft sentences are linked not merely with **que** but rather with a nominalizer **el que** or **(el) qui** (agreeing in number and gender with the noun antecedent; see **31.6.2, 31.7**):

Són aquestes joguines les que vam comprar ahir.
*Són aquestes joguines que vam comprar ahir.
It is these toys that we bought yesterday./These toys are the ones . . .

Va ser la manera en què va xisclar el que em va posar els pèls de punta.
*Va ser la manera en què va xisclar que em va posar els pèls de punta.
It was the way she screamed that made my hair stand on end.

Differences between Catalan and English versions of this type of cleft sentence centre on two aspects as described in the following sections: the use of prepositions, and the behaviour of the copular verb.

35.1.1.1   *Cleft sentences with prepositions*

If the focused phrase is the object of a preposition, then in Catalan the preposition must also appear in the focus position. As in all other constructions, and in contrast to English, prepositions may not be left stranded. Thus to focus on Jaume in **He d'escriure a en Jaume** 'I must write to Jaume' we have to say **És a en Jaume a qui he d'escriure** 'It's to Jaume that I must write/It's Jaume that I must write to'. For the second part of such sentences, though, the option exists either to use the stressed relative with the same preposition (**a qui** in the last example) or just the weak relative pronoun **que**: **És a en Jaume que he d'escriure**. No difference in meaning is involved, although with **a** or **de** the repeated pronoun + stressed relative is generally felt to be more formal.

Hem d'entregar aquest paquet al secretari.
We have to deliver this parcel to the secretary.
→ **És al secretari a qui hem d'entregar aquest paquet.**
= **És al secretari que hem d'entregar aquest paquet.**

* És el secretari a qui hem d'entregar aquest paquet.
It's the secretary that we must give this parcel to.

Tothom parlava d'una cosina seva.
Everybody was talking about a cousin of his.
→ **Era d'una cosina seva de qui parlava tothom.**
= **Era d'una cosina seva que parlava tothom.**
* **Era una cosina seva de qui parlava tothom.**
It was a cousin of his that everybody was talking about.

With prepositions other than **a** or **de**, and where inanimate complements are involved, preference seems to be for **que** rather than for the repeated preposition.

Va ser amb el nostre permís que ho varen fer.
It was with our permission that they did it.

Deu ser per això que no em vol veure més.
That must be why she doesn't want to see me again.

Clauses of place, time, or manner may use **on**, **quan**, or **com**, although **que** is again preferred in informal speech:

Va ser en aquest carrer on/que se'l van carregar.
It was this street that they wiped him out in.

Serà demà potser quan/que ens ho faran saber.
It'll perhaps be tomorrow that they'll let us know.

És entrenant-se cada dia com/que ha arribat a ser campió.
It's by training every day that he has become champion.

35.1.1.2 *Agreement of the copular verb in cleft sentences*

The Catalan copular verb in these structures agrees in number and gender with the focused phrase (if it is nominal; third-person singular if it is not, as in the last example of **35.1.1.1**). The English equivalent always begins with 'it is', 'it was', etc.:

Sóc jo el qui ha dit que vinguéssiu.
It is I who told you to come.

Ets tu el qui posa emperons a la nostra voluntat.
It's you who are putting difficulties in the way of what we want.

No era la Maria la qui plorava?
Wasn't it Maria who was crying?

Person agreement of the verb in the relative clause may also occur when, as in the examples above, this is in the singular (**Sóc jo el qui *he* dit . . .**, **Ets tu el qui** *poses* ...); strict person agreement of the verb in the relative clause *must* occur when it has a plural subject.

> **Som nosaltres els qui hem acusat els perjurs.**
> ***Som nosaltres els qui han acusat els perjurs.**
> It is we who have accused the perjurers./We are the ones who . . .

> **Sou vosaltres els qui viviu bé.**
> ***Sou vosaltres els qui viuen bé.**
> It is you who live well./You are the ones who . . .

> **Són ells els qui fan la feina bruta.**
> It is they who do the dirty work./They are the ones who . . .

Consequently care must be exercised when translating English 'it is'/'it was'/ 'it will be' at the beginning of a cleft sentence with an original plural subject, as **ser** remains plural in such constructions:

> **Eren els de la dreta els que insistien més en aquesta política.**
> It was those on the right who were insisting most on this policy.

> **Són les seves manies el que m'irrita.**
> It's his obsessions which irritate me. (more literally: His obsessions are what irritates me.)

The preceding example illustrates the important point mentioned earlier: that unlike in the English cleft pattern the Catalan structure has to involve two noun phrases. Here the second is the neuter free relative **el que m'irrita** 'what irritates me'. Similar examples are:

> **Fou la seva fe el que la va salvar.**
> It was her faith that saved her.

> **–Què duia? –Si no m'equivoco, era una camisa rosa el que portava aquell dia.**
> 'What was he wearing?' 'If I'm not mistaken it was a pink shirt he was wearing that day.'

Tense of copula in clefts

Several examples already given show how the tense of the copular verb is frequently attracted by that of the verb in the relative clause. While Catalan has more latitude in using the present tense at the head of the cleft sentence (**És la Maria la qui ha telefonat** = **Ha estat la Maria la qui ha telefonat** 'It is Maria who phoned', **És amb tu amb qui vaig parlar** = **Va ser amb tu amb qui vaig parlar** 'It is/was you that I spoke to'), the copula more often matches the tense of the original main verb, especially when this is in the past:

> **Serà/És amb ell que hauràs de parlar.**
> It will be/is him that you will have to speak to.

Va ser en aquell poble que es van conèixer.
* Era en aquell poble que es van conèixer.
It was in that town that they met.

Era captant pel carrer que mantenien la família.
*Va ser captant pel carrer que mantenien la família.
It was by begging in the street that they kept their families.

35.1.2   PSEUDO-CLEFT SENTENCES

Relative to the cleft construction, the pseudo-cleft construction (i) inverts the
order of the focused phrase and the relative clause: relative clause + copula +
focused phrase. Thus, for example, **El que em fa falta és un mapa de la regió**
'What I need is a map of the region'. The reverse pseudo-cleft (ii) has the
order: focused phrase + copula + relative clause: **Un mapa de la regió és el que
em fa falta** 'A map of the region is what I need'. Pragmatic circumstances of
communication can give rise to reinforcement, by these means, of either the
focused phrase component of the sentence or the relative clause. Note the
possible translations of Catalan cleft sentences in **35.1** and **35.1.1** by English
reverse pseudo-clefts.

(i)   pseudo-cleft:

(El) qui ha dit això és en Miquel.
(The person) who said this was Miquel.

(El/La) qui ha fet taques en terra ets tu.
(The one) who made a mess on the floor was you.

Amb qui vaig fer el tracte va ser amb tu.
The person who I made the deal with was you.

A qui he de consultar és a en Mateu.
The person (who) I must consult is Mateu.

(ii)   reverse pseudo-cleft:

En Miquel és (el) qui ha dit això.
Miquel is the one who said this.

Tu ets (el/la) qui ha fet taques en terra.
You are the one who made a mess on the floor.

Amb tu va ser amb qui vaig fer el tracte.
You are the one I made the deal with.

A en Mateu és a qui he de consultar.
Mateu is the one (who) I must consult.

Caminar aviat és el que ens cal fer.
Walk quickly is what we must do.

35.1.2.1   Prepositions in pseudo-cleft sentences

When the focused term is a prepositional complement, repetition of the preposition is always required (see **35.1.1.1**), so that, for the example used in **35.1.2**, **Amb qui vaig fer el tracte va ser amb tu**, we cannot have *Qui vaig fer el tracte va ser amb tu/*Amb qui vaig fer el tracte va ser tu, and for **Amb tu va ser amb qui vaig fer el tracte** we cannot have *Tu va ser amb qui vaig fer el tracte/ *Amb tu va ser qui vaig fer el tracte.

Other examples:

Per on han vingut és pel camí de dalt.
The way they have come is along the high route.

D'aquells col·legues era de qui havíem d'extreure la informació.
Those colleagues were the ones who we had to extract the information from.

35.1.2.2   Agreement of the verb in pseudo-clefts

In comparison with the cleft construction, the pseudo-cleft pattern (**35.1.2i**) shows a strong tendency towards the non-agreement of the verb in the relative clause with the subject of the copular verb:

(El/La) qui ha fet taques en terra ets tu.
?**(El/La) qui has fet taques en terra ets tu.**

This tendency is less strongly felt in the plural, especially when the relative is preceded by the plural article:

Qui ha fet taques en terra som nosaltres.
= **Els qui han fet taques en terra som nosaltres.**
= **Els qui hem fet taques en terra som nosaltres.**

For the reverse pseudo-cleft examples (**35.1.2ii**) verbal agreement in the relative clause is usual when the preceding phrase contains the actual subject of the copular verb:

Tu ets (el/la) qui ha fet taques en terra.
= **Tu ets (el/la) qui has fet taques en terra.**

As in cleft sentences (**35.1.1.2**), the tense of the copular verb is often attracted by that of the verb in the relative clause, so that for the example used in **35.1.2** there are alternatives:

Amb qui vaig fer el tracte va ser amb tu.
= Amb qui vaig fer el tracte és amb tu.

Amb tu va ser amb qui vaig fer el tracte.
= Amb tu és amb qui vaig fer el tracte.

Other examples:

Contra els liberals era contra qui sempre despotricava.
The liberals were the ones he was always ranting on against.

El que ens va impressionar més va ser l'eloqüència d'aquell home.
What most impressed us was that man's eloquence.

Vosaltres sereu els qui haureu de salvar la pàtria.
You will be the ones who will have to save our homeland.

35.2   MISCELLANEOUS POINTS ON CLEFT STRUCTURES

Translating 'that's why'

The regularly used cleft construction in English 'that's why . . . ' does not transfer directly into Catalan. A variety of alternatives is available.

Va ser per això que ho vam fer.	That's/That was why we did it.
Per això t'ho dic. = És per això que t'ho dic.	That's why I'm telling you.
Aquest és el motiu pel qual no hi han assistit.	That's why they didn't attend.

Style and the use of clefting

The complexities of some cleft sentences (especially those involving long prepositional phrases) can lead to a cumbersome style in writing. This may be avoided by introducing emphasis in alternative ways within the unmarked sentence:

Va ser tenint en compte aquestes objeccions que vam madurar el nostre projecte.
It was with these objections being taken into account that we rounded out our plan.
→ **Així, tenint en compte aquestes objeccions, vam madurar el nostre projecte.**

This general stylistic advice may be particularly appreciated by English speakers on account of uncertainty over 'who'/'whom', the overlap in function of 'that' (demonstrative/conjunction/relative) and the radical difference of Catalan with respect to preposition stranding. Nevertheless, sentences like:

'It's not that that I meant.'
'The one who we must be grateful to is Frederic.'
'It's Frederic that we must be grateful to.'
'It was that sort of expression that he always came out with/out with which he always came.'

which are not particularly comfortable in English, have Catalan equivalents that are formed spontaneously in very neat 'cleft' constructions:

No és això el que jo volia dir.
A qui hem de donar les gràcies és a en Frederic.
És a en Frederic que (= a qui) hem de donar les gràcies.
Era aquella mena d'expressió la que sempre amollava.

These simple examples provide a convenient summary of some main points to be borne in mind about Catalan syntax in this area: the function of the relative link, the repetition of prepositions, tense agreement (especially affecting past tenses).

36 WORD ORDER

This chapter discusses the order of the main elements in declarative sentences. For the position of attributive adjectives, see **4.2**; for order in questions, see **27.1**; for cleft constructions see Chapter 35.

Catalan shares with English the basic word-order pattern, in transitive main clauses, of subject + verb + object + remainder. However, in general, word order in Catalan is freer, and it is by no means unusual to deviate from the pattern mentioned. An important reason for this is that, in Catalan, it is the end position in a sentence that carries the information focus; it is the place where the major pitch movement takes place in speech, and it is the place where the most informative element of the sentence goes. Elements of the basic word-order sequence may have to be dislocated to achieve this. (In English, information focus is often indicated, in the spoken language, at least, by a special intonation contour placed on the focused word or phrase, which need not be at the end of a clause, as it must in Catalan.)

36.1 BASIC WORD ORDER

The normal unmarked word order of Catalan has elements (when present) in the following order

'frame' or sentential adjunct
subject
no 'not'
verb
short adverbial
direct object or predicative phrase
indirect object or other complement phrase
adverbial adjunct

For example:

Quant a la ràdio, els periodistes han donat avui un avís a la direcció sobre la vaga proposada per a dimecres.
As regards radio, the journalists have today given notice to the management about the strike planned for Wednesday.

Note in this example that, whereas, in English, a short adverbial may precede the lexical verb (following an auxiliary, if any): ' . . . have today given . . . ', in

Catalan such an element comes between verb and direct object: **. . . han donat avui un avís . . .**

36.2   BASIC WORD-ORDER VARIANTS: VERB + SUBJECT

An important variant of basic word order, with intransitive verbs whose subjects are not 'agents' (also known as 'unaccusative' intransitives), has the subject following the verb. This is particularly likely when the subject, rather than the verb (or some other element) carries most of the 'new' information (or bears the information focus). Impersonal reflexives typically follow this pattern also.

> **Ha arribat el tren.** *The train* has arrived.
> information focus on 'the train' (what you might say while waiting in the station, when the train is a (relative) novelty).

> **El tren ha arribat.** The train has *arrived*.
> information focus on 'has arrived' (What you might say on the train, when its arrival is the (relative) novelty.)

> **Els meus pares van arribar ahir.** My parents arrived *yesterday*.
> information focus on 'yesterday'

> **Ahir van arribar els meus pares.** *My parents* arrived yesterday.
> information focus on 'my parents'

> **Avui només serveix l'acció.** Nowadays only *action* is effective.
> information focus on 'action', as indicated by 'only'

> ??**Avui només l'acció serveix.** (an abnormal variant which would need information focus on **serveix**)

> **Fan falta vint cadires.** Twenty chairs are needed.
> **Vindran moltes persones a veure això.** Many people will come to see that.
> **Han passat quinze dies.** A fortnight has passed.
> **S'ha arreglat aquell assumpte.** That matter has been sorted out.

A recent approach to thematic structure, or information structure, proposes that an utterance in discourse has a *focus* and a *ground*. The focus is what we have been calling information focus, that is, that part of an utterance which contains information which is new to the hearer. (This may sometimes be the whole utterance, such as a news item out of the blue.) The ground is not new information but includes elements that guide the hearer how to process the new information – how to relate it to older information. The ground may consist of one or more *links*, and one or more *tails*. A noun phrase which is a pointer to an 'address' where the new information is to be filed is called a link, and necessarily comes at the beginning of an utterance. (What we call a link here is often referred to as a topic; but unfortunately *topic* also has many other senses in linguistics, including some which conflict with the one in question here.) In the sentence in **36.1.** there are two links, **quant a la ràdio** and **els periodistes.** Subject noun phrases are often links though not necessarily so. In intransitive sentences like those above it seems that Catalan prefers to delay the noun phrase subject to indicate that it is not a link. As some of the examples above show, indefinite noun phrases, which are most unlikely to be links, almost always follow the verb.

> **S'ha proposat aquesta solució.**
> *This solution* has been suggested./People have suggested this solution.
> (Expect more information coming up on the solution.)

> **Aquesta solució s'ha proposat.**
> This solution has been *suggested.*
> (**Aquesta solució** is a link – hearers can identify what solution is under consideration, but, for example, it hasn't been put into practice; **s'ha proposat** is the focus.)

The question of tails will be taken up in **36.4–5.**

36.3 'HEAVY NP SHIFT'

Another pattern that deviates from the 'norm' of **36.1** is sometimes called 'Heavy (noun phrase) Shift'. A long (or heavy) subject or direct object noun phrase is placed to the right of its normal position, moving towards the end of a sentence. It is no doubt an aspect of this same phenomenon that allows short adverbials to precede objects/complements in the standard order of **36.1.** For example:

> **Em va donar el paquet un senyor molt alt amb un bigoti petitet.**
> A very tall man with a little moustache gave me the parcel./I was given the parcel by a very tall man with a little moustache. (verb + object + long subject)

> **La Maria ens va donar a tots uns pastissos de xocolata que hi cantaven els àngels.**
> Maria gave all of us some chocolate cakes that were delicious. (verb + indirect object + long direct object)

> **Ahir van visitar les ruïnes de la ciutat més antiga de Catalunya els representants de diverses nacions europees.**
> Yesterday the ruins of the oldest city in Catalonia were visited by representatives of several European nations. (Note verb + object + subject in Catalan corresponding to the English passive.)

Comparteixen aquestes característiques altres sistemes tridimensionals, biplanars, icònics o simbòlics.
These characteristics are shared by other three-dimensional, biplanar, iconic or symbolic systems. (Note verb + object + subject corresponding to the English passive.)

In Catalan, it is almost certainly not the 'heaviness' itself of such phrases that provokes their movement, but rather informativeness or information focus, as mentioned before. Similar reordering can occur, for example, with quite short phrases which contain most of the new information, as in:

Em va donar el paquet en Pere.
Pere gave me the parcel./It was Pere who gave me the parcel.

The order here, verb + object + subject, indicates that **el paquet** is not part of the focus. Likewise, in the following example, the indirect object, **a la Conselleria de Treball**, which is not part of the focus, precedes the direct object, **diverses cartes**, which is the focus:

Hem enviat a la Conselleria de Treball diverses cartes.
We have sent several letters to the Employment Ministry.

And a heavy phrase does not have to be moved if there is another phrase whose informativeness predominates:

La Maria ens va donar uns pastissos de xocolata que hi cantaven els àngels a tots nosaltres.
Maria gave some chocolate cakes that tasted delicious to *all of us.*

36.4   LEFT DETACHMENT

We have mentioned that the last or rightmost position in a sentence is the position associated with focus on new information. The position associated with old or given information, that is, the link as defined in **36.2** or 'what the sentence is about', is the first or leftmost position. The subject of a sentence often appears in leftmost position and fulfils the role of link (see **29.1.4** on the 'be' passive construction which ensures that a link is a subject). Another (non-subject) noun phrase which is a link may appear in the leftmost position, however. If this is a verbal argument (a direct or indirect object, or another required complement), then a pronominal clitic corresponding to it is required next to the verb. (This phenomenon is often called left detachment, or left dislocation, or topicalization.) If the link element is not a verbal argument, a clitic is not required, though one may be found; this usage of a clitic after a detached non-argument is regarded by some grammarians as non-standard (see **12.8** on redundant clitics). A comma often follows the detached element, but usage is very variable in this matter.

Left detachment is all-pervasive in the spoken language; it is not always easy to render it idiomatically in written English, though sometimes English uses a similar order.

El ganivet, el fiquem al calaix.
The knife, we put in the drawer.

Les tovalloles, deixa-les al balcó.
The towels? Leave them on the balcony./Leave the *towels* on the balcony.

Al balcó, deixa-hi les tovalloles.
On the balcony leave the towels./It's the towels you should leave on the balcony. (It is the balcony which is already prominent in the discourse.)

A Roma, no hi podem anar, enguany.
Rome we won't be able to go to this year.

Amb aquest tros de paperet ja no hi comptava. (written on aerogram, first line on the extra space overleaf)
I wasn't counting on this little bit of paper.

Quant al Joan i la Isidora no t'ho sé dir, que el Joan el veiem ben poc.
As for Joan and Isidora, I can't say, as Joan we see very little of.

El Pep, no crec que vulgui peix.
Pep I don't think will want fish. (Here it is the subject of the subordinate clause which has been detached.)

(D')intel·ligent, la Maria n'és força.
Very intelligent, Maria is.

Intel·ligent, la Maria ho és força.
Very intelligent, Maria is.

(The above two examples are more or less equivalent, and hard to render adequately in English; **intel·ligent** is the link, and **força** 'very' is the information focus; but in English we cannot separate a degree word from its complement in a comparable way.)

Left detachment is not quite so common in more formal styles, though by no means excluded from them. The grammarians' rule that a clitic should not be used after a detached non-argument apparently leads to hypercorrection, where the clitic is omitted after a detached sentence argument. Part of the problem is that it is not easy to decide in every case whether a phrase is an argument or not. Here are some examples illustrating patterns of left detachment and clitic usage.

Argument with clitic:

Convé aclarir que aquest ús *el* retrobem en totes les regions.
It should be pointed out that this use is found in all regions. (Note English passive representing the object + active verb order of Catalan, in this and following examples.)

Que el nostre escriptor tenia consciència de marcar una distinció sintàctica *ho* mostra una frase com . . .
The fact that our writer was aware of marking a syntactic contrast is shown by a phrase such as . . .

Apèndix I. En aquest apèndix *hi* hem inclòs les espècies no estudiades per l'equip d'investigació durant la primera fase del projecte.
Appendix I. In this appendix are included the species not investigated by the research team during the first phase of the project.

Dels funcionaris de carrera, només *n'*han admès quatre.
Of the career civil servants only four have been accepted. (Here **dels funcionaris de carrera** is not strictly an argument of **admetre**, but rather of **quatre** which is itself an argument of **admetre**.)

Argument without clitic (technically non-standard, because 'hypercorrect'):

A la pregunta de quin era l'entorn literari habitual del nostre poeta no podem contestar sinó amb notícies parcials → . . . no hi podem contestar . . .
The question of what the habitual literary context of our poet was we can answer only with partial information. (**Contestar** 'answer' takes a prepositional argument **a** + noun phrase.)

El llibre s'ocupa de totes les variacions territorials d'Europa fins a la segona guerra mundial. De la segona guerra mundial l'autor diu ja ben poca cosa → . . . l'autor en diu . . .
The book deals with all the territorial variations in Europe up to the Second World War. Of the Second World War the author says very little.

Xile ha retornat a l'ortografia «normal». I a l'ortografia «normal» tornaran els «dissidents», o els seus alumnes, més tard o més d'hora → . . . hi tornaran . . .
Chile has returned to the 'normal' orthography. And the 'dissidents', too, or their pupils, will return to the 'normal' orthography, sooner or later.

Aquest costum de la tórtora no es troba en els bestiaris . . . De la castedat de la tórtora parla Hug de Sant Víctor → . . . en parla . . .
This habit of the turtledove does not occur in the bestiaries . . . The chastity of the turtledove is mentioned by Hugh of St. Victor.

Non-argument with clitic (technically non-standard):

A les llars d'hostal, *hi* perdura encara la germanor . . . dels clans. (Prudenci Bertrana)
At the fireside of an inn the brotherhood of the clan persists even now. (non-argument topic + clitic)

Ens van donar una relació de restaurants de tipus mitjà: el Gargantua, el Parellada, l'Agustí, el Set Portes, Ca la Maria, Darío, etc. «Al Set Portes», ens van advertir, «no *hi* dinareu per menys de 5.000 ptes.»
They gave us a list of medium-priced restaurants . . . 'In the *Set Portes,*' they added, 'you won't pay less than 5,000 pesetas for lunch.'

Non-argument without clitic:

En les llars d'hostal els homes es revelen a penes arribats. (Prudenci Bertrana)
At the fireside of an inn men reveal themselves as soon as they have arrived. (non-argument topic, no clitic, from the same paragraph as the Bertrana example above)

Però si en la prosa actual trobem tan abundosament tota mena d'inversions . . .
But if in contemporary prose we find so abundantly all kinds of inversions . . .

36.5 RIGHT DETACHMENT

As well as left detachment Catalan also makes use of right detachment. Right detachment is predominantly a phenomenon of spoken style. One modern approach refers to a right-detached element as a *tail*. A tail is an additional element supplied by the speaker to ensure or confirm that the hearer will properly identify elements already alluded to. Right detachment is sometimes referred to as an afterthought construction; this label is appropriate in some cases but not in all. Right-detached phrases (tails) that correspond to sentence arguments always have a related clitic in the main part of the sentence.

A comma preceding the right-dislocated element is normal in written usage; the information focus/intonational prominence of the sentence comes before the comma. (It is in this prosodic sense, at least, that we can think of right-detached elements as afterthoughts.)

El fiquem al calaix, el ganivet.
The knife, we put in the drawer./We put it in the drawer, the knife, that is.

Els pagesos ja l'hi van enviar, el bròquil, a l'amo.
The farmers have already *sent* the broccoli to the boss.

Here 'the farmers' is the link – the 'address' where the new information is to be filed – which appears first, in this case as sentence subject, and 'sent' is the focus, which in Catalan must end the main part of the sentence structure; with these information requirements, the full noun phrases corresponding to the direct and indirect objects have to appear in right-detached position. Note that the order of right-detached elements is quite free: **L'hi van enviar, a l'amo, el bròquil** would be quite acceptable.

Sap molt bé el que vol, el teu germà.
He knows what he wants, your brother.

T'hi acostumaràs aviat, a la nova feina.
You'll soon get used to it, your new job.

Avui n'hi ha per donar i per vendre, de restaurants.
Nowadays, (as for) restaurants, they are two a penny.

The following dialogue (from Vallduví) is about **ametllons** 'green almond fruits'; morphologically the word is understood (incorrectly) by B as consisting of **ametlla** 'almond' with an augmentative suffix:

A –Saps què són, ametllons?
B –Ametlles grosses, suposo.
A –Bueno, són semblants, sí. Però aixís amb la closca i tot.
B –Les ametlles també en *tenen*, de closca.

A 'Do you know what *ametllons* are? (Note virtually obligatory detachment of the subject in a question.)
B 'Big almonds, I suppose.'
A 'Well, they're similar, yes. But like with the shell and all.'
B 'Almonds have got a shell, too.' (lit. Almonds, too, *have* one, a shell.)

(**Les ametlles**, the link, re-establishes almonds as the topic of B's utterance; **tenen** is the focus, appropriately because A's utterance implies that almonds do not have a shell; the direct object **closca** is obliged to become a tail.)

A –Vet aquí la veu de l'autoritat, això cal, això no cal: aquesta és la realitat.
B –Ah, carall, que n'*és*, de dura, de vegades, la realitat!

A 'Here's the voice of authority, you must do this, you mustn't do that: this is reality.'
B –'Oh hell, how tough reality *is* sometimes!'

(Vallduví; 'normal' order **La realitat és dura** would be less appropriate here; **la realitat** is already salient, having just been mentioned by A, and B wishes to place information focus on **és**; the subject and the adjective complement thus become tails, along with the temporal adverbial adjunct **de vegades**. **La realitat** doesn't strictly need to be spelt out again, but perhaps B realizes that he might be taken to be saying that it is authority that is tough.)

One type of structure that has sometimes been taken as a special type of left detachment is really, it can be argued, an example of right detachment. Here a noun or adjective phrase precedes the remainder of the sentence, which has no clitic copy of the detached phrase. In terms of surface order on the printed page this does look very like left detachment, but in speech focal stress falls on the initial phrase. The English translation is likely to have an 'it'-cleft.

Els problemes de la companyia, discutirà el consell en la seva propera reunió.
It is the company's problems that the board will discuss at their next meeting.

El ganivet, vaig ficar al calaix de dalt.
It's the *knife* I put in the top drawer.

La Núria, té molts amics.
It's Núria that has a lot of friends.

Cansats, van arribar.
They were *tired*, when they arrived.

Demà, arribaran els meus amics.
It's tomorrow my friends arrive.

A **–Hòstia! S'hem acabat la botella, eh! Que som . . . que som . . .**
B **–Les dues botelles ja!**
A **–Dues botelles, s'hem polit!**

A 'My God! We've finished the bottle! We are . . . we are . . .'
B 'The two bottles already!'
A '*Two bottles*, we've polished off!'

Whereas left-detached structures have the form link + focus, it can be plausibly argued that these structures have the form focus + tail, where the tail happens to include the main verb.

36.6 WORD ORDER IN RELATIVE CLAUSES

Catalan avoids placing a noun phrase other than a clitic pronoun between a relative pronoun and a verb (**31.1.3**). This means that in relative clauses object + verb + subject order is quite frequent. In this context English and Catalan differ radically in order of constituents.

Tot està disposat perquè dissabte vinent s'inicïi aquí el carnaval d'hivern que organitza el Departament de Turisme.
Everything is ready for the inauguration here next Saturday of the winter carnival organized by the Department of Tourism. (lit. . . . which the Department of Tourism organizes)

Així diu la carta que ens va enviar ton pare.
That's what it says in the letter your father sent us.

He vist el policia a qui havien trucat els segrestadors.
I have seen the officer whom the kidnappers telephoned.

(**El policia a qui els segrestadors havien trucat** is possible, but corresponds only to a rather formal style.)
This word order requirement may produce ambiguity:

He vist el policia que havia apallissat el lladre.
I have seen the officer who beat up the thief./I have seen the officer who the thief beat up.

36.7   WORD ORDER IN ADVERBIAL CLAUSES

In an adverbial clause it is quite normal for a subject to follow a verb, though other orders are possible. The preferred place for a subject seems to be immediately after the verb. Thus (a) below appears more natural than (b):

(a)   **Un cop va haver tret en Pere els diners de la caixa, va sonar l'alarma.**
(b)   **Un cop va haver tret els diners de la caixa en Pere, va sonar l'alarma.**
(c)   **Un cop en Pere va haver tret els diners de la caixa, va sonar l'alarma.**
As soon as Pere had taken the money out of the safe, the alarm went off.

Segons que han revelat els treballadors del sector, no hi haurà vaga.
According to what workers in the industry have revealed, there will not be a strike.

36.8   THE POSITION OF ADVERBIALS

Generally speaking, adverbials (adverbs, prepositional, and adverbial phrases and clauses) are placed either immediately before or immediately after the word(s) they modify. This can produce an un-English order of verb + adverbial + object as in the examples below.

Han complert molt atentament els requisits.
They have fulfilled the requirements carefully./They have carefully fulfilled the requirements.

Fregirem en una paella els alls fins que estiguin daurats.
Fry the garlic in a pan until golden.

Hem de triar amb decisió i fermesa el moment d'oferir la nostra resignació.
We must choose the moment to offer our resignations decisively and firmly.
(i.e. . . . choose decisively and firmly . . .)

Fou inútil que els rectors advertissin en els pobles a les dones que els seus marits les abandonarien si arribava la llei del divorci.

It was no use the parish priests warning women in the villages that their husbands would leave them if the divorce law were introduced.

Un d'aquells desgraciats havia fugit a Mysore, on havia pintat en un palau la figura del tigre.

One of those unfortunates had fled to Mysore, where he had painted the figure of the tiger in a palace.

37 SPELLING, ACCENT RULES, AND PUNCTUATION

37.1 ALPHABET

The Catalan alphabet is basically the same as the English one, with the following additional letters: ç (*ce trencada*) which represents the sound [s] in certain words, such as **feliç** 'happy', **raça** 'race', and the digraph l·l (*ela geminada*) a symbol unique to Catalan, which represents a double l [ll]. *Ce trencada* (ç) has no special place in alphabetical order; words with ç are found among words with **c**, though when everything else is the same **c** precedes **ç**, so **coca** 'cake' comes before **coça** 'kick'. Likewise *ela geminada* has no special place, though, with words otherwise identical in spelling, **ll** precedes **l·l**: **cella** 'eyebrow' comes before **cel·la** 'cell'. The letters **k** and **w** are found only in certain foreign words and their derivatives, such as: **karate, wagnerià**. Except in certain proper names (e.g. **Ruyra, Nova York**) the letter **y** is found only in the combination **ny**: **Catalunya** 'Catalonia', **Espanya** 'Spain', **any** 'year'. The vowels have variants with written accents (see **37.5**) which also have no serious effect on alphabetical order.

37.2 CAPITALIZATION

Catalan makes rather less use of capital letters than English does. They are not used for the pronoun **jo** 'I', for the names of days or months, or for nouns or adjectives derived from proper names.

el primer divendres de gener	the first Friday in January
Catalunya	Catalonia
català	Catalan
el català	Catalan (language), Catalan (person)
catalanòfil	Catalanophile
estudis lul·lians	studies on Llull (Ramon Llull)
el lul·lisme	Lullism

In titles of books, films, and so on, normally only the first letter is a capital, so *Diccionari general de la llengua catalana* is 'General Dictionary of the Catalan Language'.

37.3   SPELLING ALTERNATIONS

There are a number of spelling conventions, rather like English 'lilies' versus 'lily', or 'rubber', 'rubbing' versus 'rub' which affect derived forms in Catalan.

37.3.1   CONSONANT SPELLING DETERMINED BY FOLLOWING VOWEL

qu before **e** or **i**, pronounced /k/, corresponds to **c** in other positions:

> **vaca**, 'cow', plural **vaques**; **cercar** 'to seek', **cerco** 'I seek', **cercava** 'I sought', **cerqueu** 'you seek', **cerqui** 'seek' (1st- or 3rd-person singular present subjunctive); **sac** 'bag', **saquet** 'little bag'.

gu before **e** or **i**, pronounced /g/, corresponds to **g** in other positions:

> **botiga** 'shop', plural **botigues**; **castigar** 'to punish', **castigo** 'I punish', **castiguem** 'we punish', **castiguin** 'they punish' (3rd-person plural present subjunctive), etc.; **figa** 'fig', **figuera** 'fig tree'.

c before **e** or **i**, pronounced /s/, corresponds to **ç** in other positions:

> **adreça** 'address', plural **adreces**; **caçar** 'to hunt', **caço** 'I hunt', **caces** 'you (*sg.*) hunt', **caçant** 'hunting', **cacés** 'hunt (1st- or 3rd-person singular past subjunctive), etc.; **plaça** 'square', **placeta** 'small square'; **feliç** 'happy', *f. pl.* **felices**.

g before **e** or **i**, pronounced /ʒ/, corresponds to **j** in other positions:

> **monja** 'nun', plural **monges**; **envejar** 'to envy', **envegen** 'they envy', **envejaré** 'I shall envy', **envegí** 'I envied', etc.; **platja** 'beach', plural **platges**; **boja** 'mad (*f.*)', **bogeria** 'madness'.
>
> Note that **j** does also occur before **e** though in relatively few words, such as **objecte** 'object', **injecció** 'injection', **jeure** 'to lie', **jersei** 'sweater', **majestat** 'majesty' and biblical names like **Jeremies** 'Jeremiah', **Jerusalem**, etc.

qü before **e** or **i**, pronounced /kw/, corresponds to **qu** in other positions:

> **obliqua** 'oblique (*f.*)', plural **obliqües**, **obliqüitat** 'obliqueness'; **adequar** 'to adjust', **adeqüem** 'we adjust', **adequava** 'adjusted' (3rd-person singular imperfect), **adeqüi** 'adjust' (1st- or 3rd-person singular present subjunctive), etc.

gü before **e** or **i**, pronounced /gw/, corresponds to **gu** in other positions:

> **llengua** 'tongue', plural **llengües**, **llengüeta** 'tab'; **aigua** 'water', **aigüera** 'sink'.

37.3.2 SPELLING ALTERNATION: WORD-FINAL VERSUS WORD-INTERNAL POSITION

Some contrasts in consonant pronunciation which are observed in word-internal position are obliterated word-finally; so the distinction between [z] in **casos** 'cases' and [s] in **passos** 'steps' is lost in the singular of these words: **cas** and **pas** respectively. If we start from the dictionary form of such words, then we have to learn which words undergo a spelling change when a suffix is added. (Good dictionaries provide this information.) There are elements of pure convention involved, too. Where we might expect **j** or **tj** to occur word-finally, **ig** (or just **g** if the preceding stem vowel is **i**) is used.

Word-final **-s** corresponds to word-internal **-s-** ([z]) in many words, but to **-ss-** ([s]) in many others. There are large numbers of both kinds:

cas	case	**casos**	cases
pis	flat	**pisos**	flats
francès	French (*m.*)	**francesa**	French (*f.*)
afectuós	affectionate (*m.*)	**afectuosa**	affectionate (*f.*)

pas	step	**passos**	steps		
esbós	sketch	**esbossos**	sketches	**esbossar**	to sketch
gros	big (*m.*)	**grossa**	big (*f.*)		
progrés	progress	**progressos**	(*pl.*)		
rus	Russian	**russos**	Russians		

With a few exceptions **b**, **d**, and **g** are not written after a vowel or diphthong in word-final position in a stressed syllable, but are replaced by **p**, **t**, and **c** respectively (also before inflectional **-s**). (**B**, **d**, and **g** are, however, written after consonants and unstressed vowels, as in **corb** 'curved', **verd** 'green', **llarg** 'long', **àrab** 'Arabic', **vàlid** 'valid', **teòleg** 'theologian'.)

llop	wolf (*m.*)	**lloba**	female wolf
sap	knows	**saber, sabia, sabem**	know, I/he/she/it/knew, we know
salut	greeting	**saludar**	greet
buit	empty (*m.*)	**buida**	(*f.*)
estimat	loved (*m.*)	**estimada**	(*f.*)
abric	shelter	**abrigar**	to shelter
dic	I say	**digueu**	say (2nd-person plural imperative)
poruc	timorous (*m.*)	**poruga**	(*f.*)

As in the case of word-final **-s**, if we start from the dictionary form, there is no straightforward way of telling which words will undergo a spelling change in inflected or derived forms and which will not, for there are also non-alternating **p**, **t**, **c** (note that the alternation between **c** and **qu** is entirely regular; see above). For example:

tip	full (*m.*)	**tipa**	(*f.*)		
tap	stopper	**tapar**	to stop up, cover		
eixut	dry (*m.*)	**eixuta**	(*f.*)		
promet	promises	**prometre, prometem**	to promise, we promise		
ric	rich (*m.*)	**rica**	(*f.*)	**riquesa**	riches
duc	duke	**duquessa**	duchess		

Most dictionary words in **-t** have inflected or derived forms with prevocalic **d** rather than **t**; the situation for dictionary words in **-p** and **-c** is more evenly balanced.

Final **-ig** may correspond either to prevocalic **-j-/-g-** or to prevocalic **-tj-/-tg-** in inflected or derived forms. The following group of examples illustrates alternation between **-ig** and **-j-**. The nominal suffix **-eig** regularly corresponds to **-ejar** in related verbs.

boig	mad (*m.*)	**boja** (*f.*)	**bogeria**	madness
passeig	walk	**passejar**		take a walk
raig	trickle	**rajar**		to trickle
fuig	runs away	**fugir**		run away

The following is a complete list of **-ig** words that make their derivatives in **-tj-/-tg-**:

bolig	sweepnet, jack (at bowls)	**bolitjada**	sweepnet catch, throw of jack
desig	desire	**desitjar**	to desire
enuig	bother	**enutjar**	to bother
estoig	box, case	**estotjar**	put away in a case/box
llebeig	south-west wind	**llebetjol**	light south-west wind
lleig	ugly (*m.*)	**lletja** (*f.*)	
mig	middle (*m.*)	**mitja** (*f.*)	
rebuig	rejection	**rebutjar**	to reject
safareig	sink	**safaretjada**	sinkful
trepig	tread	**trepitjar**	to tread

Alternations involving written accents are mentioned below (**37.5**).

37.4   THE DIAERESIS

The diaeresis ¨ occurs over **i** (replacing the dot) and **u** (both upper- and lower-case); it has two functions:

(i)   In the groups **güe, güi, qüe, qüi** it indicates that the **u** is pronounced, that is, that **gu, qu**, are not to be read as digraphs; see **37.3.1**. Thus **següent** 'following', **ambigüitat** 'ambiguity', **qüestió** 'question', **obliqüitat** 'obliqueness'. Exceptionally, in the verb **argüir** the diaeresis indicates not [w] but [u] – as ***arguir** would be read */argi/.

(ii) Over **i** or **u** following a vowel, the diaeresis indicates that **i** or **u** is pronounced as a syllabic vowel (not, as would otherwise be the case, as a semivowel [j] or [w] forming a diphthong with the preceding vowel, or a semiconsonant [j], [w], between vowels):

veïna	neighbour(ing) (*f.*)	cf. **reina**	queen
agraïa	thank	cf. **atzagaia**	javelin
	(1st- or 3rd-person		
	singular past imperfect)		
fruït	enjoyed	cf. **fruit**	fruit
evacuï	evacuate (1st- or 3rd-person	cf. **avui**	today
	singular present subjunctive)		
diürn	daily	cf. **diumenge**	Sunday
peüc	bedsock	cf. **meuca**	prostitute

By convention the diaeresis is not used, even though its use would be justified according to the above principle, in the following contexts:

(a) after a prefix, e.g. **auto-, co-, contra-, pre-, re-: autoimmunitat** 'auto-immunity' (six syllables), **coincidir** 'coincide', **reunir** 'collect';

(b) in the suffixes **-isme** and **-ista: altruisme** 'altruism' (four syllables), **panteista** 'pantheist', **arcaisme** 'archaism';

(c) in words containing the Latin endings **-us** or **-um: Màrius, harmònium, linòleum**;

(d) in the infinitive, gerund, future, and conditional of verbs ending in **-ir**: e.g. **influir** 'influence', **influint, influiré**, etc., **influiria**, etc. Other forms of such verbs have the diaeresis where expected: **influïa** (past imperfect), **influïren** (3rd-person plural preterite), **influït** (participle), and so on.

37.5 WRITTEN ACCENT: ACUTE ´ AND ` GRAVE

37.5.1 BASIC FUNCTION OF WRITTEN ACCENTS

The acute and grave accents are used on vowel letters, both upper- and lower-case. The basic function of these signs is to indicate, in a word of more than one syllable, that the stressed syllable is not that which would be expected by the general rules.

The general stress rules are:

(i)   Stress falls on the next to last syllable of:

    (a)   a word ending in a vowel (but not a diphthong): **fe_s_ta**, **ind_i_co**, **ref_i_a**, **ta_x_i**, **ret_re_ure**

    (b)   a word ending in a vowel (not a diphthong) + s: **o_s_tres**, **v_i_cis**, **t_i_pus**, **recre_ï_s**, **des_i_tjos**

    (c)   a word ending in -en or -in: **or_i_gen**, **ref_i_en**, **des_i_tgin**, **andr_o_gin**

(ii)   Stress falls on the last syllable otherwise; that is, in:

    (a)   a word ending in a diphthong or a diphthong + s: **esp_ai_**, **esp_ai_s**, **est_iu_**, **est_iu_s**, **enren_ou_**

    (b)   a word ending in -an, -on, -un: **est_an_**, **volar_an_**, **seg_on_**, **alg_un_**

    (c)   a word ending in any other single consonant except s, any group of consonants: **fin_al_**, **estim_at_**, **unic_orn_**, **desp_atx_**, **cost_ums_**

In all cases which depart from the general stress rules above the stress is indicated with a written accent on the vowel of the stressed syllable. Two accent marks are used: only the acute is used on **í** and **ú** and only the grave on **à**. On the other vowels, **e** and **o**, the acute and grave accents mark phonemic distinctions. (These phonemic distinctions are not represented at all when a written accent is not required.) Thus **é** corresponds to /e/, **è** to /ɛ/; **ó** corresponds to /o/, **ò** to /ɔ/.

All words whose stress falls on the antepenultimate syllable bear a written accent: **màquina** 'machine', **església** 'church', **pèrdues** 'losses', **síl·laba** 'syllable', **fórmula** 'formula', **anònimes** 'anonymous' (*f.pl.*).

Other examples, with final syllable stressed, by exception to the general stress rules:

sofà	sofa	**entén**	understands (3rd-person
puré	purée		singular present of
ressò	echo		**entendre**)
espès	thick (*m.sg.*)	**pliocèn**	Pliocene
abús	abuse	**esplín**	spleen

Because of the regular application of the accent rules it is quite common for a noun or adjective which has a written accent in the (masculine) singular to lack one in the plural or the feminine, for example:

sg.	*pl.*	
camí	**camins**	path
serè	**serens**	serene (*m.*), and thus **serena**, **serenes** (*f.sg.* and *pl.*)
pagès	**pagesos**	farmer
oportú	**oportuns**	timely (*m.*), and thus **oportuna**, **oportunes** (*f.sg.* and *pl.*)

Much less often a noun or adjective which lacks an accent in the (*m.*) singular requires one in the plural or feminine. These are words ending in **-en** or **-in**, singular stress rule (i)c:

fenomen	**fenòmens**		phenomenon
origen	**orígens**		origin
misogin	**misògins**	**misògina**	misogynous (*m.sg., m.pl., f.sg.*)

Adverbs in **-ment** which are derived from adjectives bearing an accent retain the accent, corresponding to secondary stress:

críticament	critically
fàcilment	easily

Except in this case, the position of secondary stress is not indicated in compounds written without a hyphen: <u>contra</u>sentit 'contradiction', <u>fisi</u>coquímic 'physico-chemical', **his<u>pa</u>noamericà** 'Hispano-American', **<u>ra</u>rament** 'rarely'.

When an accent (acute) and a diaeresis are both justified on the same vowel, the accent takes precedence, thus giving rise to alternations between í and ï, as in:

país	**països**		country, countries
veí	**veïns**	**veïna**	neighbouring (*m.sg., m.pl., f.sg.*)

Both a diaeresis and an accent can occur on the same word on different vowels, as in **traïció** 'treason', **aïllàvem** 'we isolated' (imperfect), **lingüística** 'linguistics'.

37.5.2   DIALECT DIFFERENCES IN WRITTEN ACCENTS

In western dialects (Northwest Catalan, Valencian) there are a considerable number of words that are pronounced with /e/ where eastern dialects have /ɛ/. Consequently, writers from these regions may use an acute accent on words where the eastern-based norm requires a grave: hence W: **conéixer** E: **conèixer** 'know', W: **alé** E: **alè** 'breath', W: **anglés** E: **anglès** 'English', W: **encés** E: **encès** 'lit', W: **seté** E: **setè** 'seventh'. Some western writers and publishers stick to the eastern accentuation conventions despite their own pronunciation.

37.5.3   DIACRITIC ACCENTS

While the major function of the acute and grave accents is to indicate the position of stress in words that do not follow the general stress rules, they have a second function of distinguishing between homographs (different words with the same spelling). The list of words with diacritic accents runs to about fifty; it includes several rare words, as well as a good number of common ones. Many other pairs of homographs are not distinguished with a diacritic accent (e.g. **sa** 'healthy', **sa** 'his/her/its/their'; **sou** 'wage', **sou** 'you (*pl.*)

are'; **moll** 'marrow', **moll** 'quay', **moll** 'mullet', **moll** 'soft', **molls** 'tongs'). The following list is of the most common words bearing a diacritic accent, alongside the words they are distinguished from:

bé	well	**be**	lamb, letter B
béns	goods	**bens**	lambs
bóta, bótes	cask, vat	**bota, botes**	boot
Déu **déu, déus** also **adéu, semidéu**, etc.	God god(s)	**deu** **deus**	ten, must (3*sg.*), spring must (2*sg.*), springs
dóna, dónes	give (2*sg.*, 3*sg.* present)	**dona, dones**	woman, wife
és	is	**es**	(reflexive clitic pronoun 3rd person), (definite article)
féu also **reféu, satisféu**, etc.	make (3*sg.* preterite)	**feu**	make (2*pl.* present), fief
fóra	would be (**ser** 3*sg.* conditional)	**fora**	out, outside
jóc, jócs	roost(s)	**joc, jocs**	game(s)
mà	hand (*pl.* **mans**)	**ma**	my (*f.*)
més	more	**mes**	month, but, put (*m.sg.* participle of **metre**), my (*f.pl.*)
mòlt, mòlta, mòlts, mòltes (participle of **moldre** 'grind')		**molt, molta, molts, moltes**	many, much
món also **rodamón**	world (*pl.* **mons**) globetrotter	**mon**	my (*m.sg.*)
móra, móres **Móra**	blackberry/-ies (place name)	**mora, mores**	Muslim (*f.sg.*, *f.pl.*)
nét, néta, **néts, nétes** also **besnét**, etc.	grandchild	**net, nets,** **neta, netes**	clean
ós, óssos	bear	**os, ossos**	bone
óssa, ósses	she-bear	**ossa, osses**	skeleton

pèl, pèls also **repèl**, etc.	hair	**pel, pels**	(contraction of **per** + **el, els**)
què	what (also stressed relative pronoun after preposition: **amb què**, etc.)	que	which, that (unstressed relative pronoun or complementizer)
sé	I know	se	(reflexive clitic pronoun 3rd person)
sí, sís	yes(ses)	si	(reflexive pronoun 3rd person), if, bosom, sinus, B (note of scale)
sóc	I am	soc	stump, clog
sòl, sòls	soil	sol, sols	(3*sg.*, 2*sg.* present **soler**), sun, alone (*m.*), G (note of scale)
té	has (3*sg.* present of **tenir**)	te	(2*sg.* pronoun), tea, letter T
ús	use (plural **usos**)	us	(2*pl.* pronoun)
véns, vénen (**vénga/véngui, véngues/ vénguis, vénguen** also **revéns**, etc.	come (2*sg.*, 3*pl.* present of **venir**) Bal. 1*sg.*/3*sg.*, 2*sg.*, 3*pl.* present subjunctive of **venir**)	vens, venen venga/vengui, vengues/ venguis, venguen	sell (2*sg.*, 3*pl.* present of **vendre**) 1*sg.*/3*sg.*, 2*sg.*, 3*pl.* present subjunctive of **vendre**)
vés	go (2*sg.* imperative)	ves	see (2*sg.* imperative)
véu	saw (3*sg.* preterite of **veure**)	veu	sees (3*sg.* present of **veure**), voice
vós	you (stressed polite form)	vos	(2*pl.* unstressed pronoun)

37.6 HYPHEN

The official *Diccionari de la llengua catalana* published by the Institut d'Estudis Catalans in Barcelona in 1995 significantly reduced the number of compound words which were to be written with a hyphen. Generally speaking a hyphen is now required only when both parts of the compound are independent Catalan words (and not always then). A hyphen is no longer used in words like **arximilionari** 'multi-millionaire', **exministre** 'ex-minister', **vicepresident** 'vice-president', **grecollatí** 'Greco-Latin', 'classical', **democratacristià** 'Christian democrat', **audiovisual** 'audiovisual'. It *is* used in reduplicative forms like **bum-bum** 'rumble', **fer la gara-gara** 'suck up to', **ziga-zaga** 'zigzag line' despite the elements involved not being independent words.

The hyphen is used:

(i)   In numbers from twenty-one to twenty-nine: **vint-i-un** . . . **vint-i-nou**, and the related ordinals **vint-i-unè** . . . **vint-i-novè**;

in numbers from 31 to 99: for example, **trenta-dues, quaranta-quatre, noranta-vuit**, and the related ordinals **trenta-dosè**, etc.;

in compounds involving **-cents, -centes** 'hundred', **dos-cents, dues-centes, tres-cents** . . . **nou-cents**. The ordinals likewise have a hyphen: **set-centè** 'seven-hundredth', but other derived forms do not: thus **la música setcentista** 'seventeenth-century music'.

(ii)   When an unstressed pronoun, containing a vowel letter (**a, e, i, o, u**), follows a verb: **retireu-vos** 'withdraw', **dóna-me-la** 'give me it (*f.*)', **enviant-hi** 'sending there', **veure-les** 'to see them (*f.*)'. (Pronouns consisting of one or more consonants have an apostrophe: **treure'n** 'to take some away', **menja'l** 'eat it'; see 12.1.2. Note **-us** [-ws], as in **veure-us** 'to see you', with a hyphen because the pronoun contains a vowel letter **u**, despite its being pronounced as a semiconsonant.)

(iii)   In compounds including a compass point: **nord-est** 'northeast', **sud-africà** 'South African'.

(iv)   In nouns containing the element **no** 'non-': **no-violència** 'non-violence', **no-alineament** 'non-alignment', **no-res** 'nothing'. Before an adjective, however, **no** is written separately: **no violent** 'non-violent', **els països no alineats** 'non-aligned countries'.

(v)   In a small group of irregularly derived compounds, for example: **a corre-cuita** 'in a hurry', **fer suca-mulla** 'dunk', **abans-d'ahir** 'the day before yesterday', **despús-demà** 'the day after tomorrow', **qui-sap-lo** 'tremendously, enormously many'.

(vi)   In a compound composed of Catalan words, when there is an element that begins with **r-, s-**, or **x-**. The point of this exception is to avoid mispronunciations of these letters, which, internally, might be taken as representing /r/, /z/, or /gz/ respectively, instead of /r/, /s/, and /ʃ/ as required. Hence **guarda-robes** 'cloakroom', **pit-roig** 'robin', **busca-raons** 'troublemaker', **penya-segat** 'cliff', **gira-sol** 'sunflower', **cul-de-sac** 'dead end', **cara-xuclat** 'hollow-cheeked'. (Note the presence of the first hyphen in **cul-de-sac**; as the second hyphen is required because of the following **s**, the first is required to avoid the strange or confusing *culde-sac.)

(vii) In a compound when the first element has a written accent, for example: **pèl-curt** 'short-haired', **més-dient** 'highest bidder'. Exceptions: **adesiara** 'every now and then' (from **adés i ara**), **usdefruit** 'usufruct' (from **ús de fruit**).

Compound words like the following have no hyphen: **guardaespatlles** 'bodyguard', **capicua** 'palindrome number', **pocavergonya** 'cad', **setciències** 'know-all'.

37.7   PUNCTUATION

The majority of Catalan punctuation conventions are the same as those in English. There are a few differences, though. (On conventions relating to commas after long relative clauses and after conditional clauses, see **31.1.2** and **34.1**.) *Cometes baixes* « . . . » are a form of double inverted commas, quite often used to mark titles of works, or phrases used as proper names, as in, **el bar «El Molino»** 'the "El Molino" bar'. In texts containing dialogue, it is usual to set off the quoted speech with a dash, rather than inverted commas; a dash closes the speech only when an indication of saying, replying, etc. follows:

–**Què proposes, doncs?**
–**El que hauríem de fer**– **s'atreví a suggerir** – **és anar a . . .**
'What do you propose, then?'
   'What we should do,' she ventured to suggest, 'is to go and . . .

Until recently the inverted question mark ¿ was widely used to indicate the beginning of a direct question, particularly if it did not begin with a question word, or if it extended over more than one line of print (**27.1.1**), e.g. ¿**És Blanes aquella vila que surt al darrere d'aquest sorral, entremig d'aquells dos penyals arramats d'heura i arbrissam?** 'Is it Blanes, that town which appears behind that sandbank, between those two crags covered with ivy and bushes?' Some writers and publishers used ¿ consistently before all direct questions, including short ones with question words ¿**Què vols?** 'What do you want?' In 1993 the Institut d'Estudis Catalans recommended that, in line with the rest of the world's languages (other than Spanish), the inverted question mark should no longer be used in Catalan in any circumstances.

FURTHER READING

Atrian i Ventura, S., *et al.* (1982–83) *Som-hi! Català per a adults*, 2 vols, Barcelona: Barcanova.

Brumme, J. (1997) *Praktische Grammatik der katalanischen Sprache*, Wilhelmsfeld: Egert.

Busquets, L. (1988) *Curs intensiu de llengua catalana*, Barcelona: Abadia de Montserrat.

Cavaller, R. (1984–85) *Anem-hi tots!: textos i exercicis de català fàcil*, 2 vols, Palma de Mallorca: Moll.

Gili, J. (1993) *Introductory Catalan Grammar*, (5th edn), Llangrannog: Dolphin.

Poole, S. (1995) *Catalan in Three Months*, Woodbridge: Hugo.

Puig, G. *et al.* (1984) *Sempre endavant: català per a adults no catalanoparlants*, Barcelona: Barcanova.

Tió, J. (1986) *Curs de català per a estrangers*, Vic: Eumo.

Yates, A. and Ibarz, T. (1992) *A Catalan Handbook: Working with 'Digui, digui'*, Sheffield: Botifarra (with subsequent 1993 edition (Barcelona: Departament de Cultura) of this companion to *Curs de català per a estrangers*, adaptation of the multimedia *'Digui, digui'* method by Mas *et al.*).

The above titles are all tried and tested familiar tools for the teaching of Catalan as a second language. Many other language-teaching and study materials, produced for the Catalan educational market, are available and complement substantially the items listed. The range is constantly being extended. A convenient (although incomplete) guide to these materials is provided in the *Bibliografia per aprendre català* (5th edn, 1997) issued by the Departament de Cultura of the Generalitat de Catalunya.

Several English–Catalan/Catalan–English dictionaries are available. Oliva & Buxton (2 vols) is the largest.

Català–Anglès/English–Catalan, Mini (1996) Barcelona: Enciclopèdia Catalana.

Catalan Dictionary, English/Catalan–Catalan/English (1994) London: Routledge.

Diccionari Oxford Pocket, Català–anglès anglès–català (1997) Oxford: University Press.

Oliva, S. and Buxton, A. (1983) *Diccionari anglès–català*, Barcelona: Enciclopèdia Catalana.

Oliva, S. and Buxton, A. (1986) *Diccionari català–anglès*, Barcelona: Enciclopèdia Catalana.

BIBLIOGRAPHY

Badia i Margarit, A. M. (1962) *Gramática catalana*, 2 vols, Madrid: Gredos.
Badia i Margarit, A. M. (1995) *Gramàtica de la llengua catalana. Descriptiva, normativa, diatòpica, diastràtica*, Barcelona: Proa.
Butt, J. and Benjamin, C. (1988) *A New Reference Grammar of Modern Spanish*, London: Arnold.
Cuenca, M. J. (1988–91) *L'oració composta*, 2 vols, València: Universitat de València.
Fabra, P. (1956) *Gramàtica de la llengua catalana*, Barcelona: Teide.
Fabra, P. (1968) *Introducció a la gramàtica catalana*, Barcelona: Edicions 62.
Hualde, J. I. (1992) *Catalan*, London: Routledge.
Institut d'Estudis Catalans (1990–96) *Documents de la Secció Filològica, I–III*, Barcelona: IEC.
Institut d'Estudis Catalans (1995) *Diccionari de la llengua catalana*, Barcelona/Palma de Mallorca/València: Enciclopèdia Catalana.
Institut d'Estudis Catalans (1997) *Documents normatius 1962–1996*, Barcelona: IEC.
Lacreu, J. (1992) *Manual d'ús de l'estàndard oral*, València: Institut de Filologia Valenciana, Universitat de València.
Mascaró, J. (1986) *Morfologia*, Barcelona: Enciclopèdia Catalana.
Mestres, J. M., Costa, J., *et al.* (1995) *Manual d'estil. La redacció i l'edició de textos*, Vic: EUMO.
Moll, F. de B. (1982) *Gramàtica catalana referida especialment a les Illes Balears*, Palma de Mallorca: Moll.
Morant, R. and Serra, E. (1987) *Els modificadors intraoracionals i interoracionals*, València: Universitat de València.
Payrató, L. (1990) *Català col·loquial (aspectes de l'ús corrent de la llengua catalana)*, València: Universitat de València.
Pérez Saldanya, M. (1988) *Els sistemes modals d'indicatiu i de subjuntiu*, València: Institut de Filologia Valenciana/Publicacions de l'Abadia de Montserrat.
Ruaix i Vinyet, J. (1986) *El català*, 3 vols, Moià: Ruaix.
Ruaix i Vinyet, J. (1989) *Punts conflictius de català. Deu estudis sobre normativa lingüística*, Barcelona: Barcanova.
Ruaix i Vinyet, J. (1994–95) *Observacions crítiques i pràctiques sobre el català d'avui*, 2 vols, Moià: Ruaix.
Solà, J. (1972–73) *Estudis de sintaxi catalana*, 2 vols, Barcelona: Edicions 62.
Solà, J. (1987) *Qüestions controvertides de sintaxi catalana*, Barcelona: Edicions 62.
Solà, J. (1990) *Lingüística i normativa*, Barcelona: Empúries.
Solà, J. (1994) *Sintaxi normativa: estat de la qüestió*, Barcelona: Empúries.
Vallduví, E. (1990) 'The informational component', unpublished PhD thesis, University of Pennsylvania.

Valor, E. (1977) *Curs mitjà de gramàtica catalana referida especialment al País Valencià*, València: 3 i 4.

Yates, A. (1975, 12th impression 1998) *Teach yourself Catalan*, London: Hodder & Stoughton.

INDEX

English words as main entries are in *italics* and Catalan words are in **bold**. References are to chapters and sections, not pages. Reference to a main section generally subsumes all subsections within: e.g. 14.3 refers to 14.3.1–14.3.3, etc. Irregular verbs are not listed separately here: *see* chapter 16.

a (atonic preposition)
  a *vs.* **en**, forming verbal complements 14.1.1.4, 20.3.1.1; in expressions of place 14.1.1.3; in time expressions 14.1.1.5, 20.4
  contraction with definite article 3.1.1, 14.1
  forming idioms with the infinitive 14.1.1.6, (requests) 28.4, (conditional) 34.8ii
  introducing direct objects 14.1.1.1, 23.2.5, 25.3
  introducing indirect objects 14.1.1.2
  introducing infinitive complement of **venir** and **sentir** 20.3
abans que (no) 19.4.7, 33.2.2.5
acabar de + infinitive 18.2.1
Accents *see* Written accents, Diaeresis, Diacritic accents
açò 6.5
Address forms 11.3
Adjectives Chapter 4
  agreement 4 para 1, 8.1; with coordinated nouns 4.2.3; with nouns of fixed gender 1.1.6
  comparison of Chapter 5
  complements of 4.2.4
  compound 4.1.7
  demonstrative 6.2–3
  diminutive, augmentative and evaluative suffixes 4.1.5
  formation by conversion 4.1.6
  indefinites 8.3
  morphology 4.1
  negative prefixation 4.2.5
  nominalization of 9.1, (abstraction) 9.2.1
  order of multiple adjectives 4.2.2
  plural forms 4.1.4

  position with noun 4.2.1
  possessive 4.1.2.6, 7.1–2
  quantifiers (degree adjectives) 8.2
  relative 31.9
  singular forms 'with two endings' 4.1.1–2.7; 'with one ending' 4.1.3
  syntax and usage 4.2
  synthetic comparative forms 5.2.2
  used adverbially 4.2.5, 13.1.2
  with **ser/estar** 30.5
Adjuncts (adverbial or prepositional phrases) 25.7, 36.1
adonar-se 23.9iv
adormir(-se) 23.10.8
Adverbial adjuncts (adverbial/ prepositional phrases) in sentence patterns 20.3.1.2, 25.7, 36.7–8
Adverbial clauses Chapter 33
  subjunctive in 19.4.1–7
Adverbial pronouns 12.6–7
Adverbs and adverbials Chapter 13
  adjectives used adverbially 4.2.5, 13.1.2
  adverbs ending in **-ment** 13.1.1, 13.4
  articles in adverbial phrases 3.1.4i(b)
  comparison of Chapter 13 introd., Chapter 5
  degree 13.6
  of manner 13.4
  of place and direction 13.2
  of qualification and inclusion 13.5
  of time 13.3
  prepositions used 'adverbially' 11.5.2iii
  quantifying 8.2.2, 13.6
  sentence adverbs/adverbials 13.7
  sentence position of 17.2.1.2, 36.8 (short adverbials) 36.1
  with compound tenses 17.2

Agent, passive 29.1.2
  with 'reflexive passive' 29.1.3iv, 29.2.1i
ago 13.3, 33.2.2.4i
agradar 3.1.4.3, 25.4
Agreement *see* Adjectives, Numerals,
  Past participle, Possessives
això 6.5, 9.2.1, 12.5
  i això que (concessive conjunction)
    33.3.3
ajeure's 23.10viii
ajudar a 25.5
algo (non-standard) 8.6v
algú 8.5
algun 8.3, 8.6
alhora que (= al mateix temps que)
    33.2.2.2
allò 6.5, 9.2.1, 9.2, 12.5
Alphabet 37.1
altre 8.3
altri 8.5
amb 14.1.2
  absence of indefinite article after
    3.2.3iv
  amb que 32.4.2, 33.3.3.1
  replaced before an infinitive 14.1.2,
    20.3.1.1
  (or **en**) with modes of transport 3.2.3iv
ambdós 8.2
a mesura que 32.2.2.2
Analytic (periphrastic) preterite 16.5.6.2,
    17.1.2
  see also Preterite tense
anar and **anar-se'n** 23.6.1
  anar a 18.2.1
Anglicisms 17.2.2, 18.1.1, 18.1.3iv–v
aquí 6.3
a penes (temporal conjunction) 32.2.2.6
Arguments (of verbs) 25.1, 25.6, 36.4
Arithmetical expressions 10.7
arribar a ser 30.6vi
article salat 3.1.2
Articles *see* Definite article, Indefinite
  article, 'Intensifying article',
  Neuter article **el**, Personal article
as (temporal) 32.2.2.2
Aspect 17.1.2.1, 17.1.3.1, 17.2.4
  affecting use of passive 29.1.3v
Augmentative suffixes 2.3.2, 4.1.5
Auxiliary verbs 16.5.6.2, 16.5.10.2,
    16.5.12, 17.2.1.2, 18.1
  modal auxiliary with infinitive 18.2.1,
    20.2.1iii

  modals allowing clitic raising 12.2.3

Balearic usage Preface p. xii
  specific features of 3.1.2, 3.3.2, 5.3.2,
    7.2, 8.2.1, 11.4.1, 12.1.1, 12.1.2vi,
    12.5, 12.9.3.2, 16.1.1, 16.2.3,
    16.5.5, 16.5.9, 16.5.11, 17.2.1.2,
    20.1.3, 24.1, 25.3, 26.1.9, 28.2,
    28.3, 29.1.2
bastant 8.2
  introducing clause with **perquè** 33.3.2.1
bé/ben 13.4
be Chapter 30, 23.10ii–iii, vi, *see also*
    estar, haver-hi, ser
become 23.1iii, 30.6
bo/bon 4.2.1
both . . . and 15.1.3.1

ç (*ce trencada*) 37.1
ca (= casa de) contraction with definite
    article 3.1.1, 14.1
cada 8.3
  cada u/cadascú 8.5
  cada un/cadascun 8.3
  cada vegada que 33.2.2.3
caldre 25.2.2
cap 8.3, 8.4, 8.6, 26.1.5
Castilianisms 3.2.3vi, 9.2.1, 17.1.4i,
    17.1.5ii, 18.1.1, 29.2.1, 31.4.3,
    32.1, 34.6.3
cert 8.3
Clauses
  adverbial Chapter 33, 19.4; cause
    19.4.1, 33.3.1; concession 19.4.2,
    33.3.3 (*see also* Concessive
    expressions); manner 19.4.6,
    33.2.3; of place 33.2.1; purpose
    19.4.4, 33.3.2; purpose/result/
    cause indicated by verbal mood
    33.3.2, 33.3.4; result 19.4.5,
    33.3.4; time 19.4.7, 33.2.2
  as objects of prepositions 32.4.1–2
  comparative 5.1–3
  complement Chapter 32, 19.2
    object 32.2
    subject 32.1
    with noun or adjective 32.3
  conditional Chapter 34, 15.3
  indirect question 27.1.2, 27.1.3.8
  non-finite (with infinitive) Chapter
    22, (with participle) 21.1.3, (with
    gerund) 22.2.3–4

relative *see* Relative clauses
see also Conditional sentences,
   Conjunctions, Subjunctive
Cleft sentences Chapter 35
   agreement of copular verb 35.1.1.2,
      35.1.2.2
   cleft and pseudo-cleft constructions
      35.1
   prepositions in 35.1.1.1, 35.1.2.1
   stylistic issues 35.2
Clitics *see* Pronominal clitics
ço 6.5
com 13.4, 15.4, 33.2.3
   adverbial relative 31.7, 31.8, 35.1.1.1
   com a (*vs.* com) 14.3.1
   com . . . de (in indirect questions)
      27.1.3.9 (in exclamations)
      27.2.2.2ii, 27.2.3
   com (que) 33.3.1ii
   com si 34.7.2
   in exclamations 13.6, 27.2.2, 27.2.3
   interrogative 20.3.1.3, 27.1.3.2,
      27.1.3.9
Combination of weak (object) pronouns
   see Pronominal clitics
cometes baixes 37.7
Comma 27.1.3.6, 31.1.2, 34.1.1, 36.4,
   36.5, 37.7
   with numerals 10.3, 10.9
Commands *see* Imperative
Comparison Chapter 5
   and adverbial clauses of manner
      33.2.3ii
   constructions expressing equality 5.1
   constructions expressing inequality 5.2
   correlative constructions ('the more/
      less . . . the more/less') 5.4
   del que (= 'than') 5.2.3, 31.6.2
   expletive no/no pas ('than') 5.2.2
   relative superlative 5.3.1
   synthetic forms (major, menor, millor,
      pitjor) as adjectives and adverbs
      5.2.1, 13.4
Complementizers 15.2–4
Compound nouns (plural forms of) 2.16,
   (with or without hyphen) 37.6
Compound tenses 16.5.12, 17.2
   auxiliary verbs in 17.2.1.2, 21.1.2
   coordination of 17.2.1.4
   pronominal clitics in 17.2.1.2
Concessive expressions 17.1.4iii, 19.4.2,
   20.4.1, 22.2.4.1, 33.3.3

overlap with conditional meaning 34.8
position of concessive clause 33.3.3.2
verbal mood in 19.4.2, 33.3.3
Conditional perfect tense 16.5.12, 17.2.6
   alternative forms 34.6
   with modal verb 34.6.5
Conditional sentences Chapter 34, 17.2.6
   basic patterns 34.1.1–2
   constructions other than with si 34.8.2
   fulfilled conditions 34.3
   hypothetical and remote conditions
      34.5
   miscellaneous variations 34.10
   non-standard constructions 34.8.1
   open conditions 34.2
   unfulfilled conditions 34.4
Conditional perfect tense 16.5.12, 17.2.6
Conditional tense 16.5.8
   alternative forms 16.5.8, 34.6.1
   use of 17.1.5 (as polite request) 28.4
   see also Conditional sentences
Conjunctions Chapter 15, Chapter 33,
      Chapter 34
   additive 15.1.6
   adversative 15.1.5
   causal 33.3.1
   compound 15.2.2
   concessive 33.3.3
      with indicative/subjunctive 19.4.2
   conditional 15.3, Chapter 34
   coordinating 15.1
   distributive 15.1.3
   illative 15.1.7
   manner 33.2.3
   purpose 33.3.2
   subordinating Chapter 33
      (conditional) Chapter 34
   temporal 33.2.2
   see also Adverbial clauses,
      Complement clauses,
      Conditional sentences
convertir-se (en) 30.6vi
Copular sentences Chapter 30
   see also haver-hi, *become*

Dash (showing quoted speech) 37.7
Dates 10.11
   'on' with days of the week 13.3
de 14.1.3
   contraction with definite article 3.1.1,
      14.1
   in comparative constructions 5.2, 5.3.1

in conditional expressions (with
    infinitive in 'if' clause) 34.8.1ii
    (without verb: 'if I were you'
    etc.) 34.9
introducing complements of adjectives
    4.2.4
introducing infinitive 20.2.1
linking noun to partitive **en** 12.6v
passive agent 7.5, 29.1.2
with quantifiers 8.2.1
Definite article 3.1
    absence or presence of 3.1.4
    article salat 3.1.2
    contraction with prepositions 3.1, 14.1
    idioms with feminine articles 3.4
    in distributive expressions 13.3
    in geographical names 3.1.4.5
    in relative clauses 31.6.2, 31.7
    in time expressions 3.1.4.4iii, 10.11,
        13.3
    morphology 3.1.1
    syntax of 3.1.3
    with nominalized infinitive 20.5
deixar (governing infinitive) 25.5
Demonstrative adjectives and pronouns
        Chapter 6
    as nominalizers 9.2.1
    deictic functions 6.2–3
    forms 6.2
    in relative clauses 6.4, 6.5, 6.6, 31.6,
        31.7
    neuter pronouns 6.5
    position of adjective 6.3.1
    pronominal use 6.4
    syntax 6.6
    translation issues 6.6
    use with perfect tense 17.2.2
d'ençà que 33.2.2.4
descuidar-se 23.7
Desiderative sentences 27.2.4
després que 17.2.4, 19.4.7, 33.2.2.6
des que 33.2.2.4
Déu n'hi do! 12.9.3.4, 24.1.1
deure
    in expressions of inference 17.1.4i,
        17.1.5ii, 17.2.5, 17.2.6, 18.2.1
Diacritic accents 16.1.4, 37.5.3
Diaeresis 16.1.3, 37.4
Digraphs (**l·l, ny**) 37.1
Diminutive suffixes 2.3.1, 4.1.5
Direct object 25.3, 25.4.1, 25.5
    pronouns *see* Pronominal clitics

Dislocation 25.3, 25.4; *see also* Left
        detachment, Right detachment
Distributives ('one each') 2.2.2
    distributive expressions (temporal)
        13.3, with **per** 14.1.4.1
diu que 25.2.2
diversos 8.3
dolent 4.2.1
doncs 15.1.7

el *see* Definite article, Neuter
el qual (compound relative) 31.4
    after a preposition 31.4.2
    as possessive relative (**del qual**) 31.2.2,
        31.5
    used instead of **que** 31.4.1
    vs. **el que** 31.4.3
els hi 12.9.3.5
en (adverbial pronoun) 12.6
    see also Pronominal clitics
en (preposition) 14.1.1
    absence of indefinite article after
        3.2.3iv
    in prepositional phrase adjuncts and
        complements 14.1.1.7
    vs. **a** 14.1.1.3–5, 20.3.1.1, 20.4
    with infinitive in temporal (and causal)
        expressions 14.1.1.5, 20.4
en absolut 26.1.6
encara que (and equivalent concessive
        conjunctions) 33.3.3
enlloc 26.1.5
ensenyar a/de 25.5
entendre('s) 23.9vi
es (3rd-person reflexive clitic) 12.4,
        Chapter 23
    see also Pronominal verbs, 'Reflexive
        passive' construction
esdevenir 30.6i
ésser *see* **ser**
estar
    compared with **ser** Chapter 30
    estar per + infinitive 18.2.1
    estar(-se) 23.10vi, 30.3
    estar-se de 30.1
    idiomatic phrases with 30.4
    some special uses 30.1
    with adverbial complements 30.4
    with gerund (in progressive tenses)
        18.1.1
    with past participle or adjective
        complement 30.5

Ethic dative 12.3.2.3vi, 12.9.3.7, 23.1, 25.4
Evaluative suffixes 2.3.3, 4.1.5
everything 8.2vi, 12.8.1, *see also* tot
Exclamation 27.2
  absence of indefinite article 3.2.3iv
  exclamation mark ¡ 27.2.1
  intonation 27.2.1
  miscellaneous idioms 27.2.5
  with question words 27.2.2
Expletive **no** 19.2.4v, 33.2.2.5 (in
    comparisons) 5.2.2

fer
  causative governing infinitive 18.2.1,
    25.5
  expressing weather conditions 25.2.2
  fer-se 30.6iv
  translating 'ago' 13.3, 33.2.2.4i
fins (a) 14.2.3
  fins i tot 33.3.3.1
  fins que 33.2.2.4ii
força 8.2
former/latter 6.4, 11.5.2i
Future perfect tense 16.5.12, 17.2.5
Future tense 16.5.7
  use of 17.1.4
  vs. present subjunctive in subordinate
    clauses 17.1.4.1, 19.3, 19.4.7

gaire 8.2, 8.4, 13.6, 26.1.5
Gender
  of nouns Chapter 1; of abbreviations
    and acronyms 1.2.7; of animal
    names 1.1.7; of compound nouns
    1.2.3 (*see also* 1.1.5); of foreign
    words 1.2.8; of nouns ending in -a
    1.2.1; of nouns ending other than
    in -a 1.2.2; of inanimate objects
    and non-domestic animals 1.2;
    common gender 1.1.5; derivation
    of feminine forms 1.1.1–2;
    irregular gender pairs 1.1.4;
    metonymic gender 1.2.6 (*see also*
    1.1.5); nouns of fixed gender
    1.1.6; typical feminine endings
    1.2.1, 1.2.2.2; unexpectedly
    feminine nouns 1.2.2.4; variable
    or doubtful gender 1.2.5
  homonyms with different gender 1.2.4
  of adjectives 4.1, 4.2.3
  of definite article 3.1
  of demonstratives 6.2
  of indefinite adjectives 8.3
  of indefinite article 3.2.1
  of numerals 10.2
  of (past) participle 21.1.2
  of personal article 3.3.1
  of possessives 7.1, 7.2
  of pronominal clitics 12.1
  of quantifiers 8.2
  of stressed pronouns 11.1, 11.2
  see also Neuter
gens 8.2, 8.2.1, 8.4, 8.6, 13.6, 26.1.5
  (**no . . .**) **gens ni mica** 13.6, 26.1.6
gent, la (indefinite/impersonal) subject
    29.3iv
Gerund 16.5.2, Chapter 22
  absolute (adverbial) phrases with
    22.2.3, 22.2.4.1
  compound (**havent** + participle) 22.1
  expressing condition 22.2.4.1iii, 34.8.2
  modifying direct object of verbs of
    'encountering', representation,
    perception 22.2.4.3
  negation of 26.2.1.1ii
  progressive constructions with 18.1.1,
    18.1.3
  pronominal clitics with 12.2–3, 22.2.1
  subject of 22.2.2–3, 22.3.2
  syntactic functions of, adverbial
    22.2.4.1; adjectival 22.2.4.2
  with **tot (i)/bo i** (temporal and
    concessive phrases) 22.2.4.1
gran 4.2.1
gros 4.2.1
guanyar-se 23.10iv

haver (auxiliary) 16.5.12, 17.2.1.2
  alternative conditional form 16.5.8,
    34.6.1
  haver de + infinitive 18.2.1, 20.2.1
haver-hi ('there is') 12.7v, 25.2.2, 30.1,
    31.10i
  number agreement with noun phrase
    argument 25.2.2, 30.1
  alternating with **ser-hi** 30.1
  'Heavy (Noun Phrase) Shift' 36.3
hi (adverbial pronoun) 12.7
  see also Pronominal clitics
ho (neuter pronoun) 12.3.2.1, 12.5
hom 25.2i, 29.3i
  un hom 29.3ii
home! 24.1.1
Homographs 37.5.3

how 13.6; interrogative 27.1.3.9; in
    exclamations 13.6, 27.2.2
Hyphen(ation) 26.2.1.1, 37.6
    with numerals 10.3, 37.6i

i 15.1.1
i tant! 24.1.1
Ideophones 24.2
idò 13.6
igual (a/de) 5.1, 8.3
    igual que 33.2.3
Imperative Chapter 28
    alternative ways of ordering and
        requesting 28.4
    forms 16.5.11; coincidences with
        subjunctive 28.1–2
    indirect 19.2.3, 32.2
    negative 28.2
    positive 28.1
    pronominal clitics with 12.2.2,
        12.9.3.2, 28.3
    'toned down' 15.2.3v, 19.6, 28.4, 32.2
Imperfect subjunctive 16.5.10.1
    alternating with imperfect indicative in
        conditions 34.4–5
    -ra forms 34.6.2
Imperfect tense 16.5.6.1
    contrasted with preterite 17.1.3.1
    use of 17.1.3.1; in conditional clauses
        17.2.6, 34.4–5; in consequence
        clauses (for conditional) 34.6.4
Impersonal constructions
    denoting weather conditions 25.2.2
    other impersonal constructions
        29.3
    with **es** 25.2.1, 29.2
    with 'subjectless' verbs 25.2.2
    see also **es**, Pronominal verbs,
        'Reflexive passive' construction
Indefinite article 3.2, 8.3, 8.6ii
    absence or presence of 3.2.3, 30.2
    appreciative use of 3.2.5
    as antecedent of relative construction
        31.6.2
    as impersonal subject 29.3iii
    morphology 3.2.1
    special uses of plural **uns/unes** 3.2.4–5,
        8.3, 8.6ii
    syntax of 3.2.2
Indicative mood Chapter 17
Indirect object 12.3.2.3, 25.4, 25.5
    pronouns *see* Pronominal clitics

verbs taking either direct or indirect
    object 25.4.1
Indirect questions 20.3.1.3, 27.1.2,
    27.1.3.8–9
    (with **si**) 15.3.2
Infinitive 16.5.1, Chapter 20
    after adverbial adjuncts 20.3.1.2
    after **en** in temporal phrases 14.1.1.5,
        20.4
    after verbs of permitting/prohibiting,
        etc. 25.5
    after verbs of request or command
        20.2.1i
    as verbal noun 20.2, 22.3.2
    compound 17.2.1.2, 20.1, 20.4,
        34.6.5
    in conditional clauses 34.8
    in conditional perfect with modal
        verbs 34.6.5
    in indefinite relative clauses and
        indirect questions 20.3.1.3,
        31.10ii
    introduced by **de** 20.2.1
    modifying direct object of verbs of
        perception 20.3, 22.2.4.3iii, 25.5
    negation of 26.2.1.1ii
    nominalized 20.5
    non-pronunciation of final **-r** 16.5.1
    passive 20.2, 20.2.1i
    prepositions before infinitive
        complement 20.3.1.1
    pronominal clitics with 12.1.2, 12.2,
        16.5.1
    subject of 20.2.2
Infinitive phrases
    as elements of finite clauses 20.3;
        phrases with **de** alternating with
        que clauses 20.3.1.2
Information focus, affecting word order
    36.2–5
-ing forms 21.1.3, 21.2.1, 22.1.2, 22.2.4.2,
    22.3
'Intensifying' article 27.1.3.9, 27.2.3
Interjections 24.1
Interrogation *see* Questions
Irregular verbs
    of conjugation II 16.6.1
    of conjugation III 16.6.2
    of mixed conjugation 16.3

ja 13.3
    ja no 26.1.9

Left detachment 36.4
    in questions 27.1.3.6
    in relation to passive 29.1.4ii
    see also Word order
l'hi 12.9.3.4
l·l (*ela geminada*) 37.1
llur(s) 7.1.1.1
lo (dialect variant for *m.* definite article)
    3.1.1 (non-standard neuter
    article) 9.2.1, 27.2.3, 31.6.2
    see also Neuter

mai 26.1.5
major 5.2.1
mal (adjective) 4.2.1
    mal/malament (adverb) 13.4, mal
    formulating negative wishes
    27.2.4ii
manco (Bal. = menys) 5.2, 8.2, 13.6
mant 8.3
massa 8.2, introducing clause with perquè
    33.3.2.1
mateix 8.3, 11.4.2, 23.2iv–vii
Measurements 10.12
menor 5.2.1
mentre (que) 33.2.2.2, 33.3.3.1, 34.8
menys 5.2, 8.2
més 5.2, 8.2
mi (strong first-person object pronoun)
    11.4.1
mig 3.2.3vi, 8.2, 10.9
millor 5.2.1, 13.4
Modals
    modal with infinitive 18.2.1, 20.2.1iii
    modals allowing clitic raising 12.2.3
molt 8.2
mon (unstressed possessive adjective) 7.2
Mood *see* Indicative, Subjunctive
morir 21.1.1
    morir(-se) 23.10i

Negation Chapter 26
    negative raising 26.2.1.2
    particular negation (of individual
        lexical items) 26.2.1.1
    poc/gens + adjective 13.6
    scope of 26.2.1
    translating *un-* 4.2.6
Negative polarity items 26.1.5; *see also*
    individual word entries
Neuter
    article el (lo) 9.2, as antecedent

of relative clause 9.2.2,
    27.1.3.9, 31.6.2, 31.7, 35.1.1–2;
    in indirect questions and
    exclamations 27.1.3.9, 27.2.3;
    el *vs.* lo 9.2.1, 9.2.2, 9.2.3,
    27.2.3, 31.6.2; preceding
    adverbs 5.3.1
    demonstratives 6.5
    pronoun ho 12.5
    relative pronoun 9.2.2
never 26.1.5, 26.1.6
n'hi 12.9.4.3
ni 15.1.2, 26.1.2
    ni . . . ni . . . 15.1.2–3, 26.1.2
    ni que 33.3.3
    ni (tan sols) 15.1.6, 26.1.6, 33.3.3.1
ningú 8.5, 26.1.5
ningun (= cap) 8.3, 26.1.5
no simple negation 26.1; *see also*
    Negation
    expletive no 19.2.4v, 33.2.2 5, or no pas
    in comparisons 5.2.2
    no . . . gota/no . . . mica = no . . . gens
    26.1.6
no more/no longer 26.1.9
nomenar 30.6vi
només que 33.3.3.1, 34.8
    només . . . que 33.2.2.6
Nominalization Chapter 9
    of (adjectival) relative clauses 9.1.1,
        9.2.2, 31.6.2
    of adjectives 9.1.1, 21.1 (abstraction)
        with neuter article el 9.2.1
    of infinitives 20.5
    of prepositional phrases 9.1.1.1, 9.2.3
    of present participles 21.2, 21.2.1
North Catalonia Preface ps. xii–xiii
    specific features of usage in 7.1.1.1,
        11.3iii, 17.2.1.2, 22.2.1, 26.1.8
nós 11.3i
Nouns Chapter 1
    abbreviations and acronyms 1.2.7
    abstract nouns 3.1.4ii
    compound nouns 1.1.5, 1.2.3
    count and non-count 2.2.3, 3.1.4.2,
        8.6, *see also* cap, gens
    plural of Chapter 2; collective nouns
        2.2.1; distributives 2.2.2; plural
        formation 2.1; uses of the plural
        2.2
    pronominalization of inanimates
        11.5.2

suffixation (diminutive, augmentative and evaluative) 2.3
verbal 20.2, 22.3.2
see also Gender
Number agreement (of verb with collective nouns) 2.2.1
Numerals
arithmetical expressions 10.7
cardinal numbers 10.1
collective 10.10
decimals 10.9
fractions 10.9
gender agreement of 10.2
hyphenation 10.3, 37.6i
in time expressions 10.11
'millions, billions, trillions' 10.4
musical intervals 10.9
ordinal numbers 10.8, 3.1.4i(a)
percentages 10.9
punctuation in 10.3
telephone numbers 10.1
u ('one') 10.5

o 15.1.4
o sia 15.1.4.1
o . . . o . . . 15.1.4.2
Object *see* Direct object, Indirect object, Pronominal clitics
oblidar(-se de) 23.7
obligar a 25.5
oi? (in tag questions) 27.1.1.2
oi que? reinforcing a question 27.1.1.2
on (subordinating conjunction) 33.2.1
adverbial relative 31.7, 31.8, 35.1.1.1
(interrogative) reinforced with **a** or **de** 27.1.3.2
one(s), the 9.1.1
Orders and requests *see* Imperative

Participle *see* Past Participle, Present Participle
pas in negative constructions 26.1.8, in negative imperatives 26.1.8
expletive **no (pas)** 5.2.2
passar(-se) 23.10vii
Passive agent 29.1.2
with 'reflexive passive' 29.1.3iv, 29.2.1i
Passive voice 29.1–4
formation 29.1.1
long passive (with agent expressed) 29.1.3iv

'passive avoidance' 29.1.3i–iii, 29.1.4, 29.2.1ii
pseudo-passive (with **veure's, trobar-se, quedar** + participle) 29.1.4ii(e)
true passive *vs.* adjectival participle constructions with **ser/estar** 21.1, 29.1.3vi, 30.5
use of 29.1.3
Past anterior tense 17.2.4
Past participle 16.5.3, 18.2.2, 21.1
absolute clauses with 21.1.3, 33.3.1ii
adjectival function 21.1
agreement in compound tenses 17.2.1.2, 21.1.2
expressing condition or concession 21.1.3, 34.8.2
for English '-ing' form 18.1.3ii, 21.1.3, 21.2.1
forming participle phrases 21.1.3
in passive constructions 21.1.2i; *see also* Passive voice
in periphrases with modal 18.2.2
negation of 26.2.1.1ii
with **ser/estar** 30.5
Past subjunctive 16.5.10.1
perfective (analytic form) 16.5.10.2, 19.2.4iii–v
pensar + infinitive 18.2.1
per
contraction with definite article 3.1.1, 14.1
vs. **per a** 14.1.4
see also Agent, passive
per més/molt que 33.3.3.1
per part de 29.1.2
per què? 27.1.3.2
per tal com 33.3.1(i)
Perfect tense 16.5.12, 17.2.2
contrasted with preterite 17.1.2.1, 17.2.2
and see Compound tenses
Periphrastic preterite 16.5.6.2, 17.1.2
però 15.1.5.1
però *vs.* **sinó** 15.1.5.2
perquè ('because') 33.3.1i, ('in order that') 33.3.2
contrasted with **per què?** 27.1.3.2
Personal article 3.3
morphology 3.3.1
usage of 3.3.2
per'xò 15.1.5.1, 33.3.3.1
petit 4.2.1

pitjor 5.2.1, 13.4
please 28.4
Pleonastic pronouns (redundant) 12.8,
    23.7, 29.2.1i(d), 31.2.2, 33.3.4.1,
    36.4–5
Pluperfect tense 17.2.3
    pluperfect subjunctive for conditional
        perfect in consequence clauses
        34.6.3
Plural formation
    basic rule 2.1.1
    of adjectives 4.1.4; gender-marked in
        plural 4.1.3.4
    of compound nouns 2.1.6
    of definite article 3.1
    of demonstratives 6.2
    of indefinites 8.3
    of indefinite article 3.2.1
    of possessives 7.1–2
    of pronominal clitics 12.1
    of proper names 2.1.8
    of quantifiers 8.2
    of stressed pronouns 11.1–2
Pluralia tantum (plurals without
    singular) 2.1.7, 3.2.4iii, 8.6iii
poc 8.2, 26.1.6
poder + infinitive 18.2.1
posar-se 30.6ii
Possessives Chapter 7
    adjectival and pronominal functions
        7.1.1, 7.3
    agreement of 7.1
    complement of prepositions and
        participles 7.5, 14.2.3
    forms of 7.1
    inanimate or non-personal possessors
        7.4.2
    other possessive constructions 7.4,
        12.3.2.3v, 25.4
    position and use of 7.1.2
    possession via dative clitics 7.4.1, 25.4
    propi 8.3
    relative 31.2.2, 31.5
    unstressed adjectives (**mon/ton/son**)
        7.2
prendre('s) 23.10vii
Preposition stranding 31.1.3, 35.1.1,
    35.2
Prepositions
    atonic (**a, amb, de, en, per/per a**) 14.1;
        see also **a, a** *vs.* **en, per** *vs.* **per a**
    compound 14.3

contraction with definite article 3.1,
    14.1
dropped before conjunction **que** 4.2.4,
    14.1.5, 32.3–5
governing infinitives 20.3.1–2, 25.6
governing possessives 7.5
in cleft sentences 35.1.1.1, 35.1.2.1
tonic 14.2; non-derived 14.2.1; derived
    from gerunds/participles 14.2.2;
    simple forms or alternative
    compounds (with **de**) 14.2.3;
    used as adverbs 11.5.2iii
with stressed pronouns 11.5.2ii
Present indicative tense 16.5.5
use of 17.1.1; as future 17.1.1,
    17.1.4; as polite request 28.4;
    demonstratives with historic
    present 6.3; in temporal
    expressions, for English past
    tense 17.2.2
simple *vs.* progressive (continuous)
    forms 17.1.1, 18.1 1, 18.1.3
Present participle 21.2
    nominalization of 21.2, 21.2.1
    vs. gerund 21.2.1
Present perfect tense *see* Perfect tense
Present subjunctive 16.5.9
Preterite (past perfective indicative) tense
    16.5.6.2, 17.1.2
use of (contrasted with perfect)
    17.1.2.1, 17.2.2, (contrasted with
    imperfect) 17.1.3.1
Progressive (continuous) verb forms
    18.1
    imperfect 17.1.3v, 17.1.3.1
    perfect 17.2.2, 18.1.3v
    preterite 17.1.2.1ii, 18.1.1iii
Pronominal clitics Chapter 12
    adverbial pronouns 12.6–7
    clitic raising (mobile object pronouns)
        12.2.3, 18.2.1.1, 20.2.1iii, 34.6.5;
        affecting pronoun groups 12.9.4
    clitic doubling 25.3, 25.4, with left/
        right detachment 36.4–5; *see also*
        Pronominal clitics: redundant
        pronouns
    direct and indirect objects 12.3.1.1,
        12.3.2.1–3, 25.3–4
    els hi in colloquial *vs.* normative usage
        12.9.3.5
    en 12.6, 25.2.1, 25.6–7; with 'unaccusa-
        tive' verbs 25.2.1

groups of more than two pronouns
    12.9.5–6
hi 12.7, 25.6–7; as indirect object
    (animate) 12.9.3.3 (inanimate)
    12.3.2.3, 12.7ii, 25.4; idioms with
    12.7vi–vii
ho (neuter) 12.3.2.1, 12.5
in compound tenses 17.2.1.2
in verbal periphrases 18.2.1.1
non-standard forms 12.1.2, 12.3.2.2,
    12.9.3.5
position 12.2, 22.2.1, 28.3; before verb
    12.2.1; after verb 12.2.2
redundant pronouns 12.8, 23.7,
    29.2.1i(d), 31.2.2, 33.3.4.1, 36.4–5
reflexive 12.3.1.2, 12.4
single pronoun forms 12.1.1–2
two-pronoun groups 12.9; 1st- and
    2nd-person forms combined
    12.9.3.6; 3rd-person combin-
    ations 12.9.3.3; **els hi** 12.9.3.5;
    impossible combinations 12.9.3.9;
    involving pronominal verbs
    12.9.3.7; **l'hi/n'hi** 12.9.3.4;
    mobility of 12.9.4; order of
    combination 12.9.2 (table),
    12.9.3.1 (pages 204–205);
    phonetic contact in groups
    12.9.3.8; with 'reflexive passive'
    29.2.1i(d)
see also **es**, Pronominal verbs
Pronominal verbs Chapter 23
denoting change of state 23.5iii, 30.6
reciprocal meaning 23.3
reflexive meaning 23.2; emphasis
    of reflexive subject or object
    23.2iv–v
'reflexive passive' function (with
    inanimate subjects) 23.4, 29.2
special uses involving verbs of motion
    23.6; remembering/forgetting
    23.7; consumption 23.8;
    knowledge/perception 23.9; and
    others 23.10
transitivity/intransitivity, 'detransitivi-
    zation' 23.1ii, 23.4
variant patterns in translation 23.5
verbs with pronominal form only
    23.5ii
with clitic groups 12.9.3.7, 23.1
with prepositional objects 23.5iii,
    23.7

Pronominalization of adjective phrases
    4.2.4
Pronouns
adverbial (**en**, **hi**) 12.6–7
demonstrative 6.4, in relative clauses
    6.6, 31.6.1–2
indefinite 8.5
neuter **ho** 12.3.2.1, 12.5
personal (stressed) Chapter 11; as
    subject 11.1–3, use and omission
    11.5, 25.2.1; with imperative 28.3;
    duplication with unstressed clitics
    25.3–4; 'strong' (prepositional
    objects) 11.4, use and omission
    11.5.2; **si** (3rd-person reflexive)
    11.4.2, 23.2v
possessive 7.3
relative Chapter 31; forms following
    prepositions 31.3, 31.4.2; *see also*
    Relative clauses
weak (object) pronouns
    see Pronominal clitics
Proper names 2.1.8, 3.3.2
propi 8.3
prou 8.2, introducing clause with **perquè**
    33.3.2.1
Pseudo-cleft sentences 35.2.2
'Pseudo-relative' constructions 27.1.3.9,
    31.10iii
puix que 33.3.1i
Punctuation 37.7
in numerals 10.3
pus 5.2, 8.2, 26.1.5, 26.1.9

qualcú 8.5
qualque 8.3
    qualque cosa 8.3, 8.6
qualsevol 8.3, 8.5, 8.6
quan (subordinating conjunction)
    33.2.2.1, 33.2.2.6
adverbial relative 31.7, 31.8, 35.1.1.1
interrogative 27.1.3.2
quant 8.2
exclamatory 27.2.2.1–2
interrogative 27.1.3.3
Quantifiers 8.1–2
as degree adjectives and adverbs 8.2.2,
    13.6
idiomatic use of **la de/una de**
    expressing quantity 3.4iii
uns/unes 3.2.4i–iii
with **de** 8.2.1

que (subordinating conjunction/
  complementizer) 15.2, Chapter 32
  as colloquial subordinator/
    coordinator 15.2.3iii, 33.2.2.6,
    33.3.1i
  as degree adverb 13.6, 27.2.2.2
  as subordinator in result clauses
    33.3.4.1
  heading a main clause 15.2.3
  in cleft sentences 35.1 esp. 35.1.1.1
  in compound conjunctions 15.2.2,
    Chapter 33
  in exclamations 8.2, 13.6, 27.2.2.1–2
  introducing direct questions 15.2.3i;
    27.1.1.1; indirect questions
    27.1.3.8; echo questions 27.1.1.1
  with subjunctive in 'toned down'
    requests 15.2.3v, 19.6, 28.4, 32.2
que (relative) Chapter 31 esp. 31.1–2
  in relative clauses of time 31.2.1
  non-standard/colloquial constructions
    with 31.2.2, 31.5
què (interrogative) 27.1.3.1, 27.1.3.3
què (relative) 31.3
quedar(-se) 30.6v
quelcom 8.5, 8.6v
Questions 27.1
  adverbial interrogative words 27.1.3.1
  direct 27.1.1
  emphasis in 27.1.3.7
  indirect (with **si**) 27.1.2
  partial (with *wh-* words), direct 27.1.3;
    indirect 27.1.3.8; prepositions
    with *wh-* words 27.1.3.5
  'pseudo relatives' in questions
    27.1.3.9
  question mark ¿ 27.1.1, 37.7
  rhetorical (with conditional tense)
    17.1.5ii
  word order in 27.1.1
qui (interrogative) 27.1.3.1
qui (relative) 31.3
  a qui for **que** 31.2ii
  in headless relative clauses 31.7
  with pronoun or article antecedent
    31.6.1–2
quin (interrogative) 27.1.3.4
  (exclamatory) 27.2.2.2ii

rai 24.1.1
recordar(-se de) 12.6iv, 23.7
Reflexive verbs *see* Pronominal verbs

Reduplicative forms 37.6; *see also*
  Ideophones
'Reflexive passive' construction 23.4,
  25.2 1, 29.1.3ii, 29.1.4, 29.2
  constraints on use (grammatical)
    29.2.1i (stylistic) 29.2.1ii, 29.3
  number agreement of verb in 29.2.2
  overlap with other impersonal
    constructions 29.2 esp. 29.2.1
  pronoun groups with 29.2.1i(d)
  see also Pronominal verbs, **es**
Relative clauses Chapter 31
  alternative English constructions
    22.1.2, 22.3.1, 31.10
  ambiguity in 31.4.4
  antecedent of 31.1.1, 31.6
    (non-specific) 9.2.2, 31.6.2
  headless (free) 20.3.1.3, 31.7
  in cleft sentences 35.1.1
  in comparative constructions (**del que**
    = 'than') 5.2.3, 31.6.2
  neuter **el** as antecedent 9.2.2, 31.6.2
  nominalization of 9.1.1
  non-standard constructions 31.2.2
  ordinal as antecedent 10.8
  possessive 31.2.2, 31.5
  prepositions in 31.1.3, 31.3, 31.4.2–3,
    35.1.1, 35.2
  redundant pronominal clitics in 12.8.2,
    25.4, 31.2.2
  related to adverbial clauses (of
    manner) 33.2.3i (of result)
    33.3.4.1
  restrictive and non-restrictive types
    31.1.2
  subjunctive in 19.3
  temporal 31.2.1
  word order in 31.1.3, 36.6
  see also Infinitive, Pseudo-relative
    constructions, individual word
    entries
Requests 17.1.1ii, 17.1.3ii, 17.1.5ii
  28.4
res 8.5, 8.6, 26.1.5
Right detachment 36.5
  see also Word order
riure('s) 23.10v

saber + infinitive 18.2.1
Salutations 24.1
segons com 33.2.3
sempre que 33.2.2.3, 33.3.3.1

sengles 8.3
sense 26.1.3
  absence of indefinite article after
    3.2.3iv
  sense que 19.2.4iv, 26.1.3, 33.2.3, 34.8
Sentence composition: elements and
    grammatical relations Chapter 25,
    Chapter 36
  see also Adjuncts, Word order
ser Chapter 30
  absence of indefinite article in
    complements of 3.2.3i–ii
  alternative conditional form 16.5.8,
    34.6.1; alternative past participle
    21.1.1
  as auxiliary in compound tenses
    17.2.1.2, 21.1.2
  choice between **ser** and **estar** with
    adjectival complements (animate
    subjects) 30.5.1 (inanimate
    subjects) 30.5.2
  impersonal use 25.2.2, 29.4ii, 30.1
  in cleft sentences Chapter 35
  indicating identity, set membership,
    profession 30.2
  with past participle 21.1, 30.5 (passive
    construction) 29.1
  vs. **estar** with location/time predicates
    30.3
si ('if') 15.3, Chapter 34 esp 34.7–8
  see also Conditional sentences,
    Indirect questions
si (strong 3rd-person reflexive pronoun)
  11.4.2, 23.2v
si us plau/sisplau 28.4
since 32.2.2.4
sinó 15.1.5.2, 26.1.4
  sinó *vs.* **però** 15.1.5.2
  sinó *vs.* **si no** 15.3i
som-hi?/! 24.1.1
some, any, something (translation) 8.6
son (unstressed possessive adjective)
  7.2
sort que 19.2.2
Spelling Chapter 37 (verbs) 16.1
  alternations **c/qu, g/gu, ç/c, j/g, qu/qü,**
    gu/gü 16.1.2, 37.3.1
  alternations in word-final *vs.* word-
    internal position 1.1.1iv, 2.1.3,
    2.1.5.2–3, 4.1.2, 37.3.2
  forms of pronominal clitics in groups
    12.9.6

  forms of single pronominal clitics
    12.1.1
Stress 37.5.1
Subject 25.2
  impersonal 25.2, 29.2
Subjunctive mood Chapter 19, 16.5.9–10
  and indicative mood, general remarks
    19.2.1–2
  alternating with indicative mood
    17.1.4.1, 17.2.5, 19.2.4iii–v, 19.3,
    19.4.7, 33.2.2.5, 33.3.2–4, 34.4–5
  vs. indicative mood, in various types of
    adverbial clause 19.4.1–7: causal
    19.4.1; concessive 19.4.2, 33.3.3;
    conditional 33.2.2.3, Chapter 34;
    manner 19.4.6, 33.2.3; purpose
    and result 19.4.4–5, 33.2.3,
    33.3.2, 33.3.4; temporal 19.4.7;
    in expressions of supposition or
    appearance 19.2.4iii; request *vs.*
    statement 19.2.3; 'waiting' *vs.*
    'hoping' 19.2.4v
  in clauses dependent on verbs of
    emotion or evaluation 19.2.2
  in clauses dependent on verbs of doubt
    or denial 19.2.4iv, 26.2.1.2
  in complement clauses 19.2, 32.1–3
  in conditional sentences Chapter 34
  in desiderative sentences 19.6, 27.2.4
  in exhortations and 'toned down'
    imperatives 15.2.3v, 19.6, 32.2
  in imperatives 28.1–2
  in main clauses 19.6, 34.6.3
  in negative imperatives 28.2
  in negative wishes 27.2.4ii
  in relative clauses 17.4.1ii, 19.3
  in temporal clauses 17.1.4.1, 19.4.7,
    33.2.2 esp. 33.2.2.5–6
  optative (relating to wish, desire,
    intention, request, cause or
    achievement) 19.2.3; 'hoping' *vs.*
    'waiting' 19.2.4v
  potential (relating to necessity,
    possibility/probability,
    appearance, doubt/denial,
    fear) 19.2.4
  thematic 19.2.1
Subordinate clause *see* Clauses
Suffixation
  absolute superlative **-íssim** 5.3.2
  applied to nouns 2.3
  applied to adjectives 4.1.5

diminutive **-et** applied to adverbs 13
    (introduction)
Superlative 5.3
    absolute suffix **-íssim** 5.3.2
    applied to adverbs 13 (introduction)
    relative superlative 5.3.1
    subjunctive after 19.3
Synthetic preterite tense 16.5.6.2
    alternating with analytic (periphrastic)
        form 17.1.2
    see also Preterite tense

Tag questions 27.1.1.2
tal 3.2.3vi, 8.3 (adverb) 33.2.3ii
talment (com) 33.2.3ii
tampoc 26.1.7
tanmateix 33.3.3.1
tant 8.2, 33.3.4
    distinguished from **tan** 5.1, 13.6
    tant de bo que 19.6, 24.1, 27.2.4
Temporal expressions 13.3, 15.2.3iii,
    17.2.2, 33.2.2.4
tenir
    as auxiliary in compound tenses
        21.1.2
    in possessive expressions 7.4
Tense of verbs 16.5.5–10, Chapter 17
    compound *see* Compound tenses
    in conditional sentences 34.2–5,
        34.6.3–4
    in cleft sentences 35.1.1.2
    progressive (continuous) 18.1.1–3
    sequence in subjunctive clauses 19.5
    see also individual tense categories
that's why 35.2
there is/there are 12.7v, 25.2 2, 30.1
they (impersonal) Chapter 29 esp. 29.2.1ii,
    29.3vi
Time expressions 3.1.4.4iii, 10.11
    asking time 27.1.3.4
    use of demonstratives 6.3
Topicalization *see* Left detachment
ton (unstressed possessive adjective) 7.2
tornar a + infinitive 18.2.1
tornar-se 30.6iii
tot
    as adjective 8.2, 8.3
    as adverb 13.6
    as pronoun 8.5
    tot i in non-finite concessive clauses
        20.4.1, 22.2.4.1
tothom 8.5

transformar-se (en) 30.6vi
trobar(-se) 23.10ii, 29.1.4ii(e)
tu (impersonal subject) 29.3v
tu! (interjection) 24.1.1

u *vs.* **un** 10.5
un- (negative prefix) 4.2.6
un/una (impersonal subject) 29.3iii
    see also Indefinite article, Numerals
'Unaccusative' (intransitive) verbs 25.2.1,
    36.2
unless 34.1.2, 34.8i

va- auxiliary (in analytic preterite)
    16.5.6.2
Valencian usage preface p. xiii–xiv
    specific features of 2.1.4, 4.1.4, 6.2,
        6.2.7, 6.5, 7.1, 12.7.1, 12.9.3.3,
        13.2, 14.1.4, 16.2.3, 16.3, 16.5.5,
        16.5.9, 16.5.10.1–2, 16.5.11,
        16.5.12, 30.3, 34.6.2, 37.5.2
Valency 25.5
Verbal nouns 20.2, 22.3.2
Verbal periphrases Chapter 18
Verbs Chapter 16
    auxiliary 16.5.6.2, 16.5.10.2, 16.5.12,
        17.2.1.2, 18.1
    conjugation classes (regular
        inflectional paradigms) 16.2;
        conjugation I (infinitive in **-ar**)
        16.2.1; conjugation II (infinitive
        in **-re**, unstressed/stressed **-er**,
        vowel-final stem + **-r**) 16.2.2;
        conjugation III (IIIa with
        'inchoative' stem extension, IIIb
        without extension) 16.2.3, 16.5.5;
        mixed conjugation 16.2.4
    dative subject verbs 25.4
    diacritic written accents 16.1.3–4
    irregularity in inflection 16.4, 16.6
    modal auxiliary with infinitive 18.2.1,
        20.2.1iii
    modals allowing clitic raising 12.2.3,
        34.6.5
    mood and aspect 16.5, Chapter 17; *see
        also* Aspect
    non-finite 16.5; *see also* Infinitive,
        Gerund, Past participle
    periphrases Chapter 18; *see also*
        Analytic preterite
    person/number endings 16.5.4
    spelling alternations 16.1

syncretisms or ambiguous forms 16.3
taking 'non-object' complements 25.6
taking prepositional phrase
  complements 20.3.1.1, 25.6
unaccusative 25.2.1, 36.2
see also individual tense categories,
  Pronominal verbs, Tenses of
  verbs, Subjunctive
ves (per on)! 24.1.1
voler + infinitive 18.2.1
vós 11.3iii
  in polite imperatives 29.2.1i(c)
vostè(s) 11.3ii
  impersonal 'you' 29.3v

Weak (object) pronouns *see* Pronominal
  clitics
Weather (impersonal expressions denoting conditions) 25.1, 25.2.2
what (= 'that which') 9.2.2, 31.6.2
what? 27.1.3.1, 27.1.3.4
Wishes 19.6, 27.2.4
Word order Chapter 36
  basic pattern 36., verb + subject
    variants 36.2; 'Heavy Shift'
    (long subject or object placed
to right of normal position)
  36.3; position of adverbials 36.8;
  position of causal clauses 33.3.1;
  position of concessive clauses
  33.3.3.2
in adverbial clauses 36.7
in exclamations 27.2.2.2
in non-finite constructions 20.2.2iv,
  21.1.3, 22.2.3
in questions 27.1.1, 27.1.3.5–6,
  36.5
in relative clauses 31.1.3, 36.6
position of adjectives 4.2.1
position of demonstratives 6.3.1
position of possessives 7.1.1
position of pronominal clitics 12.2,
  12.9.2, 12.9.4
relating to passive 29.1.4ii, 29.3
see also Cleft sentences, Left
  detachment, Right detachment
Written accents (and stress rules) 1.1.1i,
  2.1.1, 16.1.4, 37.5.1;
  distinguishing homonyms/
  homographs 16.1.4, 37.5.3

xe! 24.1.1

Printed in the United Kingdom
by Lightning Source UK Ltd.
131045UK00001BA/3/A